Time Was...

Program Authors
Richard L. Allington
Camille L. Z. Blachowicz
Ronald L. Cramer
Patricia M. Cunningham
G. Yvonne Pérez
Constance Frazier Robinson
Sam Leaton Sebesta
Richard G. Smith
Robert J. Tierney

Instructional Consultant
John C. Manning

Program Consultants
Jesús Cortez
Alfredo Schifini
Robert E. Slavin

Critic Readers
Sister Charles Mary Hanlan
Pamela R. Hoagland
Lisa Isaacks
Theresa O'Bee

Scott, Foresman and Company

Editorial Offices:
Glenview, Illinois

Regional Offices:
Sunnyvale, California
Tucker, Georgia
Glenview, Illinois
Oakland, New Jersey
Carrollton, Texas

Scott, Foresman Reading: An American Tradition

Gold Medal Printing

Acknowledgments

Text

Page 9: From *Mr. Mysterious and Company* by Sid Fleischman. Copyright © 1962 by Albert S. Fleischman. By permission of Little, Brown and Company, in association with the Atlantic Monthly Press, and Curtis Brown Ltd.

Page 20: Excerpts from *Wild Courage* by Robert Franklin Leslie. Copyright © 1974 by Robert Franklin Leslie. Reprinted by permission.

Page 23: From *Zia* by Scott O'Dell. Copyright © 1976 by Scott O'Dell. Reprinted by permission of Houghton Mifflin Company and Oxford University Press.

Page 37: "The Quarrel" from *Eleanor Farjeon's Poems for Children* by Eleanor Farjeon (J. B. Lippincott). Copyright 1933, 1961 by Eleanor Farjeon. Reprinted by permission of Harper & Row, Publishers, Inc. and Harold Ober Associates.

Page 38: Adaptation of "Of Chinese Kites and Associations" by Jade Snow Wong from *No Chinese Stranger*. Copyright © 1975 by Jade Snow Wong. Reprinted by permission of Curtis Brown, Ltd.

Page 47: From "The Worst Thanksgiving in the Entire History of the Universe" by Bill Conklin. Reprinted by permission from the November, 1977 issue of *Yankee* Magazine, Dublin, N.H. 03444, Copyright 1977.

Page 57: "A Word" by Emily Dickinson. Reprinted by permission of the publishers and the Trustees of Amherst College from *The Poems of Emily Dickinson*, edited by Thomas H. Johnson, Cambridge, Mass.: The Belknap Press of Harvard University Press, Copyright 1951, © 1955, 1979, 1983 by The President and Fellows of Harvard College.

Page 76: "Go With The Poem" from *Go with The Poem* by Lilian Moore. Copyright © 1979 by Lilian Moore. Used by permission of the author. All rights reserved.

Page 77: From *The Oxford Book of American Light Verse* edited by James Thomas Fields, pp. 74–76. Oxford University Press, Inc., 1979.

Page 80: "Water Picture" by May Swenson is used by permission of the author from *New & Selected Things Taking Place*, copyright © 1956, renewed 1984 by May Swenson. The poem first appeared in *The New Yorker*.

Page 81: "It's Hot in the City" by Peter West from *Voices of Literature, Book 1*, compiled by Dr. Marshall McLuhan and Dr. Richard J. Schoeck, Holt, Rinehart and Winston of Canada, Limited, 1964. Reprinted by permission.

Page 82: Edwin A. Hoey. "Foul Shot," from *Read* magazine. Copyright © 1962 by Xerox Corporation. Special permission granted by *Read* magazine, published by Xerox Education Publications, this agreement is assignable to any successor organization of Xerox Education Publications.

Page 83: "Joy" by Clarissa Scott Delaney from *Caroling Dusk: An Anthology of Verse by Negro Poets* edited by Countee Cullen. Copyright 1927 by Harper & Row, Publishers, Inc. Copyright renewed 1955 by Ida M. Cullen. Reprinted by permission of Harper & Row, Publishers, Inc.

Page 84: "The Unwritten" by W. S. Merwin, *Writings to an Unfinished Accompaniment*. Copyright © 1971, 1973 by W. S. Merwin. Reprinted with the permission of Atheneum Publishers, Inc. and David Higham Associates Ltd.

Page 87: "Hinky-Pinky" adapted from *Arrow Book of Word Games*. Copyright © 1964 by Scholastic Magazines, Inc. Reprinted by permission of Scholastic, Inc.

Page 88: Adapted from *My Life with Martin Luther King, Jr.* by Coretta Scott King. Copyright © 1969 by Coretta Scott King. Reprinted by permission of Holt, Rinehart and Winston, Publishers.

Page 95: Quotation by Coretta Scott King from book jacket of *My Life with Martin Luther King, Jr.* by Coretta King. Copyright © 1969 by Coretta Scott King. Reprinted by permission of Holt, Rinehart & Winston.

Page 96: Excerpt from "I Have a Dream" by Martin Luther King, Jr. Reprinted by permission of Joan Daves. Copyright © 1963 by Martin Luther King, Jr.

Page 106: 2000-word summary from throughout *Felisa Rincón de Gautier: The Mayor of San Juan* by Ruth Gruber, (Thomas Y. Crowell). Copyright © 1972 by Ruth Gruber. Reprinted by permission of Harper & Row, Publishers, Inc.

Page 114: Adaptation from *Michael Naranjo* by Mary Carroll Nelson. Copyright © 1975 by Dillon Press, Inc. Reprinted by permission.

Page 118: Excerpt from "Blind sculptor touches the spirit of Michelangelo" by Marcia Dunn, *Chicago Tribune*, August 15, 1985. Reprinted by permission of The Associated Press.

Page 121: "Mother to Son" reprinted from *Selected Poems* by Langston Hughes, by permission of Alfred A. Knopf, Inc. Copyright © 1926 by Alfred A. Knopf, Inc. and renewed 1954 by Langston Hughes.

Page 122: Adapted from *Philip Hall Likes Me, I Reckon Maybe* by Bette Greene. Text copyright © 1974 by Bette Green. A Dial Books for Young Readers book. Reprinted by permission of E. P. Dutton, a division of New American Library, and the author.

Page 136: "The Last of the Dragons" by E. Nesbit reprinted with permission of Macmillan Publishing Company from *The Complete Book of Dragons* by E. Nesbit. Copyright © 1972 by Hamish Hamilton Ltd.

Page 152: From *Scott, Foresman: Earth Science* by Jay M. Pasachoff, Naomi Pasachoff and Timothy M. Cooney, pp. 396–397. Copyright © 1983 by Scott, Foresman and Company.

Page 158: From *Scott, Foresman: Earth Science* by Jay M. Pasachoff, Naomi Pasachoff and Timothy M. Cooney, pp. 402–404. Copyright © 1983 by Scott, Foresman and Company.

Page 161: From *People on Earth: A World Geography* by D. Drummond and R. Drummond, pp. 59–61, 63, 534, 535. Copyright © 1983 by Scott, Foresman and Company.

Page 172: Adapted from *Octopus and Squid: The Soft Intelligence* by Jacques-Yves Cousteau and Philippe Diole. Translated from the French by J. F. Bernard, copyright © 1973 by Jacques-Yves Cousteau. Used by permission of Doubleday & Company, Inc.

Page 178: Adaptation of "Bizarre Sharks Come to Light" by Walter Sullivan from *New York Times*, October 25, 1983. Copyright © 1983 by The New York Times Company. Reprinted by permission.

Page 181: From "The Great Shark Hunt" by Erla Zwingle, *American Photographer*, June 1982. Copyright © 1982 by CBS Publications, the Consumer Publishing Division of CBS Inc. Reprinted by permission.

Page 214: Dramatization of *Three Strong Women: A Tall Tale from Japan* by Claus Stamm. Copyright ©1962 by Claus Stamm. Adapted by permission of Viking Penguin, Inc.

Page 244: From *Sister* by Eloise Greenfield (Thomas Y. Crowell). Copyright © 1974 by Eloise Greenfield. Reprinted by permission of Harper & Row, Publishers, Inc. and Marie Brown Associates.

Page 248: From *Winter Thunder* by Mari Sandoz. Adapted by permission of The Westminster Press and McIntosh & Otis, Inc. Copyright, MCMLI by The Curtis Publishing Company, copyright, MCMLIV by Mari Sandoz.

Page 262: Four haiku from *Flower, Moon, Snow: A Book of Haiku* by Kazue Mizumura (Thomas Y. Crowell). Copyright © 1977 by Kazue Mizumura. Reprinted by permission of Harper & Row, Publishers, Inc.

Page 264: "The Midnight Visitor" adapted by permission of Random House, Inc. from *Mystery and More Mystery* by Robert Arthur. Copyright 1939 and renewed 1967 by Robert Arthur.

Page 268: From *Everybodies* by O. Henry. London: 1902.

Page 274: From *The Hobbit* by J. R. R. Tolkien. Copyright © 1966 by J. R. R. Tolkien. Reprinted by permission of Houghton Mifflin Company and George Allen & Unwin.

Page 302: From *Choosing Good Health*, grade 7 by Merita Lee Thompson et al., pp. 180, 210–211 and 220–221. Copyright © 1983 by Scott, Foresman and Company.

Page 306: Adaptation of "Japan's Passionate Affair with Baseball" by Robert Whiting from *Asia*, September/October 1982. Reprinted by permission of the author.

Acknowledgments continued on page 632

Contents

What could be more surprising than seeing a magician stumped when something unexpectedly disappears?

by Sid Fleischman

It was a most remarkable sight. Even the hawks and buzzards sleeping in the blue Texas sky awoke in mid-air to glance down in wonder.

A covered wagon was lurching west along the barren trail to Cactus City, but it was like no other wagon seen in those parts before. To begin with, it was the wrong color. Its canvas was bright red and could be seen for miles. The wheels were painted gold, like a circus wagon, and the horses (if seeing was believing) were as white as swans.

The man driving this most remarkable wagon and these white horses was himself a most remarkable man. He wore a stovepipe hat, as tall as Abe Lincoln's and just as black, and had a smiling red beard even sharper than the letter V. If the hawks and buzzards could have read, they would have seen his name in golden letters a foot high on the sides of the wagon:

MR. MYSTERIOUS & COMPANY

The day was hot and the hour was noon. The gentleman (for even at this distance you could tell he was a gentleman) led the horses to the shade of a lone oak tree and pulled back on the leather reins.

The moment the wagon came to a halt, three young faces, in an assortment of ages from six to twelve, appeared in the puckered canvas opening behind the driver's seat. Two girls and a boy had been doing their school lessons farther back in the wagon.

Mama had once been a schoolteacher, and now she taught the youngsters their lessons as the wagon traveled from town to town. She also played the small portable piano inside the wagon and could sing all the Stephen Foster songs. "We're almost out of water, Andrew," she said.

"We'll get water and supplies in Cactus City," he nodded.

His name was not, as one might suppose, Andrew Mysterious. It was simply Andrew Perkins Hackett—which hardly sounded mysterious enough for a man who could pluck coins from the air and turn hens' eggs into silk handkerchiefs. He had, therefore, adopted a stage name, according to the custom among show folks. As Mr. Mysterious & Company, the family entertained settlers and pioneers in the small towns of the Old West, which at the time was Brand New.

The brightly painted show wagon carried all the tricks and props of their trade. It was full of lacquered boxes with trap doors and secret compartments, colored scarves and silk ribbons. There were velvet tables with gold fringes, cabinets and strange vases. Tucked in a corner was a hutch of white rabbits, waiting to be pulled out of hats. On occasion Mr. Mysterious had pulled rabbits out of ten-gallon cowboy hats, Mexican sombreros, coonskin caps, and even ladies' bonnets.

Pa printed up handbills on a small hand press. These were sent ahead to be posted on walls and fences to announce the show's arrival. Handbills had already been sent to Cactus City, where Mr. Mysterious & Company would present its show at seven o'clock sharp—unless the wagon got stuck in the mud. It hadn't got stuck in the mud since last February in Iowa.

"Let me make the sourdough biscuits, Mama," Jane said, adjusting the yellow ribbon in her hair. She looked rather plain in her dark calico dress, but on show nights she was able to wear her pink gingham and float through the air. She looked enchanting behind the footlights. Pa would pass a barrel hoop around her to prove there were no wires holding her up. It amazed everyone, except Jane herself, who quite naturally knew how the trick was done. Pa had sworn her to secrecy, and she had never told a soul. But then, she hardly knew a soul outside the members of her family.

"Do we have to have biscuits again?" Paul groaned. Jane had recently learned to make sourdough biscuits and it seemed as if the family ate them three times a day.

"Come along, my lad," Pa called. "We'll need to root up some wood for the fire."

Paul had already climbed onto the stilts he had patiently whittled out of old wagon boards. He practiced every time the wagon stopped, and sometimes he took his meals standing as long-legged as a young giraffe. The stilts made him almost as tall as Pa himself, but of course Paul didn't have a smiling red beard as sharp as the letter V. But one day he would have, for he dreamed of becoming a magician like his father. Pa had already taught him to palm coins and small balls. He could untie knots in a rope with his toes. But it would take years of hard practice to master the difficult feats Pa did before the kerosene footlights.

Pa had brought along a shovel and began to dig for mesquite roots. "My lad," he smiled, "you can't dig roots from up there on stilts."

Reluctantly, Paul jumped back to earth and brushed the hair out of his eyes. He began hunting a mesquite root. Firewood was rarely found lying on the prairies and badlands. Wood was so hard to find that houses were often built of adobe or sod, and after a rain you could see new grass growing on the roofs. But there was mesquite to be found, and the roots made a good fire. Nothing else was at hand except Paul's stilts, and they didn't count.

"Pa," he said, pulling up a fat root and shaking the dirt out, "I wish we didn't have to go to California. Settle down, I mean."

"You'll like living on a cattle ranch," Pa said. "I grew up with cattle. Ranching is the only other trade I know."

"I'd rather travel around just the way we do. Seeing things and having adventures—why, we have adventures every day. Sometimes twice a day."

Pa shook his head. "The matter is settled, my lad. Your mother and I have talked it over from front to back and side to side. You young 'uns ought to have a regular house to grow up in and be getting a regular schooling."

"Mama's the best schoolteacher there is, I bet."

"No doubt about it," Pa said. He stepped on the shovel with his dusty boot. "But a show wagon is no place to get your schooling. No, my lad, we're going to homestead some land and raise beef, like your Uncle Fred in San Diego. And your mother will have a house with a real kitchen and curtains on the windows. No two ways about it—this is going to be the last tour of Mr. Mysterious & Company."

Paul fell silent.

"Come Christmas," Pa said, "this family is going to settle down for good, like other folks."

There were times when Paul noticed a certain sadness come into his father's eyes at the thought of laying aside his magic wand. Pa loved entertaining folks and making them laugh, but once he made up his mind, it stayed made. "I hope Christmas never comes," Paul said under his breath.

He didn't really mean that. He liked Christmas as much as the Fourth of July and birthdays and Abracadabra Day. Sometimes he thought Abracadabra Day was the best holiday of all. It was listed in no almanac and printed in no calendar. It was a secret holiday that belonged to the show family. They had invented it, and no one else knew about it.

The secret was this: no matter how bad you were on Abracadabra Day or no matter what pranks you pulled, you would not be spanked or punished. It was the one day in the year, in the Hackett family at least, on which you were supposed to be bad.

As Pa had once explained it to them, "The way we live, moving about all the time, you young 'uns have got to be good. But no young 'uns ought to have to be good three hundred and sixty-five days in the year. So you each have one day to be bad."

There was only one rule about Abracadabra Day. You must not tell anybody the day you had chosen to be bad. The children sometimes planned for weeks or months just what prank they would pull on Abracadabra Day. No matter what it was, they couldn't be spanked, which was why they had named it Abracadabra Day. It was like magic to do something naughty and not get punished.

Paul was digging out another mesquite root when there came a shouting and a commotion behind them at the show wagon. He turned and saw Mama and Jane and Anne, all three, waving their arms like windmills.

"Andrew—come quick!" shouted Mama.

"Pa! Hurry!"

Pa dropped his shovel and whipped off his hat so he could run all the faster. Paul dropped a root and climbed on his stilts, but tripped over the shovel. To add to the confusion, it must be admitted at this point that horses and rabbits were not the only livestock traveling with Mr. Mysterious & Company. There was Madam Sweetpea. Madam Sweetpea didn't perform in the show; she tagged along behind. Madam Sweetpea was a black and white cow. Despite her name, there was nothing very sweet about Madam Sweetpea except the fresh milk she provided for the three Hackett youngsters. She was by nature proud, ornery, and the laziest cow north of the Rio Grande River (and south of the Rio Grande as well). She walked very slowly, and since she was tied to the rear of the show wagon by a rope, the wagon could never go any faster than Madam Sweetpea walked.

"Pa!" Jane said. "Look!"

"Calm down now. Look at what?"

"Behind the wagon," Mama exclaimed. "Madam Sweetpea! She's gone!"

"Vanished into thin air!" Jane added.

"The cow jumped over the moon," Anne said.

Jane watched Pa tap the stovepipe hat firmly on his head and stride on his long legs to the rear of the show wagon. It was true: Madam Sweetpea was gone. Her rope was gone. The flies she switched with her tail were gone.

Even her hoofmarks had vanished from the earth.

"A splendid mystery," Pa mused. He stood sharpening the point of his beard and wondered how a full-grown, ornery cow could disappear into thin air.

"Pa, it's *impossible*," Jane said.

"Nothing is impossible, sister," Pa said. "Not if we put our minds to it."

Jane brushed a wisp of hair from her forehead and tried to put her mind to it. She knew that Pa needed mirrors or threads or trick boxes to make things disappear. But she had never seen a mirror or trick box large enough to hide a cow. And Madam Sweetpea, who weighed more than half a ton, could hardly have been plucked out of sight with threads.

"Andrew," Mama said gently. She was very worried. "What are we going to do? Poor Madam Sweetpea. There'll be no milk for the children."

"A splendid mystery," Pa said again, staring hard at the place where Madam Sweetpea should have been, but wasn't.

Even her fat shadow was gone.

"What's all the fuss?" Paul said, hurrying up on his stilts.

"Now that we have all assembled," Pa said, "let us get at the bottom of this mystery. Is anyone carrying a grudge against Madam Sweetpea?"

"She kicks," Jane said. "She kicked you when you weren't looking, Pa—just last Tuesday."

"How well I remember," Pa nodded with a look of pain and sorrow.

"She ate Mama's hat," Anne said. "Her Sunday-go-to-meeting hat. The one with the wax cherries on it."

"That cow will even eat rusty nails," Paul put in. "She's got no sense at all."

"Maybe so," Pa admitted. "Madam Sweetpea eats straw hats and rusty nails and kicks grown men. Those are ornery traits in a cow—or in a horse or a mule, for that matter. But she gives milk, and I suppose we'd better overlook her bad habits."

Jane glanced at Paul, and it seemed to her he was almost glad that now she wouldn't be able to make sourdough biscuits for the noon meal. But he wasn't old enough to make a cow disappear. He wasn't a magician, like Pa.

Pa lifted his hat to scratch his head. "Who last heard a sound from Madam Sweetpea?"

"She went *moo,*" Anne said.

"When?"

"When we crossed the dry creek, Pa."

"Thank you, sister." A twinkle was coming into Pa's eye. "Then she was last heard about five minutes ago—just before she vanished into thin air."

"Pa!" Jane exploded. "Maybe Madam Sweetpea just ran away."

"But she was tied to the wagon. A good stout knot too. I tied her myself."

All eyes suddenly turned to Paul, who remained on stilts and was casting a shadow as long as his father's. Paul, they knew, had been practicing untying knots with his toes.

"Young man," Pa said. "Did you untie Madam Sweetpea's rope as we were crossing the dry creek?"

Paul straightened his shoulders and said evenly, "Yes, Pa."

"So I couldn't make biscuits!" Jane said.

"In that case," Pa declared, "the mystery is solved. Madam Sweetpea is just behind that small hill at the dry creek bed."

And at that moment they all heard a *moo* from the other side of the hill. It was Madam Sweetpea's voice, as loud and clear as a foghorn on the Mississippi River.

"Paul!" Mama said. "How could you do such a naughty thing?"

"You walk yourself behind the wagon there," Pa said, "and I'll administer a first-rate spanking."

Paul, who had kept a perfectly straight face, now burst out, "Abracadabra Day!" And then he began to laugh so hard he almost lost his balance high up on the stilts. "Abracadabra Day!"

There was a stunned silence from Pa and Mama and Jane and Anne. He had taken them all by surprise.

"So that's what you've been up to, you rascal!" said Pa, starting to laugh himself.

Mama forgot her anger and found herself joining in the laughter. A moment later all five of them stood merrily on the bare Texas badlands, laughing as hard as at a circus—which woke the hawks and the buzzards again as they napped on the high winds in the sky.

"By gosh and by golly," Pa said. "I can't very well give you a hiding on Abracadabra Day, so why don't you and I go fetch Madam Sweetpea?"

They walked back over the hill, still chuckling, and found the cow munching a tuft of buffalo grass. She was standing right over her shadow, switching flies with her tail, and her rope dragged in the dust. Paul, on his stilts, walked her back to the wagon—or rather, pulled and tugged on her rope, for she didn't want to leave the dry creek bed. He had planned his prank for more than a week. He had heard Pa call out that they would stop for the noon meal at the shade tree up ahead. That was when he had untied Madam Sweetpea with his toes. Now he had surprised them all—and he had even fooled Pa, for a moment or two at least. It had been like a magic trick.

The red covered wagon creaked and lumbered over the trail, and Madam Sweetpea walked along behind, with her rope well knotted to the tail gate. The family rode together on the wooden seat, watching the passing sights.

Most of the time they chuckled about Paul's Abracadabra Day. They would laugh many times, and even for years to come, over the day Paul made a cow disappear!

1

Family Matters

A variety of pictures can come to mind when you hear or read the word *family*. Families come in an assortment of sizes and can include people of all ages. There is no typical family, and matters that concern families are just about as different as you can imagine.

Seeking a lost relative, restoring ancient traditions, or even surviving a family get-together—frequently there is nothing that concerns a family that is ordinary or predictable.

Understanding Comparisons

If you were choosing a family pet, which puppy would you take home? How would you compare them? That big, fuzzy puppy with the deep black eyes seems friendly but not too active. The little brown mutt—the one chewing on its tail—is full of sass and looks like a playful pup. The smallest of all, peeking out from behind those floppy ears, looks a little scared and very sleepy. Do you want a friendly, sassy, or shy puppy? Which will you take home?

Just as you compared the puppies, you can also make comparisons when you read. Authors often make **comparisons** and tell you directly how two things are alike and different by using clue words such as *alike*, *different*, *but*, or *whereas*. But sometimes there are no clue words. In order to make comparisons for yourself, think about the subjects, identify the characteristics, and note how the characteristics make the subjects alike or different. When comparing the puppies (the subject), you could identify their size and behavior (the characteristics) to explain which one you would choose.

When you read, keep in mind that people, animals, places, and things can be compared. When you compare subjects, ask yourself, "How are the subjects alike or different?" "Do they look, feel, or act the same?" and "How does the author show this?"

In the paragraphs below from *Wild Courage* by Robert Franklin Leslie, the author observes a family of wild coyotes. Think about how the coyotes are alike and different.

I sat on a log near the fire pit and held the pups gently but firmly against my chest until they stopped squirming. Four wide-eyed, button-nosed little faces peered curiously into mine. As they gradually quieted down, I glanced from time to time at the mother. She lay unmoving, stretched out on her side, eyes closed. I thought that she was dying.

The pups began to whine and I knew that they must be hungry. Anchoring them securely under my arms, I clumsily opened a can of condensed milk and a package of raisins. The smell of food swiftly put to rest any remaining fear of me. As soon as I put them down they wiggled, snapped, and cuffed at each other, and whined for shoulder room around the aluminum pan into which I mixed the sticky milk with water and raisins.

As they ate, I looked them over more closely. They seemed to be about three months old. Each lanky pup appeared different from the next. The larger male probably weighed about four pounds. The other male was the runt of the litter, little more than half the size of his brother. The big male and the two females constantly nipped at him, muscling him out of line when I offered bits of cheese and peanut-butter crackers.

1. Describe how the pups act differently from their mother.

In answering question 1, did you compare the behavior of the mother with that of her pups? The pups are active but the mother is motionless and seems to be dying. If you had difficulty, reread and note that the mother "lay unmoving" and compare her to her pups.

2. Do the pups look the same or different? Explain.

Did you notice the characteristics that describe how the pups look? All of them are about three months old and are lanky. Two are male and two are female. The large male weighs four pounds whereas the younger male is half that size. If you had difficulty, reread and note the characteristics the author gives you that describe how the pups are alike and different.

3. Do the pups behave the same with each other? How do you know?

Practicing Comparisons

As you read more about the family of coyotes from *Wild Courage*, compare the mother's—Sandy's—goal to that of a pack of other coyotes that is threatening her. Also think about how Sandy and her pups are changing.

More gaunt, haggard, and weedy each day, the spindle-shanked mother was clearly starving in order to feed her family. On the other hand, the coyote pack now enjoyed the rewards of team hunting. They seemed now to almost carelessly await the inevitable when hunger, weakened reflexes, and a broken spirit would make Sandy the easiest of victims.

Each evening when she arrived with the pups her tongue seemed to hang farther from her long, panting muzzle. Her ears, so efficiently pointed earlier, now drooped. Her foot pads had accumulated heavy clods of sticky autumn resin that she no longer bothered to chew away.

In spite of diminished rations, the pups underwent a sudden spurt of growth. Their short, stubby legs stretched out like spindly asparagus shoots. Gray guard hairs grew into their winter pelage. Rib cages expanded, but no cushion of fat padded their ribs. The soft, mink-like puppy touch was soon gone, replaced by rough, saggy hide so loose on the two females that it looked as if they might inadvertently jump out of their skins or turn around in them.

1. How is Sandy's goal different from that of the coyote pack?
2. How has Sandy's appearance changed?
3. Compare the appearance of the pups before and after their growth spurt.

Tips for Reading on Your Own

- Try to find characteristics about subjects that show how they are alike and different.
- Pay attention to how subjects act, think, look, feel, and to what they do that shows if they are alike or different.

Alone on a voyage out in the ocean, a teenage girl and her brother find themselves in conflict. Think about the way they act and what they are like to help you compare their goals and their personalities in this story.

ZIA

by Scott O'Dell

It is the mid-1800s. Zia Sandoval, a fourteen-year-old girl living on the southern coast of California, has learned that her aunt Karana has been seen alive on the Island of the Blue Dolphins— sixty miles out in the Pacific Ocean. Aunt Karana had been accidentally left behind on the island when the rest of the family was rescued from there eighteen years ago, before Zia was born. After finding an abandoned rowboat, Zia and her younger brother, Mando, set out to bring Aunt Karana to the mainland.

Mando found a piece of cloth for a square sail and made a small mast, but on the night we left, with the moon shining on the water and the sea calm, the sail blew away before we had gone a league.

We rowed all night, rowing together and one at a time, resting when our hands began to hurt. We followed the line of the surf that showed white in the moon. At dawn we were down the coast, near Mission Ventura.

The surf was heavy here. Off in the west I could see the cliffs of Santa Cruz and Santa Rosa. Mando caught a *dorado* near the surf but he was too tired to clean it, so we ate a strip of jerky and two tortillas apiece.

There was no wind, only swells coming from the northwest. Rowing was easy in the smooth water and we reached the kelp bed on the south point of Santa Cruz. We worked our way through the kelp into a quiet cove. We moored our boat with strands of kelp instead of the heavy anchor and waded ashore, carrying the fish Mando had caught.

We climbed the cliff, while it was still light. Off to the southwest I could see the outline of the Island of the Blue Dolphins. It looked near to us and clear, but I noticed that the water was not so calm between Santa Cruz and the Island of the Blue Dolphins as it was along the shore we had traveled during the night. On the horizon there were humps that looked like hills, but were really big waves.

I put the compass on a rock and turned it until the needle pointed to "N," as Captain Nidever[1] had told me to do, and read the direction where the island lay.

We went back down the cliffs and built a fire of sticks and brush. We ate the fish and boiled mussels we pried off the rocks in the pot I had. We had a good meal, but the blankets I had brought were not heavy enough to keep us warm. It was cold and my hands hurt. I was glad to see the sun come up far across the channel.

It took Mando an hour, or so it seemed, to get his fishing line together. He tied the big hook he had made in the workshop to a piece of thin chain, and the chain to the lines

---

1. Captain Nidever, the person who sighted Karana on the Island of the Blue Dolphins.

and ropes he had gathered during the past month and strung together and coiled in a wine barrel. None of the lines were the same size or length, but they were all very heavy.

"I'll catch a *pez espada*[2] as big as the boat," he said as we made our way out of the kelp and started off toward the island. I kept the compass in my lap while we rowed and looked at it from time to time to make sure we were going in the right direction, for we could no longer see the Island of the Blue Dolphins.

The wind was light and the waves had not built up yet. Dolphins came and played around the boat, back and forth across our bow. We saw five whales moving south, blowing fountains of mist in the air. Two flying fish came crashing aboard and Mando fastened one on his big hook and let out some of his line from the barrel.

"I'll catch an *espada* as big as the boat," Mando said.

"What will you do with one that big?"

"Tow it home and haul it up on the beach for everyone to see."

"You forget that we are headed for the island, not for home," I reminded him. "Nor to catch *espadas*."

It was clear to me that he thought of our voyage as a chance to fish and of little else.

He picked up the whaling harpoon, which he had brought along, and stopped rowing to brandish it over his head like a sword.

Far out, behind us, as he was brandishing the harpoon, I saw a fin. It was large and shining and caught the morning sun. It was moving slowly toward us, smoothly, like a knife cutting through the water. Then it slowly sank and I thought of it no more.

Mando put his harpoon down in a handy place, should he need it.

The sun was warm and a light wind came up, which felt good. My hands hurt and I tried different ways of holding the oar. Mando did the same and we went along very slowly for a while. But I watched the compass and kept it pointing right, as Captain Nidever had explained to me.

---

2. *pez espada* (pās' es pä'ᖴHä), swordfish.

Mando had a bare foot on the line where it ran out from the barrel. The line began to move and he took his foot away and grabbed hold of it.

"I think," he said and stopped suddenly. The line was moving in his hand. "I think I have something. Maybe Señor[3] Espada."

"I saw a fin a while ago," I said.

"Where?"

"Behind us."

"Why did you not say you saw a fin?"

"Because it disappeared before I could speak."

"That is no reason."

"We are not here to fish for *espadas*. That is a reason."

As I spoke, Mando pitched forward, holding tightly to the line.

"Let go!" I shouted.

The line was ripped from his grasp or else he would have been yanked overboard.

"Espada!" he gasped.

The barrel that held the coiled line began to jump. Then it turned over. I reached out and wrapped my arms around it. Mando wrapped his arms around me. The line made a hissing noise as it came out of the barrel.

"How much is left?" Mando said.

My face was close to the barrel and I could see the coils of line clearly. "Less than half."

The boat, as we stopped rowing, began to rock. It turned its beam to the waves that had come up and that made it rock worse.

"I'll hold the barrel," I said to Mando. "Take the oars and turn the bow into the wind."

He unloosened his hold on me and took up the oars. The boat righted itself.

The line was singing now. There was less than a third of it left.

"Brace yourself," I shouted to Mando.

At the same time I wedged the barrel under the forward thwart and held it there, with my feet braced against an oak rib.

---

3. Señor (sā nyôr'), Mr.

Before we left Mando had bored a hole in the bottom of the barrel, passed the line through the hole and tied a double knot. There was no way the line could come free.

The last loop whirred past my ear. There was a jar and the whole boat shivered, as if we had struck a rock. The line was taut as iron but it did not break. I clung to the barrel that was wedged against the thwart, using all my strength. Mando kept our bow into the wind. The pull on the line grew steady and now we were moving slowly toward the island.

"Maybe he will tow us to where we want to go," Mando said. "I'll speak to Zando[4] and he will speak to Señor Espada."

He said something under his breath and made a sign with three fingers. The great fish moved toward the island in a straight line. He was swimming deep but straight for the Island of the Blue Dolphins.

To ease the strain I asked Mando to throw a double rope around the barrel and tie it down. Then I let go of the barrel and took hold of the line. It was as thick through as my little finger and big and rough.

The wind shifted and the waves grew stronger. We started to take water aboard. We bailed as best we could and kept the water ankle deep.

The sun was overhead. It was hot and bounced off the sea. We were moving slower than we could row, but we moved. Then the line slanted at a different angle. It moved straight down and swung the boat around. We were now headed in the direction of Santa Cruz, which we had left at dawn.

After a time the line slackened. I pulled on it, putting a dozen coils and more back in the barrel again. Then a dozen more.

"We have lost him," said Mando.

"No, he is coming up. He is coming toward the boat."

The fish came on. The barrel was half full of line now. But there must have been three hundred feet out.

"Does he come still?" Mando asked.

"Still, but not fast."

---

4. Zando (zän′dō), an Indian god.

"It is big," he said.

"Maybe a marlin?"

"Too early for the señor. I have never seen him here in June. Nor has anyone. He comes from the south only when the sea is warm."

"How big do you think he is?"

We had now been hooked up to him since soon after dawn and now the sun was on its way into the west.

"He must be immense, Zia."

"How immense?"

"As big as three big men. If he was not, he would not pull us all over the ocean."

Mando knew more about the *pez espadas* than any fisherman at the Mission. He could tell them just by their fins when they lay far off sunning themselves.

The heavy line quit coming. I braced my feet against the ribs of the boat and pulled. We pulled together. But the fish slowly took the line out of our hands and then out of the barrel again.

"There is no more line left and he now pulls us," I said. "There has been a strain on the barrel all day. It might collapse sometime."

"I selected a barrel I have used before and have faith in," Mando said. "It is made of oak that is an inch in thickness. And it has five iron bands around it. It will hold as long as the line holds and that will be a long time. Make yourself comfortable and have patience. He will tire before we do."

I was tired already. My hands were bleeding.

"Place them in the water," Mando said. "But one at a time. I have a heavy load up here." He was braced at the bow, with the line looped once around the bit. "The salt water makes them feel better. Worse for a while, then better."

"I do not feel them at all," I said. "They are numb. They are not mine. They belong to someone else."

"Not to me. I already have a pair that are numb."

We rounded the kelp bed at the south point of Santa Cruz, moving slowly. It was better now. The sun was on my back and not in my eyes, and the water was not so rough. But I was tired and very angry.

"Remember again we did not come to fish for *espadas*," I said. "I am going to cut the line. Then we will turn around and go ashore and in the morning start for the island once more."

"You will cut the line with what?" Mando asked. "I have the knife. I have it in my belt. Perhaps you can cut the line with your teeth. They are big like the fish's teeth and you have many of them."

The drag stopped and the line no longer slanted out.

"He is going down. That is a good sign," said Mando.

He unloosened the line looped on the bit and we both took it in hand over hand.

"He is under us now," Mando said. "And coming up. Slow. But he comes."

We peered over the side of the boat and watched for him in the water that was clear but a deep blue.

Nightfall had come on gently. There was no wind and the sky was clear except for pink streaks in the west where the sun had been. I was trailing one hand in the cool water. Then I shifted across the thwart and trailed my other hand. They were still numb but they did not hurt so much and the blood had stopped.

Mando's cry must have been heard by those at the Mission, even by those who were asleep. I heard the cry before I saw the fish.

"Grande!"[5] shouted Mando. "Un gran pez espada."[6]

When I saw it first it was in the air about fifty yards off to our right. It seemed to be standing on its scythelike tail. The hook that Mando had made and polished in the workshop had gone into the bone of the fish's underjaw. His sword was longer than my arm and he thrashed it from side to side in an attempt to throw off the hook.

With a great splash he fell back in the water, into the same hole he had come from.

"Hold tight," Mando shouted. "But not too tight. Give him a chance to run."

The fish took out some line and jumped again and thrashed his sword. But he did not come in. He took out more line and we tied it to the bit and gave him the boat again to carry.

It was too dark to see now. By the evening star and then by the position of the Big Bear, the only constellation I knew, I thought we must be moving north and toward the

---

5. *Grande!* (grän′dä), Great!

6. *un gran pez espada* (ün grän′ päs′ es pä′ŦHä), a large swordfish.

coast. But I was not sure, though the compass pointed in the right direction. Even in the channel, the night wind was sharp and full of spray.

"Do we have tortillas?" Mando asked.

"Four apiece," I said and handed them up to him.

"And water."

I gave him the jug, which was half empty. "Do not drink like a camel," I cautioned him.

"How does a camel drink?" he asked.

Mando felt very good. He was thinking of all the praise he would receive when he got back to the Mission.

"The camel drinks all the water he can hold," I said. "And then he goes without water for weeks. Sometimes he bursts himself wide open after he drinks so much at one time."

"The fish will not last for weeks," Mando said. "He will last through the night. He will go slow now and wait for daylight. Then he will thrash about and put on a big fiesta and it will be his last."

Mando ate the four tortillas, taking his time, and drank one long swig of water. Then he sat for a while. Then he talked and by the time the moon was overhead he was asleep, snoring. He was without a worry.

I was too tired to sleep and afraid that we would run ashore, either on Santa Cruz Island or the coast. I was not sure where we were. We seemed to be following along the kelp bed that rimmed the island, but I could be wrong. The sea is not a good place to be when you are tired and hungry and worried. At no time is it a place to do foolish things.

At the first false dawn, a pearly gray in the east, I was aware that we were no longer moving. We were, as I had thought, near the kelp beds. The line was slack as if it had been broken. At some time during the night I could have fallen asleep and the fish could have broken free.

I began to take in the line, cautiously at first, and then hand over hand. As it came in I coiled it carefully in the big barrel. Mando lay in the bow, one hand trailing in the water, asleep as if he had never slept before.

The sun was up by the time that I caught sight of the big fish. He was about five boat lengths away and scarcely moving. Only his tail moved and very slowly. The way the rising sun slanted he was in the shadow of the boat, but I could see that he was about three arms' lengths away. My hands still bled and I guided the fish up to us, not forcing him. I crouched in the bottom of the boat, keeping out of sight, and making as few movements as possible.

I had the line wrapped around my left wrist as I brought him up, a foot at a time, putting my knees on the line as each strip came in. The sun was in Mando's face, but he did not move. He had a wonderful look as if he were listening to some heavenly music. All I could hear was the surf beating against the shore and then the sounds of the waves washing back from the cliffs and caves.

The big fish was not a *pez espada,* as Mando had thought it to be. His bill was a round spear, very long, and curved upward a little. His back was a purple blue and light blue bands ran from his back to his undersides, which were silver. I had seen marlin before and this was a marlin, a big one, the size of three large men and almost as long as the boat.

The fish stopped and I held the line softly, not moving, trying not to breathe. The hook was there in his lower jaw and looked solid. He came forward so that his pointed bill was even with the bow of the boat. His tail was barely moving. The big fin on his back caught the sun and showed violet and blue spots.

I crouched, watching him. His eyes moved, looking up at the boat and then at me. They were immense and once they had found me they did not shift away. In the sun they looked golden, but they were of different colors, some of the colors that were on his back.

His gaze did not move from me. It was strange to look into the eyes of a fish that looked back at you. It seemed to me, as I crouched there, that in his mind he knew that I was the cause of the hook in his mouth and the long fight through the day and the dark. And yet I saw no hatred in them. Only a sort of wonderment and surprise and besides all a look of submission.

Mando was sleeping, fighting off a cloud of gnats, but still in his sleep. I was close enough to him to touch his outstretched foot with mine. I thought of waking him, but feared that he would jump and arouse the fish into a last effort to free itself.

The harpoon and a gaff made of a long bamboo rod and iron lay within my reach. I could use either one. Or if I thought and planned carefully I would be able to use both on the great fish.

He was now even with the boat, leaning against it as if to rest. I could not see the marlin's eyes any longer. Only his purple back and the blue bands running down his sides. But I remembered his eyes and their look of surprise and submission. I could think of nothing else but his eyes looking at me.

Mando was asleep on his side. Leaning forward, I slipped his long knife from its sheath. I unloosed the line from my wrist and set it down squarely on the gunwale. The knife was sharp and it went through the line quickly.

The big fish had not moved. He did not know yet that he was free. I stood up and as I did the boat rocked against him. He started to move away. I tossed the severed line over the side. The fish saw the movement and began to edge away from the boat. He slanted downward, his fins barely moving. He became a long shadow and then a small shadow and was gone.

The iron hook in his jaw and the line would be eaten away in time by the sea, which ate everything. I sat back and for a while watched Mando sleeping. Then I picked up the oars and began to row.

The morning was clear and there was no wind. I headed back, up the coast toward the Mission of Santa Barbara. In one part of me I was glad the marlin had come between us and the ocean.

Mando was still asleep when we rounded Santa Cruz. It was midmorning. I gave him a kick in the shins and he came awake, staring about as if he had no idea where he was, on land or on the sea. But in one glance he saw that the big fish had gone.

He jumped to his feet. "What happened? *Qué pasa?*[7] My *pez espada.* Where is he?"

The line I cut lay at his feet beside his knife. Mando glanced at the line, at his knife, then at me.

"He is gone," I said. "He left while you were asleep."

Mando picked up the line I had cut and looked at it. "The line did not fray. It did not break from the fish's strength. The line was cut." He picked up his blade. "It was cut with a sharp knife. Like this one. I did not know that the *pez espada* carries a knife."

"They do not carry knives. Only people carry knives," I said. "When did we hook the fish?"

"Yesterday, in the morning."

---

7. *Qué pasa?* (kä pä′sä), What's happening?

"Then he was with us for almost a day," I said. "How would you like to be with a boat for almost a day at the end of a line—with an iron hook in your mouth? Would you like that, Señor fisherman? How would you like half a day? Or perhaps an hour would suit you better."

"I am not a fish."

"If you were, amigo, would you like an iron hook in your mouth?"

"You talk foolish talk," Mando said. "People are not fish."

"But fish also bleed. How would you like the blood for an afternoon and a night and a morning? How would the *sangre* taste, brother Mando?"

"*No tiene nada en la cabeza,*"[8] Mando said, put his knife back in its sheath, and stretched out to sleep again. "Next time I fish among fishermen," he said with great disgust.

"I have enough in my head," I answered, "to know that you are a poor sailor and when I go anywhere again it will be alone."

"I am still here," he said, looking at me through half-closed eyes. "I am still a sailor."

"About to fall asleep."

"I am still here, I repeat. We have lost more than a day, but the weather is good. We have enough food. Let us continue what we have begun."

I nodded my head, yet I was afraid of the wind and the wild seas I had seen. I was afraid all over—in my stomach and in my head.

Zia and Mando did not reach the Island of the Blue Dolphins. However, Zia persuaded Captain Nidever to rescue Aunt Karana when he next sailed to the island. Aunt Karana left the island willingly to live with Zia on the California coast.

---

8. *No tiene nada en la cabeza* (nō tyā′nä nä′ᵮHä än lä kä bä′sä), You have nothing in your head. You don't know anything.

Comprehension Check

See your Thinker's Handbook for tips.

Think and Discuss

1. Compare Zia's and Mando's goals and explain what their conflict is about.
2. Why do you think Mando wants to catch the big fish?
3. How does Mando react to Zia's letting the fish go?
4. How is Mando's personality different from Zia's?
5. If you had been Zia, would you have cut the fish loose? Explain.

Comprehension Skill: Comparisons

Communication Workshop

Talk

Zia narrates this story and we learn most of what we know about Mando from what Zia says and feels about him. If Mando were telling the story perhaps he would describe the events differently and tell us how he feels about them. Work with a partner to retell some incidents from Mando's point of view. One of you could retell the part in which Mando hangs onto the marlin. The other might choose the part when Mando realizes Zia has freed the marlin.

Speaking/Listening: Role-playing

Write

Pretend you are Scott O'Dell and have decided to rewrite some of the story from Mando's point of view. Write a paragraph about one of the incidents you have discussed. Tell what happened and how Mando felt about it. Read your paragraph to your partner and see if you both understand Mando better.

Writing Fluency: Paragraphs

The Quarrel

by Eleanor Farjeon

I quarreled with my brother,
I don't know what about,
One thing led to another
And somehow we fell out.
The start of it was slight,
The end of it was strong,
He said he was right,
I knew he was wrong!

We hated one another.
The afternoon turned black.
Then suddenly my brother
Thumped me on the back,
And said, "Oh, *come* along!
We can't go on all night—
I was in the wrong."
So he was in the right.

Jade Snow Wong tells the true-life events of a major incident in her family's life—the renewing of an ancient Chinese tradition. Pay attention to the sequence of these events. Notice in particular the steps that detail how the family re-created this ancient Chinese art.

The
PHOENIX

by Jade Snow Wong

Toward the end of February when the winter rains temporarily halted, we took the children for a Sunday drive. Near San Francisco's long Marina Green, Ming Tao (ming dou) noticed a number of flying kites—the kind made of two crossed sticks covered with printed plastic. "Daddy, will you buy me a kite like those?" he asked.

Woody was scornful. "They are so simple, and the plastic stretches. See how they flap? See how some keep diving for lack of balance? So they fly, but are they beautiful or graceful?"

To help Ming Tao understand that kites could be more than toys, I explained, "Kites have been a great Chinese pastime. By the old lunar calendar, kite flying began in the seventh month.[1] On the ninth day of the ninth month, after a great feast, the season's kites were released to the skies. Each season, a family created another new kite."

---

1. The seventh month, about September 1.

Ming Tao was fascinated. "I didn't know all that."

Woody picked up the subject. "You know, those old kites ranged in shape from a dragon to a centipede. They might carry decorations like mirrors, feathers, or tassels. I've heard of some small enough to fit into your palm and others large enough to lift a person."

"But, Daddy, you were born in San Francisco. Did Grandfather tell you about them?"

"As you know, I was born at Brenham Place and Clay Street, facing Portsmouth Square," Woody began. "There I noticed flying kites with fantastic shapes, maneuvered by a white-haired, white-mustached man. Finally I talked him into teaching me his tricks."

When we got to Grandmother's apartment, Woody explained our new interest.

Grandmother exclaimed with surprising excitement, "Don't tell me that Ming Tao is going to take up kites!"

Woody was astonished. "I was only telling him *about* kites. Who said anything about flying them?"

"Please, Daddy, you know so much about kites. I want to learn how to make and fly one too," begged Ming Tao.

Woody replied, "It isn't that easy. Chinese kites can be made only from select bamboo and a special paper. It's been so many years since I made a kite, I don't know where I can get those things."

Our son was unconvinced. "I see bamboo all over Chinatown."

"Any bamboo won't do. Kite bamboo should be large in diameter and straight, with its joints or nodes some inches apart."

"But if you made a kite, can't I try too? Please help me," Ming Tao begged.

"I'll think about it," Woody promised. So, one Saturday, after Ming Tao had learned his lessons, Woody offered to search for kite materials.

With our young daughters Lai Yee (lī yē) and Lai Wai (lī wī) and our sons Ming Tao and tiny Ming Choy (ming choi), we went to a small shop which specialized in bamboo accessories and furniture. Woody greeted the store's proprietor, Mr. Kong, and explained our quest. Mr. Kong disappeared into his basement and returned with several lengths of bamboo, from half an inch (1.3 cm) to two inches (5 cm) in diameter.

Mr. Kong picked out a straight, refined-looking length.

"This is what you want, Tonkin bamboo from China. I have a limited supply imported prior to 1950."

Woody examined it and marveled, "The nodes are as widely spaced as any I have seen—over a foot apart."

Woody counted three dollar bills, but Mr. Kong refused. "I don't want you to pay me. Take these samples with my good wishes for fun ahead."

With this partial success, we were encouraged to begin our search for kite paper. We went to a store on Grant Avenue, and Woody asked about kite paper.

"It is this kind of paper," replied the clerk. "I use small squares to wrap the slippers which I sell."

He produced a square of light buff paper with a visible vertical grain. "You can tear off many strips of this paper along its grain, but you cannot tear horizontally. Its lightness, softness, and strength come from its unique fiber content," he explained.

At home, our family gathered to design our kite, and I wondered, "I have never seen a dragonfly kite. Will that work?"

"Why not?" asked Woody. "Strange, neither have I. Ming Tao, go get your book on insects."

In the illustrated section on the dragonfly family, there was a "May Fly." I liked its wider wing formation and long, graceful tail. "Let's try to make a 'May Fly.'"

Woody sketched a design. He got our ax and a sharp, stout boning knife, and put on a pair of working gloves.

"Let's go downstairs to the garden room," he said.

The family watched as he achieved the first split. With the second split, he obtained a straight piece about three-eighths of an inch (0.9 cm) wide.

Woody said, "I am working on the three most important structural parts: the two front ribs for the wings and the body. These lengths must be sound and straight."

Seated on a stool, Woody whittled until the sticks were free of splinters. As he worked, he told us, "Kites have long been a Chinese family project. An adult starts teaching the children."

He continued to show our son. "You can whittle and work as much as you want. Then we will all make the bamboo as smooth as possible with fine sandpaper. But for now this is good enough. Let's go to the kitchen and shape these sticks."

Woody held the bamboo length of the May Fly body so that its midpoint was over an open pot of boiling water. After the steam softened the bamboo, he gradually bent it until both ends met, and he fastened this loop with an elastic.

Woody was searching. "Where is the paste I asked you to make?"

It is possible to use store-bought white glue, but as a part of our home product, I had made the paste. Woody tore off half-inch-wide (1.3 cm) strips of the kite paper; after moistening them with the paste, he lashed and overlapped them around each kite joint. Then Ming Tao took over, following his father's example.

Slowly, over a series of hours, the skeleton of the kite evolved. The wing stretch of four feet (1.2 m) was attached to the center hollow body frame. Woody instructed Ming Tao to attach cross-bracing at various points of the body frame. Then using two quarter-inch-deep (0.6 cm), two-inch-diameter (5 cm) bamboo rounds for eyes, Woody drilled holes straight so they would rotate around a ten-inch (25 cm) bamboo skewer. Our son became excited as he saw the kite taking shape. Carefully, he lashed the skewer across the head. Sections of plastic conduit kept the eyes in place.

Woody surveyed its looks. "It's too complicated to fasten the May Fly's second pair of lower wings. This would look better and handle more easily if we added a tail section." So he redesigned and constructed the tail, which was hinged to the body with two twine loops. The frame was finished.

"OK," Woody said. "It's all yours."

Ming Tao was dismayed. "I haven't covered a kite before."

"You have the paper. All you do is lay the frame on it and draw the outline, cut, and glue it to the bamboo. You've been cutting and gluing ever since I can remember."

When his son occasionally had trouble, Woody relented to give him a hand. When the tissue wrinkled, a fine spray of water tightened the slack. At the lower edges of the wings, Ming Tao pasted double thicknesses of tissue for reinforcement. What started to be a May Fly looked more like a gigantic bird, too big to handle at home, so it was transported to my studio.

The fun part for Ming Tao was painting the bird. He used poster colors in swirls of magenta, yellow, orange, and blue. One side of the tissue-covered eyes was red and the other side green. Painting was Ming Tao's forte. The kite was named "Phoenix."[2]

The job of searching and working, on and off, had taken months, during which Ming Tao doubted and Woody remained confident. At last they would fly it, Ming Tao still doubting, and Woody still confident. From his tackle box, Woody took a saltwater fishing-reel. He said to me, "Bring some strips of rags for the tail of the kite. I am not sure how many I need, depending on the air currents and how this goes up."

"I'm not going to bring any old rags. Let me find something that would look nice in the air," I replied. Black, natural, white, and red raw silk left over from pajamas made an artistic partnership. We put the kite, the fabric, and the reel in the car. Our daughters Lai Yee and Lai Wai got in the back seat with their brothers Ming Tao and Ming Choy.

We drove to the Marina Green. Woody pierced two tiny holes in the kite about midpoint on each of the forward wing frames and another hole at the end of the body. He cut off enough twine from his fishing-reel to form a triangular bridle. Then he fastened the reel line to the bridle. Some strips of raw silk were tied to the tail.

The moment Phoenix was lifted from the car it was eager and restless, catching the slightest wind movement and reaching for heights. Woody remarked, "Wind currents are tricky; although not apparent at ground level, higher up they may be strong." The kite went up, but soon it swooped and darted. Woody looked at it critically. "More tail," he muttered, and reeled it in.

We attached more tail, but the kite would not gain height; again, it was pulled in. The younger children wandered off, but Ming Tao became anxious as I attached more cloth. Finally, I gave up and tied a whole yard (0.9 m) of red silk at the end.

Thank goodness, that gave it weight. The kite rose like the mythical phoenix, up and up. Its powerful wing span in brilliant waves of color soared against the pale blue sky. Its revolving red and blue eyes gazed downward at the world. The wings flapped continuously in lively fashion at an angle to its body.

---

2. Phoenix (fē′niks), a bird of Greek mythology that every five hundred years or more destroyed itself by fire and then arose from the ashes with restored youth and beauty.

Ming Tao was enchanted. "Let me hold the reel now."

Then each daughter returned, wanting to hold the reel. Even tiny Ming Choy was successful with his turn. The bird seemed to hypnotize casual onlookers into a captive audience. Drivers stopped their cars for a better look.

After we had our fun, the kite was brought to the studio and hung by its beak, waiting to be flown again, the only one of its kind in all the world. If Phoenix could talk, it would have told of a Chinese-American family re-creating a Chinese art more than two thousand years old.

Meet the Author

Jade Snow Wong is the daughter of Chinese immigrants and was born in San Francisco in 1922. She has written two books about her dual Chinese-American heritage—*Fifth Chinese Daughter* (1950) and *No Chinese Stranger* (1975). In 1976 she received the Silver Medal for nonfiction from the Commonwealth Club of San Francisco. She has also been the owner of a ceramics gallery in San Francisco for over forty years and has won several awards for her pottery.

Jade Snow Wong, when asked about the events in "The Phoenix," said, "The Phoenix hangs at the loft on my ceramics studio, being too large to be accommodated in the average home. It was flown once again by Ming Choy when he was older, as a one-time repeat, since Ming Choy remembered when his brother flew it. Phoenix is a strong flyer, and high up the currents rip the fragile paper, making it necessary to mend it each time it was flown. We didn't build other kites. The construction of Phoenix became a complete family historical episode."

Comprehension Check

Think and Discuss

1. What ancient Chinese tradition do Jade Snow Wong and her family renew?
2. Why doesn't Mr. Kong charge Woody for the bamboo?
3. What characteristics does Woody display as he teaches Ming Tao how to make the kite?
- 4. At the same time that Ming Tao doubts that the kite will fly, how does Woody feel?
- 5. Put the following steps for making Phoenix in order. You may wish to refer to parts of the selection.
  a. Attach the wing stretch to the body frame.
  b. Whittle the sticks free of splinters.
  c. Split the bamboo into straight pieces.
  d. Sketch a design of the kite.
  e. Soften and bend the bamboo.
  f. Cut and glue the paper to the frame.
  g. Attach silk to make a tail.
- Comprehension Skills: Time sequence, Steps in a process

Communication Workshop

Talk

Work with two other classmates to gather information from the story about the different shapes, sizes, and decorations of ancient Chinese kites. Have each member of your group choose one of these areas and be ready to talk about it to the other two. After each person has presented his or her facts to the others, decide for yourself how you would combine the elements of size, shape, and decoration to make the ideal kite of your choice.
Speaking/Listening: Cooperative learning

Write

Write a short paragraph that describes your ideal kite. Use specific words to describe its size, shape, and how it is decorated. Illustrate your paragraph and display it with those of your classmates on the bulletin board.
Writing Fluency: Paragraphs

Using PQ2R

You have just learned how to follow a sequence of steps to make an ancient Chinese kite. You can also follow a sequence of steps, called PQ2R, to get the most from what you read and to organize your study time.

PQ2R has four steps: Preview, Question, Read, and Review. To preview, you take a quick look ahead at a story or an article to get a general idea of the contents. To question, ask yourself what you expect to learn. Then read the story or article with your questions in mind and look for the answers. After reading, review to see if your questions were answered and then reread or skim if they weren't. When you take a test, it is especially helpful to review by making a list of the main points in an article or by writing down the plot of a story.

Before you read the next selection, you can begin to use PQ2R. Preview the pages. What do you think the selection will be about? Write two questions you think the selection might answer. Then when you do read the selection, keep your questions in mind. After the reading, review to see if your questions were answered.

Ever since Cousin Edward has come to live with the narrator's family, something incredible has happened every Thanksgiving. In fact, several members of the family have come to dread this time of the year. Notice the cause and effect relationships in this humorous story that help you realize what causes this year's celebration to be the most incredible yet— even by this zany family's standards.

The WORST Thanksgiving in the Entire History of the Universe

by Bill Conklin

The worst Thanksgiving in the entire history of the universe occurred during my senior year in high school. It began with a note from my mother's sister Carrie, inviting us from our house in Duxbury to her house in Boothbay Harbor for "the best Thanksgiving ever."

Mother accepted at once, saying it would do her frail and awkward cousin Edward, a student of photography who boarded with us at the time, a world of good. Mother was always concerned about Edward at Thanksgiving because he was afraid of it. I don't mean depressed by it, as some people are by certain holidays; I mean scared silly of it. And with good reason. Edward maintained that "something awful" had happened to him every Thanksgiving of his otherwise uneventful life. We could definitely vouch for the two Thanksgivings he'd lived with us.

On the first one, Edward went for a walk before dinner, and a cow drove him deeper and deeper into the salt marshes behind our house. He found temporary sanctuary in an old dinghy, but the mooring lines parted and we found him floating and screaming down the inlet. The cow stood stiff-legged, defiantly bellowing bon voyage. The glint in my father's eye as he watched Edward drift away indicated he was of two minds about going after him. But Mother prevailed.

The following Thanksgiving the whole family was awakened by more Edwardian screams. We raced to his room. He was standing up wild-eyed in the middle of the bed, shouting that "something awful" had bitten him.

There were certainly signs of it; three ugly red welts had appeared on his stomach, and they grew larger as we stared. Mother's mother, Grandma Bell, said, "if they meet around his middle, he's a goner."

It wasn't what Edward wanted to hear. He clutched his stomach and began a wild dance on the bed. Father summoned our neighbor Doctor Peters, who came at once. He gave Edward some ointment to heal the welts.

In my opinion, the only thing worse than spending Thanksgiving at home with Edward was having Thanksgiving dinner in Maine with Aunt Carrie and Uncle Warren. Aunt Carrie was probably the worst cook in New England. Added to that, she loved to cook. Carrie's kitchen was her castle. She shared it with another cook whose culinary skills closely matched her own—her husband, Warren.

Every Thanksgiving Warren roasted a monstrous thing he called "The Twenty-four-Hour Turkey." His preparations began at six o'clock on Thanksgiving Eve, and with the aid of an alarm clock that woke him every hour for what he called "The Bastings," he produced "The T-Bird at Six of T-Day." Nobody in our family had actually sampled his turkey, but unsettling rumors about it trickled down to us. We heard it emerged from the oven in a charred shell that had to be cracked open.

As for my father, he agreed to spend Thanksgiving away from home only after several long, thoughtful looks at Edward. If he considered the trip the lesser of two evils, it was because Mother managed to suppress all the bad news that arrived in subsequent letters from Maine. Warren, we learned, was going to attempt the biggest Twenty-four-Hour Turkey ever, while Carrie was planning a gourmet menu of Thanksgiving dishes from around the world. (In her mind, Pilgrims and Plymouth Rocks apparently stretched from Austria to Australia.)

The most suppressible news by far, however, was that Carrie and Warren had decided to combine Thanksgiving with a family reunion; "everybody" was coming.

When we arrived, Uncle Warren in white chef's hat and apron descended on my father and called him "Old Sock from Sockertown." Father fled to the front piazza. Edward backed up to a wall in the study. Mother, Grandma Bell, and I went in search of Aunt Carrie. We found her in the kitchen, laboring over a long harvest table piled high with concave pies, soggy salads, and at least ten casseroles best described as burnt efforts. Small foreign flags were stuck in them. On the flags were printed the names of the dishes, in languages known only to Carrie.

In the center of the table was a huge chocolate tower rising unsteadily toward the ceiling. I knew it was a THANKSGIVING CAKE because Carrie had emblazoned these words on it in scarlet frosting. The cake was strangely pockmarked, and in some places shot clean through with Swiss-cheese holes. It brooded ominously over the whole buffet, a science-fiction confection which I felt could double its mass at any time and destroy us all.

One part of the kitchen was entirely off limits. That was the giant wall oven that held Uncle Warren's Twenty-four-Hour Turkey. Warren had rigged an old shower curtain to protect the area from public view, and from time to time he'd disappear behind it to slam things about.

As the afternoon wore on, more of Mother's relatives arrived to poke bony fingers in Father's ribs and thump him between the shoulder blades. If he sought refuge in the kitchen, Warren would leap at him from behind the curtain.

Six o'clock came and went. At seven, people began to whisper about a Twenty-five-Hour Turkey. They also began to mill about, circle each other warily, and stand in sullen groups.

The front doorbell rang. It was my Aunt Joan and Uncle Dave. Dave was carrying something that made Father smile for the first time that day: a big turkey, crisply browned, plump, aromatic, beautiful.

Mother hurried forward, her hand raised in some secret warning, and tried to shoo Dave out the door. But just then Uncle Warren came out of the kitchen.

"You call that a turkey?" he snorted. We all studied the bird solemnly. It was difficult to call it anything else, I thought. Then Uncle Warren uttered a line which has become a family classic. "Put away your turkey," he declared. "Your turkey's no good here. You want to see a *turkey,* follow me!"

We trooped to the kitchen. Cousin Edward was already there. Carrie and Warren had arranged for him to take a picture of the Twenty-four-Hour Turkey presentation. Edward stood behind one of those old-fashioned box cameras mounted on a wooden tripod. I'd watched Edward operate a variety of cameras in the last two years. His pictures had one thing in common. Few of them ever came out. At Warren's command, he stuck his head resolutely under the black cloth at the back of the camera, and stood ready. Warren yanked down the shower curtain, slowly opened the oven door, and stepped proudly to one side.

There are conflicting opinions about what happened after that. The consensus is that Warren lost his hotmitt grip on the enormous roasting pan, and the turkey fell to the floor and skidded to the center of the room. What Father and I say is, twenty-five hours is too long to cook a Twenty-four-Hour Turkey. We think some potent combination of gases built up within the bird and catapulted it forward—a turkey cannonball.

In any event, a turkey was loose amongst us, wreathed in smoke, coated with a dense charred crust, sinister, vengeful, the symbol of all doomed Thanksgiving turkeys past. We stood transfixed as the creature began to hiss and pulsate. Soon it was revolving in a slow circle on the floor. Then it angled itself upward like some incredible cannon. It was aimed precisely at the spot where Edward crouched, frozen, behind the camera.

A low murmur swept the room. The turkey sputtered and sizzled and rocked back and forth once. Then suddenly the air was filled with flying bits and pieces of Uncle Warren's T-Bird.

Some say it exploded. Some say it imploded. One thing is certain: a great many people were diving for cover, and Edward led all the rest.

Clutching camera and tripod to his chest, head still buried under the cloth, Edward bounced backward, bucking and screaming, into Aunt Carrie's buffet table. For a long moment the THANKSGIVING CAKE seemed equal to him, but then his quivering body broke its resistance and sliced through it, collapsing the table into a V beneath his supine form. Dish after dish gathered momentum and crashed down on Edward.

When the smoke began to clear I managed to get Edward upstairs to a hall bedroom where he huddled uncomforted beneath a comforter, muttering "something awful" over and over again.

I returned to the kitchen to find Grandma Bell and Father (both of them had remained standing throughout the entire fracas, watching the scene with unabashed delight) organizing a cleanup squad. Mother had disappeared into the stormy night with most of her relatives. They came back from the cars with a brand-new Thanksgiving dinner.

Although Aunt Joan and Uncle Dave had prematurely displayed their turkey, it hadn't been prepared by chance. Mother had instructed everybody to bring a Thanksgiving dish, and hold it in reserve. She told Carrie tactfully it was "in case more people came than you'd expected." Mother was always a person of great resource. As she said at the time, "Expect the worst and when it comes, it won't be."

It was close to twelve o'clock before we washed and finished stacking dishes. Mother prepared a tray for Edward. I took it up to Edward, but he was in a deep sleep. I couldn't rouse him. He moaned once, the moan of a man who might possibly have a photo of an exploding turkey in his camera, and then a big smile crossed his face.

His smile puzzled me for a moment before I figured it out. The grandfather clock in the hall was striking midnight. The worst Thanksgiving in the entire history of the universe was over, and Edward was smiling because it would be a whole year before "something awful" happened to him again.

Comprehension Check

Think and Discuss

- 1. What causes this Thanksgiving to be incredible?
  2. How does the narrator feel about celebrating Thanksgiving at Carrie and Warren's home? Why?
  3. The narrator says that Warren's line "You want to see a *turkey*, follow me!" became a family classic. What does the narrator's statement foreshadow, or lead you to think might happen next?
  4. Do you think the relatives are sorry the dinner was ruined? Why or why not?
- 5. What do you think would probably have been the effect if the narrator's mother had not arranged for the extra food?
- Comprehension Skill: Cause and effect relationships

Communication Workshop

Talk

    Have a group discussion about how the narrator, his father, his mother, and Edward will remember this Thanksgiving in Maine. Imagine that an outsider has listened to the story and has said, "What a disaster *your* Thanksgiving turned out to be!" Then take turns being each of the characters and try to find something good, positive, or even entertaining to talk about that makes the day seem less of a disaster.
Speaking/Listening: Group discussion

Write

    Combine what you have read and discussed with your own ideas and imagine that you are one of the four characters. Write a four- or five-sentence "Thank You" note to Uncle Warren and Aunt Carrie that includes something about the holiday that you can honestly thank them for. Read your notes to your classmates. Did you agree or disagree about what was honestly positive?
Writing Fluency: Thank you notes

LOOKING BACK

See your Thinker's Handbook for tips.

Prewriting

Thinking and Writing About the Section
You have just read about three families: a sister and brother on an ocean trip, a family re-establishing a tradition, and a wild family holiday. Imagine how an incident in one story might be different if a character from another story was present. You can write a narrative paragraph for your classmates to describe such an incident. First think about the different characters you read about. Then copy the chart and talk with a partner to fill in the missing information.

Characters	Traits	Favorite Incident
Mando		catching big fish
Woody		
Carrie		
Edward	sickly, excitable	

Writing

Use the information in your chart to write a narrative paragraph to describe an incident in one story that includes a character from another story. For instance, what might happen if Edward, rather than Zia, were in the boat with Mando? Your paragraph should tell about the events in the order in which they happened. For more information on narrative paragraphs, see your Writer's Handbook.

Revising

Read your first draft to a partner. Does it tell about all the events that took place in order? Does it tell about the part each character played? Make changes if necessary. Then proofread for spelling and punctuation errors. Write your final copy.

Presenting

Read your paragraph aloud to your classmates. Ask if they agree about how the different character you chose would have acted in the incident you wrote about. If they do not agree, ask how they would have written the scene.

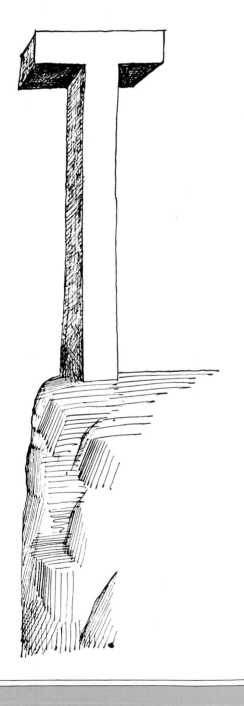

The Power of Words

A word is dead
When it is said,
Some say.

I say it just
Begins to live
That day.

Emily Dickinson

Words are powerful tools that have a life of their own. The power of words is especially evident in each of the selections you will read in this section. You'll see how spoken and written words are used to persuade, to paint mental pictures, to inform, and to inspire. Perhaps some of these words will be kept alive in your mind for many years to come.

Understanding Character

Have you ever seen a play acted out on a stage before an audience, such as the one shown in the photograph above? Perhaps you have seen one in school or at a theater. You may have even taken part in a play yourself. When you see a play, you learn about the characters by watching how the actors and actresses act and use gestures, by listening to their tone of voice, and by noticing what the other actors and actresses say to them. When you read a play, you learn about characters by reading their written parts and the stage directions they follow.

Characters in stories and plays are very important elements. **Characters** are the people and, sometimes, the animals in a story. The most important character is called the **main character** and there can be more than one main character.

When you read, do you try to get to know the characters? Do you try to figure out what they are like? Doing so will make the characters seem to come alive and can make a story or a play more enjoyable for you.

One way an author lets you know about a character is through the character's words, actions, and thoughts. Authors may also give a physical description to help you picture the character. Or they may show what other characters in the story think or feel, and what they say to or about the character.

Read this part of a play below. As you read, see what you can learn about the characters. Think about what they say, think, and do. Then decide how they feel and what kind of people they are.

On the Fence

by Marcia Moray Beach

CHARACTERS

    MRS. MILES

    TOM MILES

TIME: *Saturday morning*

PLACE: *A backyard with a picket fence*

AT CURTAIN RISE: *Mrs. Miles is hanging out some washing while Tom paints the fence.*

TOM: Jeepers, Mom! Why did you have to pick today to make me paint this old fence?

MRS. MILES: You've been putting it off for the past week, Tom. As far as I can see, any day would be wrong. You might as well settle down and get it over with.

TOM: But there's baseball practice this morning! And our big game with Central is next week.

MRS. MILES: You had baseball practice all *last* week too. I doubt if a big-league player spends as much time at practice as you do. Now get on with that painting, Tom.

TOM *(muttering):* What a break! Stuck here all day.

MRS. MILES: What's that you're saying, Tom?

TOM: Nothing, Mom. *(He starts painting with exaggerated speed.)*

MRS. MILES: Not so fast, there! You've skipped a place. Maybe someone will come along and help you. Remember how it happened in *Tom Sawyer?*

TOM: Who was he?

MRS. MILES: Tom Miles, don't tell me you've never heard of *Tom Sawyer!*

1. How does Tom feel about painting the fence?

When answering, did you look both at what Tom says as well as at the stage directions that show how he acts? Tom feels unhappy about painting the fence. If you had difficulty, reread and note that Tom says he wants to go to baseball practice and feels "stuck." Also notice the stage directions that state that Tom is "muttering" and "painting with exaggerated speed."

2. What kind of a person do you think Mrs. Miles is? Why?

Did you look to see what Mrs. Miles says to Tom? She is kind, yet determined that he will paint the fence because she says such comments to Tom as, "settle down and get it over with," and "get on with that painting, Tom." If you didn't answer correctly, reread and notice what Mrs. Miles says to Tom that shows you how she reacts to him not wanting to paint the fence.

3. Which of these words—hardworking, lazy, or cheerful—describe Tom? Why?

Practicing Character

Reread the pages from "Zia" indicated below and think about the characters.

1. Describe the marlin in "Zia" by using the details that tell about its physical appearance. (page 32)
2. What kind of a person is Zia? Use examples of what she thinks and does when she sees the fish gazing at her. (pages 32–34)
3. Why does Mando want to catch "an *espada* as big as a boat"? What does this tell you about the kind of person he is? (page 25)

Tips for Reading on Your Own
• Get to know characters by paying attention to what they say, think, and do; and by seeing if the author gives physical descriptions.
• Think about what the other characters think or say about the character.

Welcome to Natalia's parlor wherein sits Lomov, her suitor. Lomov, beset by arguments and fainting spells, tries to find the words to ask for her hand in marriage. Will he ever propose and win her hand? As you read, pay attention to what the characters think, say, and feel.

A Proposal of Marriage

by Anton Chekhov
adapted by Paul T. Nolan

CHARACTERS

 MR. STEPANOVITCH, *an old farmer*

 NATALIA, *his daughter*

 LOMOV, *their bachelor neighbor*

TIME: *The late nineteenth century.*

SETTING: *The formal, nineteenth-century parlor of* STEPANOVITCH's *home in rural Russia. There is one entrance up center,[1] and another at left center. A draped window is up right of the upstage entrance. In front of the window is a stiff-looking love seat. Everything about the room suggests that it is used only for formal occasions.*

AT RISE: STEPANOVITCH *is standing up center, peeking through the drapes,* NATALIA *is sitting in chair down right, knitting.*

---

1. Theater terms: center, the center of the stage; up, toward the back of the stage; down, toward the audience; right, left, an actor's right or left as he or she faces the audience.

STEPANOVITCH: I think I see him coming.

NATALIA (starting to gather up her knitting): I'll go to the kitchen.

STEPANOVITCH: Don't you like our good neighbor, Lomov?

NATALIA: I like Lomov well enough, but he's such a big baby. There is always something wrong with him—his heart, his liver, his lungs, his right arm, his left arm, his right eye, his left ear. Fifteen minutes with Lomov is like reading a medical book for an hour.

STEPANOVITCH: Men get like that when they live alone too long.

NATALIA: He doesn't have to be a bachelor. Of course, I would feel sorry for any woman married to a big baby like that. And then, he has too many opinions too.

STEPANOVITCH (still looking out window): Aha, he almost slipped and fell into the ditch.

NATALIA: He is also clumsy.

STEPANOVITCH: I like Lomov. He is an easy man to beat in an argument.

NATALIA: Good, then you talk to him.

STEPANOVITCH: I just thought. Suppose he has come to borrow money!

NATALIA: He's your friend, Papa.

STEPANOVITCH: I won't give him any.
(There is a knock on door up center.)
He's here.

NATALIA: I'm gone. (She exits left center.)

STEPANOVITCH (opening door): Who is this I see at my own door? Why, Lomov! I am so glad to see you. (as LOMOV enters) How are you?

LOMOV (coming down center, carrying his hat): Thank you, Mr. Stepanovitch. I am all right, I guess. Hot and tired from the walk, but all right, I guess. How are you?

STEPANOVITCH: All right, I guess. Please sit down. (LOMOV sits stiffly in love seat.) It isn't right for people to forget their neighbors. (Sits in chair down right, rises quickly, holding knitting needle.) Natalia's needle. Women are forever leaving things around where they shouldn't be.

LOMOV: Yes, yes. How is your daughter?

STEPANOVITCH: All right, I guess. But tell me, my good friend, what is the reason for such a formal visit? Coat and tie and your hat in your hand? Are you on your way to give a lecture or preach a sermon?

LOMOV: No, I have no engagement with anyone but you, Mr. Stepanovitch.

STEPANOVITCH: Then why are you all dressed up? This isn't New Year's Eve, you know.

LOMOV: Well, it's . . . it's just . . . (Rises, looks straight ahead.) I have come to you Stepan Stepanovitch, to trouble you with a request. It is not the first time I have had the honor of turning to you for assistance, and you have always—(his voice breaks)—excuse me. I beg your pardon, I am a little excited. Could I have a glass of water?
(STEPANOVITCH goes down left to table with water pitcher, and pours a glass of water.)

STEPANOVITCH (aside): He has come to borrow money. I should have fled with Natalia. But he won't get a cent from me. (Giving water to LOMOV.) What is it you are asking of me, my good friend?

LOMOV: Well, you see, my dear Mr. Stepanovitch, my good friend, my old neighbor, my . . . my . . . *(Drains glass and hands it back to* STEPANOVITCH.*)* I am terribly nervous, as you can probably see.

STEPANOVITCH: To be sure. To be sure. Sit down, old fellow.

LOMOV *(sitting)*: What I mean to say is . . . You are the only man in the world who can help me. To be sure, I don't deserve it, and I have no right—no right at all—to make this request of you.

STEPANOVITCH: My dear Lomov, I have no idea what you are talking about. What is it you want from me?

LOMOV: I shall get to that. Immediately. In a minute or so.

STEPANOVITCH *(going back to chair and sitting)*: How about now?

LOMOV: Here it is, then: I have come to ask for the hand of your daughter, Natalia Stepanovitch, in marriage.

STEPANOVITCH *(rising; pleased)*: My dear friend, my good neighbor, dear Lomov, would you mind repeating that? I didn't quite hear you.

LOMOV: I have the honor to request the hand . . .

STEPANOVITCH: Of course, of course. My dear, dear man. *(He goes to* LOMOV, *who rises.)* I am so happy that everything is . . . so . . . so everything. *(Hugs him.)* I have wanted this to happen for so long. It has always been my dearest wish. It was Natalia's mother's dearest wish.

LOMOV: I didn't think Mrs. Stepanovitch liked me.

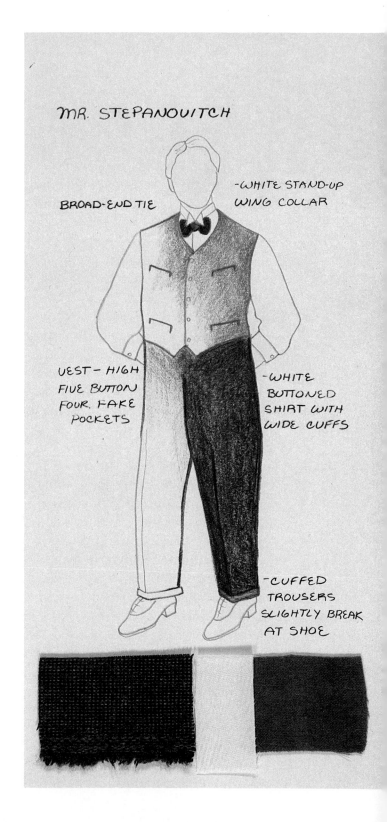

MR. STEPANOVITCH

BROAD-END TIE

-WHITE STAND-UP WING COLLAR

VEST - HIGH FIVE BUTTON FOUR FAKE POCKETS

-WHITE BUTTONED SHIRT WITH WIDE CUFFS

-CUFFED TROUSERS SLIGHTLY BREAK AT SHOE

STEPANOVITCH: She loved you. If she were alive today she would tell you so. And I have always loved you, too, my dear friend. I've loved you like my own son. I've always wanted this marriage to take place. *(Moves away.)* But why am I standing here like a fool? I am overcome with pleasure, completely overwhelmed. This is the moment of the greatest happiness of my life. I'll call Natalia. *(Starts for door, left.)*

LOMOV: But Mr. Stepanovitch, just a minute. What do you think? Will Natalia accept me?

STEPANOVITCH *(turning)*: A good-looking handsome fellow like you? What do you think? Natalia was telling me, just this very morning, how much she admires you. I think she has always loved you. But I shall fetch the lady herself. *(Exits center.)*

LOMOV *(sitting, standing, then sitting)*: I'm cold. My whole body is trembling as though I were here for a medical examination. But I'll wait it out. The important thing is to be settled. If a person thinks too much or waits for the ideal love, he never gets married. But I'm cold. Natalia is an excellent housekeeper, not bad-looking, and well-educated. What more can I ask? I'm so excited that my ears are ringing. *(Goes to table with water, pours a glass of water, and starts to drink it.)* It doesn't do for a man to stay single. I'm thirty-five years old, a critical age, so to speak. I must have a well-regulated life. I have a weak heart, continual palpitations, and I am very sensitive and always get excited. *(Takes sip of water, sets glass down, returns to love seat.)* My lips are trembling. The pulse in my right temple throbs terribly. Sleep is worst of all. Every night when I lie down to sleep, my arms, my legs, my head—they all start aching. Ah, poor me. *(Sits.)*

NATALIA *(entering right)*: Oh, it's you, Lomov. Papa said there was a dealer out here who had come to buy something. He must have been joking. How have you been, Lomov?

LOMOV *(starting to rise)*: Very well, Natalia, and you?

NATALIA: No, no, keep your seat. *(Sits in chair down right.)* I can only stay a few minutes. I have a cake in the oven.

LOMOV: A few minutes will be fine.

NATALIA: I see that you are all dressed up. You will have to excuse my wearing my apron and this old dress. We are working here today.

LOMOV: No, that is fine. Very fine.

NATALIA: Why don't you come around and see us more often? Would you like something to eat?

LOMOV: No, thank you. I just had my lunch.

NATALIA: Then rest. It's a fine day today. Only yesterday it was raining so hard that the workmen couldn't do a stroke of work in the meadows. How are you coming with the wheat harvest? I was so anxious to have the hayfields mowed that I had the men work overtime, and they got everything out. Now I'm sorry they did. With the rain we've been having, the hay may rot. It would have been better if I had waited. (*Looks at him.*) Why are you all dressed up? You look like a city salesman or something. Are you on your way to a dance? (*Observes him closely.*) You know, Lomov, you're better-looking when you're dressed up. You really are. But what's the occasion?

LOMOV (*rising, pacing nervously*): Well, you see, my dear Natalia Stepanovitch, it's . . . it's simply this. (*Looks at ceiling.*) I have decided to ask you to . . . to listen to me. Of course, it will be a surprise. Indeed, you might be angry. It's getting very cold, is it not? (*Blows on his hands.*)

NATALIA: I hadn't noticed, but then, of course, I have been working. (*Pauses.*) What is it exactly that you want?

LOMOV (*sitting*): Well, er . . .

NATALIA (*folding her arms; impatiently*): Well?

LOMOV: I'll try to be brief. My dear Natalia, as you know, for many years, since we were children, I have been a family friend. Longer than that. My poor aunt and her husband, from whom, as you know, I inherited the farm, were friends of your family. Our families have been friends for many years. (*Wipes his brow.*)

NATALIA (*impatiently*): Where is all this leading?

LOMOV: What? Oh, yes. Well, as you know, our families have not only been friends, but neighbors.

(*Smiles.*) Our land runs right next to your land. My meadows, for example, stand right next to your birch woods.

NATALIA (*with irritation*): What did you say? Your meadows?

LOMOV: Yes, you know. My meadows down east of your birch woods.

NATALIA: That's nonsense.

LOMOV (*rising*): I mean the meadows by the birch woods.

NATALIA (*turning away*): I know what meadows you mean. (*Raises her voice.*) They are ours, not yours.

LOMOV (*sitting; calmly*): I am afraid you are mistaken, Natalia. Those are my meadows.

NATALIA (*going toward him*): You must be confused. People who inherit property on which they were not born are often confused about such matters.

LOMOV: I am not confused. I looked at the will, and it is quite clear. Those meadows belong to my farm. (*He folds his arms and stares straight ahead.*)

NATALIA (*speaking through clenched teeth*): You'll pardon my saying so, but it just isn't true.

LOMOV (*still staring off*): It's all a matter of legal record. It's true that at one time there was some question of who owned them, but now everybody knows I own them. There really is no room for discussion. My aunt's grandmother, it is true, let your grandfather use them for a time.
(*With emphasis.*) But it was just for a time.

NATALIA: There's not a word of truth in what you're saying. *(Raises her voice and points her finger at him.)* My grandfather—yes and my great-grandfather—knew that his farm ran all the way to the swamp. *(Folds her arms.)* You are not going to say that the meadows are on the other side of the swamp, are you?

LOMOV: Certainly not. My meadows are on this side of the swamp, but . . .

NATALIA *(walking away):* Really, there is no room for any further discussion. You are just trying to annoy me.

LOMOV *(rising; with anger):* I'll show you the papers. It's all legal.

NATALIA: Bah! You are either joking or trying to make me angry. *(Turns away.)* I don't consider this at all neighborly. It isn't as if they were worth anything, but it's the injustice of your taking them that bothers me.

LOMOV *(going toward her):* Would you listen to me for a minute? My aunt's grandmother allowed your grandfather . . . .

NATALIA: Grandfather! Grandmother! *(Turns and faces him.)* The meadows belong to me, and that's the end of the matter. *(Sits in chair and folds arms.)*

LOMOV *(returning to his chair):* They belong to me.

NATALIA: You can shout until you are blue in the face, and put on ten new suits, and it won't change matters. The meadows are mine.

LOMOV *(turning toward her):* Natalia, I don't need the meadows. I am only concerned with what is right. If you want the meadows, I beg you to take them as a gift.

NATALIA *(calmly):* How can you give me what's already mine? Until now, Lomov, I considered you a good friend. Just last season, we helped you harvest your crops. Now, you offer to give me my own meadows. Good neighbors don't treat each other this way.

LOMOV *(gripping his chair and leaning toward her):* Do you think I'm a thief? I never took anything that wasn't mine. And I don't let people call me names.

NATALIA *(shouting):* The meadows are mine!

LOMOV *(shouting):* Mine!

NATALIA *(shouting):* Mine!

LOMOV *(rising):* Mine!

NATALIA *(settling back in her chair):* Really, you needn't scream. If you want to yell and scream and carry on in this fashion, you may do it in your home.

LOMOV *(sitting):* Excuse me.

NATALIA *(with very proper tone):* While you are in my house, I'll thank you to behave yourself decently.

LOMOV *(trying to control his temper):* I said I'm sorry. *(Wipes his brow.)* If it weren't that I am suffering from palpitation of the heart, I would deal with this whole matter differently. *(Shouts.)* The meadows are mine!

NATALIA *(shouting):* Ours!

LOMOV *(shouting):* Mine!

STEPANOVITCH *(entering left):* What's all the yelling about? This is no way to . . . .

NATALIA (*rushing to her father*): Papa, would you tell this person whether the east meadows belong to us or to him?

STEPANOVITCH (*puzzled*): They are of no value, but they are ours.

LOMOV (*turning away*): You too? I thought at least you would be reasonable. (*Rises, trying to be calm.*) My aunt's grandmother gave the use of the meadows—free of charge, I might add—to your grandfather. It is true that your family was allowed to use the meadows for forty years, but later when . . . .

STEPANOVITCH (*going toward* LOMOV): My dear friend, you are forgetting the lawsuit. Besides, everyone knows the meadows are ours. Haven't you ever looked at a map of your property?

LOMOV: I can prove the meadows belong to me. I can take this matter to court.

STEPANOVITCH (*glaring at* LOMOV): I wouldn't try anything like that if I were you.

LOMOV (*nervously*): I certainly will.

STEPANOVITCH: My dear friend, what are you so upset about? I don't ask for anything that doesn't belong to me. But I don't intend to be robbed. I'd rather give the meadows away than let you steal them.

LOMOV (*angrily*): What's that! What right have you to give my meadows away? You can't do that.

STEPANOVITCH (*calmly; looking off*): I can do whatever I like with my own property. (*With rising anger.*) And I want to tell you something. I am

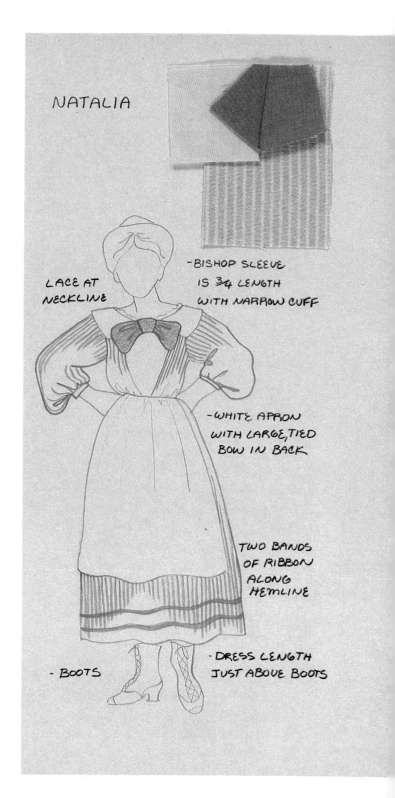

NATALIA

LACE AT
NECKLINE

-BISHOP SLEEVE
IS 3/4 LENGTH
WITH NARROW CUFF

-WHITE APRON
WITH LARGE, TIED
BOW IN BACK

TWO BANDS
OF RIBBON
ALONG
HEMLINE

- BOOTS

-DRESS LENGTH
JUST ABOVE BOOTS

not used to having people address me in that tone of voice. *(Draws himself up.)* I, young man, am twice your age, and I'll thank you to treat me with proper respect.

LOMOV *(sitting):* That's it. You think I'm a fool because I'm young. *(Pouts.)* You're making fun of me. You call my property yours, and you think I'll stand for it. *(Attempts to be calm.)* Mr. Stepanovitch, this is not the way good neighbors behave. *(Shouts.)* You're a land rustler, that's what you are.

STEPANOVITCH *(slowly; with great anger):* What did you say?

NATALIA *(going to her father):* Papa, send the workers to protect our meadows right now.

STEPANOVITCH *(ignoring* NATALIA*):* Young man, what was that you called me?

NATALIA *(to her father):* The meadows are ours, and I won't give them up. I won't. I won't. I won't.

LOMOV *(a little frightened):* I'll take this to court.

STEPANOVITCH *(with quiet contempt):* You can sue me if you like. I knew it would come to this. Your family always looked for an excuse to drag things into court, where they could plot and quarrel with their betters. *(Shouts.)* Your whole family were always plotters.

LOMOV: Don't insult my family. We don't have any embezzlers like your uncle.

STEPANOVITCH: The whole Lomov family was insane.

NATALIA: Every one of them.

STEPANOVITCH: Your grandmother dipped snuff, and your great-aunt Natasia ran off with a salesman.

LOMOV: And your mother was a lousy cook. *(Puts hand over his heart.)* My heart. My palpitations. *(Holds his head.)* My head is bursting. I need water. Water.

STEPANOVITCH: And your grandfather was a gambler and a glutton.

NATALIA: And your aunt was a gossip.

LOMOV: And you are schemers! Oh, my heart. And it's commonly known that you cheat in elections. Where is the door? I'm getting faint. My legs won't hold me. I'm going to have an attack. *(Staggers to door up center and starts out.)*

STEPANOVITCH *(following him, shouting):* And don't ever come back!

NATALIA *(shouting):* I hope you do bring this suit to court. It will show the whole world what a grasping schemer you are!

LOMOV: My heart, my head! I'm dying. *(Exits.)*

STEPANOVITCH: A loafer, scarecrow, monster.

NATALIA: A swindler. A weakling.

STEPANOVITCH: The nerve of such a man. He came here to propose marriage to you.

NATALIA *(aghast):* What did you say, Papa? Lomov came to propose marriage . . . to me?

STEPANOVITCH: Yes, yes, the puppy.

NATALIA: Why didn't you tell me this before?

STEPANOVITCH: That's why he was all dressed up. The puppy.

NATALIA (dropping into chair): Propose to me? Oh! Oh! Papa, Papa, bring him back.

STEPANOVITCH: What?

NATALIA: Run, Papa, run and bring him back. (Groans.) Or I shall die.

STEPANOVITCH: Bring him back? Are you crazy too?

NATALIA: I'm dying. Bring him back. (Wails loudly.)

STEPANOVITCH: All right, all right, I'll get him. Don't cry. (Starting out.) A man with a marriageable daughter should hide in the hills. (Exits up center.)

NATALIA: Bring him back. Bring him back! (She looks up, sees her father is gone, straightens her hair and collar, takes off her apron and folds it, and sits demurely.)

STEPANOVITCH (entering): All right, he's coming back . . . . We insult the man, throw him out, tell him not to come back—and five seconds later, I'm asking him to please come and call. It's all your fault, Natalia.

NATALIA: It's not my fault. It's yours, Papa. You're hard on people. If it hadn't been for you, he wouldn't have left.

STEPANOVITCH: Of course, I'm to blame. The father is always to blame. Ask any young girl who is to blame. She'll tell you, "My father." (LOMOV appears in doorway.) There he is. There's the great lover. You talk to him. (Exits through door left.)

LOMOV (staggering into room): Palpitations. My leg is paralyzed. My side hurts. I feel faint.

NATALIA: (helping him to love seat, then sitting next to him): You must excuse my father, Lomov. He is so unreasonable. I remember now that the meadows are yours.

LOMOV: My heart is beating terribly. My meadows ache. I mean my head aches. It wasn't the meadows I cared about. It was only the principle of the thing.

NATALIA: Of course, the principle. Let's forget the whole thing.

LOMOV: I have proof . . . in writing.

NATALIA: I know, but let's talk about something else. Are you going hunting soon?

LOMOV: I hope to, after the harvest. But I don't know. My dog, Blue, is limping.

NATALIA: That is too bad. How did it happen?

LOMOV: I'm not sure. (Sighs.) And he was the best dog I ever had. I paid one hundred and twenty-five for him.

NATALIA: One hundred and twenty-five! You're joking.

LOMOV: Indeed, I am not. And he was a bargain.

NATALIA: We only paid a hundred for our Rover, and Rover is a much better dog than your Blue.

LOMOV: Rover better than Blue! You're joking, of course. (Laughs.) That's really very funny.

NATALIA: Of course, Rover is better. It's true Rover is young, but for pointing game or following, he's the best dog in the whole area.

LOMOV: Rover has a short lower jaw, and a dog with a short lower jaw can't snap.

NATALIA: A short lower jaw? Our Rover? Nonsense.

LOMOV: I've seen your Rover. His lower jaw is shorter.

NATALIA: Have you measured it?

LOMOV: As a matter of fact, I have. I will admit he runs well.

NATALIA: Rover is purebred. Your Blue is a mongrel. Nobody could even figure out his pedigree. He's old and ugly and as skinny as a starving weasel.

LOMOV: He's not old. He's mature. I wouldn't take five of your Rovers for one Blue. Anyone can pick up a hound like your Rover on the streets. And it would be a public service to get rid of him.

NATALIA: Lomov, I must say that you are in a bad humor today. First, you say that you own our meadows. And now you're trying to pretend that your Blue is better than our Rover. I didn't think you were the kind of person who went around saying things he didn't believe. Our Rover is worth a hundred of your Blue, and you know it.

LOMOV: I can see, Natalia, that you think I'm either a blind man or a fool. Look, will you admit your Rover has a short lower jaw?

NATALIA: No, I will not.

LOMOV: Rover has a pug jaw.

NATALIA: He has not!

LOMOV: He has!

NATALIA: He has not!

LOMOV: What are you shouting about? I thought you didn't like shouting.

NATALIA: When people talk nonsense, it's enough to make sane people shout. Rover is a better dog than Blue.

LOMOV: I don't wish to discuss this any further. I have palpitation of the heart.

NATALIA: A great hunter you are. Palpitation of the heart!

LOMOV: I ask you to be quiet, Natalia. I may have a heart attack.

NATALIA: No, you won't. Not until you admit that our Rover is worth a thousand of your old Blue.

STEPANOVITCH (entering): Well, I see that it has started again. Forget the meadows.

NATALIA: This has nothing to do with the meadows, Papa. We'll leave it to you. Which is the better dog—our Rover or Lomov's Blue?

LOMOV: First, answer this question, Mr. Stepanovitch. Does Rover have a pug jaw or does he not?

STEPANOVITCH: What if he has? A pug jaw is a good thing in a dog. It shows courage. Our Rover is the best dog in the whole country.

LOMOV: But not better than my Blue. Now, tell the truth.

STEPANOVITCH: Don't get excited. We can discuss these things like sensible people. Your Blue certainly has his good points—he's from a good breed and has a good stride. But he has two faults. First, he is old. Secondly, he has a long lower jaw. He's buck-toothed.

LOMOV: Buck-toothed! (Rises.) I feel faint. (Puts his hand on his heart.) Palpitations, I can feel them. (Takes a deep breath.) All right, let's keep to the facts. Do you remember at the last hunt that Blue ran away from your Rover?

STEPANOVITCH: But he ran in the wrong direction.

LOMOV: He did not. The game circled. If your Rover hadn't become confused and made so much noise, Blue would have found the game.

STEPANOVITCH: Your Blue should be retired.

NATALIA: Or you should get crutches for him. The poor dog should be put out of his misery.

LOMOV: Palpitation. My leg is lame. I'm blacking out.

NATALIA: Palpitation! What kind of hunter are you? You and your old Blue should sit on the porch and keep out of the way of real hunters with real dogs. Palpitation.

STEPANOVITCH: Yes, what kind of hunter are you? A man with your diseases ought to stay at home where it is safe. If you were a hunter, you'd know that Rover is a better dog than Blue. I really am very much upset. Let's drop the whole subject. It's foolish to talk to you. You are no hunter.

LOMOV (*feeling his chest*): It's happened. I'm having an attack. I can feel it. My heart's breaking into little pieces.

STEPANOVITCH: You're not only not a hunter, but your housekeeper tells you what to do. You're not even the head of your own house.

LOMOV: I'm dying. That's what's happening. (*Staggers downstage and falls into chair.*)

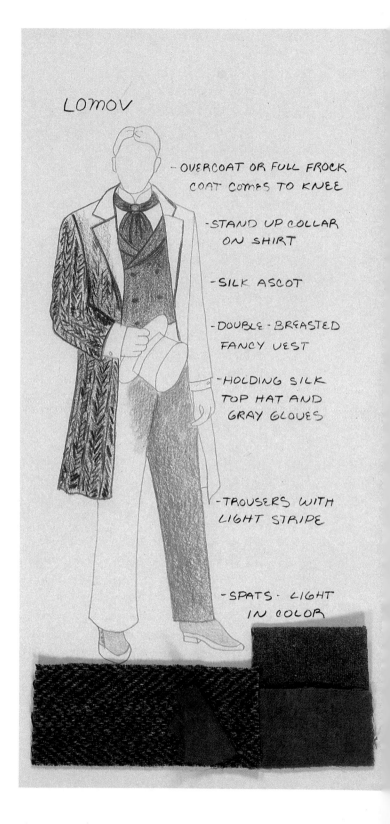

LOMOV

- OVERCOAT OR FULL FROCK COAT COMES TO KNEE
- STAND UP COLLAR ON SHIRT
- SILK ASCOT
- DOUBLE-BREASTED FANCY VEST
- HOLDING SILK TOP HAT AND GRAY GLOVES
- TROUSERS WITH LIGHT STRIPE
- SPATS-LIGHT IN COLOR

STEPANOVITCH: Baby! Weakling. Milk toast.

LOMOV: I can't breathe. Air! Air! *(He flops back in chair.)*

NATALIA *(going to him):* He is dead! *(Shakes him.)* Lomov. Lomov! *(turns toward* STEPANOVITCH.*)* What have we done? He is dead. *(Sinks into chair.)* The doctor. The doctor. *(Stands up, shouting.)* Somebody call a doctor!

STEPANOVITCH: And now what's the matter with you? You're as bad as he is.

NATALIA: He's dead. Dead.

STEPANOVITCH *(going down and pouring glass of water):* That's nonsense. He's not dead. Why would he be dead? Just because we were having a quiet discussion. *(Goes to* LOMOV *and tries to pour water into his mouth.)* Drink. Come on, be a good fellow and drink the water. *(He lets* LOMOV's *head fall back.)* He won't drink. He is dead! This is a terrible situation. Why didn't I shoot myself when I thought of it this morning? It would have saved the whole day. Why don't I do it now? What am I waiting for? *(Again puts glass to* LOMOV's *lips.)* Come on, don't be difficult. Drink the water. All right, be hard to get along with. Go ahead and stay dead. A fine neighbor you are. *(He throws water in* LOMOV's *face.)*

LOMOV *(leaping up):* I'm being drowned! Help, I'm going down for the third time! *(Looks around.)* Where am I?

STEPANOVITCH: You just passed out—with joy, I guess. You proposed to my Natalia, and she accepted. I give you my blessing. Now, please, let's have a little peace and quiet around here.

LOMOV: What? What are you saying? Did I propose?

STEPANOVITCH: Yes, and Natalia is willing. Go ahead, kiss the bride.

NATALIA: He lives. He lives. My Lomov lives! Yes, Lomov, I will marry you.

STEPANOVITCH: Well, go ahead. Kiss her.

LOMOV: Who? Oh. *(Takes* NATALIA's *hand and kisses it.)* Oh yes. Now, I think I remember. I am very happy. I am very happy, Natalia.

NATALIA: I am happy, too, Lomov.

LOMOV: But my leg. It is paralyzed.

NATALIA: Sit down, my darling. Rest.

LOMOV *(sitting):* That's the important thing, to rest.

STEPANOVITCH: Well, now it is all settled. No more problems. This certainly takes a load off my back.

NATALIA: And now, my darling, that it is all settled about our marrying, you will do one thing for me.

LOMOV: Anything, my love.

NATALIA: Admit Rover is a better dog than Blue.

LOMOV: He's not.

NATALIA: He is.

LOMOV: Not!

NATALIA: Is!

STEPANOVITCH *(starting off up center):* Don't go away. I'll go and bring the preacher. *(Fast curtain.)*

Think and Discuss

See your Thinker's Handbook for tips.

1. How does the "proposal of marriage" actually happen?
• 2. What do you learn about Lomov from what Natalia says about him at the beginning of the play?
3. Why do you think Stepanovitch might be so anxious to have Lomov marry Natalia?
4. What reasons does Lomov give for wanting to marry Natalia?
• 5. What do you learn about Stepanovitch from what he says and does at the end of the play?
• Literary Skill: Character

Communication Workshop

Talk

Imagine that Stepanovitch awakens Lomov and does *not* trick him. Would Lomov leave in anger again? Would Natalia or Stepanovitch calm him down and convince him to stay? Would Lomov then find the courage to propose to Natalia? Work in groups of three to make up a conclusion to the scene and choose characters to play. Make up words for each character to say and act out the scene. Switch roles, make up a different ending, and act out the scene again with different dialogue.
Speaking and Listening: Role-playing

Write

Write a dialogue between Lomov and Natalia in which he proposes and she accepts. Read your dialogue to your group members. In which dialogue is Lomov the most enthusiastic? In which is Natalia the most hesitant?
Writing Fluency: Play dialogue

Using Context to Figure Out Unfamiliar Words

Carla and Gary were visiting the city zoo when they came to the sign shown in the picture above. "What's *fauna?*" asked Gary. The word was completely unfamiliar to him.

Carla replied, "I'll give you a clue. The kangaroo and the koala bear are two kinds of fauna of Australia."

"Oh," exclaimed Gary, "then *fauna* must mean animals."

Gary was able to figure out the meaning of a word he had never seen before by using a helpful clue from Carla. When you read, you sometimes come across a word whose meaning you don't know. When this happens, you can often use clues given in the context—the words and sentences around the word—to help you figure out the meaning of the word.

Sometimes the context contains specific clues such as a definition, explanation, or a synonym or antonym for an unfamiliar word. When the context does not define, explain, or give a synonym, you can use the other words and sentences around the word and your own common sense to figure out the word's meaning. Can you figure out the underlined words below?

Pam wanted to buy a <u>canoe</u>, a kind of light boat. She placed an <u>advertisement</u>, or notice, on the supermarket bulletin board, asking if anyone had a canoe to sell. Three people called the next day. Pam was surprised that she got so many <u>responses</u> that soon.

The context defines the word *canoe* for you as "a kind of light boat." The synonym *notice* gives the meaning of *advertisement*. The context does not give a definition, explanation, or synonym for the word *responses*. But by using your common sense together with the context clue "called" you should be able to figure out that *responses* means "answers."

What do each of the underlined words in this paragraph mean?

By ten o'clock the rain had changed to sleet, a half-frozen rain. Weather reports warned motorists that driving conditions were hazardous because of the ice-covered roads. Ted realized that the sagacious, or wise, thing to do was to stay home.

Did you see that the context explains *sleet* in the second sentence with the clue "ice-covered," and gives the synonym *wise* for *sagacious?* Common sense and context clues, "reports warned motorists" and "ice-covered roads," should tell you that *hazardous* means "dangerous."

If using context clues and common sense doesn't help you enough to figure out a word's meaning, use the dictionary.

Practicing Context

Use context to get the meanings of the underlined words.

1. Linda wants to study ornithology, a branch of science dealing with the study of birds, when she goes to college.
2. Signs along the trail warned hikers to stay on the trail. Ed, not heeding the warnings, wandered off and became lost.
3. Practicing in the hot sun lowered the team's energy. Their vitality was gone by noon.
4. The desolate countryside was described in detail by the poet in the poem, "The Barren Hills."

Tips for Reading on Your Own
• Look for context that defines, explains, or gives a synonym or antonym for an unfamiliar word. If none are given, use the other words and sentences around the unfamiliar word as well as your common sense to get the meaning.
• Use a dictionary when context and common sense are not enough.
• For other tips on figuring out words, see your Word Study Handbook.

The pleasure of poetry can be found on these pages as you share the experiences and feelings of poets. As you read, notice the different kinds of poems and the power of the poets' words to produce images that help you see, hear, smell, and feel. Think about the words and images to help you decide which poem is your favorite.

THE PLEASURE OF POETRY

Go with the Poem

by Lilian Moore

Go with the poem.
Hang glide
above new landscape
into other weather.

Sail the poem.
Lift.
Drift over treetops
and towers.

Loop with the poem.
Swoop, dip.
Land.
Where?
Trust the poem.

The Owl Critic

by James Thomas Fields

"Who stuffed that white owl?" No one spoke in the shop,
  The barber was busy, and he couldn't stop;
  The customers, waiting their turns, were all reading
  The "Daily," the "Herald," the "Post," little heeding
  The young man who blurted out such a blunt question;
  Not one raised a head, or even made a suggestion;
    And the barber kept on shaving.

"Don't you see, Mr. Brown,"
  Cried the youth, with a frown,
"How wrong the whole thing is,
  How preposterous each wing is,
  How flattened the head is, how jammed down the neck is—
  In short, the whole owl, what an ignorant wreck 'tis!
  I make no apology;
  I've learned owl-eology.
  I've passed days and nights in a hundred collections,
  And cannot be blinded to any defections
  Arising from unskillful fingers that fail
  To stuff a bird right, from his beak to his tail.
  Mister Brown! Mister Brown!
  Do take that bird down,
  Or you'll soon be the laughing-stock all over town!"
    And the barber kept on shaving.

"I've *studied* owls,
  And other night-fowls,
  And I tell you
  What I know to be true;
  An owl cannot roost

With his limbs so unloosed;
No owl in this world
Ever had his claws curled,
Ever had his legs slanted,
Ever had his bill canted,
Ever had his neck screwed
Into that attitude.
He can't *do* it, because
'Tis against all bird-laws.
Anatomy teaches,
Ornithology preaches,
An owl has a toe
That *can't* turn out so!
I've made the white owl my study for years,
And to see such a job almost moves me to tears!
Mr. Brown, I'm amazed
You should be so gone crazed
As to put up a bird
In that posture absurd!
To *look* at that owl really brings on a dizziness.
The man who stuffed *him* don't half know his business!"
    And the barber kept on shaving.

"Examine those eyes.
I'm filled with surprise
Taxidermists should pass
Off on you such poor glass;
So unnatural they seem
They'd make Audubon scream,
and John Burroughs laugh
To encounter such chaff.
Do take that bird down;
Have him stuffed again, Brown!"
    And the barber kept on shaving.

"With some sawdust and bark
I could stuff in the dark
An owl better than that.
I could make an old hat
Look more like an owl
Than that horrid fowl,
Stuck up there so stiff like a side of coarse leather.
In fact, about *him* there's not one natural feather."

Just then, with a wink and a sly normal lurch,
The owl, very gravely, got down from his perch,
Walked around, and regarded his fault-finding critic
(Who thought he was stuffed) with a glance analytic,
And then fairly hooted, as if he should say:
"Your learning's at fault *this* time, anyway;
Don't waste it again on a live bird, I pray.
I'm an owl; you're another. Sir Critic, good day!"
    And the barber kept on shaving.

Water Picture

by May Swenson

In the pond in the park
all things are doubled:
Long buildings hang and
wriggle gently. Chimneys
are bent legs bouncing
on clouds below. A flag
wags like a fishhook
down there in the sky.

The arched stone bridge
is an eye, with underlid
in the water. In its lens
dip crinkled heads with hats
that don't fall off. Dogs go by,
barking on their backs.
A baby, taken to feed the
ducks, dangles upside-down,
a pink balloon for a buoy.

Treetops deploy a haze of
cherry bloom for roots,
where birds coast belly-up
in the glass bowl of a hill;
from its bottom a bunch
of peanut-munching children
is suspended by their
sneakers, waveringly.

A swan, with twin necks
forming the figure three
steers between two dimpled
towers doubled. Fondly
hissing, she kisses herself,
and all the scene is troubled:
water-windows splinter,
tree-limbs tangle, the bridge
folds like a fan.

It's Hot in the City

by Peter West

White light glares on car rails, cobbles,
Swirling dust, and scraps of paper
Stirred by baked enamel autos.
Shirt-sleeved drivers, forearms upright
Sweat and swear and steer one-handed.
Sickly-sweet, warm, wafted smells—from
Joe's Place and the Lucky Garden—
Mingling, bring no invitation.

Lolling dogs droop in dead doorways.
Children seek the soiled and struggling
Patch of earthy grass between the
Bus stop and the supermarket;
Lining up to bow and gasp in
Turn at the delicious shock of
Water gushing from the fountain.

Damp, red men and moist, pale women
Feel the grilling sidewalks reach up,
Suck vitality through shoe soles
Down toward the earth's hot centre.
Old folk, wise, released from tension,
Rock, or fan themselves on porches
By front steps of teeming houses.

But
Nobody hurries.

Friday: and man flies, gasping
From what he has made
Out, off and away
To the cool wood,
The sweet turf
Or the limpid lake—
To breathe. . . .

It's HOT in the city.

Foul Shot

by Edwin Hoey

With two 60's struck on the scoreboard
And two seconds hanging on the clock,
The solemn boy in the center of eyes,
Squeezed by silence,
Seeks out the line with his feet,
Soothes his hands along his uniform,
Gently drums the ball against the floor,
Then measures the waiting net,
Raises the ball on his right hand,
Balances it with his left,
Calms it with fingertips,
Breathes,
Crouches,
Waits,
And then through a stretching of stillness,
Nudges it upward.

The ball
Slides up and out,
Lands,
Leans,
Wobbles,
Wavers,
Hesitates,
Exasperates,
Plays it coy,
Until every face begs with unsounding
   screams—

And then
        And then
                And then,

Right before ROAR-UP
Dives down and through.

Joy

by Clarissa Scott Delany

Joy shakes me like the wind that lifts a sail,
Like the roistering wind
That laughs through stalwart pines.
It floods me like the sun
On rain-drenched trees
That flash with silver and green.

I abandon myself to you—
I laugh—I sing.
Too long have I walked a desolate way,
Too long stumbled down a maze
Bewildered.

The Unwritten

by W. S. Merwin

Inside this pencil
crouch words that have never been written
never been spoken
never been thought

they're hiding

they're awake in there
dark in the dark
hearing us
but they won't come out
not for love not for time not for fire

even when the dark has worn away
they'll still be there
hiding in the air
multitudes in days to come may walk through them
breathe them
be none the wiser

what script can it be
that they won't unroll
in what language
would I recognize it
would I be able to follow it
to make out the real names
of everything

maybe there aren't
many
it could be that there's only one word
and it's all we need
it's here in this pencil

every pencil in the world
is like this

Comprehension Check

Think and Discuss

1. Which poem is your favorite? What are some of the poet's words and images that you particularly like?
2. Compare what you learn about the owl at the beginning of "The Owl-Critic" with what you learn about it at the end.
• 3. What examples of alliteration do you find in "It's Hot in the City"?
• 4. What does the poet want you to feel while reading the image "squeezed by silence" in the fourth line of "Foul Shot"?
• 5. What does the poet who wrote "Joy" compare her feeling of joy to? Does she use similes or metaphors?
• Literary Skills: Figures of speech, Imagery, Alliteration; Poetry

Communication Workshop

Talk

Have a group discussion about your favorite place, sport, season, pet, holiday, or any subject about which you or a classmate has strong feelings. Discuss the images that come to your mind when you think of each activity or thing and compare them with your classmates' choices and descriptions.
Speaking/Listening: Cooperative learning

Write

Choose your favorite subject of those you discussed and write a few sentences or phrases that could be used in a poem that describes the subject. Use strong and colorful images so that others can see and feel what you write about. Without naming the subject, read some of your writing to your classmates and see if they can guess what you are writing about.
Writing Fluency: Poem

Learning to Paraphrase

While waiting for his dentist appointment, Sam read these words in a magazine, "Wood interdental stimulators." Curious (and confused), Sam continued reading, "are now composed of plastic to prevent damage to the teeth."

"Aha!" thought Sam. "All these words really mean is that there are plastic toothpicks!"

Sam was able to understand the words he read because he knew how to paraphrase. Paraphrasing is putting someone else's words into your own words. Being able to paraphrase difficult passages when you read fiction and nonfiction allows you to check your comprehension and helps you understand as well as remember what you've read. To paraphrase, first figure out what the words mean. Then put them in your own words—you can move words around if it helps—but be sure no ideas are missing.

Can you paraphrase the following passage? The words are from a speech given in 1872 by Susan B. Anthony, a leader of the woman's suffrage movement. She spoke these words before women could vote.

"The only question left to be settled now is: Are women persons? And I hardly believe any of our opponents will have the hardihood to say they are not. Being persons, then, women are citizens; and no State has a right to make any law, or to enforce any old law, that shall abridge their privileges or immunities. Hence, every discrimination against women in the constitutions and laws of the several States is today null and void . . ."

Paraphrasing can help you understand the words in every kind of reading you encounter: magazines, newspapers, books, articles, and speeches.

Play with Words

Can you make a pair of rhyming definitions? For example, a chubby feline is a *fat cat.*

Write your rhyming definitions on a separate piece of paper.
1. A seafood platter is a *fish* ____.
2. Alaska is a *great* ____.
3. The skinny one of two is a *thin* ____.
4. A thin young horse is a *bony* ____.
5. A tiny insect is a *wee* ____.

Now complete these on your paper.
6. A happy father is a ____ ____.
7. A great baseball team is a ____ ____.
8. A girl from Switzerland is a ____ ____.
9. A rodent's home is a ____ ____.
10. A sixth-month satellite is a ____ ____.

Can you think of one yourself?

Dr. Martin Luther King, Jr., was a great American who inspired others with his words. In 1964, he learned he was to receive one of the world's highest honors. In this excerpt from her autobiography My Life with Martin Luther King, Jr., *Coretta Scott King gives her personal account of how her husband felt when he learned he was to receive this honor.*

KING: Nobel Laureate

by Coretta Scott King

Martin Luther King, Jr., was born on January 15, 1929, in Atlanta, Georgia. He devoted most of his adult life to working for racial justice and full civil rights for all people. Partly as a result of his leadership in promoting peaceful protests, Congress passed the Civil Rights Act of 1964 and the Voting Rights Act of 1965.

In 1964, King was nominated for the Nobel Prize for Peace, one of the world's most respected awards. On the prize medal is the motto "For Peace and Brotherhood of Nations." King believed that before there could be a brotherhood of nations, there must be a brotherhood of people. His brief life was given to this effort.

The summer of 1964 had been very difficult for my husband, Martin Luther King, Jr. The calls upon him were staggering and his life was filled with great pressures. He was away from our home in Atlanta, Georgia, much of the time, working for voter registration and helping to open public facilities to all people. He had also taken a trip to Germany. He was working in the presidential campaign, and he had many other difficult tasks.

I was worried about him. In October, soon after he returned from Germany, I encouraged my husband to go to St. Joseph's Hospital in Atlanta for a checkup, hoping that he would in that way be able to get a few days' rest.

At about nine o'clock in the morning after Martin went to the hospital, the telephone rang; it rang most of the time in our house. Many of the calls were from people with whom Martin worked or who wanted to give support to his work or who wanted help from him. But many times the telephone brought unpleasant things.

This time when I answered, the voice on the line said, "This is the Associated Press. I would like to speak to Dr. Martin Luther King."

I explained that Dr. King was not at home, and the reporter said, "Is this Mrs. King?"

When I explained that it was, he said, "We have just received word from Norway that your husband has been given the Nobel Peace Prize for 1964."

It was too much to fully comprehend, but I tried to act calmly. We had heard, of course, that Martin was high on the list of possible winners, but Martin and I both had thought these reports were merely rumors.

"This year the prize is worth fifty-four thousand dollars," the reporter said. "What do you suppose Dr. King will do with all that money?"

"Knowing him," I answered, "I'm sure he will give it all to the work he is now doing."

"How do you feel about that?"

"I think that is where the money should go. I believe in it wholeheartedly." Later, my husband did give all the money to the civil-rights movement, as I said.

As soon as the reporter hung up, I called Martin at the hospital. When he answered in a sleepy voice, I said gaily, "How is the Nobel Peace Prize winner for 1964 feeling this morning?"

"What's that?" Martin asked.

"Martin, the Associated Press just called to tell us that the announcement has been made and you are the winner." After a long silence, Martin said, "I'd better check to see if this is true."

Martin told me later that he had fallen asleep after his early-morning breakfast at the hospital. When I called him with the news, he was stunned. He thought he was still dreaming.

Later we began asking why. Why was Martin's work considered of international importance? What was the deeper meaning of all this? For this was not just a prize for civil rights, but for contributing to world peace. Though we were very happy, both Martin and I understood the great responsibility that this placed on him. This was, of course, the greatest recognition that had come to him, but we both knew that to accomplish what the prize really implied, we still had a long way to go. It was a great tribute, but an even more awesome burden. As he later said, he felt that the prize was "a commission to go out and work even harder for the things in which we believe."

Our solemn thoughts did not mean we were not joyful. Getting ready for our trip to Norway was great fun. The first question was whom we could take with us. Martin felt that the prize was not for him alone but also for those who had worked at his side.

Some of Martin's friends gave money so that his mother, Alberta Williams King, and his father, the Reverend Martin Luther King, Sr., could go on the trip. Martin's father had, by that time, been pastor of Ebenezer Church on Auburn Avenue in Atlanta for thirty-three years. He is a big man, physically and spiritually. He stands strong and broad in his pulpit. He is afraid of no one, telling it like it is.

At that time, Martin was his co-pastor at Ebenezer, and the two of them were very close. Daddy King, as we called him, was very proud of his son's winning the Nobel Peace Prize. At the same time, he was truly humble. He, too, was awed by the new responsibilities that had fallen on Martin's shoulders.

I wanted to take my two oldest children. Yolanda, whom we call Yoki, was almost nine, and Martin Luther King, III, or Marty, was seven. I thought it would be good for them to see their father receive the world's highest humanitarian award. But the Nobel Committee advised us against bringing children younger than twelve years old. The children were very disappointed when I told them they could not go though they understood the reasons.

Early in December our party of about thirty people left Atlanta for New York. In New York several special activities had been planned for us by Ralph Bunche, United Nations diplomat, and the president of that organization's General Assembly. We met representatives from Norway and Sweden, from England, and from some of the African countries. We began to feel that our trip abroad had already started.

Then we took off for London, where Martin had several speaking engagements. On Sunday he preached a sermon in St. Paul's Cathedral. Except for the Nobel ceremony itself, this was the high moment of the trip.

While Martin was speaking, his father sat among us, completely carried away. Members of our party teased Daddy King afterward, saying that he was muttering under his breath a favorite phrase he would have used in our own church. He was saying, "Make it plain, son, make it plain."

On December 8, we took off for Oslo, Norway. Though we landed fairly early in the afternoon, the sun was setting. In that month of the shortest days, there were only about four or five hours of sunlight in Oslo. This we had to get used to, and also to the intense, crisp cold we felt as we stepped from the plane.

On December 10, 1964, Martin received the Nobel Prize. We had quite a time getting him ready. He had to wear formal dress—striped trousers and a gray tailcoat. While several of us were working on the ascot, Martin kept fussing and making funny comments about having to wear such a ridiculous thing. Finally he said, "I vow never to wear one of these things again."

He never did.

But I must confess that when he was finally dressed, he looked very handsome—so young and eager and excited, almost like a boy going to his first dress-up party.

The ceremony was held in Aula Hall of Oslo University. The hall held about seven hundred people, and it was crowded to capacity.

Dr. Gunnar Jahn presents the Nobel Peace Prize to Dr. King.

After King Olav and Crown Prince Harald arrived, the orchestra played the Norwegian national anthem. The King's party sat in special chairs close behind us, and the ceremony began.

Dr. Gunnar Jahn, who headed the Nobel Committee, read the beautiful citation and presented Martin with the cash prize, a gold medal, and the scroll. Then Martin stepped up to make his acceptance speech.

He said in part . . . "I conclude that this award, which I receive on behalf of the (civil-rights) movement, is a profound recognition that nonviolence is the answer to the crucial political and racial questions of our time . . . .

"I accept this award today with an abiding faith in America and an audacious faith in mankind . . . ."

The next day Martin gave the Nobel Foundation lecture in Aula Hall. Then he went to Stockholm for the great reception for all the other Nobel Prize winners, who had received their prizes in Sweden.

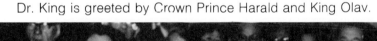

Dr. King is greeted by Crown Prince Harald and King Olav.

From Stockholm we all went to Paris. By then Martin was tired out. All the excitement, the many speeches he had to make, the receptions, the press conferences, and most important, being always at the center of things, had worn him down.

However, our trip home was wonderful. The strain was over and the tension eased. For the moment we put away our solemn thoughts.

New York gave Martin a hero's welcome. Fireboats on the Hudson River jetted streams of water. The mayor received Martin at City Hall and gave him the key to the city, and the governor and his wife entertained us at a luncheon in their New York apartment.

That night Martin had spoken at a huge gathering in Harlem. He said, "For the last several days I have been on the mountaintop and I really wish I could just stay on the mountain, but I must go back to the valley . . . ."

Dr. King and Mrs. King arrive in New York.

After a reception at the White House, we were met at the Atlanta airport by a large number of people most of whom were from Ebenezer Church. We were driven directly to our church for another reception. It did not have the glamor and the splendor of the other receptions Martin had been given, or was to be given, but it had the sincerity and humility of real love. These were the home folk who had shared with his parents the agonies and joys of his childhood, youth, manhood, and maturity. They had watched his development from Auburn Avenue, where he was born, to Boston University, where he received his Ph.D. at twenty-five. They had seen him go on to Montgomery, Alabama, where he had begun his career in the ministry. They had seen the accolades of the world showered upon him. Finally, they were sharing with him, perhaps as no other group of people could, this pinnacle of recognition, the Nobel Peace Prize.

Meet the Author
The following dedication appears in Coretta Scott King's autobiography *My Life with Martin Luther King, Jr.:*

"This book is dedicated to the memory of my late husband whose noble life of unselfish devotion to love, justice, and truth I was privileged to share, and from that sharing derived immeasurable fulfillment—and to our four children Yolanda, Martin III, Dexter, and Bernice who may live to see the realization of that dream."

Coretta's book became an award-winning best seller. It has been printed in many foreign languages and read throughout the world.
Coretta King has become one of the best known and loved women in the world. She has twice been named "Most Admired Woman" by American college students. In 1968 she won the "Woman of the Year Award" given by the National Association of Radio and Television Announcers.
Since her husband's assassination in 1968, Coretta has assumed the role of a civil rights leader herself. She has presented over thirty freedom concerts in which she sings, recites poetry, and lectures.
In a speech celebrating Dr. King's birthday, Coretta once told children of the best birthday present they could give him. "Keep caring and keep trying to love one another," she said. "Martin Luther King had a dream that you would do this, and we all want to make his dream come true."

On August 28, 1963, in one of the most memorable speeches in history, Dr. King addressed more than 200,000 people in Washington, D.C., as millions more watched on television. A part of that speech appears on the next page. As you read it, think about what Dr. King says and how the people listening to him might have felt as they heard his words.

"I Have a Dream"

by Dr. Martin Luther King, Jr.

CLASSIC

I have a dream today.

I have a dream that one day "every valley shall be exalted and every hill and mountain shall be made low. The rough places will be made plain and the crooked places will be made straight, and the glory of the Lord shall be revealed, and all flesh shall see it together."

This is our hope. This is the faith with which I return to the South. . . . With this faith, we will be able to hew out of the mountain of despair a stone of hope. With this faith, we shall be able to transform the jangling discords of our nation into a beautiful symphony of brotherhood. With this faith, we will be able to work together, to pray together, . . . to struggle together, to stand up for freedom together, knowing that we will be free one day. This will be the day when all of God's children will be able to sing with new meaning: "My country 'tis of thee, sweet land of liberty, of thee I sing. Land where my fathers died, land of the pilgrim's pride, from every mountainside, let freedom ring." And if America is to be a great nation, this must become true.

- Into what does Dr. King want to transform "the jangling discords of our nation"?

- Do you recognize the song in the third paragraph?

So let freedom ring from the prodigious hilltops of New Hampshire. Let freedom ring from the mighty mountains of New York. Let freedom ring from the heightening Alleghenies of Pennsylvania! Let freedom ring from the snowcapped Rockies of Colorado! Let freedom ring from the curvaceous slopes of California! . . . Let freedom ring from Stone Mountain of Georgia! Let freedom ring from Lookout Mountain of Tennessee! Let freedom ring from every hill and molehill of Mississippi! From every mountainside, let freedom ring.

When we let freedom ring, when we let it ring from every village and every hamlet, from every state and every city, we will be able to speed up that day when all God's children, black men and white men, Jews and gentiles, Protestants and Catholics, will be able to join hands and sing in the words of the old Negro spiritual: "Free at last. Free at last. Thank God Almighty, we are free at last."

- Tell in your own words what Dr. King's dream is.

Comprehension Check

Think and Discuss

1. How does Dr. King feel when he first learns he has won the Nobel Prize for Peace?
2. What does Dr. King's father mean when he mutters, "Make it plain, son, make it plain"?
- 3. What characteristics of an autobiography and/or speech make them different from a story or a biography?
- 4. What kinds of information does Mrs. King provide in her autobiography that would probably not be found in an encyclopedia article about Dr. King?
- 5. How do you think Dr. King's speech made people feel? Why?
- Literary Skills: Autobiography, Speech

Communication Workshop

Talk

Mrs. King's autobiography is a first-hand account that helps you feel as if you are sharing the Kings' life, or as if you had been with them on important occasions. Work with a classmate and discuss how you felt when you read about these important events in Dr. King's life: the day he learned he had won the Nobel Prize; the day he accepted the prize; the receptions at which the Kings were honored.

Speaking/Listening: Discussion

Write

Choose one of the events you discussed and write a paragraph that describes what happened. Also tell how you felt when you read about the event for the first time. Include quotes from the autobiography if you wish. Read your paragraph to your partner. Did you have the same feelings about the same events? If not, how were your feelings different?

Writing Fluency: Paragraph

LOOKING BACK

*See your Thinker's
Handbook for tips.*

Prewriting

Thinking and Writing About the Section
In this section you have read selections in which words are used to persuade, to create sensory pictures, or to inspire. You can write a letter to a friend to tell him or her about a time when words have persuaded you, created a picture in your mind, or inspired you. First copy the chart below. Then fill in the missing information.

Selection	What Happens	How I Felt
A Proposal of Marriage		
Foul Shot		
King: Nobel Laureate	King wins Nobel Prize.	I felt happy for him.
I Have a Dream		

Writing

Use the information in your chart to help you think of a time when you felt the power of words. Write a letter to a friend. Describe what happens in one selection and tell your friend how you felt about it. Use everyday language, as if you were actually speaking to your friend. Remember to refer to your Writer's Handbook if you need to.

Revising

Read your first draft to a partner. Does your letter tell what happened and how you felt about it? Does your letter contain all five parts? Make changes if necessary and then proofread for spelling and punctuation errors. Write your final copy.

Presenting

Send your letter to your friend. Remember to include the mailing address and the return address on the envelope.

National Air and Space Museum, Smithsonian Institution

3

Breakthroughs

When Neil Armstrong described his first step on the moon as a "giant leap for mankind," he was describing a type of breakthrough. Not all breakthroughs are as dramatic as walking on the moon, but they all have two things in common— overcoming obstacles and opening new worlds for exploration.

All kinds of people make breakthroughs. Some famous people had to overcome traditional roles or handicaps in order to achieve their breakthroughs. For others, simply learning to understand themselves is a breakthrough. Breakthroughs *seem* like great leaps because of the way they open up our worlds, but you'll find that most breakthroughs are really the result of many small, determined steps.

Finding the Main Idea and Supporting Details

If you were asked to write about the photograph, what would the topic be? The topic would be the Olympics. What would be the main idea about the Olympics and some details that would lead you to the main idea? Such details as the medals, the flowers, and the expressions on the faces, tell you about the main idea—winning an Olympic event is an emotional experience.

When you read an article, focus on the topic, main idea, and supporting details and you will increase your understanding of the article. The **topic** is what the article is about; it can sometimes be found in the title. The **main idea** is the most important idea about the topic. **Supporting details** are pieces of information from the article that tell about the main idea.

Sometimes the main idea is easy to find because it is stated directly, often at the beginning, but also in the middle or at the end of an article. When the main idea is not stated, you need to decide what is the most important idea that most of the sentences in the article present about the topic. You can put that idea into a sentence. To check yourself, ask "Does my main idea make sense?" and "Do all (or most) of the important details support my main idea?"

Read the article about Pierre de Coubertin (pyer′ də kü ber taN) and look for the topic, main idea, and supporting details.

Pierre de Coubertin's Olympic Challenge

The flame of the ancient Olympic Games burned from 776 B.C. to about A.D. 400, when the problems of politics and war combined to extinguish it. Fifteen centuries later, the Olympic spark was rekindled in the imagination of a young French nobleman, Pierre de Coubertin.

Born in 1863, Baron de Coubertin gave up an army career to study political science and education. Inspired by reports of archaeological excavations of the site of the ancient Olympics, de Coubertin believed that reviving the Olympic Games could foster better relations between nations. To promote his idea, de Coubertin began to produce a series of speeches and articles in praise of athletic competition. In 1892, he presented his Olympic plan to a gathering of French sportsmen, but they showed little interest in the idea.

De Coubertin refused to give up. Two years later, he organized an elaborate banquet for an international meeting of sports enthusiasts, at which he gave them a "taste" of the Olympic Games. The banquet was lit by a thousand torches and there were horse races, mock battles, and fireworks. The participants were won over. De Coubertin's dream became reality in 1896 when the Olympic flame was rekindled in Athens, Greece.

1. In a few words, what is the topic of this article?

In answering this question, did you pay attention to what the article is about? The topic is de Coubertin's revival of the Olympics. If you didn't answer the question correctly, you could go back and reread the article.

2. What is the main idea of the article?
   a. Pierre de Coubertin's planning and persistence led to the rebirth of the Olympic Games.
   b. Pierre de Coubertin staged a "preview" of the Olympics for a gathering of sports enthusiasts.

In answering question 2, did you remember to look first for a main idea sentence? When you didn't find a main idea sentence, you should have asked yourself what was the most important idea presented in the article. The main idea is *a*. If you had difficulty in answering the question, reread the article, keeping in mind that the most important idea about the topic is the main idea. Then you could check yourself by asking, "Does my main idea make sense?" and "Do all (or most) of the important details support my main idea?"

3. What details support the main idea? How did you decide?
4. What details do not support the main idea? How did you find the answer?

Practicing Main Idea and Supporting Details

Read the article below about Babe Didrikson. Remember to look for the topic, main idea, and supporting details.

Babe Didrikson

It was July 16, 1932, and the Women's National Championship for track and field was getting underway in Evanston, Illinois. Teams of twelve to twenty-two members had been sent from all over the country to compete; the winners would go to the 1932

Olympic Games. The huge stadium resounded with cheers as the favored twenty-two member Illinois team was introduced. When the team from Dallas, Texas, was introduced, the cheers turned into laughter; the "team" had only one member—Babe Didrikson.

But Babe's will to win was a match for any team. At eighteen, through a combination of single-minded determination, careful study of techniques, and *practice, practice, practice,* Babe had conquered every sport she had tried. Now, more than anything, she wanted to go to the Olympics. Babe ignored the crowd and focused on her goal. Dashing from one event to another, she proceeded to take first place in the broad jump, the shot-put, the baseball throw, the hurdles, and the javelin toss—setting world records in the last two. When the scores were added up, the astonished crowd gave Babe a standing ovation. The one-girl "team" from Dallas had accumulated thirty points to win first place. The Illinois team came in second with twenty-two points—one point per person. "I never just wished for something," Babe once said, "I went to work to get it."

1. What is the topic of the article?
2. What is the main idea of the article?
   a. Through hard work and determination, Babe achieved her Olympic goal.
   b. Babe set two world records in the 1932 Women's National Championship.
3. Give one detail that supports the main idea.
4. Give one detail that does not support the main idea.

Tips for Finding the Main Idea
- Ask yourself what—in a few words—the article is all about. This is the topic of the article.
- Look for a main idea sentence that sums up the information in the article and details that support the main idea.
- If there is no main idea sentence, decide for yourself what the most important idea about the topic of the article is.
- Then ask yourself if your main idea sentence makes sense and is supported by all (or most) of the important details.

Felisa Rincón de Gautier's[1] greatest joy in life came from helping others. She knew that the only hope for Puerto Rico's desperately poor people was strong political action. But the Spanish cultural tradition limited women's role to home and the family. It was a barrier that Felisa was unwilling to break through. Then one day a hurricane threatened the tiny island and Felisa was forced to make an important decision that would change her life. Look for the main idea and supporting details that tell you about Felisa's breakthrough.

Felisa Rincón de Gautier

based on the book by Ruth Gruber
adapted by Maryann Davitt

Felisa Rincón, or, as she came to be known, Doña Felisa, was born in Puerto Rico in 1897, the first child of Doña Rita and Don Enrique Rincón. While most Puerto Ricans at that time suffered grinding poverty, the Rincón family belonged to a well-to-do minority on the island. Don Enrique was a successful attorney and was able to provide a very comfortable life for his large family.

---

1. Felisa Rincón de Gautier (fe lē′ sä rēn kon′ de gout yer′)

Felisa attended the local school, where she was a quick learner and an able student. On Saturdays, in keeping with Spanish tradition, Felisa was taught "the womanly arts" of cooking, sewing, embroidery, and dancing. Sometimes, to her mother's dismay, Felisa would steal away to indulge in a favorite pastime—the very untraditional, "unladylike" game of American baseball. But Felisa began to develop another interest that soon took up much of her free time—working in her Uncle Paco's drugstore.

In Puerto Rico, the drugstore was much more than just a pharmacy. Like the old-time General Store in the United States, the drugstore was a central meeting place where people would gather and discuss the issues of the day. As she listened attentively to the spirited discussions of political intrigue and power, Felisa was also learning to read prescriptions and to treat minor ailments. She loved helping people and seemed to have a natural talent for working with the sick. Felisa began to dream of becoming a pharmacist.

Unfortunately, Felisa's dream was not to be. The Rincón family's happiness was shattered when Doña Rita died in childbirth. The family of eight needed looking after, and tradition dictated that the oldest daughter take on the responsibilities of mother. Only one year away from graduation, Felisa left school, heartbroken, never to return.

Her new responsibilities kept her so busy that Felisa had little time to think about lost dreams. Don Enrique had moved the family to a farm about thirty-five miles from San Juan. In addition to caring for the children, Felisa was in charge of the household servants and the farm workers. It was here, on the farm, that she first became aware of the desperate poverty of the jíbaros—the country people. Most of the jíbaros worked for the owners of a huge sugar plantation, earning only about eleven cents an hour. The work was seasonal; there were jobs only in the spring, for planting, and in the winter, for harvesting. The rest of the time there was no work and the people went hungry. They suffered from malnutrition and the diseases that poverty seems to breed—hookworm, malaria, tuberculosis. The jíbaros learned about Felisa's background in pharmacy and began to come to her for first aid and medical advice. Felisa became something of a "nurse-godmother" to them. She nursed the sick, listened to their problems, delivered babies, and prepared simple breakfasts for the workers to eat on their way to the fields each morning.

Felisa developed great respect for the jíbaros; they were proud people with strong values and traditions that went back to Spain in the Middle Ages. There was no welfare on the island; there were no social services to help the jíbaros, but they took care of each other as best they could, sharing what little they had.

When Felisa was seventeen, Don Enrique moved the family back to San Juan. World War I was raging in Europe, and the United States had just granted citizenship to Puerto Ricans. The political leaders who were Don Enrique's frequent dinner guests held endless discussions about Puerto Rico.

Felisa listened to these discussions with interest, but there was another issue that excited her more. She read in the newspapers that women in the United States were organizing and marching for the right to vote. They won their battle in 1920, when the Nineteenth Amendment was passed by Congress. But the amendment would have to be ratified by the Puerto Rican legislature before it could take effect on the island. Traditional ideas about the role of women were very difficult to overcome, and it took twelve more years for Puerto Rican women to be granted the right to vote. When it finally happened, Felisa, now thirty-five years old, announced to her father that she had decided to register to vote.

Don Enrique was shocked. He held many liberal political views, but when it came to the role of women, he was still very traditional. He felt that women should not concern themselves with politics. But Felisa argued her point so well that finally Don Enrique agreed and even offered to take her to the polls to register.

Felisa believed that drastic political change was the only hope for Puerto Rico's poverty-stricken majority. Their situation had been steadily worsening. Most of the profits from the huge sugar and tobacco plantations were going to outside owners in the United States. Corrupt government officials accepted bribes from the rich, who would go for years without being taxed, while the poor struggled under heavy tax burdens and worked for practically nothing.

Felisa joined the reform party headed by Muñoz Marín. The party promised a "quiet revolution"—a revolution that would be fought with votes—to unseat corrupt government officials and improve the quality of life on the island. Felisa helped register women voters for the 1932 election, and she worked so hard that within a few weeks she was appointed a member of the Executive Committee of the party.

The election was disappointing to Felisa because the reform party failed to gain enough power to effect any real changes. But the party's leader, Muñoz Marín, did win a seat in the Senate. The primary reason for the party's failure was that many of the poor had sold their votes to other parties for a few dollars. Felisa believed her party would be successful in the next election if they could convince the poor that their votes really could make a difference. She decided to take her party's message to the San Juan slums.

Felisa began her work in La Perla, the worst barrio in San Juan. The conditions were appalling. Families were crowded into thousands of wooden shacks, cardboard huts, and tin shelters. Barefoot children scampered through the shallow rivers of garbage and raw sewage that ran through the streets. The air was thick with the stench from the nearby slaughterhouse and it echoed with the shrieks of dying cattle. Felisa was shaken by the experience. No one should have to live in such conditions. She was more determined than ever to work for change.

Felisa became a familiar figure in La Perla and the other slums of San Juan. The people began to recognize her and to welcome her. They were irresistibly drawn to this kind, aristocratic woman who spoke so passionately about helping them.

In 1936, when Felisa was thirty-nine, she was asked to run for the Senate; but her father, still the traditionalist, disapproved of a woman holding public office, so she declined. Instead, she threw herself into the campaign to register voters for the 1940 election. This time, she thought, they really did have a chance of getting power.

During this campaign Felisa met Jenaro Gautier, a lawyer who worked with her in the slums, visiting shacks and registering voters. Jenaro shared Felisa's deep concern for the people in the barrios. Felisa and Jenaro were married in March, 1940. There was no time for a honeymoon—they could spare only one day away from their work. But their campaign efforts were well rewarded in the election: Marín's party won a smashing victory.

That same year, Felisa, now popularly known as "Doña Felisa," accepted the presidency of the San Juan committee of the party. The post had been offered to several men and was rejected by them because it seemed to lack any real power.

In the next few years, the results of "the quiet revolution" began to show. The government began to industrialize the island and to improve living conditions for the jíbaros and the slum dwellers. There were new medical facilities; and there was a new emphasis on education. Doña Felisa was proud of the part she had played in making these changes. They had accomplished a great deal, but she knew that there was still much more to be done.

In 1944, the party delegates asked Doña Felisa to run for mayor. But, like Don Enrique, Felisa's husband still had very traditional ideas about women's roles. Felisa was torn—she wanted to accept, but part of her was still bound by the Spanish code. She declined—she wasn't yet ready to break tradition.

Felisa was determined to clean up slums such as this one.

On September 25, 1945, warning flags went up all over the island—a hurricane was on the way. Felisa and Jenaro were safe enough in their large second-floor apartment, but she worried about the people who lived in the flimsy shacks of the barrios. Already the wind and rain were pounding the island. She knew that their shacks would be flooded. What would happen to the people? Would they be swept into the sea? Where would they go if their homes were destroyed?

It wasn't long before Felisa's questions were answered. A mob of people appeared at her door, pleading for her to let them in. She recognized many of them from the slums just behind her house. They were dripping wet; some were carrying babies; others were carrying their possessions. Some were hysterical, having already lost their homes, everything they owned, to the devastating wind and tides. Doña Felisa brought them in, gave them food and dry clothing, and tried to calm them. As the wind and rain battered the windows, the radio announced that the full force of the hurricane was expected to hit Puerto Rico the next day. By now there were nearly three hundred people packed into the apartment, and

Low-cost housing made it possible for many families to leave the slums.

there was a steady stream of new arrivals. Doña Felisa decided that something would have to be done about finding a safe place for these people to stay until the storm had passed.

Felisa and Jenaro set off in the car for the office of Civil Defense. She explained the situation to the manager and asked that a school or public building be opened for the homeless people. The manager refused. He was sorry, but the storm hadn't been declared an official hurricane and, until it was, he had no legal power to open a public building.

Next they tried the Red Cross. They got the same response. Felisa decided to try the governor. He was a good friend and a compassionate man; surely he would help. But his answer was the same as the others.

Felisa had to do something. She went back to the apartment and recruited a few strong young men. They trudged a few blocks to a large school building and Doña Felisa instructed them to kick the door open. Then they went back to the apartment and led the frightened people into the building. Doña Felisa went out into the storm again, bought food enough for everyone, and took it back to the school.

Back in her apartment, having settled everyone comfortably, Felisa did some serious thinking. She was disappointed in

Felisa urges the garbage collectors to have pride in their work and their city.

public officials who adhered rigidly to the letter of the law and ignored its spirit. She saw that even in her position as President of the Municipal Committee, she had no real power to do anything. To really help people, she needed political power. Without that power, the best she could do would be to patch things over without ever getting to the source of the problem. The hurricane had forced Doña Felisa to take bold action for her people; now she was ready to challenge tradition. In the next election, Felisa Rincón de Gautier would run for mayor of San Juan.

On December 5, 1946, Felisa Rincón de Gautier began her first day as mayor of San Juan, the first woman ever to hold such an important post on the island. She held office for twenty-two years, retiring at the age of seventy. Under her guidance, the dirty, neglected city of San Juan became a model for urban renewal. Low-income housing began to replace the slums, new parks were created, new streets and roads were built, and job training programs helped people find work. Doña Felisa had indeed achieved her goal.

Felisa at her desk in city hall.

Blindness struck Michael Naranjo before he had a chance to think about what he wanted to do with his life. Michael desperately wanted to be independent—to make it on his own. Would he be able to achieve independence? Look for the main idea and supporting details in this true account of Michael's breakthrough.

The Spirit of Michael Naranjo

by Mary Carroll Nelson

Michael Naranjo is a Pueblo Indian who was born in Santa Clara, California. Michael's family moved to Taos, New Mexico, when he was nine, and there he developed interest in the ceremonies of the Taos Pueblos.

When Michael finished high school, he couldn't decide what to do. He was drafted into the army in 1967. He had been in Vietnam only two months when an explosion left him blind and unable to move his right arm and shoulder. While he was in the hospital, Michael began to create small figures out of modeling clay. Physical therapy helped him regain partial use of his right hand and arm and he began working on more complicated figures. After his release from the hospital, Michael went to a special school for the blind in Palo Alto, California. There he was taught to walk with a cane, to read Braille, and to handle small appliances and kitchen gadgets. But he wasn't taught any career skills. Michael knew that it was up to him to find his own path in the world.

For artists, vision is the most precious ability one has; to lose it would be such a blow that the artist's creative life might end. Famous artists such as Mary Cassatt, Edgar Degas, and Camille Pissaro have become nearly blind in old age. These artists, however, had already achieved their goal of creating beautiful work before they lost their sight.

Michael Naranjo was blinded before he had even chosen his goal, let alone reached it. He had always been attracted to art. He had sketched and studied, enjoying his talent and sharing it generously, but it was not his profession. Michael's untimely injury could have stopped him before he got started.

While he was in the school for the blind in Palo Alto, a photograph of Michael Naranjo with some of the sculptures he had made in the hospital was sent out over the news wires. People started writing to him from all over the country. They told him he was an inspiration to them and even asked him to visit them in their homes. And they asked for pieces of his sculpture. Such requests were a source of comfort to Michael; if his sculpture was good enough for people to ask for, maybe he could be a sculptor. He was considering this possibility when it came time for him to leave the shelter of the school to begin a new life in the outside world.

Although Michael was grateful for the love and support of his family, he felt that he had to get away from other people's feelings about his blindness. Michael wanted to try and make it alone. He moved to an apartment in Santa Fe in January,

1969. Within a few days, Michael knew the apartment well enough to find his way around it and to locate all the things in it that he needed. He began his new life.

Gradually, Michael developed a way of working as a sculptor. With wax, his hand, and an inner picture of what he wanted to model, he could create a sculpture. The sculptor's part is to model in wax. From that model, the foundry can cast the piece in bronze. This is what Michael eventually decided to do: to create works in wax to be cast in bronze.

Throughout 1970 he worked very hard on a large figure of an eagle dancer wearing the huge wings of the costume and the beaked headdress that identifies the dance. The eagle dance is one of the most dramatic of all the Southwest Indian ceremonies. High up on Puyé Cliff the spectacular dance is performed each July. Up near the very place where eagles live, the Indians dance in honor of this brave bird. Michael recaptured the motion of the eagle dancer with his left arm low to the ground as he swoops down into a hovering position. The right arm is raised. All the details were lovingly executed. For a time, Michael felt he was the eagle dancer.

The finished bronze was cast at Shidoni foundry in Tesuque, a village just north of Santa Fe. With this piece and the publicity that it received, Michael's career took an upward turn; indeed, it soared much as the eagle itself might do.

In the next few months, Michael Naranjo and his *Eagle Dancer* received a lot of publicity. Then in 1971, Michael's bronze sculpture called *Hopi Dancer* won second prize at an all-Indian show. The name of the sculptor was becoming known to art collectors. When the award was announced, the President wrote Michael a letter of congratulations.

It was the Feast of San Geronimo, September 30, 1971, in Taos Pueblo. All around him were the Taos people, excited by the feast day, but quiet as they usually are in public. It was pleasantly warm beside the shady side of the pueblo. Michael heard the drums and felt the beat of the dancing feet on the earth beneath his own feet. He smelled the bread baking in the outdoor earthen ovens. The smell of roasting meat and bubbling chili was in the air.

There were many visitors. Michael heard the Taosians speaking quietly and the louder voices of the English-speaking onlookers. Everyone seemed to be expecting something. The Chifonetti were coming. He felt their arrival in the movements of the people and the laughter in the crowd. The day was incomplete without these free-spirited clowns. Michael wondered if they would tease him.

He saw the Chifonetti in his mind—the costume, the hairstyle, and their whirling, exhausting race through the feast day. This was their day of power. Soon he felt a commotion near him and realized that a Chifonetti was teasing those standing by. Sure enough, the Chifonetti came to him too. The Chifonetti's words were comforting and funny. He made Michael share his gaiety. Then he was gone.

An idea began to form in Michael's mind. He thought of how much the Taos Indians looked forward to the feast day and the fun everyone had watching the clowns. He thought of the deep respect the people had for the clan that added so much to the cultural life of the Pueblo. Only the members of one clan are able to be Chifonetti. They remind people that there is both good and bad in everyone. Michael decided to capture the spirit of the Chifonetti in a sculpture. More than anything else, he wanted the figure to look free.

He could hardly wait to get started. A few days later, back in his home in Santa Fe, he twisted some wire into an armature. This little stick figure made of wire would support the wax he would use to model a sketch. The sketch is a small trial study of the planned piece. He tore a few chunks of the wax from a big chunk in his warming pan. The wax was kept in a deep electric frying pan set on warm. He pushed tiny pieces of the wax into place along the wire armature, building up the figure with his fingers. He steadied the piece with his right hand. Within a few hours he had made a rough sketch. Over and over again he kept thinking about the Chifonetti and making more sketches. He decided to make the figure upright and bigger than others he had tried.

At last, after several months of this work, he began to model the final figure. The armature he made was for a figure twenty-two inches high. He spent months on the process of modeling. His main effort was to give the figure a feeling of motion, one of the hardest tasks a sculptor can set. If there is a tension or twist in a sculpted figure, it is called torsion. The upper trunk in Michael's figure is turned a little away from the lower trunk so that torsion gives a lively feeling to the work.

To add to the grace of the figure, Michael decided to stretch out the arms of the Chifonetti with the hands suspended as though he had just whirled around rapidly and was still moving. Cornhusks in the Chifonetti's hair are flung out by his twist. He has his face turned up and back. His face is much like Michael's own face. His eyes are not shown, and that makes him appear to be deep in thought.

How does the blind sculptor make a realistic form? He sometimes hires a model. Though he cannot see the model, he can touch the person to check the position of the body and the way it is balanced. It is a slow process. Naranjo usually depends instead on his memory and his instinct for form.

It was nearly six months after the idea came to him that Michael felt the Chifonetti was becoming a sculpture. His left hand got blisters on it that later broke and turned sore. He had to wait a few weeks for his hand to heal, and then he pushed on.

The Chifonetti became more real to the artist. It had a character separate from its creator. The wax figure seemed to tell Michael when he added something wrong; it would make him feel good when he added something right. He decided the name of the piece would be *Spirit*.

For Michael, working at night when the whole world was asleep had become a habit. He would awaken at two or three in the morning and begin to work on his sculpture. When *Spirit* was finished, Michael knew it instinctively. There was nothing left for him to do on it. He talked to the statue and felt a companionship with it. The connection between him and his statue had lasted close to a year.

Before he made the first casting, Michael had decided to make only twelve copies of *Spirit*. This total number is called an *edition*.

Michael has an emotional attachment to his work. He feels that every piece has a life of its own. It will have a different history. Different collectors will buy it and pass it on to others. The life of a bronze statue is far longer than that of a person. So when Michael finishes a piece, he has made something real that will live into the future. It is fitting that he named his Chifonetti *Spirit* and sent it out to find its way into history. Each *Spirit* carries with it a memory of Taos Pueblo on the Feast of San Geronimo.

Michael Naranjo has now sculpted about seventy-five pieces. His limited editions sell for anywhere between $250 and $30,000, and his sculptures have made their way into museums around the country. Each time he casts a new sculpture, Michael keeps one copy for himself. "It's a very personal kind of thing. I still get sad when I sell them," he says. "A little bit of me goes with them."

Eagle and Fish

Buffalo Dancer

Summer Hawk

Comprehension Check

See your Thinker's Handbook for tips.

Think and Discuss

1. What decision does Doña Felisa make that changes her life?
2. What is the main idea of the article?
   a. Felisa's father does not want her to be in politics.
   b. Felisa realizes that for her, helping people is more important than following tradition.
3. List at least three details that tell how Felisa helps the people who flock to her apartment during the storm.
4. Doña Felisa becomes mayor of San Juan; what does Michael Naranjo become?
5. What is the main idea of "The Spirit of Michael Naranjo"?
   a. Through hard work and determination, Michael achieves his goal of independence and artistic recognition.
   b. Michael's inspiration comes from the ceremonies of the Taos Pueblos.

• Comprehension Skill: Main idea and supporting details

Communication Workshop

Talk

Work with a classmate to take turns being the characters of Doña Felisa and Michael Naranjo. Talk about how the obstacles in your lives helped make you more determined to achieve your goals. Imagine how you might have felt about each of the scenes or objects pictured in the selections.
Speaking/Listening: Role-playing

Write

Imagine that you are making scrapbooks for Doña Felisa and Michael Naranjo and you are going to use the photographs from the two selections. Choose one photograph from each selection and write a caption to accompany it. Your caption should include a brief description and information about the strength and determination of the character in the selection. Read your captions to your classmate and compare your ideas about each of the two characters.
Writing Fluency: Captions for photographs

Mother to Son

by Langston Hughes

Well, son, I'll tell you:
Life for me ain't been no crystal stair.
It's had tacks in it,
And splinters,
And boards torn up,
And places with no carpet on the floor—
Bare.
But all the time
I'se been a-climbin' on,
And reachin' landin's,
And turnin' corners,
And sometimes goin' in the dark
Where there ain't been no light.
So, boy, don't you turn back.
Don't you set down on the steps
'Cause you finds it kinder hard.
Don't you fall now—
For I'se still goin', honey,
I'se still climbin',
And life for me ain't been no crystal stair.

Beth Lambert wants to become a veterinarian, but first she must earn money for college. Resourceful Beth comes up with a money-making plan, but will she be able to make a success of it? As you read about Beth's breakthrough, think about the theme of the story. What does Beth learn about business—and about herself?

Philip Hall Likes Me, I Reckon Maybe

by Bette Greene

If I'm the number-one best student now, it's because of what Doc Brenner told me, and I don't mean what he said about my outgrowing my allergies either. I'm talking about when he patted my wrist and told Ma and Pa, "Whole town is proud of this youngun."

He went on to tell us about this "smart young fellow" who went through four years of agricultural school with some assistance from him and his friends. Then he said that I had "undeniable talent" and when I was ready for college, he'd be pleased to help me get there too.

The doctor thought they could come up with at least half the money if Pa could manage the other half.

Fancy Annie brought Baby Benjamin out on the porch, sat down next to me, and without so much as I beg your pardon, interrupted my thoughts. As I played with his two-month-old nibbly toes, I told her, "I've decided to become Randolph County's first veterinarian."

"Miss Elinor Linwood's already beat you to it," said Anne. "'Cause she hasn't had a piece of meat in her mouth since that time she got a hunk of pot roast lodged in her throat."

I sighed. Being smart can sometimes be a burden. "Folks who don't eat meat are called vegetarians. I'm going to study in college to become an animal doctor—a *veterinarian.*"

Anne got up and I followed her into the kitchen, where Ma was standing over the cookstove. Anne spoke to her back. "Would you listen to your younger daughter! Being a farmer's wife isn't good enough for our Beth. No sir! She's got to be more special than that. She's going to go to college to become a *vegernarian!*"

"Veterinarian," I corrected.

"There's nothing wrong with ambition," said Ma, placing a cover over the cast-iron skillet.

After supper I overheard Ma talking proudly about what I had decided to become. Pa remarked that half of a heap of money is still a heap of money, "And I don't know any way to earn that kind of money."

For days after that I asked everybody I knew how to go about earning college money. My own teacher said right off that it's easier to earn money if you "first acquire a good education." When I told her that I needed the money first so I could become educated with it second, Miss Johnson was silent for a spell before replying, "That would make it considerably more difficult."

When days went by without a single money-making idea worth thinking about, I began to get more and more discouraged. It was Anne, of all people, who began encouraging me. "For a long time now," she said, "folks've been getting me madder than a wet hen saying that when brains were passed out little Beth stayed around long enough to get an extra helping. Well, are you going to prove all those folks wrong? Don't reckon you are."

"Well, those same people've been making me just as mad," I admitted, "by telling me that you are the prettiest thing ever."

For a moment Anne and I stared at each other just as though we saw—or understood—something that we had never understood before. Together we drifted out on the front porch and sat down on the steps. We sat for a long spell, not saying anything, just watching the plow from Pa's tractor turning rows of lime-green grass into rich chocolate earth.

Then I remembered something. On the cover of the very last issue of the *Saturday Evening Post* was a painting of a roadside vegetable stand, and crowding around to buy were some right fancy-looking folks from the city.

The next picture that I saw didn't come from remembering, cause what I was seeing had never yet been. Not as yet been. My friend Philip Hall and I were selling vegetables from behind our own roadside stand. A sign read: THE ELIZABETH LORRAINE LAMBERT & FRIEND VEG. STAND.

When I told my sister what I was "seeing," she began beating my shoulder. "Oh, Beth baby, you've done it again."

I jumped off the porch and started running to where Pa and his tractor were opening up the Arkansas earth. "Plant more!" I called to him in my loudest voice. "Plant more! Much *more!*"

For days and days after the planting I waited for the first green leaves to pop through the earth. First I worried that the seeds weren't going to sprout in such a dry soil. Then we had some rain, and I got to worrying that the moisture was sure to rot the roots. Even Ma noticed my concern, 'cause one day when she was helping me weed, she said that I was fretting more over my garden than my brother Luther does over his "precious pigs."

Still, with all the work I put in, it wasn't until the first seedlings broke earth that I began to believe, really believe, that vegetables were going to grow and that those vegetables were going to make a veget—a veterinarian out of me.

After the seedlings appeared, we got what Pa said was "good growing weather," but that doesn't mean exactly what it sounds like it means. Since farmers are afraid to ever do even the tiniest bit of bragging—thinking that might change their luck for the worse—they say "bad" when what they really mean is "not bad." And when farmers say "good growing weather," then that's their way of saying it couldn't be more perfect.

Well, the good growing weather brought forth worthy vegetables. Lovely tomatoes, crunchy corn, and melons sweeter than candy.

And on the first free day of summer vacation my friend Philip and I built a stand on the gravelly shoulder of the highway by placing some barn boards over a couple of rickety orange crates. When I began to nail on the sign that I had so carefully painted the night before, Philip read out loud: "The Elizabeth Lorraine Lambert & Friend Veg. Stand" in a voice so high that it actually cracked, probably from lack of oxygen. "That's not fair!"

I moved Philip's finger to the word *Friend.* "See, I didn't leave you out."

He shook his head. "Not fair!"

"It is *too* fair," I insisted. "Whose idea was it? Who did the planting? The weeding? The picking? You are nothing but a Philip-come-lately."

Philip only gave me a quick look that I couldn't quite read before going on about his business of arranging the tomatoes, melons, and corn in the shape of pyramids on the counter.

"Sure does look nice," I said, hoping that a little appreciation would perk him right up. Philip's face flashed something that could be mistaken for a smile, and just when I was deciding whether or not to count that as progress, a dark blue car came to a stop in front of our stand. Our first customer! Now that was progress, sure enough.

The bald head that poked itself out of the car window belonged to the bushy-eyed owner of the Busy Bee Bargain Store.

" 'Lo Mr. Putterham," I called as he came over to look. "Want to buy some farm-fresh vegetables today?" When he didn't answer, I added, as a sort of extra attraction, "At a bargain?"

Mr. Putterham seemed to take a fancy to one of the ears that was in the dead center of Philip's pyramid. As he gave it a quick yank, it caused the great triangle of corn to level. Philip watched the destruction of his labor with obvious pain, but Mr. Putterham took no more notice of my partner's pain than he did of the great corn leveling. For one thing, he was too busy sniffing the corn, peeling down the shucks, and sniffing some more. Then he looked down at me just as though he had appointed himself as judge. "Thought you said you were selling *fresh* vegetables?"

"An hour ago that corn was still growing on its stalk."

When Mr. Putterham finally drove off, I was one dollar and ninety-five cents richer and a whole lot happier. Philip and I threw our arms around each other, jumped into the air, and made loud and joyful noises.

THE ELIZABETH LORRAINE LAMBERT & FRIEND VEG. STAND

After the celebrating, I told Philip to mind the store while I made a trip back for more vegetables. Not only had Mr. Putterham bought every last ear of our corn, but he also bought the best two of our three melons.

At first I got to figuring that he probably bought that second melon to give to a friend, but that was before I got to remembering what it is that folks in these parts say about Mr. Cyrus J. Putterham. "Old Putterham is so cheap he wouldn't give anybody anything, not even a kind word."

I packed the cart, whose long-time missing wheel Luther had replaced as a going-in-business present to me, with a couple dozen ears of corn and four of our biggest melons. But I couldn't get over thinking how peculiar it is that some folks would pay out good money for the same vegetables that they could grow themselves.

As I pulled the rolling produce back along the dusty road, I could see up ahead that a car was parked near our stand. Another customer! I wanted to see him. Wanted to be there when he reached down into his pocket to bring out the money that was going to help pay my way through college.

Running when a person has to play steam engine to a cargo on wheels isn't the easiest thing to do. So while I couldn't exactly run, I did walk just as fast as I could. When I finally reached the highway, the car with a man and woman inside was just driving off.

I gave Philip Hall a congratulating pat on the back. "Reckon you must have sold them a good amount," I said, noticing that the last melon was now gone.

He shook his head no.

"What do you mean *no*?"

"What I mean to say," said Philip, pretending great patience, "is that they didn't buy anything. And they didn't spend any money. Do you understand now what I mean when I say no?"

"No," I said. " 'Cause I don't see the melon. Who bought that?"

His head swirled to look at the place that was now made vacant by the missing melon. "Oh, that one," he said.

"Yep, that one. Who bought it?" I asked just at the moment I caught sight of some melon rinds (and only the rinds) lying in the gully. I didn't have to ask another question 'cause now

I understood everything. "You good-for-nothing, low-down polecat of a Philip Hall! Those folks stopped to buy a melon, didn't they?"

He looked too surprised to answer, so I just went on telling what I knew to be the truth. "But you didn't have a melon to sell, did you? 'Cause you already ate it!"

Philip called me "crazy" and then he stopped talking. And if that wasn't bad enough, the cars too seemed to have stopped stopping. A couple of times, they slowed down and I thought for sure they were going to stop, but they didn't. Don't know why, unless maybe they caught a look at Philip's sourer-than-a-lemon-ball face.

Another thing about this day that wouldn't stop was the sun. One of the real hot ones. I reckon I could've drunk a gallon of ice water. Reckon I could've even drunk a gallon of water without the ice.

Then I heard Philip's voice actually speaking. "We have another customer." He pointed across the road to Al's red tow-truck with the words WALNUT RIDGE GAS STATION neatly painted on its door.

After Al, the baseball-capped garageman, paid me for one melon and a half dozen ears of corn, I asked him if he knew my grandmother, Mrs. Regina Mae Forde. "She lives on Route 67 just north of Walnut Ridge."

"No, but," he smiled a dimpled smile, "I'm going to be going right past her house to fetch a battery, so I reckon I can take you there and back if you've a mind to do some visiting."

I thought about the lemonade that Grandma makes with exactly the right number of sugar granules. I thought about the shade trees that circle her little house. And most of all I thought about Grandma.

I would have gone on thinking, but I was interrupted by my partner's voice. "Let's go, Beth. Please?"

As we walked up Grandma's now grassless path, I had a sudden thought, "If she sees me so unexpectedly at her door, she'll right away think I'm bringing bad news."

So I stayed hidden in the bushes while friend Philip walked up the front step and knocked hard against the wood door. After a moment's wait he knocked even harder. And when she didn't answer that one, I came out of hiding long enough to ask him to walk around back to see if she was out hanging clothes. Well, he did, but she wasn't.

We sat on a piece of shady grass by the side of the road making bets on who would be coming along first: Grandma or Al. Just as I said, "Grandma," as though there wasn't room enough in this world for one speck of doubt, I saw Al's arm waving at us through his truck's open window.

About fifteen minutes later, when we came within viewing distance of our stand, I stabbed at the windshield. "What are those fool cows doing bunched around our stand?"

"They're our dairy cows," explained Philip as though that was the most natural explanation in the world. "Being brought back from the west pasture for milking."

Al hadn't come to a one hundred percent complete stop before I was out of that truck flailing my arms as though they had been set into revolving sockets. "Shoo! Shoo, you dumb cows! Shoo! Would you look at what you've done to my business!"

All the cows moved leisurely on except one rust-and-white spotted Jersey, who took the only remaining ear of corn into her mouth without even bothering to see what my displeasure was about.

"You're dumb," I yelled at the Jersey. "Dumb, *dumb, dumb!*"

Then just as if to show me how she felt about my name-calling, she backed into the stand, sending all three melons to the ground. Two of them cracked, but the largest melon miraculously made the fall intact.

"*Dumb!*" I screamed, and the cow lifted her head as though to demonstrate her complete contempt at my shockingly bad behavior before sending her front foot through the last surviving melon. "Ohhh . . ." I said, feeling violent about the destruction of The Elizabeth Lorraine Lambert & Friend Veg. Stand.

"Her name's Eleanor," said Philip, with what sounded like pride. "She's one cow that's always had a mind of her own."

I pointed my finger at him. "You and Eleanor are exactly alike! 'Cause neither of you has any sense!"

At the supper table I told Pa, Ma, Luther, and Anne about how my vegetable stand was destroyed when Philip Hall made me go with him to Walnut Ridge.

Pa put down his glass of buttermilk. "Show me your scars."

"My what?"

"Your scars," he said again. " 'Cause I never knew anybody who could make my Beth do what she hadn't a mind to do." Pa leaned his head back just like he always does when he laughs. "So show us your scars." He wasn't laughing alone either. They were all laughing their fool heads off. All excepting me.

I jumped up, slapping my hand down upon the oilcloth. "Reckon I should have known you folks would rather take sides with Philip Hall than with your own flesh and blood."

Ma gave my hand little taps saying, "Now, now, nobody in this world is taking sides against you."

Tears were coming on, coming on too strong for stopping. I ran into my room to throw myself across my bed. I cried as quietly as I could, wondering why I hadn't seen it before. How they all love Philip Hall better'n me. Well, let them! I don't mind.

After a while I had to quit crying 'cause it was giving me a headache and I was, truth to tell, plumb tired of lying across the bed. So I tiptoed out the front door so quietly that I didn't have to face a single solitary Lambert.

I passed Pa's garden of the good growing weather, admired the corn stalks which seemed to grow taller and prouder with each sunrise. And on each stalk I saw ears—lots of corn-ripened ears—ready for the picking. Plenty there for a heap of selling. And in the next rows were the tomatoes that should be able to win a blue ribbon at anybody's country fair. But the bluest ribbon should be saved for the melons. The sweetest melons in all of Randolph County.

THE ELIZABETH LORRAINE LAMBERT & FRIEND VEG. STAND

The sun was lowering, but there was still light enough on the rutty back road that I followed out to the highway. When I reached what remained of The Elizabeth Lorraine Lambert & Friend Veg. Stand, I surveyed the damage. The corn was muddied and bruised; mashed tomatoes littered the gravel shoulder; and the burst melons had become a feast for ants and flies. The boards and the crates were unbroken although the company sign did suffer from a muddy hoofprint directly across the word *Friend.*

As I replaced the boards across the crates I began thinking about what really happened. I thought about the good growing weather, about Pa's extra planting, about Ma's taking the time to help me weed my garden. I thought about Luther's repairing the cart, Anne's encouragement, and I even thought about Philip Hall who had always been better at talking than at working. And isn't that what I really wanted him for? For company?

Sweet Philip. Did he really force me to go to Walnut Ridge? Although I didn't come close to smiling, I did come closer to understanding what Pa and the rest of the family found funny.

I threw the feast-for-flies melons across the road into the gully and swept away the tomatoes with a willow branch. Then with only one mighty swing of a roadside rock, I nailed the company sign onto the stand again.

As I stepped back to look it all over, I saw only one thing still needed doing. So with my hand I brushed away—carefully brushed away—the mud from the word *Friend.*

Meet a Reader

Shawn Cokus, a seventh-grader in New York, especially liked the ending of "Philip Hall Likes Me, I Reckon Maybe." Shawn says, "I like what Beth learned about friendship—she learned to trust her friends and not to blame her friends for her own mistakes."

Shawn enjoys reading science fiction and short fiction; he spends much of his spare time writing computer programs, and trading programs, and building electronic parts for his computer.

1. What does Beth learn about business and about herself?
2. What is Beth's goal and what plan does she think of to try to reach her goal?
3. Whom does Beth blame for the damage to the stand? What reason does she give?
4. Do you think that Beth ever earned enough money to go to college? Why or why not?
• 5. Any of the following themes could fit the theme of the selection. Choose the one that means the most to you and give a reason for your choice.
   a. In reaching a goal, we must rely more on ourselves than on others.
   b. Friendship means accepting both the good and the bad traits of our friends.
   c. Learning from our mistakes helps us understand ourselves.
• Literary Skill: Theme

Communication Workshop

Beth's plan to earn money nearly failed because she didn't consider what would happen if she left the vegetable stand unattended. If Beth had planned ahead and made a list, perhaps one of the entries on the list would have been: "Enough volunteers to attend stand at all times". Discuss with your classmates plans you would have to make for a car wash. What would you list?
Speaking/Listening: Cooperative learning

You have decided to hold your car wash and need to make a sign to advertise the event. Write a list of information that you think should go on the sign. Include those from your discussion. Then make a model of the sign and display it on the bulletin board. Does it include all the important points?
Writing Fluency: List

Setting Your Own Purpose

Ann wanted to think of a new way to earn money. After discarding the usual ways her friends used to earn money, Ann kept thinking and finally worked out a new idea. Ann decided to make popcorn to sell at the school football games. By setting her own purpose—to find a new idea—she was able to earn some money.

Like Ann, you also set purposes in your everyday life when you study for a test, try out for sports, or when you read. You may have more than one purpose when you read because you read for information as well as for pleasure. When you read an article or a textbook, you usually want to find the main idea, facts, or information, but you may also want to satisfy your curiosity. In stories, you may also want to satisfy your curiosity. In stories, you may want to find out what happens to a character as well as to be entertained.

Look through pages 136–147, and pages 158–167. What purposes might you set for reading each story? For reading the textbook lessons? You may find it helpful to write down your purposes before you read. After reading, ask yourself if you found what you were looking for. If so, you have achieved your purpose.

In the usual dragon-rescue story, the helpless princess is rescued from the fearful dragon by the courageous prince and they ride off on his trusty steed to live happily ever after. But this is not your usual dragon-rescue story. In this classic story, everyone breaks the pattern. The princess is far from helpless, the prince drives around in a motor car, and the dragon—well, the dragon . . .

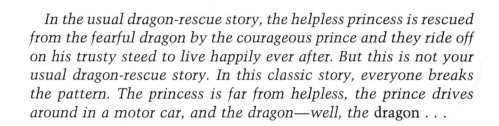

THE LAST OF THE DRAGONS

CLASSIC

by E. Nesbit

Of course you know that dragons were once as common as motor-omnibuses are now, and almost as dangerous. But as every well-brought-up prince was expected to kill a dragon, and rescue a princess, the dragons grew fewer and fewer till it was often quite hard for a princess to find a dragon to be rescued from. And at last there were no more dragons in France and no more dragons in Germany, or Spain, or Italy, or Russia. There were some left in China, and are still, but they are cold and bronzy, and there were never any, of course, in America. But the last real live dragon left was in England, and of course that was a very long time ago, before what you call English History began. This dragon lived in Cornwall in the big caves amidst the rocks, and a very fine big dragon it was, quite seventy feet long from the tip of its fearful snout to the end of its terrible tail. It breathed fire and smoke, and rattled when it walked, because its scales were made of iron. Its wings were like half-umbrellas—or like bats' wings, only several thousand times bigger. Everyone was very frightened of it, and well they might be.

Now the King of Cornwall had one daughter, and when she was sixteen, of course she would have to go and face the dragon: such tales are always told in royal nurseries at twilight, so the Princess knew what she had to expect. The dragon would not eat her, of course—because the prince would come and rescue her. But the Princess could not help thinking it would be much pleasanter to have nothing to do with the dragon at all—not even to be rescued from him. "All the princes I know are such very silly little boys," she told her father. "Why must I be rescued by a prince?"

"It's always done, my dear," said the King, taking his crown off and putting it on the grass, for they were alone in the garden, and even kings must unbend sometimes.

"Father, darling," said the Princess presently, when she had made a daisy chain and put it on the King's head, where the crown ought to have been. "Father, darling, couldn't we tie up one of the silly little princes for the dragon to look at—and then I could go and kill the dragon and rescue the prince? I fence much better than any of the princes we know."

"What an unladylike idea!" said the King, and put his crown on again, for he saw the Prime Minister coming with a basket of new-laid Bills for him to sign. "Dismiss the thought, my child. I rescued your mother from a dragon, and you don't want to set yourself up above her, I should hope?"

"But this is the *last* dragon. It is different from all other dragons."

"How?" asked the King.

"Because he *is* the last," said the Princess, and went off to her fencing lessons, with which she took great pains. She took great pains with all her lessons—for she could not give up the idea of fighting the dragon. She took such pains that she became the strongest and boldest and most skilful and most sensible princess in Europe. She had always been the prettiest and nicest.

And the days and years went on, till at last the day came which was the day before the Princess was to be rescued from the dragon. The Prince who was to do this deed of valour was a pale prince, with large eyes and a head full of mathematics and philosophy, but he had unfortunately neglected his fencing lessons. He was to stay the night at the palace, and there was a banquet.

After supper the Princess sent her pet parrot to the Prince with a note. It said:

"Please, Prince, come on to the terrace. I want to talk to you without anybody else hearing.—The Princess."

So, of course, he went—and he saw her gown of silver a long way off shining among the shadows of the trees like water in starlight. And when he came quite close to her he said: "Princess, at your service," and bent his cloth-of-gold-covered knee and put his hand on his cloth-of-gold-covered heart.

"Do you think," said the Princess earnestly, "that you will be able to kill the dragon?"

"I will kill the dragon," said the Prince firmly, "or perish in the attempt."

"It's no use your perishing," said the Princess.

"It's the least I can do," said the Prince.

"What I'm afraid of is that it'll be the most you can do," said the Princess.

"It's the only thing I can do," said he, "unless I kill the dragon."

"Why you should do anything for me is what I can't see," said she.

"But I want to," he said. "You must know that I love you better than anything in the world."

When he said that he looked so kind that the Princess began to like him a little.

"Look here," she said, "no one else will go out tomorrow. You know they tie me to a rock and leave me—and then everybody scurries home and puts up the shutters and keeps them shut till you ride through the town in triumph shouting that you've killed the dragon, and I ride on the horse behind you weeping for joy."

"I've heard that that is how it is done," said he.

"Well, do you love me well enough to come very quickly and set me free—and we'll fight the dragon together?"

"It wouldn't be safe for you."

"Much safer for both of us for me to be free, with a sword in my hand, than tied up and helpless. *Do* agree."

He could refuse her nothing. So he agreed. And next day everything happened as she had said.

When he had cut the cords that tied her to the rock they stood on the lonely mountain-side looking at each other.

"It seems to me," said the Prince, "that this ceremony could have been arranged without the dragon."

"Yes," said the Princess, "but since it has been arranged with the dragon—"

"It seems such a pity to kill the dragon—the last in the world," said the Prince.

"Well then, don't let's," said the Princess; "let's tame it not to eat princesses but to eat out of their hands. They say everything can be tamed by kindness."

"Taming by kindness means giving them things to eat," said the Prince. "Have you got anything to eat?"

She hadn't, but the Prince owned that he had a few biscuits. "Breakfast was so very early," said he, "and I thought you might have felt faint after the fight."

"How clever," said the Princess, and they took a biscuit in each hand. And they looked here, and they looked there, but never a dragon could they see.

"But here's its trail," said the Prince, and pointed to where the rock was scarred and scratched so as to make a track leading to a dark cave. It was like cart-ruts in a Sussex road, mixed with the marks of sea-gulls' feet on the sea-sand. "Look, that's where it's dragged its brass tail and planted its steel claws."

"Don't let's think how hard its tail and its claws are," said the Princess, "or I shall begin to be frightened—and I know you can't tame anything, even by kindness, if you're frightened of it. Come on. Now or never."

She caught the Prince's hand in hers and they ran along the path towards the dark mouth of the cave. But they did not run into it. It really was so very *dark*.

So they stood outside, and the Prince shouted: "What ho! Dragon there! What ho within!" And from the cave they heard an answering voice and great clattering and creaking. It sounded as though a rather large cotton-mill were stretching itself and waking up out of its sleep.

The Prince and the Princess trembled, but they stood firm.

"Dragon—I say, dragon!" said the Princess, "do come out and talk to us. We've brought you a present."

"Oh, yes—I know your presents," growled the dragon in a huge rumbling voice. "One of those precious princesses, I suppose? And I've got to come out and fight for her. Well, I tell you straight, I'm not going to do it. A fair fight I wouldn't say no to—a fair fight and no favour—but one of these put-up fights where you've got to lose—no! So I tell you. If I wanted a princess I'd come and take her, in my own time—but I don't. What do you suppose I'd do with her, if I'd got her?"

"Eat her, wouldn't you?" said the Princess, in a voice that trembled a little.

"Eat a fiddle-stick end," said the dragon very rudely. "I wouldn't touch the horrid thing."

The Princess's voice grew firmer.

"Do you like biscuits?" she said.

"No," growled the dragon.

"Not the nice little expensive ones with sugar on the top?"

"*No*," growled the dragon.

"Then what *do* you like?" asked the Prince.

"You go away and don't bother me," growled the dragon, and they could hear it turn over, and the clang and clatter of its turning echoed in the cave like the sound of the steam-hammers in the Arsenal[1] at Woolwich.

The Prince and Princess looked at each other. What were they to do? Of course it was no use going home and telling the King that the dragon didn't want princesses—because His Majesty was very old-fashioned and would never have believed that a new-fashioned dragon could ever be at all different from an old-fashioned dragon. They could not go into the cave and kill the dragon. Indeed, unless he attacked the Princess it did not seem fair to kill him at all.

"He must like something," whispered the Princess, and she called out in a voice as sweet as honey and sugar-cane:

"Dragon! Dragon dear!"

"WHAT?" shouted the dragon. "Say that again!" and they could hear the dragon coming towards them through the darkness of the cave. The Princess shivered, and said in a very small voice:

"Dragon—Dragon dear!"

And then the dragon came out. The Prince drew his sword, and the Princess drew hers—the beautiful silver-handled one that the Prince had brought in his motor-car. But they did not attack; they moved slowly back as the dragon came out, all the vast scaly length of him, and lay along the rock—his great wings half-spread and his silvery sheen gleaming like diamonds in the sun. At last they could

---

1. An arsenal is a factory.

retreat no further—the dark rock behind them stopped their way—and with their backs to the rock they stood swords in hand and waited.

The dragon drew nearer and nearer—and now they could see that he was not breathing fire and smoke as they had expected—he came crawling slowly towards them wriggling a little as a puppy does when it wants to play and isn't quite sure whether you're not cross with it.

And then they saw that great tears were coursing down its brazen cheek.

"Whatever's the matter?" said the Prince.

"Nobody," sobbed the dragon, "ever called me 'dear' before!"

"Don't cry, dragon dear," said the Princess. "We'll call you 'dear' as often as you like. We want to tame you."

"I *am* tame," said the dragon—"that's just it. That's what nobody but you has ever found out. I'm so tame that I'd eat out of your hands."

"Eat what, dragon dear?" said the Princess. "Not biscuits?" The dragon slowly shook his heavy head.

"Not biscuits?" said the Princess tenderly. "What, then, dragon dear?"

"Your kindness quite undragons me," it said. "No one has ever asked any of us what we like to eat—always offering us princesses, and then rescuing them—and never once, 'What'll you take to drink the King's health in?' Cruel hard I called it," and it wept again.

"But what would you like to drink our health in?" said the Prince. "We're going to be married today, aren't we, Princess?"

She said that she supposed so.

"What'll I take to drink your health in?" asked the dragon. "Ah, you're something like a gentleman, you are, sir. I don't mind if I do, sir. I'll be proud to drink your and your good lady's health in a tiny drop of"—its voice faltered—"to think of you

asking me so friendly like," it said. "Yes, sir, just a tiny drop of puppuppuppuppupetrol—tha–that's what does a dragon good, sir—"

"I've lots in the car," said the Prince, and was off down the mountain like a flash. He was a good judge of character and he knew that with the dragon the Princess would be safe.

"If I might make so bold," said the dragon, "while the gentleman's away—p'raps just to pass the time you'd be so kind as to call me Dear again, and if you'd shake claws with a poor old dragon that's never been anybody's enemy but his own—well, the last of the dragons'll be the proudest dragon that's ever been since the first of them."

It held out an enormous paw, and the great steel hooks that were its claws closed over the Princess's hand as softly as the claws of the Himalayan bear will close over the bit of bun you hand it through the bars at the Zoo.

And so the Prince and Princess went back to the palace in triumph, the dragon following them like a pet dog. And all through the wedding festivities no one drank more earnestly to the happiness of the bride and bridegroom than the Princess's pet dragon—whom she had at once named Fido.

And when the happy pair were settled in their own kingdom, Fido came to them and begged to be allowed to make himself useful.

"There must be some little thing I can do," he said, rattling his wings and stretching his claws. "My wings and claws and so on ought to be turned to some account—to say nothing of my grateful heart."

So the Prince had a special saddle or howdah made for him—very long it was—like the tops of many tramcars fitted together. One hundred and fifty seats were fitted to this, and the dragon, whose greatest pleasure was now to give pleasure to others, delighted in taking parties of children to the seaside. It flew through the air quite easily with its hundred and fifty little passengers—and would lie on the sand patiently waiting till they were ready to return. The children were very fond of it, and used to call it Dear, a word which never failed to bring tears of affection and gratitude to its eyes. So it lived, useful and respected, till quite the other day—when someone happened to say, in his hearing, that dragons were were out-of-date, now so much new machinery had come in. This so distressed him that he asked the King to change him into something less old-fashioned, and the kindly monarch at once changed him into a mechanical contrivance. The dragon, indeed, became the first aeroplane.

Meet the Author

The story you have just read was taken from the book *Five of Us—and Madeline*, a collection of short stories that was published in 1925, after the author's death. Edith Nesbit, born in 1858 in London, began publishing her work in 1885. She wanted to be a poet or a serious novelist, but she really wasn't very good at these forms of literature. Because of her husband's illness and bad business sense, Edith had to work very hard to support their family of five children. She wrote verses and stories for children's magazines and eventually realized that she had a special gift for writing about young people. She began to draw upon memories of her own happy childhood adventures for her stories.

Some of Nesbit's most famous books are *The Story of the Treasure Seekers* (1899), *The Wouldbegoods* (1901), *Five Children and It* (1902), and *The Phoenix and the Carpet* (1904).

LOOKING BACK

Prewriting

Thinking and Writing About the Section

You have just read about people who needed to make a breakthrough in order to overcome obstacles and achieve their goals. Some obstacles, such as cultural or traditional barriers, are caused by others, and some may be caused by a disability. You can write a narrative paragraph to share with a partner about one of these characters and the way in which he or she used a breakthrough to achieve his or her goal. First copy the chart. Then fill in the missing information.

See your Thinker's Handbook for tips.

Character	Goal	Obstacle	Breakthrough
Doña Felisa		culture	
Michael Naranjo	to be a sculptor		replaced sight with touch and memory
Princess	to marry Prince without killing dragon	fairy-tale tradition	joined with Prince to outwit tradition

Writing

Use the information from the chart to write about the goal, the obstacle, and the breakthrough made by one of the characters. Put the events in order. For more information on narrative paragraphs, see your Writer's Handbook.

Revising

Read your first draft to a partner. Did you tell about your character's goal and how he or she used a breakthrough to achieve it? Did you write about the events in order? Make changes if necessary. Then proofread for spelling and punctuation errors. Write your final copy.

Presenting

Read your paragraph to your partner. Ask if he or she has other suggestions about a breakthrough your character might have used.

Books to Read

P.S. Write Soon by Colby Rodowsky. Franklin Watts, © 1978.

You'd think Tanner's biggest challenge in life would be her family—her "zilch" sister and an intruding sister-in-law. But her real problem is the fantasy-filled letters she's written to her pen pal.

The Young Writer's Handbook by Susan and Stephen Tchudi. Scribner's Sons, © 1984.

Did you ever want to write a great school paper, keep an interesting journal, or even become a professional writer? This guide with its helpful suggestions can help you improve your writing skills.

Word Play by Joseph T. Shipley. Hawthorn Books, Inc. © 1972.

From riddles to anagram twisters, from double words to charades, this book presents a wide assortment of word games to challenge you and to expand your power of language and words.

The Brooklyn Bridge; They Said It Couldn't Be Built by Judith St. George. G. P. Putnam Sons, © 1982.

The remarkable story of the Roeblings— John, Washington, and Emily—achieving a seemingly impossible goal of engineering and building the Brooklyn Bridge.

American Library Association

4

The Seas Around Us

How proud a thing to fight with wind
and wave!

Arthur Hugh Clough

This line mirrors the fascination we have always had for the open sea. Beyond its beauty, we are also attracted to the sea's freedom. It knows no boundaries and obeys no master. It acts and we react.

While a study of the sea can reveal numerous facts about its life forms, continents, and islands, the sea still retains surprises and mysteries. We'll never know everything about the sea—and maybe that is its supreme fascination.

Reading Science and Geography Textbooks

As you read about "The Seas Around Us," you will be reading textbook material, just as you do in your science and geography classes. Reading textbooks is these classes is different from reading stories, poetry, and novels. Science and geography textbooks contain factual information, difficult terms, and graphic

Chapter and/or Lesson number.

Title announces the topic.

Introductory material gives you an idea of what the topic will be about and may include important questions.

Graphic aids illustrate or add to the information in the text. Graphic aids include graphs, tables, charts, diagrams, maps, and pictures.

Captions and labels identify different details in graphic aids.

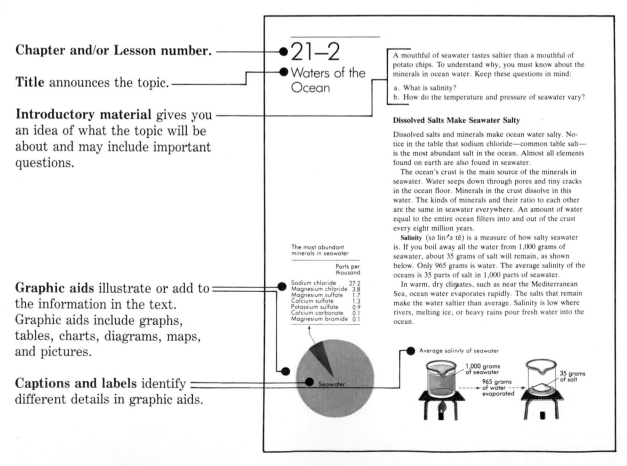

21–2
Waters of the Ocean

A mouthful of seawater tastes saltier than a mouthful of potato chips. To understand why, you must know about the minerals in ocean water. Keep these questions in mind:

a. What is salinity?
b. How do the temperature and pressure of seawater vary?

Dissolved Salts Make Seawater Salty

Dissolved salts and minerals make ocean water salty. Notice in the table that sodium chloride—common table salt—is the most abundant salt in the ocean. Almost all elements found on earth are also found in seawater.

The ocean's crust is the main source of the minerals in seawater. Water seeps down through pores and tiny cracks in the ocean floor. Minerals in the crust dissolve in this water. The kinds of minerals and their ratio to each other are the same in seawater everywhere. An amount of water equal to the entire ocean filters into and out of the crust every eight million years.

Salinity (sə lin′ə tē) is a measure of how salty seawater is. If you boil away all the water from 1,000 grams of seawater, about 35 grams of salt will remain, as shown below. Only 965 grams is water. The average salinity of the oceans is 35 parts of salt in 1,000 parts of seawater.

In warm, dry climates, such as near the Mediterranean Sea, ocean water evaporates rapidly. The salts that remain make the water saltier than average. Salinity is low where rivers, melting ice, or heavy rains pour fresh water into the ocean.

The most abundant minerals in seawater

	Parts per thousand
Sodium chloride	27.2
Magnesium chloride	3.8
Magnesium sulfate	1.7
Calcium sulfate	1.3
Potassium sulfate	0.9
Calcium carbonate	0.1
Magnesium bromide	0.1

Seawater

Average salinity of seawater

1,000 grams of seawater
965 grams of water evaporated
35 grams of salt

aids. Such textbooks organize this information in a special way to help you understand it more easily.

When you have a reading assignment in your science or geography textbook, **preview** the pages first to get a quick idea of the contents. Notice the various features: title, introductory information, subheads, terms in dark type, graphic aids, and questions at the end.

Previewing takes a few minutes but saves you time by helping you see how the information is organized, what the content is about, and what the important points are. Look at the features in the example below from Chapter 21, Lesson 2, of *Earth Science*. Notice that you can use the questions in the introductory material to help you set a purpose for reading.

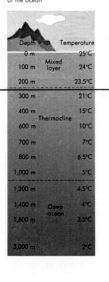

Temperature and Pressure of Ocean Water

Temperature The sun warms the water on the ocean's surface. Wind and waves mix the heated surface water with cold water beneath it. Notice in the diagram that water temperature is almost the same throughout the top layer of water. The temperature of this layer—the **mixed layer**—is different in different parts of the ocean. At the poles, it is usually colder than 0°C. Near the equator, surface water can be as warm as 30°C. In the middle latitudes, the surface temperature changes with the seasons. The mixed layer is 100 to 300 meters deep.

Beneath the mixed layer is the **thermocline** (thèr′mō klīn)—a layer of water that rapidly gets colder with increasing depth. Seawater at the bottom of the thermocline is very cold. Even near the equator, the bottom of the thermocline is colder than 5°C. The thermocline can be as deep as 1,000 meters.

Below the thermocline, temperatures drop slowly. The freezing point of seawater of average salinity is −2°C. The temperature of deep ocean water is always near freezing.

Pressure Air above the earth presses on the earth's surface. The air pressure that results can be measured in "atmospheres." Average air pressure at sea level is one atmosphere. In the same way that air presses on the earth's surface, water presses on the ocean's bottom. Pressure becomes greater with depth. Water pressure on the sea floor increases by an amount equal to one atmosphere of pressure for every increase of 10 meters beneath the ocean's surface. Forty atmospheres of water press on objects 400 meters below the surface. Deeper in the ocean, pressures are even greater.

Review It

1. What is the average salinity of seawater?
2. What is the thermocline?
3. How many atmospheres of pressure would the ocean put on an object 6,000 meters beneath the surface?

Temperature of layers of the ocean

Depth	Temperature
0 m	25°C
100 m	Mixed layer 24°C
200 m	23.5°C
300 m	21°C
400 m	15°C
Thermocline	
600 m	10°C
700 m	7°C
800 m	6.5°C
1,000 m	5°C
1,200 m	4.5°C
1,400 m	Deep ocean 4°C
1,600 m	3.5°C
3,000 m	2°C

Subheads are like titles for the paragraphs that follow. They tell what those paragraphs are about.

Dark type or some other special print within a paragraph calls your attention to new, important words or terms to learn. Sometimes pronunciation is included.

Questions, along with summaries or other review features, let you check your understanding of a lesson. They often restate the ideas brought out in the introductory material.

Using Your Reading Skills

Now that you have previewed the science textbook pages, you are ready for more careful reading of the material. As you might expect in textbooks of this type, one major focus of your reading will be learning unfamiliar terms and concepts. Two of the features that will assist you in understanding these terms and concepts are the graphic aids and words in dark type.

Look at the first page of the lesson "Waters of the Ocean," shown again at the right. In question **a** of the headnote, you can see that you are being asked to learn a new term—*salinity*—and from the subhead, you can see the new concept—*dissolved salts*—that will be the focus of the rest of the page.

The first paragraph under the subhead refers you to the table at the side of the page, which shows the breakdown of the most abundant minerals (salts) in seawater.

1. What does the full, blue circle graph represent? What does the dark wedge represent?

In answering the first part of the question, did you notice the label in the circle graph? The full, blue circle graph represents a sample of seawater in a total of 1,000 parts. To answer the second part of the question, notice the arrow pointing from the wedge to the table of minerals in seawater. The dark wedge shows the amount (parts) of dissolved minerals found in that 1,000-part sample of seawater.

2. What is salinity? What helps you know how to say the term?

In answering the first part of this question, did you remember from your previewing to look again to see if *salinity* was in dark type? Salinity is a measure of how salty seawater is. If you had difficulty answering the question, remember that unfamiliar and important terms you are expected to know are often highlighted in dark type. To answer the second part of the question, notice that the pronunciation of *salinity* is given right after the dark type.

3. What does the diagram directly below the text help illustrate? Does the diagram show one glass beaker used in two situations or are there two separate beakers? Explain.

21-2
Waters of the Ocean

A mouthful of seawater tastes saltier than a mouthful of potato chips. To understand why, you must know about the minerals in ocean water. Keep these questions in mind:

a. What is salinity?
b. How do the temperature and pressure of seawater vary?

Dissolved Salts Make Seawater Salty

Dissolved salts and minerals make ocean water salty. Notice in the table that sodium chloride—common table salt—is the most abundant salt in the ocean. Almost all elements found on earth are also found in seawater.

The ocean's crust is the main source of the minerals in seawater. Water seeps down through pores and tiny cracks in the ocean floor. Minerals in the crust dissolve in this water. The kinds of minerals and their ratio to each other are the same in seawater everywhere. An amount of water equal to the entire ocean filters into and out of the crust every eight million years.

Salinity (sə lin′ə tē) is a measure of how salty seawater is. If you boil away all the water from 1,000 grams of seawater, about 35 grams of salt will remain, as shown below. Only 965 grams is water. The average salinity of the oceans is 35 parts of salt in 1,000 parts of seawater.

In warm, dry climates, such as near the Mediterranean Sea, ocean water evaporates rapidly. The salts that remain make the water saltier than average. Salinity is low where rivers, melting ice, or heavy rains pour fresh water into the ocean.

The most abundant minerals in seawater

	Parts per thousand
Sodium chloride	27.2
Magnesium chloride	3.8
Magnesium sulfate	1.7
Calcium sulfate	1.3
Potassium sulfate	0.9
Calcium carbonate	0.1
Magnesium bromide	0.1

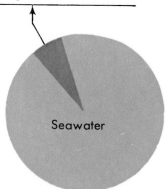

Seawater

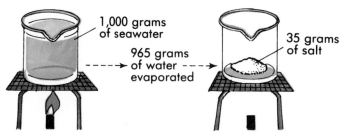

Average salinity of seawater

1,000 grams of seawater
965 grams of water evaporated
35 grams of salt

Practicing Textbook Reading

On the right is the second page of the lesson. Read the page, noticing how the text uses a graphic aid and dark type to help you understand important information and to give that information more emphasis.

1. What is the diagram about?
2. What is the mixed layer?
3. Answer **Review It** question 2.
4. What are the three layers of the ocean? What is the only textbook feature that directly lists all three?
5. Compare the temperature range in each layer. Which layer has the greatest range? Where did you find your answer?

After carefully reading an assignment, be sure to review it. Thinking of the answers to the questions at the end will show you how well you learned and understood the important facts and ideas. Going back over the lesson and taking notes will keep you prepared for class or for tests.

Tips for Reading on Your Own
- Preview your textbook reading assignments by looking at the features.
- Use the introductory questions and review questions to help you set a purpose for reading.
- Use the graphic aids and notice the important new terms in dark type.
- Read the entire assignment carefully. Make sure you understand each paragraph.
- Make notes that will help you remember important facts and ideas. Write down any questions you still have.
- Review the main points of the assignment. Reread any parts that you do not understand.

Temperature and Pressure of Ocean Water

Temperature The sun warms the water on the ocean's surface. Wind and waves mix the heated surface water with cold water beneath it. Notice in the diagram that water temperature is almost the same throughout the top layer of water. The temperature of this layer—the **mixed layer**—is different in different parts of the ocean. At the poles, it is usually colder than 0°C. Near the equator, surface water can be as warm as 30°C. In the middle latitudes, the surface temperature changes with the seasons. The mixed layer is 100 to 300 meters deep.

Beneath the mixed layer is the **thermocline** (thėr′mō klīn)—a layer of water that rapidly gets colder with increasing depth. Seawater at the bottom of the thermocline is very cold. Even near the equator, the bottom of the thermocline is colder than 5°C. The thermocline can be as deep as 1,000 meters.

Below the thermocline, temperatures drop slowly. The freezing point of seawater of average salinity is −2°C. The temperature of deep ocean water is always near freezing.

Pressure Air above the earth presses on the earth's surface. The air pressure that results can be measured in "atmospheres." Average air pressure at sea level is one atmosphere. In the same way that air presses on the earth's surface, water presses on the ocean's bottom. Pressure becomes greater with depth. Water pressure on the sea floor increases by an amount equal to one atmosphere of pressure for every increase of 10 meters beneath the ocean's surface. Forty atmospheres of water press on objects 400 meters below the surface. Deeper in the ocean, pressures are even greater.

Temperature of layers of the ocean

Depth		Temperature
0 m	Mixed layer	25°C
100 m		24°C
200 m		23.5°C
300 m		21°C
400 m	Thermocline	15°C
600 m		10°C
700 m		7°C
800 m		6.5°C
1,000 m		5°C
1,200 m		4.5°C
1,400 m	Deep ocean	4°C
1,600 m		3.5°C
3,000 m		2°C

Review It

1. What is the average salinity of seawater?
2. What is the thermocline?
3. How many atmospheres of pressure would the ocean put on an object 6,000 meters beneath the surface?

As you study the seas around us in the following two lessons, notice the important ideas that would help you if you had to take a test. Preview and then read this first lesson, from the textbook Earth Science. *Notice the terms in dark type and the pictures that aid you in remembering different points about life in the sea.*

21–4
Ocean Life

When you think of organisms that live in the ocean, you probably think of whales or sharks. But most organisms in the ocean are so small they can only be seen through a microscope. As you read about ocean life, ask yourself:

a. What organisms in the ocean need sunlight?
b. What organisms exist in the dark?
c. How is the ocean important as a source of food?

Sunlight and Ocean Life

Sunlight reaches only about 100 meters into the water. Because plants need energy from the sun, ocean plants live only as far down as the sunlight reaches. Most sea animals live in or just below this layer of sunlit water. Fish, squid, porpoises, and whales are some organisms that swim in the surface waters of the ocean.

Plankton (plangk′tən) are organisms that drift with ocean currents. Most plankton, such as the ones below, are less than 1 millimeter long. They are an important food for many sea animals. Many kinds of plankton make their own food. Some kinds of plankton feed on others.

Plankton

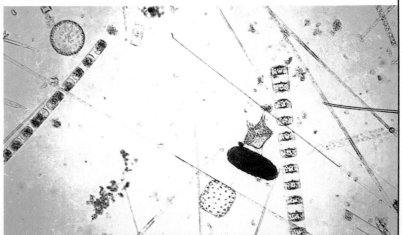

Some fish eat seaweed and plankton. Many kinds of fish eat other fish. These, in turn, are eaten by still larger fish. The relationship among organisms that feed on each other is a food web.

Life in the Depths

The deep parts of the ocean are dark and cold. No plants can grow there and the pressure is enormous. Yet some life exists even in the deepest parts of the ocean.

Almost all complex organisms need oxygen to release energy from food. Surface water contains oxygen from the air and from plants that live in the water. Water sinking from the surface carries oxygen down to deeper levels. Organisms in deep water need this oxygen to survive.

Some fish and other organisms live at great depths and adapt to the pressure. Most of them could not survive near the surface where the pressure is lower. Some animals that live in the depths eat the bodies of plankton and other organisms that die and sink to the bottom. Other animals digest the decayed remains of organisms in sediment on the ocean floor. Still others prey on the living organisms that swim in the cold, dark water.

Have You Heard?

Fireflies flicker like sparks in the dark night sky. In the same way, some animals that live in the continuous darkness of the deep ocean glow in the dark water. Bioluminescence (bī′ō lü′mə nes′ns) is the ability of an organism to give off light. Scientists think the light helps the animals attract food or mates.

Life in dark waters

Food from the Ocean

Plants of the ocean are important as food for fish. But people also eat sea plants, such as seaweed. Chemicals taken from some kinds of seaweed are used to make ice cream and salad dressing. Kelp, an ocean plant, can grow more than 80 meters in height. It is harvested for food, iodine, and potassium.

Sea animals such as fish are an important food for many people. Fish make up 90 percent of the sea life caught each year. The picture at the left shows a day's catch of fish. Whales and crabs, shrimp, oysters, and their relatives are also caught. More than half the fish caught in the oceans are used to feed poultry and livestock.

One way to increase the production of food from the sea is sea farming. The number of fish that live in an area will increase if more food is provided for them. Minerals that plankton need for life could be brought up from the deep waters. Other sea life that eat the plankton could then grow in greater numbers.

Problems arise as people depend more and more on sea life for food. One problem is **overfishing**—or the removal of so many fish from an area that the fish population cannot reproduce itself. Overfishing for just one year means there will not be enough fish for years to come.

Pollution of the ocean is another problem for people who depend on fish for food. Most of the fish we eat live in waters above the continental shelves. Insecticides and toxic wastes wash off the land into the water. Some fish in these polluted waters die, and some produce eggs that cannot hatch. Poisons stored in the bodies of other fish make them unsafe for people to eat. Oil spills from ships at sea or from oil drilling on the continental shelves can also pollute fishing areas.

The day's catch

Review It

1. What are plankton?
2. How do fish living deep in the ocean get their food?
3. How does pollution of ocean water affect sea life?

As you learn more about the seas around us, continue to note the important ideas. Preview and then read this second lesson, from the textbook People on Earth: A World Geography. *Pay attention to the terms and graphic aids in the "Vocabulary" and "Building Skills" section of the* **Lesson Review** *at the end.*

2/Continents, Islands, and Oceans

From space, the earth looks like a nearly round blue and white ball. It is outlined against a black background. The white clouds make earth look like a big marble. Much of the earth's surface appears to be quite smooth. Elsewhere, it is marked with rough areas. The smooth areas usually represent the **ocean.** The ocean is the huge body of salt water that covers more than 70 percent of the earth's surface. The rough areas are the large land masses.

Photographs from space also show that land makes up only a small part of the earth's surface. Water is much more widespread. We live on a watery planet.

Continents and Islands

The largest land masses are continents. In reality, continents are the largest of **islands.** Although there are six large land masses, there are seven continents. Find them on the World—Elevation of Land map in the Atlas.

The land mass of Eurasia includes two continents. On the west is Europe. On the east is Asia. There is no clearcut boundary between the two parts. On the map, you can see that northeast of the Caspian Sea there is a range of mountains running north to the Arctic Ocean. This range is known as the Ural Mountains. For convenience, we shall consider that the continent of Europe extends eastward to the Urals.

The boundaries of the other continents are more clearly defined. Antarctica, centering on the South Pole, is separate from all the other continents. Australia is also separate. North America and South America are connected by a narrow piece of land, known as the Isthmus of Panama. The **isthmus** has been cut through by the Panama Canal. In effect, the Panama Canal makes an island of both North America and South America.

Africa, too, is clearly defined. The Mediterranean Sea and the Straits of Gibraltar separate Africa from Europe. In the northeast, the Red Sea and the Suez Canal form Africa's boundary with Eurasia. The Suez Canal, connecting the Mediterranean Sea with the Red Sea, makes an island of Africa.

There are other masses of land that rise out of the oceans. However, these land masses are much smaller than continents. These smaller land masses are islands.

North and South America are two of the world's seven continents. They are joined by the Isthmus of Panama.

NORTH AMERICA

Isthmus of Panama

SOUTH AMERICA

Look at the map again to locate some of the largest islands. Southeast of North America is a group of islands known as the West Indies. Of these the largest are Cuba, Hispaniola, Jamaica, and Puerto Rico. In the northern part of the Atlantic Ocean is the large island of Greenland and the small island of Iceland. Off the eastern coast of Africa is the island of Madagascar. South of India is the island of Ceylon, or Sri Lanka. South of Australia is Tasmania. The two islands that make up the country of New Zealand lie to the southeast of Australia. Off the eastern coast of Asia, there are several island groups. These include the islands of Japan, Taiwan, the Philippines, and the islands of Indonesia.

Oceans

The world's oceans are really one continuous body of water. For convenience, we give separate names to different parts of the world ocean. Water surrounding Antarctica separates northward into the Pacific, Indian, and Atlantic oceans. The Pacific and Atlantic oceans join with the Arctic Ocean. In its frozen form, the Arctic Ocean covers the North Pole.

Near the shores of the continents the arms of the oceans have names that begin with **"Gulf"** or **"Bay"** or end with **"Sea."** Some examples are the Gulf of Mexico, the Bay of Bengal, and the Coral Sea. Find these places on the map. Can you find some others?

Look at the pie graph that shows the sizes of the oceans and the continents. Which ocean is about as large in area as all the other oceans put together? Which ocean is greater in area than all seven continents put together?

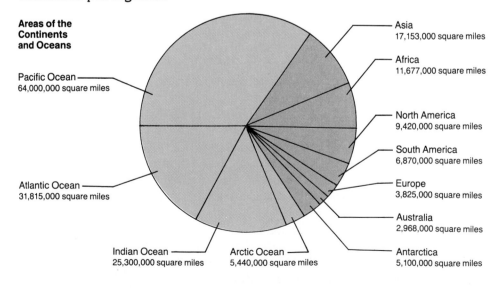

Areas of the Continents and Oceans

Asia 17,153,000 square miles

Africa 11,677,000 square miles

Pacific Ocean 64,000,000 square miles

North America 9,420,000 square miles

South America 6,870,000 square miles

Atlantic Ocean 31,815,000 square miles

Europe 3,825,000 square miles

Australia 2,968,000 square miles

Indian Ocean 25,300,000 square miles

Arctic Ocean 5,440,000 square miles

Antarctica 5,100,000 square miles

Ocean Currents

Within the oceans are strong **currents.** A current is like a river, always flowing. The currents are an important reason why people are able to live on the earth. Pushed by **prevailing winds** and the spinning of the earth, the currents flow in a circular pattern within the world's oceans. These great circular currents move clockwise in the Northern Hemisphere and counterclockwise in the Southern Hemisphere. These currents help to transfer some of the heat of the equatorial regions to the polar regions. And, these currents bring the cold of the polar regions towards the equator. As you might expect, some of the currents are warm and some are cold. Find both kinds of currents on the map showing the major ocean currents.

Ocean currents influence the climate of the lands along the coasts. Look at the map of ocean currents again. Note how the North Atlantic Drift carries warm water from the Caribbean Sea

World — Major Ocean Currents

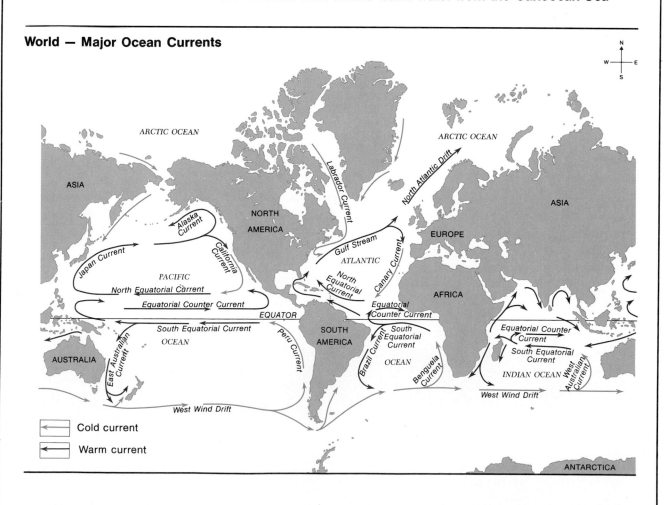

northeastward across the Atlantic Ocean. It helps to give Europe a mild climate, even though Europe has a far more northerly latitude than our country.

Tides

Ocean water also moves up and down. A **tide** is a rise or fall in the level of the surface of the ocean. This is caused mainly by the pull of the moon's gravity on the earth. As a general rule, there are two high tides and two low tides every day. The difference in water level between a high tide and a low tide is called the **tidal range.** In the open sea, the range is only about 2 or 3 feet (.6 or .9 meters). Along the shorelines, the range can be from as little as 2 feet (.6 meters) to as much as 50 feet (15 meters).

People who live along the shore and designers of buildings and bridges have to take the tides into account. In a few areas of the world, where the tidal range is great, tides can be used as a source of power.

The Earth's Land and Water Hemispheres

The two global diagrams on page 165 show some important facts about the distribution of the earth's continents and oceans. Each diagram shows a special hemisphere.

The first one shows the globe turned so that you are looking at Western Europe. With the globe turned in this way, you can see all of Europe, Africa, and North America. You can also see nearly all of Asia and most of South America. From this point of view, you can see most of the earth's large land masses. This is called the **land hemisphere.**

Tides in the Bay of Fundy, Nova Scotia, sometimes rise and fall more than 50 feet (15 meters). The tides determine when the work day begins and ends for the fishermen. They leave or enter the harbor at high water.

Now look at the other globe. It is turned so that you are looking at New Zealand in the Pacific Ocean. Now, you can only see Antarctica, Australia, and a small part of South America. You are looking at the **water hemisphere.** It has been given this name because more than 90 percent of it is covered by water.

Land and water hemispheres are important when you remember that most of the world's people live on the land. Ninety-four percent of them live in the land hemisphere. Events that take place in the land hemisphere usually affect more people than do events that take place in the water hemisphere.

Lesson Review

Vocabulary: ocean, island, isthmus, gulf, bay, sea, ocean current, prevailing wind, tide, tidal range, land hemisphere, water hemisphere

Recalling the Main Ideas

1. Why is it said that we live on a watery planet?
2. Describe the boundaries of the continents.
3. How are continents different from islands?
4. Explain how the ocean currents move in the Atlantic, Pacific, and Indian oceans.
5. Why do the people who live along the shore have to take the tides into account?
6. What is the difference between the land and water hemispheres?

Building Skills

1. Use a globe to demonstrate how the world's oceans are really one continuous body of water.
2. Use the graph showing the areas of the oceans and continents. List the continents according to size, from largest to smallest.

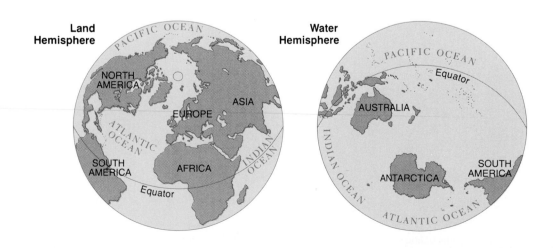

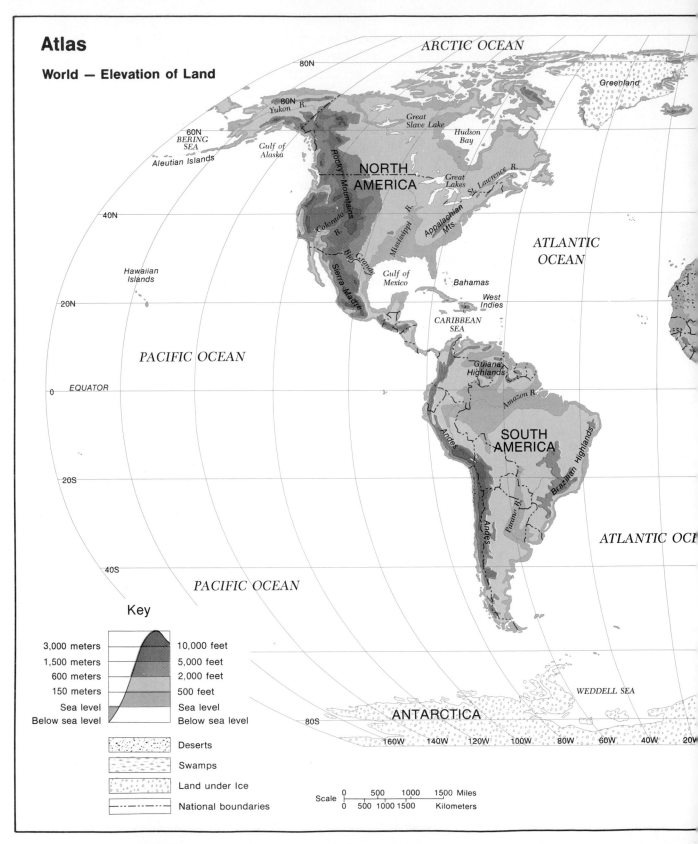

Atlas

World — Elevation of Land

ARCTIC OCEAN

Greenland

80N

80N
Yukon R.

60N
BERING
SEA

Gulf of
Alaska

Great
Slave Lake

Hudson
Bay

Aleutian Islands

Rocky Mountains

NORTH
AMERICA

Great
Lakes

St. Lawrence R.

ATLANTIC
OCEAN

40N

Colorado
R.

Mississippi

Appalachian
Mts.

Hawaiian
Islands

Rio Grande

Sierra Madre

Gulf of
Mexico

Bahamas

West
Indies

20N

PACIFIC OCEAN

CARIBBEAN
SEA

Guiana
Highlands

0   EQUATOR

Amazon R.

Andes

SOUTH
AMERICA

Brazilian Highlands

20S

Paraná R.

Andes

40S

PACIFIC OCEAN

ATLANTIC OCE

Key

3,000 meters	10,000 feet
1,500 meters	5,000 feet
600 meters	2,000 feet
150 meters	500 feet
Sea level	Sea level
Below sea level	Below sea level

Deserts

Swamps

Land under Ice

National boundaries

WEDDELL SEA

80S

ANTARCTICA

160W   140W   120W   100W   80W   60W   40W   20W

Scale
0   500   1000   1500 Miles
0 500 1000 1500   Kilometers

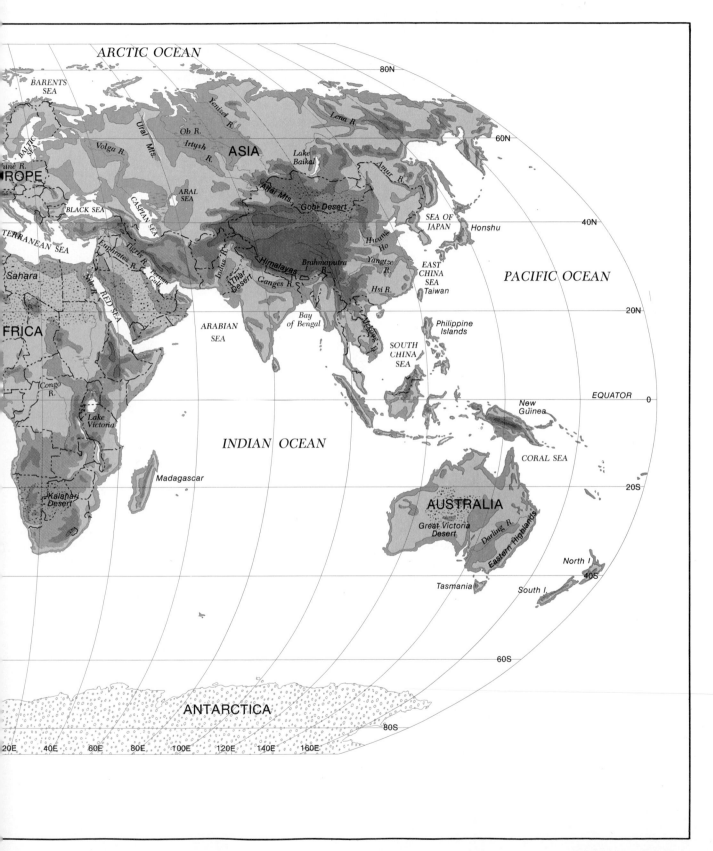

ARCTIC OCEAN

BARENTS
SEA

BALTIC
SEA

Yenisei R.

Ob R.

Irtysh
R.

Lena R.

80N

60N

Ural Mts.

Volga R.

ine R.

ROPE

ASIA

Lake
Baikal

Amur R.

ARAL
SEA

Altai Mts.

Gobi Desert

SEA OF
JAPAN

Honshu

40N

CASPIAN SEA

BLACK SEA

TERRANEAN SEA

Sahara

Tigris R.

Euphrates R.

Persian
Gulf

Indus R.

Thar
Desert

Himalayas

Ganges R.

Brahmaputra
R.

Hwang
Ho

Yangtze
R.

Hsi R.

EAST
CHINA
SEA

Taiwan

PACIFIC OCEAN

FRICA

Nile R.

RED SEA

ARABIAN
SEA

Bay
of Bengal

Mekong R.

SOUTH
CHINA
SEA

Philippine
Islands

20N

Congo
R.

Lake
Victoria

INDIAN OCEAN

New
Guinea

EQUATOR 0

CORAL SEA

Madagascar

Kalahari
Desert

AUSTRALIA

Great Victoria
Desert

Darling R.

Eastern Highlands

20S

North I.

40S

Tasmania

South I.

60S

ANTARCTICA

80S

20E   40E   60E   80E   100E   120E   140E   160E

Comprehension Check

See your Thinker's Handbook for tips.

Think and Discuss

1. What are three important ideas you should remember from the lessons when you prepare for a test?
• 2. Answer the first **Review It** question on page 160. What textbook feature helped you find the answer to the question?
3. According to the geography lesson, the ocean makes up what percent of the earth's surface?
• 4. What textbook feature lets you see quickly that the Pacific Ocean is about one-third of the area of the earth?
5. What is the difference between currents and tides?
• Study Skills: Textbook reading techniques

Communication Workshop

Talk

Work with a small group of classmates. Look over the graphic aids in the two textbook lessons you have just read. Discuss how the aids helped you understand the text and also added to your knowledge. For example, what did you find out about plankton from the picture that you did not learn from the text?
Speaking/Listening: Group discussion

Write

Use the ideas you discussed above to write four test questions for the others in your small group. Construct each question so that you have to use one of the graphic aids in order to answer it. Then exchange test questions within your group. Are all the questions clear? Can they be answered by using one of the graphic aids you discussed? Answer one or more of the questions that you did not write.
Writing Fluency: Test questions

Oceans of Laughs

"We never know what to expect after a violent hurricane."

Drawing by B. Petty;
©1964 The New Yorker
Magazine, Inc.

"Are you sure this species has never faced a camera before?"

Using Context to Find Appropriate Word Meaning

In the geography textbook lesson you just read, "Continents, Islands, and Oceans," you learned that a *current* is a flow of water in the ocean. You also know other meanings for the word *current*. What does it mean in the phrase, "current events"? If you said it means "present," you were right. You know many meanings for a word.

As you read, you will often come across words that have a special meaning depending on the context in which they are found. Think about the word *pie*. You would expect the word *pie* to refer to a kind of food but it refers to a type of graph called a "pie graph" in a geography lesson, such as the one you just read.

To find the appropriate, or correct, meaning of a word, keep in mind the type of reading in which you find the word. When you come to a word that has several meanings, read the context—the other words and sentences around the word—to help you find clues to figure out which meaning makes the best sense. If you cannot figure out the meaning after rereading, look up the word in a dictionary to find the meaning that makes the best sense.

Can you figure out the appropriate meaning for these underlined words below?

Some fish eat seaweed and plankton. Many kinds of fish eat the decayed *remains* of other fish or prey on living fish. These fish, in turn, are eaten by still larger fish. The relationship among organisms that feed on each other is a food *web*.

The context shows you that *remains* means the "dead bodies" of other fish and that *web* means a "relationship." Why doesn't *remains* mean "stays" and *web* refer to something that is woven? These words are used in a paragraph about fish in the ocean, such as you would find in a science or geography textbook. Thus, the words will have meanings appropriate for that context.

What do each of the underlined words in this paragraph mean?

As a *general* rule, there are two high tides and two low tides every day. The difference in water level between a high tide and a low tide is called the tidal *range*. In the open sea, the range is only about 2 or 3 feet (.6 or .9 meters). Along the *coasts*, the range can be from as little as 2 feet (.6 meters) to as much as 50 feet (15 meters).

In this context, the appropriate meaning for *general* is "usual" and the meaning for *coasts* is "shorelines." The word *range* is used here in reference to tides and the context explains that a tidal range refers to the different levels of water between high and low tides.

Practicing Context

Use the context of the sentences to help you find the meanings of the underlined words below.

1. The teacher brought in some small octopuses in a <u>tank</u>.
2. Some octopuses are sixty feet <u>long</u>.
3. An octopus has strong, hard jaws. The jaws come to a <u>point</u> like a parrot's <u>bill</u>.
4. Octopuses are members of a group of shellfish and belong to the <u>class</u> *Cephalopoda*.

Tips for Reading on Your Own
- Remember that the meaning of a word may depend on the type of reading in which you find the word.
- When you come to a word for which you know more than one meaning, continue reading for clues that will help you decide on the appropriate meaning.
- Use a dictionary if you cannot figure out a meaning that makes sense.
- For other tips on figuring out words, see your Word Study Handbook.

Are cephalopods[1]—more commonly known as octopuses and squids—merely slimy, terrible monsters of the open sea? Or are they little-understood creatures worthy of more attention from us? In an essay, world-famous French undersea explorer Jacques-Yves Cousteau shares his thoughts on these creatures. What is his opinion about them? What different type of information can you learn about octopuses in the encyclopedia article following the essay?

Dark and Misunderstood Waters

by Jacques-Yves Cousteau

• Set your purpose for reading. What do you want to find out by reading this essay?

Cephalopods are astounding. They have a freedom in the sea and two ways of moving—swimming and jet propulsion. And, as far as their intelligence goes, we have only begun to suspect its breadth. So, at the risk of sounding like science fiction, we might say that if any group of animals without backbones can one day rise to unexpected heights, cephalopods are that group.

Because of this, the gifts and talents of cephalopods deserve better than our scorn. Observation of them in an aquarium will not erase the falsehoods. What is needed is contact in the open sea. Octopuses and squids should have the same kindly attention that we give to animals on land. But then, we have never known more than three elements: air, land, and fire. Water, the sea, has been a mystery to us until the middle of this century. Just as the octopus knows nothing of fire, so we know nothing of water. The ocean was closed to us, and it has only just been opened.

Exploration of the sea offers us many new animals to study, understand, and appreciate. The most striking example of this has been that of the cephalopods.

We have been able to determine that the curiosity of the octopus is virtually without limits. Their sole misfortune is that they lack the means to hear and to speak. Sound, beyond a doubt, is the best contact between us and animals. The only senses common to us and the octopus, however, are touch and sight. And these must be enough to establish a mutual understanding.

---

1. cephalopods (sef′ə lə podz).

Aboard *Calypso,*
Captain Cousteau and
Andrew Packard watch
octopuses in a tank.

Before long, friendship between cephalopods and divers will become one of the pleasures of life in the sea. Even then, of course, we will have to remember not to disturb the cephalopods or interfere with their lives. People can be very ignorant. They feel that all animals must be their subjects, regardless of the effects upon the animals themselves.

It is the next generation that will finally put aside all the legends about the monsters which sink ships and drown divers. I have already had an experience which has been very enlightening in that respect, at the Lindero Canyon School in Aguora, California. There I sat in on a natural history class. The teacher had brought in a group of small octopuses in a tank. We asked the pupils if they would put their hands into the tank and touch the octopuses. At first, they were slightly uneasy, but, after only a moment, they put their hands into the tank and touched them.

I then had an interesting conversation with one of the pupils, a girl named Debbie. "You see that little octopus," I said. "I bet that it is able to show affection. Why don't you shake hands with it?"

Debbie hesitated a bit, and giggled a little, but bent over the tank and put her arm into the water. The octopus, naturally, put out an exploratory arm of its own.

"It's funny," Debbie said. "It has so many hands to shake. It's kind of sticky."

"Are you afraid?"

"Oh, no. Of course not."

Debbie and her friends did not believe the old legends. I showed them the engravings that had been used to illustrate Jules Verne's novel *Twenty Thousand Leagues Under the Sea.* I asked them what they thought about them. Everyone answered that they were fairy tales and that people shouldn't be fooled by them.

And yet, one must admit that not all cephalopods are like the friendly little Pacific octopuses that the pupils saw and touched. At the bottom of the sea, there are giants which, if we can judge from the pieces found on the surface, are sixty feet (18.29 m) long and weigh four tons. So as imaginary as the old stories may be, they do have a basis in reality. But until the present time, the giant cephalopods seen on the surface have all been either dead or dying. Until it is proved otherwise, we may assume that these "monsters" do not leave deep water.

I myself, from the minisub, saw an unidentified cephalopod which, while not a giant, was of considerable size. How is it, then, that we see these animals so rarely? For the past fifteen years,

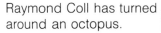
Raymond Coll has turned around an octopus.

dives have been undertaken in increasing numbers by the Russians, the French, and the Americans. These dives have been made by experienced observers. One would think that they would have seen giant squids if there were such animals.

The explanation may be that their devices are slow, and they move within a very small area. Also, the squids are rather timid animals. We may well frighten them and awaken a desire to escape—which they have all the time in the world to do. This was the reaction of the only large cephalopod that I have ever met underwater.

Despite all the progress that we have made in discovering the secrets of the sea, those of the deep still escape us. We must learn to explore those depths. It is, after all, only a question of technology. The future may well reveal to us those great and mysterious beings at the bottom of the sea. That alone is an expectation that makes life worth living.

• Was your purpose-setting question answered? If not, reread the selection before answering the questions on page 182.

Meet the Author

Jacques-Yves Cousteau is perhaps best known for his adventures on the *Calypso,* which have been dramatized on the television series, "The Undersea World of Jacques Cousteau." But Cousteau's contributions to undersea exploration also include the invention of important technology, such as the aqualung, and underwater diving stations and vehicles.

Captain Cousteau was the first person to take underwater color photographs. He has made several films of his underwater discoveries, three of which have won Academy Awards. Cousteau's books about the sea have been translated into many languages and include *The Silent World, The Living Sea,* and *Octopus and Squid: The Soft Intelligence,* from which the selection you have just read was taken.

Douglas P. Wilson

Many Octopuses Find Their Prey on the Ocean Bottom.

OCTOPUS is a sea animal with a soft body and eight arms called *tentacles*. The word *octopus* comes from two Greek words that mean *eight feet*.

Some people call octopuses *devilfish*, probably because of the animal's frightening appearance. An octopus has large, shiny eyes, and strong, hard jaws that come to a point like a parrot's bill. The octopus uses its arms to catch clams, crabs, lobsters, mussels, and other shellfish, and to break the shells apart. It cuts up food with its horny jaws. Some kinds of octopuses inject a poison that paralyzes their prey. Octopuses rarely attack people.

There are about 50 kinds of octopuses, and most are only about as big as a man's fist. The largest ones may measure 28 feet (8.5 meters) from the tip of one tentacle to the tip of another on the other side of the body.

Octopuses live chiefly in the China and Mediterranean seas, and along the coasts of Hawaii, North America, and the West Indies. Many people in these regions eat octopus meat. Octopuses belong to a group of shellfish called *mollusks*. This group includes clams, oysters, and snails. Like squid and cuttlefish, octopuses are mollusks that have no outside shells. See MOLLUSK.

An octopus has no bones, and no inside shell as squid and cuttlefish do. A tough protective wrapper called a *mantle* covers the body and gives it shape. The tentacles are joined to the body and to one another by a web of tissue at their bases. Rows of round muscles

R. Tucker Abbott, the contributor of this article, holds the du Pont Chair of Malacology at the Delaware Museum of Natural History, and is the author of American Seashells *and* Sea Shells of the World.

BODY OF AN OCTOPUS

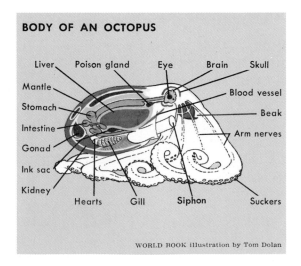

WORLD BOOK illustration by Tom Dolan

on the underside of each tentacle act much like suction cups. These suckers can fasten tightly to any object, and may hold on even if the tentacle is cut off. If an octopus loses a tentacle, a new one grows in its place.

An octopus has two eyes and sees well. It has the most highly developed brain of all the *invertebrates* (animals without backbones). It has three hearts that pump blood through its body. The animal breathes by means of gills, somewhat as fish do. An octopus swims by drawing water into its body. Then the animal squeezes the water out through its *siphon*, a funnel-shaped opening under the head. The force of the expelled water moves the animal backward. The octopus can also squirt a black fluid from the siphon. This fluid forms a dark cloud that hides the animal so it can escape from sharks, whales, human beings, and other enemies.

The skin of an octopus contains small bags of *pigments* (coloring matter). The pigment bags connect with the animal's nervous system. When an octopus becomes excited, it changes color—becoming blue, brown, gray, purple, red, white, or even striped. Many octopuses change color to blend with their surroundings.

A female octopus lays a cluster of as many as 180,000 nearly transparent eggs. The eggs are attached to rocks and hatch in about two months. The female tends the eggs and does not eat during this period. The young begin to find their own food as soon as they hatch.

Scientific Classification. Octopuses are members of the phylum *Mollusca*, and belong to the class *Cephalopoda*. They make up the genus *Octopus*.   R. TUCKER ABBOTT

See also CUTTLEFISH; MOLLUSK; NAUTILUS; SQUID.

OCULAR. See MICROSCOPE; TELESCOPE.

OCULIST is a physician who treats eye disorders and diseases. See OPHTHALMOLOGY.

ODD FELLOWS, INDEPENDENT ORDER OF, is one of the largest fraternal and benevolent orders in the United States. The order was founded in England. The date of its founding is not known, but Odd Fellows' groups probably existed in the early 1700's. The members founded a system of benefits and helped one another in time of misfortune. Branches called *lodges* grew up in the various English cities, but each branch refused to admit the superior rank of any other. Adjustments were finally made, and in 1814 the Manchester Unity of the Independent Order of Odd Fellows was organized. It has branches in various countries but has no present connection with the order in the United States.

The American Order. In 1819, the Washington Lodge of Odd Fellows was organized in Baltimore. The next year, Washington Lodge became a subordinate lodge in the Manchester Unity. Other American lodges were established later and assumed a like position.

But in 1843 the American lodges separated themselves from the parent order in England. The United States grand lodge became the head of the order in America and reserved for itself the right to found new lodges in Europe. The Canadian branch operated under a separate charter until 1852. In that year the society in Canada was merged with the grand lodge of the United States. The Order of Odd Fellows in the United States has a membership of 1,250,000.

Purpose and Organization. The chief purpose of the Order of Odd Fellows is to give aid, assistance, and comfort to its members and their families. It is a secret society and has its own system of rites and passwords. The three links in its symbol represent friendship, love, and truth. The skull and crossbones speak of mortality, and the single eye represents the all-knowingness of God.

A local lodge can confer three degrees of membership upon an Odd Fellow. When a member has reached the highest of these three grades he is ready for membership in an encampment. The encampment also has three degrees of membership, the Patriarchal, the Golden Rule, and the Royal Purple. The Patriarchal is an English degree. Since 1884, there has also been a military or uniformed degree called the Patriarch Militant.

The Rebekah lodges in Odd Fellows are chiefly for women, although some men belong. Rebekah assemblies were organized in 1851 and have more than 1 million members. Headquarters are at 16 W. Chase St., Baltimore, Md. 21201.

Critically reviewed by the INDEPENDENT ORDER OF ODD FELLOWS

ODE, *ohd,* a poem of moderate length, usually expresses exalted praise. Greek dramatists wrote *choral odes* that had three parts. Two parts, a *strophe* and an *antistrophe*, had identical meter. The third part, called an *epode*, had a contrasting meter. Pindar, of ancient Greece, wrote odes in praise of athletic heroes. He used the strophic form, which came to be called *Pindaric* (see PINDAR). Horace, of ancient Rome, wrote odes made up of uniform stanzas, called *stanzaic* form.

English poetry, from the time of Ben Jonson, included a variety of Pindaric odes, stanzaic odes, and *irregular* odes, or those with no particular stanza structure. John Dryden wrote two irregular odes in praise of St. Cecilia. "Ode to Evening," by William Collins, is a notable stanzaic ode. The great irregular and stanzaic odes of the 1800's include William Wordsworth's "Ode: Intimations of Immortality," Percy Bysshe Shelley's "Ode to the West Wind," John Keats' "Ode on a Grecian Urn," and Alfred, Lord Tennyson's "Ode on the Death of the Duke of Wellington." CHARLES W. COOPER

See also GREEK LITERATURE (Lyric Poetry).

O'DELL, SCOTT (1903-   ), an American author, became known for his historical novels for children. Most of his works are set in Mexico, southern California, and the Southwest. O'Dell began his writing career in 1934, but his first children's book was not published until 1960. That book, *Island of the Blue Dolphins*, won the 1961 Newbery medal. O'Dell's other children's books include *The King's Fifth* (1966), *The Black Pearl* (1967), *Sing Down the Moon* (1970), and *The Treasure of Topo-el-Bampo* (1972). O'Dell received the 1978 Regina medal for his contributions to children's literature. He was born in Los Angeles.   ELLIN GREENE

ODELSTING. See NORWAY (Parliament).

ODER RIVER is an important waterway of central Europe. It is 550 miles (885 kilometers) long and drains more than 43,000 square miles (111,000 square kilometers), which is about the area of Tennessee.

The Oder rises in the Carpathian Mountains of Czechoslovakia. It then flows northward across western Poland where it joins the Neisse River to form the boundary between Poland and East Germany. It empties into the Baltic Sea by way of the Oder Lagoon (see POLAND [terrain map]).

Another misunderstood creature of the sea is the shark. We seem to know a great deal about sharks from books, movies, and television shows. Sharks are about ten-foot long "killing machines" that roam the coastal waters of the United States, right? But maybe we don't know everything about sharks yet. The following newspaper article is from The New York Times. *What makes these sharks newsworthy? Notice the type of information the newspaper article contains to help you answer the questions.*

Bizarre Sharks Come to Light

by Walter Sullivan

The great white shark, man-eating star of movies, television, and nightmares, is losing some of its popularity with scientists. Taking its place, under dark waters and nearly unknown, are some other, rarely seen sharks.

Once in a while, some accidental discovery brings a bizarre shark up to the ocean's surface. In 1976 a 15-foot monster was dragged up off Hawaii. It was quickly named "megamouth." It had a 4-foot mouth with which, it is believed, it swam the deep, scooping in tiny plants and animals drifting in the sea.

This 1,653-pounder is so far one of a kind. But there must be more. Since megamouth is a male, and female sharks are usually bigger than males, a number of even larger such sharks probably roam the ocean depths. Such areas are one of the few places on earth where human explorers can still expect surprises.

One of the most fascinating of all deepwater sharks is the grotesque goblin shark. It has a long, spearlike snout and vicious-looking teeth. According to Dr. Eugenie Clark of the

University of Maryland, who has studied sharks for 28 years, no one has ever seen a live goblin. Pieces of several dead goblins have come up in fishermen's nets. Two of these are preserved at the American Museum of Natural History in New York. So even dead, a whole, intact goblin shark has never been recovered. In common with many of the deepwater sharks, they lack the tough skin that helps hold many of these boneless creatures together. But from bits and pieces, it appears they may reach 15 or 20 feet in length.

The goblins live at great ocean depths. However, a Japanese fisherman says he knows where, at certain times of the year, they come up to within 800 feet of the surface to feed. Not long ago Japan built a small submarine. Some people hope it can be used to capture one for exhibition at an aquarium.

Dr. Clark wants to go down in the craft and have a look at living goblins. She doubts, however, that they could survive a trip to the surface. In any case, no one even knows how to bait a hook for them. Their eating habits are unknown.

Similar unknowns apply to the diet of the frilled shark, which has an eel-like body and frills on its neck. Its eating habits are little known, although sharp ridges on its lips may enable it to hold onto slippery prey, such as squid.

The one and only megamouth was caught 26 miles northeast of Oahu in the Hawaiian Islands. A navy craft doing ocean research dropped two large parachutes 545 feet down as sea anchors, to avoid drifting with surface winds and currents. When the chutes were hauled up, one of them contained megamouth.

The fish was brought aboard with great difficulty. Then it was taken to the Naval Undersea Center at Kaneohe[1] Bay, where it was stored overnight next to a pier. When a crane was used to lift it out of the water the next day, its long tail fin broke off.

1. Kaneohe (kä′nä ō′hä).

Megamouth

The monster was kept frozen until a special preservation tank could be built. A study of the remains has been published in California.

The report reveals that the huge mouth is used for filtering small organisms from the sea, as many whales do. The stomach of megamouth was found to be filled with "a thick, reddish soup." The soup contained tiny shrimp of a species that dives deep by day but at night comes up to the 545-foot depth at which the shark was caught.

Megamouth's hide bore two wounds that looked like those made by the "cookie-cutter"

shark. Only about 16-inches long, these little sharks have big teeth in comparison to their body size. They can scoop deep chunks of flesh from larger fish by first clamping themselves to their prey with suction-cup lips. There are reports that cookie-cutter sharks have attacked nuclear submarines, biting chunks out of the plastic covers on their sonar domes.

Tiny sharks, hardly larger than a minnow, have been newly found far below the surface of the Caribbean Sea. They are being studied and catalogued in Florida by Stewart Springer and George Burgess. Mr. Springer, 78 years

old, has spent most of his professional life on the study of sharks. The new species are being found chiefly in very deep water off Colombia and Venezuela. Some, such as the cigar shark, have been netted off Japan.

Some 14 species have already been identified. Mr. Springer thinks there may be as many as 20. When one shark is caught, there are often several in the net. This leads Mr. Springer to believe they hunt in packs, like wolves. In this way they can kill prey much larger than themselves. They rarely survive the great pressure change when brought to the surface.

Above: Cigar Shark. Right: Cookie-cutter

Many of the Caribbean minisharks are brightly colored. But Mr. Springer is at a loss to explain what purpose color serves in the total darkness where they feed. Their glowing spots, however, may help them keep together during an attack. He has found octopus beaks in their tiny stomachs—evidence of their ability to kill animals far larger than themselves.

All of this is evidence of a growing interest in sharks, of which at least 350 species are known. Most sharks are not aggressive. Nor are they, according to Dr. Clark, "stupid unpredictable eating machines." She has found them to be rather quick learners.

Meet the Photographers

David Doubilet is considered by many to be the best underwater photographer in the world. Anne Doubilet, David's wife, is also a photographer, and they often work as a team. The photographs in the article you just read were taken by the Doubilets. Photographing sharks has been a speciality of the Doubilets since they undertook a study of sharks for the *National Geographic* in 1979. The two-year expedition took them from the Great Barrier Reef to Japan's Bonin Islands to the Yucatan Peninsula and, more than once, to the Red Sea.

Photographing sharks requires great patience as well as great courage. Often there can be days, even weeks, of waiting for sharks to appear. And when they do appear, the drama begins. "We anchored about midday off Dangerous Reef and a great white came roaring in, the biggest I'd ever seen. He ate a 60-pound chunk of meat off the stern. Then he stuck his head out of the water by the swim platform of the boat and snapped his teeth, then he bit the propellor and shook the boat. It was unbelievable."

The Doubilets tend to downplay the danger of their work. "It's okay to risk your life, as long as you're home by 5:00," David deadpans, to which Anne adds, "We like to go back to nature, but we also like to go back to the hotel."

David regards his work as a nice combination of science and art. The chance to find yet another piece of the underwater puzzle, whether scientific or photographic, is very appealing to the Doubilets, and more than makes up for the long days spent waiting for the sharks to appear.

Think and Discuss

1. What feature of the sea prevents us from knowing more about cephalopods and unusual sharks?
2. What is Cousteau's viewpoint about cephalopods?
 • 3. Did the essay or the encyclopedia article tell you that octopuses can change color? Why is this source better for learning about the physical characteristics of something?
4. What makes the sharks in the newspaper article newsworthy?
5. Explain why it is fair to say that sharks exist in a wide variety of sizes and physical features.
 • 6. Why is a newspaper article a better source for finding out information about fish than a story such as "Zia"?
 • Study Skills: Reference sources

Communication Workshop

Talk

Work with a classmate and take turns being a student who lived in an earlier historical time and a student of today. Discuss cephalopods from your different vantage points. For instance, whomever plays the eighteenth-century student might say, "Oh, squids are known to be very dangerous monsters," while the modern-day student might counter with "That's nonsense. Squids are highly intelligent animals who have more reason to fear *us*."
Speaking/Listening: Role-playing

Write

Pretend that your local aquarium wants to capture more cephalopods to keep in captivity. Using material from your discussion and your reading, write a letter to the editor of the local newspaper telling why you believe that octopuses should be left in their natural home, the open sea, and be studied there. Read your letter to your partner and listen to his or hers. Which is more convincing?
Writing Fluency: Letter to the editor

LIMERICKS

An octopus—"Casey the Great"—
Brought a bat in each hand to the plate.
    But the pitcher stayed cool
    And was glad for the rule
Giving Casey three strikes, and not eight!

There once was a mean shark named Phil
Whose "toothaches" were not at all real.
    When the dentists stopped by,
    Unaware of the lie,
They were eaten before they could drill.

Special Reference Sources

You have just read an encyclopedia excerpt to find out information about the octopus. An encyclopedia is one kind of reference source that has useful information. You can also find information in many other special reference sources. These sources can give you practical information you can use every day as well as particular information to make your school reports more interesting, accurate, and complete.

To find information quickly and to save time, rather than looking *through* many sources of information, learn to look for sources of information to suit your specific purpose. The descriptions below will help you learn what kinds of information some special reference sources offer.

An **atlas** is a book of maps. World atlases contain maps of the continents, oceans, and countries of the world—like the one you used on pages 166–167. Some atlases feature maps of each American state. A road atlas shows highways and routes between towns on each map, as well as area attractions such as state parks. Other atlases have certain kinds of maps such as those showing city streets, average rainfall in various locations, the surface of the moon or planets, or historical boundaries of some areas. Many atlases also have population figures listed in an index or appendix.

A **dictionary** gives information about words. In a dictionary you can find the meaning, pronunciation, and spelling of a word, as well as information about the origin of most words.

Newspapers are daily or weekly publications. They contain information on current events, cultural affairs, weather, sports, and entertainment as well as provide feature stories, editorials, and advertisements.

Telephone directories include "white pages"—phone books that list alphabetically addresses and phone numbers of families, individuals, and businesses—and "yellow pages"—directories of businesses and services classified alphabetically by kind of business. Many stores, companies, and services use advertisements in the yellow pages to inform you of their hours, specialized services, and other details. Many telephone directories also carry local emergency numbers, area codes for many states and cities, local maps and Zip Code lists, and other information.

To make the best use of reference sources, it is important to go to the most appropriate one for your needs. Think of which source you would examine to find answers to the following questions.

- What is the origin of the word *cephalopod?*
- Between what two oceans is the Indian Ocean located?
- What stores have tropical fish for sale?
- What is the extended outlook for the weather this weekend?

No matter what reference book you wish to use, you can judge how up-to-date the information is by checking to see when it was published. The year of copyright is printed on a page near the front of most books. Using the latest edition allows you to have more confidence in facts and information that may change, such as sports records, population figures, and descriptions of computers. You can also evaluate the information by deciding how reliable it is, whether it is based on facts or opinions, and if it tells all that you need to know.

Kodiak
Island

Outer
Banks

Channel
Islands

Hawaiian
Islands

Padre
Island

Have you ever been on an island—in the open sea? If you haven't, then you haven't really been on an island, according to the author of this magazine article. You will travel with her to five islands in the sea. Which will be your favorite? Maps of the islands will help you picture them and locate them in relation to the United States.

ISLANDS IN THE SEA

CONTENT-AREA READING

by Carolyn Pantazelos

There is something that draws me to an island, especially an island in the open sea. Islands in the sea are usually far more interesting than islands found in rivers and lakes, which are mostly flat, wooded, and much the same. But, cut off from the large land areas, islands in the sea are shaped by strong waves and winds in unusual ways. The contrasts between the islands can be extreme, and therein lies much of the fun in exploring them. It does not matter where they are found—north, south, east, or west. Each has a personality all its own and offers unexpected things to see and do. Let's visit five American islands that, I think you'll agree, are quite special. We'll begin with one of the least known and end with the most famous of all.

Kodiak Island

Alaska still remains unknown to most Americans, especially the 100-mile-long Kodiak Island southwest of Anchorage. During the 1800s the island was a headquarters for Russian fur traders. (Russia had founded the first non-Indian settlement on the island in 1784.) Russia's sale of Alaska and all its islands to the United States in 1867 for about two cents an acre allowed our country to acquire one of the most incredible regions of the world. You won't find those famous, towering Alaskan glaciers at Kodiak Island. But you'll find an unspoiled wilderness.

Kodiak Island can be reached from Anchorage by either the Kodiak Island Ferry or by plane. The ferry ride takes about thirteen hours, but the awe-inspiring views of forested hillsides, rocky beaches, and glistening water make the time pass quickly. As the ferry glides into the crowded but scenic harbor at Kodiak, the largest city on the island, you will see many fishing boats. Kodiak, with a small population of only about 5,000, boasts the largest fishing fleet in Alaska. Fish are processed at local canneries, and you can tour them on request.

A good time to visit Kodiak Island is during the summer months. Then the temperatures may be in the 70s in the day. Daylight hours extend into the late Arctic evening. In early August of each year *Cry of the Wild Ram*, a pageant play, is presented several times in an outdoor theater there—Alaska's only one. This drama, which tells of the late 18th-century founding of this area, is a popular tourist attraction.

The island has a rough landscape and very few roads. You travel on foot, on horseback, or by plane into a wilderness where animal life is plentiful. There are numerous species of birds to observe, including the great bald eagle—our rarely seen national emblem. Alaskan brown bears, also known as Kodiak bears, live in the Kodiak National Wildlife Refuge, which takes up nearly 80 percent of the island. These 9-foot bears are the largest of the meat-eating land animals. Quite a few travelers come here just to see these huge beasts.

If you stay near the northern shore, in Kodiak, you can visit the Baranof Museum and see its collection of traditional Aleut, Russian, and American artifacts. You can also rent a kayak and explore the shoreline in complete silence without startling the birds and animals. This soundless and unhurried experience is typical of Kodiak Island, still as fresh as when we bought it over 100 years ago.

The Outer Banks

Nowhere can the extremes in ocean islands be seen more dramatically than in leaving the ruggedness of Kodiak Island for the soft, sandy shores of the Outer Banks. This chain of narrow barrier reefs lies in the Atlantic Ocean off the coast of North Carolina and follows the state's coast for 175 miles. The Outer Banks can be reached by car over two causeways near the north end. Airline and boat service also connect the Outer Banks with the mainland. But to explore the islands, you will need a car. The distances between places are great, and the roadways are not suitable for walking or bicycling. The climate is mild, with average winter temperatures in the 50s and summers in the 80s.

Part of the beauty and wonder of the Outer Banks is that they are never the same. The sea pounds against their shores, forming new inlets and destroying old ones. The shoreline is always changing.

The most populated section of the Outer Banks is near the area reached by the causeways. Here the resort towns of Kitty Hawk, Kill Devil Hills, and Nags Head offer much to the history buff or air adventurer. It was on a narrow beach of sandy dunes called Kill Devil Hills, just south of Kitty Hawk, that the Wright brothers made their important first motor-powered flights on December 17, 1903. The Wright Brothers National Memorial Park is found in Kill Devil Hills. A building there houses a replica of their first airplane. At the park you can experience the thrill of walking from a marker at their take-off spot to the marker where each of the four flights the Wrights made that day ended. The farthest marker is only 852 feet away. You will be amazed to see that the history of aviation began with four such short flights!

Jockey's Ridge State Park in Nags Head is an area of huge dunes. These dunes, which are the highest in the United States, are constantly moving. But now that the island is more developed, the dunes do not move as much as they used to. Then they were known to bury houses and trees.

A popular pastime from the tops of the dunes is hang gliding. It is breathtaking to watch the fliers dash down a dune into the wind. They are lifted into the air. Then by leaning to one side or the other, they steer the gliders into the wind for more lift. You can take hang-gliding lessons and rent

equipment for your flight. I have been told that there is nothing to compare to the feeling of being airborne over the dunes with the bright sea in the distance. If you lose your courage once you are in the air, don't panic. Landings tend to be fairly safe in the deep sand.

A tamer sport related to flight is kite flying. You can make your own or buy one there. As you race along a deserted beach to launch your kite, ocean breezes will make a successful kite-flier out of even a beginner. Look how those winds helped the Wright brothers.

By driving your car south, you will reach Hatteras Island by crossing the last bridge on the Outer Banks. As much of the north part of Hatteras Island is undeveloped, you will go by mile after mile of grass-covered dunes before you reach a good stopping point—Cape Hatteras. This area of the island sticks out in the ocean like a bent elbow. It has been nicknamed the "graveyard of the Atlantic" because of the large numbers of ships that have run aground in its shallow waters. Parts of two ships that were wrecked in 1878 and in 1948 can still be seen along the beaches. Over the years the shifting sands have buried and uncovered these wrecks many times.

The Cape Hatteras Lighthouse is the tallest on the Atlantic coast. It is 208 feet above sea level. You can climb to the top and be treated to an almost limitless view of the island and the surrounding ocean.

Hatteras Island is the center for sportfishing in the Outer Banks. The warm-water Gulf Stream is mainly responsible for making this a major fishing area. You can enjoy fishing from bridges, piers, beaches, and boats.

Don't skip Ocracoke[1] Island. You can take your car there on the ferry from Hatteras. Ocracoke has an interesting history. English naval hero Sir Richard Grenville ran aground on Ocracoke in 1585. It is thought that the sturdy wild ponies on the island may be related to some that escaped from Grenville's ship. The once-large herd of ponies now numbers only about a dozen. These remaining ponies are protected by the park service and can be seen at the Ocracoke Pony Pens.

Fortune may await you on Ocracoke. During the 1700s it was an active base for pirates. It is said that the famous pirate Blackbeard terrorized ships all along the Outer Banks until he was killed in a battle in 1718. Nobody has ever located the pirate's fabled treasure, but many people think it is buried somewhere on Ocracoke. To start your own treasure hunt, you need only walk the beaches, coves, and inlets with a metal detector.

A trip to the Outer Banks will certainly bring surprises. Who knows what the sand will have uncovered for your visit.

Padre Island

Padre Island is a fascinating ribbon of white sand in the Gulf of Mexico off the coast of Texas. It extends from Corpus Christi in the north to Brownsville in the south, near the Mexican border. It was named for Padre José Nicholás Balli, a priest who built a mission there for the Indians in the early 1800s. It is warm and damp on Padre Island, even in the winter, because of the winds from the Gulf.

The island can be reached by causeways that cross the narrow strip of water—the

---

1. Ocracoke (ō′krə kōk).

Laguna Madre—that separates Padre Island from the mainland. There is a causeway at each end of this 113-mile sandbar because you cannot drive from one end to the other.

As recently as 30 years ago, the island was virtually undeveloped. Now the South Padre end of the island (only a half-mile wide) has modern hotels, tennis courts, pools, and other tourist comforts. But it also has some unusual things to do for those who do not want to spend their vacation beside a pool. There is a miniature train, The Coast Line, that takes visitors around the area. On its route is Ocean Safari, a park where you can see wild animals and birds. The train also stops at an old paddlewheel boat. You can take a sightseeing cruise on this boat across the Laguna Madre.

North Padre has only a few motels. This part of the island attracts people who are interested mainly in camping. Many of these people pitch tents along the shore. The sand on the island is soft, but it is so firm that you can drive an automobile or ride a bicycle on it.

Padre Island National Seashore was founded by Congress in 1962. It covers the island from the Gulf of Mexico to the Laguna Madre and stretches southward for eighty miles. During the day you can walk for miles along the Gulf side, climbing dunes and stepping around colorful beach flowers that grow wild in this area. On the Laguna Madre side, there is less vegetation. The dunes there are constantly moving with the winds, much to the delight of photographers.

The beaches on the Gulf side of north Padre draw shell collectors. Hundreds of different kinds of shells are washed ashore on Little Shell Beach and Big Shell Beach after storms. On a walk along these beaches, you will probably find shells that you have never seen before. The shallow, marshy areas on the Laguna Madre side of North Padre are ideal for bird watching. Hundreds of kinds of birds feed there.

The two halves of Padre Island—North and South—are a study in contrasts all by themselves. They offer an island-in-the-sea vacation of either activity or leisure—or you can divide your time between both.

The Channel Islands

Off the western coast of the United States are California's Channel Islands. Here there are no gentle, rolling dunes and sandbars like those on the Outer Banks and Padre Island. These eight Channel Islands are mountain peaks that were thrust above the surface of the Pacific Ocean by volcanic action. The five northernmost islands were made into a national park in 1980. The waters around the islands are now a marine shelter, keeping the waters in their natural state. The forming of the park has also helped control the visitor traffic to the islands and protect the wildlife.

A good place to begin a visit to the Channel Islands is at the Channel Island Harbor park headquarters in Ventura, on the California mainland. Here you can gather information about the park, its animals, plants, and camping grounds. I must warn you that there are no fancy hotels or restaurants here. The islands are strictly places to "rough it," to spend a leisurely day or weekend exploring their grand sights.

As the islands can be reached only by water, you will have to take a tour boat or hire a private one. So, grab a sweater (sea air can be very cool), binoculars, camera, hiking shoes, and swim fins, and you'll be ready to begin your adventure. During your boat trip across the Santa Barbara Channel, you may see flying fish skimming the waves, graceful dolphins leaping

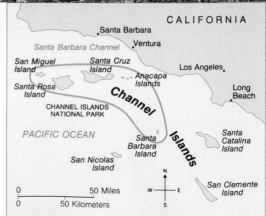

playfully, or gray whales spouting proudly. The boat ride is not very long, for the most distant of the Channel Islands is only about 60 miles from shore.

The island of San Miguel has a large population of California sea lions and northern fur, harbor, and elephant seals. Their loud barking fills the air, and their antics in the water are enjoyable to watch. Here you can visit the "ghost forests" that make one area of this island unusual. The "ghosts" are actually calcified coverings that have formed over plants. The plants have since died, but their strange shapes remain.

Some of the island cliffs rise almost straight up from the sea. Many have been pounded so violently by the surf that arches and tunnels have been cut into them. Most of the island beaches are rocky, a fact that will discourage sunbathers. The lack of silt from sand, however, makes these waters especially clear for scuba diving and snorkeling. Underwater visibility is excellent, so plant and animal life can be easily viewed. For those who do not enjoy swimming, tidepooling is a fabulous pastime. By visiting a tidal pool at low tide, you can better view various sea plants and animals.

Many plants and animals are worth seeing on these islands because they have developed into forms that are found nowhere else. Among these are the island fox, the spotted skunk, and the ironwood tree. A trip to any one of the Channel Islands in the park is a wonderful escape from the fast pace of city life. Here the animals are the year-round residents and the humans merely visitors. There is time to enjoy the mild climate, ocean breezes, surging sea, and beautiful landscape. There is also an opportunity to exercise by hiking over mountain paths.

So, now, when you think of California, think about including the Channel Islands on your trip.

The Hawaiian Islands

Our fifth and final visit is to the Hawaiian Islands. These famous volcanic mountain tops unfortunately are often taken for granted. But nothing is ordinary here. Unlike the Channel Islands, many of the Hawaiian volcanic peaks have been pounded smooth by the action of wind and waves, creating legendary sand beaches. Some, though, still have lofty peaks and steep cliffs. The eight main islands are at the southwestern end of the island chain. They lie about 2,000 miles southwest across the Pacific Ocean from the California coast. You can't get a truer island-in-the-sea experience that you can here.

The climate is pleasant, with air temperatures averaging in the 70s all year. Water temperatures are somewhat warmer than that. But what you might remember most is color. To experience Hawaii is to experience color.

The Hawaiian Islands, of course, can be reached only by ship or plane. Most travelers arrive at Honolulu, the capital city on the island of Oahu.[2] Here they may be met by natives who hang leis of lavender and white flowers around their necks. Honolulu is a busy port, whose chief attraction is Waikiki Beach. Waikiki is really a series of fine sand beaches rimmed with towering palms and modern hotels. Here you can take part in surf events, sand-castle contests, and kite-flying contests. You can enjoy the water by joining the surfers and riding the long breakers on a brightly colored surfboard. Or you might wish to rent a sailboat or an outrigger canoe, take a picnic cruise around the island, or ride in a glass-bottom boat. Don't miss strolling along the beach at either sunrise or sunset. You'll find the sky is radiant with orange, pink, blue, and gold, which are mirrored in the ocean.

You can explore Honolulu on foot or in an open-air pedicab. You can attend a free hula show and try to learn this famous island dance. A visit to the Honolulu Zoo and the nearby Waikiki Aquarium will let you closely observe the forms of wildlife found on the islands.

Travelers who want to be away from the city environment prefer to visit some of the less populated islands. Besides flying directly to them, you can take a cruise ship that stops for day trips on the various islands. Traveling this way will give you a chance to see some of each island's attractions while enjoying the incredible views of an ocean voyage.

On Hawaii, the largest island, you can visit Hawaii Volcanoes National Park. A highway leads near the edge of the crater known as Kilauea.[3] From a roped-off platform, you can peer into the crater of this still active volcano and see the blazing-red, bubbling, awesome lava. The charcoaled trees nearby prove how destructive volcanic eruptions can be.

---

2. Oahu (ō ä'hü).

3. Kilauea (kē'lou ä'ə).

Down the coast from the park is the Kaimu[4] Black Sand Beach, a beach made up of crushed lava rock. It is a visual treat to see a beach of black sand contrasted against green palms and deep-blue water. There are also many beaches of white sand on the island. You can swim in the water around the island or go fishing.

Kauai[5] is called Hawaii's garden island. Pineapples and sugar cane grow well in its fertile soil. Large ferns line the walls of a cave at Fern Grotto. Exotic flowers grow in abundance on both the dry hills and in the forests. A mountain, rising more than 5,000 feet above sea level, towers over the landscape. It is the wettest spot on earth, getting more than 400 inches of rain each year.

Kauai was the first of the Hawaiian Islands visited by the explorer Captain James Cook, who landed there in 1778. You can drive from the monument commemorating his visit into the mountains of Kokee State Park. From lookouts along the roadway, you can view the Waimea[6] Canyon. This deep, colorful, and rocky valley has been nicknamed the "Grand Canyon of the Pacific." You can enjoy your lunch in the picnic grounds, hike over trails, or fish for trout.

Our visits to these special islands in the sea are over. From the almost totally unknown Kodiak Island to the well-known Hawaiian Islands, Americans can find island experiences of unequaled variety. What doesn't vary is the delight you will find in vacationing on any one of them. Start planning today.

---

4. Kaimu (kī′mü).
5. Kauai (kou ī′).
6. Waimea (wī mä′ə).

Comprehension Check

Think and Discuss

1. Which island in the article would you most like to visit? Why?
2. Name at least two things you can see or do on Kodiak Island.
3. Name three similarities between the Outer Banks and Padre Island which can be noted from looking at the maps alone.
4. Hawaii is said to be an "experience" in color. What are some of the examples that describe its colorful beauty?
5. Look at the map on page 186. Which of the five islands is closest to where you live?

• Study Skills: Maps and Globes

Communication Workshop

Talk

Almost everyone dreams about "getting away from it all" by escaping to an island. Discuss with a group of four classmates the special features of the islands you read about. What makes each island a particularly interesting place to visit? What slogan might appear on a travel poster advertising each island? Write the suggestions from the discussion on the board.

Speaking/Listening: Cooperative learning

Write

Write a slogan for each island that you would like to visit. Then make a travel poster by taking a large piece of paper, drawing a picture of one of the special features of the island, and adding your slogan. Exchange posters with classmates. Which islands are the most popular? Why do you think this is so?

Writing Fluency: Advertising slogan

LOOKING BACK

See your Thinker's Handbook for tips.

Prewriting

Thinking and Writing About the Section
In this section you have read about the vast ocean, some islands in the ocean, and many fascinating creatures of the deep. You can write a descriptive paragraph for a classmate that creates a word picture of one of the topics you have read about. First copy the chart below and fill in the missing information.

Topic	Details (Sight, Hearing, Taste, Smell, Touch)
Ocean	
Octopus or Shark	large, shiny eyes, sticky arms
Island	

Writing

Use the information from the chart to write a paragraph to describe one of the topics on the chart. Use colorful and vivid details that appeal to your reader's sense of sight, hearing, smell, taste, or touch. For more information on descriptive paragraphs, refer to your Writer's Handbook.

Revising

Read your first draft to a partner. Did you describe several sensory details about your topic? Did you use words that let your reader see and feel the things you wrote about? Make changes if necessary. Then proofread for spelling and punctuation errors. Write your final copy.

Presenting

Read your paragraph aloud. Have your listener tell which sensory details he or she thought were the most vivid.

5

From Here to There

The theater can take you from here to there—to anywhere in the world. When the curtain goes up, you could be in Nigeria, or Japan, or France. Wherever the theater takes you, even though the culture and customs may be totally foreign, you'll find that the characters and situations are familiar. This is because plays all over the world express the same ideas about wisdom, the same hopes for success and love, and the same foolish flaws that we all experience at some time in our lives.

Recognizing Theme

In the theater, one special type of performer is called a *mime*. A mime gives a message or makes a point by using motions and facial expressions instead of words. What point is the mime in the picture making? How might he use each of the hats in the picture to express a different idea?

Just as a mime can express an important point in a performance, an author can express an important point in a story, novel, or play. The underlying meaning in a piece of literature is called the **theme.** Sometimes an author may choose to develop more than one theme.

Finding the theme or themes in a piece of literature is not always easy. Authors usually don't state a theme in a single sentence. Instead, they plan the events and actions of the characters carefully to express the theme.

To figure out the theme in a play, story, or novel, be sure to read the entire selection first. Then think about what goal the main character or characters wanted to achieve. Review how they tried to reach that goal and whether they were successful. Notice what the characters' attitudes were toward the goal and the outcome. Going over all these things in your mind can help you recognize the theme or themes.

For example, keep in mind what you have just read as you think back over the story "The Last of the Dragons." In that story, a princess is supposed to be rescued from a dragon; a prince is supposed to rescue her; and a dragon—the very last dragon on earth—is supposed to come after the princess and be slain by the prince. But the prince and princess do not want to follow those foolish traditions. They decide to find some sensible way to keep themselves and the dragon safe, and they accomplish that goal by making the dragon their pet and taking him to the palace, where he gives dragon-back rides to the children.

One theme of "The Last of the Dragons" is that breaking with old traditions can sometimes be beneficial. Can you see how the characters and events in the story illustrate that theme? Since the tradition had never really helped anyone, the prince and princess want to find an acceptable way to avoid having to slay the dragon. They discuss the situation with the dragon, and the three of them decide on a way to achieve that goal. The outcome shows that everyone—even the village children—benefits from breaking with tradition.

In Section Two you read "A Proposal of Marriage." You will probably remember that in the play Lomov goes to the Stepanovitch home to ask for Natalia's hand in marriage. But instead of offering a marriage proposal, he seems to do all the wrong things: he gets into arguments, exchanges insults with the family, and even leaves the house in a huff. Yet at the end of the play, Lomov and Natalia are engaged, and Mr. Stepanovitch rushes off to find a preacher to marry them. How does this peculiar engagement come about? The following questions will help you think over the play and decide what its theme is.

1. What is Lomov's goal? How do Stepanovitch and Natalia feel about it?

You are right if you said that Lomov wants to propose marriage and that Natalia and her father both like that idea.

2. How does the "marriage proposal" actually happen?

Lomov, after many arguments and emotional words, simply passes out. When he revives, quick-thinking Stepanovitch tells Lomov that he has proposed and that Natalia has accepted.

3. Both of the following statements express themes of the play. Why is statement **a** a theme? Support your answer with information from the play.
   a. Quick thinking can save a nearly lost cause.
   b. Love conquers all.

The hope that Natalia and Lomov will marry seems like a lost cause until Stepanovitch tricks Lomov into thinking that Lomov has proposed and Natalia has accepted.

4. Why is statement **b** also a theme? Support your answer with information from the play.

Practicing Recognizing Theme

Read this summary of a Japanese play by Kanze Motokiyo Zeami to discover its theme.

The Reed Cutter

A noblewoman from the Capital City travels to the village of Kusaka, hoping to find an old friend. In Kusaka she learns that her friend once lived there but now is gone. He has somehow lost all his money and is ashamed to have people see him in poverty.

The noblewoman is extremely sad to hear the news. She decides to continue the search because, as she says, she and the friend once made many vows together.

One day the woman encounters a reed cutter who makes a meager living by cutting reeds that people buy to make hats. The woman recognizes the reed cutter as her long lost "friend," actually her husband. He left home long ago to see the famous scenery of the region around Kusaka. Then, with all his money gone, he was ashamed to return home. Now, embarrassed by his poverty, he runs and hides in his hut.

The noblewoman goes to the hut and persuades him to come out, assuring him that she still loves him and that he is not in disgrace. At last he realizes that he is still welcome in his home, and the two agree to return together to the Capital City.

1. For what purpose does the noblewoman go to Kusaka?
2. Does she accomplish her goal? How?
3. Why hadn't her husband returned to the Capital City?
4. How do you know he is glad to be welcomed back?
5. Both of the following statements express themes of the play. Which one means the most to you? Use information from the play to support your choice.
   a. Love and friendship are more important than money.
   b. True love accepts people as they are.

Tips for Reading on Your Own
- Think about what the main character or characters want, how they try to reach their goal, and what the outcome is.
- Ask yourself what the underlying meaning is.
- Support your theme with information from what you read.

How can you get to Nigeria? Take a front-row seat in the theater and when the curtain goes up, you will be in Nigeria. You will meet Olog and Tanya, who think they will find wisdom, and Cashew, their wise-cracking camel, who thinks he knows it all. As you discover what Tanya and Olog learn about wisdom, notice how the setting—where they go—plays a part in what they learn.

Hi! I'm Cashew

A SEARCH FOR WISDOM

by Peter Grahame
Adapted from a Nigerian folktale

CHARACTERS

OLOG, *a poor farmer*   VILLAGERS, *1 and 2*
TANYA, *his daughter*   SELLERS, *1, 2, and 3*
CASHEW, *the camel*   FARMERS, *1, 2, and 3*
NEIGHBORS, *1, 2, and 3*   A TRAVELER

TIME: *The Harvest Season, long, long ago.*
PLACE: OLOG's *small home-village in the bush country, as well as several other villages along the road, in Nigeria.*

SCENE ONE: *The front of* OLOG's *little farmhouse. We see a wooden fence, beyond which is a small garden. Carrying baskets of yams,* OLOG *and his daughter* TANYA *enter from behind the garden fence. They speak as they walk and set the baskets down by the door of the house.*

OLOG: This is the last of the yams, my daughter. Oh, I am weary, but now the harvest is done for another season.

TANYA: Sit, my father. I will get you some water.

OLOG *(sitting on a low stool by the door):* Thank you, my precious one. You are so good to your old father.

TANYA *(smiling, as she opens the door):* You are not so old, Father, you just work too hard. *(Exits into house.)*

OLOG: So do you! And what do we have to show for it? A few bushels of yams, this poor farm, and Cashew, our camel.

TANYA *(entering with a gourd cup of water, handing it to him):* But we are alive and well. What more do we want?

OLOG *(drinks, looks at* TANYA*):* Me? I don't want much any more. I am old. But you are young! Surely you must want to go and see the wide world outside this tiny village.

TANYA: Oh yes, Father, I would very much like to go!

OLOG *(smiles):* To tell the truth, so would I. Ah, what must the rest of the world be like, I wonder?

TANYA: Perhaps it is peaceful and full of flowers. Or perhaps it is strange and frightening, with many odd creatures running about! *(Laughs.)* We can only imagine.

OLOG: You know, so often I have heard from travelers that the world is very big and full of wonders. Most important, there is much wisdom to be learned in the world, they say. Ah, it would be very good for both of us to go and learn and see.

TANYA: Father! I have a splendid idea! Let us go out into the world. Let us see these wonders. Let us learn this wisdom!

OLOG: But how can we? It is far—and the expense!

TANYA: We will ride Cashew, our camel. I have saved a little money. We can take along some food. We will travel for only a few days and no more. It will be so exciting!

OLOG: Oh, I don't know . . . What of the garden and the house?

TANYA: The harvest is over. Our neighbors will watch the house. Please, Father, it is now or never. It is our chance!

OLOG: It would be good. But I'm old and tired.

TANYA *(happily):* Dear Father, you are strong like an ox! Here is my plan. Tonight we will rest. Then we will leave fresh, first thing in the morning. It will do us both a world of good to get away for a while. And think what we will learn!

OLOG *(thinks, stands up):* Very well, Tanya. For your sake, I will make this supreme effort. We shall do as you say.

TANYA *(with delight, hugs* OLOG*):* Oh, Father, thank you! We won't be sorry! Come now, let us prepare. *(Both exit into house.)*

SCENE TWO: *The next morning.* CASHEW *the camel enters from behind the house. Two sacks of provisions lean against the wall of the house. Note:* CASHEW's *voice can be heard only by the audience, not the other characters.*

CASHEW *(walking slowly to center):* Oh me, oh woe. Oh what a peculiar turn of events. All my farm work is *done,* I thought. Now time for a nice long *rest,* I thought. But oh, nooooo! *They* want to go off to see the *world*—to find *wonders,* to learn wisdom, no less. It'll be a wonder if this old camel makes it through the *gate,* let me tell you. And as for *wisdom,* here's what I think of the wisdom of the world. *(Sticks out tongue and rolls his eyes.)*
(Enter OLOG *and* TANYA *from the house. They are dressed in their best clothes.* OLOG *carries* CASHEW's *bridle.* TANYA *has a little sack purse.)*

TANYA: Oh, Father! I'm so excited! At last we're going off to see the world! It will be wonderful, don't you think?

CASHEW: If they could hear me, I'd be happy to tell them what *I* think! *(Rolls his eyes again.)*

OLOG: You see how our camel makes a noise? That is what I think, Tanya. I think we are making a big mistake.

CASHEW: Oh good! Maybe we won't have to go. Please? *Please?*

TANYA: Oh no, Father! We must not back away now!

OLOG: I know, my daughter. It is for your sake as well as mine that we do this. Yes, the time is now or never.

CASHEW (*shifting about*): I say "nuts to that!"

OLOG (*bringing* CASHEW *center*): Steady yourself now, Cashew, my camel. We'll both make the best of this.

CASHEW: That's easy for *you* to say.

TANYA: Look, Father, our neighbors are coming to say good-bye!

CASHEW: Augh! I hate crowds.

> (*Several* NEIGHBORS *enter talking, laughing, calling "Olog!" "Tanya!"* TANYA *and* OLOG *"mount" the camel by merely stepping behind the beast. The three can stoop down, then come up.* CASHEW *groans with the movement and remains bending over.*)

NEIGHBOR 1: All ready, are you? Off to see the world?

TANYA: Yes! Is it not grand? I wish you could come.

NEIGHBOR 2: Not me, I've seen enough right here. You two going off to see the world and learn wisdom. Ha!

NEIGHBOR 3: Don't be rude! You'd love to go and you know it! (*To the riders.*) Take care, you two. Don't worry about a thing here. We will count the days until you return. (*The camel and the two riders pantomime moving off, but they stay at center. At the same time, the* NEIGHBORS, *calling and waving, walk backwards, moving off the house and fence, left. Worked out, this business will give the illusion that the camel and riders are moving right.*)

NEIGHBORS: (*ad lib*): Good-bye! Come back safe! (*Exit.*)

SCENE THREE: *Continues from previous scene. A tree and a rock move slowly across stage, right to left. The tree moves behind and the rock in front of the camel and riders, as they continue to pantomime moving at center.*

TANYA: Well, here we are, Father, traveling at last!

OLOG: Yes, my sweet. Have you seen any wonders yet?

TANYA: No, Father, only that tree over there. It looks much the same as trees in our village, and yet . . . (*Looking ahead.*) Oh, Father! Look there! We are coming to a big town!

OLOG: Oh, what wonders will we find there, I wonder?

SCENE FOUR: *The town appears as several* VILLAGERS, *carrying baskets, move a market cart on stage and surround the camel. The camel and riders stop moving.*

CASHEW: More crowds! Is that all the world is? Crowded?

OLOG: It must be market day in this town. Look at all the wonders! Surely there is much wisdom to learn here.

TANYA: Yes, Father! Let us ask them some questions!

OLOG: An excellent idea! *(To a* VILLAGER.*)* Excuse me, do you have any wisdom to impart to us? You see, we . . .

VILLAGER 1: Wisdom! I should think so! Look at you! *(To another* VILLAGER.*)* Can you believe what you see?

VILLAGER 2: They're absolutely disgusting in every way.

OLOG: We? Disgusting? What do you mean by this insult?

VILLAGER 1: Look what you are doing! A grown man and a healthy young girl—*both* riding this *one* camel.

OLOG and TANYA: So?

VILLAGER 2: So? You make this poor, tired old beast carry *two* persons at once. It's worse than disgusting. It's cruel!

CASHEW: Tired old beast . . . Who, me? Now wait a minute . . .

VILLAGER 1: One of you must get down at once.

TANYA: Yes, I see. This is wisdom. I will get down.

OLOG: No, my daughter. You ride. I will walk.

TANYA: Please, Father, let me follow this wisdom. Down, Cashew. (CASHEW *groans and lowers.* TANYA *gets off, comes to the front and takes the bridle to lead* CASHEW *onward.)*

VILLAGER 1: That's better. And don't do it again.

TANYA *(bows):* Thank you for your wisdom. We will go now. *(As they continue moving on in pantomime,* OLOG *riding, the* VILLAGERS *back off left with cart and so on, talking.)*

SCENE FIVE: *Back on the road. The three continue to pantomime moving. Same rock and tree move across, front and back.*

TANYA: Well, we have seen and learned much so far, Father.

OLOG: Yes. Never again will two of us ride poor Cashew!

CASHEW: I really didn't mind so much, you know. But to call me a tired old beast! Indeed! *(Rolls his eyes.)*

TANYA: Stop making that awful noise, Cashew. I know you are annoyed. But look! There is yet another town ahead!

SCENE SIX: *Town appears as* SELLERS *bring on a market stall and colorful banners. Camel and riders stop.*

OLOG: Well, now. This must be a bazaar—a big market! I have heard of such things! See the colors! Smell the smells!

CASHEW *(nose up in disgust):* Phew-ie!

SELLER 1 *(wide-eyed, to* OLOG*):* Can you believe it!?

OLOG: What, what, my friend. Is there some new wonder?

SELLER 1: The only wonder here is *you,* old man.

TANYA: You there, why do you speak to my father this way?

SELLER 1: Poor child, how could you know? So innocent.

CASHEW: Get to the point, you bizarre creature. Oh, hee-hee! I made a pun! This is a *bazaar*. And he is a *bizarre* creature! Oh, hee-hee. I'm too good for this. I should be on the stage. *(Looks at audience.)* Oh, I am on the stage. Well, I *am* the star of this, you know. Which reminds me of another story . . .

OLOG *(to* SELLER 1*):* Get to the point!

CASHEW: That's what *I* said.

SELLER 1: Look everyone! Look how the father rides while he makes his worn-out daughter walk. Is it not a shame?

SELLER 2: Worse than a shame! It is a scandal! This man has no love for his child. He has no heart. He is unjust!

OLOG: No heart? Unjust? But, but, but . . .

SELLER 3: There are no ''buts'' about it sir. If you want to pass safely through this town, you'd better get off at once and let this poor girl ride. Who do you think you are? A king? And your daughter is your servant, I suppose!

OLOG: A servant? No, no, she is my beloved child!

SELLERS *(all together):* Then let her ride!

CASHEW *(stooping down, groaning):* Here we go again! (OLOG *gets off,* TANYA *gets on.)*

CASHEW *(groans, resumes position):* There, are you satisfied?

SELLER 1: Ah, there now, we are satisfied.

OLOG *(coming around to front to lead* CASHEW*):* My friends, what can we say? You have bestowed great wisdom upon us. We are grateful. But now, we must be going. Good-bye. *(The* SELLERS *talk among themselves and move everything off left. The three pantomime moving at center as before.)*

Phew-ie!

SCENE SEVEN: *Once more, the open road. The same tree and rock are seen moving across, right to left, as before.*

TANYA: Well, Father, we are getting wisdom, yes?

OLOG: Yes, I suppose so.

TANYA: Father, have you noticed? The tree we passed looks very much like the tree we passed before—and the one before that. And they all look much like the trees in our village.

OLOG *(lost in thought):* Hmm!? Yes, I suppose they do.

TANYA: Yet, somehow, the trees in our village seem more special than the ones we see in the world. Why is that?

CASHEW: I'm sure there's a message in all this.

OLOG: Look! Another town! New wonders! More wisdom!

CASHEW: Please, I can't take any more wisdom.

TANYA: Yes, Father, and yet there is something . . . not right.

FARMER 1: That's it! That's it! Now we're surely lost.

FARMER 2: Lost? What do you mean lost?

FARMER 1: Don't you see? When the young no longer have any respect for the elderly, the end is surely in sight.

FARMER 3: What do you mean? Where is there no respect?

FARMER 1 *(pointing at* TANYA*):* There! There! A young, healthy girl sits there so smug on that camel while her poor, old, decrepit father must hobble along on the ground.

OLOG: What!? Old? Decrepit? I am not!

CASHEW: See? How do *you* like being called names?

OLOG *(to* FARMER*):* Look, a while back, some other people said . . .

FARMER 2: Enough! Don't defend her, old man. That child is proud and stubborn—and ungrateful, too!

OLOG: But, but, but . . .

CASHEW: More "buts?"

FARMER 2: No "buts!" *(To* TANYA.*)* Who do you think you are, young woman? Off! Off with you! *(The* FARMERS *pull* TANYA *down. She screams.)*

OLOG: Unhand my daughter. How dare you!

FARMER 3: Can you not see? She has no respect for you.

OLOG: She has nothing *but* respect for me!

TANYA: Father, please, do not anger yourself. *(To* FARMERS.*)* If what you say is true, then so be it. But instead, neither my father nor I will ride. We shall both walk side by side.

CASHEW: At last. *I* sure could use the rest.

FARMER 1: As you wish. But show respect!

TANYA: Yes, I will. Thank you. Good day to you now. *(The three resume walking. The noisy* FARMERS *disappear.)*

SCENE EIGHT: *Once more, the road. All are silent, thinking. From right, a* TRAVELER *enters, whistling. All stop.*

TRAVELER: Well, now. I have been here and there. I have been up and down. I have been all over this world and I thought I had surely seen it all.

OLOG: Good day to you. That's what we're doing. Going here and there, up and down. We hope to see it all, too.

TRAVELER: If you'd like to see it all, you only have to look at yourselves. I mean, here are two people who have been traveling long. They are obviously tired, worn-out—and yet . . .

TANYA: Yes, yes, and yet? And yet?

TRAVELER: There stands a big strong camel with nobody on it!

CASHEW *(sarcastically):* Thank you.

TANYA and OLOG *(look at each other):* But, but, but, but . . .

CASHEW: What are you, a couple of goats? "Butt, butt, butt!"

TRAVELER: "But, but, nothing!" If you are tired and worn out, it's just plain common sense that you *both* should *ride!*

CASHEW: Isn't this where I came in?

OLOG: We *both* should ride Cashew? Are you sure?

TRAVELER: Yes! Now, *that* would be wise indeed! *(Exits laughing.) (*TANYA *and* OLOG *look at each other. They start to laugh. They both mount* CASHEW *as before.* CASHEW *groans. This time, all three, laughing, actually do exit off stage right.)*

Isn't this where I came in?

SCENE NINE: *Back home. The front of the house, the fence and so on come on with the* NEIGHBORS *from left.*

NEIGHBORS *(ad lib):* Here they come! Tanya and Olog! Hooray!
  (Applause as camel and riders enter from right.)
NEIGHBOR 1: Back so soon? Well, tell us what happened in the big wide world. What did you see? What did you learn?
NEIGHBOR 2: Yes! Tell us of the wonders!
OLOG *(as he and* TANYA *get down from the camel):* Well, in the end, one place is very much like another. But the wonders that are truly special are right here at home!
NEIGHBOR 3: Oh, this is good news. But what of wisdom?
TANYA: That is simple. Wisdom is all well and good, but the most important thing is common sense. But we had common sense in the beginning, even though not everyone agrees.
CASHEW: And that, as they say, is that! *(Rolls his eyes. Everyone exits laughing.)*

Meet the Actor

In addition to his memorable performance as Cashew in "A Search for Wisdom," nineteen-year-old Thomas Greene has an impressive list of acting credits. While in high school, Tom performed with the Piven Theater Workshop in Evanston, Illinois. One of Piven's most popular productions was a show that the students developed based on their best improvisational skits. The production was aired on local television.

A favorite role of Tom's was that of Charles Carter in a play called "The Roommate," which was about college students in the 1950s. "I liked playing Charles Carter because he was good-natured and fun-loving, yet he had a sharp edge that made him interesting. And the baggy fifties' clothes and big old cars were great fun." The play has been taped by PBS network for *Great Performances.*

Think and Discuss

• **1.** What do Olog and Tanya learn about wisdom?
  2. What goals do Olog and Tanya have and how do they plan to reach them?
  3. Why are Tanya and Olog so willing to accept the advice of strangers as wisdom?
  4. If you were Tanya, how would you have responded to the farmers who accused you of being proud, stubborn, and ungrateful?
• **5.** Either of the following themes could fit the play; choose the one that means the most to you and explain your choice.
  a. You can't please everyone.
  b. Different people have different ideas about wisdom.

See your Thinker's Handbook for tips.
• Literary Skill: Theme

Communication Workshop

Talk

Work with your classmates to discuss the view Tanya would have had of the world outside her village. Would she have found it peaceful, strange, or would she have used some other adjective to describe it? Think about where you live as well as some of the places you have traveled. Discuss how you would describe the world to Tanya.
Speaking/Listening: Class discussion

Write

If you could travel to anyplace in the world, what place would you choose? Write two paragraphs which explain why you would like to go there and what you think you might learn. Read your paragraph to your classmates and listen to theirs. Who has the most interesting reason for wanting to travel somewhere?
Writing Fluency: Explanatory paragraphs

Islands of Matsushima (Detail) Ogata Korin, (1658–1716) Edo Period, early 18th c. Fenollosa-Weld
Collection Courtesy, Museum of Fine Arts, Boston

You can now travel to Japan, where you will meet Oyama, called Forever Mountain, because he is the strongest man in Japan. Or is he? Can the Mountain be moved by a pretty young woman, her mother, and her aged grandmother? What does he learn from these women? Notice how the author develops the plot by weaving together the characters' goals, problems, and actions.

Three Strong Women

A tall tale from Japan
by Claus Stamm

adapted for the stage by Donald Abramson

CHARACTERS

OYAMA *("Forever Mountain"), a famous wrestler*
MARUMI, *a country girl*
MOTHER, *Marumi's mother*
GRANDMOTHER, *Marumi's grandmother*
THE EMPEROR *of Japan*
LORD CHANCELLOR, *the Emperor's right-hand man*
MASTER OF CEREMONIES
ONAMI *("Big Wave"), another wrestler*
WRESTLER 1
WRESTLER 2
WRESTLER 3
LORDS *and* LADIES *of the Emperor's court*
SPECTATORS

SCENE ONE
A path in the woods. A stream flows nearby upstream, but it cannot be seen. There are many trees and some rocks. OYAMA *is heard offstage before he appears over a rise and strolls down the path.*
OYAMA *(singing):* Forever Mountain, that's what they call me,
　　　For when I face the other wrestlers in the ring

I loom above them, so they can't maul me
Because a mountain's far stronger than anything.
Sometimes I rumble, like a volcano
Then when I stamp my foot like this—*(He stamps his foot)*
     —they have to blanch
I make the earth quake to make sure *they* know
Who's going to fall upon them like an avalanche!
(Speaking) Ah, what a fine day—I think I'll sit under this tree for a while and listen to the birds and the water in that stream. I'm not tired, of course, but I don't have to be anywhere in a hurry. The Emperor's wrestling tournament isn't for three months yet, and I'm in such good shape I'm bound to win it. Hmmm, I wonder if I could train a bird to sing my song. Listen, little bird, here's how it goes: "Forever Mountain, that's what they—" Oh, someone's coming. I wonder who it is. If it's another wrestler, maybe I'll challenge him. (MARUMI *comes over the rise and down the path, carrying a wooden bucket on her head.)* Why, it's a young woman! A pretty one too. She must be after some water from that stream. I'll just hide here. (MARUMI *reaches the bottom of the path and climbs down to the stream upstage to fill her pail with water. That done, she climbs back up and starts back the way she came.)*

OYAMA: Hello, there, Miss. Won't you give me a drink of water?

MARUMI: Hello yourself. Why don't you get your own drink? The stream's right there. If I give you some water, I'll have to refill my pail again.

OYAMA: But I want *you* to give me a drink. I could steal it from you, after all. In fact, I could steal a kiss from you, and you wouldn't be able to do anything about it.

MARUMI: Oh, you think so, do you?

OYAMA: Or if I tickled you, you'd surely drop the whole pail of water, and then I'd have to refill it for you and probably carry it home for you as well.

MARUMI: You seem to have quite an opinion of yourself.

OYAMA: I'm Oyama—Forever Mountain—the famous wrestler. You've probably heard of me. I'm on my way to prove my strength before the Emperor.

MARUMI: Well, I'm Marumi, and I know you haven't heard of me. Mother and Grandmother and I don't have much to do with the goings-on at court. As for your proving your strength—

OYAMA: Come on, now—are you going to give me a drink, or am I going to tickle you?

MARUMI: Tickle away, if it pleases you.

OYAMA: Kochokochokocho! (*He reaches for her side, but* MARUMI *merely brings one arm down to trap his hand against her side.*) Oh! Hoho! You've caught me, have you? I can't move at all! (*He laughs.*)

MARUMI (*smiling quietly*): I know.

OYAMA (*trying to pull his hand away*): Well you can let me go now, Marumi. I'm a very powerful man. If I pull too hard, I might hurt you.

MARUMI: Pull away. I admire powerful men. (*He tries harder, but cannot free his hand.*) No? Well, then, I guess you'll have to come with me. (*She starts away up the path, dragging* OYAMA *along behind her.*)

OYAMA: Now, wait—you can't do this to me. I am the famous Forever Mountain.

MARUMI (*smiling sweetly*): Oh, yes? When word gets out that you let a young woman drag you away, they may call you "Hardly Ever Mountain!"

OYAMA (*squirming and looking uncomfortable*): Why are you doing this? Why won't you let me go?

MARUMI: I only want to help you. Now, I'm sure if you went on to the Emperor's court you'd have no more trouble than any of the others. You'd win, or else you'd lose. But aren't you afraid you might meet a really strong man someday?

OYAMA: Well, no, to tell you the truth. I've won a lot of wrestling matches in my time, after all. I haven't really been afraid of meeting any stronger—um—man.

MARUMI: I just thought, why not bring you to my mother's house and let us make a really strong man of you? The wrestling won't begin for another three months. I know, because Grandmother thought she'd like to go.

OYAMA: But they're expecting me—

MARUMI: You'll just be spending all your time in bad company and wasting what little power you have— No, it's best that you come along with me. (*She starts dragging him off.*)

OYAMA (*struggling in vain*): No, wait—I don't want to go—ow!— you're hurting my hand! (*They disappear over the rise.*)

SCENE TWO

MARUMI's *house. The simple farmhouse is partly seen down right. A rude wooden fence with a gate runs along the back of the stage. There are a few trees, a large rock or two, and flowers. OYAMA is heard offstage, still complaining; then MARUMI appears at the gate, still dragging him.)*

MARUMI: Oyama, will you stop complaining? What a big baby you are, after all. *(This shuts him up.)* Here we are at my house. If I let you go, you won't run away, will you? If you do, I'll chase you and carry you back here. Promise?

OYAMA *(chastened and shamefaced):* I won't run, I promise.

MARUMI: Fine. Then would you please open the gate for me? *(She releases him; he does so.)* Thank you. *(She enters the courtyard, sets down her pail, and looks back at him. Rather sheepishly he enters and closes the gate. Then he collapses on the ground.)* Oh, poor Oyama, are you tired? Shall I carry you inside where you can rest?

OYAMA: No, I don't want to rest. I want to go away so I can forget I ever met you. I'll never be able to show my face again—

MARUMI: Relax. You'll thank me for this someday. Now, I wonder where Grandmother is. Oh, she's probably taking a nap; she's very old. But Mother should be here. *(The "Moo-oo-oo" of a cow is heard in the distance.)* Ah, there she is now, bringing our cow home from the pasture. *(Over the top of the fence a cow's head is seen bouncing along, as if it is being carried.)* Mother—here I am! *(The cow's head disappears with another "Moo-oo-oo," and MOTHER appears at the gate. She enters, notices OYAMA, and bows to him, all smiles. He bows back.)*

MOTHER: Hello. Excuse me, these mountain paths are full of stones that hurt the poor cow's feet, so I just carry her back and forth to pasture. It's only a couple of miles. And who is this nice young man, Marumi?

MARUMI: He's a famous wrestler, named Oyama, Mother. I brought him home because—well, he's strong, but he could still benefit from a little extra training. You know what I mean. But we only have three months—

MOTHER: Three months! That's not long enough to do much, but we might still manage something. *(She feels OYAMA's muscles; he flinches at her touch.)* Hmmm. Well, it's a start.

MARUMI *(calling into the house):* Oh, Grandmother! Wake up!

雲も修鞘
不ぢ掾ヶ
ふいの山

芳月ゟ宇
丹鳥齋前　奥村文角政信正筆一

Scene from a Kabuki Play, 1750
Okumura Masanobu
Courtesy, Museum of Fine Arts, Boston.

MOTHER: I'm sorry, but you do need toughening up—and a lot of good food. Then when you're stronger you can help with some of the easy work around the house.

MARUMI: Yes, that's a good idea. *(Calling louder.)* Grandmother! Grandmother, we have a visitor. Come out and meet him!

GRANDMOTHER *(from within):* I'm coming, I'm coming! *(She totters out the door, leaning on a stick.)* I'm just slow, that's all. I'm an old woman, don't forget.

MARUMI: Grandmother, here is someone I'd like you to meet—

GRANDMOTHER *(stumbling over a huge rock):* Ow! Oh, excuse me, my eyes aren't what they used to be. That's the fourth time this month I've bumped into that rock. I should have gotten rid of it long ago! *(She picks up the rock easily and tosses it over the fence.)*

MARUMI: You should have let me do that for you, Grandmother.

GRANDMOTHER: Ah, how clumsy! I meant to throw it over the mountain. It's probably blocking the path now. Well, I'll move it later. Hmmm, I hope I didn't hurt my poor old back.

MOTHER: Mother, Marumi has brought home this young man she wants us to meet. Oyama, this is my mother.

OYAMA: *(bowing):* I'm honored to meet you.

GRANDMOTHER: Hello, hello, young man. Welcome to our house.

MARUMI: He's a famous wrestler, Grandmother, but he still needs a little more training.

MOTHER: Yes, we'll start with the diet. *(to OYAMA)* Now, every day I'll prepare your rice with a little less water, and then a little less, and after a while you'll be eating rice with no water at all. That ought to toughen you up some.

MARUMI: And you can help around the house, and carry the cow—

GRANDMOTHER: I'll help, too. I know—I can be your wrestling partner. I'm so old and feeble I'm not quite so likely to hurt you accidentally. Besides, the exercise might be good for my rheumatism. We can start now, if you like. I'm feeling quite rested after my nap. *(She grabs his hand and drags him toward the gate.)*

OYAMA: Well, I'm not sure—we don't have to start right away, perhaps—I don't want to inconvenience you, after all—

GRANDMOTHER: Oh, it's no bother. Glad to do it. *(to him privately)* Besides, I think our Marumi's a bit stuck on you. Tell you what, though, we'll just go outside here, away from the house. We don't want to knock anything over accidentally. *(She drags him out through the gate.)*

MARUMI: Oh, Mother, isn't he a fine man? I think maybe I've found someone worthwhile at last—

MOTHER: Yes, my daughter, I think he just might do—*(From behind the fence, OYAMA is heard grunting and groaning. Then he is seen tossed above the fence, yelling, his arms and legs flailing. Again, even higher. After a moment of silence, GRANDMOTHER appears at the gate, grinning broadly.)*

GRANDMOTHER: Yes, yes—but he needs a lot of work, all right!

SCENE THREE

MARUMI's *house, three months have gone by.* MOTHER *is sitting by the door preparing vegetables. Noises are heard behind the fence, and* OYAMA *is seen flying through the air once more.* MARUMI *appears at the gate with her buckets, watches the wrestling match for a moment, and then enters.)*

MARUMI: Oh Mother, today's the last day. Do you think he'll be ready?

MOTHER: Well, he's been working hard, and he *has* been improving. Your grandmother told me yesterday he actually held her down for a few seconds. If we had more time—who knows? But he'll be strong enough to show off in front of the Emperor, I suppose. *(with a meaningful smile)* Do *you* think he is strong, my Marumi?

MARUMI *(blushing and looking away):* Oh, Mother! *(A tremendous growl is heard from OYAMA, and this time GRANDMOTHER is seen flying through the air.)*

MARUMI: Why—that was Grandmother! *(She runs to the wall, climbs on a bench, and looks over.)* Oyama's holding Grandmother down now—she's struggling—he's still holding her—*(She runs back.)* Mother, he's stronger than Grandmother!

(A roar of triumph is heard from OYAMA. GRANDMOTHER comes tottering through the gate, grinning broadly.)

GRANDMOTHER *(chuckling):* Half a minute! He held me down for half a minute! I would never have believed it!

(OYAMA comes through the gate, exhausted but happy. MARUMI and MOTHER applaud him; then MARUMI throws her arms around him.)

MARUMI: Oh, Oyama, I knew you could do it!

MOTHER: Very good, young man, very good indeed.

GRANDMOTHER: You've been a good student. Of course, I'm an old woman and not nearly as strong as I used to be—

MOTHER: But I think we agree that now your training is complete and you're ready to show some real strength before the Emperor.

OYAMA: Yes, today is the day I must leave, isn't it? I'm sorry I have to go. I'm going to miss you, all of you. I want to thank you for what you've done for me—

GRANDMOTHER: Oh, tut, tut, young man—it was a pleasure. You help me get the kinks out of my old back.

MARUMI: Oyama, we all agree—you should take the cow with you.

OYAMA: The cow! But what am I to do with a cow?

MARUMI: Sell her and buy yourself a silken belt—the fanciest one you can find—as a token from us. We want you to look splendid when you appear before the Emperor.

OYAMA: Why, I wouldn't think of taking your only cow. You'll need her to plow the fields, won't you?

MOTHER (laughing): You don't think we put our cow to work, do you? Why, any of us is stronger than five cows!

MARUMI: The cow is our pet. She has such lovely brown eyes.

MOTHER: But it's really tiresome to carry her back and forth every day so that she gets enough grass to eat.

OYAMA: Then you must let me give you all the prize money I win.

MOTHER: No, we couldn't think of it. You're still a stranger.

OYAMA: But if I were—a member of the family?

MOTHER: Well, maybe that would be all right.

OYAMA: Then when I win, I'll come right back here and ask Marumi to be my wife!

GRANDMOTHER: *If* you win. Remember, somewhere in Japan there might be three strong women teaching other wrestlers—

OYAMA (laughing in agreement): If I win, then.

MOTHER: Well, it's time you were on your way.

OYAMA: Yes, I'll go now. Thank you for the cow, and thank you for—everything. (He pauses at the gate.) Marumi, I will be back! (He exits. A tremendous "Moo-oo-oo" is heard, then the cow's head appears above the fence as he picks her up and carries her away. From the distance his voice is heard singing.) Forever Mountain, that's what they call me—

MARUMI (climbing on the bench, to wave after him): Goodbye! (climbing down) Grandmother, you said before that you'd like to go and see the tournament, didn't you—?

(They all look at each other, nod, and then burst out laughing.)

SCENE FOUR

A palace courtyard. A low stone wall runs along the back, behind which SPECTATORS *are gathering for the tournament. In front of the wall,* LORDS *and* LADIES, *dressed in their finest, sit on mats or low stools. Banners on standards lend a festive air. A screen with a pierced design encloses the* EMPEROR's *private viewing area, down left. The* EMPEROR *is seated on a low stool in front of a table, writing on a scroll. He thinks for a moment, dips his brush in the ink, writes a word, and then thinks some more. The* LORD CHANCELLOR *enters behind him.*

CHANCELLOR: Your Excellency, the tournament is about to begin.

EMPEROR: Yes, yes, I just—ah!—wait a minute! *(He writes one final word, then leans back to study the scroll.)* What do you think of this, Lord Chancellor? *(reading)*
"Sad, little moon?
Your tears again this morning
on all the flowers."

CHANCELLOR: It's a lovely haiku, Your Excellency. But there's a time for poetry and a time for wrestling, and right now—

EMPEROR *(sighing):* Oh, I know, I know—but I don't like wrestling very much. I'd much sooner write poetry.

CHANCELLOR: Well, it won't last *that* long. All the lords and ladies are assembled, I believe. *(He peeks through the holes in the screen.)* Yes, they all seem to be here.

EMPEROR: At least behind the screen like this, no one can tell whether I'm watching with interest or with boredom.

CHANCELLOR: The screen, Your Excellency, is there for a traditional purpose. You are far too noble for ordinary people to look at.

EMPEROR: Yes, well—things may have a dual purpose. Hmmm, I might write a poem about that.

CHANCELLOR: Your Excellency, not now—it's time to begin.

EMPEROR: Very well, give the signal to start the tournament.

*(*THE LORD CHANCELLOR *disappears behind the screen. A large gong sounds three times. All the* WRESTLERS *file in and take their places equidistantly around the ring. A* MASTER OF CEREMONIES *enters.)*

MASTER OF CEREMONIES: Lords and ladies of the court and all loyal subjects of His Excellency, the Emperor of Japan, the tournament is about to begin. The wrestlers have already been chosen by lot. The first to exhibit their strength will be—*(He consults a scroll.)*—Onami and Oyama.

(The SPECTATORS *applaud politely. The* LORDS *and* LADIES *wave their fans.* ONAMI *and* OYAMA *step to the center of the ring.)*

ONAMI *(scattering some salt):* I scatter this salt to dispel whatever evil spirits might attend upon us.

*(*OYAMA *does the same thing, using the same words.)*

MASTER OF CEREMONIES: And now, let the wrestling begin!

(A hush of anticipation falls upon the crowd. ONAMI *and* OYAMA *bow ceremoniously to each other; then they circle each other, looking fierce and making grunting noises.)*

ONAMI *(irreverently):* So you're Oyama, the Forever Mountain, are you? I've never heard of you. How's this—? *(He raises his foot and brings it down with a tremendous stamp; then he puts his hands on his hips and smiles at* OYAMA *with disdain.)*

OYAMA: So you're Onami, the great wave of the sea. I *have* heard of you. You're supposed to be one of the best wrestlers in all Japan. However—

*(*OYAMA *raises his foot, but before stamping he notices* MARUMI, MOTHER, *and* GRANDMOTHER *in the audience and gives them a little wave. Then he brings his foot down with a crash! Everyone in the audience falls down; the* LORDS *and* LADIES *are knocked off their stools, and* ONAMI *does a backward somersault. The banner standards are knocked askew and the* EMPEROR'S *screen collapses.* OYAMA *just stands there, surveying the effect. One by one, people pick themselves up, they are all dazed and in awe. The* LORD CHANCELLOR *rushes to help the* EMPEROR. *Finally,* ONAMI *gets to his feet. Trying to regain some dignity, he bows to the* EMPEROR.*)*

ONAMI: Doubtless *that* was just an earthquake and it would seem that the earth god is angry. Possibly there was something wrong with the salt I scattered. I didn't behave illegally; but, in view of this bad omen, I do not think it would be wise for me to wrestle this season. *(He bows again and leaves.)*

(The other WRESTLERS *look at each other and start murmuring.)*

WRESTLER 1: He's right—if the earth god's angry with you, you haven't a chance.

WRESTLER 2: I was going to use some of that same salt, too—

WRESTLER 3: Maybe it's just not a good year for wrestling. Some years aren't, you know.

(One by one the WRESTLERS *bow to the* EMPEROR *and leave.* OYAMA *remains stalwart. The* MASTER OF CEREMONIES *and the* LORD

CHANCELLOR *can be seen holding a hasty conference. Finally, the* EMPEROR *motions the* LORD CHANCELLOR *over.)*

EMPEROR: Is that it? Have all the other wrestlers truly withdrawn from the ring?

CHANCELLOR: It appears so, Your Excellency. There are none left. They all went out the back gate rather hurriedly.

EMPEROR: Then that young man is the winner. Good! Award him the prize money so I can go. I feel a poem coming on—

CHANCELLOR: But Your Excellency! Oh, very well. *(Raising his voice.)* Lords and Ladies of the court and all loyal subjects under our Emperor's protectorship and so on, in tribute to the outstanding show of strength and—hum—wrestling skill demonstrated by—ah—*(He looks at the* MASTER OF CEREMONIES *who consults his scroll and whispers to him.)*— Oyama, the Emperor has directed me to award this prize money—

(SERVANTS *wheel on large bags of money. The crowd goes wild.)*

OYAMA *(bowing low):* Thank you, Your Excellency.

EMPEROR: Young Man, I would strongly advise you not to wrestle any more. With you in the ring, there'd be no reason ever to hold another tournament, and people are sure to miss all that tugging and grunting. They do like their tournaments, I'm afraid.

OYAMA: Your Excellency, I had already made up my mind to retire from wrestling. There's always sure to be someone— somewhere—just a little stronger. I am going to become a farmer.

EMPEROR: That's very wise, young man. Did you ever consider writing poetry? Well, goodbye. Good luck. *(He exits.)*

(MARUMI, MOTHER, *and* GRANDMOTHER *appear beside* OYAMA.)

OYAMA *(giving* MARUMI *a hug):* Marumi, will you marry me now?

MARUMI: Of course I will. I'm so proud of you. Will you let me honor you by carrying your money?

OYAMA: Surely. *(She picks up the large bags easily and starts off.)* In fact, you carry the money, and I'll carry *you.* *(He starts off after her.)*

MOTHER: Ah well, in honor of the occasion, I'll carry Marumi, the money, and Oyama. *(She starts off after them.)*

GRANDMOTHER: And in honor of the occasion—*(winking at the audience and chuckling)*—I'll carry them all! *(She exits.)*

Comprehension Check

Think and Discuss

1. What does Oyama learn from Marumi, her mother, and her grandmother?
2. What different goals do Marumi and Oyama have?
3. What obstacle stands in the way of Oyama's goal? How does the obstacle Oyama faces help Marumi achieve her goal?
• 4. In a few sentences, state the plot of the play.
5. Do you like Oyama better at the beginning of the play or at the end? Why?

• Literary Skill: Plot

Communication Workshop

Talk

Work in a small group. Choose a member to play Oyama, who wants to write an article about how he prepared for and won the Emperor's tournament. The article must be short. The rest of the group can help Oyama decide what to include by discussing the main events in the play and then deciding which details are important and which are not. For example, was Oyama's rice diet important to the outcome? Was the mother's habit of carrying the cow important?

Speaking/Listening: Cooperative learning

Write

Help Oyama organize his article by writing a paragraph that describes the events which lead up to his retirement. Tell about the events in the order in which they occurred. Then have Oyama read each group member's paragraph aloud, choose the one he or she thinks is best, and tell why.

Writing Fluency: Paragraph

What kind of battle goes on in a French village? You can find out by going there in this play. What kind of characters are Jean and Jeanette? Notice the details in the setting that tell you more about them.

Who Speaks First

a French folk tale
dramatized by Donald Abramson

CHARACTERS

JEAN MOREL, *a shoemaker*
JEANETTE MOREL, *his wife, a weaver*
SIMONE, *a neighbor*
PIERRE, *a neighbor*
MADAME CARTIER, *a rich villager*
MONSIEUR DUPONT, *the mayor of the village*
COACHMAN *for the Prince*
THE PRINCE *of Dauphiné*

A modest cottage in a small French village, long, long ago. There is a large stone fireplace, right. A shoemaker's bench sits in front of it. In the back wall is a window and a door, the top and bottom of which open separately. Another door leads to a bedroom. A spinning wheel sits in front of another window, left. There is a table and a few chairs. JEAN *and* JEANETTE *are just finishing supper.*

JEAN: Well, Jeanette, I surely got a superb cook when I married you.

JEANETTE: You haven't gotten tired of my cooking, then, Jean, after almost a year we've been together?

JEAN: Oh, no, no! Just keep on cooking the way you do now.

JEANETTE: I'm pleased you like it, but why don't you ever compliment anything else I do—like my weaving?

JEAN: Why, I don't notice it, I guess. It just seems as though you do what you're supposed to do. After all, women have their work, and men have theirs.

JEANETTE: Supposed to—? Yes, that's a man's way of looking at it. However, I'll wash the dishes now—since somebody has to do it—if you'll fetch me a pail of water from the well.

JEAN: Now then, don't be annoyed, Jeanette. We haven't yet had any cross words between us. Why, I've often remarked to the fellows down at the inn how even-tempered you are—

JEANETTE: What? You discuss me with those good-for-nothings?

JEAN: Why, I don't mean any harm by it, I'm sure. Somebody says, "My wife did this, and my wife said that!" and then I say, "Ah, friends, but *my* wife—now, she knows when to hold her tongue."

JEANETTE: Hold my tongue? I'll hold *your* tongue for you!

JEAN: Well, I won't mention you any more. And so that there'll be no hard feelings, I'll go and get the water for you now, as you asked. *(He picks up a bucket and starts for the door.)*

JEANETTE: Thank you. Oh—and while you're going—*(Quickly she searches beside the fireplace.)* Do you remember when we got married and moved in here? We had hardly any furniture—not even plates to eat from—and we borrowed things from all the neighbors—including a kettle from Madame Blanchard down the road? Well, this is funny, but it's embarrassing, too—we never did return it. *(She places a good-sized cooking kettle on the table. Sweetly:)* Would you take it back to her now?

JEAN: What's that? We never returned this to Madame Blanchard?

JEANETTE *(laughing):* No, when we got our new kettle, this got misplaced, somehow—and I forgot all about it!

JEAN: And it's been almost a year now?

JEANETTE: Yes, but you can explain that to her when you—

JEAN: Well, I'm not taking it back!

JEANETTE: After all, we've got to take it back sometime, and apologize to Madame Blanchard for keeping it so long.

JEAN: Take it back yourself, then. And apologize yourself.

JEANETTE: But why can't you just stop by on your way to the well?

JEAN: Why should I be the one to be embarrassed in front of Madame Blanchard, with Monsieur Blanchard there too, no doubt? No, it's you who must take it back.

JEANETTE: But you're the one who borrowed it in the first place. Naturally you're the one who should return it.

JEAN: Yes, I borrowed it, but you're the one who used it, so you should return it. Anyway, you're the one who mislaid it.

JEANETTE: So you don't mind if I'm to be humiliated. You know Madame Blanchard will tell her neighbor, Madame St. Claire, who will certainly tell her best friend, Madame Pigot, who won't attempt to keep it a secret—

JEAN: But if word of this got out, I could be ruined. Every man in the village would point at me and say, "There goes a man who can't be trusted, whose word is no good—"

JEANETTE: About me they'd say, "There goes a woman who doesn't know how to keep house, who loses a neighbor's kettle—"

JEAN: Well, that's true, after all—

JEANETTE: I only asked you to do me a little favor!

JEAN (coldly): I see now that you're willing to sacrifice my standing in the community just to save yourself embarrassment—

JEANETTE (just as coldly): I see now that you're not gentleman enough to stand up for your wife—

JEAN: Well, I shall never be the one to return that kettle!

JEANETTE: I certainly shan't be the one to take it back!

JEAN: That kettle can sit there and rust for all I care!

JEANETTE: You would, wouldn't you? You'd let a perfectly good kettle go to ruin while you just talk and talk—

JEAN: I'm through with talking! Before I return that kettle, I'll—I'll—never speak another word!

JEANETTE: And I'll never speak a word before I return it!

(They glare at each other and then turn their backs and fold their arms stubbornly. There is a long pause. JEANETTE looks around.)

JEANETTE (suddenly): Fire!

JEAN (alarmed; looking around the room): What? Where?

JEANETTE: No, I mean—what if there were a fire? I wouldn't care to be burned to death just because you're so stubborn.

JEAN: I'm stubborn! And you're not, I suppose.

JEANETTE: I just know my own mind. But look—suppose we make an agreement. We won't speak, but we ought to be able to make some sort of noise, just in case.

JEAN: Hmmm. I could whistle, perhaps. I used to be very good at whistling down the lane when I was single—and didn't have a care in the world. All the girls told me so.

JEANETTE: And I could sing. I used to be very good at singing when I sat at my spinning wheel at Mother's house and sang little spinning songs. All the boys were *very* impressed.

JEAN: Very well, then—you can sing, and I can whistle.

JEANETTE: But we won't say a word—

JEAN: Not a word. Not to each other—

JEANETTE: Not to anyone else. And whoever does speak first—

JEAN: Has to return the kettle!

JEANETTE: Agreed!

JEAN: Agreed! Well, then—when shall we start? *(JEANETTE doesn't answer but starts singing a little wordless song instead.)* Oh, so that's the way you want to play it! All right, then! *(He starts whistling—a different tune.)*

(Very nonchalantly they move around, whistling and singing and ignoring each other. JEAN *sits at his shoemaker's bench, and* JEANETTE *sits at her spinning wheel. Glancing at each other, they set about their occupations, whistling and singing with renewed vigor. Then* SIMONE *appears at the door, peering in the open top half. Throughout the following,* JEAN *and* JEANETTE *use no words, but their whistling and singing sounds like dialogue and reflects their thoughts and the conflicting emotions they feel.)*

SIMONE *(calling):* Jeanette! Oh, there you are. Listen—I've got to tell you—*(She lets herself in.)* There's going to be such a celebration. Three days of dancing and feasting! People in their finest clothes! I don't know what I'm going to wear— maybe a new bonnet—oh, Jeanette, isn't it wonderful? *(JEANETTE sings, "What is it?")* But I didn't tell you, did I? You know that Madame Cartier, so rich she barely speaks to us? Her daughter, Yvonne, is going to be married—and you'll never guess who— *(JEANETTE sings, "No, who is it?")* Only the most eligible young man in the village, the mayor's son, Albert Dupont! Isn't it exciting? What a couple they'll make! *(JEANETTE sings, "How nice!")* What's the matter, Jeanette, I thought you'd have *something* to say. Anyway, that's not all. Of course she's going to need a fabulous trousseau, and guess what—Madame Cartier wants *you* to weave the wool! It was such luck—I was in the market, and there she was putting on airs, and she asked if anyone knew of a reliable weaver. So I told her my friend Jeanette Morel weaves the most marvelous wool—and well, to make a long story short, she's on her way to see you now! *(JEANETTE, singing excitedly, starts tidying up the room.)* Jeanette, what is the matter with you? Why don't you say something? This is such a chance for you. Oh, here she is!

MME. CARTIER *(at the door):* Hello? Madame—Morel, is it? *(JEANETTE curtseys and sings, "You honor me, Madame.")*

SIMONE *(giving* JEANETTE *a strange look and opening the door for* MADAME CARTIER*):* Oh, please come in, Madame Cartier, I've just been telling Jeanette about your daughter's wedding.

MME. CARTIER: Then you will be able to furnish my needs? Everything must be of the highest quality, of course, and I'll need it in three weeks. *(JEANETTE sings "I'll do my best.")* Why, what's wrong? Can't you answer? This is serious business, young woman. Do you know whom my daughter is marrying? How important it is that everything be exactly right? *(JEANETTE sings that she understands.)* And yet you make no reply. All you do is sing that idiotic song. *(to* SIMONE*)* You're sure this is the reliable weaver you were telling me about?

SIMONE: Of course, Madame Cartier. I don't know what's wrong with her. She was perfectly all right when I saw her yesterday.

MME. CARTIER: Well, I have no intention of dealing with someone who is either attempting to make fun of me, or who is—quite mad! *(She starts to go;* JEANETTE *runs after her, singing.)*

SIMONE: Please Madame, don't go—I'm sure there's some explanation! *(But* MME. CARTIER *is gone.)* Oh, Jeannette, how could you? What must she think of you, now? *(with horror)* What must she think of *me?* Oh! *(JEANETTE sings despondently.)* And still you sing! Well, if you won't even give me a civil word, I'm certainly not going to speak to you! Goodbye!

(SIMONE flounces out and slams the door. JEAN, *enjoying this enormously, whistles at* JEANETTE *mockingly. She sings back at him angrily and stalks back to her spinning wheel.* JEAN *strolls about the room, whistling brightly. Then* PIERRE *appears at the door.)*

PIERRE *(calling):* Jean! Oh, there you are. Listen, I've got to tell you—*(He lets himself in.)* Have you heard about Yvonne

Cartier and Albert Dupont getting married? (JEAN *whistles that he has.*) Well, Monsieur Dupont wants new clothes for his entire family, of course. I was in the market just now when he asked if anyone knew a really skillful shoemaker, and I mentioned my friend, Jean Morel—and to make a long story short, he's on his way to see you now. (*Now it is* JEAN's *turn to fuss about, whistling excitedly.* JEANETTE *can't resist a few mocking notes, and* JEAN *responds angrily.*) Why, Jean, what's the matter with you? Why don't you say something? This is such a chance for you. It's as much money as—Oh, here he is!

M. DUPONT (*at the door*): Excuse me, is this the abode of one—ah—Monsieur Morel, the shoemaker? I've come on an important business matter. (JEAN *whistles and bows to invite him in.*)

PIERRE (*giving* JEAN *a strange look and opening the door*): Yes, yes, this is the place, Monsieur Dupont. Do come in—

M. DUPONT: Good day to you, Monsieur. I take it you have heard of the impending marriage of my son? Well, naturally, as mayor of this village, I am sparing no expense. I wish to order new shoes for my entire family—that is, for myself, my wife, and our three daughters—as well as for my son. Naturally they must be of the highest quality leather, the stitching must be impeccable, and the fit must be perfect. None of your, "Oh they'll stretch out in a month or so." Are you capable of accepting such a commission? (JEAN *whistles, "I certainly am!"*) And all this must be ready in three weeks' time, do you understand? I say, is there something wrong with you? (*To* PIERRE.) Is he quite all right, do you think? I'm trying to discuss business, and he keeps—er—whistling at me!

PIERRE: Oh, Jean's just in high spirits—ah—naturally—ah—because of your upcoming happiness, Monsieur.

M. DUPONT: No doubt. Still, I don't expect happiness from my tradespeople, I expect service. Now, how's he going to provide service if he whistles all the time? It hardly suggests seriousness of purpose. Are you sure he's competent?

PIERRE: I swear I don't know what might be wrong with him, Monsieur Dupont. He was perfectly all right yesterday.

(JEAN, *a little panicky, grabs* M. DUPONT's *foot as if to measure it. This throws* M. DUPONT *off balance.*)

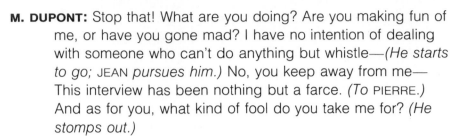

M. DUPONT: Stop that! What are you doing? Are you making fun of me, or have you gone mad? I have no intention of dealing with someone who can't do anything but whistle—*(He starts to go;* JEAN *pursues him.)* No, you keep away from me—This interview has been nothing but a farce. *(To* PIERRE.*)* And as for you, what kind of fool do you take me for? *(He stomps out.)*

PIERRE: Oh, but Monsieur Dupont, I assure you—*(But* M. DUPONT *is gone.* JEAN *whistles despondently.)* And still you whistle! Have you no sense, man? You've just lost your biggest order in years, you've antagonized our mayor, and you've made *me* look like an idiot! Well, I'm not going to waste any more time with you! Goodbye! *(He stalks out and slams the door.)*

*(*JEANETTE, *enjoying this turnabout, sings mockingly. They begin to argue back and forth, blaming each other. Finally they are face to face, singing and whistling furiously. Suddenly there is a knock at the door. A* COACHMAN *appears, carrying a lantern.)*

COACHMAN: Hello! Excuse me, I'm the Prince's coachman, and I'd like to– Mind if I come in? *(Taking their silence as consent, he lets himself in.)* The Prince is waiting in his coach just down the road. We're on our way back to the palace, but as it's getting dark, we stopped to light our lanterns—if I could please have a light from your fireplace? *(Their silence puzzles him. To* JEANETTE.*)* Madame? *(*JEANETTE, *almost in tears from frustration, still sings.)* What's that? I can't understand you. Perhaps you don't speak French, after all? *(To* JEAN.*)* Monsieur? *(*JEAN, *equally frustrated, still whistles.)* What? You whistle at me? Monsieur, I am attached to the royal household as personal coachman to the Prince, and it's he who requests a light, not I—*(*JEAN *whistles, "Light your lantern!")* Well, you're an insolent couple, I must say!

*(*PIERRE *and* SIMONE *have crept into the doorway, burning with curiosity about who the visitor is. Now they let themselves in.)*

PIERRE: Psst! You! Coachman!
COACHMAN: Yes, what is it? Do you know these people?

SIMONE: Yes, we do. They're our friends, Jeanette and Jean—

COACHMAN: Well, I came in here to light the Prince's lantern—

SIMONE *(excited):* The Prince? Here? Where?

COACHMAN: Just down the road, but these two refuse to answer my simple request. What's the matter with them?

PIERRE: We don't know. Usually they're as talkative as anyone else. I can't imagine why they're not speaking today.

COACHMAN: The Prince doesn't like to be kept waiting, but even worse, if he thought these two were trying to insult him—

(Now SIMONE and PIERRE, frightened for their friends, hover over JEANETTE and JEAN, earnestly trying to reason with them.)

SIMONE: Listen, Jeanette, you've got to speak now. This is the Prince's coachman, here to light his lantern from your fireplace— you'll be famous in the village!

PIERRE: For heaven's sake, Jean, this is serious. You can't afford to insult the Prince. He could be a powerful friend—or a powerful enemy. Don't deny him a light!

Together

(JEAN and JEANETTE whistle and sing at the same time, however, so the effect is that of four people speaking at once. In the midst of all this confusion, the PRINCE appears in the doorway. He surveys the hubbub with growing irritation.)

PRINCE *(finally):* Will you all stop this infernal racket!

(PIERRE and SIMONE shut up immediately, but JEAN and JEANETTE don't realize at first what is going on.)

PIERRE *(in a hushed whisper, nudging JEAN):* It's the Prince!

(The COACHMAN rushes to open the door, and the PRINCE enters.)

PRINCE: Now what is all this? Coachman, where is that lantern? What on earth is taking you so long?

COACHMAN: Your Highness, this man, this woman, they refuse—

SIMONE: Your Highness, it's not their fault, I swear to you—

PRINCE *(looking at them suspiciously):* My Coachman is only here, after all, on a simple errand from me. If these people have insulted my servant, they've insulted me. Now I want to hear about it from them.

PIERRE: Oh, Your Highness, that's just it, you see, they can't—

PRINCE *(thundering):* Silence! *(To* JEAN *and* JEANETTE.*)* Now, I want an explanation from you, and it had better be good.

(Frightened, JEAN *and* JEANETTE *start haltingly, quaveringly, to whistle and sing. The* PRINCE *listens to them intently. Finally they fade out in embarrassment, and there is a long silence. When the* PRINCE *speaks, he is rather amiable.)*

PRINCE: Oh, well—now I see the problem. *(To the* COACHMAN.*)* I think we need not worry about any deliberate insult. Go ahead and light your lantern. *(The* COACHMAN *does so, using a stick from the fireplace. The others relax visibly.)* Now, what are we to do about these two, however? It's clear to me that she—*(He points to* JEANETTE*)*—is suffering from some rare disease, but that he—*(He points to* JEAN*)*—has quite lost his wits. One or the other. Fortunately for them, we have very learned doctors at court who will be able to tell us which one—or if both—belongs in a hospital. Fear not, my friends, we'll find help for you. Now, we'll start with the woman. *(To* PIERRE.*)* Would you help my man carry her out to the coach?

*(*PIERRE *and the* COACHMAN *take* JEANETTE *by the shoulders and attempt to raise her, but she grasps the chair and wraps her legs around it. They look to the* PRINCE *for advice.)*

PRINCE: Well, then—take her, chair and all!

(They lift the chair with JEANETTE *in it; she screams.)*

JEAN *(finally breaking his long silence):* Stop! Don't take my wife! *(*PIERRE *and the* COACHMAN, *startled, set the chair down.)* I—I love her, and I—I—*(*JEANETTE *smiles triumphantly and points an accusing finger at* JEAN. *He looks at her and at the group in frustration, and finally snatches up the disputed pot from the table.)*—I'll take back the kettle!

(All the other characters show their amazement. JEANETTE *gives* JEAN *a fond and thankful smile.)*

Think and Discuss

1. What kind of characters are Jean and Jeanette? Select the adjectives below that describe each of them and support your answer with examples from the play:

   easygoing   stubborn   self-sacrificing
   quick-tempered   insecure   selfish

• 2. Which details in the setting help you find out more about Jean and Jeanette?

3. Why don't either Jean or Jeanette want to return Madame Blanchard's kettle?

4. Who finally breaks the silence? Why?

5. Do you think Jean and Jeanette gained anything from their experience? Explain your answer.

• Literary Skill: Setting

Communication Workshop

Talk

Divide into groups of four. Within each group assign people to play the parts of Jean, Jeanette, Madame Cartier, and Monsieur Dupont. What would Jean and Jeanette do or say to persuade Madame Cartier and Monsieur Dupont to bring their business back to the store? How would Cartier and Dupont respond?
Speaking/Listening: Role-playing

Write

Now have each member of each group pretend to be Jean and write a brief note of explanation to Monsieur Dupont to try to convince him that he should bring his business back. Each group member should then read his or her notes aloud. What arguments were used to convince Mr. Dupont? Which do you think are the most effective and why?
Writing Fluency: Personal note

Get Up and Bar the Door

It fell about the Martinmas time,
    And a gay time it was then,
When our goodwife got puddings[1] to make,
    And she's boild them in the pan.

The wind so cold blew south and north,
    And blew into the floor;
Quoth our goodman to our goodwife,
    "Go out and bar the door."

"My hand is in my housewife's work,
    Goodman, as ye may see;
And it should not be barrd this hundred year,
    If it's to be barrd by me."

They made a pact between the two,
    They made it firm and sure,
That the first word who'er should speak,
    Should rise and bar the door.

Then by there came two gentlemen,
    At twelve o'clock at night,
And they could neither see house nor hall,
    Nor coal nor candle-light.

"Now whether is this a rich man's house,
    Or whether is it a poor?"
But ne'er a word would one o' them speak,
    For barring of the door.

---

1. *puddings,* sausages.

And first they[2] ate the white puddings,
 And then they ate the black;
Tho much thought the goodwife to herself,
 Yet ne'er a word she spake.[3]

Then said the one unto the other,
 "Here, man, take ye my knife;
Do ye take off the old man's beard,
 And I'll kiss the goodwife."

"But there's no water in the house,
 And what shall we do then?"
"What ails ye[4] at the pudding-broth,
 That boils into the pan?"

O up then started our goodman,
 An angry man was he:
"Will ye kiss my wife before my eyes,
 And wi' pudding-broth scald me?"

Then up and started our goodwife,
 Gave three skips on the floor:
"Goodman, you've spoken the foremost[5] word,
 Get up and bar the door."

2. *they*, gentlemen.
3. *spake*, spoke.
4. *What ails ye*, why not use.
5. *foremost*, first.

Learning to Visualize

When you read plays, it's natural to try to visualize—or picture in your mind—how the characters look and act and what the setting is like. This helps you bring the play to life. For example, picture the wrestling scene in "Three Strong Women," when Oyama brings his foot down with a crash:

> *Everyone in the audience falls down; the* LORDS *and* LADIES *are knocked off their stools, and* ONAMI *does a backward somersault. The banner standards are knocked askew and the* EMPEROR's *screen collapses.* OYAMA *just stands there, surveying the effect. One by one, people pick themselves up: they are all dazed and in awe.*

Notice how the details that you "see" help you feel the force of Oyama's stamping.

You can also bring stories, novels, and poems to life by visualizing. It's like making a movie in your mind, and *you* are the director.

When you read "Winter Thunder" in the next section, try these different ways of visualizing the story:

- Close your eyes and imagine the scene or character being described.
- Think about what you would see, hear, touch, taste, and smell in a similar setting.
- Draw a picture, map, or diagram if it will help you sort out the details of what you are reading.
- Ask yourself questions to clarify what the author tells you: Why does the food have to be rationed? Does Lecia think they will be rescued soon?

Preview the story now and notice the side notes that will help you picture the setting.

LOOKING BACK

See your *Thinker's Handbook* for tips.

Prewriting

Thinking and Writing About the Section

You have just traveled from here to different places in the world through the magic of the theater. You can write a description to show how the plays are alike and different to share with a partner. For instance, you might compare and contrast the characters' searches or the setting of the plays. First copy the chart below and talk with a partner to fill in the missing information.

Characters	Searching for	Setting: Country and Region
Olog and Tanya	wisdom	Nigeria: small village
Oyama, Marumi, Mother, Grandmother		: woods, farm
Jean and Jeanette	acceptance, love	France:

Writing

Now use the information on your chart to write a comparison-contrast description about two of the plays. Show the ways they are alike and the ways they are different. Include sensory details so your partner can visualize what you describe. For more information about comparison-contrast descriptions, see your Writer's Handbook.

Revising

Read your first draft to a partner. Did you point out how the two plays you chose are alike and how they are different? Did you use sensory details? Make changes if necessary. Then proofread for spelling and punctuation errors. Write your final copy.

Presenting

Read your paragraph to your partner. Ask him or her to listen for the similarities and differences.

6

Encounters

From the time your feet first touch the floor in the morning until you bury your head in the pillow at night, you will experience many different encounters. Some encounters may surprise you and "sweep you off your feet." Others may open your eyes to new ideas, change your way of thinking, or help you understand yourself.

In this section, you will read about people who encounter the force of nature, which threatens their survival and tests their strength. You'll see characters who encounter other people and find themselves in puzzling or dangerous situations. And you'll witness an encounter between two fanciful characters that leads to a game of wits, where one character dares not lose.

Appreciating Author's Style

These artists both drew pictures to show a ship encountering danger at sea. You can better appreciate these different drawings by looking at the techniques the artists used to express their ideas. In the first, the artist's technique is to use thin, sketchy lines. In the second drawing, the artist's technique is to use lines as well as shading. Which gives you more of a feeling of danger?

Authors also have different styles. The techniques they use to express their ideas makes one author's way of telling a story different from another's. Two techniques are foreshadowing and mood. Authors use **foreshadowing** when they place clues or hints that suggest what will happen before it happens. Later in the story when that something *does* happen, you recognize how the clues worked. Authors use foreshadowing to make you curious or give you a sense of how the story may develop.

Mood is the feeling of a selection that the author tries to give you—such as fearful, romantic, or humorous. Authors choose specific settings, details, and words to create the mood of a selection. Often the mood of a selection changes. A selection may begin in a hopeless mood and change later to a joyful mood.

Read the following story, "The Flute," by Eloise Greenfield. Look for two clues that foreshadow something Doretha realizes and think about the mood.

Doretha didn't know just what it was, but there was something different about Mrs. Anderson today. When Doretha went up on the porch, Mrs. Anderson was sitting kind of squeezed into the green metal chair, as she was every Sunday afternoon in the fall. She had on the same bulky-knit sweater, and her short gray hair was brushed back and bobby-pinned at her ears.

Maybe her plump brown hands were lying extra still in her lap, or maybe her eyes were looking too far away. Whatever it was made Doretha pause before disturbing her.

"Mrs. Anderson?"

"Yes? Oh, hello, Doretha, I didn't see you come up. How are you today?"

"Fine. Mama said Mr. Anderson wanted to see me."

"He certainly does. Go right on in. I think he's in the living room."

Mr. Anderson met Doretha at the door. "I thought I heard you, Doretha," he said. He was cheerful, smiling behind his rimless glasses and under his thin, mixed-gray mustache, but the house seemed to have taken on Mrs. Anderson's mood. He led Doretha into the front room. "Sit right down there in the big chair. I have a present for you."

"But my birthday's not until February," Doretha said.

"Now, could I forget when your birthday is?" Mr. Anderson said. He pushed at the sides of his glasses. "The way your father was bragging the day you were born? But this is something I want you to have now." He slid a long black leather case from behind the sofa, opened it, and took out the silver instrument. He put it in Doretha's lap.

"Your flute?" she said. She held the flute with one hand to keep it from rolling off her lap.

"I want you to have it," Mr. Anderson said. He stood with his back swayed like a man with a big stomach, but he had hardly any. "Remember when you were little and you used to sit there and listen to me play? And you called me Mr. Flute, remember? I might not have been the best musician in the world, but I'll bet I had the best audience. You and Mrs. Anderson."

Doretha was too surprised to think of being glad. She couldn't imagine Mr. Anderson without his flute. "You giving me your flute?"

"I have to go away soon, and I can't take many things with me. I know you'll take good care of it."

"I will!" Doretha said. Now she felt the excitement of the cool metal in her hands. "But why you *giving* it to me? You need it when you get back."

"I won't be coming back," Mr. Anderson said. "I can't come back this time."

"Oh."

"Here, let me put it back in the case for you, so you can take it home. And if your mother says it's all right, I'll give you a lesson every Saturday until I go away."

"I know Mama'll say okay," Doretha said. "Can we start this Saturday?"

"This Saturday is fine. Oh, I almost forgot." He picked up a bag from the coffee table and handed her the record album that was in it.

"Here's something I bought especially for you." On the cover was a dark, slender-faced girl, set back in deep brown shadows. She was holding a blue-silver flute. "That's Bobbi Humphrey. Beautiful girl like you, not too much older than you, either. Plays black music." He looked out the window. "If I could turn the clock back, that's the kind I'd play too."

Doretha stood up. Through the window she saw Mrs. Anderson sitting just the way she had left her. "Is Mrs. Anderson sick?" she asked.

"No, she's worried. She's worried about my trip. She was always with me when I traveled before, and I'll be going alone this time. But I'll be all right. I'll be all right."

Going home, Doretha carried the flute up in her arms, instead of by the handle. She would take care of her flute the way her mother took care of the piano. She would love it as much as she loved Mr. Anderson.

He hadn't told her very much about his trip. She wondered when he was leaving. And where he was going all by himself. And why he couldn't ever come back.

And then she knew.

She held the flute tighter, but she kept walking and didn't cry.

1. What does Doretha realize? What two clues foreshadow this?

Doretha realizes that Mr. Anderson is seriously ill and did not expect to live much longer. One clue is Mrs. Anderson's behavior—she was sitting unusually still with a faraway look in her eyes. Another clue is when Mr. Anderson says he has to go away soon and won't be coming back. If you had difficulty, reread and notice the words "her eyes were looking too far away," "I can't come back this time."

2. How would you describe the mood—fearful, frightening or tender? What words does the author choose to create the mood?

The mood is a tender one because even though Mr. Anderson did not expect to live much longer, he gave his flute to Doretha as a special gift of friendship and remembrance. The author creates this mood by using such words as Mr. Anderson being "cheerful" and Doretha saying she would love the flute "as much as she loved Mr. Anderson." If you had difficulty, reread and notice the author's words to help you appreciate how she creates a mood of tenderness.

3. To Doretha, the house seemed to take on Mrs. Anderson's mood. What do you think Doretha meant?

Practicing Author's Style

Reread "The Worst Thanksgiving in the Entire History of the Universe," on pages 47–53. Think about the author's style—how he uses foreshadowing and mood.

1. What clue does the author use on page 47 that foreshadows that Cousin Edward may have a horrible Thanksgiving?
2. What clues does the author give you on page 49 and page 50 that foreshadow that the food would be terrible?
3. How would you describe the mood of this story—humorous, serious, or suspenseful?
4. Name three details that the author chose to create the mood.

Tips for Reading on Your Own

- Look for clues an author uses that foreshadow what happens later.
- Think about the mood of a story and how the author's choice of details or words creates the mood.

Lecia had no way of knowing when she and her small band of pupils boarded the school bus one Monday morning that they soon would encounter a life-or-death situation. As you read, pay attention to the author's style. Notice how she uses foreshadowing and what mood she creates in this story, which is based on a real life event in her own life.

WINTER THUNDER

by Mari Sandoz

The light snow flurries turned into a severe blizzard, covering the lonely countryside in deep drifts of snow, and blotting out any trace of the road. Suddenly, the wheels lost traction and the bus skidded and overturned. Lecia helped the terrified children from the smoky interior of the bus. Then she grabbed the blankets and lunches and followed them, urging Chuck, the teenage driver, to do the same.

As they hurried away, they heard the explosion of the gas tank. They stopped only long enough for Lecia to line up the sobbing children from youngest to oldest and to secure one to the other by their coat sleeves. Chuck went to the end of the line to make sure no one became separated in the blizzard that surrounded them.

For over five hours, they searched desperately for some kind of shelter. Then, frozen and worn out, Lecia spotted a clump of bushy willows through the blinding snow. She and Chuck made a partial shelter by pulling the willows together at the top, fastening them together with belts, and using blankets to close the gap between the willows. Chuck found a few dry matches in his shirt pocket and was able to start a small fire with some dead wood, some dry inner bark, and a piece of waxed paper. With the fire to warm them and thaw their numb hands, they set about building a wall of snow around the willows to block out the bone-chilling wind and blowing snow. They would be safe and warm—as long as the shelter could withstand the ferocity of the blizzard.

Now they tried to plan for what was to come, but here they were as blind as in the flight through the storm. There would be sickness, with the noses already running, Joanie coughing deep from her chest, and, worst of all, Maggie's feet that seemed to be dying. Besides, the fire must be kept going and the food spread over three, perhaps four days.

Suddenly Calla and Eddie's younger brother, Fritz, shouted, "I'm hungry! I want my lunch!"

Matter-of-factly the teacher washed her raw hands with snow and held them over the fire. Then she spread her napkin on her lap and set out all there was in the eight lunches now—fourteen sandwiches, most of them large; six pieces of Sunday cake; a handful of cookies; a few pieces of candy; and six apples and two oranges, frozen hard. There were two thermos bottles of milk, and these Lecia pushed away into the snow wall. "We'll keep them in case somebody gets sick and can't eat solid food," she said to the owners.

The frozen fruit she handed Chuck, and he set it around the coals for toasting, to be eaten now because it would not keep well. In the meantime Lecia set one lunch box filled with snow near the fire and packed away all except four of the big sandwiches into the others. Then she divided the four sandwiches into halves and passed them around.

"Eat very slowly," she cautioned. "Blizzards usually last three days, so we must make what we have here last too, probably clear to Thursday, or longer."

There was silence all around the fire now, the storm seeming to rise, the children edging closer to each other, glancing fearfully over their shoulders as though toward night windows with terrible things stalking outside. Thinking of a five-day storm, the teacher looked around at the frightened, sooty faces, the children coughing and sniffling, their pocket tissue gone, the few handkerchiefs hung to dry, and wondered if any, even the hearty Chuck, would be here by then.

• How does visualizing the setting help you sense the children's fear?

But Olive, the newcomer, was unconcerned. "I should like another sandwich, Miss Terry. From my own lunch, please," she said. "I won't need the remainder. My father will come for me when it is time."

"He won't find you," Maggie said as she rubbed at her feet.

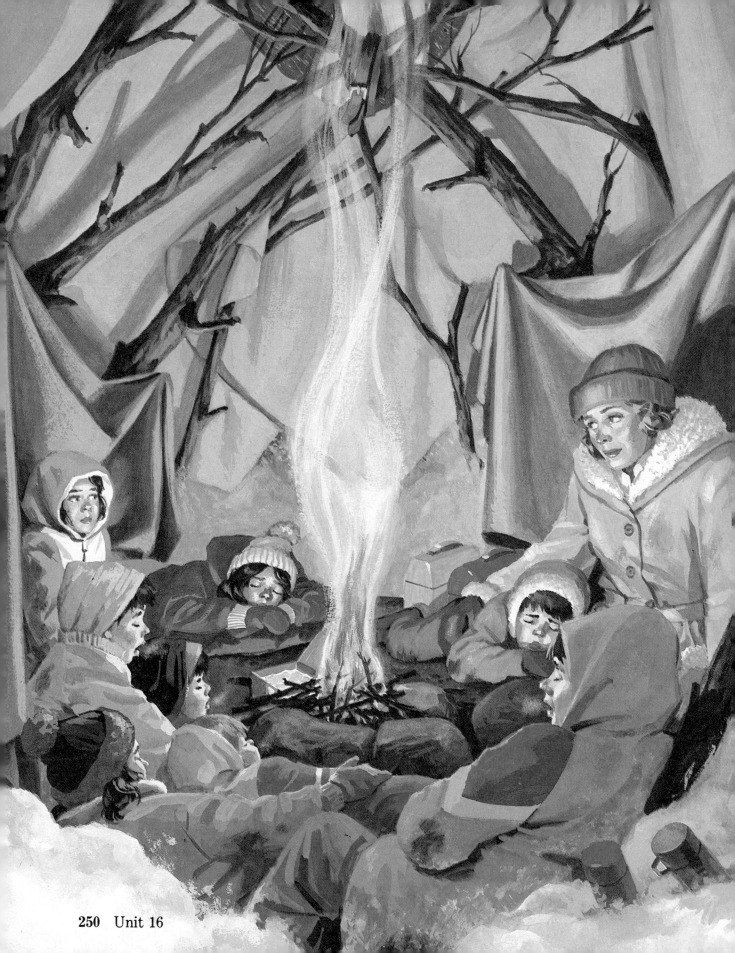

"We must save the rest of the sandwiches," Lecia said as she busied herself hanging up everything loose. Then with Chuck's knife she slit the remaining blanket down the middle and fastened half around each side against the snow wall. By the time the white blizzard darkness came, the smaller children had all been taken outside for the last time and lay in fretful, uneasy sleep.

Finally, even Joanie was asleep, her feverish head in the teacher's lap, her throat raw and swelling, with nothing except hot snow water to ease the hollow cough. There were half a dozen lozenges in Lecia's pocket, but those must be saved for the worse time that would surely come. The children were packed around the fire like little pigs or puppies on a very cold night. The older ones lay nearer the wall, their arms over the younger to hold their restlessness from the fire.

Several times before midnight, Lecia started to doze but jerked herself awake at each creak of the frozen willow shelter to push the out-tossed arms back and replenish the fire. Eddie's cough began to boom deep as from a barrel. He turned and moaned, digging at his chest, Calla helpless beside him, her sleep-weighted eyes anxiously on the teacher. Maggie too was finally crying now. Her feet had puffed up and purpled dark as jelly bags. Yet all Lecia could do was turn the girl's feet from the fire and push them behind the blanket against the snow to relieve the pain and the itching a little—perhaps only freeze them more. The teacher wondered how many days it might be before help could get through. Suddenly their plight here seemed so hopeless, the strength and wisdom of her twenty-three years so weak and futile, that she had to slip out into the storm for calm. And finally Maggie slept, worn-out, but still tearing at her feet.

Toward morning the weary teacher knew that she could not keep awake. She had stirred Chuck to sit up a while, but he was unable to shake off the weight of sleep. Trying to remember how to carry fire—something about moss and damp, rotted wood—Lecia pulled old dead roots from the willows and laid them into the coals with the ends sticking far out. Even with waxed paper handy it would be a desperate chance. Willows burned fast as kindlings, and there were only five matches left and no telling how many spoiled by dampness.

Even so, it was sweet to let herself sink into darkness, but it seemed that she awoke at once, stiff and cold from the nightmare that reached into the waking black, even the ashes of the fire pile cold. With the waxed paper held ready, Lecia blew on the ends of the unburnt roots her hands found, carefully, breathless in her fear. At last a red spark glowed deep in one, and when the fire was going again, she slipped outside for calm in the cold that was like thin, sharp glass in the nose.

There was still no earth and no sky, only the white storm of late dawn blowing hard. But the wood had lasted, and now Lecia put on a few extra sticks and heated water to wash the inflamed eyes of the children. She started a rousing song, "Get up! Get up, you sleepyhead!" But even before it was done, Joanie began to whimper, "I'm hungry."

So the teacher laid out four sandwiches on sticks over the coals and then added another half for herself. "There won't be anything more today except a pinch of cake unless the sun breaks through."

Soon the teacher started as for a school day except that the arithmetic was rote learning of addition and multiplication tables and a quick run through some trick problems. In history and nature study, they talked about the Indians that had roamed the sand hills when Lecia's grandfather came into the country.

That night Joanie was delirious, and once Maggie slipped past the teacher out into the storm to relieve the fire of her feet. By midnight she couldn't stand on them, the swelling creeping above the girl's thin ankles, with red streaks reaching almost to the knees. Her eyes glistened, and her cheeks were burning.

Lecia tried to remember all that she had read of frostbite, and she had to make a desperate decision. She dug two holes deep into the snow wall and laid Maggie with her feet in them almost to her knees, wishing they had something waterproof for covering. The cold would probably freeze the girl more, but it would numb the nerves and perhaps slow the congestion and tissue starvation. Later, when the girl was restless again and crying, Lecia bathed her feet and bound them in the sleeves torn from Lecia's white shirt blouse and thrust them back into the snow. Then she gave Maggie half a cup of milk, very quietly, hoping none would awaken to see, although none needed it more. Almost at once the girl was asleep.

But the next time Lecia returned with firewood, she saw the thermos bottle half out. She jerked it from the hole. The milk was all gone, and across the little fire Olive stared at her teacher. "It was mine," the girl said flatly. So the time had come when the little food left must be hidden. Now, with all but Olive sleeping, was the time.

All the third day there was watching out of the smoke hole for the sky that never appeared. When night finally came without star or stillness, even Lecia, who had tried to prepare herself for this eventuality, felt that she could not face another day of blizzard. Maggie no longer sat up now, and both Joanie and Eddie were sick.

The fourth day was like the rest, colder, with the same white storm outside, the children hunching silent upon themselves inside. Sometimes a small one sobbed a little in sickness and hunger, but it was no more than a soft moaning now, even when Lecia divided most of the little food that was left. The children, even Chuck, took it like animals, and then sat silent again, the deep-socketed eyes watching, some slyly gnawing at willow sticks and roots hidden in the palm.

Everybody around the fire was coughing and fevered now, it seemed to Lecia. Quarrels began. Only Maggie with her poor feet was quiet, and Olive, sitting as though stunned or somewhere far away. The teacher knew that she should do something for this girl, only eight, yet apparently so self-contained. Too weary to think about it, and knowing she must keep awake in the night, Lecia stretched out for a nap.

When she awoke, Olive was sitting exactly the same, but the places of Chuck and Eddie were empty—Eddie out in the blizzard after his night of sweating. Then the boys returned with wood, weak, dragging, almost frozen, and with news that Lecia had to be told outside. There seemed to be only one willow clump left.

Friday morning the sun came out toward ten o'clock, a cold, pale disk, with the snow still running along the earth, running higher than the shelter or Chuck, shutting out everything except the veiled sun. The boy came in, looked around the starved, listless circle, at the fire, at the teacher too, with her face gaunt

and sooty now. He laid two red-tipped matches, half of all he had, in Lecia's lap. "I'm getting out," he said. Without a protest from anyone he crawled through the hole and was gone.

After a long time there seemed a dull sound outside. Then Chuck was suddenly back, crawling in almost as though he had not left, panting in his weakness from the fight against the wind that had turned north again, and colder. "Scared an eagle off a drift out there," he finally managed to say. "And there's a critter stuck in the snow—beyond the far willows. Small spring calf. Frozen hard, but it's meat."

Then the realization that Chuck was back struck Lecia. She was not alone with the children, and he too was safe for now.

"Oh, Chuck!" the teacher exclaimed. Then what he said reached her mind. "A calf? Maybe we could build a fire there so we can cut some off, if we can't get it all out." She reached for her boots. "But we'll have to go work at it one at a time."

"I'll go with Chuck, Miss Lecia," Bill said softly. "He can show me and I'll show you. Save time hunting."

"He can make it," Chuck said. "It's not over an eighth of a mile, and I found more willows farther along the way, the drifts mostly frozen hard too. I blazed the willows beyond our poles."

"You'll be careful—mark everything," Lecia pleaded.

"We've got to. It's snowing again, and the sun's gone."

It seemed hours since the boys went out. Finally the teacher had to go after them, appalled that the younger ones had to be left alone. Yet it must be done. She moved very carefully, feeling her way in the new storm, going sideways to it, from pole to pole. Then she came to a place where the markers were gone, probably blown down and buried by the turning wind. The boys were out there, lost, in at least fifteen, perhaps twenty, below zero. Without sticks to guide her way back, Lecia dared go no farther. She crouched there, bowed before the wind, cupping her mouth with her mittens, shouting her hopeless, "Boys! Chuck! O-hoo!"—the wind snatching it away. She kept calling until she was shaking and frozen and then felt a frightening warmth.

But now she had to keep on, for it seemed that she heard something, a vague, smothered sound, and yet a little like a reply.

• Visualize the scene. Can you picture how difficult it is to move?

She called again and again until suddenly the boys were at her feet. For a few minutes they crouched together in desperate relief. Then, together, they pulled themselves up and started back. When they finally reached the shelter, out of breath and frozen, they said nothing of what had happened nor spoke at all for a while.

As soon as the teacher was warmed a little, she started out alone, not certain that she could make it against the storm, but knowing that she must try to get meat. She took Chuck's knife, some dry bark, waxed paper, the two matches in her shirt pocket, and a bundle of poles pulled from their shelter. Moving very carefully beyond the gap in the willow markers, she set new sticks deep, and tipped carefully with the new storm. She found the farther willow clumps with Chuck's blazing and the brush pile the boys had made, and beside it the ice-covered head of the calf still reaching out of the snow. The hole they had dug around the red hindquarters was drifted in loosely but easily dug out. Lecia set a fire pile there and felt for a match with her numb fingers, fishing in the depths of her pocket. She got the match and lighted the fire under her shielding sheepskin coat. For a long time she crouched protectively over the flame. As the skin thawed, she hacked at it the way people must have done here a thousand years ago, their stone knives sharper and more expertly handled.

As the heat penetrated the meat, she cut off one slice after another until she had a little smoky pile. Not much for nine people who had lived five days on one lunch apiece, but enough to bring tears that were not all from the storm. In this meat, perhaps three pounds, might lie the lives of her pupils.

Lecia headed sideways into the storm. Numb and frightened, she managed to hold herself, not get hurried or panicked, never move until the next broken willow, the next marker was located. She got back to find Chuck out near the shelter digging wood from the old clumps, watching, uneasy.

It was hard for the children to wait while the thinner slices of meat roasted around the sticks. When the smell filled the little shelter, Lecia passed out toasted bits to be chewed very slowly and well. It tasted fine, and none asked for bread or salt—not even Olive, still silent and alone.

By now the white blizzard darkness was coming back. But before they slept there was a little piece of boiled veal for each and a little hot broth. It was a more cheerful sleeping time, even a confident one.

The next morning, the sixth, Bill helped Lecia with the smaller children, washing at the grime on their faces that would never yield except to soap, and took them out into the storm and back while the teacher soaked Maggie's swollen feet. The air was thick and white with new snow whipped by a northwest wind when Lecia went out for a little wood and to watch for Eddie and Chuck who had gone for more meat. But they were once more within touching distance before she could see them—very cold and backing awkwardly into the storm through the soft, new drifts, but dragging a whole hindquarter of the calf.

By the time Eddie and Chuck were warm, they knew they had eaten too much roasted veal while they worked. Next Olive became sick, and Fritz, their deprived stomachs refusing the sudden meat. During the night Lecia became ill. Then sometime toward morning the wind turned and cut into the southeast corner of the shelter, crumbling the whole side inward.

The boys crawled out to patch it with brush and snow softened at the fire. Lecia was helping dry off the children as much as she could. Then when they were done, she heard a coyote's thin, high howl and realized that the wind was dying. Through the smoke hole she saw the running snow like pale windows of cloud against the sky and between them stars shining, far pale stars. As one or another awoke, she directed sleepy eyes to look up. Awed, Joanie looked a second time. "You mean they're really stars?"

"Yes, and maybe there will be sunshine in the morning."

Dawn came early that eighth day. It seemed that nothing could be left alive in the cold whiteness of the earth that was only frozen scarves of snow flung deep and layered over themselves. But the meadow was not completely empty, for out of a little white mound of drifted willows a curl of smoke rose and spread thin and blue along the hill. There was another sound too, a sound seeming to come from all around and even under the feet.

"A plane!" Chuck shouted hoarsely, bursting out into the blinding sunlight.

Several other dark figures crept out behind him into the frosty air, their breath a cloud about them as they stood looking northward. A big plane broke from the horizon over the hills, seeming high up, and then another, flying lower. Foolishly, Chuck and Eddie started to shout. "Help! Hello! Help!" they cried, waving their arms as they ran toward the planes, as though to hasten their sight, their coming. But almost at once the sky was empty, the planes circling and gone. For a long time the boys stared into the broad, cold sky, pale, with nothing in it except wind streaks that were stirring along the ground too, setting feather curls of snow to running.

"Quick! Let's make a big smudge!" Lecia called out, her voice loud and fearful in the unaccustomed quiet. She threw water on the fire inside, driving smoke out of the hole while the boys set the snowy woodpile to burning.

Before the smoke could climb far, there were planes up over the north hills again, coming fast. Maggie was lifted up by Lecia to watch through the smoke hole as something tumbled from the higher plane. Then it opened out like the waxy white bloom of the yucca and settled toward the snow, with several other smaller chutes, bright as poppies, opening behind.

• Visualize what the people in the plane saw as they circled overhead.

There was shouting and talk outside the shelter, and while Lecia was hurrying to get the children into their caps and boots, a man came crawling into the shelter with a bag—a doctor. In the light of the fire and a flashlight he looked swiftly at Joanie and then at Olive, considered her unchanging face, lifted the lids of her eyes, smiled, and got no response. Then he examined the poor feet of Maggie.

The doctor nodded reassuringly to Lecia and smiled down at Maggie. "You're a tough little girl!" he said. "Tough as the barbed wire you have out in this country. But you're lucky somebody thought to try snow against the gangrene.

"All nine of you alive, the boys say. Amazing! Somebody got word to a telephone during the night, but we had no hope for any of you. Small children lost eight days without food, with fifty inches of snow at thirty-eight below zero. I don't see how you managed here."

The doctor smiled into Maggie's fearful eyes, as people carrying a stretcher broke into the front of the shelter. When they got outside, the air was loud with engine roar, several planes flying around overhead, two with skis already up toward the shelter and a helicopter, hovering like a brownish dragonfly. People in uniform were running toward the children, motioning where they should be brought.

They came along the snow trail broken by the stretcher carriers, but walking through it as through the storm. Lecia, suddenly trembling, shaking, her feet unsteady on the frozen snow, was still in the lead, the others behind her, and Chuck once more at the end. Bill, limping awkwardly, carried little Joanie, who clung very close to her brother. They were followed by Calla and Eddie, with Fritz between them, and then the stretcher with Maggie. Only Olive, of all the children, walked alone, just ahead of Chuck, and brushing aside all help.

There were people running toward the bedraggled, sooty little string now, some with cameras and others, among them some who cried, joyous as children. But for now, for this little journey back from the smoke-holed shelter of snow, the awkward queue stayed together.

Meet a Reader

Oliver Wei, a seventh-grade student in Washington, thinks that "Winter Thunder" is a story that appeals to all ages. He feels that "the author developed the characteristics of the characters very well."

Oliver likes to read classics, war history, and science fiction. In his spare time he enjoys jogging, tennis, biking, and making model planes.

Comprehension Check

Think and Discuss

1. Why is the situation that Lecia, the children, and Chuck encounter a life-or-death situation?
• 2. On their first day in the shelter, Lecia, thinking of a five-day storm, wonders if anyone—even the hearty Chuck—would be here then. How does this foreshadowing add to the suspense of the story?
3. What discovery does Chuck make on Friday that may make the difference between life and death for everyone in the shelter?
4. How are the characters finally rescued from their eight-day nightmare?
• 5. Any of the following words could describe the mood of the story: *inspiring*, *desperate*, *hopeless*. Choose one and explain how the author creates the mood you chose.

See your Thinker's Handbook for tips.

• Literary Skills: Foreshadowing, Mood

Communication Workshop

Talk

Have a group discussion about courage and fear. Recall the main characters in the story "Winter Thunder." Which character do you think shows the most courage and why? Which character is the most frightened? Put yourself in the story as one of the children in the shelter. How would you feel?

Speaking/Listening: Cooperative learning

Write

Again, pretend you were in the shelter during the storm. Write a diary entry for each of the eight days, telling what happened and how you felt. Read your entries to your group and listen to theirs. Did their entries talk about similar feelings and experiences? Which entries did you think were the most interesting? Why?

Writing Fluency: Diary entries

HAIKU

by Kazue Mizumura

Snow makes a new land.
One step, two steps. I explore
The way to my school.

All through the long night,
Snow is falling and falling
Upon the snowman.

With the frenzied wind
Snowflakes dancing, whirl and whirl
Then die at my door.

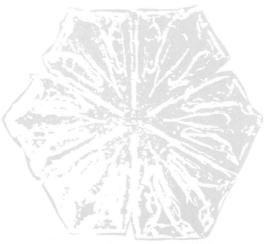

The spring snowflakes tickle
The lilac buds and
Ride off with the gentle wind.

SURVIVAL FOOD

1½ cups whole-wheat flour
¼ cup all-purpose flour
¼ cup sesame seeds
¾ teaspoon salt
⅓ cup oil
½ cup water

Stir the flours, seeds, and salt together. Add the oil and blend
well. Add enough water so that the dough can be kneaded into a
soft ball and can be rolled easily to a thickness of ⅛ inch. Cut the
dough into cracker shapes and place on an ungreased sheet. Bake
at 350 degrees for about 15 to 20 minutes or until the crackers are
crisp and golden. Yield: 3 to 4 dozen crackers.

This survival food stays fresh and is good to take on camping
trips or when you may need a nutritious food in case of an
emergency.

It is midnight. Fowler is about to witness a tense and unexpected encounter between two secret agents, each of whom wants the same secret report. What will be the ironic outcome of this dangerous situation? Notice the author's style, especially the point of view and irony he uses.

THE MIDNIGHT VISITOR

by Robert Arthur

Ausable did not fit any description of a secret agent Fowler had ever read. Following him down the musty corridor of the gloomy French hotel where Ausable had a room, Fowler felt let down. It was a small room, on the sixth and top floor, and scarcely a setting for a figure of romantic adventure. But Ausable, in his wrinkled business suit badly in need of cleaning, could hardly be called a romantic figure.

He was, for one thing, fat. Very fat. And then there was his accent. Though he spoke French and German passably, he had never altogether lost the New England twang he had brought to Paris from Boston twenty years before.

"You are disappointed," Ausable said wheezily over his shoulder. "You were told that I was a secret agent, a spy, dealing in espionage and danger. You wished to meet me because you are a writer, young, with your head in the clouds. You envisioned mysterious figures in the night, secret wiretaps, clever disguises.

"Instead, you have spent a full evening in a French music hall with a sloppy fat man. And instead of having messages slipped into his hand by dark-eyed beauties, he gets only a prosaic telephone call making an appointment in his room. You have been bored!"

The fat man chuckled to himself as he unlocked the door of his room and stood aside to let his discomfited guest enter.

"You are disillusioned," Ausable told him. "But take cheer, my young friend. Presently you will see a paper, a quite important paper for which several people have risked their lives. It comes to me in the next-to-the-last step of its journey into official

hands. Some day soon that paper may well affect the course of
history. In that thought there is drama, is there not?"

As he spoke, Ausable closed the door behind him. Then he
switched on the light.

And as the light came on, Fowler had his first authentic thrill
of the day. For halfway across the room, a mocking look on his
face, stood a man.

Ausable blinked a few times.

"Max," he wheezed, "you gave me a start. I thought you
were in Berlin. What are you doing here in my room?"

Max was slender, a little less than tall, with features that
suggested slightly the crafty pointed countenance of a fox.
There was about him an air of authority, leaving no doubt that
he had the upper hand.

"The report," he murmured. "The report that is being brought
you tonight. I thought it would be safer in my hands than in
yours."

Ausable moved to an armchair and sat down heavily.

"I'm going to give the management a piece of my mind this time," he said grimly. "This is the second time in a month somebody has gotten into my room off that hateful balcony!"

Fowler's eyes went to the single window of the room. It was an ordinary window, against which now the night was pressing blackly.

"Balcony?" Max said, with a rising inflection. "No, a passkey. I did not know about the balcony. It might have saved me some trouble had I known."

"It's not my balcony," Ausable said with extreme irritation. "It belongs to the next apartment."

He glanced at Fowler and went on to explain.

"You see," he said, "this room used to be part of a large unit, and the next room—through that door there—used to be the living room. *It* had the balcony, which extends under my window now.

"You can get onto it from the empty room two doors down— and somebody did, last month. The management promised me to block it off. But they haven't."

Max glanced at Fowler, who was standing stiffly a few feet from Ausable, and waved an arm commandingly toward a chair.

"Please sit down," he suggested. "We have a wait of half an hour at least, I think."

"Thirty-one minutes," Ausable said moodily. "The appointment was for twelve-thirty. I wish I knew how you learned about that report, Max."

The other smiled without mirth.

"And we wish we knew how it has gotten this far," he replied. "However, no harm has been done. I will have it back—What's that?"

Unconsciously Fowler, who was still standing, had jumped at the sudden rapping on the door. Ausable yawned.

"The gendarmes," he said. "I thought that so important a paper as the one we are waiting for might well be given a little extra protection tonight."

Max bit his lip in uncertainty. The rapping was repeated.

"What will you do now, Max?" Ausable asked. "If I do not answer, they will enter anyway. The door is unlocked, and they will not hesitate to arrest you."

Max backed swiftly toward the window; with his hand behind him, he flung the window up to its full height and swung a leg over the sill.

"Send them away!" he rasped. "I will wait on the balcony. Send them away, or I'll make you sorry you didn't."

The rapping on the door became louder, and a voice was raised.

"M'sieu! M'sieu Ausable!"

Keeping his body twisted so that he still could watch the fat man and his guest, Max grasped the frame to support himself. He rested his weight on one thigh and then swung his other leg up and over the sill.

The doorknob turned. Swiftly Max pushed with his left hand to free himself from the sill and drop to the balcony outside. And then, as he dropped, he screamed once, shrilly.

The door opened and a waiter stood there with a tray, a pitcher, and two glasses.

"M'sieu, the iced coffee you ordered for when you returned," he said. He set the tray upon the table, deftly poured the coffee over ice cubes in the glasses, and retired.

Fowler stared after him.

"But—," he stammered, "the police—"

"There were no police." Ausable sighed. "Only Henri, whom I was expecting."

"But won't that man out on the balcony—," Fowler began.

"No," Ausable said, "he won't return. You see, my young friend, there is no balcony."

Miss Fairchild, like Fowler, is about to have an unexpected encounter. Her encounter with two men, while traveling on a train in the old West, will lead to an ironic outcome. How does the author make the outcome ironic, and what point of view does he use to tell the story?

CLASSIC

Hearts and Hands

O. Henry

At Denver there was an influx of passengers into the coaches on the eastbound B. & M. express. In one coach there sat a very pretty young woman dressed in elegant taste and surrounded by all the luxurious comforts of an experienced traveler. Among the newcomers were two young men, one of handsome presence with bold, frank countenance and manner; the other a ruffled, glum-faced person, heavily built and roughly dressed. The two were handcuffed together.

As they passed down the aisle of the coach the only vacant seat offered was a reversed one facing the attractive young woman. Here the linked couple seated themselves. The young woman's glance fell upon them with a distant, swift disinterest; then with a lovely smile brightening her countenance and a tender pink tingeing her rounded cheeks, she held out a little gray-gloved hand. When she spoke her voice, full, sweet, and deliberate, proclaimed that its owner was accustomed to speak and be heard.

"Well, Mr. Easton, if you *will* make me speak first, I suppose I must. Don't you ever recognize old friends when you meet them in the West?"

The younger man roused himself sharply at the sound of her voice, seemed to struggle with a slight embarrassment which he threw off instantly, and then clasped her finger with his left hand.

"It's Miss Fairchild," he said, with a smile. "I'll ask you to excuse the other hand; it's otherwise engaged just at present."

He slightly raised his right hand, bound at the wrist by the shining "bracelet" to the left one of his companion. The glad look in the girl's eyes slowly changed to a bewildered horror. The glow faded from her cheeks. Her lips parted in a vague, relaxing distress. Easton, with a little laugh, as if amused, was about to speak again when the other forestalled him. The glum-faced man had been watching the girl's countenance with veiled glances from his keen, shrewd eyes.

"You'll excuse me for speaking, miss, but I see you're acquainted with the marshal here. If you'll ask him to speak a word for me when we get to the pen he'll do it, and it'll make things easier for me there. He's taking me to Leavenworth prison. It's seven years for counterfeiting."

"Oh!" said the girl, with a deep breath and returning color. "So that is what you are doing out here? A marshal!"

"My dear Miss Fairchild," said Easton, calmly, "I had to do something. Money has a way of taking wings unto itself, and you know it takes money to keep step with our crowd in Washington. I saw this opening in the West, and—well, a marshalship isn't quite as high a position as that of ambassador, but—"

"The ambassador," said the girl, warmly, "doesn't call any more. He needn't ever have done so. You ought to know that. And so now you are one of these dashing Western heroes, and you ride and shoot and go into all kinds of dangers. That's different from the Washington life. You have been missed from the old crowd."

The girl's eyes, fascinated, went back, widening a little, to rest upon the glittering handcuffs.

"Don't you worry about them, miss," said the other man. "All marshals handcuff themselves to their prisoners to keep them from getting away. Mr. Easton knows his business."

"Will we see you again soon in Washington?" asked the girl.

"Not soon, I think," said Easton. "My butterfly days are over, I fear."

"I love the West," said the girl, irrelevantly. Her eyes were shining softly. She looked away out the car window. She began to speak truly and simply, without the gloss of style and manner; "Mamma and I spent the summer in Denver. She went home a week ago because Father was slightly ill. I could live and be happy in the West. I think the air here agrees with me. Money isn't everything. But people always misunderstand things and remain stupid—"

"Say, Mr. Marshal," growled the glum-faced man. "This isn't quite fair. I'm needin' a drink and haven't had a smoke all day. Haven't you talked long enough? Take me in the smoker now, won't you? I'm half dead for a pipe."

The bound travelers rose to their feet, Easton with the same slow smile on his face.

"I can't deny a petition for tobacco," he said, lightly. "It's the one friend of the unfortunate. Good-bye, Miss Fairchild. Duty calls, you know." He held out his hand for a farewell.

"It's too bad you are not going East," she said, reclothing herself with manner and style. "But you must go on to Leavenworth, I suppose?"

"Yes," said Easton, "I must go on to Leavenworth."

The two men sidled down the aisle into the smoker.

The two passengers in a seat near by had heard most of the conversation. Said one of them: "That marshal's a good sort of chap. Some of these Western fellows are all right."

"Pretty young to hold an office like that, isn't he?" asked the other.

"Young!" exclaimed the first speaker, "why—Oh! didn't you catch on? Say—did you ever know an officer to handcuff a prisoner to his *right* hand?"

Think and Discuss

• 1. Both of the stories you read have ironic outcomes. What are the outcomes of "The Midnight Visitor" and of "Hearts and Hands"? Why are the outcomes ironic?
• 2. How does the author of "The Midnight Visitor" make the physical appearance of Ausable ironic?
• 3. How does the author of "Hearts and Hands" make the physical appearances of the marshal and Mr. Easton ironic?
• 4. Both authors used the third-person omniscient point of view. How does this make the stories more interesting for you?
  5. Which story did you enjoy more? Why?
• Literary Skills: Irony, Point of view

Communication Workshop

Talk

Work in small groups. Start with the story "The Midnight Visitor" and take turns playing the characters of Fowler and Ausable. How might each tell the story? Then move on to "Hearts and Hands." Play the characters of Mr. Easton, the marshal, and Mrs. Fairchild. How would each of these characters tell the story? What parts in each story might change from these different points of view—the characters, their appearances, the events, the outcomes?

Speaking/Listening: Role-playing

Write

Choose one of the characters from either story and write a summary of the story from his or her point of view. Read your summary to your group. Do others in the group agree that the summary fits the character who is telling the story?

Writing Fluency: Summary

Standard Book Features

Learning about standard book features need not be a puzzling or mysterious encounter for you. You can use the following information to help you locate and evaluate information you need to find.

The **copyright date** tells you the year a book was published. A copyright gives an author or publisher the exclusive right to publish a book or other work. You can find the copyright date on the copyright page which usually follows the title page in most books. Noting the copyright date (and copyright symbol ©) helps you judge how current the information in a book is. Most books published today also include a **sample catalog card** on the copyright page which summarizes the book and provides information that can help you prepare bibliographies for a report.

A **preface** is an introduction to a book, article, or speech. Prefaces are usually found in nonfiction books, but sometimes before fiction as well. By skimming or reading the preface of a book, you can get an idea of why the author wrote the book and of the kinds of information the book contains. This can help you decide if the book is useful for your purposes and if you want to read it.

A **table of contents** is a list of chapters, articles, or stories in a book or magazine. A table of contents is located near the front of a book or magazine. It shows the page on which each chapter or selection begins and often lists authors' names. You can use the contents to get a general idea of what a book or magazine contains and to locate a specific chapter or selection.

An **index** is an alphabetical list of subjects covered in a book. It tells what pages have information about each subject. An index usually comes at the back of a book. In an index, words in dark

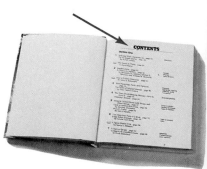

type are called main topics. Listed below many main topics are subtopics, which are smaller parts of a big subject. A direction that tells you to *See* or *See also* is called a cross-reference which leads you to another related topic for information. When you look something up in an index, first think of a key word or words to look for. The key word will often be listed as a main topic.

You use an index when you are looking only for information on a specific subject. You use a table of contents to get a general idea of what's in a book or to find selection titles.

A **glossary** is a short dictionary that gives the meanings of certain words used in a textbook or reference book. It is located at the back of a book.

An **appendix** is a section at the end of a book or article that gives additional information. Appendices often take the form of a table, chart, list, or graph. If you need more facts about a topic covered in a reference book, check the appendices to see if the information is given. Often footnotes or other references within a book will direct you to see the appendix.

To make the best use of standard book features, it is important to know the kind of information you can find in each one. Think of what standard book feature you would use to find answers to the following questions.

1. What is the title of the next section in this book? What are the selections in Unit 19 about? On what page does "The Samaritan" begin?
2. Where could you look to find out how Winston Churchill felt about writing his autobiography, *My Early Life?*
3. In what year was this reading book published?
4. Where would you look to find out if a book you want to use for a computer report is recent?
5. What is the meaning of the word *encounter?*

Remember to use what you know about standard book features to help you find and evaluate the information you need.

The hill : hobbiton-across-the Water

Bilbo Baggins, a shy, unadventursome hobbit, encounters a clever and dangerous opponent—a strange, slimy creature—who challenges Bilbo to a game of riddles. Will Bilbo be able to outwit this creature? How?

Riddles in the Dark

from *The Hobbit*
by J. R. R. Tolkien

Bilbo Baggins, the hobbit, is a little person, about half the size of a human and smaller than a dwarf. Hobbits "are inclined to be fat in the stomach; they dress in bright colours (chiefly green and yellow); wear no shoes, because their feet grow natural leathery soles and thick warm brown hair like the stuff on their heads (which is curly); have clever brown fingers, good-natured faces, and laugh deep fruity laughs." They live in comfortable, well-furnished hobbit holes in the side of a hill: Hobbiton—across—the Water.

Bilbo Baggins had no use for adventures. He considered them "nasty disturbing uncomfortable things that made you late for dinner," and eating was what Bilbo most liked doing. Bilbo was a well-to-do and respected hobbit—"respected because he never had any adventures or did anything unexpected"—until, that is, Gandalf the wizard arrived at Bilbo's door. Then Bilbo's uneventful life went topsy turvy. Gandalf had chosen Bilbo to join an expedition of dwarves who were going on an adventure to reclaim their riches from the greedy dragon, Smaug.

To reach the Lonely Mountain in the East where Smaug slept on their treasure, Bilbo and the dwarves had to cross through the Misty Mountains. While they were in the mountains, a terrible thunder storm forced them to seek shelter in a cave, where they were attacked by goblins. Gandalf and the dwarves escaped, but poor Bilbo "bumped his head on a hard rock and remembered nothing more" until he awoke and found himself in a dark tunnel. He groped about on all fours "till suddenly his hand met what felt like a tiny ring of cold metal lying on the floor." He put it in his pocket, and tried to decide what he must do. He did not know where he was or what had happened, but he picked up his sword and finally determined that he must go on alone.

On and on he went, and down and down; and still he heard no sound of anything except the occasional whirr of a bat by his ears, which startled him at first, till it became too frequent to bother about. I do not know how long he kept on like this, hating to go on, not daring to stop, on, on, until he was tireder than tired. It seemed like all the way to tomorrow and over it to the days beyond.

Suddenly without any warning he trotted splash into water! Ugh! It was icy cold. That pulled him up sharp and short. He did not know whether it was just a pool in the path, or the edge of an underground stream that crossed the passage, or the brink of a deep dark subterranean lake. The sword was hardly shining at all. He stopped, and he could hear, when he listened hard, drops drip-drip-dripping from an unseen roof into the water below; but there seemed no other sort of sound.

"So it is a pool or a lake, and not an underground river," he thought. Still he did not dare to wade out into the darkness. He could not swim; and he thought, too, of nasty slimy things, with big bulging blind eyes, wriggling in the water. There are strange things living in the pools and lakes in the hearts of mountains: fish whose fathers swam in, goodness only knows how many years ago, and never swam out again, while their eyes grew bigger and bigger and bigger from trying to see in the blackness; also there are other things more slimy than fish. Even in the tunnels and caves the goblins have made for themselves there are other things living unbeknown to them that have sneaked in from outside to lie up in the dark. Some of these caves, too, go back in their beginnings to ages before the goblins, who only widened them and joined them up with passages, and the original owners are still there in odd corners, slinking and nosing about.

Deep down here by the dark water lived old Gollum, a small slimy creature. I don't know where he came from, nor who or what he was. He was Gollum—as dark as darkness, except for two big round pale eyes in his thin face. He had a little boat, and he rowed about quite quietly on the lake; for lake it was, wide and deep and deadly cold. He paddled it with large feet dangling over the side, but never a ripple did he make. Not he. He was looking out of his pale lamplike eyes for blind fish, which he grabbed with his long fingers as quick as thinking. He liked meat too. Goblin he thought good, when he could get it; but he took care they never found him out. He just throttled them from behind, if they ever came down alone anywhere near the edge of the water, while he was prowling about. They very seldom did, for they had a feeling that something unpleasant was lurking down there, down at the very roots of the mountain. They had come on the lake, when they were tunnelling down long ago, and they found they could go no further; so there their road ended in that direction, and there was no reason to go

The Misty Mountains looking West from the
Eyrie towards Goblin Gate

that way—unless the Great Goblin sent them. Sometimes he took a fancy for fish from the lake, and sometimes neither goblin nor fish came back.

Actually Gollum lived on a slimy island of rock in the middle of the lake. He was watching Bilbo now from the distance with his pale eyes like telescopes. Bilbo could not see him, but he was wondering a lot about Bilbo, for he could see that he was no goblin at all.

Gollum got into his boat and shot off from the island, while Bilbo was sitting on the brink altogether flummoxed and at the end of his way and his wits. Suddenly up came Gollum and whispered and hissed:

"Bless us and splash us, my precioussss! I guess it's a choice feast; at least a tasty morsel it'd make us, gollum!" And when he said *gollum* he made a horrible swallowing noise in his throat. That is how he got his name, though he always called himself 'my precious.'

The hobbit jumped nearly out of his skin when the hiss came in his ears, and he suddenly saw the pale eyes sticking out at him.

"Who are you?" he said, thrusting his dagger in front of him.

"What iss he, my preciouss?" whispered Gollum (who always spoke to himself through never having anyone else to speak to). This is what he had come to find out, for he was not really very hungry at the moment, only curious; otherwise he would have grabbed first and whispered afterwards.

"I am Mr. Bilbo Baggins. I have lost the dwarves and I have lost the wizard, and I don't know where I am; and I don't want to know, if only I can get away."

"What's he got in his handses?" said Gollum, looking at the sword, which he did not quite like.

"A sword, a blade which came out of Gondolin!"

"Sssss," said Gollum, and became quite polite. "Praps ye sits here and chats with it a bitsy, my preciousss. It like riddles, praps it does, does it?" He was anxious to appear friendly, at any rate for the moment, and until he found out more about the sword and the hobbit, whether he was quite alone really, whether he was good to eat, and whether Gollum was really hungry. Riddles were all he could think of. Asking them, and sometimes guessing them, had been the only game he had ever played with other funny creatures sitting in their holes in the long, long ago, before he lost all his friends and was driven away, alone, and crept down, down, into the dark under the mountains.

"Very well," said Bilbo, who was anxious to agree, until he found out more about the creature, whether he was quite alone, whether he was fierce or hungry, and whether he was a friend of the goblins.

"You ask first," he said, because he had not had time to think of a riddle.

So Gollum hissed:

> *What has roots as nobody sees,*
> *Is taller than trees,*
> *Up, up it goes,*
> *And yet never grows?*

"Easy!" said Bilbo, "Mountain, I suppose."

"Does it guess easy? It must have a competition with us, my preciouss! If precious asks, and it doesn't answer, we eats it, my precioussss. If it asks us, and we doesn't answer, then we does what it wants, eh? We shows it the way out, yes!"

"All right!" said Bilbo, not daring to disagree, and nearly bursting his brain to think of riddles that could save him from being eaten.

> *irty white horses on a red hill,*
> *First they champ,*
> *Then they stamp,*
> *Then they stand still.*

That was all he could think of to ask—the idea of eating was rather on his mind. It was rather an old one, too, and Gollum knew the answer as well as you do.

"Chestnuts, chestnuts," he hissed. "Teeth! teeth! my preciousss; but we has only six!" Then he asked his second:

> *Voiceless it cries,*
> *Wingless flutters,*
> *Toothless bites,*
> *Mouthless mutters.*

"Half a moment!" cried Bilbo, who was still thinking uncomfortably about eating. Fortunately he had once heard something rather like this before, and getting his wits back he thought of the answer. "Wind, wind of course," he said, and he was so pleased that he made up one on the spot. "This'll puzzle the nasty little underground creature," he thought:

> *An eye in a blue face*
> *Saw an eye in a green face.*
> *"That eye is like to this eye"*
> *Said the first eye,*
> *"But in low place,*
> *Not in high place."*

"Ss, ss, ss," said Gollum. He had been underground a long long time, and was forgetting this sort of thing. But just as Bilbo was beginning to hope that the wretch would not be able to answer, Gollum brought up memories of ages and ages and ages before, when he lived with his grandmother in a hole in a bank by a river, "Sss, sss, my preciouss," he said. "Sun on the daisies it means, it does."

But these ordinary aboveground everyday sort of riddles were tiring for him. Also they reminded him of days when he had been less lonely and sneaky and nasty, and that put him out of temper. What is more they made him hungry; so this time he tried something a bit more difficult and more unpleasant. . . .

> *This thing all things devours:*
> *Birds, beasts, trees, flowers;*
> *Gnaws iron, bites steel;*
> *Grinds hard stones to meal;*
> *Slays king, ruins town,*
> *And beats high mountain down.*

Poor Bilbo sat in the dark thinking of all the horrible names of all the giants and ogres he had ever heard told of in tales, but not one of them had done all these things. He had a feeling that the answer was quite different and that he ought to know it, but he could not think of it. He began to get frightened, and that is bad for thinking.

Gollum began to get out of his boat. He flapped into the water and paddled to the bank; Bilbo could see his eyes coming towards him. His tongue seemed to stick in his mouth; he wanted to shout out: "Give me more time! Give me time!" But all that came out with a sudden squeal was:

"Time! Time!"

Bilbo was saved by pure luck. For that of course was the answer.

Gollum was disappointed once more; and now he was getting angry, and also tired of the game. It had made him very hungry indeed. This time he did not go back to the boat. He sat down in the dark by Bilbo. That made the hobbit most dreadfully uncomfortable and scattered his wits.

"It's got to ask uss a quesstion, my preciouss, yes, yess, yesss. Jusst one more quesstion to guess, yes, yess," said Gollum.

But Bilbo simply could not think of any question with that nasty wet cold thing sitting next to him, and pawing and poking him. He scratched himself, he pinched himself; still he could not think of anything.

"Ask us! ask us!" said Gollum.

Bilbo pinched himself and slapped himself; he gripped on his little sword; he even felt in his pocket with his other hand. There he found the ring he had picked up in the passage and forgotten about.

"What have I got in my pocket?" he said aloud. He was talking to himself, but Gollum thought it was a riddle, and he was frightfully upset.

"Not fair! not fair!" he hissed. "It isn't fair, my precious, is it, to ask us what it's got in its nassty little pocketses?"

Bilbo seeing what had happened and having nothing better to ask stuck to his question. "What have I got in my pocket?" he said louder.

"S–s–s–s–s," hissed Gollum. "It must give us three guesseses, my preciouss, three guesseses."

"Very well! Guess away!" said Bilbo.

"Handses!" said Gollum.

"Wrong," said Bilbo, who had luckily just taken his hand out again. "Guess again!"

"S–s–s–s–s," said Gollum more upset than ever. He thought of all the things he kept in his own pockets: fishbones, goblins' teeth, wet shells, a bit of bat-wing, a sharp stone to sharpen his fangs on, and other nasty things. He tried to think what other people kept in their pockets.

"Knife!" he said at last.

"Wrong!" said Bilbo, who had lost his some time ago. "Last guess!"

Now Gollum was in a much worse state. . . . He hissed and spluttered and rocked himself backwards and forwards, and slapped his feet on the floor, and wriggled and squirmed; but still he did not dare to waste his last guess.

"Come on!" said Bilbo. "I am waiting!" He tried to sound bold and cheerful, but he did not feel at all sure how the game was going to end, whether Gollum guessed right or not.

"Time's up!" he said.

"String, or nothing!" shrieked Gollum, which was not quite fair—working in two guesses at once.

"Both wrong," cried Bilbo very much relieved; and he jumped at once to his feet, put his back to the nearest wall, and held out his little sword. He knew, of course, that the riddle-game was sacred and of immense antiquity, and even wicked creatures were afraid to cheat when they played at it. But he felt he could not trust this slimy thing to keep any promise at a pinch. Any excuse would do for him to slide out of it. And after all that last question had not been a genuine riddle according to the ancient laws.

But at any rate Gollum did not at once attack him. He could see the sword in Bilbo's hand. He sat still, shivering and whispering. At last Bilbo could wait no longer.

"Well?" he said. "What about your promise? I want to go. You must show me the way."

"Did we say so, precious? Show the nassty little Baggins the way out, yes, yes. But what has it got in its pocketses, eh? Not string, precious, but not nothing. Oh no! gollum!"

"Never you mind," said Bilbo. "A promise is a promise."

"Cross it is, impatient, precious," hissed Gollum. "But it must wait, yes it must. We can't go up the tunnels so hasty. We must go and get some things first, yes, things to help us."

"Well, hurry up!" said Bilbo, relieved to think of Gollum going away. He thought he was just making an excuse and did not mean to come back. What was Gollum talking about? What useful thing could he keep out on the dark lake? But he was wrong. Gollum did mean to come back. He was angry now and hungry. And he was a miserable wicked creature, and already he had a plan.

Not far away was his island, of which Bilbo knew nothing, and there in his hiding-place he kept a few wretched oddments, and one very beautiful thing, very beautiful, very wonderful. He had a ring, a golden ring, a precious ring.

"My birthday-present!" he whispered to himself, as he had often done in the endless dark days. "That's what we wants now, yes; we wants it!"

He wanted it because it was a ring of power, and if you slipped that ring on your finger, you were invisible; only in the full sunlight could you be seen, and then only by your shadow, and that would be shaky and faint.

"My birthday-present! It came to me on my birthday, my precious," so he had always said to himself. But who knows how Gollum came by that present, ages ago in the old days when such rings were still at large in the world? Perhaps even the Master who ruled them could not have said. Gollum used to wear it at first, till it tired him; and then he kept it in a pouch next to his skin, till it galled him; and now usually he hid it in a hold in the rock on his island, and was always going back to look at it. And still sometimes he put it on, when he could not bear to be parted from it any longer, or when he was very, very, hungry, and tired of fish. Then he would creep along dark passages looking for stray goblins. He might even venture into places where the torches were lit and made his eyes blink and smart; for he would be safe. Oh yes, quite safe. No one would see him, no one would notice him, till he had his fingers on their throat. Only a few hours ago he had worn it, and caught a small goblin-imp. How it squeaked! He still had a bone or two left to gnaw, but he wanted something softer.

"Quite, safe, yes," he whispered to himself. "It won't see us, will it, my precious? No. It won't see us, and its nassty little sword will be useless, yes quite."

That is what was in his wicked little mind, as he slipped suddenly from Bilbo's side, and flapped back to his boat, and went off into the dark. Bilbo thought he had heard the last of him. Still he waited a while; for he had no idea how to find his way out alone.

Suddenly he heard a screech. It sent a shiver down his back. Gollum was cursing and wailing away in the gloom, not very far off by the sound of it. He was on his island, scrabbling here and there, searching and seeking in vain.

"Where is it? Where iss it?" Bilbo heard him crying. "Losst it is, my precious, lost, lost! Curse us and crush us, my precious is lost!"

"What's the matter?" Bilbo called. "What have you lost?"

"It mustn't ask us," shrieked Gollum. "Not its business, no, gollum! It's losst, gollum, gollum, gollum."

"Well, so am I," cried Bilbo, "and I want to get unlost. And I won the game, and you promised. So come along! Come and let me out, and then go on with your looking!" Utterly miserable as Gollum sounded, Bilbo could not find much pity in his heart, and he had a feeling that anything Gollum wanted so much could hardly be something good. "Come along!" he shouted.

"No, not yet, precious!" Gollum answered. "We must search for it, it's lost, gollum."

"But you never guessed my last question, and you promised," said Bilbo.

"Never guessed!" said Gollum. Then suddenly out of the gloom came a sharp hiss. "What has it got in its pocketses? Tell us that. It must tell first."

As far as Bilbo knew, there was no particular reason why he should not tell. Gollum's mind had jumped to a guess quicker than his; naturally, for Gollum had brooded for ages on this one thing, and he was always afraid of its being stolen. But Bilbo was annoyed at the delay. After all, he had won the game, pretty fairly, at a horrible risk. "Answers were to be guessed not given," he said.

"But it wasn't a fair question," said Gollum. "Not a riddle, precious, no."

"Oh well, if it's a matter of ordinary questions," Bilbo replied, "then I asked one first. What have you lost? Tell me that!"

"What has it got in its pocketses?" The sound came hissing louder and sharper, and as he looked towards it, to his alarm Bilbo now saw two small points of light peering at him. As suspicion grew in Gollum's mind, the light of his eyes burned with a pale flame.

"What have you lost?" Bilbo persisted.

But now the light in Gollum's eyes had become a green fire, and it was coming swiftly nearer. Gollum was in his boat again, paddling wildly back to the dark shore; and such a rage of loss and suspicion was in his heart that no sword had any more terror for him.

Bilbo could not guess what had maddened the wretched creature, but he saw that all was up, and that Gollum meant to murder him at any rate. Just in time he turned and ran blindly back up the dark passage down which he had come, keeping close to the wall and feeling it with his left hand.

"What has it got in its pocketses?" he heard the hiss loud behind him, and the splash as Gollum leapt from his boat. "What have I, I wonder?" he said to himself, as he panted and stumbled along. He put his left hand in his pocket. The ring felt very cold as it quietly slipped on to his groping forefinger.

The hiss was close behind him. He turned now and saw Gollum's eyes like small green lamps coming up the slope. Terrified he tried to run faster, but suddenly he struck his toes on a snag in the floor, and fell flat with his little sword under him.

In a moment Gollum was on him. But before Bilbo could do anything, recover his breath, pick himself up, or wave his sword, Gollum passed by, taking no notice of him, cursing and whispering as he ran.

What could it mean? Gollum could see in the dark. Bilbo could see the light of his eyes palely shining even from behind. Painfully he got up, and sheathed his sword, which was now glowing faintly again, then very cautiously he followed. There seemed nothing else to do. It was no good crawling back down to Gollum's water. Perhaps if he followed him, Gollum might lead him to some way of escape without meaning to.

"Curse it! curse it! curse it!" hissed Gollum. "Curse the Baggins! It's gone! What has it got in its pocketses? Oh we guess, we guess, my precious. He's found it, yes he must have. My birthday present."

Bilbo pricked up his ears. He was at last beginning to guess himself. He hurried a little, getting as close as he dared behind Gollum, who was still going quickly, not looking back, but turning his head from side to side, as Bilbo could see from the faint glimmer on the walls.

"My birthday-present! Curse it! How did we lose it, my precious? Yes, that's it. When we came this way last, when we twisted that nassty young squeaker. That's it. Curse it! It slipped from us, after all these ages and ages! It's gone, gollum."

Suddenly Gollum sat down and began to weep, a whistling and gurgling sound horrible to listen to. Bilbo halted and flattened himself against the tunnel-wall. After a while Gollum stopped weeping and began to talk. He seemed to be having an argument with himself.

"It's no good going back there to search, no. We doesn't remember all the places we've visited. And it's no use. The Baggins has got it in its pocketses; the nassty noser has found it, we says."

"We guesses, precious, only guesses. We can't know till we find the nassty creature and squeezes it. But it doesn't know what the present can do, does it? It'll just keep it in its pocketses. It doesn't know, and it can't go far. It's lost itself, nassty nosey thing. It doesn't know the way out. It said so."

"It said so, yes; but it's tricksy. It doesn't say what it means. It won't say what it's got in its pocketses. It knows. It knows a way in, it must know a way out, yes. It's off to the back-door. To the back-door, that's it."

"The goblinses will catch it then. It can't get out that way, precious."

"Ssss, sss, gollum! Goblinses! Yes, but if it's got the present, our precious present, then goblinses will get it, gollum! They'll find it, they'll find out what it does. We shan't ever be safe again, never, gollum! One of the goblinses will put it on, and then no one will see him. He'll be there but not seen. Not even our clever eyeses will notice him; and he'll come creepsy and tricksy and catch us, gollum, gollum!"

"Then let's stop talking, precious, and make haste. If the Baggins has gone that way, we must go quick and see. Go! Not far now. Make haste!"

With a spring Gollum got up and started shambling off at a great pace. Bilbo hurried after him, still cautiously, though his chief fear now was of tripping on another snag and falling with a noise. His head was in a whirl of hope and wonder. It seemed that the ring he had was a magic ring: it made you invisible! He had heard of such things, of course, in old old tales; but it was hard to believe

The Mountain-path

that he really had found one, by accident. Still there it was: Gollum with his bright eyes had passed him by, only a yard to one side.

On they went, Gollum flip-flapping ahead, hissing and cursing; Bilbo behind going as softly as a hobbit can. Soon they came to places where, as Bilbo had noticed on the way down, side-passages opened, this way and that. Gollum began at once to count them.

"One left, yes. One right, yes. Two right, yes, yes. Two left, yes, yes." And so on and on.

As the count grew he slowed down, and he began to get shaky and weepy; for he was leaving the water further and further behind, and he was getting afraid. Goblins might be about, and he had lost his ring. At last he stopped by a low opening, on their left as they went up.

"Seven right, yes. Six left, yes!" he whispered. "This is it. This is the way to the back-door, yes. Here's the passage!"

He peered in, and shrank back. "But we durstn't go in, precious, no we durstn't. Goblinses down there. Lots of goblinses. We smells them. Ssss!"

"What shall we do? Curse them and crush them! We must wait here, precious, wait a bit and see."

So they came to a dead stop. Gollum had brought Bilbo to the way out after all, but Bilbo could not get in! There was Gollum sitting humped up right in the opening. And his eyes gleamed cold in his head, as he swayed it from side to side between his knees.

Bilbo crept away from the wall more quietly than a mouse; but Gollum stiffened at once, and sniffed, and his eyes went green. He hissed softly but menacingly. He could not see the hobbit, but now he was on the alert, and he had other senses that the darkness had sharpened: hearing and smell. He seemed to be crouched right down with his flat hands splayed on the floor, and his head thrust out, nose almost to the stone. Though he was only a black shadow in the gleam of his own eyes, Bilbo could see or feel that he was tense as a bowstring, gathered for a spring.

Bilbo almost stopped breathing, and went stiff himself. He was desperate. He must get away, out of this horrible darkness, while he had any strength left. He must fight. He must stab the foul thing, put its eyes out, kill it. It meant to kill him. No, not a fair fight. He was invisible now. Gollum had no sword. Gollum had not actually threatened to kill him, or tried to yet. And he was miserable, alone, lost. A sudden understanding, a pity mixed with horror, welled up in Bilbo's heart: a glimpse of endless unmarked days without light or hope of betterment, hard stone, cold fish, sneaking and whispering. All these thoughts passed in a flash of a second. He trembled. And then quite suddenly in another flash, as if lifted by a new strength and resolve, he leaped.

No great leap for a man, but a leap in the dark. Straight over Gollum's head he jumped, seven feet forward and three in the air; indeed, had he known it, he only just missed cracking his skull on the low arch of the passage.

Gollum threw himself backwards, and grabbed as the hobbit flew over him, but too late: his hands snapped on thin air, and Bilbo, falling fair on his sturdy feet, sped off down the new tunnel. He did not turn to see what Gollum was doing. There was a hissing and cursing almost at his heels at first, then it stopped. All at once there came a bloodcurdling shriek, filled with hatred and despair. Gollum was defeated. He dared go no further. He had lost: lost his prey, and lost, too, the only thing he had ever cared for, his precious. The cry brought Bilbo's heart to his mouth, but still he held on. Now faint as an echo, but menacing, the voice came behind:

"Thief, thief, thief! Baggins! We hates it, we hates it, we hates it forever!"

Then there was silence. . . .

Meet the Author and Illustrator

The idea for *The Hobbit* grew out of the stories that the author, J. R. R. Tolkien, used to tell his sons at bedtime. Tolkien was a natural storyteller, and when his sons expressed a keen interest in his tales, he decided to put the stories on paper.

Someone suggested to Tolkien that there was a good deal of similarity between Tolkien and the hobbit—to which Tolkien responded, "I am in fact a hobbit, in all but size. I like gardens, trees, unmechanized farmlands; I smoke a pipe and like good plain food. I am fond of mushrooms (out of a field); have a very simple sense of humor; I go to bed late and get up late (when possible). I do not travel much."

The Hobbit was only the first of several books that Tolkien wrote about the small, imaginary people who inhabited the English countryside. It was so popular—winning the Children's Spring Book Award—that Tolkien's publisher urged him to write more hobbit adventures. *The Lord of the Rings*, a trilogy comprised of *The Fellowship of the Ring*, *The Two Towers*, and *The Return of the King*, was published nearly twenty years later. The hero of this legend is a hobbit named Frodo, and his mythical adventures became so popular that Tolkien and Frodo clubs were founded where members meet to study and discuss Tolkien's books. *The Lord of the Rings* received the International Fantasy Award.

Tolkien was also a talented illustrator. The drawings in "Riddles in the Dark" are by Tolkien.

LOOKING BACK

See your Thinker's Handbook for tips.

| Prewriting |

Thinking and Writing About the Section
In this section you have met several characters who experienced different encounters. By looking at each character's behavior, you can tell what kind of person he or she is and you can write a paragraph for your classmates that describes a character's behavior during an important encounter. First copy the chart below and fill in the missing information.

Character	Encounter	Character's Traits
Lecia	trapped in blizzard with children	strong, selfless, brave
Ausable		
The marshal		compassionate, understanding
Bilbo	lost in Lonely Mountain, meets Gollum	
Gollum	meets Bilbo, tries to keep ring	frightened, grasping

| Writing |

Write a paragraph that uses the information from the chart to describe one character's encounter and how his or her traits show what kind of person he or she is. Use specific words to describe the character's traits. For more information on descriptive paragraphs, see your Writer's Handbook.

| Revising |

Read your first draft to a partner. Have you used specific words to describe your character's traits? Make changes if necessary. Then proofread for spelling and punctuation errors. Write your final copy.

| Presenting |

Read your paragraph to the class. Have listeners tell which specific words you used were especially effective.

Books to Read

The Shark: Splendid Savage of the Sea
by Jacques-Yves and Philippe Cousteau.
Doubleday and Company, Inc., © 1970.

How does it feel to confront a shark
with only a camera as protection? Why
does a shark die if it is taken from the sea,
if only for a moment? The Cousteaus
discover the answers to these and many
other questions.

Discovering the Sea by Sandra Smith.
Stonehenge, © 1981.

Did you know there are floods and
hurricanes—*under* the water? Explore the
geography, weather, plant and animal life
that exists under the stretch of blue we
call the sea.

Dramatized Folk Tales of the World
edited by Sylvia E. Kamerman. Boston:
Plays, Inc., © 1971.

Have you ever wanted to star in, direct,
or design costumes for a play? If it seemed
too big an undertaking, take a look at this
book which contains fifty one-act plays
taken from folk tales of many lands.

Archer's Goon by Diana Wynne Jones.
Greenwillow Books, © 1984.

The trouble started when Howard came
home from school and encountered a
"goon" sitting in the kitchen. Seven sibling
wizards soon involve Howard's entire
family in a struggle for power.

7

A Sense of Direction

Imagine your journey through life as an adventure in a giant maze of freeways. Do you have a good sense of direction? Some people spend their lives wandering aimlessly, with no particular direction. They have no sense of where they've been or where they are going, and they often find that the road they've been traveling is a dead end. Other people set goals for themselves, like trying to reach a special place. These are people with a sense of direction—they know where they've been and where they want to go. If they find that the road is blocked, their sense of direction will help them find a better way.

In this section, you will read about different kinds of goals that can give meaning and direction to people's lives— from teamwork to business success to the ultimate goal—self-knowledge.

Finding and Evaluating Generalizations

cathy

by Cathy Guisewite

EXERCISE! I MUST EXERCISE! RUN! WORKOUT! DANCE! GET IN SHAPE!!

COOK! FIBER...SPROUTS ...ORGANIC GOURMET! I MUST PAMPER MY HEALTHY BODY WITH HEALTHY FOOD!!

RELATE! COMMUNICATE!! OPEN UP!! WE MUST CREATE A HEALTHY, LOVING ENVIABLE RELATIONSHIP!!

WHAT BRINGS YOU IN SO EARLY, CATHY??

MY RELAXATION TIME HAS BECOME MORE STRESSFUL THAN MY WORK TIME.

Cathy's goal is to control stress in her life. She's doing a number of things to help her relax—she's exercising, watching her diet, and creating healthy relationships. Yet, Cathy says her relaxation time has become more stressful than her work time. Why? Perhaps this generalization will explain: Overdoing things—even the right things—generally increases stress instead of reducing it.

A **generalization** is a broad statement that is reached after thinking about a number of facts. You could reach the generalization about Cathy by thinking about the facts that show that she overexercises, is frantic about her diet, and is anxious about her relationships.

Sometimes authors make generalizations based on facts they present in their writing or in graphs and charts that appear in their writing. The ability to identify and evaluate an author's generalizations is very important because it helps you understand the information presented. It will also help you decide how much to trust or rely on a point of view that is presented.

To identify a generalization, look for a broad statement. (Generalizations often sum up the information or state the main idea.) A generalization may contain clue words such as *generally* or *many;* or clue words may be implicit—that is, they may not be stated, but could be added without changing the meaning of the generalization. For example: In northern cities there are (generally, usually) more outdoor sports activities in the summer than in the winter.

To evaluate an author's generalization in a selection you are reading, look to see if there are facts that support the generalization. Think about these facts as well as any others you already know about the topic. If there are enough specific facts in the selection to support the generalization, it is a valid generalization. If there aren't enough facts to support it, the generalization is faulty.

Look for the generalization in the following paragraph from *Choosing Good Health*, a health textbook, and decide whether it is valid.

> There are many benefits to regular participation in physical activity. Regular physical activity can help you lose unwanted body fat. It can help release tension and help your muscles relax. Regular physical activity can help you maintain good posture. It also can help reduce your chances of developing certain health problems, such as cardiovascular diseases, diabetes, and ulcers.

1. How do you know that the following statement from the paragraph is a generalization? "There are many benefits to regular participation in physical activity."

Did you remember that a generalization is a broad statement? The generalization above is a broad statement and also includes the clue word *many*.

2. Is the generalization valid or faulty? How do you know?

Did you look for facts? The generalization is valid because it is supported by enough specific facts. Regular physical activity can (1) help you lose unwanted fat, (2) help your muscles relax, (3) help you develop firm muscles and maintain good posture, and (4) reduce your chances of developing certain health problems.

If you had difficulty, reread the paragraph and pay attention to these facts. You can also use what you know about the benefits of regular physical activity to help you decide if the generalization is a valid one.

3. Why aren't the other statements in the paragraph generalizations? How are they used?

Practicing Generalizations

Now read this paragraph from *Choosing Good Health*. Remember to look for a broad idea that is supported by specific facts.

Some physicians advise moderation in eating foods containing saturated fats. Saturated fats generally are solid at room temperature. Meat, cheese, butter, and lard are foods high in saturated fats. Some saturated fats are liquid at room temperature. Whole milk, cream, coconut oil, and palm oil are examples of such saturated fats.

1. What generalization is made in this paragraph?
2. Is the generalization valid or faulty? How do you know?

Read the following paragraph and think about the facts you already know about the topic.

Cardiovascular diseases are diseases of the heart and blood vessels. Long periods of tension can increase your chances of getting cardiovascular diseases. Eating too many saturated fats may also contribute to the development of cardiovascular diseases. You can prevent cardiovascular disease by eliminating all saturated fats from your diet.

3. Is the generalization "You can prevent cardiovascular disease by eliminating all saturated fats from your diet" valid or faulty? How do you know?

Study the following chart from a health magazine and evaluate the generalizations listed below it.

Recommended Calories per Day

		Age	Wt. (Lbs.)	Ht. (In.)	Calories
Children		1–3	28	34	1,300
		4–6	44	44	1,800
		7–10	66	54	2,400
Females		11–14	97	62	2,400
		15–18	119	65	2,100
		19–22	128	65	2,100
		23–50	128	65	2,000
		51+	128	65	1,800
Males		11–14	97	63	2,800
		15–18	134	69	3,000
		19–22	147	69	3,000
		23–50	154	69	2,700
		51+	154	69	2,400

4. Which statements are valid generalizations?
   a. There are several factors that determine the recommended number of calories per day.
   b. In general, the recommended number of calories per day is the same for males and females.
   c. For most people, caloric needs decrease after age twenty-two.
5. List the facts that support your choice(s).

Tips for Finding and Evaluating Generalizations
- To find a generalization, look for broad statements.
- Look for clue words. When a clue word is not used, add one. If the meaning does not change, the statement probably is a generalization.
- To evaluate a generalization, look for facts and think about facts you already know about the topic. If there are enough facts to support the generalization, it is valid. If there are not, the generalization is faulty.

One goal you should set for yourself is physical fitness. But if jogging just isn't your thing and you'd rather self-destruct than do aerobics, don't despair. In this excerpt from Choosing Good Health, *a health textbook, look for the generalization that will guide you in the right direction to help you build physical fitness through sports.*

12-1 Building Physical Fitness Through Sports

· What is a sport?
· How can you build physical fitness through sports?
· How do time and effort affect the level of fitness you can achieve through sports?

Glenda enjoys volleyball practice after school. She thinks the drills and games help build some parts of physical fitness. Remember that physical fitness is the ability of the body to do the most activity with the least amount of effort.

Volleyball is one of several physical activities that can build certain parts of physical fitness. You actually need a variety of activities to build all parts of physical fitness.

Before you choose activities, you should be aware of exactly what parts of skills fitness and health fitness the activities build. Also, you should realize that the amount of time and effort you put into the activities affects the level of fitness you can build.

Sports Can Build Different Parts of Physical Fitness

You can build parts of physical fitness through a variety of activities. One kind of physical activity is a sport. A sport is an organized, competitive activity. A sport usually has specific rules, player positions, and playing areas.

Sports can be played individually or in teams. Team sports are activities played by two or more people on a team. Softball and field hockey are team sports. Individual sports are activities that you can play by yourself. Golf and archery are individual sports.

Different sports build different parts of skills fitness and health fitness. To build all parts of physical fitness, you need to participate in a variety of sports. Refer to the chart on pages 304 and 305 to determine exactly what parts of physical fitness each sport builds.

Parts of Physical Fitness

Skills Fitness	Health Fitness
speed	flexibility
coordination	muscular strength
power	muscular endurance
agility	cardiovascular fitness
balance	body fatness
reaction time	

Building Physical Fitness Requires Time and Effort

Chuck and Jim are trying out for the basketball team. Chuck practices free throws in the schoolyard every once in awhile. He believes he will make the team since he makes most of his shots. However, Chuck does not realize one important thing. Playing basketball involves more than shooting baskets. Basketball players need several parts of fitness to play the game.

Jim, on the other hand, plays basketball with his friends each day after school. This regular practice has helped Jim build and improve various parts of his physical fitness.

For example, running has improved Jim's speed, cardiovascular fitness, and muscular endurance. Running also has helped control his body fatness. Shooting lay-ups has improved Jim's coordination. Pivoting has helped develop his agility. Guarding his opponents has improved Jim's sense of balance and reaction time.

So who do you think will have a better chance of making the basketball team, Jim or Chuck? Of course, Jim will. Jim realizes that achieving physical fitness through sports requires time and effort. The more time and effort a person puts into a sport, the greater chance a person has of building the parts of physical fitness.

But Jim cannot develop all parts of physical fitness by participating in only one activity. Jim must participate in other activities in order to build these parts of fitness.

What Do You Remember?

1. What kind of an activity is a sport?
2. How do sports help you develop physical fitness?
3. How are time and effort related to building parts of fitness through sports?

Physical Fitness and Lifetime Activities

Health Fitness	Archery	Back-packing	Bad-minton	Bowling	Canoeing	Cross-Country Skiing
Develops Cardiovascular Fitness	Poor	Good	Good	Poor	Fair	Excellent
Develops Muscular Strength	Fair	Good	Poor	Poor	Fair	Fair
Develops Muscular Endurance	Poor	Excellent	Fair	Poor	Fair	Good
Develops Flexibility	Poor	Fair	Fair	Poor	Poor	Poor
Helps Control Body Fat	Poor	Good	Good	Poor	Fair	Excellent

Skills Fitness

	Archery	Back-packing	Bad-minton	Bowling	Canoeing	Cross-Country Skiing
Develops Balance	Fair	Fair	Fair	Good	Good	Good
Develops Coordination	Good	Fair	Excellent	Good	Good	Good
Develops Reaction Time	Poor	Poor	Excellent	Poor	Fair	Poor
Develops Agility	Poor	Fair	Good	Fair	Fair	Fair
Develops Power	Poor	Fair	Poor	Fair	Good	Good
Develops Speed	Poor	Poor	Fair	Fair	Poor	Fair

Downhill Skiing	Hiking	Jogging	Roller-Skating	Social Dancing	Swimming	Tennis	Walking
Fair	Good	Excellent	Fair	Fair	Excellent	Good	Good
Fair	Fair	Poor	Poor	Poor	Fair	Fair	Poor
Good	Excellent	Good	Fair	Fair	Excellent	Good	Fair
Fair	Fair	Poor	Poor	Poor	Fair	Fair	Poor
Fair	Good	Excellent	Fair	Fair	Excellent	Fair	Good

Downhill Skiing	Hiking	Jogging	Roller-Skating	Social Dancing	Swimming	Tennis	Walking
Excellent	Good	Fair	Excellent	Fair	Poor	Fair	Poor
Excellent	Fair	Poor	Good	Good	Good	Excellent	Poor
Good	Poor	Poor	Poor	Fair	Fair	Excellent	Poor
Excellent	Good	Fair	Excellent	Good	Good	Good	Poor
Good	Good	Poor	Fair	Poor	Good	Good	Poor
Poor	Poor	Fair	Good	Fair	Good	Good	Poor

The national sport of Japan is played by teams of nine players who take turns swinging a bat at a ball that is pitched from a mound in the center of a diamond-shaped field. Sound familiar? It should . . . it's baseball. As you read this article about the direction that Japanese players have taken, decide whether the generalizations the author makes are valid.

BASEBALL IN JAPAN: NO SLIDING BY

by Robert Whiting

"This country has got its national flag all wrong," said one visitor from New York recently during his brief stay in Japan. "Instead of the Rising Sun in the center, there should be a baseball." American tourists who annually visit Japan find the same amazing situation: a nationwide passion for *besuboro* (bes'ù bō rō: baseball).

The Japanese first learned how to play the game in 1873 from an American missionary. It has been played professionally since 1936. Today there are twelve teams in two leagues (the Central and Pacific), over thirteen million fans each year, and several modern stadiums with electronic video scoreboards and artificial grass.

Baseball, not sumo or judo, is Japan's national sport. What is also apparent at a closer look is a "Made in Japan" stamp on this game: *besuboro* and baseball are two different things.

What really sets baseball, Japanese-style, apart is the single-minded dedication with which its players attack the game. Consider first how American major-league teams approach baseball. They start spring training March 1, allowing themselves five weeks to prepare for the six-month season. They spend three to four hours on the field each day before heading for the nearest golf course.

The Japanese, on the other hand, begin "voluntary" training in the freezing cold of mid-January. This routine of daily workouts is designed to get them ready for the usual February 1 opening of camp. Camp itself is made up of daily six- to seven-hour outdoor workouts followed by indoor practice in the evening.

During the season the hard training continues. Whereas American players reduce their pregame mid-summer workouts as a means of saving energy for the games, the Japanese often step theirs up. They believe that extra work is the only way to beat the heat.

The Japanese game is strictly organized around a number of rules meant to train both the body and the mind. Players report to practice fifteen minutes early, do not have private conversations on the field, encourage teammates in a loud voice, and run when moving from place to place.

Clubhouse walls are covered with slogans to spur the players on: "without self-sacrifice there can be no real team"; "you are the master of your own fate"; "cry in practice, laugh in the games"; "fulfill your destiny—exercise your best efforts."

To Americans used to the notion that a player is responsible for himself and that performance on the field is the only thing that matters, the Japanese system seems very confining. Charlie Manuel, a former Minnesota Twin who played in Japan from 1976 to 1981, said, "I've never experienced anything like it in all my years of baseball. One manager I had used to call me up at night to make sure I was in bed. Then he'd call me in the morning to tell me what to eat for breakfast. He even told me when to change my athletic socks."

For American professionals baseball is a job. For the Japanese it is a way of life. From the younger players who live in the team dormitory year-round to the older veterans who may organize workouts in the brief off-season, the story is the same: total commitment. To say the players eat, sleep, and think baseball every day of the year would be no exaggeration.

The attitude of Sadaharu Oh (sä dä′hä rủ ō), now the Yomiuri (yō mē′ủ rē) Giant assistant manager and the man who topped Hank Aaron's record with 868 career home runs, is typical. "I achieved what I did because of my coaches and my

willingness to work hard," he says. When Oh signs autographs for young fans, he signs *doryoku* (dō′ryō kù), "effort."

Oh's view of himself is typical. The Japanese view is that nothing in life comes easily, that only through *doryoku* can one achieve success. Indeed, in a recent survey, the word *doryoku* was chosen as the "most-liked" word by those polled. The rest of the top ten were *patience, thanks, sincerity, endurance, love, harmony, kindness, friendship,* and *trust.*

The capacity for *doryoku,* Japanese coaches will tell you, must be gotten through practice. Thus, a major part of spring training routines are *gattsu* ("guts") drills designed to push a player to his limits. One year's most noted example was a veteran player who, in two hours and fifty minutes one day in camp, took nine hundred ground balls at first base before dropping from exhaustion.

Another area of the game that reflects a clear difference of cultural values is that of team harmony—*wa* (wä). Many things Americans accept as displays of individualistic spirit—"letting it all hang out" as it were—are not welcomed by the Japanese. No long hair or beards are allowed, nor are violent displays of temper in the clubhouse and on the field. There is no place for practical joking, and, above all, no contract holdouts are allowed. A player's behavior is considered just as important as his batting average. In addition, bad behavior is seen as a sign of character weakness. In Japan a "real" man is one who keeps his emotions to himself and thinks of others' feelings.

The Japanese hope that their approach to baseball will eventually bring them equality with the American game. After all, hard work and group cooperation helped to make Japan an economic power. It would seem to follow that if the same dedication is applied to baseball, a world championship should eventually result.

Yomiuri Giant owner Toru Shoriki (tō′rû shō′rē kē) is one who feels the time has already come. Recently Shoriki met with the United States baseball commissioner to formally request the establishment of a "Real World Series" between the American and Japanese baseball champions. The U.S. commissioner replied that he would form a committee to study the question.

Regardless of what eventually happens, one thing at least seems certain. The American and Japanese systems will remain culture-bound. An American manager who tried to use Japanese methods on his baseball team would definitely have a mutiny on his hands. At the same time, a Japanese manager who took the American way would find himself with a group of confused players.

Indeed, when a former major leaguer named Don Blassingame took over as manager of the 1979 Hanshin Tigers and tried, to a certain degree, to Americanize things, he was met with much opposition. The players complained that they were not getting enough practice. The press complained that Blassingame was not keeping team harmony intact.

Says Blassingame, who is now managing the Nankai Hawks, "Knowing how and when to make changes in the existing system is probably the hardest thing about managing over here. I see players doing things that I know aren't good for them physically. But if I make them change, then it upsets them so much that it just makes the situation even worse. It's a completely different world."

Think and Discuss

- 1. In the selection from the health textbook, what generalization about time, effort, and physical fitness does the author make at the end of the article?
  2. Name the two types of physical fitness and give an example of each. Where did you find your answer?
  3. Answer the questions under **What Do You Remember?** at the end of the textbook article.
- 4. The main idea of "Baseball in Japan" is a generalization. Is it **a** or **b** below? Support your answer with facts from the article.
  a. What really sets baseball, Japanese-style, apart is the single-minded dedication with which its players attack the game.
  b. The Japanese view is that nothing in life comes easily.
  5. Do you think that American baseball teams would benefit from adopting some of the Japanese ideas about team spirit? Why or why not?

See your Thinker's Handbook for tips.

- Comprehension Skill: Generalizations

Communication Workshop

Talk

Work with a small group. Choose one member of your group to be the moderator and have a panel discussion on the health benefits and skills fitness to be gained from each of the sports on the chart on pages 304–305. Appoint one member of the panel to contribute ideas from the article on Japanese baseball.
Speaking/Listening: Panel discussion

Write

Select your favorite sport from the chart on pages 304–305 and pretend you are the captain of this team and need to recruit players. Prepare a one-page flier to encourage your teammates to sign up for the team. Mention the health and skills benefits of the sport. Display your flier to your group and examine theirs. Which team sounds the most interesting to you? Why?
Writing Fluency: Flier

Learning About Etymologies

Well, the graham cracker was actually named after Mr. *Graham*. Sylvester Graham lived from 1794–1851. His goal was to reform the way people ate and he was certainly successful. A graham cracker is made from whole-wheat flour and not only tastes good but is good for you.

Every word has an origin and a history. Learning about etymologies—the origins and histories of words—can give you a sense of wonder as you discover that many of the words you speak today have been used by people throughout time.

Many of our words come from languages other than English. The word *slim*, for example, came from the Dutch language and meant—believe it or not—"bad." It's not bad to be slim today. In fact, the information below will tell you how to be slim. As you read, note the underlined words and then read their etymologies.

To be slim, it's best not to eat chocolate.
Cookies and salty pretzels should also be avoided.

Chocolate is a Mexican word that came from *chocolatl* (chō′kō lä tl) which meant "sour water"; and the word *cookie* came from the Dutch word *koekje* (ku′kya) which meant "little cake." The word *pretzel* has an amazingly long history. It is traced to the German word *Brezel* (brāt′səl), and still sounds a little like this word. But *Brezel* itself can be traced back to an even older Latin word *brackitum*, meaning "folded arms." Pretzels do look a bit like folded arms, even today!

Notice that the meaning of some words has changed, such as *slim* and *chocolate*. Other words still retain much of their original meanings, such as *cookies* and *pretzels*. Etymologies like these as well as others can be found in glossaries and dictionaries.

Reading Etymologies

Read below to learn about the history of several words as well as what they mean today. Which meanings have changed and which mean almost the same thing?

incline   The word comes from the Latin word *inclinare* (in′kle nä′rā) which was made up of two parts—*in-* which meant "in" and *clinare* (klə nä′rā) that meant "to bend." Incline can mean "bending" or "willing" as in this sentence: *Although the young man didn't know much, the manager was inclined to hire him.*

zero   The word comes from the Italian word *zero* (tsā′rō), which came from the older Arabic word *sifr* (sē′fər) that meant "empty" and the Arabic word *cipher* which referred to the number *0*. Zero refers to the temperature represented by the zero mark on a thermometer. *An ice storm drove the temperature down to zero.*

salary   The word comes from the Latin *salarium* (sä lä′rē üm) which meant "a soldier's allowance for salt." *Sal* (sal) was the word for "salt." In ancient times, soldiers were paid with salt because it was rare and, as now, necessary for life. Salary means "a fixed payment made to a person for work." *I got a good salary for my work.*

clamor   The word comes from the Latin word *clamare* (klä mä′rā) which meant "cry out." *Clamor* means "a loud noise." *The church bells set up a loud clamor to alert the people to the fire.*

Tips for Understanding and Appreciating Language
- Learning about etymologies helps you appreciate language.
- Many words come from languages other than English or from names.
- The meanings of words can stay the same or change over time.
- Glossaries and dictionaries are sources for etymologies.
- For other tips on figuring out words, see your Word Study Handbook.

"Going to be a lawyer like your brother, eh?" Why couldn't people understand that Cyrus Field had his own plans? A business career was what he wanted, and he believed that he was headed in the right direction. But would he be prevented from reaching his goal? Look for details to help you draw conclusions about the kind of person Cyrus Field was.

YOUNG MAN IN A HURRY

by Jean Lee Latham

Cyrus Field was born in 1819 in Springfield, Massachusetts, and grew up in a family of achievers. When he left home to seek his fortune in New York City, few people thought he would be able to make his living.

The following excerpt from Young Man in a Hurry *tells about Cyrus Field's initiation into the world of business. His brother Dudley, a successful New York lawyer, has offered to look after Cyrus. Fifteen-year-old Cyrus arrives in New York with little more than eight dollars given to him by his father and a new suit made by his mother. But he also has a vision of the future that is all his own.*

"I want to see Mr. Stewart, please!"

Heads jerked; clerks and customers turned to stare at him. Confound it, what had made him shout?

The clerk, as though to reprove him, spoke very softly. "Your name, sir?"

"Cyrus Field."

The clerk smiled. "Oh! Any relation to David Dudley Field?"

"I'm his brother. But he's not—I mean I'm not—I'm getting a job on my own!"

After a wait that seemed forever he was in Mr. Stewart's office.

"So you're David Dudley Field's brother?"

"Yes, sir, but I'm getting my own job, myself."

"So? Sit down, my boy, and tell me what experience you've had."

Cyrus explained how he had kept the family accounts for three years—ever since he was twelve.

"I see. Do you know double-entry bookkeeping?"

"Uh—no, sir."

"Hmm . . . . Well, we can use another errand boy. How well do you know New York City?"

"I don't. I just got here this morning, Mr. Stewart."

Mr. Stewart's eyebrows went up. "And you're applying for a job the first thing?"

"No, sir. The first thing I got a room over on Murray Street."

Mr. Stewart's eyebrows stayed up. "You must have been quite sure you'd get a job here."

Cyrus hesitated, then blurted out, "No, sir. I was really stalling around, getting up the nerve to come in."

Mr. Stewart's eyes twinkled. "Cyrus, I believe you'll get along all right. I don't generally hire an errand boy who doesn't know the city, but I'm inclined to try you. Here's a map of New York. If you study it—"

"I'll learn it by heart!" He was going to get the job! Wouldn't Dudley be surprised when he strolled in and said, "Sorry I'm a little late, but I stopped to talk to Mr. Stewart." Wouldn't everybody—

"And even though you don't know the city," Mr. Stewart went on, "I'm going to start you at the usual salary for new errand boys. Fifty dollars."

Fifty dollars! His heart hammered. Of course, Mr. Stewart didn't mean fifty dollars a week—no boy could earn that much—but just to think of making fifty dollars a month!

"Do you want to start tomorrow, or wait till Monday?"

"I'll start tomorrow, sir!" As soon as he got his first month's pay he could send that eight dollars straight back to Father, and another eight besides. He could—

Mr. Stewart jotted something on a card. "Give this to the man at the door when you come in tomorrow morning. Our errand boys report at six-thirty and work until we close at night. But you'll get an hour off for dinner and forty-five minutes for supper, so it's really not much more than a twelve-hour day."

Cyrus took the card and got up grinning. "I'll be here bright and early, sir!" He could help Father out all the time with money for Stephen and Henry. He could—

"By next year," Mr. Stewart said, "if you turn out well—and I have a feeling you will—we'll raise you to a hundred. By the time you've been here three years, you'll probably be making a dollar a day."

"A—dollar a day?"

Mr. Stewart beamed. "Surprises you, eh? I've seen bright hard-working boys get ahead that fast; start at fifty dollars a year and work right up to a dollar a day in three years."

"Yes, sir. Thank you, sir." He managed to keep the smile on his face as he left Mr. Stewart's office. He even managed to smile all the way through the store until he reached the street.

Again Cyrus was alone in the crowd on Broadway. Two hours ago he had been scared; now he was heartsick. His board and room over a hundred dollars a year, his salary fifty dollars—if he worked out all right.

I'd better start learning the city! he told himself.

Map in hand he wandered south, then east, trying to memorize the tangle of streets. He didn't remember how many times he got lost. When he reached Dudley's house that evening supper was over.

Dudley shook hands and slapped him on the back. "So you went right after a job? Good for you! Get washed up and eat; then come on in the library and tell me about it!"

He dawdled over his supper. He knew he was stalling, trying to put off the minute when he'd have to tell Dudley what a failure he was. At last he got up and went slowly toward the library.

Two strangers were talking with Dudley.

"So," the older man said, "going to be a lawyer like your brother, eh?"

"No, sir. I'm going into business." Cyrus tried to sound brisk and confident. "I have a position with A. T. Stewart's."

"A position? Well, well! Clerk? Or bookkeeper?"

"Errand boy," Cyrus admitted. He sat down, suddenly so sleepy he had to fight to keep his eyes open, and waited for the visitors to leave. It seemed they would never stop talking.

They were asking Dudley's advice. Cyrus tried to follow the conversation, but the tangle of "whereas" and "wherefore" and "party of the first part" was worse than the tangle of New York streets. At last the visitors got up, said good night, and started toward the door.

The younger man paused. "Oh, did you hear about that electrical contraption Samuel Morse is working on? Calls it his 'magnetic telegraph.' Says he's going to send messages through wires. Any distance. New York to Washington, even! Instantly!"

The older man snorted. "Bah! I don't know what's the matter with Samuel Morse. Good blood in him. His brothers turned out all right. But that one! Why the son of a fine minister like Mr. Morse . . . What a disappointment that one must be to his family!"

Cyrus felt a hot flush crawling to his face. He shot a quick glance around, but nobody was paying any attention to him. I'd like to meet Samuel Morse, he thought. I'd tell him, "I know just what you've been through!"

"Maybe Morse's telegraph is a crackbrained scheme," the younger man said, "but what if it would work? Think what it would mean! Remember last December when one of our newspapers arranged to rush President Jackson's speech to New York? Used the fastest express service—I heard it cost them seven hundred dollars to do it—and it took fourteen hours and a half! Just think! If Morse could send messages instantly!"

The older man said, "Humph!"

They argued a while longer; at last they were gone.

Dudley said, "So you went right after your job and got it, eh?"

"Yes, sir, I—" Might as well tell it all and get it over with. "Errand boy. Fifty dollars a year. And my room and board—" He clenched his teeth to keep his chin from shaking. At last he managed to finish.

Dudley only nodded. "Of course you'll need a little help at first. I'll make up the difference between board bill and salary till you're earning your keep. How about other expenses? Can you handle them?"

"Oh, yes! Father gave me some money before I left home."

Dudley smiled. "Better spend part of it on shoe-blacking and a pair of brushes, hadn't you?"

Cyrus looked down at his shoes and flushed.

"Do you have a better suit?" Dudley asked.

"A brand-new one. The last thing before I left home—!" He stopped again.

"Better wear it."

"I was saving it for Sunday."

"Maybe Mother can make you another one for Sunday. You'll need to look spick-and-span at Stewart's."

"Yes, sir."

Dudley studied him for a moment. "What's the matter, Cyrus?"

"I—I thought I'd be on my own. But I won't be earning enough to—"

Smiling, Dudley shook his head. "Young man in a hurry, aren't you? The important thing right now isn't what you'll earn; it's what you'll learn. It's this way, Cyrus—"

Another man came to see Dudley; another man shook hands with Cyrus and said, "So! going to be a lawyer, eh?"

"No, sir. I'm going to be a businessman. I've got a—a job at Stewart's. Errand boy." He excused himself and went to his room.

Tired as he was, he lay staring into the dark. How long would he be a nobody? Just the brother of David Dudley Field? The one who wasn't going to be a lawyer? All this year he'd have to depend on Dudley for half of his board bill. More than half. But he'd see that he didn't have to ask for anything else. With six whole dollars left of the eight Father had given him, he'd get along.

By mid-June he stared at his account book, appalled. Only fifty cents left! How had he spent five dollars and fifty cents in such a short time?

One pair shoebrushes	25 cents
One box shoe-blacking	12½ cents
Haircut	12½ cents
Turpentine (to get spots out of coat)	6¼ cents
Shoes mended	18¾ cents

On and on and on! Easy enough to see where the money went. It certainly cost a lot to live in New York and keep neat and well dressed.

For a long time he sat with his head on his hands. He was a big success, he was! Dudley helping with his room and board— Mother making his clothes. And everybody disappointed in him. He knew that. Especially Dudley. No matter what Dudley said, Cyrus could feel what he wasn't saying. "Too bad Cyrus doesn't want to be a lawyer."

A drop of water hit the page and made a blot on "haircut." I'm just tired, he told himself. I'll be all right tomorrow.

All the next day he found himself fighting a lump in his throat and a hollow feeling in his stomach. He left the store at closing time that night dragging his heels.

Mr. Jackson, an elderly clerk, fell in step with him. "Had about enough of it?"

"Sir?"

"Wish you were home again, sleeping in your own bed, eating your mother's cooking?"

The truth hit Cyrus in the midriff. He was homesick! Homesick and scared!

"What'd you be doing right now," Mr. Jackson asked, "if you were home?"

Cyrus hunted frantically for something to say—anything—to change the subject. "Oh, I'm all right. It's just the heat. Errand boys really have it easy. But a clerk—you must have your hands full all the time, don't you?"

"Do I! Why, just this morning . . ."

Cyrus walked five blocks out of his way, listening to Mr. Jackson's woes. Finally he said, "I'm sorry, but I'd better say good night."

"Eh? Oh, too bad. Hope we'll have a chance to talk again, Cyrus. You're a mighty interesting lad. Got a head on your shoulders. If there's ever anything I can do to help, just let me know."

You've helped already! Cyrus thought. He went back to the airless, sticky heat of his room. Instead of tossing, turning, trying to sleep, he lay thinking of Mr. Jackson and his problems.

All at once it was morning. He got up smiling. The next time I can't stand thinking, he told himself, I'll start somebody talking!

All through the sweltering morning he whistled on his errands. By afternoon the whistle died. Just dried up, he decided. Down on South Street he stopped in the shade of a store, took off his hat, and mopped his sweating face.

A clerk was standing in the doorway. He said nothing. He just stood. Cyrus got uneasy. At home it was all right to stop in the shade to cool off. Wasn't it all right in New York?

"I just stopped to cool off," he said.

The clerk glanced at him. "Eh? Help yourself."

A carriage drew up and a well-dressed young man got out and sauntered toward the entrance.

"I've been watching for you, Mr. Taylor!" the clerk said. He lowered his voice. "Mrs. You-Know-Who is here, and she won't deal with anybody but the boss."

Mr. Taylor laughed, winked at Cyrus as though to include him in the joke, and went into the shop.

"Does he *own* this store?" Cyrus asked.

"He certainly does!" the clerk said. "And not yet thirty! That young man's made his mark!" He followed his boss inside.

If Mr. Taylor can do it, Cyrus told himself, *I can, too. I'll have my own business before I'm thirty!* He looked about him at the rows of stores. "Some day," he whispered, "you'll have to move over, gentlemen! You'll have to make room for Cyrus W. Field."

For almost a week he didn't have to fight the lump in his throat and the hollow feeling in his stomach. Then they came back again. More and more often he hunted for someone to talk with. More and more often he said, "You really have a job on your hands, don't you?" and listened. Listening seemed to help more than anything else. At night, when he was alone, he tried to think of the future, when he'd get out of a carriage and walk into his own store. By August all he could think of was the heat. If only winter would come!

It came. In December a gale howled in and drove temperatures down to zero. By day Cyrus waded snowdrifts and shivered. At night he shivered, too. No matter what he piled on top of the covers the cold crept up through the thin, hard mattress. He tried not to think of home—of heating bricks on the hearth and wrapping them in pieces of blanket to warm his bed. But the lump in his throat was an ache that would not go away.

He was plodding back to his room one mid-December night when the bell on City Hall clanged. *Fire!* He looked toward the tower to see which way the watchman swung the lantern to guide the firemen. Southeast.

A yelling mob in their red shirts came tearing down the middle of the street dragging their fire engine. In a few moments the bell clanged again. Two more yelling fire companies passed.

When Cyrus reached the boardinghouse half a dozen men were in the parlor, crowded around the hearth.

"Come on in, Cyrus, and thaw out!" one called. They made room for him.

He had not been there long enough to get warm when all the church bells in the city set up a frantic clamor. The boarders looked at one another.

"It's a bad one!"

Someone banged on the door and yelled, "Turn out! Turn out! We'll need every able-bodied man in the city!"

Cyrus picked up his coat again and followed the others to the street. On Broadway he stopped with a gasp, staring south. A red glare lighted the sky.

When they got to the fire twenty buildings were blazing.

"Move back!" a fire chief shouted. "We can't save those! We've got to keep the fire from spreading!"

The red-coated men dragged their engines back, and tried to train streams of water on roofs just beginning to smolder. Faster and faster they pumped. When they stopped, exhausted, others took their places. Men in top hats and evening coats toiled by workmen in corduroys.

But it was hopeless. The streams of water froze in mid-air. Flames leaped the narrow streets. Sixty buildings blazed—a hundred.

Unless they stopped the fire the whole city was doomed. But how could they stop it? The firemen were helpless, the engines useless, the hose frozen and burst. The howling wind carried embers three blocks from buildings already ablaze.

Desperately they planned. If they could blow up buildings in the path of the fire—flatten them—make a fire check . . . But they must have gunpowder—kegs of it—from the Brooklyn Navy Yard. What chance did a boat have to cross that stormy water tonight? A boat pushed off. People watched—waited—prayed— and gave up hope.

Three hundred buildings blazed—four hundred—five hundred. Long after hope was gone, the boat came from Brooklyn with gunpowder.

People cheered; then the cheers died in their throats as they watched the sailors start ashore into the burning city with the kegs of gunpowder. Time and again an ember fell on a blanket-wrapped keg and smoldered. The sailor paused only long enough to knock it off and beat out the fire. He marched on, carrying salvation for the city on his shoulder—or his own death. Depending on whether or not he got rid of the keg before it exploded.

One dull boom after another. Walls toppled. The fire check worked. But seven hundred buildings lay in smoking ruins. Only the burning of Moscow had ever destroyed that much property in a single fire.

Cyrus wandered into the burned-out region a week later and did not know where he was—there were no landmarks—until he heard a man ask, "Did you save anything, Mr. Taylor?"

The young man "who had made a mark for himself" shook his head. "Nothing."

"But you were fully insured, of course?"

"That won't help. The insurance companies are ruined, too."

"Then you—"

"I'm wiped out."

"But—but what will you do?"

Mr. Taylor stared at the blackened ruins, shrugged, and straightened. "Charge it to profit and loss and start over."

Cyrus walked away slowly. *If Mr. Taylor can do it, I can, too.* That was what he had been saying to himself. It was one thing to have the dogged stick-to-itiveness to climb inch by inch up your mountain to success. But to have an avalanche of disaster sweep you from your goal—to be wiped out and have to begin over . . . He wondered. The next spring he was still wondering.

"Cyrus, Mr. Stewart wants to see you. Right away."

His heart lurched. Wasn't he working out all right? Was Mr. Stewart going to fire him? Was he . . .

But Mr. Stewart was smiling. "Cyrus, I've been hearing very good reports about you. Quite a few of the clerks—especially Mr. Jackson—tell me you have a head on your shoulders. They've recommended that we try you out as a clerk."

Cyrus didn't have a bit of trouble smiling when he left Mr. Stewart's office. The clerks were smiling at him, too.

Mr. Jackson shook hands. "Don't know how you found your feet so fast, my boy, but you've done it!"

It's being a preacher's son in Stockbridge, Cyrus thought, and learning to listen! But he didn't go into that.

All he knew was that the homesickness was gone, and New York was his city. By the fall of '36, just a year after the fire, bigger, finer buildings had sprung from the ruins. Cyrus felt as proud of them as though he had built every one of them by himself. You can't stop us New Yorkers! That was what he liked to say.

His city! How it was growing! Lots marked out—on maps— clear up to what men said would some day be Seventy-second Street! Land! That was the thing! Men bragged of buying lots at one hundred dollars and selling them for two thousand. Here a man had made eighty thousand on a piece of property he had bought only three years ago; there a man had made two hundred thousand!

Cyrus listened and smiled. One of these days he'd be investing. One of these days he'd . . .

The spring of 1837 the bubble burst. He saw a disaster greater than the fire sweep the city. Panic. No blackened ruins. Fine buildings stood—with FOR SALE signs on them. Banks closed. Businesses failed. Month after month, one failure after another.

"It's worse than the fire!" Cyrus told Dudley. "That was awful, but we stopped it in two days. We made a fire check. But how can you stop a panic? What can a man depend on, Dudley?"

Dudley's square jaw looked a little squarer. "His energy and his integrity. His ability to come back fighting! The only man who leaves his mark on the world is a fighter! Do you understand?"

"Yes . . . sir."

But New York had lost its savor. It was no longer the city where a boy could dream big dreams. When Cyrus got a letter from his brother in Lee, Massachusetts, he thought long and hard.

At last he went to talk it over with Dudley. "Matthew wants me to work for him in his paper mill."

"Matthew with a paper mill," Dudley said. "An odd business for him. His real love is engineering."

"You mean I shouldn't go?" Cyrus asked.

"I didn't say that."

"He's offering me two hundred and fifty a year and my board and room and washing. That's more than I'm making here."

Dudley only said, "Well?"

"What do you think?"

"That's your problem." Dudley's smile took the sting out of his words. "Young men in a hurry have to learn to make their own decisions."

Cyrus Field left New York to work as a salesman for his brother's paper company. By the time he was thirty, he owned his own business, and by the time he was thirty-five, he was able to retire from that business. He then devoted more than twelve years to a project that many people thought was crazy—the laying of a telegraph cable across the bottom of the Atlantic Ocean. Field raised the funds and held the project together through many disappointments. Finally, in 1866, he supervised a dramatic mid-ocean splice of the cable that revolutionized communication by linking the Old World and the New.

Meet the Author

The selection you have just read is from Jean Lee Latham's biography, *Young Man in a Hurry.* Asked how she gets all the facts for her books, Miss Latham replies: "If a book is based on history, I get all the facts by research. I travel, I study maps, and I read, read, read! I probably read about a pound of books for every paragraph in a story."

Miss Latham went to Nova Scotia to research Cyrus Field because she knew that was where she could find many details of his most famous exploit—the laying of the Atlantic Cable: "First I consulted the archives in Halifax. I used a tape recorder to take notes. Then I went to Canso, where the cable lines begin. *Before I went there I had learned everything I could about cables.* I wanted to be ready to understand what I saw." Miss Latham's preparation paid off. The head of the cable station was so impressed with her knowledge of submarine cables that he gave her valuable help with her research.

Miss Latham has written many books on historical subjects, including the Newbery Award winning *Carry On, Mr. Bowditch, Medals for Morse: Artist and Inventor,* and *This Dear Bought Land.*

Think and Discuss

1. What is Cyrus Field's goal and what disappointments does he encounter in trying to reach it?
2. "The important thing right now isn't what you'll earn; it's what you'll learn." Do you think this is good advice for someone beginning a career today? Why or why not?
3. Compare the two encounters Cyrus has with the young, successful Mr. Taylor. How do these encounters affect Cyrus?
• 4. How does Cyrus feel about his future when he is promoted? How do you know?
• 5. Do you agree that Cyrus is a "young man in a hurry"? Support your answer with details from the selection.
• Comprehension Skill: Drawing conclusions

Communication Workshop

Talk

Have a small group discussion about how communication has changed over the years. Consider these points: In the 1880s it took two weeks to get messages from London to New York by steamer; from New York to California by wagon train the message could then take up to nine months; however, sending the message by steamer around Cape Horn would take only four months. Discuss how communication would be different today without telephones, radios, computers, and satellites.
Speaking/Listening: Cooperative learning

Write

Keep track of your use of electronic communication during several days or over a weekend. Record your use of the telephone, television, or stereo. Include the number of times you use each type and for what reason, such as recreation or information. Display your chart and compare your use of electronic communication with your group's.
Writing Fluency: Records

Learning How to Take Notes

In "Meet the Author," Jean Lee Latham explained how she gathered the information she needed to write *Young Man in a Hurry*. When she visited the archives in Halifax, Miss Latham used a tape recorder to take the notes that were eventually written down and organized into the biography of Cyrus Field.

Taking notes can help you understand and remember what you read as well as help you gather information before you write. There are two situations in which taking notes may be useful: when you especially want to remember what you've read (as for a test) or when you read an article that is difficult and you want a way to reorganize the information. There is no single correct way to take notes.

Reread page 315 of "Young Man in a Hurry" and then look at the note card at the right.

> "Young Man in a Hurry," p. 315
> 1. Cyrus Field was born in 1819 in Springfield, Massachusetts.
> 2. Cyrus grew up in a family of achievers and went to New York at the age of fifteen to work.
> 3. His brother Dudley was a famous lawyer.

Notice how the notes help make the important points about Cyrus clear and help you understand the information. Notice that the notes did not include any mention of the long wait to see Mr. Stewart because that information is not an important detail.

In Section 8, you will read about Phillis Wheatley and you will be asked to outline the information about this famous poet. To do this, it will be helpful for you to take notes as you read. Use these tips to help you when you take notes:

- First, preview the article. If it's complicated, you may want to read it first and take notes as you read it a second time.
- Be selective: make notes of the main ideas and important details.
- Keep the notes brief. Use key words, phrases, and short sentences.
- Keep in mind your purpose for taking notes and make sure your notes reflect that purpose.
- Record the source of your notes in case you need to refer back to it later.

Six men, a million miles from nowhere, are hurtling into the unknown reaches of space. Commander Max Landin will soon face two difficult decisions. One could alter the direction of his spaceship, the other could alter the direction of his life. As you read this science-fiction story, see if you can predict what impels Max to decide as he does.

The Samaritan

by Richard Harper

The spaceship was in deep space, traveling with sleek mechanical precision at nearly the speed of light, its computer and drives all functioning automatically, moving it along a predetermined course toward a certain planet of a certain star still four light-years away.

Commander Max Landin had the watch. Strapped in the deep, cushioned chair of the control room, he monitored the maze of instruments set in banks around him while Edward Haverson, the watch officer, prepared food in the starboard compartment. Raul Barrios, the watch medic, was busy in the aft compartment, giving the weekly sustenance injections to the other three crew members, the relief watch, who were sleeping soundly in a state of suspended animation.

Two weeks of monitoring the course and actions of the spaceship—then two weeks of sleep, like a long weekend. Six light-years had passed since leaving Earth, although for them the passing of time was only a few months, and they were right on schedule with no complications and everything going according to plan.

Yet they were beginning to feel the remoteness of their situation, the complete and utter isolation that was sometimes frightening. Max had noticed the strain first in Haverson, who was beginning to worry about little things. Medic Barrios had assured him that all was in order, but even Barrios was showing the effects of the awesomeness of prolonged flight.

In spite of being picked for special space aptitudes and trained for years in flights to the moon and to Mars, a person never seemed to get used to the uncanny detached feeling of complete aloneness. And now, for the first time, human beings were venturing beyond Earth's solar system toward an unseen goal that existed only on their instruments.

A buzzer sounded on the console, and moments later Ed Haverson pulled himself into the compartment to take over. Max floated back along the passageway to his quarters for a few hours' sleep. But he lay there, sleepless, thinking about his life and this spaceship and this flight, wondering what they were really doing a million miles from nowhere like a bubble on an endless sea. What were they really looking for? What did they expect to find? Space conquest was his life, but he was beginning to wonder if it was all worth it.

He dozed fitfully, and awakened startled at the sound of the intercom calling him forward to the control room.

He found Ed busy checking and rechecking the instrument data and finding the readings hard to believe. Haverson said, "You check it out, Skipper. I don't trust my readings."

Max Landin checked the control board—deciphering and monitoring the information. He let out a slow breath. There was no mistake. The instruments were registering a large mass, evidently an asteroid. But what was incredible to them both was that the mass was sending out a signal—a constant, beamed signal.

Ed Haverson was frowning. "Then I wasn't wrong? The instruments aren't malfunctioning?"

Max shook his head slowly. "No, you weren't wrong. The instruments aren't wrong."

"But, Skipper, what—"

"Call Raul up here," Max said quietly.

Barrios pulled himself into the control room. "What is it?"

Max handed him the data book and Barrios, after studying it a moment, stared at the scope, fascinated. He asked, "And it checks out? It's a *bona fide* signal, not some freak of space?"

"It checks out," Max Landin said.

"But—who's sending it?"

Seconds later the signal was coming in stronger, and Max knew the time had come for a decision. And the decision was his alone. As commander of the watch, he had complete jurisdiction over the spaceship. But altering the course was planned for only in case of an emergency, and, as near as he could tell, the ship was in no danger. He could stay on course and ignore the signal. He had no authorization for landing anywhere short of their fixed goal. It could lead to complications: it meant risking the ship, the personnel, the entire expedition. And according to all their data, they were nowhere. Yet there was no denying the signal. He had double-checked everything.

• What will Max do?

His curiosity alone was almost overwhelming, but curiosity couldn't be the basis for a decision—a decision he would have to make soon or they would be out of range. Already the signal had grown noticeably weaker. He looked at Haverson and Barrios. They waited, watching him, and there was nothing in their expressions to aid him in his choice.

And, for all his arguments and logic, he knew with a terrible certainty what his decision would be. He felt it, as he felt now the reasons for their being out here at all: to seek and find and learn whatever there was to be found and learned. The ship's computer could store a great deal of knowledge, but there were some things the computer couldn't do. It couldn't wonder about things, and it couldn't make decisions. Max Landin could.

"Secure for landing," he said. "We're altering course."

With the new course coordinates fed into the computer, the ship homed in on the beamed signal, roaring into the thin, hostile atmosphere of the mass, retrorockets decelerating as it circled the mass twice before coming down on the guiding signal. As the ship came to rest, they lay quietly for several minutes—gradually adjusting to the light gravity of the mass. It was then that they heard the tapping on the ship's hull.

• Was your prediction about what Max would do correct?

They looked around, first at each other and then at the sealed port of the cabin that separated them from the airlock and the outer port of the ship. The tapping came again, loud and insistent. For a moment nobody moved; then Max recovered enough to switch on the ship's floodlights and step to the view-scope.

The floodlights barely penetrated the absolute darkness around the ship, revealing a little barren rocky ground, and the scope couldn't be trained along the now vertical sides of the ship. The tapping came again, louder.

"Help me break out a suit, Raul," Max said.

"You're not going out there?" Ed Haverson interrupted.

Max gave him a hard look. "What would you suggest? Let whatever it is in here?" Certain now that only some form of intelligent life could have sent out the signal they had received, he didn't let himself even speculate as to what type of creature it might be. But whoever or whatever it was, it was waiting just outside the ship, and to leave without attempting contact was unthinkable.

He threw a switch, pressurizing the airlock, and as Raul Barrios helped him into a suit, the tapping came again.

"Shouldn't one of us go with you?" Raul suggested.

"No," Max answered thoughtfully. "If they're hostile, I don't think two of us would be any better off than one. And the ship needs its crew. Besides, it's my responsibility."

They tested the suit and the communicator in the helmet, and when the green light showed above the sealed cabin door, Max nodded. Ed Haverson handed him a thermal pistol and a solar torch and opened the airlock port.

Inside the lock, the tapping on the outer hull port was louder, as Max waited for the light above the cabin port to glow red when the chamber had depressurized. When the light turned red, it was several moments before he could bring himself to give the order over the communicator: "Open the outer port." His voice shook with suppressed excitement.

The outer port slid open, and Max's torch illuminated the man who was standing on the ship's ladder looking in. Suited in close-fitting glossy-smooth material, his face was clearly visible through the transparent globe that covered his head. As he raised a gloved hand to shield his eyes from the light, Max lowered his torch so that it shone on the deck of the chamber but still reflected on the alien in the open portway.

It was incredible. Except for a completely hairless face and head, the man was almost identical to themselves. And Max was aware that the alien was speaking. A voice was coming through the communicator—the sounds human but unintelligible.

Then Barrios cut in, "Max? You all right?"

"Yes, yes, I'm all right."

"Well, what is it?"

"It's a man," Max Landin said.

The alien was talking freely now and motioning with his arm. He had not attempted to enter the ship.

"Listen," Max spoke hurriedly, "is Ed listening to this? He's the linguist; see if he can make any of it out."

Haverson's voice came in, "Can't read him. It's like nothing we've got on Earth. Does he really look human?"

"He's human," Max said. "He's motioning with his arm—I think he wants me to go with him."

Haverson's voice came back at him. "Skipper, he's got a language. I can crack it sure, but it'll take time."

Max had been watching the alien closely. The expression in the man's eyes was one of urgent need. "I'm afraid we don't have time, Ed," he said. "And he doesn't either. I'm going with him."

There was no answer on the communicator.

"Did you read me? Ed? Raul?"

"We read you."

"I'll maintain contact," Max said. "If anything happens, reset the course coordinates and continue the voyage." He nodded to the alien, motioning him down. Hooking his torch and pistol on his belt,

Max climbed through the outer port and descended down the ship's ladder to the ground.

Activating the magnetic locator on his belt so he could find his way back, he followed the alien, who was shining his own lamp ahead of him and seemed to know where he was going.

As they moved in silence across the dead mass, weird-shaped rock formations rose like grotesque giants around them. Just beyond the small tight circles of their lights pressed the formless dark of perpetual night. Max, hurrying along behind the alien, felt a growing and profound respect for the whole fantastic experience.

"Are you reading us, Skipper?" Haverson's voice came over the communicator, interrupting his thoughts.

"I read you," Max answered. "We're still moving away from the ship. Nothing to see but rocks and darkness."

But moments later the alien stopped and pointed his lamp off to the right. Up on a ledge, the light illuminated the broken, mangled

wreckage of a spaceship, a ship almost twice the size of Max Landin's. Then the alien's lamp left the wreckage in darkness and shone ahead of him to where two more aliens in spacesuits waited—one of them standing, but the other lying motionless on the ground.

Stunned by the sight, Max approached them cautiously, whispering into his mouthpiece. "Ed? Raul? There are two more of them. And a ship, or what's left of one. They don't belong here either; they crashed."

Moving to the alien on the ground, he knelt and peered through the globe. The man's features were ashy and there was blood in one corner of his mouth. His eyes were closed, but he was still alive. His breath was coming in shallow gasps. "One of them is hurt. Hurt bad."

Rising, he looked at the other two. The three of them, the man from Earth and the two from somewhere out beyond, stood there in their circles of brightness, staring at each other.

Max knew of course what should be done, and what the aliens expected him to do. They had crashed, and somehow these three had survived. And he saw now the instrument that had evidently been sending out the distress signal. It was lying on the ground, silent now that it had brought help. Only that was the tragic irony of it—there was no help he could give.

Barrios's voice said, "They expect us to help them, Max."

"I know what they expect!" Max snapped. It was getting to him now, the inner turmoil of an impossible situation. Barrios knew, and Haverson too, that there was nothing he could do. Nothing any of them could do. He shivered involuntarily, to think that the first contact with other beings—a chance meeting and maybe the only one they would ever have—should result in this.

"What are you going to do?" Barrios's voice was tense.

"You know the answer to that," Max's voice was harsh with the strain of command. "The oxygen and food replenishers were all calculated for six people, not nine. There's nothing we can do." But he didn't really believe that; he wouldn't let himself believe it. Somehow there must be something . . . .

The alien who had led him here was motioning toward himself and the others and then pointing in the direction of Max's ship. Max slowly shook his head. Then, with motions and with signs scratched on the hard ground, he tried to explain their numbers and how three more would be too many; and he seemed to be getting it across. The two aliens looked at each other and then back at the man from Earth and their eyes burned with grim horror. Then one of them knelt and scratched three lines on the ground and carefully rubbed out two of them. He pointed to the remaining line and then to the injured alien lying beside him.

Haverson's voice demanded, "Skipper? What's happening?"

"He wants to know if one of them can go—the injured one."

It just might be possible, Max was thinking. Maybe, by making a few fine adjustments of the instruments, a few compensations, they could take on one more man. But only one.

"We might be able to compensate for one," he said. "We'd be taking a chance."

"I think we ought to try, Max," Barrios's voice cut in.

Max looked down at the alien on the ground. If there were only more time, they could find a way to communicate. They could find out who they were and where they came from. So many questions would remain unanswered—unless they could get one of them away alive. He didn't want to take on an injured man, but he felt the choice was theirs. He had to give them that much.

Stooping, he scratched a single line on the ground and nodded. The aliens bent over their companion, then straightened suddenly, shock and hurt in their expressions.

Max knelt beside the injured man. He was no longer breathing. Raul Barrios's voice came over the communicator, "Max? What's the decision?"

"The injured one is dead," Max answered.

"Then we'll take one of the others?"

"Yes," Max said, and he showed the aliens with signs and motions that one of them could still go. But only one. A terrible choice, he knew, but what else could they do? What they did almost unnerved him.

They looked at each other, and then at the man from Earth, and they shook their heads. And kneeling slowly, they put out their lamps and bowed their heads inside their transparent globes. He could hear their voices over his communicator, murmuring softly in their strange tongue.

Max stared, almost unbelieving. Then he realized for the first time the real purpose of his life in space, the meaning of it, and reason for it. Now he knew what it was he had to do.

• What decision will
Max make?

As the aliens rose, turned on their lamps, and stood in their meager pools of light, enclosed by the blackness of a world alien to them all, Max made his last decision quickly, while the courage and the dream were there. Stooping, he drew two lines on the ground and pointed at the aliens and then toward the ship. Unfastening the locator on his belt, he handed it to one of them and motioned again toward the ship.

"Skipper?" Haverson's voice asked. "Have they decided?"

"They've decided," Max said. "They're coming."

"You mean both of them?"

"Listen," Max's voice was tight with emotion. "Listen closely. One of them wouldn't go without the other, and we need them. We just can't afford to lose this contact. Take them on board. Both of them."

"But, Max, that means—"

"I know what it means."

"Max, you can't do it!"

• Was your prediction
about Max's decision
correct?

"You're wrong," Max countered. "I can't do anything else. They're on their way. Take them. That's an order."

Reaching up to his helmet, he turned off his communciator and stood there, watching the aliens' lights melt away in the blackness. Then he looked down at the dead one at his feet and a quick cold terror gripped him. For a moment he was near panic. He wanted to run after them, to cry out. But he forced himself to look at the sky, to realize that to die was not the worst that could happen to a person.

And a strange calmness came over him. Here for the first time was something besides black voids, minerals and metals, and cold dead worlds. Here was another race of people, and this way there would be time. He was giving them time to decode the alien tongue and to establish a common ground for communication, understanding, and knowledge. Switching off his solar torch, he stood looking up at the eternal brilliance of the farthest stars.

Max Landin no longer felt the terrible aloneness. Instead, he felt he really belonged. For the first time in his life, he really belonged in space.

Comprehension Check

1. What are the two decisions Max Landin makes and why does he make them?
2. What kind of person is Max Landin? Support your answer with examples from the story.
3. What is the conclusion of the story?
4. Do you think Max's solution was the best solution? Why or why not?
● 5. What do you predict will happen after the spaceship leaves with the aliens?

● Comprehension Skill: Predicting outcomes

Communication Workshop

Talk

Work with a partner. Pretend you are a two-person crew assigned to a spaceship which is exploring beyond the solar system. You plan to be on board the ship for two years. Discuss the few personal items you would take with you and why.
Speaking/Listening: Discussion

Write

Pretend that you, like Max Landin, must stay behind on an asteroid. Your ship has not left yet. A computer-controlled satellite will bring you additional supplies in two months, but you will probably have to stay on the asteroid for up to a year. Write a letter for the crew to take back to your family in which you describe five personal items you would like to have sent. Explain why you need them. Share your letter with your partner. Were any of the items you chose similar or totally alike? Which ones? What different choices did you make?
Writing Fluency: Friendly letter

The Road Not Taken
by Robert Frost

Two roads diverged in a yellow wood,
And sorry I could not travel both
And be one traveler, long I stood
And looked down one as far as I could
To where it bent in the undergrowth;

Then took the other, as just as fair,
And having perhaps the better claim,
Because it was grassy and wanted wear;
Though as for that, the passing there
Had worn them really about the same,

And both that morning equally lay
In leaves no step had trodden black.
Oh, I kept the first for another day!
Yet knowing how way leads on to way,
I doubted if I should ever come back.

I shall be telling this with a sigh
Somewhere ages and ages hence:
Two roads diverged in a wood, and I—
I took the one less traveled by,
And that has made all the difference.

LOOKING BACK

Thinking and Writing About the Section

In this section you have read about people whose goals give direction to their lives. You've read about physical fitness, Japanese baseball, a young man's success, and a generous man's sacrifice. You can write an explanatory paragraph for a classmate, using facts to explain one of these topics. First copy the chart below. Then fill in the missing information.

See your Thinker's Handbook for tips.

Topics	Facts
Physical Fitness	sports—individual and team each builds different skills and health fitness
Japanese Baseball	
Cyrus Field's Success	started working at age 15 earned $50.00 per year

Writing

Write an explanatory paragraph about one of the topics on your chart, using the facts to explain it. Also use words such as *for example*, *first*, *next*, and *as a result* to connect ideas. For more information about explanatory paragraphs, see your Writer's Handbook.

Revising

Read your first draft to a partner. Have you used facts and words such as *for example* to explain your topic? Make changes if necessary. Then proofread for spelling and punctuation errors. Write your final copy.

Presenting

Read your paragraph to a classmate. Have him or her identify two specific facts in your paragraph that help explain your topic.

8

Americans All

America is as vast and varied as her people—people of all ages, races, and creeds. People new to the shores of America and those who are native-born all leave their mark on our nation.

In this section, you will read about two famous people—one whose contributions to literature captured the spirit of the American Revolution; another whose achievements in modern technology are changing the way we do things. You will also read a story about the lives of two ordinary people who are a part of America too. Famous or not, we are Americans all.

Learning to Outline from More Than One Source

You know that Thomas Jefferson was a colonial statesman, author of The Declaration of Independence, and the third President of the United States. But did you also know that he was an inventor? When Jefferson attended the Second Continental Congress in 1776, he took with him a plan for a portable desk he had designed. He gave the plan to a cabinetmaker, Benjamin Randolph, so Randolph would understand how to make it.

In a similar way, a plan can help you understand an article. An **outline** is a plan that shows the important points of an article and how the points are related to each other. Often you may want to outline from more than one source so that you can get a more complete understanding of a topic. When you outline, you should group, or **classify**, related information and ideas together.

On the following page are two articles about Thomas Jefferson. Read the articles. As you work through the questions on pages 346–347 you will learn step-by-step how to make an outline from these two sources. The first article is "Thomas Jefferson: Man of Many Talents."

Thomas Jefferson: Man of Many Talents

Thomas Jefferson is remembered as a great president. He is also honored as the author of The Declaration of Independence, which lives as one of the most eloquent papers of all time. His original draft was so well done that it was approved with few changes. Yet Jefferson's talents went beyond patriotism.

Inventor

Among Jefferson's many talents was that of inventor. He created the basis for our monetary system. Jefferson's system was a decimal system based on tens. He proposed that all the colonies use this same decimal system because the different systems the various colonies were using caused confusion. He also improved a device to help him copy his letters.

Designer

Jefferson designed furniture. He created a portable writing desk which had a folding shelf that could be used as a reading stand or small table. He also designed a swivel chair and made a music stand that held music for four people.

As you read the next article, keep in mind what you read in the first article about Jefferson's patriotism.

Thomas Jefferson: Patriot

Thomas Jefferson was one of the outstanding patriots of the American Revolution. The leaders of the independence movement constantly asked for Jefferson's help. They asked him to write a recommendation that the colonies write to each other so they could share ideas about independence. Later, as relations with England worsened, they asked him to serve on a committee to arm Virginia. Jefferson is also known as the author of The Declaration of Independence in which he set forth the views of the American Revolutionaries. Jefferson said his object in writing it was to show "the common sense of the subject, in terms so plain and firm as to command their assent. . . ."

1. Who is the subject of both articles?

The subject of both articles is Thomas Jefferson. In an outline, the subject of the article is often used as the **title** of the outline.

2. What main points do the articles cover?

Did you notice that although there are two articles, there are really three main points? The three main points are: Jefferson was a patriot, an inventor, and a designer. If you had difficulty, look at the articles again and notice that Jefferson's patriotism is the first topic of the first article and the main topic of the second article. The other two main points are found in the two subheads of the first article. In an outline, these main points are called **main topics.** Here is how you might begin to make an outline of these articles:

Thomas Jefferson
   I. Patriot
  II. Inventor
 III. Designer

3. What important points can you add about Jefferson, the patriot?

Skimming the first article will show you that Jefferson wrote The Declaration of Independence. Skimming the second article will show you that he also helped the independence leaders. In an outline, the important points that tell you more about the main topics are called **subtopics.** Here is how to show these subtopics in the outline:

Thomas Jefferson
  I. Patriot
    A. Wrote Declaration of Independence
    B. Helped independence leaders
 II. Inventor
III. Designer

4. What are some facts that tell more about Jefferson writing The Declaration of Independence?

Jefferson's original draft was used, he set forth the views of Americans, and he stated his purpose. To find the information you need, remember to read for details about the main topics. In an outline, the facts that tell more about subtopics are called **details.** Here is how this outline looks when these details are added:

Thomas Jefferson
    I. Patriot
        A. Wrote Declaration of Independence
            1. Original draft used
            2. Set forth views of Americans
            3. Said purpose was to clearly show "common sense" of the cause
        B. Helped independence leaders
   II. Inventor
  III. Designer

As you worked through this part of the outline, did you notice that although the information about Jefferson as the author of The Declaration of Independence was in both sources, it was classified together under Roman numeral I?

5. Where will you classify the information about Jefferson as inventor and as a designer? Why?

Look at the outline above. The information in an outline is organized in a certain form or style. Notice how Roman numerals, capital letters, and Arabic numerals—all followed by periods—are lined up in an outline. Also notice that the title, main topics, subtopics, and details each begins with a capital letter.

6. If one of the sources went on to describe how Jefferson built his home, Monticello, under what letter or numeral would you give this information in the outline?

Practicing Outlining

Look at the partial outline on Thomas Jefferson below. Reread the articles and use the questions below to help you fill in the outline. Then complete the outline and copy it on a separate piece of paper.

Thomas Jefferson
I. Patriot
    A. Wrote Declaration of Independence
        1. Original draft used
        2. Set forth views of Americans
        3. Said purpose was to
           clearly show "common sense"
           of the cause
    B. Helped independence leaders
        1.
        2.
II. Inventor
    A.
        1. Based on a decimal system
        2. Proposed all colonies use same system
    B.
III. Designer
    A.
    B.
    C.

1. What are two details that tell how Jefferson helped the independence leaders?
2. What are two subtopics that tell about Jefferson as an inventor?
3. What information do you need in order to complete the outline?

Tips for Reading on Your Own
- Before you begin to outline, read all of the information to see what it is about and how it is organized.
- First, look for the main topics of the article. Then look for the subtopics.
- Next look for details about the subtopics.
- Classify information about the same points together.

Abducted from her home and sold as a slave, Phillis Wheatley held dear a love of freedom. What would she achieve despite being a slave and a woman in colonial America? As you read about Phillis Wheatley in this article and the next one, pay attention to the organization to help you outline the information.

Phillis Wheatley

by Chet Martin

Early Years

A slender, frail black child of seven or eight arrived in Boston in August of 1761 to be sold as a slave. She had been kidnapped from her home somewhere on the west coast of Africa and crowded into a slave vessel sailing for America.

On that August day Susanna Wheatley, the wife of John Wheatley, a successful Boston tailor, came to the docks looking for a domestic—a slave to help with household chores. For whatever reason, it was Susanna Wheatley that bought the girl, described as "suffering from a change in climate," from the auctioneer.

Back at the Wheatley home, the child's health improved eventually. Soon the family named her Phillis and gave her the family name, as was the custom for slaves.

But Phillis was not destined for a life of manual labor. The Wheatleys had a teenage daughter named Mary. She was well educated, which was unusual for a girl, black or white, in colonial America. Girls were usually taught only cooking and needlecraft. But Mary had a twin brother, Nathaniel, who shared his books and learning with Mary, and now she was determined that Phillis Wheatley should be educated.

So, thanks mainly to Mary, Phillis began a variety of studies. Before Phillis had lived in Boston for two years, she was reading and writing. In 1767, at the age of thirteen, she had one of her poems published for the first time, in a Rhode Island newspaper.

It is very likely that from this time on, Phillis did very little housework. Her reputation as a poet spread around the Boston area, and many writers and clergymen are said to have visited her, some bringing her books.

Career

Many of Phillis's poems were composed as words of comfort to someone who had suffered the loss of someone close. Phillis received much attention in 1770 for a poem she wrote entitled "On the Death of the Rev. Mr. George Whitefield, 1770." English-born George Whitefield was an extremely popular preacher of the day. He spent much time in the American colonies, though living most of his life in England. In 1748 Whitefield had been appointed as chaplain at the castle of the Countess of Huntingdon, a wealthy English supporter of religious causes. Phillis dedicated her poem on Whitefield to the Countess, an action that later proved of great benefit for Phillis.

When in 1771 Mary, Phillis's devoted friend, married and left the Wheatley household, Susanna Wheatley took over guidance of Phillis's career. In 1772 Susanna attempted to get a collection of Phillis's poems printed in Boston. But an effort to sign up enough subscribers to pay for the printing failed. Then Susanna enlisted the help of the Countess of Huntingdon in getting an English publication of the collection. The Countess had been very moved by Phillis's poem for Whitefield two years earlier. So she actively worked to find Phillis an English publisher.

John Wheatley soon got involved. To quiet any accusations that a slave could not have written the poems, he arranged for some of Boston's most influential citizens, including John Hancock, to judge Phillis's talents. The eighteen men presiding over this "examination" of Phillis all signed a statement in defense of Phillis's authorship of her poetry. This statement was sent to England.

During this time, Phillis's health declined, and doctors recommended sea air. As it happened, Nathaniel, now a grown man, had already planned a business trip to England in May of 1773, and Phillis was sent on the boat with him.

While in England in the early summer of 1773, Phillis met several important persons, but it is believed that she did not get to meet the Countess. However, Phillis's health did improve somewhat, and her stay was a great success. Plans for publishing her book of thirty-eight poems, now entitled *Poems on Various Subjects, Religious and Moral*, were finalized. The volume was to include an engraving of Phillis, a dedication to the Countess, a Preface from John Wheatley telling readers who Phillis was, the statement signed by the eighteen Boston men, and the poems.

It was at this time, near Phillis's moment of triumph, that the first of several disappointments occurred. Phillis and Nathaniel received word in July that Susanna Wheatley was gravely ill. She requested Phillis's immediate return. Phillis did not hesitate and was quickly on a boat heading back to Boston. Thus Phillis was not present for the actual publication of

---

To the PUBLICK.

AS it has been repeatedly fuggefted to the Publifher, by Perfons, who have feen the Manufcript, that Numbers would be ready to fufpect they were not really the Writings of PHILLIS, he has procured the following Atteftation, from the moft refpectable Characters in *Bofton*, that none might have the leaft Ground for difputing their *Original*.

WE whofe Names are under-written, do affure the World, that the POEMS fpecified in the following Page, * were (as we verily believe) written by PHILLIS, a young Negro Girl, who was but a few Years fince, brought.............................. from *Africa*, and has ever fince been, and now is, under the Difadvantage of ferving as a Slave in a Family in this Town. She has been examined by fome of the beft Judges, and is thought qualified to write them.

His Excellency THOMAS HUTCHINSON, *Governor*,

The Hon. ANDREW OLIVER, *Lieutenant-Governor.*

The Hon. Thomas Hubbard,	*The Rev.* Charles Chauncy, *D. D.*
The Hon. John Erving,	*The Rev.* Mather Byles, *D. D.*
The Hon. James Pitts,	*The Rev* Ed. Pemberton, *D. D.*
The Hon. Harrifon Gray,	*The Rev.* Andrew Elliot, *D.D.*
The Hon. James Bowdoin,	*The Rev.* Samuel Cooper, *D.D.*
John Hancock, *Efq;*	*The Rev. Mr.* Samuel Mather,
Jofeph Green, *Efq;*	*The Rev. Mr.* John Moorhead,
Richard Carey, *Efq;*	*Mr.* John Wheatley, *her Mafter.*

N. B. The original Atteftation, figned by the above Gentlemen, may be feen by applying to *Archibald Bell*, Bookfeller, No. 8, *Aldgate-Street.*

---

* The Words " *following Page,*" allude to the Contents of the Manufcript Copy, which are wrote at the Back of the above Atteftation.

Statement on Phillis's poetry in *Poems on Various Subjects, Religious and Moral* signed by eighteen of "the most respectable Characters in Boston." Notice the "f"-like symbol often taking the place of an "s," which was common in printing at that time.

her book that September. (Nathaniel stayed behind in England, never to return to America again.)

Phillis found Mrs. Wheatley bed-ridden and not improving. In March of 1774, Susanna died. Two other events from about this time were overshadowed by her death: Phillis's being officially freed from slavery by the Wheatleys and the appearance in Boston of her *Poems*. The book, now recognized as the first book of poetry published by an American black author, was reprinted several times in the eighteenth century.

When Phillis returned to America the situation between the colonies and England was worsening. In June of 1775, the outnumbered colonists retreated from the Battle of Bunker Hill near downtown Boston. The war effort looked bleak, but in July, General George Washington took command of the colonial troops outside Boston. Most Bostonians now felt confident that Washington would somehow defeat the British.

At that time Phillis was living outside of Boston—in Providence, Rhode Island, with Mary and her husband. On October 26, 1775, Phillis wrote a poem praising General Washington and had it sent to him. It remains her single most famous poem. The following is the conclusion of the poem:

> Shall I to Washington their praise recite?
> Enough thou know'st them in the fields of fight.
> Thee, first in peace and honours,—we demand
> The grace and glory of thy martial band.
> Fam'd for thy valour, for thy virtues more,
> Hear every tongue thy guardian aid implore!
>
> . . . .
>
> Proceed, great chief, with virtue on thy side,
> Thy ev'ry action let the goddess guide.
> A crown, a mansion, and a throne that shine,
> With gold unfading, WASHINGTON! be thine.

For months Phillis heard nothing from Washington. Then in March of 1776 she received a letter from him. He thanked her for the lines she had written and regretted that he could not publish them, because he did not want people to think him vain.

Washington's Letter to Phillis Wheatley

Cambridge, February 28th, 1776

Miss Phillis:

Your favor of the 26th of October did not reach my hands till the middle of December. Time enough, you will say to have given an answer ere this. Granted. But a variety of important occurrences continually interposing to distract the mind and withdraw the attention, I hope will apologize for the delay and plead my excuse for the seeming but not real neglect. I thank you most sincerely for your polite notice of me in the elegant lines you enclosed. However undeserving I may be of such encomium and panegyric, the style and manner exhibit a striking proof of your poetical talents; in honor of which, and as a tribute justly due to you I would have published the poem had I not been apprehensive that while I only meant to give the world this new instance of your genius, I might have incurred the imputation of vanity. This, and nothing else, determined me not to give it place in the public prints.

If you should come to Cambridge, or near headquarters, I shall be happy to see a person so favored by the Muses, and to whom Nature has been so liberal and beneficent in her dispensations. I am, with great respect, Your obedient humble servant,

George Washington

However, by a set of circumstances still not known today, Phillis's letter and poem to Washington did get published, in the April, 1776, issue of *The Pennsylvania Magazine*. It is not known for certain, either, whether Phillis ever did meet with Washington in Cambridge.

Closing Years

After the letter and poem to Washington, Phillis's writing slowed down considerably. Some facts of her life are unclear during this period, though certain tragic events are known. She probably continued receiving support from John Wheatley, but he died in March of 1778. A month later Phillis married a free black, John Peters. He owned a small grocery, but, like many during the war years, he had built up debts and soon he was desperate for money. In September of 1778, Mary died, and with her passing, Phillis's last contact with the Wheatley family disappeared. Peters deserted Phillis for long periods of time and eventually was put into debtor's prison.

Phillis tried unsuccessfully to support herself and failed to get a second volume of her poetry published. Finally, she hired herself out as a scrubwoman. The work was hard and the pay poor. The Boston winters were bitterly cold and took their toll on her slight body. Phillis became ill and could not go out. With little food and no wood, she grew steadily weaker and finally died—alone and impoverished in 1784.

Before and after the American Revolution, Phillis Wheatley wrote poems of comfort and inspiration for people who had lost loved ones. Yet her poetry went beyond these ideas. How did they reflect the patriotic hope and spirit of her times? As you read this social studies lesson, find the main points to help you outline.

PHILLIS WHEATLEY: COLONIAL POET

CONTENT-AREA READING

Phillis Wheatley (c. 1753–1784) was the first black American poet to be published. She was brought from Africa to Boston in 1761 in a slave ship and sold to the Wheatley family. They taught her English, encouraged her to write, and even defended her when authorship of her poetry was disputed. The verses Phillis wrote often reflected the goal of the thirteen colonies to be free and independent from the British. It is not surprising that Wheatley, to whom freedom was denied in her early years, should express so well the spirit of colonial America.

During the 1760s the American colonies were protesting several taxation laws that England had enacted in the colonies which colonists felt were unjust. Then in 1766, the British Parliament repealed the Stamp Act, which had forced the colonists to buy stamps and put them on almost all printed materials—bills, legal papers, newspapers, and magazines. When the Stamp Act was repealed, the colonists rejoiced and for a few years the colonists' relations with England's King George improved.

In 1768 Wheatley wrote a poem in honor of King George, praising him as a beloved ruler, mainly because of his repeal of the Stamp Act nearly two years earlier. Notice in the last of the lines reprinted from the poem on the next page how Wheatley manages to get in the idea of freedom while honoring the king.

The Battle of Bunker Hill.

> May George, belov'd by all the nations round,
> Live with heav'ns choicest constant blessings
>   crown'd!
>
> . . . .
>
> And may each clime with equal gladness see
> A monarch's smile can set his subjects free!

In 1772, three years before the first major battle of the Revolutionary War at Bunker Hill in Boston, the king appointed the second Earl of Dartmouth to be Secretary of State for the colonies. Because Wheatley had great hopes that Dartmouth would be sympathetic to the colonists' cause, she composed a poem honoring the Earl. In the poem, from which the lines on the next page are taken, Wheatley expresses the origin of her love of freedom:

No more, America, in mournful strain
Of wrongs, and grievance unredress'd complain,
No longer shalt thou dread the iron chain,
Which wanton Tyranny with lawless hand
Had made, and with it meant t' enslave the land.
    Should you, my lord, while you peruse my song,
Wonder from whence my love of Freedom sprung,
Whence flow these wishes for the common good,
By feeling hearts alone best understood,
I, young in life, by seeming cruel fate
Was snatch'd from Afric's fancy'd happy seat:
What pangs excruciating must molest,
What sorrows labour in my parent's breast?
Steel'd was that soul and by no misery mov'd
That from a father seiz'd his babe belov'd:
Such, such my case. And can I then but pray
Others may never feel tyrannic sway?

In 1784, the year of her death, Wheatley issued two poems
in pamphlet form, having published only one other poem in the
last seven years of her life. One of the poems, "Liberty and
Peace," celebrated the American victory over England. In the
following patriotic lines, the conclusion of the poem, Wheatley
depicted a prosperous America (which she calls Columbia)
showing off its newly won freedom for all the world to see.

    From every Tongue celestial Peace resounds:
As for the East th' illustrious King of Day,
With rising Radiance drives the Shades away,
So Freedom comes array'd with Charms divine,
And in her Train Commerce and Plenty shine.
. . . .
Auspicious Heaven shall fill with fav'ring Gales,
Where e'er Columbia spreads her swelling Sails:
To every Realm shall Peace her Charms display,
And Heavenly Freedom spread her golden Ray.

Think and Discuss

1. What does Phillis Wheatley achieve and why is it remarkable?
2. Summarize the hardships that Phillis underwent in her closing years.
3. According to the social studies lesson, what is a recurring theme in Phillis's poetry?
• 4. Listed below are some categories under which Thomas Jefferson and Phillis Wheatley could be classified. List each of them under the correct category. You may list them under more than one.

   Patriot   Writer   Poet   Inventor

• 5. Look at the outline below and on page 359. Some of the outline has already been filled in. Use your answers to the questions below to help you complete the outline. Remember to use the information from both articles.
   a. What are two subtopics and one detail that tell about Phillis's early life?
   b. What is the main topic for II? What are two details about the poem honoring Dartmouth? What is the subtopic and a detail about a publishing event that happened between the writing of the poems to Dartmouth and Washington? What are two details about the poem to Washington?
   c. What is the main topic for III? What is a detail that tells about a difficulty Phillis encountered?

See your Thinker's Handbook for tips.

• Study Skills: Outlining and Classifying

Phillis Wheatley
   I. Early Years
      A.
      B. Bought by Susanna Wheatley
      C.
         1.
         2. Published first poem at age 13

II.

    A. Wrote poem to King George in 1768

    B. Wrote poem in memory of Whitefield

    C. Wrote poem honoring Dartmouth in 1772

        1.

        2.

    D. 1.

        2. Proved she was an author

    E. Wrote poem to General Washington in 1775

        1.

        2.

    F. Wrote poem to celebrate American victory

III.

    A. Encountered difficulties

        1.

        2. Married and deserted

        3. Published only 3 poems

    B. Died in 1784

Communication Workshop

Talk

    Discuss the nature of freedom with a small group. Talk about Phillis Wheatley, who wrote about freedom in a very personal way. Discuss what you have learned about Phyllis's life and the way in which these events contributed to her expressions about freedom. Do you think her words have any application today? How?

Speaking/Listening: Cooperative learning

Write

    Write a poem or a paragraph that describes what you think and feel about freedom. Your poem may or may not rhyme and it may be as long or short as you like. Read your poem to your group. Do they understand your feelings on freedom? What parts of your poem or paragraph do they particularly like?

Writing Fluency: Poem or Paragraph

As a young girl, Grace Murray Hopper was punished for taking apart seven clocks to see how the alarms worked. Yet such natural curiosity led her to become an American computer pioneer and to contribute two major computer inventions. As you read this article, use the graphic aids to help you understand more about computers.

Grace Hopper

AMERICAN COMPUTER PIONEER

by B. L. McGinnis

The clock in Grace Hopper's office at the Pentagon runs backwards, with the numbers painted in reverse order. It keeps perfect time, and Hopper's response to curious onlookers is a question: "Who said a clock has to run clockwise?"

Grace Hopper's grandfather was the senior civil engineer for New York City and she used to follow him around when he was surveying city streets. Hopper wanted to be an engineer, but in the late twenties and early thirties, when she attended college, there weren't any opportunities for women in the engineering field. Hopper did the next best thing and put her study of mathematics to work. After attending first Vassar, then Yale, she returned to Vassar as a professor of mathematics.

In 1943, while still a professor at Vassar, Hopper joined the Naval Reserve as a lieutenant junior grade. Thus she began her career in the navy. The following year, the navy assigned her to the Harvard team that designed the Mark I—the first all-purpose American computer.

While working on the Mark I, Hopper soon decided that there must be an easier way of feeding information into the computer than the codes that were being used at that time. Hopper was determined to change the way information was fed into a computer and she invented the first practical compiler. A compiler is a computer program or language that allows a user to feed a computer instructions in the English language, rather than in a code. The computer then changes the English instructions into a machine language that it can process. Hopper says that no one thought of such a compiler earlier because they weren't as lazy as she was.

Hopper continued to work with computers, and during the late fifties, she invented another computer language that was easier for humans to write and understand. This new computer language was called COBOL.[1] Today, COBOL is the most widely used business-computer language.

Hopper is not only well known for inventing computer programs or languages that have simplified the use of computers. She is also given credit for coining the term "bug" to describe something that makes a computer program malfunction. When her team was working on the Mark I, they traced a problem in the program to a two-inch moth caught in the circuitry. So, since 1945, a problem in the proper working of a computer program has been called a "bug."

When Hopper turned sixty, she retired from the navy. She says it was the saddest day of her life. Several months later, however, the navy realized they couldn't get along without her. They called her back to standardize the navy's computer programs and languages. During her short-lived retirement, the payroll program had been rewritten 823 times.

Now at age seventy-nine, Hopper is the navy's oldest officer on active duty, and that only by a special act of Congress. When Hopper came out of retirement, she was too old for a regular promotion, so Congress passed a special act that allowed the navy to raise Hopper's rank first to Captain, then later to Commodore.

---

1. COBOL, Common Business Oriented Language.

Though Hopper is officially assigned to the Naval Data Automation Command in Washington, D.C., she spends over three hundred days a year traveling and lecturing to students, business groups, and military personnel. She tells her audiences: "Get in, start learning, get as much computer time as you can."

Hopper delivers that message to her audiences because she has seen many changes in computers since the development of the Mark I, and she believes that future changes will be even more rapid. The Mark I was a huge computer. It was nearly 58 feet long, 8 feet high, and had close to a million parts. In the mid-1940s when it was designed, it was thought to be the most advanced computer available because it could add three numbers a second. Today's microchip computers can do the same addition in a nanosecond, or a billionth of a second.

This line graph illustrates the rapid changes in computer technology over the last forty years.

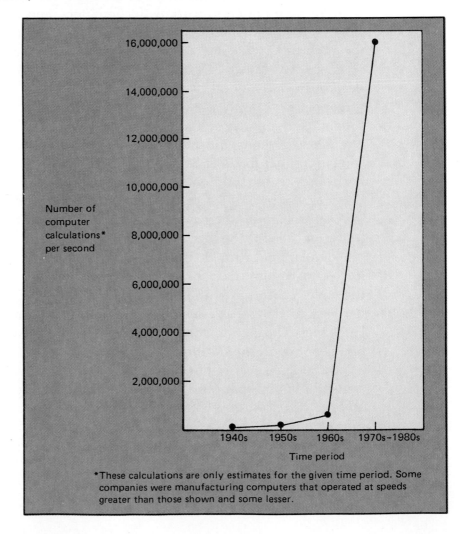

When Hopper lectures, she hands out samples of nanoseconds. She says, "I didn't know what a billion is. So how could I know what a billionth is? I'm an extremely annoying employee because I won't do anything until I understand it. I could see a second go by, but darned if I could see a billionth of a second. I asked them to please cut off a nanosecond and send one over." What Hopper hands out is 11.8 inches of copper wire—the maximum length electricity can travel in a billionth of a second.

To further demonstrate to her audiences the advances in computer design and efficiency, Hopper will show them a thick yellow coil 984 feet long, which is the distance electricity can travel in a millionth of a second or a microsecond.

To get home her message about the rapid changes in computer capabilities, Hopper points out that even the computers that measure speed in nanoseconds will eventually be outdated. Tomorrow's computers will be driven by light, not electricity. The new computers will help make long-range weather predictions to aid farmers in growing enough food to support the rapidly expanding world population. They will also aid in managing our shrinking water resources.

This chart projects what putting more power on computer chips will mean by the dawn of the twenty-first century.

WHAT PACKING MORE POWER ON A CHIP WILL BRING

	1980	1985	1987	1990	1995
CIRCUIT SIZE:	4 MICRONS	2 MICRONS	1 MICRON	0.5 MICRON	0.25 MICRON
MEMORY CAPACITY:	64K	256K	1,024K	4,096K	16,384K
POWER RANGE:	DESKTOP MICROCOMPUTER	MINICOMPUTER	MAINFRAME COMPUTER	SUPERCOMPUTER	ULTRACOMPUTER
APPLICATIONS:	DIGITAL WATCHES, VIDEO GAMES, PERSONAL COMPUTERS	LAP COMPUTERS, ENGINEERING WORK STATIONS, PROGRAMMABLE APPLIANCES	POCKET COMPUTERS, ELECTRONIC MAP-NAVIGATORS, HIGH-RESOLUTION TVs	ROBOTS THAT CAN SEE, FREEZE-FRAME TVs, COMPUTERS THAT RECOGNIZE AND USE NATURAL LANGUAGES	STAR WARS SYSTEMS, PERSONAL ROBOTS, COMPUTERS WITH HUMAN-LIKE LOGIC

DATA: BW

Anyone who listens to Hopper soon knows that she thinks the computer is a wonderful tool. When questioned about problems created by computers, Hopper replies, "A computer can't do anything somebody doesn't tell it to do." If your report card or standardized test score is incorrect, don't blame the computer. In short, computers are only as good as the people using—or misusing—them. Hopper likes to point to Apollo 13 as an example of the relationship between people and computers. Apollo 13 was sent into space in 1970 to land on the moon. It never arrived because of an explosion that destroyed the electricity and oxygen supply lines. According to Hopper, Apollo 13 would never have made it back to Earth, despite all the computers on board, if people had not been on board to make the decisions and pilot the craft back safely.

The following list illustrates the wide and varying uses of home computers. The list shows the different uses and percentage of home-computer owners surveyed who said that they used their computers for a particular task (owners were able to give multiple responses). By reading this information you will have a better understanding of the need for computer programs and languages that are easy to read and understand.

Leading Uses of Home Computers

Video games	51%
Business or office homework	46
Child's learning tool	46
Adult's learning tool	42
Balancing checkbook or budget	37
Business-in-home uses	27
Word-processing	18
Mailing lists	16
Information retrieval[*]	14
Appointment calendar	9
Storing recipes	9
Calorie counting	4

[*] Includes information on investing, travel, and account balances as used in paying bills by phone.

What Hopper does worry about is keeping computer records private. She will mention the case four years ago when students at New York's Dalton School tapped into computer systems belonging to several Canadian companies and universities.

Another concern of Hopper's is computer phobia, or fear of computers. She remembers when the telephone was first brought out and people were afraid to use it because they thought they might be electrocuted. Hopper sees the same type of fear toward computers. During an interview, she asked a photographer if his camera had a computer in it. He replied, "Yes, but I don't use it." Hopper says that's the trouble. People are afraid of change—afraid of trying something new.

The parts of a floppy disk. Information is stored on the diskette surface.

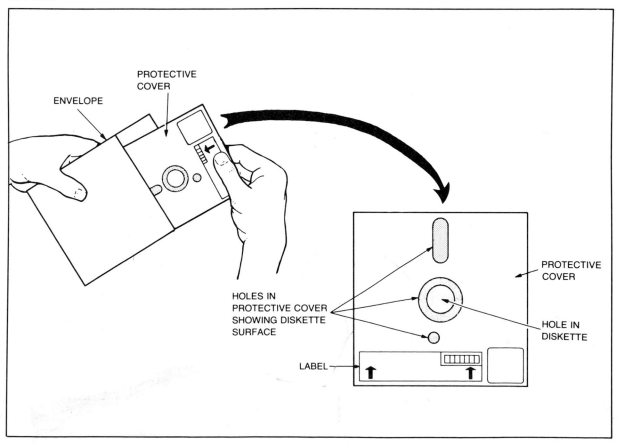

Hopper believes that the future of computers lies with young people because they are not afraid of change or of new technology. Today's preschoolers play with educational computers and think of them as little black boxes with a friend inside. "Young people are our greatest natural resource," proclaims Hopper. "They will ask all the questions in the future."

The special act of Congress that brought her out of retirement expired in the summer of 1985, ending Hopper's forty-two year naval career. "I've loved every minute of it," says Hopper. "I've received the highest award anybody can give me, and that is the privilege and the honor of serving proudly in the United States Navy."

Hopper ended her career as a celebrity. Her many years with the navy and her contributions to the computer field gained the attention of a national news program. Hopper was interviewed on national television, and now people stop her at airports. Hopper says she never intended to be a celebrity—she feels she was very lucky the navy ordered her to work on that first computer over forty years ago.

Meet a Reader

One reader of this article is Steve Kuppenheimer, age thirteen, of Illinois. Steve says, "I liked this article. It shows how Grace Hopper contributed to the development of computers and the many uses of computers. I wasn't surprised that it was an older woman who invented COBOL because good ideas can come from all people—men, women, or young people. I was surprised to learn the size of the Mark I and the amount of calculations possible today. At my junior high school, we have special computer classes where we learn about word processing and programming. Right now, I like using computers for games and reports. I hope that all students will have a chance to learn about computers because computers can help you think and are critical for the future."

In addition to Steve's interest in computers, he also likes to play baseball and soccer and to read. His favorite books are *The Hobbit* and the trilogy, *The Lord of the Rings,* by J. R. R. Tolkien.

Think and Discuss

1. What two things did Grace Hopper invent for computers?
2. Why does Hopper show her audiences samples of microseconds and nanoseconds?
3. What do you think is Hopper's greatest concern about computers? Why?
• 4. After reading the line graph on page 362, what conclusion can you draw about the change in how fast computers work?
• 5. Use the information in the list on page 364 to answer the following questions:
   a. What is the biggest use of home computers?
   b. What percentage of home computers is used as a child's learning tool?
6. What would you like to use a computer for? Why?
• Study Skills: Graphic aids

Communication Workshop

Talk

Work with a partner to discuss Grace Hopper's character. Give examples to illustrate her manner of never accepting things as they are but looking for new and better ways of doing them. What do you think she meant by her motto "A ship in port is safe. But that is not what ships are built for."
Speaking/Listening: Discussion

Write

Write Grace Hopper's motto and give an explanation of what it means. Or, think of a different motto for Grace Hopper and explain why you think it describes her. Read your new motto to your partner. Does he or she agree that it fits Grace Hopper? Why or why not?
Writing Fluency: Motto

Computer Terms

Many computer terms may sound very technical. The terms below do not sound very technical at all—in fact, they're kind of fun. What do these terms mean? Read to find out. (The terms were printed by a computer, so you'll be reading about them in the same form that you would see if you used a computer and a printer.)

BASIC An easy-to-learn computer language (Beginner's All-purpose Symbolic Instruction Code).

Bit A single digit in the binary system of numbering, which uses only the two digits, 0 and 1.

Byte Four bits. When you read that a computer has an 18K memory, that means it can hold 18,000 bytes.

Chip A very small piece of silicon that carries electronic circuits.

Floppy disk A soft, coated disk used to store information mechanically.

GIGO (Garbage in/Garbage out) Errors entered by the user that result in false answers.

Hardware The physical equipment that makes up the computer system.

Interpreter A chip that turns BASIC words into computer numbers.

RAM Chips that can memorize instructions and can be changed (Random-Access Memory).

ROM Chips that can store information and cannot be changed (Read-only Memory).

Tape drive A piece of equipment on which information to be worked on by the processor is stored, recorded on magnetic tape.

How to Read Word Problems in Mathematics

Imagine that your school has a new computer and your class wants to buy some disks. A set of 10 double-sided disks costs $25.00. To earn the money, your class sold 100 team buttons at the football games. Your class paid 5¢ each for the buttons and sold them for 25¢ each. How much money did your class earn?

The paragraph above is an example of a math word problem. You need to read word problems in a different way than you read stories or articles. Use the following tips to help you:

- Read the problem carefully. Ask, "What is the question?"
- Decide how to solve the problem. Ask, "What should I do first?"
- Solve the problem.
- Answer the question. Then reread the question and ask, "Does my answer make sense?"

Use these tips to solve the math word problem.

- Read   Reread the problem in the first paragraph. What is the question? The question is, "How much money did your class earn for the disks?"

- Decide

Price Your Class Sold Buttons for	−	Price Your Class Paid for Buttons	=	How Much Money Class Earned

- Solve

100×25¢	$- \; 100 \times 5$¢	$= x$
($25.00)	− ($5.00)	= $20.00

- Answer   Your class earned $20.00.

How much money does your class need to buy 10 disks? How many buttons would your class have to sell to earn enough money?

Jenny arrived in America excited and eager to meet her grandmother Smith—but things were not exciting at all—they were difficult. Mrs. Smith resented the fact that Jenny's father had married a Japanese woman and settled in Japan and that her other son was killed during World War II in the war against Japan. Will Jenny and her grandmother be able to change their relationship? As you read, think about their goals to help you summarize this modern realistic story.

Jenny Kimura Smith Meets Grandy

by Betty Cavanna

Jenny stirred in the strange bed. Very slowly she awakened to a consciousness that this was not Tokyo. This was Kansas City, U.S.A.

Fatigue had blurred her mind last night. She had transient memories of a fast taxi ride through empty city streets, of a carpeted hall and curving stairs in a house that seemed more like a hotel than a home, and of a woman who had wept—then greeted her with solicitude.

Jenny got dressed and went downstairs. She encountered her grandmother coming in from the terrace wearing Bermuda shorts, a sleeveless shirt, and gardening gloves.

"Hello, dear!" Mrs. Smith called with quick gaiety. "I'm so glad you slept late. Never have I seen such a tired child!" There was something about the use of the word *child* that disturbed Jenny. Or was it that the greeting was so casual—almost too casual, considering that she had just flown halfway across the world?

An orange-and-white cat appeared in the hall. "This is Freddy," Jenny's grandmother explained, as she bent to pick the animal up. "Freddy is a member of the family."

"Hello, Freddy." Jenny moved forward to stroke the cat's head, but her grandmother was hurrying on.

"You must be hungry. Come, I'll give you some breakfast. Let's take it out on the terrace, and you can watch while I prune the shrubs," she said.

This corroborated Jenny's first impression that her grandmother was a person of great vigor. She was always doing something. She worked in the garden and seemed to enjoy it, although she came back into the house with her hair tousled, her arms scratched, and her forehead beaded with perspiration.

When Jenny finished breakfast, her grandmother said, "Now come and see the pool. It's just off the terrace."

"Do you swim?" Jenny asked in astonishment.

"Of course," said her grandmother, as though this were a very peculiar question. "I usually go in for a dip before breakfast. You must join me—any time you like."

"I'm sorry," said Jenny, feeling rather inadequate, "but I don't know how to swim."

"You don't know—?" Her grandmother swung around, obviously appalled. "What have you been doing all your life?"

Jenny gulped, but took the question seriously. "Living in Tokyo," she replied. "Going to school." She added, "Playing tennis sometimes."

Her grandmother seemed to recover. "You do play tennis then. Well, that's good. I'll teach you how to swim," she promised.

One thing struck Jenny as odd, a habit her grandmother had of quickly sliding her eyes away whenever their glances met. She would examine her granddaughter quickly, but her eyes never lingered in affection, as the eyes of Jenny's parents did. "But of course we're strangers, really; it will take time to get to know one another," Jenny thought. "Daddy warned me that things might be awkward at first."

What exactly had he said? That his mother was a woman of high principles and strong prejudices. "Just be yourself and she'll grow to love you, but it may take a while."

Love was a word Jenny couldn't yet associate with her American grandmother. Jenny had expected all sorts of preliminaries— questions about her father, some mention at least of her mother, inquiries about her school. She had anticipated a gradual building up of an acquaintanceship, but apparently all that was to be skipped.

As the day wore on, Jenny found herself trotting at her grandmother's heels, trying to find out what was expected of her. It was a distinct relief when Mrs. Smith announced after lunch that she must attend an important committee meeting, but would be back about five.

Going up to her room, Jenny sank down into a chair and took stock of the situation. Mrs. Smith apparently spent a great deal of time away from the house. She was vice-president of her garden club, a hospital Gray Lady—whatever that might be!—and a committee member of all sorts of charities.

Some of this information Jenny Kimura had gleaned from bits and pieces of overheard telephone calls. Indeed, the phone seemed to ring almost constantly during the late morning hours, and her grandmother kept turning the pages of an engagement book with one hand while she held the receiver in the other, making now a commitment, then an excuse. "My granddaughter has just arrived, you see."

"Don't worry about me," Jenny was impelled to say. "I'll be all right."

"Of course you will, dear," her grandmother had answered. "But I want to see you get acquainted first." Not "we" get acquainted? Shouldn't that be the first consideration?

Perhaps there were things that she should do, Jenny thought, gestures she must make. First of all, the presentation of gifts. She felt that this might be done most appropriately at the evening meal. So at dinner time, refreshed from the promised dip in the pool and the discovery that it was quite easy to stay afloat, she came downstairs bearing an armful of beautifully wrapped packages.

After dinner, Jenny presented them ceremoniously. "These are sent by my mother and father with deep affection and many thanks for your kindness to me." Then she knelt by her grandmother's chair while Mrs. Smith exclaimed in delight at the beautiful Imari bowl, expressed surprise at the compactness of a pocket-size transistor radio, and admired the luster of the pearls her son had chosen.

"Now she'll ask about my father, now we'll start getting acquainted," thought Jenny. But instead her grandmother suddenly straightened her back and said with unexpected briskness, "I've asked some children over to meet you on Saturday night—for a cookout by the pool."

Was this her grandmother's return gift? Jenny wondered, uncertain of American customs. "That will be very nice," she said politely. "A cookout means hamburgers? I do like American hamburgers! Daddy sometimes makes them for Saturday lunch."

"Hamburgers and hot dogs," murmured Mrs. Smith absently, as she let the pearls trickle back into the little silk envelope in which they had arrived. Freddy came into the room and, seeing his mistress occupied, leaped into Jenny's lap.

"I think he likes me," Jenny said, and suddenly there was a lump in her throat and she felt very, very far away from home and her parents and the familiar house in which she had been raised. Trying to conquer the emotion, Jenny sat looking down at the cat, pride coming too slowly to her aid. She began to perceive how much her grandmother resented her father's marriage. Then why had the invitation to visit been extended, and why had Daddy allowed her to accept? When he must have realized—he must have known!

She felt betrayed—by her father, who expected so much of her and by her grandmother, whose heartiness too lightly cloaked a deep resentment from which she had never recovered. Jenny wished she could call on some magic to whisk her straight back home where she was loved and cherished.

Jenny calmed herself. Her father would expect it of her. At this thought, Jenny realized that her father hadn't betrayed her, really. He'd tried to forewarn her. And he'd said, quite clearly, that it wouldn't be easy. She couldn't be a quitter; she'd just have to do her best.

So it was with outward poise, the smooth, impenetrable good manners she had learned from her mother, that Jenny behaved warmly toward her grandmother.

In spite of all of her efforts, Jenny did not overcome her grandmother's resentment of her. Toward the end of the summer, Mrs. Smith took Jenny and her other grandchild, Dick Smith, to Cape Cod, Massachusetts. It was Dick's father who had been killed in the war. Through Dick's eyes, Jenny was now to discover something new about her grandmother.

Dick took Jenny bicycling, escorted her to the summer theater, and spent long hours on the beach just talking with her. Jenny began to feel that Dick was a person of considerable depth. He felt a deep responsibility for his grandmother, which Jenny didn't quite understand.

She questioned him about it one morning when he seemed especially restless. "Have you enjoyed coming here with Grandmother, summer after summer?"

"Not really. I get a lot of reading done, but I feel useless as though I should be working," Dick admitted. "Next year I want to go abroad, but I scarcely know how to tell her. Since my grandfather died, I'm the only one she has left."

"Our grandfather," Jenny corrected gently. "I've seen his picture. He looks as though he must have been a wonderfully vigorous old man."

"Oh, he was!" Dick said. "And he wasn't half as pigheaded as Grandy—about your father, I mean."

"I wonder," Jenny murmured. "I suppose inviting me here was a great concession. She still seems to resent me."

"Anyway," continued Dick, "Grandy has taken one big step forward, and—who knows—maybe she'll take another someday."

"Be friendly with Daddy, you mean?"

Dick nodded. "I was born after my father left for the Pacific," Dick said. "He never even saw me. I guess it was pretty tough for Mom, as well as for my—*our* grandmother."

Jenny nodded. "My Japanese grandparents were also very unhappy that my mother married an American," she said.

"They were? Why?"

"In their village they are looked down upon because they have a foreign son-in-law. They wouldn't attend the wedding, and my

parents have never had a single meal in my Japanese grandparents' house."

"You're kidding!" breathed Dick, in such amazement that Jenny could tell this was an idea so strange that it was utterly baffling.

"It makes my mother very sad," Jenny continued. "Once a year on New Year's Day we always go to the village to pay our respects. When we leave, Mother always cries a little, because her parents remain so stern and unyielding, even after all these years."

"What's wrong with the Smiths?" Dick asked so pugnaciously that Jenny burst out laughing.

"Suppose I ask Grandmother, 'What's wrong with the Kimuras?' There isn't any answer to a question like that."

Dick gave a long sigh and scratched his head ruefully. "It beats me," he said. "It really does." Then, as though he was tired of wasting time on an insoluble problem, he said abruptly, "I heard Mother talking to you about coming back to the States for college. You ought to consider it seriously, Jenny. Then you could spend holidays with Grandy. She *needs* you, actually."

But Jenny shook her head. "I think Grandmother is very self-sufficient. I don't think she needs anyone."

"That's where you're wrong," objected Dick immediately. "She just gives that impression. At heart Grandy's an old softie, and if she could only bring herself to it, a reunion with your dad would be the greatest thing ever. She needs him too."

Need. It was a word that Jenny would never have associated with her grandmother. Thinking about it later, she tried to imagine what urgent need could not be satisfied, and only then did she fully realize Dick's meaning. Her grandmother needed the love of her family—of her own son and her two grandchildren. She had Dick's affection, certainly, but one out of three was not enough.

Some days later Jenny, wearing a life belt, almost drowned in a water-skiing accident. While skiing, Jenny had seen her grandmother enter the beach and had taken one hand off the tow rope to wave to Mrs. Smith. Then Jenny fell into the water. Forgetting that she should let go of the rope anytime she fell, Jenny clung to the tow rope. She was dragged by the boat until her lungs were full of water. When Jenny finally let go of the tow rope, she could not breathe.

"A miracle," her grandmother said. "Jenny's rescue has been a miracle." Out of the nausea and pain of returning to consciousness, Jenny could remember only this one word. How long they had worked over her on the beach, giving her artificial respiration, Jenny would never know. Mercifully, yesterday was no more than a bad dream, and today, the doctor had ordered, she must remain in bed.

"Jenny? Jenny, dear, are you awake?" Mrs. Smith's voice was hushed, her expression still full of concern as she came toward the bed with a breakfast tray. "I've brought you a glass of orange juice, and some toast and milk."

"Thank you, Grandmother," she murmured.

Mrs. Smith continued to fuss around Jenny's bedroom for several minutes, tucking odds and ends into bureau drawers, adjusting the blinds, bringing a chair close to the bed. She took the breakfast tray away, brought a glass of water and a damp washcloth from the bathroom, and began gently bathing her granddaughter's face.

Such ministrations seemed so unnatural that Jenny Kimura smiled again, humor quickening in her eyes. "You don't have to wait on me, Grandmother. I'll be all right." Then, quite without meaning to, she slid down into her pillowed nest once more and fell asleep.

When she awakened the next time, Jenny felt considerably more alert. Once again her grandmother was hovering about, looking anxious. "Hi," Jenny said.

"It's almost noon," her grandmother responded. "Do you want some lunch?"

"Oh yes!" Jenny pulled herself straight up in bed, started to push her hair back from her face, and said, "Ugh! It's full of salt water."

"So were you," her grandmother replied tartly, then smiled.

Jenny nodded. "I ought to apologize," she said after a moment. "I saw you coming down the steps to the beach, and I was waving when—"

"You don't have to tell me. I know the rest."

"I'm terribly sorry." Weakness made Jenny's eyes fill with tears.

"Sorry? You should be glad! As glad as I am. You had a close call. I didn't think you'd make it," she confessed. "For nearly an hour I didn't think you'd make it, and I promised myself, if you pulled through, that I'd try to be a bigger person—a better grandmother."

"But you're a wonderful grandmother!" Jenny said. She stretched out a hand. "And you've given me a wonderful summer."

"A summer to remember perhaps. But wonderful?" Mrs. Smith shook her head. "I've been a bitter old woman, Jenny, but you've made me love you. Please believe that."

"And I love you too," said Jenny.

Tears stood, unshed, in Mrs. Smith's eyes. "I remember a letter you sent me," she said, "a month before you came. You had no idea what you were biting off, Jenny, what you'd have to learn to chew. And you wrote, with the most complete innocence, 'My heart is already in your home.' "

Jenny didn't speak, because she didn't quite understand.

"I'm just being overly sentimental," Jenny's grandmother said gruffly. "It's not like me. It's more like your father. Is he still very put out with my attitude, or do you think he'd listen to reason and let bygones be bygones?"

Jenny could scarcely believe her ears. "I think he misses you terribly," she whispered. Then she added, "Oh, Grandy, you'd adore my mother! Truly you would!"

The tears in Mrs. Smith's eyes suddenly overflowed, and she reached for a tissue in the box on the bedside table.

"I'm sorry. I didn't mean—"

"Foolish!" snorted Mrs. Smith, getting up abruptly and blowing her nose. "It's just that you've never called me Grandy before."

"I won't if—"

"Nonsense. I like it. After all, you're just as much my grandchild as Dick is!"

Late that night a full moon rode over the ocean. Jenny, who had slept too much during the day, could not sleep now. "Will I come back to the United States to attend college?" Jenny wondered. Her heart leaped at the very idea.

Think and Discuss

1. Compare the relationship between Jenny and Grandy at the beginning and end of the story.
2. How does Jenny feel when her grandmother doesn't ask about Jenny's father after Jenny presents the gifts?
3. What conclusion does Jenny come to about how she should behave toward her grandmother?
4. Both of the following themes fit this story. Which do you like better and why?
   a. Seeing a situation through someone else's eyes will help you understand things more clearly.
   b. Prejudice can cause much personal pain and suffering.
 • 5. Think about Jenny's and Grandy's goals and summarize the story.
 • Comprehension Skill: Summarizing

Communication Workshop

Talk

Work with a partner to discuss the difficulty Jenny had in establishing a close relationship with her grandmother. Talk about how their relationship changed. Imagine that Jenny decides to write to her father about the new closeness between her and Grandy. Take turns playing Jenny and her father. What would each one say to the other?
Speaking/Listening: Role-playing

Write

Pretend you are Jenny. Write a letter to your father and tell him about the closeness you and Grandy now share. Be sure to mention Jenny's thoughts about college. Will she return to America to go to school? Read your letter to your partner and listen to hers or his.
Writing Fluency: Friendly letter

LOOKING BACK

Thinking and Writing About the Section

In this section you have read about famous and ordinary Americans. You can write two paragraphs to explain how two of them are alike and different to share with your social studies class. For instance, in a paragraph of comparison, you might mention that they are Americans. In a paragraph of contrast, you might show that Jefferson and Hopper lived in different times. First copy the chart below. Then fill in the missing information.

See your Thinker's Handbook for tips.

People	Jenny Kimura Smith	Phillis Wheatley	Grace Hopper
Comparisons	ordinary American	American patriot wrote poems about freedom	American
Contrasts		poet	inventor

Writing

Now write two paragraphs. One should explain how two of the people are alike. The other should explain how they are different. Use details from your chart and special comparison and contrast words such as *similarities* and *unlike*. For more information on explanatory paragraphs, see your Writer's Handbook.

Revising

Read your first draft to a partner. Does each paragraph have a topic sentence? Have you shown how the people were alike and different? Have you used words that signal likenesses and differences? Make changes if necessary. Then proofread for spelling and punctuation errors. Write your final copy.

Presenting

Read your paragraph to your social studies class. Ask them to listen to find out how the people are similar or different.

FLYING AND SOMERSAULTING THROUGH THE AIR.

Taking a Chance

Do you take chances? Can you picture yourself somersaulting through the air or taking part in a mad race like the Sisters La Rague?

In Section Nine, you'll meet characters who would probably answer *yes* to these questions, for these characters take chances. One boy takes a chance that tests his opinion of himself. A girl risks losing a race that has important consequences, and another boy takes a chance that could save—or end—his life. Still another character takes a chance on love. Not all their results are successful. Yet none of these characters will have to say "I didn't try."

Recognizing Types of Literature

Meet three girls quite different from one another. Each one is preparing to eat her supper. The one at the top is Tanya-Z who lives in the year 2070. Tanya-Z has just entered her height, weight, and age into the "Nutritional Computer System," which in turn has issued her an entire meal—within one capsule. The girl in the middle, Rachel, is a Pilgrim who lives in the year 1683. She's going to eat soup that she has prepared over a fire. The one at the bottom is Jessica. She lives today, and hamburgers are her favorite meal. Which girl would you like to read about most?

You would read about each girl in a different type of fictional story. As you may recall, **fiction** is made up, or imagined. Tanya-Z could be a character in a **science**-fiction story. Rachel could appear in **historical** fiction. And Jessica could be in a story of **modern realistic** fiction.

Let's take a look at the three different types of fiction to learn more about them.

Science fiction is a story that includes both scientific fact and fantastic ideas. Science-fiction stories often tell about life in the future and they often occur in space.

Historical fiction is a story based on historical facts although the story itself is fiction. It tells what real life was like in the past. Historical fiction usually contains real descriptions of the clothes that people wore, what the homes were like, and the standard way of life. However, most events, dialogue, and characters are made up by the author.

Modern realistic fiction is a story about things that could happen in the present. The characters, events, and places are all true-to-life in our present time.

When you read a story, it helps to identify what kind of fiction it is. Then you have a basic groundwork for understanding the characters and events. **Setting** is the biggest clue for identifying what type of fiction a story is. Remember that setting is the time and place a story occurs.

1. Turn back to pages 370–379 and skim the story, "Jenny Kimura Smith Meets Grandy." What type of literature is the story? How do you know?

Did you answer that the story is modern realistic fiction? If not, notice the details that show how Jenny and Grandy act like true-to-life people do today.

2. Go back to pages 330–338 and skim the story, "The Samaritan." What type of literature is the story? How do you know?

"The Samaritan" is a science-fiction story. Is that what you answered? Notice that the first paragraph identifies outer space as the setting of the story. It also has examples of things that could not happen today such as the crew being in "suspended animation."

3. Skim the story, "The Worst Thanksgiving in the Entire History of the Universe," beginning on page 47. What type of fiction is it? How can you tell?

Practicing Types of Literature

Skim these two stories in order to determine what kind of fiction each one is: "Philip Hall Likes Me, I Reckon Maybe" (pages 122–133) and "Hearts and Hands" (pages 268–270).

1. What type of fiction is "Philip Hall Likes Me, I Reckon Maybe"? How can you tell?
2. What kind of fiction is "Hearts and Hands"? Why?
3. What type of fiction did neither of the above stories represent? How do you know?

Tips for Reading on Your Own
- Look for clues about the setting to help you identify what type of fiction a story is.
- Notice if the story is based on science, on history, or on present-day reality.

Twelve-year-old John Sumner has cerebral palsy, a disorder which causes lack of muscle control. Until today, John has lived in two worlds—a fantasy world in which he can do anything, and the real world that is full of "don'ts" and "can'ts." Now, left all alone for the first time in his life, John Sumner struggles with whether he should take a daring chance and test his own dreams. He seeks to prove to his parents (and, more important, to himself) that he can do something he has never done before—except in his imagination. As you read about John's struggle, decide what type of literature this story is.

Let the Balloon Go

by Ivan Southall

John Clement Sumner stood on the open driveway looking up at branches and leaves and sky, with his blood running wild, and with that busy little car of Mum's completely gone, bustling far away through the hills down to Melbourne.[1] For this one day he had waited all his life. Every day lived had been counted simply as one more along the road to this one. Oh, it was fierce; it was crazy.

He would run like the wind, he would leap and dance, he would cartwheel and swing from trees. All these things he would do because there was no one to tell him that he could not do them, no shrill voice; "John, get down from there!" "John, walk, don't run!" Mum's voice, Dad's voice, every blooming voice a fellow ever heard.

They were wrong, all of them but one.

He could do anything that any boy could do: kick a football, hit a cricket ball out of sight, swim a hundred yards, dive into deep water, dig a dirty great hole, fight fist and tooth and claw, climb a tree, sit on the topmost branch and shriek at the sky.

---

1. Melbourne (məl'bərn), seaport in SE Australia.

It was only the look in their eyes and the things they said that stopped him. He couldn't do them because he never tried, because they frightened him with looks and words, because they said, "You mustn't. No, John. Don't."

An operation wasn't going to make any difference. Someone had said that once, in a roundabout way: some unknown, gentle-eyed man who had spoken to him on a city street.

John had been standing there trembling, trying to fight off the shakes, waiting for Mum who never seemed to be coming. The man's head had come down, his eyes had come down, and then his voice like a quiet fire: "You'll do it, son. Don't let anything stop you from being the boy you want to be. The answer's inside you. A balloon is not a balloon until you cut the string and let it go."

"Aw h-heck," John said now, "I'd b-b-better do that blooming old model."

Then the explosion came. Bang.

He felt like a billion bits blasting off in all directions. "I'm not goin' back inside; I'm not."

He didn't know that his hand was beating his thigh, that he was stammering aloud.

"I'm going to do what I want to do. I'll—I'll climb a tree. That's what I'll do."

The idea shocked him. It came so suddenly it could have dropped from the morning sky.

John turned to run, but stumbled, and fell bewildered on the coarse gravel of the driveway.

He lay there stinging for several seconds before he moved (hurt more inside than outside), then discovered that he was trembling all over. "Oh, golly," he moaned, and shifted awkwardly to the grassy bank below the fence. There, after a few tries, he managed with a shaking hand to dislodge the pieces of gravel that stuck to him. There was not much blood but he had skinned his knee-cap and grazed an elbow.

"It's not fair. Other kids don't fall."

Little by little he straightened his legs and tried to relax before the stupid old shakes had a chance to set in properly. He had got himself too excited; the grown-ups were always telling him not to, but what did they know about it? It was like telling a tree not to grow or a seed not to send up a shoot.

John pleaded with the shakes to go away. "Not today. Please."

"I'm not going inside," he announced to the treetops. "No fear. I'm not dead yet, not on your life."

He strode round the side of the house with increasing confidence (it was terrific), then strode back again calling the beat: "Left, right, left, right. Lift your feet there."

He crossed the front of the house, then marched cockily down the far side. "At the double now. One two, one two."

It was marvelous; he pranced with his knees lifting high, then stopped at the foot of a peppermint gum, a tree thirty years old, huge, graceful, with the first branch fifteen feet from the ground; the sort of tree that every boy and girl wanted to climb.

"If only I *could*."

He looked up, and up, and up. From way up there, seventy feet, eighty feet up, he'd see for a mile. He'd look down on to roads and gardens and unsuspecting people who would never dream that John Clement Sumner was way up there. He couldn't do it, could he?

"No . . ."

The first branch was only twelve feet from the ground; it wasn't fifteen feet at all.

With a bit of luck he could chuck a rope and loop it over the bough. Then he could shin up, hand over hand. He shivered. Other boys could do it. Girls could climb. Even babies could climb.

There was a house in the sky up there. There was a flagpole; a ship with a tall mast. A lighthouse. There was a tower. A chimney stack. There was a whole new world up there.

He'd say, "Hi-ya, bird. Hi-ya, cloud. Hi-ya, Mr. Sun." Any kid worth his salt could shin up a rope with his eyes shut.

But there wasn't a rope in the shed or behind the fowl-house or in the laundry or even under the back verandah, where in moments of crisis things had been known to be pushed out of sight. Rope was like rusty nails and old paint tins, and broken window-glass; other people always had it lying around. But Dad wasn't other people. Dad was so neat and tidy it was enough to drive a fellow nuts. It was *infuriating*.

It was a beaut word that; infuriating! But it would be horribly hard to say out loud.

Of course he had known all along he wouldn't find any rope. He had known he wouldn't be able to toss it up to the branch anyway. And if he did manage to toss it up, how was he to tie it so it wouldn't slip? It wouldn't stop there just because he wanted it to. The whole idea was stupid from the start. Whoever heard of a little spastic kid like John Clement Sumner sittin' up a gum-tree?

There was always the garden hose, but how could a fellow lift it twelve feet into the air and loop it over the bough?

Twelve feet? Fifteen feet if it was an inch.

There was always the ladder on a rack under the back verandah. Dad pulled it out every June when he scraped the dead leaves out of the gutters and cleaned the chimneys. It was a long ladder. It was a strong ladder. It was older than John himself, but still looked like new. It was painted red at the tips and the rest of it was varnished all over.

John got his hands on the ladder and started dragging it out. It weighed about a ton and he had to heave like mad. It came out from under the house.

How would he ever push it in again? The thought hit him just as the far end teetered over the edge of the rack, pivoted sharply from his grasp, and whacked with a splitting sound to the ground.

He froze with eyes shut and fists clenched, hoping for the ladder to say, "I remain sound in wind and limb. What are you in a fizz about?" But the ladder said nothing so John had to look for himself. There lay all fourteen feet of it prostrate on the grass, bruised a bit perhaps, aching a bit perhaps, but with not a break in sight.

He walked in a circle, then stopped in his stride and regarded first the tree, then the ladder and finally the rack under the verandah.

"It's a certain thing if I *can* get it up to the tree, liftin' it back on the rack'll be a pushover."

So he dragged it across the lawn and placed the top rung against the bottom of the trunk, round the far side where no one could see it from the house, then looked up, and up, and up.

He heaved the ladder up a couple of feet and jammed the top rung against the tree, leant on it, and panted.

He heaved again. It was a surf boat and the engine wouldn't work and he had to row like crazy to get out to the rocks before Mamie[1] was swept to sea.

"Heave!"

Maybe the ladder had arms like an octopus because somehow or other it was on top of him and he was underneath it and seas were breaking everywhere and that bloomin' tree was pushing the wrong way like something that wanted to fall down.

He flopped on his back among the fallen leaves, his chest heaving, sweat breaking out of him.

But the ladder still leant against the trunk and the top rung must have been seven or eight feet up. It was well on the way. Not real bad after all.

_____

1. Mamie, the real Mamie is a neighbor girl whom John likes a lot.

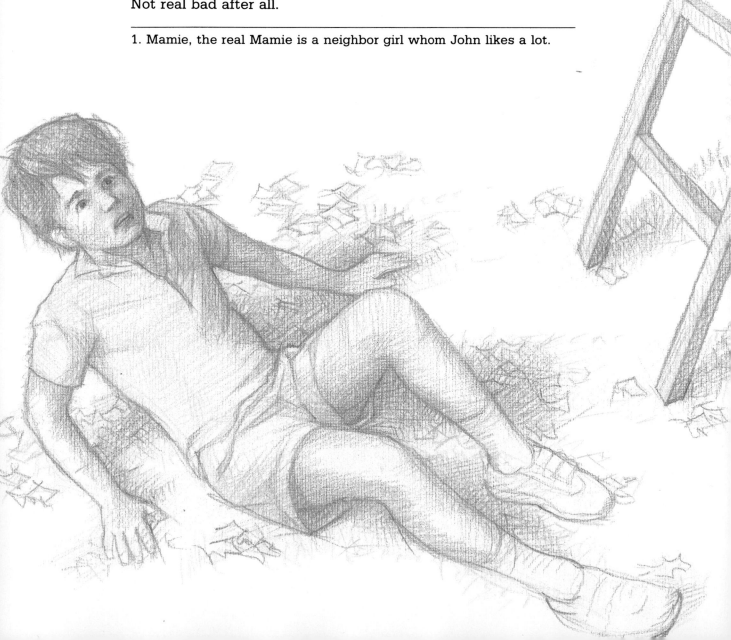

"Hang on, Mamie," he said, "I'm still coming."

He had the shakes in the knees but they were a different sort of shakes. He lurched the ladder up another couple of feet, inches at a time, but it was getting heavier and heavier and harder to manage. It was harder than rowing any silly old surf boat. Mamie was now in a tower waving a white handkerchief. "Help. Help."

"Mamie van Senden, you got yourself into it; you get yourself out of it. You'll have to jump. I can't get way up there."

He sank back to the ground at the foot of the ladder, hot and shaking, with sweat in his eyes.

After a while he went into the house, drank two glasses of water, raided the biscuit barrel, and sat outside on the verandah steps feeling lost and tearful.

Kids were having a rough-house somewhere; he could hear the shouting in a distant sort of way. That was the way his world went. The other world where kids did as they please was about a million miles away.

He cried inside himself for a few minutes, then wandered across to the ladder and sat on the bottom rung. It wasn't a comfortable seat and something moved him to try a somersault, but he made an absolute mess of it as usual and rolled on to his side. The postman's whistle blew somewhere, a forlorn, empty, lonely sound. He cried a bit more and ended up on his back looking at the sky. The sky was miles away; the top of the gum-tree was miles away. A hawk wheeled in the emptiness between. It was lonely up there, too, but different.

"Hi-ya, bird. Hi-ya, cloud. Hi-ya, Mr. Sun." Saying it made him cry again and he hated crying, even when no one else was around.

A voice came to him from a long way off; one of those *imagined* voices. It sounded rather cross. "I didn't put myself up in this tower, you know. You did, John Sumner, with your stupid make-believe. You can't expect me to jump. I'll break my neck. You've got to come up to carry me down."

It was Mamie still waiting to be rescued, but John wasn't interested any more. "I can't climb that high," he said. "I can't get the ladder up."

"I bet Harry Hitchman would get the ladder up. Save me, Harry. John Sumner can't get me down."

"You be quiet, Mamie van Senden. It's not fair bringing Harry into it."

"I won't be quiet. Save me, *Hareee!*"

"Harry can't hear you. He's gone away to do things of his own. I suppose you're going to go away, too, aren't you, Mamie van Senden?"

She went away.

Nothing was left but the sky and the gum-tree and the ladder.

"Why don't you go away too?" he snarled at the ladder.

But the ladder was real and didn't have to go away.

"I'm going to do my model. It's got 227 pieces. When it's finished it'll be a yacht for putting on the shelf. Then I'll paint it white and take it to school and all the kids'll say it's terrific. But they'll know it's only 227 pieces out of a box."

He rolled over sideways, over and over downhill into the geraniums at the fence. "I hate geraniums. They stink." But he put up with the smell because he couldn't be bothered moving. He didn't care about anything. What was the use of caring? The answer to everything was either "don't" or "can't." There was only one John Clement Sumner and he was the one who shook and jerked and smudged his pages.

The ladder began to sneer at him. He wanted to rush it and give it a good kick, or push hard from the side so that it would fall with a crash. Several times the urge came like a command, but his body wouldn't move; it wanted only to lie on the ground.

"I wish you'd go away, you bloomin' old ladder."

But the ladder leant against the tree like a tough character in a film. "I'm stayin' right where I am, see. Are you makin' somethin' of it?"

"Oh go away. You're only a ladder."

"I'm goin' no place, kid. I'm stickin' right where I am. No one pushes me around."

John edged off a yard or two from the geraniums.

"No," he cried. He felt hot and prickly and cruelly ashamed. His face twitched, his hands jerked, and on impulse he scrambled to his feet and rushed at the ladder. He grabbed it viciously near the bottom and wrenched it from the grass.

By the top rung it shot up the trunk of the tree as though propelled and struck the bough. It hit with a crack almost like a whip and jarred all the way to the ground; but it stayed there and did not fall down.

Something happened to John. A storm passed through him. There was a battlefield and he was in the middle of it flaying at heads in armor with a flat sword. There were screams and shouts and sour smells. It was savage.

Then there was absolutely nothing.

After a time he saw the ladder against the tree, butted up to the bough. It was a road to the sky and the road was open.

He was puzzled. He had not done it himself; of that he was sure. He *could* not have done it. Lifted that dirty great ladder?

Numbed, he moved aside and sat back from it on the grass with legs crossed, not sure of himself, not sure of anything.

Oddly, the ladder did not break up rung by rung, did not melt like wax, did not disappear in a puff of smoke. It would not have surprised him if it had. But it was not a ladder that he had invented; it was not fashioned of substances he had imagined; nor was the feat of strength performed in a dazzling dream.

He had been so certain that this extraordinary event could not occur, but there stood the ladder ready for his use, as though it had never stood anywhere else. But his heart-beat was becoming a thud in his head and a breath-catching pulse in his throat. He was becoming frightened, and something inside him seemed to be falling endlessly. The longer he stared the more frantic his fall became, the faster his fears tumbled one over the other like dozens of people falling head over heels into an ever-deepening hole.

Then he looked up again to the long, slender curves of branches way up high like thin arms, to the topmost twigs like hands, to the last leaves groping like blind fingers for the sky, and there was a giddiness in him and a sickening wave of alarm. There was a cliff and he was on crutches at the edge of it.

John started to race across the lawn towards the house. Then he stopped as though caught suddenly in his flight by a pair of strong arms, but nothing touched him; ahead of him was something that he saw. It was a girl.

She said, "Are you a nut or something?"

It was Mamie in blue jeans and yellow jumper and golden hair like a bright helmet. She was eating an apple and drooped a bulging shopping-bag to the ground by one handle. It was not the Mamie of the surf-drenched rocks or the Mamie of the tower, but the real Mamie who lived seven houses away on the right-hand side of Dawson Street, going up.

John stammered at her but it was a sound that meant nothing to himself or to Mamie either.

She asked, "Isn't your mum home?"

He shook his head.

"She'll shoot you when she comes home. You're awful dirty."

He was so breathless, so distressed, so ashamed. He was dust and grass and sweat and dirt from head to foot. He tried to speak, but couldn't, and realized that his hand was beating his thigh. It was a painful effort of will to stop it.

"I've been shopping," Mamie said. "Mum told me not to dawdle. But I did. She's going to be cross." She rolled her eyes. "What are you doing?"

He tried to explain, but it was a meaningless gabble.

Mamie began to look uncomfortable, began to wish she hadn't come—as she was supposed not to have done.

"I'd better be going," she said. "Mum'll scream."

"Don't go," he blurted out.

Mamie looked at her feet (she was just a bit frightened) and gathered up the stray handle of her shopping bag. "Got to," she said. "Ta-ta."

She skipped a little as she went, but not because she was happy. Mamie really wanted to run, and when she was round the side of the house, out of sight of John, she made no secret of it to herself and scuttled down the drive as fast as she could.

John still stood where his scramble to the house had halted. He was furious, mad with himself, mad with Mamie, mad with the world. He wanted to break things, wanted to jump up and down and stamp his feet. Never, never had he shaken to a fury like it. He was so ashamed, so burnt up with all the frustrations and prohibitions and failures, and *don't do this's* and *can't do that's* of a whole lifetime that he was almost beside himself.

"You lousy, rotten ladder," he screamed and started jerking about in circles and snatching at clods of dirt from the garden and hurling them at the tree.

"It's not fair, it's not fair. Other kids climb. Other kids don't make fools of themselves in front of their girls. You rotten old tree."

He rushed at it and hit it with his fist. He kicked the tree. He grabbed at the ladder and not comprehending his actions all but ran up the rungs, stumbling, clawing, fumbling, until he was at least ten feet from the ground. There he stopped, suddenly shocked.

Everything went cold and became a mist.

So suddenly it happened; cold inside; cold outside; no fury left; no violence; not even any words.

The mist cleared and his legs somewhere below were trembling like reeds and his hands up above were clenched white about the side rails. He was stretched on the ladder, frozen in the act of a stride.

John panted rapidly through his teeth, and all the world was a gigantic ache, a terrible pain, and a continuing fright.

The sweat on his hands was like grease, and his fingers were slipping down those varnished rails a fraction of an inch at a time, in tiny jerks. Each jerk was a spasm of fear that he felt in his heart as though something there had ripped.

Sweat was running into his eyes and mouth; it was creeping in horrible streams from his armpits. It was strength dripping out of him, his life dripping away. His whole body was soft, was limp, was melting. His body was becoming longer and longer and heavier and heavier. It felt like an object made of plastic stretching on a hot day, an object that in the end had to tear or break or fall apart.

He tried to go up but couldn't. He pleaded with himself, commanded his body to climb, but nothing responded. His body could have been another person a mile away for all the attention it paid. It was like calling to Mum in the middle of the night when she was asleep and all the doors had slammed shut.

He bore down on his legs, he pushed, he heaved, but nothing was there, no strength and no feeling; he could have been dead down there in his legs for all the use they were. He clung on, held on, pleaded, prayed.

Nothing answered him; nothing from the inside; nothing from the outside. It was Mamie who had driven him up here but even Mamie was gone. Only the ground was down there; way, way down there. It was hard, that ground. It hadn't rained for a month. The thick roots of the gum-tree broke the surface and they were there, too, like rods of iron, like rails. It wasn't soft grass or deep grass. It was dry grass shaved to the surface by Dad's lawnmower. There was nothing down there to fall on; only things to break on; and that ghastly slipping away through his fingers went on and on, each jolt another drop of life gone.

There were weary voices inside him, arguing. One was stern (though tired) and the other desperate. One sounded something like Mum; the other sounded like part of himself.

"I didn't mean to climb the rotten thing in the first place. Never, ever. It was only pretending. All the time I wasn't going to do it. All the time it was only *pretending*."

"It wasn't pretending."

"It was, it was. Like everything else it was only pretending."

"Getting the ladder down from the rack—was that pretending? Getting it up to the tree—was that pretending?"

"Of course it was. I'm not silly, I'm not crazy. I know I can't climb."

"Kicking the ladder. Punching it. Running away from it. Were they all pretending?"

"I don't know, I don't know."

"You got up here, didn't you? You climbed here. You couldn't have got here any other way. All the time you knew it was going to happen, but you knew that when you got here you'd fall."

"It's that rotten man telling me about the balloon."

"It was easy for him. It was nothing to him. He was only a stranger passing by."

"He had a nice face and had a nice voice. I think he was handicapped too. I *believed* him. I'm sorry I said he was a rotten man."

"He was a stranger. He didn't understand. He didn't know."

"*He did know.*"

"If he knew, you wouldn't be hanging here now; you'd be climbing up and up and up. You'd be saying hi-ya, bird; hi-ya, cloud; hi-ya, Mr. Sun. You'd be way up there looking down on Main Street and on people getting off the bus."

A whimper broke out that he had striven to hold back and with the whimper came the shakes; they came together; shakes that he could feel even in the ladder. It shook under him, throbbed under him, and nothing was left in his hands, nothing at all. They stayed there, still slipping, still sliding, but numb.

He would lie down there, perhaps broken, perhaps dead, and no one would know. People coming to the back door wouldn't see him and Mum coming home wouldn't see him because the ladder was hidden from the house. Mamie had faced the tree but had never guessed that the ladder was there.

Mum would call, "John. Where are you, darling?" And she would become more frantic; she would dash here and dash there crying out; and then after a while she would find him. "Oh, John. I knew all the time I should never have left you. All these years I have kept you safe. In one day you kill yourself."

Even now if he yelled (if there was breath enough) would anyone hear? Would they take notice? Would they come? Would they understand if they found him, not on the ground, but still sprawled grotesquely on the ladder? Would they understand why he had done it or would they say in scathing grown-up tones, "Stupid child. Get down from there?"

"I can't."

"If you can get up you can get down."

"I can't."

"Come on down at once, John Sumner."

"It's no use. I can't go up and I can't get down and I can't even fall."

He flowed like fluid into the crevices of the ladder, and hung there by the crook of an arm, by a knee bent through the rungs, and by his chin. He became hooked by the chin, his head went back, and he strained against something solid— himself—his own body fighting and crying to prevent its strangulation. There were no shakes, not now, only a war to the death against a rung of wood and his own weight.

He was not going to fall, not going to die on the ground; he was going to choke on the ladder and they would find him there strung up like a chicken. The flag was at half-mast and kids at school would say, "Did you hear about that stupid John Sumner? Couldn't even climb a ladder."

He screamed with indignation deep inside and not a sound came out, but his body of jelly turned into muscles and sinews and bones. His hands and arms moved, his legs moved, he fought off the pressure at his throat and raised himself up. He raised himself up three excruciating steps and with clawing fingers touched the bough.

He wanted to let go, to hit the ground in a heap, simply to know that it was over, but his fingernails were clawing bark and he could see this thing happening as though he stood a short distance off and something started cheering like thousands of people.

"That's the boy, John. Stick at it, John. You'll show 'em, John. Keep going, John. Don't stop now, John."

"I can't. I can't."

"You'll do it, John. It's a long way down but a short way up."

"It's *impossible.*"

"There goes the balloon. Chase that balloon, John. Fight for it, John. After it, after it."

He fought to hold the moment and keep the mood and thousands cheered. He clawed and snatched and swung and madly scrambled and suddenly was crying. He was weeping as he had never wept in his life.

Only women and girls wept for joy; that was what people said; but it was not true. Boys wept like it too.

He was sitting on the bough.

He couldn't see for tears, couldn't think, couldn't reason, couldn't look ahead or look back, but he knew what he had done.

"Hi-ya, bird. Hi-ya, cloud. Hi-ya, Mr. Sun. Here I am."

Meet the Author

When Ivan Southall was just fourteen years old, his father died and Southall was forced to quit school and get a job washing bottles. He did not abandon his love of books, however, nor his dream to become a writer, and by the time Southall was twenty, he had written four books during whatever hours he could scrape together. Today Southall is one of the most acclaimed authors in Australia (his native country), and his books are read and enjoyed throughout the world.

This story was taken from one of Southall's novels by the same title, *Let the Balloon Go.* As he wrote the book, Southall's feeling for the character of John Sumner grew strong, and he himself wept when John reached the bough. "In its modest way, (John's victory) brought home to me the tragedy and triumph of being human—" said Southall, "there being nothing new under the sun, but never anything as rewarding as discovering it for yourself."

Southall did not model the character of John Sumner after any person he knew in real life. "If John is to be based upon any *real* person," he said, "I've got to say he grows from the spirit of adventure and longing that is in all of us."

Comprehension Check

Think and Discuss

1. What daring chance does John Sumner take and why is it so important to him?
2. What is the first problem John must solve? What is the second problem he faces?
3. The story says "It was Mamie who had driven him up here (the ladder)." How had Mamie done that?
4. Compare the voices that shout inside John when he realizes that he is ten feet up the ladder.
5. What makes John move and climb to the bough?
- 6. What type of fiction is this story—science fiction, historical fiction, or modern realistic fiction? How do you know?
- Literary Skill: Types of literature

See your Thinker's Handbook for tips.

Communication Workshop

Talk

By titling his story "Let the Balloon Go," Ivan Southall is saying that you never know what you can do until you try. Work with a small group and discuss what you think the balloon means, or symbolizes. What does it stand for or represent to John? Why is the balloon a good symbol for John and his goals?
Speaking/Listening: Group discussion

Write

Write a paragraph that explains why you think the balloon is a good symbol for John and what he wanted to achieve. Then, write a paragraph about something *you* wish to achieve. Choose a symbol to represent your goal and explain why the symbol is a good one for you. Read the paragraph about *your* symbol and goal to the class. Do you agree that the symbol you chose really represents you and your goal?
Writing Fluency: Paragraph

No man in all of Greece can outrun the beautiful maiden, Atalanta. And those who try lose not only the race but their lives as well. Even though the sport is deadly, men continue to take the risk. During one race, however, Atalanta is faced with taking a chance that may cause her to lose for the very first time. Will she take the chance? Why does she even consider it? Notice the elements in this story that characterize it as a myth.

ATALANTA'S RACE

A Greek myth retold by Doris Gates

Atalanta had been born to a father whose heart was set on having a son. So disappointed was he upon seeing his small newborn daughter, that he gave orders for the babe to be exposed on a mountain side, there to die of hunger. Luckily a she-bear discovered the child and gave her nourishment. And so, among animals and kindly hunters, Atalanta grew to maidenhood, a wild creature of the woods. Somehow she and her father rediscovered each other and became reconciled. But Atalanta never abandoned her hunter's life. She roamed the woods and fields with a spirit free and fearless. Like other such maidens before her, she vowed never to marry.

Nonetheless, suitors who heard of Atalanta's great beauty flocked to her father and begged for her hand in marriage. Atalanta's father became so beseiged with her suitors that at last he begged his daughter to give consideration to his plight.

"It is useless to suppose that you can forever withstand the powers of Aphrodite.[1] Nor can I longer turn a deaf ear to the pleading of these worthy men. You must choose among them."

Atalanta answered her father. "I shall never choose among them. But if they wish to compete for my hand, I will accommodate them. Let them all line up and race against me. Whichever one of them wins the race will win my hand. But if I outrun them, then their lives will be forfeit."

---

1. Aphrodite (af′rə dī′tē), goddess of love.

Atalanta was as famous for swiftness of foot as for beauty. No man had ever outdistanced her in the hunt or in a footrace. It was a cruel offer, but so great was her beauty that suitors were willing to chance it.

Naturally, news of the contest quickly spread throughout all Greece, and one young man, Hippomenes,[2] journeyed from afar to witness it. He was curious to see men foolish enough to risk their lives for a mere woman.

He sat apart and watched as one by one the suitors took their places at the starting line.

Then Atalanta appeared.

For a startled instant Hippomenes supposed a goddess had come among them. And then he saw the girl take her place with the men. This, then, was the famed Atalanta! Hippomenes marveled that a mortal could claim such perfection.

"It is I who am the fool," he told himself. "What man wouldn't risk his life for such a woman? And I must have my chance too. May none of these win over her that my opportunity to race with her may come," he prayed.

---

2. Hippomenes (hi pom′ə nēz).

The signal was given, and the race began. Atalanta sprang forward. As if sandaled by Hermes,[3] her bare feet skimmed the ground. Her hair, loose now, floated straight behind her shoulders. Never had mortal woman appeared so beautiful.

It was soon apparent to Hippomenes that his prayer would be answered. Atalanta sped in front of her pursuers almost at once. By the time the last lap was run, she was an easy victor. The losers groaned, knowing the fate that awaited them.

Now it was Hippomenes's turn. He rose and went to meet Atalanta as she came off the field.

"Atalanta," he addressed her, "why race against men who are plainly not in condition for an athletic contest? They are slow-footed and short-winded. I am neither. And I am nobly born. Let us race, and if I win against you, you will not need to be ashamed of my blood."

As he spoke, Atalanta experienced a strange feeling. Should they race, she half-hoped that he might win. The thought frightened her, and she fought to smother it. Of course she would win! What sudden madness had hinted at any other outcome? She would win and he would die. Yet still Atalanta suffered an unaccustomed pang—regret that one so handsome and so young should have to die.

"Stranger," she said, "return safely to your home and there seek the hand of another maiden. Surely none will refuse you. You saw the many I defeated and whose lives are forfeit. You must be tired of living that you should seek to race with Atalanta."

But Hippomenes stubbornly demanded his chance against the maiden, and at last her father and the onlookers insisted that the stranger be allowed his race.

The pair walked slowly to the starting line. Atalanta was reluctant to race at all, while Hippomenes sought a few moments of time to send up a prayer to the goddess of love.

"Aphrodite," he whispered, "who has lighted this flame of love within my breast, now help me. Either quicken my feet or slow Atalanta's. Conspire to let me win this race."

Aphrodite heard his prayer and decided to help him. On the island of Cyprus, where she dwelled, there grew a most

---

3. Hermes, a messenger god who wore winged shoes.

wondrous tree. Its leaves and branches were of purest gold, and it bore golden apples. Aphrodite happened to be passing the tree when she heard Hippomenes' prayer. Quickly she plucked three golden apples from a golden bough and rushed, invisible, to Hippomenes. She continued invisible to all but him as she handed over the apples and told him what to do with them.

Again the signal was given, and the two runners darted forward as one. But instead of passing Hippomenes, Atalanta ran easily beside him the better to admire the athlete. But when the youth was about to draw ahead of her, Atalanta put on a sudden burst of speed. She was about to pass him when he drew from his tunic one of the golden apples and tossed it in front of her. Atalanta broke stride, tempted by the bright object. She measured the distance between herself and Hippomenes and, deciding she had time, swooped and seized the apple. Hippomenes darted ahead.

The crowd cheered wildly and urged him on. The cheers changed to groans when Atalanta came abreast of Hippomenes and again was about to pass him. Again a golden apple was rolled into her path, and again she slowed to get it. Hippomenes flew down the course, his speed gaining as his hopes rose.

Now the spirit of contest flamed in Atalanta. She felt chagrined that her longing for the golden fruit had threatened her victory. No longer did she feel compassion for this youth. She would run as ruthlessly as she had ever done. Soon she was abreast of Hippomenes, and though the apples gathered in her tunic hampered her efforts, she was running in front of him when Hippomenes threw the last golden apple. He tossed it far to the edge of the course, where it rolled into the grass, a bright temptation. They were nearing the end of the course and Atalanta hesitated. Should she risk it with the end so near? Was it possible that this apple gleamed more brightly than the other two? Temptation overcame her. She sped from the course, seized the apple, and returned. But Hippomenes was across the finish line. He had won the race and a bride!

Hand in hand they left the field, Hippomenes waving in triumph to the exulting crowd. Atalanta kept her eyes upon the ground, but no sullen disappointment looked out of her face. Instead, she wore a smile almost as sweet as Aphrodite's own.

In an attempt to capture two young eagles, Tonweya becomes trapped and must take a chance to save his life. What is the chance he takes? Who helps him take it? Look for elements in this story that characterize it as a folk tale.

Tonweya and the Eagles

by Rosebud Yellow Robe

Long ago in summer a band of Lakotas[1] were camping at the foot of cliffs in the Western plains. Among them was a young man whose name was Tonweya. He was not only good to look upon, but he was a great runner and hunter. He was very brave in the face of danger.

One day Tonweya went out hunting. He found a small herd of buffalo grazing near the hills, and picking out a young fat cow, sent an arrow straight into her heart. While he was skinning the buffalo, he noticed a large eagle circling above him. Watching her flight he saw that she settled on a ledge of rock projecting from a high, steep cliff. Tonweya knew there must be a nest there. He was determined to find it. If there were young eaglets, he could capture them and raise them for their feathers.

He looked carefully at the ledge. He saw it would be impossible to climb up to it from the plain below. The only way was from above and getting down would be very dangerous. He would need a strong rope.

Tonweya finished skinning the buffalo and cut the green hide into one long narrow strip. Then he stretched and twisted the strip through the dust until he had a long strong rope of hide. Coiling this about him, he made his way to the tip of the cliff right above

---

1. Lakotas: Sioux or Dakota Indians who spoke the Lakota dialect.

the eagle's nest on the ledge. Fastening one end of this rawhide rope to a jack pine, he let the other fall over the ledge. Looking down he saw that it hung within a few feet of the nest. His plan was to slide down the rope and tie the eaglets to the end. Then after he had pulled himself up again, he would draw them up after him. Great honor would be his. A pair of captive eagles would supply feathers for many braves.

Tonweya carefully lowered himself over the edge of the cliff and soon stood on the ledge. There were two beautiful young eaglets in the nest, fully feathered, though not yet able to fly. He tied them to his rope and prepared to climb up. But just as he placed his weight on the rope, it fell down beside him. The green hide had been slipping at the knot and came loose when Tonweya grabbed hold.

Tonweya realized immediately that he was trapped. Only Wakan-tanka,[2] the Great Mystery, could save him from a slow death by starvation and thirst. He looked below him. There was a sheer drop of many hundreds of feet with not even the slightest projection by which he might climb down. Neither was there handhold or foothold to climb up. The eagle had chosen well the place for her nest.

Despite his brave heart, terror gripped Tonweya. He stood looking off in the direction he knew his people to be. He cried out, "Ma hiyopo! Ma hiyopo! Help me!" But only the echo of his own voice answered.

As the sun was setting, the mother eagle returned to her nest. She screamed in rage when she saw a man with her eaglets. Round and round she flew. Now and then she charged with lightning speed toward Tonweya and the young birds. The two eaglets flapped their wings wildly and called out to her. Finally in despair the mother eagle made one more swoop toward her nest, and then screaming defiantly, flew off and disappeared. Night fell and the stars came out. Tonweya was alone on the ledge with the two little birds.

Tonweya did not sleep during the night, for the ledge was so narrow, he feared rolling off. When the sun rose, he was very tired.

All day Tonweya watched the sun high in the heavens. He was very hungry and so terribly thirsty. When the sun began its descent toward the west, Tonweya knew it would soon be night. He looked forward with dread to the lonely vigil he must again keep.

---

2. Wakan-tanka (wä′kän tang′kä).

On the next day, an idea came to Tonweya. He had noticed a small spruce growing in a cleft of rocks above him. Tonweya devised a way to tie a piece of his rope to this tree and fasten the other end around his waist. That way he would not fall off the ledge, even if he stumbled. More important still, he could chance some sleep, which he needed badly.

The next day passed as the others had: heat, hunger, unquenchable thirst. The hope that some of his people might come in search of him was gone. Even if they came, they would never think of looking for him on the cliffs. The mother of the eaglets did not return. Tonweya's presence had frightened her away.

By this time the two eaglets, seeing that Tonweya had no intention of hurting them, had made friends with him. They allowed Tonweya to touch them at will. Tonweya could see that they were as hungry as he was, so taking out his knife he cut small pieces from the rawhide rope and fed them. This act of kindness removed their last vestige of fear. They played all about Tonweya and allowed him to hold them aloft. They flapped their wings bravely as he lifted them toward the sun. As Tonweya felt the upward pull of their wings, there came to him another idea. Since he had no wings of his own, why could he not make use of the wings of his eagle brothers? Suddenly Tonweya was no longer afraid. He knew that his time to die had not yet come. He would once more see his people.

For days thereafter Tonweya fed the rawhide rope to his eagle friends. But while the eaglets thrived on it and grew larger and stronger each day, Tonweya grew thinner and weaker. It rained one day and Tonweya drank the water that gathered in the hollows of the rocks on the ledge. Still he was hungry and thirsty. He tried to think only of caring for eaglets.

Each day Tonweya held the eagles up by their legs and let them try their wings. One day the pull on his arms was so powerful, it almost lifted him from his feet. He knew the time had come for him to put his idea into action. Weak as he was, he would be unable to do it after a few more days.

The last of the rawhide was gone now; the last bit of water on the ledge was drunk. Tonweya was so weak, he could hardly stand. With an effort he dragged himself upright and called his eagle brothers to him. Standing on the edge of the ledge he called to Wakan-tanka for help. He grasped the eaglets' legs in each hand and closing his eyes he jumped.

For a moment he felt himself falling, falling. Then he felt the pull on his arms as he was lifted toward the sky. Opening his eyes Tonweya saw that the two eagles were flying easily. In a moment they had reached the ground. Tonweya lay there too exhausted, too weak to move. The eagles remained by his side guarding him.

After resting a while Tonweya slowly made his way to a little stream nearby. He drank deeply of its cool water. A few berries were growing on the bushes there. He ate them ravenously. Strengthened by even this little food and water, he started off in the direction of the camp. His progress was slow, for he was compelled to rest many times. Always the eaglets remained by his side guarding him.

On the way he passed the spot where he had killed the buffalo. The coyotes and vultures had left nothing but bones. However his bow and arrows were just where he had left them. He managed to kill a rabbit upon which he and his eagle friends feasted. Late in the afternoon he reached the camp, only to find that his people had moved on. It was late. He was very tired so he decided to stay there that night.

The sun was high in the sky when Tonweya awoke. The long sleep had given him back much strength and once more he set out after his people. For two days he followed their trail. He lived on the roots and berries he found along the way and what little game he could shoot. He shared everything with his eagle brothers, who followed him.

Well along in the afternoon of the second day he caught up with the band. At first they were frightened when they saw him. Then they welcomed him with joy.

They were astonished at his story. The two eagles who never left Tonweya amazed the people. They were glad that they had always been kind to eagles and had never killed them.

The time came when the eagles were able to hunt food for themselves and though everyone expected them to fly away, they did not. True, they would leave with the dawn on hunting forays, but when the evening drew near, they would fly back fearlessly and enter Tonweya's tipi, where they passed the night. Everyone marveled at the sight.

But eagles, like people, should be free. Tonweya, who by now understood their language, told them they could go. They were to enjoy the life the Great Mystery, Wakan-tanka, had planned for them. At first they refused. But when Tonweya said he would call for them if he ever needed their help, they consented.

The tribe gave a great feast in their honor. In gratitude for all they had done Tonweya painted the tips of their wings a bright red to denote courage and bravery. He took them up on a high mountain. He held them once more toward the sky, and bidding them good-bye, released them. Spreading their wings, the eagles soared away. Tonweya watched them until they disappeared in the eye of the sun.

Many snows have passed and Tonweya has long been dead. But now and then the eagles with the red-tipped wings are still seen. There are always two of them and they never show any fear of people. Some say they are the original sacred birds of Tonweya, for the eagle lives for many snows. Some think they are the children of the sacred ones. It is said that those who see the red-tipped wings of the eagles are sure of their protection as long as they are fearless and brave. And only the fearless and brave may wear the eagle feather tipped with red.

Meet the Author

When Rosebud Yellow Robe was a young girl in South Dakota, she often listened enthralled as her father, Chief Chauncey, told her tale after tale of the Lakota tribe. He himself had heard the stories from his father, Tasinagi, who may in turn have heard some of them from Sitting Bull, a famous Native American leader and ancestor of Rosebud Yellow Robe.

As Yellow Robe grew older, her own gift for storytelling developed. To preserve the treasured stories of her people and of her childhood, Yellow Robe wrote them down. Her collection of Lakota tales bears the same title as this story, *Tonweya and the Eagles*.

Comprehension Check

Think and Discuss

1. What chance does Atalanta take during her race against Hippomenes, and why does she take it?
2. Hippomenes also takes a chance. What is it and why is it a dangerous chance to take?
3. How does Aphrodite help Hippomenes win the race?
• 4. What elements in "Atalanta's Race" characterize it as a myth?
5. Like Atalanta, Tonweya takes a chance. What is the chance he takes and who helps him take it?
• 6. What elements in "Tonweya and the Eagles" characterize it as a folk tale?
• Literary Skills: Myth, Folk tale

Communication Workshop

Talk

Discuss with a small group of your classmates the following themes: **a)** *Love conquers all.* **b)** *Kindness and respect for all living things enable people to live in harmony with nature.* Which one fits the myth "Atalanta's Race" and which fits "Tonweya and the Eagles"? Be sure to give reasons for your choices.
Speaking/Listening: Cooperative learning

Write

Choose one of the themes above and write a paragraph about why you think it fits one of the stories. Give at least one reason or example to show why the theme fits the story. Read your paragraph to your group. Do they agree or disagree with your reasons for linking the theme you have written about to its story?
Writing Fluency: Paragraph

Understanding What You Read

Reading different types of literature gives you the chance to enter into and share the struggles of someone like John Sumner. You can also travel back through time and join in the action of ancient adventurers.

When you read different types of literature, you'll encounter different types of writing styles. Often there may be words, phrases, and ideas that are difficult. When this happens, you can help yourself by stopping and thinking about how well you are reading, and asking yourself such questions as these:

- Am I getting the point of this selection?
- Does this make sense? Do I understand what this is about?
- Are there words, phrases, or paragraphs I need to reread?
- Am I reading too fast or too slowly?

Stopping to think about how well you are reading will help you know when your understanding is sufficient and when you need to rethink and reread.

You can use this strategy with other reading hints you already know—previewing and visualizing. On the following pages, you will join Ichabod Crane in Sleepy Hollow. Before you read this classic legend, preview the headnote and the illustrations to help you visualize the nineteenth-century setting. As you read, if you don't understand any of the ideas, stop and ask yourself what the words, phrases, and paragraphs mean. Then you will be able not only to understand but to feel the flavor of Washington Irving's writing. Here is just one example that he uses to describe Ichabod. What does he look like? Ask yourself if there are any words or phrases you need to reread to answer the question.

> "He was tall but exceedingly lank, with narrow shoulders, long arms and legs, hands that dangled a mile out of his sleeves, feet that might have served for shovels, and his whole frame most loosely hung together."

Washington Irving wrote this story in 1819. It has become a classic largely because of its unlikely hero—a schoolmaster named Ichabod Crane. Ichabod wants to win the heart (and the large dowry!) of a lass named Katrina. Despite strong competition from other suitors, Ichabod is willing to take his chances. Find out what happens to Ichabod that perhaps makes him wish he had taken his chances elsewhere!

The Legend of Sleepy Hollow

CLASSIC

by Washington Irving

In the bosom of one of those spacious coves which indent the eastern shore of the Hudson, there lies a small market-town or rural port which is known by the name of Tarry Town. Not far from this village, perhaps about two miles, there is a little valley, or rather lap of land, among high hills, which is one of the quietest places in the whole world. A small brook glides through it, with just murmur enough to lull one to repose; and the occasional whistle of a quail, or tapping of a woodpecker, is almost the only sound that ever breaks in upon the uniform tranquillity.

From the listless repose of the place and the peculiar character of its inhabitants, who are descendants from the original Dutch settlers, this sequestered glen has long been known by the name of Sleepy Hollow. A drowsy, dreamy influence seems to hang over the land, and to pervade the very atmosphere. The good people there are given to all kinds of marvellous beliefs, and frequently see strange sights and hear music and voices in the air. The whole neighborhood abounds with local tales, haunted spots, and twilight superstitions.

The dominant spirit, however, that haunts this enchanted region is the apparition of a figure on horseback without a head. It is said by some to be the ghost of a Hessian trooper[1] whose head had been carried away by a cannonball in some nameless battle during the Revolutionary War and who is, ever and anon, seen by the countryfolk hurrying along in the gloom of night, as if on the wings of the wind. His haunts are not confined to the valley but extend at times to the adjacent roads, and especially to the vicinity of a church at no great distance. Indeed, certain of the most authentic historians of those parts allege that, the body of the trooper having been buried in the churchyard, the ghost rides forth to the scene of battle in nightly quest of his head. The spectre is known at all the country firesides by the name of the Headless Horseman of Sleepy Hollow.

In this by-place of nature, there abode in a remote period of American history, a worthy wight of the name Ichabod Crane, who sojourned, or, as he expressed it, "tarried," in Sleepy Hollow for the purpose of instructing the children of the vicinity. The cognomen of Crane was not inapplicable to his person. He was tall but exceedingly lank, with narrow shoulders, long arms and legs, hands that dangled a mile out of his sleeves, feet that might have served for shovels, and his whole frame most loosely hung together. His head was small, and flat at top, with huge ears, large green, glassy eyes, and a long snipe nose, so that it looked like a weathercock perched upon his spindle neck to tell which way the wind blew. To see him striding along the profile of a hill on a windy day, with his clothes bagging and fluttering about him, one might have mistaken him for some scarecrow eloped from a cornfield.

The schoolhouse stood at the foot of a woody hill with a brook running close by and a formidable birch tree growing at one end of it. From hence the low murmur of his pupils' voices conning over their lessons might be heard like the hum of a beehive,

---

1. Hessian trooper, a German soldier who fought against Americans.

interrupted now and then by the authoritative voice of the master in the tone of menace or command or, peradventure, by the appalling sound of the birch[2] as he urged some tardy loiterer along the flowery path of knowledge. Truth to say, he was a conscientious man and ever bore in mind the golden maxim "Spare the rod and spoil the child."

When school hours were over, he was even the companion of the larger boys; and on holiday afternoons would convoy some of the smaller ones home, who happened to have pretty sisters or good housewives for mothers, noted for the comforts of the cupboard. Indeed it behooved him to keep on good terms with his pupils. He was, according to country custom in those parts, boarded and lodged at the houses of the farmers, whose children he instructed. With these he lived successively a week at a time thus going the rounds of the neighborhood with all his worldy effects tied up in a cotton handkerchief.

That all this might not be too onerous on the purses of his rustic patrons, who are apt to consider the costs of schooling a grievous burden and schoolmasters as mere drones, he had various ways of rendering himself both useful and agreeable. He assisted the farmers occasionally in the lighter labors of their farms; helped to make hay; drove the cows from pasture; and cut wood for the winter fire. He found favor in the eyes of the mothers by petting the children, particularly the youngest. He would sit with a child on one knee, and rock a cradle with his foot for whole hours together.

Thus, by divers little makeshifts in that ingenious way which is commonly denominated "by hook and by crook," the worthy pedagogue got on tolerably enough and was thought, by all who understood nothing of the labor of headwork, to have a wonderfully easy life of it.

---

2. birch, a switch made from a birch tree branch.

Ichabod Crane

The schoolmaster was an odd mixture of small shrewdness and simple credulity. His appetite for the marvellous was extraordinary and had been increased by his residence in this spellbound region. No tale was too monstrous for his capacious swallow. One of his sources of fearful pleasure was to pass long winter evenings with the old Dutch wives as they sat spinning by the fire, with a row of apples roasting and spluttering along the hearth, and listen to their tales of ghosts and goblins, and haunted fields, and haunted bridges, and haunted houses, and particularly of the Headless Horseman.

But if there was a pleasure in all this while snugly cuddling in the chimney corner where no spectre dared to show its face, it was dearly purchased by the subsequent walk homeward. What fearful shapes and shadows beset his path amidst the dim and ghastly glare of a snowy night! With what wistful look did he eye every trembling ray of light streaming across the waste fields from some distant window! How often was he appalled by some shrub covered with snow, which, like a sheeted spectre, rose before him! How often did he shrink with curdling awe at the sound of his own steps on the frosty crust beneath his feet; and dread to look over his shoulder lest he should behold some uncouth being tramping close behind him! And how often was he thrown into complete dismay by some rushing blast howling among the trees, in the idea that it was the Headless Horseman on one of his nightly scourings!

All these, however, were mere terrors of the night; and he would have passed a pleasant life of it if his path had not been crossed by a being that causes more perplexity to mortal man than ghosts, goblins, and the whole race of witches put together, and that was— a woman.

Among the musical disciples who assembled each week to receive his instructions in psalmody, was Katrina Van Tassel, the daughter and only child of a substantial Dutch farmer. She was a blooming lass of fresh eighteen, plump as a partridge, ripe and melting and rosy-cheeked as one of her father's peaches, universally famed, not merely for her beauty, but for her vast expectations; and she was withal a little of a coquette.

Ichabod Crane had a soft and foolish heart toward the sex; and it is not to be wondered at that so tempting a morsel soon found favor in his eyes, more especially after he had visited her in her paternal mansion. Hard by the farmhouse was a vast barn, every window and crevice of which seemed bursting forth with the treasures of the farm. Sleek, unwieldy porkers were grunting in the repose and abundance of their pens whence sallied forth, now and then, troops of sucking pigs as if to snuff the air. A stately squadron of snowy geese were riding in an adjoining pond, convoying whole fleets of ducks; and regiments of turkeys were gobbling through the farmyard.

The pedagogue's mouth watered as he looked upon this sumptuous promise of luxurious winter fare. In his devouring mind's eye he pictured to himself every roasting pig running about with an apple in its mouth; the pigeons were snugly put to bed in a comfortable pie, and tucked in with a coverlet of crust; the geese were swimming in their own gravy; not a turkey but he beheld daintily trussed up with its gizzard under its wing.

As the enraptured Ichabod fancied all this, and as he rolled his great, green eyes over the fat meadow lands, the rich fields of wheat, of rye, of buckwheat, and of Indian corn, and the orchards burdened with ruddy fruit which surrounded the warm tenement of Van Tassel, his heart yearned after the damsel who was to inherit these domains. To gain the affections of the peerless daughter of Van Tassel, however, he had more real difficulties than generally fell to the lot of a knight-errant of yore who seldom had

Katrina Van Tassel

anything but giants, enchanters, fiery dragons, and suchlike easily conquered adversaries to contend with. Ichabod on the contrary, had to win his way to the heart of a country coquette; and he had to encounter a host of fearful adversaries of real flesh and blood, the numerous rustic admirers who beset every portal to her heart.

Among these the most formidable was Brom Van Brunt. The country round rang with his feats of strength and hardihood. From his Herculean[3] frame and great powers of limb, he had received the nickname of Brom Bones. He was famed for great skill in horsemanship, being as dexterous on horseback as a Tartar.[4] He was always ready for either a fight or a frolic but had more of mischief than ill-will in his composition. He had three or four boon companions who regarded him as their model and at the head of whom he scoured the country, attending every scene of feud or merriment for miles around.

This hero had for some time singled out the blooming Katrina for the object of his gallantries, and it was whispered that she did not altogether discourage his hopes. Certain it is, that, when his horse was seen tied to Van Tassel's paling on a Sunday night, all other suitors passed by in despair.

Such was the formidable rival with whom Ichabod Crane had to contend; and, considering all things, a stouter man than he would have shrunk from the competition and a wiser man would have despaired. To have taken the field openly against his rival would have been madness. Ichabod, therefore, made his advances in a quiet and gently insinuating manner. Under cover of his character of singing master he made frequent visits at the farmhouse.

---

3. Herculean, Hercules was a Greek hero who possessed extraordinary strength.
4. Tartar, one from the tribes led by Genghis Khan who overran Europe during the 1200s and 1300s.

Brom Van Brunt

Brom, who had a degree of rough chivalry in his nature, would fain have carried matters to open warfare and have settled their pretensions to the lady by combat; but Ichabod was too conscious of the superior might of his adversary and too wary to give him an opportunity. Brom had no alternative but to play practical jokes upon his rival. Ichabod became the object of whimsical persecution to Bones and his gang. They smoked out his singing school by stopping up the chimney; broke into the schoolhouse at night and turned everything topsy-turvy. But what was still more annoying, Brom took opportunities of turning him into ridicule in the presence of his mistress, and had a scoundrel dog whom he taught to whine in the most ludicrous manner and introduced as a rival of Ichabod's to instruct Katrina in psalmody. In this way matters went on for some time.

On a fine autumnal afternoon Icabod sat enthroned on the lofty stool whence he usually watched all the concerns of his little literary realm; the birch of justice reposed on three nails behind the throne; while on the desk before him might be seen sundry contraband articles and prohibited weapons, detected upon the persons of idle urchins, such as half-munched apples, popguns, whirligigs, and fly cages. A kind of buzzing stillness reigned throughout the schoolroom. It was suddenly interrupted by the appearance of a man clattering up to the school door with an invitation to Ichabod to attend a merrymaking or "quilting frolic" to be held that evening at Mynheer Van Tassel's.

All was now bustle and hubbub in the late quiet schoolroom. The scholars were hurried through their lessons. Books were flung aside without being put away on the shelves, inkstands were overturned, benches thrown down; and the whole school was turned loose an hour before the usual time, bursting forth like a legion of young imps, yelping and racketing about the green in joy at their early emancipation.

The gallant Ichabod now spent at least an extra half-hour brushing and furbishing up his best, and indeed only, suit of rusty black and arranging his looks by a bit of broken looking-glass that hung up in the schoolhouse. That he might make his appearance before his mistress in the true style of a cavalier, he borrowed a horse from the farmer with whom he was domiciliated, an old Dutchman, of the name of Hans Van Ripper, and thus gallantly mounted, issued forth like a knight-errant in quest of adventures.

The animal he bestrode was a broken-down plough horse that had outlived almost everything but his viciousness. He was gaunt and shagged, with a ewe neck and a head like a hammer; his rusty mane and tail were tangled and knotted with burrs; one eye had lost its pupil, but the other had the gleam of a genuine devil in it. Still, he must have had fire and mettle in his day, if we may judge from the name he bore of Gunpowder. Ichabod was a suitable figure for such a steed. He rode with short stirrups which brought his knees nearly up to the pommel of the saddle; his sharp elbows stuck out like grasshoppers'; he carried his whip perpendicularly in his hand like a sceptre, and as his horse jogged on, the motion of his arms was not unlike the flapping of a pair of wings. A small wool hat rested on the top of his nose, and the skirts of his black coat fluttered out almost to his horse's tail. Such was the appearance of Ichabod and his steed as they shambled out of the gate of Hans Van Ripper, and it was altogether such an apparition as is seldom to be met with in broad daylight.

It was toward evening that Ichabod arrived at the castle of the Heer Van Tassel, which he found thronged with the pride and flower of the adjacent country. Brom Bones, however, was the hero of the scene, having come to the gathering on his favorite steed Daredevil—a creature, like himself, full of mettle and mischief, and which no one but himself could manage.

Fain would I pause to dwell upon the world of charms that burst upon the enraptured gaze of my hero as he entered the state parlor of Van Tassel's mansion. Not those of the bevy of buxom lasses, but the ample charms of a genuine Dutch country tea table in the sumptuous time of autumn. Such heaped-up platters of cakes of various and almost indescribable kinds, known only to experienced Dutch housewives! There was the doughty doughnut and the crisp and crumbling cruller; sweet cakes and short cakes, ginger cakes and honey cakes, and the whole family of cakes. And then there were apple pies and peach pies and pumpkin pies; besides slices of ham and smoked beef; and moreover, delectable dishes of preserved plums and peaches and pears and quinces; not to mention broiled shad and roasted chicken; together with bowls of milk and cream, all mingled higgledy-piggledy, with the motherly teapot sending up its clouds of vapor from the midst.

Ichabod Crane was a kind and thankful creature whose spirits rose with eating. He could not help rolling his large eyes round him as he ate and chuckling with the possibility that he might one day be lord of all this scene of almost unimaginable luxury and splendor.

Old Baltus Van Tassel moved about among his guests with a face round and jolly as the harvest moon. His hospitable attentions were confined to a shake of the hand, a slap on the shoulder, a loud laugh, and a pressing invitation to "fall to and help themselves."

And now the sound of the music from the common room, or hall, summoned to the dance. Ichabod prided himself upon his dancing as much as upon his vocal powers. Not a limb, not a fibre about him was idle; and how could the flogger of urchins be otherwise than animated and joyous? The lady of his heart was his partner in the dance, while Brom Bones sat brooding by himself in one corner.

When the dance was at an end, Ichabod was attracted to a knot of the sager folks, who, with old Van Tassel, sat at one end of the piazza, gossiping over former times and drawing out long stories about the war. Several of the Sleepy Hollow people were present at Van Tassel's and, as usual, were doling out their wild and wonderful legends. The chief part of the stories turned upon the favorite spectre of Sleepy Hollow, the Headless Horseman, who, it was said, tethered his horse nightly among the graves in the churchyard.

Brom Bones made light of the Galloping Hessian. He affirmed that on returning one night from the neighboring village he had been overtaken by this midnight trooper; that he had offered to race with him and should have won, for Daredevil beat the goblin horse all hollow; but just as they came to the church bridge the Hessian bolted and vanished in a flash of fire. This tale and the others sank deep in the mind of Ichabod.

The revel now gradually broke up. The old farmers gathered together their families in their wagons; some of the damsels mounted on pillions behind their favorite swains. Gradually the late scene of noise and frolic was all silent and deserted. Ichabod only lingered behind to have a tête-à-tête with the heiress, fully convinced that he was now on the high road to success. What passed at this interview I will not pretend to say, for in fact I do not know. Something, however, must have gone wrong, for he certainly sallied forth, after no very great interval, with an air quite desolate and chopfallen. He went straight to the stable and with several hearty cuffs and kicks roused his steed most uncourteously from the comfortable quarters in which he was soundly sleeping.

It was the very witching time of night that Ichabod, heavy-hearted and crestfallen, pursued his travel homeward. The hour was as dismal as himself. In the dead hush of midnight he could even hear the barking of a watchdog from the opposite shore of the Hudson. Now and then too, the crowing of a cock would sound far, far off, from some farmhouse away among the hills. No signs of life occurred near him but occasionally the melancholy chirp of a cricket or perhaps the guttural twang of a bullfrog from a neighboring marsh, as if sleeping uncomfortably, and turning suddenly in his bed.

All the stories of ghosts and goblins that he had heard that evening now came crowding upon his recollection. The night grew darker and darker; the stars seemed to sink deeper in the sky, and driving clouds occasionally hid them from his sight. Ichabod had never felt so lonely and dismal. He was, moreover, approaching the very place where some of the scenes of the ghost stories had been laid. In the center of the road stood an enormous tulip tree; its limbs were gnarled and fantastic. It was connected with a tragical story of the unfortunate Major André, who had been taken prisoner hard by.

As Ichabod approached this fearful tree, he began to whistle. He thought his whistle was answered; it was but a blast sweeping sharply through the dry branches. As he approached a little nearer, he thought he saw something white hanging in the midst of the tree. He paused and ceased whistling; but, on looking more narrowly, perceived that it was a place where the tree had been scathed by lightning and the white wood laid bare. Suddenly he heard a groan. His teeth chattered and his knees smote against the saddle; it was but the rubbing of one huge bough upon another as they were swayed about by the breeze. He passed the tree in safety, but new perils lay before him.

About two hundred yards from the tree a small brook crossed the road and ran into a marshy and thickly wooden glen. A few rough logs, laid side by side, served for a bridge over the stream. On the side of the road where the brook entered the wood, a group of chestnuts, matted thick with wide grapevines, threw a cavernous gloom. It was at this identical spot that the unfortunate André was captured, and under the covert of those chestnuts and vines were the sturdy yeomen concealed who surprised him.

As Ichabod approached the stream, his heart began to thump; he summoned up, however, all his resolution, gave his horse a score of kicks in the ribs, and attempted to dash briskly across the bridge; but instead of starting forward, the perverse old animal made a lateral movement, and ran broadside against the fence. Ichabod, whose fears increased with the delay, jerked the reins and kicked lustily. It was all in vain. His steed started, it is true, but it was only to plunge to the opposite side of the road into a thicket of brambles and alder bushes. The schoolmaster now bestowed both whip and heel upon the starveling ribs of old Gunpowder, who dashed forward, snuffling and snorting, but came to a stand just by the bridge with a suddenness that nearly sent his rider sprawling over his head. Just at this moment a plashy tramp by the side of the bridge caught the sensitive ear of Ichabod. On the margin of the brook he beheld something huge, misshapen, black, and towering. It stirred not but seemed gathered up into the gloom like some gigantic monster ready to spring upon the traveller.

The hair of the affrighted pedagogue rose upon his head with terror. What was to be done? To turn and fly was now too late; and besides, what chance was there of escaping ghost or goblin, if such it was, which could ride upon the wings of the wind? Summoning up, therefore, a show of courage, he demanded in stammering accents, "Who are you?" He received no reply. He repeated his demand in a still more agitated voice. Still there was no answer. Once more he cudgelled the sides of the inflexible Gunpowder and, shutting his eyes, broke forth with involuntary fervor into a psalm tune. Just then the shadowy object of alarm put itself in motion and with a scramble and a bound stood at once in the middle of the road. Though the night was dark and dismal, the form of the unknown might now in some degree be ascertained. He appeared to be a horseman of large dimensions, mounted on a black horse of powerful frame. He kept aloof on one side of the road, jogging along on the blind side of old Gunpowder, who had now got over his fright and waywardness.

Ichabod, who had no relish for this strange midnight companion, and bethought himself of the adventure of Brom Bones with the Galloping Hessian now quickened his steed in hopes of leaving him behind. The stranger, however, quickened his horse to an equal pace. Ichabod pulled up and fell into a walk, thinking to lag behind, the other did the same. He endeavored to resume his psalm tune, but his parched tongue clove to the roof of his mouth, and he could not utter a stave. There was something in the moody and dogged silence of this companion that was mysterious and appalling. It was soon fearfully accounted for. On mounting a rising ground, which brought the figure of his fellow-traveller in relief against the sky, gigantic in height and muffled in a cloak, Ichabod was horror-struck on perceiving that he was headless! But his horror was still more increased on observing that the head, which should have rested on his shoulders, was carried before him on the pommel of the saddle. His terror rose to desperation; he rained a shower of kicks and blows upon Gunpowder, hoping by a sudden movement to give his companion the slip; but the spectre started full jump with him. Away then they dashed, stones flying and sparks flashing at every bound. Ichabod's flimsy garments fluttered in the air as he stretched his long, lank body away over his horse's head in the eagerness of his flight.

They had now reached the road which turns off to Sleepy Hollow; but Gunpowder, instead of keeping up it, made an opposite turn and plunged headlong downhill to the left. This road leads through a hollow shaded by trees for about a quarter of a mile,

where it crosses the bridge famous in goblin story, and just beyond swells the green knoll on which stands the whitewashed church.

As yet the panic of the steed had given his unskilful rider an apparent advantage in the chase; but just as he had got halfway through the hollow the girths of the saddle gave way, and he felt it slipping from under him. He seized it by the pommel and endeavored to hold it firm, but in vain. He had just time to save himself by clasping old Gunpowder round the neck when the saddle fell to the earth and he heard it trampled under foot by his pursuer. For a moment the terror of Hans Van Ripper's wrath passed across his mind, but this was no time for petty fears. The goblin was hard on his haunches; and (unskilful rider that he was!) he had much ado to maintain his seat, sometimes slipping on one side, sometimes on another, and sometimes jolted on the high ridge of his horse's backbone with a violence that he verily feared would cleave him asunder.

An opening in the trees now cheered him with the hopes that the church bridge was at hand. He recollected the place where Brom Bones's ghostly competitor had disappeared. "If I can but reach that bridge," thought Ichabod, "I am safe." Just then he heard the black steed panting and blowing close behind him; he even fancied that he felt his hot breath. Another convulsive kick in the ribs and old Gunpowder sprang upon the bridge. He thundered over the resounding planks; he gained the opposite side. And now Ichabod cast a look behind to see if his pursuer should vanish, according to rule, in a flash of fire and brimstone. Just then he saw the goblin rising in his stirrups and in the very act of hurling his head at him. Ichabod endeavored to dodge the horrible missile, but too late. It encountered his cranium with a tremendous crash; he was tumbled headlong into the dust; and Gunpowder, the black steed, and the goblin rider passed by like a whirlwind.

The next morning the old horse was found, without his saddle and with the bridle under his feet, soberly cropping the grass at his master's gate. Ichabod did not make his appearance at breakfast; dinner hour came, but no Ichabod. The boys assembled at the schoolhouse, but no schoolmaster. Hans Van Ripper now began to feel some uneasiness about the fate of poor Ichabod and his saddle. An inquiry was set on foot; and, after diligent investigation, they came upon his traces. In one part of the road leading to the church was found the saddle trampled in the dirt; the tracks of horses' hoofs, deeply dented in the road and evidently at furious speed, were traced to the bridge, beyond which was found the hat of the unfortunate Ichabod and close beside it a shattered pumpkin.

The brook was searched, but the body of the schoolmaster was not to be discovered. The mysterious event caused much speculation at the church on the following Sunday. Knots of gazers and gossips were collected in the churchyard, at the bridge, and at the spot where the hat and pumpkin had been found. A whole budget of legendary happenings were called to mind; and, when they had diligently considered them all, they shook their heads and came to the conclusion that Ichabod had been carried off by the Galloping Hessian. As he was a bachelor and in nobody's debt, nobody troubled his head anymore about him.

It is true, an old farmer, who had been down to New York on a visit several years after, and from whom this account of the ghostly adventure was received, brought home the intelligence that Ichabod Crane was still alive; that he had left the neighborhood partly through fear of the goblin and Hans Van Ripper and partly in mortification at having been suddenly dismissed by the heiress; that he had changed his quarters to a distant part of the country, had kept school and studied law at the same time, had been admitted to the bar, turned politician, electioneered, written for the newspapers, and finally had been made a justice of the Ten Pound Court. Brom Bones, who shortly after his rival's disappearance conducted the blooming Katrina in triumph to the altar, was observed to look exceedingly knowing whenever the story of Ichabod was related and always burst in a hearty laugh at the mention of the pumpkin, which led some to suspect that he knew more about the matter than he chose to tell.

Meet the Author

Washington Irving was born in 1783—just seven years after America itself was born. During Irving's youth, America was bustling with promise—*except* in the arts. No writer in America was considered to have any real merit, and well-educated Americans still turned to Europe for good literature.

Irving changed all that. He became the first American to receive recognition and popularity in Europe as well as at home. His wit and style of storytelling influenced a whole generation of writers who came after him. Irving published a famous collection of stories, called *The Sketch Book* which included "The Legend of Sleepy Hollow" and "Rip Van Winkle." *The Sketch Book* helped establish the short story as a popular literary form in America.

Irving's personality was fun-loving and lively. However, he took himself seriously as a writer even at an early age, and had his first work published when he was just a teenager. At different times in his life, Irving worked as a lawyer, businessman, and international diplomat. His most important place in history, however, remains in literature.

Windy Nights

by Robert Louis Stevenson

Whenever the moon and stars are set,
  Whenever the wind is high,
All night long in the dark and wet,
  A man goes riding by.
Late in the night when the fires are out,
Why does he gallop and gallop about?

Whenever the trees are crying aloud,
  And ships are tossed at sea,
By, on the highway, low and loud,
  By at the gallop goes he.
By at the gallop he goes, and then
By he comes back at the gallop again.

LOOKING BACK

See your Thinker's
Handbook for tips.

Prewriting

Thinking and Writing About the Section
You have read about many interesting characters who took
chances. You can write a feature story to entertain or to inform
another class about one of their stories. First copy the chart
below. Then fill in the missing information.

Story	Who?	Where?	What Happened?	Why?
Let the Balloon Go	John Sumner	Melbourne	climbed tree	
Tonweya and the Eagles		Western Plains		He befriended them.
Legend of Sleepy Hollow	Ichabod Crane		disappears after midnight ride	He was chased by Headless Horseman (Brom Bones).

Writing

Now write a feature story about one of the selections on your
chart. Use the information to answer the questions *who*, *where*,
what happened, and *why*. For more information about explanatory
writing, see your Writer's Handbook.

Revising

Read your first draft to a partner. Do you have an interesting
opening? Did you answer all of the questions? Make changes if
necessary. Then proofread for spelling and punctuation errors.
Write your final copy.

Presenting

Read your feature story to another class. See if they can answer
the questions *who*, *where*, *what happened*, and *why* from the
information you have put in your feature story.

Books to Read

North of Danger by Dale Fife. E. P. Dutton, © 1978.

Can Arne cover two hundred miles of frozen wasteland in time to reach his father? Can he trust the one man who can make it possible? You can share this true tale of courage and survival where a sense of direction is critical.

Computers: How They Work and What They Do by Patricia Fara. Pelham Books, © 1982.

Is it possible to understand the complicated workings and work of the modern computer? This exciting and colorful book helps you do just that. Find out how computers control underseas robots and aid in apprehending criminals.

Computer Languages by Christopher Lampton. Franklin Watts, © 1983.

How do you "talk" to a computer—using FORTRAN, COBOL, BASIC, PASCAL, or LOGO? Find out the differences and similarities among these languages and how to use them.

The Painter of Miracles by Cal Roy. Farrar, Straus, and Giroux, © 1974.

Will Maclovio take the chance and rise to the challenge life has presented to him? Experience what changes him from a boy who could paint miracles to a man who can live and see them.

10

Spare Time

Spare time is like spare change—most people never seem to have enough. Spare time is that free and easy time when schedules and deadlines don't matter—a time you can fill up by whim or notion. How do *you* like to spend yours?

Shopping, going to the movies, and playing sports—these are three ways of spending spare time that you'll read about in Section Ten. Shoppers will discover how to outsmart slick ads. Sports fans will have a chance to meet some vigorous soccer players who tackle all odds when they start up a team, and movie-goers will get a free ticket to revisit some film classics. In short, Section Ten presents lively ideas to add spice to your spare time!

Recognizing Propaganda

Ernie had saved just enough money to treat himself to a movie. He liked action films, and when he saw an ad that promised "action-packed adventure and stupendous special effects," he decided that was the movie to see. But the movie was a big disappointment. It was so boring that Ernie left before it was over. Ernie had "fallen for a line" in the ad. He has been a victim of propaganda.

Propaganda is a deliberate effort to persuade people to be for or against someone or something. Propaganda techniques are used in many political campaigns to persuade you to vote for a person or a law. You can also find evidence of propaganda in most of the advertising you read and hear. Advertising uses propaganda not necessarily to deceive you but to encourage you to buy a product.

The writers of advertisements use many techniques. One is called **loaded words**. In this kind of propaganda, a writer uses words that are loaded to appeal to your emotions, instead of using facts that inform. This sentence presents simple facts: "You can leave winter behind by going to Tropic Isle." Now look at the ad and notice the difference when loaded words are used instead. Words like *escape*, *miserable*, *blues*, and *paradise* are all loaded to slant your opinion in a certain direction.

Escape the miserable
WINTER BLUES!
Fly away to
Your Sunshine Paradise
TROPIC ISLE

The Super Sunglasses advertisement is an example of another technique. It's called **transfer**. Notice that this advertisement does not make claims to try to convince you that Super Sunglasses are best. Instead, it shows that kids who are wearing them are very happy and having great fun with friends. The ad writers hope that you will transfer your positive feelings about fun and friendship to buying Super Sunglasses. This technique uses things that are unrelated to the product to encourage you to buy, instead of informing you about real qualities of the product.

Another propaganda technique, called **glittering generalities**, can be seen in the GTX sports car ad. This technique makes big claims and vague promises without providing specific facts or research to back them up. In this example, the reader has no way of knowing why that sports car is "the world's most advanced." Who says so, and what proof is there? Glittering generalities often contain "permissible lies"—statements that give a misleading impression and lead people to draw false conclusions.

Get your pair of SUPER SUNGLASSES TODAY!

The New GTX Sports Car!
The Car with the World's Most Advanced Design! No Better Car on the Market

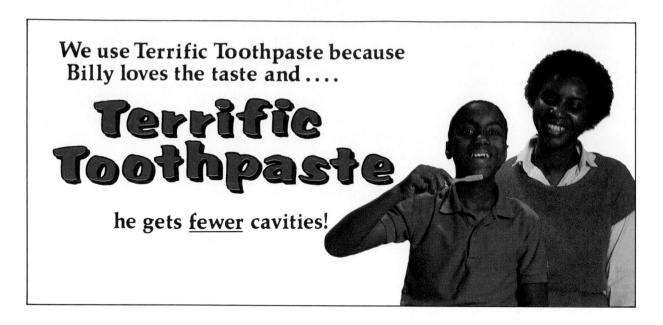

We use Terrific Toothpaste because Billy loves the taste and . . . .

Terrific Toothpaste

he gets <u>fewer</u> cavities!

Plain folks is one more technique. This type of ad uses models who look like "plain folks" you could trust and sets them in ordinary situations. Ad writers want to make you *identify* with these people and consequently buy the same products. Terrific Toothpaste is an example of a plain-folks ad.

1. What technique does the ad below use?

Our family goes for

PaNcake DeLiGHT!

This ad uses a plain-folks technique. If you had trouble identifying it, notice that the ad does not not make a big claim or promise. Instead it shows an ordinary family in an ordinary situation—eating around the kitchen table.

2. Read the ad slogan below and see if you can tell what propaganda technique it uses.

NOTHING IS MORE REFRESHING

THAN

LILLY'S LEMONADE!

Did you answer that the slogan uses *glittering generalities?* Notice that it makes a big claim, "nothing is more refreshing," without giving any real facts to back it up.

3. What kind of technique does the cereal ad below use?

EAT TROPICAL ORANGES

Practicing Recognizing Types of Propaganda

1. Identify the propaganda technique used in the Tropical Orange ad above and explain how it works.

2. What propaganda techniques are used in the ad slogans below? Explain how they work.

Leave behind the shabby look!

Join the glamorous set in clothes by FLIPSIDE.

Stay at the International Inn—the island's most luxurious hotel!

Tips for Reading on Your Own

- When you suspect that what you're reading may be propaganda, ask yourself these questions: *What* are the facts? *Where* is the evidence? *Who* is writing this, and for whom?
- If you decide the writing is propaganda, read carefully and critically, so you can decide whether or not you wish to be persuaded by it. Keep in mind facts and ideas the writer did not mention.
- Pay attention to the techniques that were used.

Millions of kids think that shopping is just about the best way to spend their spare time. In fact, kids are driven to shop—not necessarily by cars but by ads. Advertisers use powerful tricks of the trade to convince kids to spend their money on products. What eye-opening tricks of the trade will you discover in this article? As you read, notice the different kinds of propaganda that advertisers use.

Tricks of the Trade

by Ann E. Weiss

Every year, industries in America spend millions of dollars on advertising. In a single year, one large manufacturer of soaps and cleaners spent $460 million on advertising. A cosmetics company paid a comparatively tiny $80 million to advertise its cosmetics. At the same time, a toy firm bought $15 million worth of TV advertising time. This company spent the bulk of that amount in the weeks before Christmas—a bonanza season for toy makers.

How is this advertising money spent? Much of it goes into preparing the ads we see and hear. For a TV campaign to advertise a soft drink, over one hundred young performers sang and danced their way from California to New Orleans to New York City. To get one twelve-second sequence exactly right, the performers went through seventeen rehearsals and seventy-eight retakes. Finally, the shooting was over. The result—one sixty-second commercial and four thirty-second "spots"—cost nearly $1 million to produce. And that was before any money was spent to air the ads.

The cost of airing an ad, or of getting it into print, is great too. Sixty seconds of TV time can cost an advertiser $265,000 if it comes during a popular program in evening prime time. On a daytime show with a smaller audience, thirty seconds of time cost anywhere from $6,000 to $20,000. Many of the advertisers are happy to pay the higher rate for a more popular show because that means more people will see their ads.

Advertising rates in the print media are also based on the popularity of a particular newspaper or magazine and on the number of men, women, or children who will see the ads it carries.

One national magazine, with a circulation of six and one half million, charges about $44,000 for a full-page color ad. Another weekly magazine, with a circulation of over twenty million, charges $65,000 for a one-page color ad.

People in advertising do not want to run the risk of wasting the client's advertising dollars. When those dollars amount to millions each year, waste is unthinkable. So the country's leading ad agencies spend long hours laboring over every detail of the ads they prepare. Nothing escapes their notice. Every word in the advertising copy, every line in a drawing, every shadow in a photograph, every note of music— everything must contribute to the ad's overall purpose: making us want to buy the product.

One way an advertiser can get us to buy is by encouraging us to identify with the people we see using the product in the ad. That may make us want to use the product too. For example, one communications company paid for a series of TV ads that urge us to call long distance. In one ad, an Illinois woman tells us about her friend who lives in California. The two are close, almost like sisters. How wonderful it is that at a cost of only $2.60 they can talk on the telephone for ten minutes. Naturally, we identify with the people in this ad. Like them, we have faraway friends and relatives whom we miss. Suddenly, telephoning those we love seems like the right thing to do.

Some of today's ad agents aim to give their campaigns a dramatic flair. For example, in one automobile ad, a car and a beautiful woman appear to be perched atop a peak in the Rocky Mountains. Appear to be? They *were* on the peak. A helicopter carried the auto and model to the rocky summit, and an airborne camera crew photographed the scene. In one razor ad, an actor shaved his face during a demolition derby. "I was terrified," the actor confessed later. But the razor company was delighted with its attention-grabbing ad.

These advertising techniques are quite straightforward. They are designed to appeal to us and to make us want a particular product, but they do not attempt to trick us into thinking that the product is bigger or better or more useful than it really is. Other advertising tricks, however, do exactly that.

Thomas Lipton, founder of a large tea company, dreamed up one such trick when he was a boy. He suggested that when someone came into the shop for eggs, he and his father should stand aside and let Mrs. Lipton do the selling. Why? Mrs. Lipton had more delicate hands than either her husband or her son. Small eggs looked larger when she held them, and customers thought they were getting more for their money.

The Liptons didn't say anything untrue about the size of their eggs. They just set up a scene that gave a misleading impression and let people draw their own false conclusions. Today, that kind of selling technique has a name—the "permissible lie."

Modern advertising is full of carefully-worded permissible lies. It's easy to learn to spot them. "No finer kind than . . ." "The unique taste of . . ." "Nothing cleans better than . . ." But there may be several kinds that are just *as fine*. The taste may be unique, but something else may taste *better*. Many others may clean just *as well*.

Permissible lies come with many disguises. A hand cream that promises it will "keep your hands younger-looking" isn't really promising anything at all. Younger-looking than what? Than your hands looked a year ago? Twenty years ago? Younger than they'll look ten years from now? An ad for a tablet that "helps cure your cold" isn't offering you a cure, just a "help." What about a medicine that gives "fast relief" from stomach upset? How fast is "fast"?

An ad can even say that one product is superior to another without using the word *better*. In one commercial a woman is amazed at how well a particular brand of denture cleaner gets stains off a set of false teeth. She announces that she's going to switch to that brand right away. Without actually saying so, she lets us know that this denture cleaner is better than any other she's used.

Permissible lies can mislead by telling the truth—but not the whole truth. An oil company advertised that its gasoline contained *platformate*. People thought that platformate was a rare ingredient that increased their gas mileage. An ingredient that increased mileage, yes. Rare, no. Platformate, or a platformate-like substance, is part of every refined gasoline. Saying that a gasoline contains platformate, one person commented, "is like a baker advertising, 'I bake my cake with flour.'"

An ad for a pain reliever included the line "Three out of four doctors surveyed recommend . . . ." Perhaps three out of four doctors did recommend that brand. But how many were surveyed? Four thousand . . . or four? Who were they? Independent M.D.'s from reputable hospitals? People employed by the company that manufactured the pain reliever?

Whatever other techniques they use, advertisers know that their most effective selling tool is a successful appeal to people's emotions. Flip through almost any national magazine and you can see this principle at work. You might, for example, find an ad for a hotel chain that depicts a peaceful moonlit countryside. From the window of a farmhouse, light streams out into the night. "They left a light in the window . . . . It's the light that will lead you home." Pure nostalgia.

Copywriters, however, try to conceal the emotional appeal of the ads they write. How does this concealment work? Take a TV ad for a headache remedy. As the actors in the commercial talk about fast relief, soothing music plays softly in the

background. On Madison Avenue, this kind of music is called a *rug* or *carpet*. A person watching the commercial may hardly be conscious of the music. But subconsciously, it's different. Scientists know that the subconscious mind takes in far more impressions every second than does the conscious mind. Experiments prove that the human subconscious notices and remembers nearly every detail of every event of a person's life.

So there sits the viewer (let's say a man) barely noticing the ad. But with his subconscious mind, he hears and remembers every word, every note of music. In his subconscious, the name of the headache remedy is linked with the gentle soothing quality of the music. Days later, when he has a headache, his subconscious memory may direct him to select that medicine for relief.

Color can also be used to appeal to our subconscious minds. Ads for household cleaning products—soaps, detergents, and polishes—typically feature clear, bright tones with lots of clean white space. The colors in ads for products like clothes and cosmetics conform to changing fashions—glowing one year, muted the next.

The props that appear in an ad may be designed to appeal to our subconscious selves, too. The focus of a full page magazine ad for a dishwashing soap is a woman's reflection shining on a plate that has theoretically been washed in the liquid. A headline in inch-high type, "See it for yourself," appears across

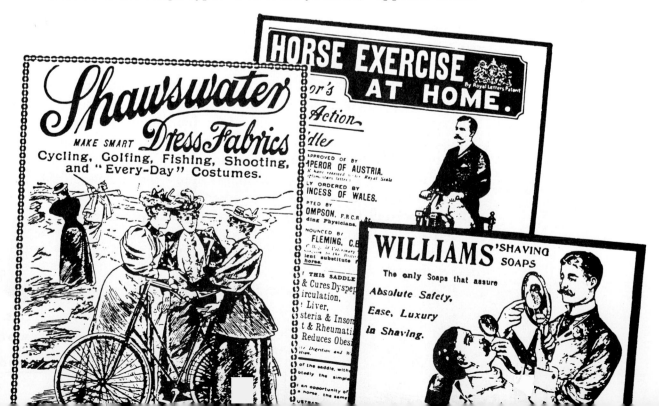

the top of the page. A photo of the soap bottle is prominent at the bottom right-hand corner.

On a conscious level, that's about all the average magazine reader will notice in this ad. Yet as the reader (let's say a woman) turns the page, she may smile slightly or feel her spirits rise. Why? Her subconscious mind, which takes in many times the number of details that her conscious mind does, has noticed the small photo above the bottle of soap. A festively set table . . . gold cloth and napkins . . . blue plates sparkling clean . . . a carved roast . . . corn on the cob . . . rolls. An attractive young woman is just setting out the salad. Around the table are another woman, two men, and two children.

To our reader's subconscious mind, that's a picture of sheer delight—at least so the person who wrote the ad hopes. The reader, of course, is supposed to identify with the attractive hostess. It's her husband who gazes attentively at her from across the table and their closest friends who are about to share her delicious dinner. Those are her well-mannered children, the little girl sitting with her hands politely folded in her lap, the baby quiet in his highchair. Naturally, our reader smiles. Part of her mind—a hidden part, but a part nonetheless—has caught a glimpse of an idyllic family scene. And this idyll is associated in her subconscious with a particular soap. Next time she goes to the supermarket her subconscious may prod her to buy that soap—and an image of domestic bliss.

If an agent can get so much across in a magazine ad, what can be accomplished in a sixty-second TV commercial? Plenty. Think of all the inviting little vignettes of harmonious family life we see in TV ads. And think of all the other visual appeals to our subconscious minds that are worked into television ads. The spotlessly neat kitchen in an ad for shortening. The beautifully dressed children in an ad for cat food. The happy faces of the women who scrub and clean with one product after another. The obviously expensive house that belongs to a man about to come down with an achy cold.

It is important that we try to look at disguised advertising, indeed at all advertising, carefully and critically. We should alway look at it with the question in mind "What is this ad really saying?"

Comprehension Check

Think and Discuss

1. What trick or tricks of the advertising trade are the most eye-opening to you? Why?
2. What are the two major ways in which advertising money is spent?
3. Do you think Thomas Lipton used dishonest methods to sell his eggs? Explain your answer.
- 4. What kind of propaganda is the hand cream ad that promises to "keep your hands younger looking"? Why?
- 5. Find an example in the article that uses *transfer* as a propaganda technique.
- Comprehension Skill: Propaganda techniques

See your Thinker's Handbook for tips.

Communication Workshop

Talk

Work with a partner to discuss the different ads you read about. Which do you think were the most effective? Then use advertising techniques to create an ad for an imaginary car called The Panther. Brainstorm with your partner to come up with an ad that is exciting or clever.

Speaking/Listening: Discussion

Write

Write an ad of your own. Use the information from your brainstorming session or create one from scratch. Read your ad to your partner. Would he or she buy your product? Why or why not?

Writing Fluency: Advertisement

Understanding Multiple Affixes

STOP GRINNING AT ME!

© 1962 United Feature Syndicate, Inc.

It might be a good idea for Linus to use his spare time practicing kicking the football. The poor fellow made a *big* mistake—he missed the ball. What word could you use to describe him? One word might be *unfortunate*. *Unfortunate* would be a good choice since you know that the prefix *un–* means "not" and "not fortunate" certainly describes him.

As you read, you may often see words you know with prefixes, suffixes, or endings added to them. Some words even have multiple affixes—more than one prefix, suffix, or ending. The meanings of these words aren't usually hard to figure out.

You know that a root word is a word from which other words are formed. You also know that a prefix is a word part added to the beginning of a root word, that a suffix is a word part added to the end of a word, and that an ending is a group of letters also added to the end of a word. When you come to a word with a prefix, break the word into the prefix and the root word to help you pronounce the word and often to figure out what the word means. When a word has an ending or a suffix, look for the root word and add the ending or suffix to pronounce the word.

Figure out what the underlined words below mean.

Advertisers often use famous athletes in their ads. These ads are pretested to be sure you will identify with these professionals and buy the products in the ad.

You know that the root word *advertise* means "sell" and you could note the suffix –*er* and the ending –*s* to figure out that *advertisers* are "people who sell." You also know that the root word *profession* refers to work that requires skill. When the suffix –*al* and the ending –*s* are added, the meaning changes to "people who work in a profession." The root word *test* means "try out." Notice that the prefix *pre–* and ending –*ed* are added to *test*. What does *pretested* mean? It means "tried out beforehand."

What do these underlined words mean? Remember to look for root words and affixes.

Some ads are <u>indescribably</u> clever. In one ad for a vacation spot, there were no <u>talkative</u> <u>tourists</u>—only the soft sound of the ocean.

The word *indescribably* means "in a manner not able to be described" and *talkative* means "given to talking a great deal." Did you notice the suffix -*ist* in *tourists?* It is like the suffix -*er* in *advertisers. Tourists* are people who tour or travel.

Practicing Multiple Affixes

Use what you know about root words and multiple affixes to figure out the underlined words below.

1. Soccer is a great <u>equalizer</u>. It gives kids with different abilities a chance to be <u>successful</u> in a sport.
2. Our team studied the strengths and <u>weaknesses</u> of the opposing team.
3. It was only a matter of time until our team's <u>disorganized</u> defense fell apart before the well-planned charge of the Tigers.

Tips for Reading on Your Own

- When you're reading on your own and you come to a word you don't know, see if it is made up of a root word and a prefix, suffix, or ending.
- Remember that a root word may have more than one prefix, suffix, or ending added to it. This may help you pronounce the word.
- Remember that prefixes and some suffixes have meanings of their own that can help you figure out the meanings of words they are part of.
- Reread the sentence to figure out what the word means.
- For other tips on figuring out words, see your Word Study Handbook.

Lots of kids at Orkney High love to play sports in their spare time—especially football. When Jamie Mitchell, a new student, fails to make the football team, he decides to organize a team of his own and he introduces a new sport to the school—soccer. Jamie's team call themselves the "Soccer Orphans." You'll soon discover why as you join them in their first game. Look for examples of biased writing as you read.

The Soccer Orphans

by William MacKellar

No doubt it was curiosity about the new Orkney team that attracted the moderate-sized crowd to the Kenyon home field. It was obvious to Jamie, as he eyed the crowd, the Spartans' band, and the cheerleaders, that in some way rumors about the Orkney Orphans had drifted across the county. Jamie would have preferred a less splashy debut. There was no sense, though, in worrying about that. There were other things to think about—like uniforms. Or rather, the lack of them.

Jamie grimaced slightly as he and his teammates trotted onto the Kenyon High School soccer field for the pregame warm-up. At least the Orphans all had shorts, though few of them matched. Shirts had been a real problem and one they had yet to resolve. In the meantime they had all agreed to wear white jerseys with a large O in the front. As for soccer shoes, only a handful of the players had them. It was a sad-looking, ragtag outfit that lined up against the Kenyon Spartans, trim in their red-and-gold jerseys and light-blue shorts.

Play had no sooner started than the Spartans mounted a blistering attack on the Orkney goal. In the space of five minutes, Kenny Harper, the Orkney goalkeeper, smothered or turned aside six powerful drives on his goal. It seemed only a matter of time before the desperate and disorganized Orkney defense would collapse before the red-and-gold attack.

"Mark him, Charlie!" Jamie hollered as he scurried to cover King, a Spartan attacker. The high pass from the wing floated in,

dead on target. King slipped past Charlie, met the ball with his head, and sent it spinning into the net, just beyond the reach of Kenny Harper's clawing fingertips. First goal for Kenyon.

Taking the ball after the kickoff, Jamie beat two tacklers and slipped it to Calvin Dobkins. Cal raced ahead and sent a low, lead pass to Red Carson who came flashing in from the wing. Red's boot sent the ball crashing goalward, and Manny Gilmore seemed to explode from nowhere. With a lightning-quick flick of his head, he met the ball in midair and nodded it into the net. First goal for Orkney!

So sudden had been the Orkney response that the Spartans seemed to be in a state of shock. They exchanged more than a few startled stares as they took their places for the kickoff. Plainly there was more to this Orkney team than showed on the surface. The Spartans, though, were too well disciplined to panic at the unexpected. Playing conservatively until it could fathom the strengths and weaknesses of the visitors, the home club swung into a classic formation. Slowly, inexorably, experience started to tell. Then, with devastating suddenness, the Kenyon offensive forces burst through. When the whistle blew for half time, Orkney's demoralized defense had been shattered for three additional goals. Trailing 4–1, Jamie gathered his disconsolate teammates around Coach Jill Huntley.

Amusement touched Coach's eyes as she said, "I've never seen such a woebegone bunch. Remember one thing. Nobody ever wins while he's feeling sorry for himself. So forget what's happened and think about what can happen. We're losing 4–1. OK. If we lose 7–1, it won't make that much difference. So we're going to beef up our offense. Sy Romano and you halfbacks, I want you to rush ahead. Keep pressure on them. Charlie and Mark, come well upfield from your fullback positions. Got it?"

"Got it," said Charlie as he chewed on an orange. "We keep them under the guns. Better them than us."

"Exactly." Coach Huntley turned to big Jeb Jennings. "Jeb, you're not getting the distance you're capable of on your throw-ins. Go back a few yards from the touchline and use a run-up approach for momentum. With your strength you should be able to heave the ball thirty-five yards at least. Center it near their goal. Jamie, Calvin, and the others will be watching for it.

It's going to surprise and confuse their defense. They've never seen anyone who could toss a ball overhead like you can."

She turned to her team captain as the whistle shrilled. "You're the key, Jamie. They're looking to you out there. And so am I. Good luck."

Play had no sooner started than Sy Romano neatly block-tackled a Kenyon striker with his good arm and sent a long grass cutter over to Monty Templeton. The English boy collected the pass, slipped past one defender, then deftly backheeled the ball to Jeb Jennings. Suddenly the whole Spartan goal was flooded with Orphans. Jamie, taking a pass from Jeb, eluded two tacklers, then sent a little chip shot to Red Carson. The goalkeeper never had a chance as the redhead blasted the ball into the net.

"Way to go, Red!" sang out Jamie. "Let's get another!"

It was easier said than done. Slowly the minutes slipped away with the score still 4–2 in favor of the home club. Then suddenly big Jeb Jennings was on the touchline for a throw-in. A few quick steps, a snap of his powerful wrists, and the ball was soaring into the goal mouth. Caught completely off guard by Jeb's incredible heave, the defenders scrambled to intercept. Too late. Jamie's left foot met the ball while it was still descending. There was the clean thud of leather meeting leather. The next moment the ball was cradled in the webbing at the top left corner of the goal.

That was the end of Orkney's scoring for the day. After a series of desperate assaults on the Kenyon goal, inexperience and lack of conditioning took their toll. In the space of five minutes from the closing whistle, the red-and-gold attackers hammered home three more goals. The electric scoreboard showed 7–3 in favor of the home team as Jamie and the others trudged off the field.

"Great game!" It was a short time later, and Jamie was about to squirm into Charlie Riley's vintage car. He turned to face the speaker, Sally Reynolds, a reporter for the school newspaper.

"We lost," was all he could say. "What happened to us?"

"Just inexperience," cut in a cool voice. Coach Huntley tossed a couple of soccer balls into the trunk of her car. "Next time we're going to do better. We really threw a scare into them before we ran out of gas. I don't think they expected what we showed them. No, I can't say I'm disappointed."

"Do you mind if I give the game a play in the *Clarion?*" asked Sally.

"Hey, Sally, you can't do that!" cried Jamie in dismay. "Not after the licking we just got!"

"But Jamie," remonstrated Sally, "all the kids were super, even if we didn't win. I'll be honest and admit I had meant to give the game a brief write-up. But now that I've seen what a great sport it is, I think it deserves more. Anyway, all we seem to have in the *Clarion* is football and more football."

"Sally's right," Coach Huntley said decisively. "I think it's a great idea. It will let our school know who we are! Sally's just the one who can do it for us."

"She can?" ventured Jamie doubtfully. "It's just that when you were hoping to win and you lose—"

Coach Huntley closed the trunk of her car. "Not everyone can win, Jamie. But when you profit from a loss, then you don't lose either. As for Sally, the publicity she gets us will be good for us. It'll sure make us play harder and tougher."

Sally suddenly looked worried. "What about Coach Mylko?" she asked. "He plays hard and tough too. Maybe he won't like it."

"Maybe." The coach smiled. "Maybe."

"Then I'll go ahead with the story," Sally sang out. "Super!"

This time Jamie kept his mouth shut. He still thought the fewer who learned about their 7–3 stomping, the better. Only it was clear that Coach Huntley didn't agree. And neither did Sally Reynolds.

When Jamie read the *Clarion* that week, the bold headline on the front page seemed to hit him between the eyes.

SOCCER DEBUTS AT ORKNEY

This may come as a surprise to most of our students. Not only does Orkney have a soccer team, but it has just played its first game—a friendly match against the Kenyon Spartans.

It may seem strange to introduce a new sport to Orkney. Yet soccer is not a new sport. In fact it is one of the oldest in the world, its origins going back to China as long ago as 200 B.C.

Soccer is also the most popular sport in the world. More people play and watch soccer, or football as it is usually called abroad, than any other sport. An estimated audience of well over one billion watched the last World Cup on television.

The rules for soccer are simple. The field is approximately the length of a football gridiron. There is a goal at each end and eleven players on each side. The object of the game is to propel the ball across the opposite goal line with the feet, head, or body. Except for a touchline throw-in, only the goalkeepers may use their hands.

Perhaps one of soccer's greatest appeals is that it can be played by men and women of average height and weight. One doesn't have to be a glandular goon to participate. In a world that puts an increasing premium on muscular development, it is comforting to know that outstanding soccer players are of average stature and weight.

So, soccer has come to Orkney High. It has a coach, too, a very fine one in Jill Huntley who studied the game in Switzerland. Still, there are a number of things that the team doesn't have yet but should have—like a field it can use for its home games, like equipment and uniforms, like your support and your interest.

But already they do have the things that matter most: determination and dedication and a bunch of the most exuberant players this reporter has seen in a long time.

Jamie put down the paper and grinned. Not bad! Sally hadn't even mentioned the score. His grin broadened. Clever girl! He was glad she had gotten in that bit about their uniforms too. Or rather, their lack of them. Well, maybe they'd get some action now.

They did. Not exactly, though, as Jamie had hoped. Coach Mylko had been more than just a little upset—first at the glandular goon reference and secondly at the remarks about the soccer boys having no place to play. "Understand one thing, Mitchell," he snapped at Jamie that afternoon after gym. "My football players need our field. It's in use every day—all day. Besides, the cleats on those soccer shoes would chew the field to ribbons in no time."

"I see."

The coach looked at him sharply. "No, you don't see. Look, if I start playing Mr. Nice Guy around here, you know what's going to happen? Once the Wildcats start losing, the alumni will be after my scalp." He ran his thick fingers over his closely cropped head and grinned sourly. "What's left of it. Anyway, you can forget about using the football field. And you can forget about your uniforms and equipment. Every penny in my budget is already spent, or will be soon."

Mylko looked at Jamie glumly. "Look, you may not believe this, but I'm just a guy trying to do a job. And sometimes it's not a nice job with all the pressures I get from the town. Anyway, just understand two things. I can't let you use the football field. And there's nothing in my budget for soccer. Sorry."

Jamie nodded. "Sure," he said. For the first time he felt a pang of pity for the square-jawed man. Maybe Coach Mylko wasn't all he appeared on the surface.

Jamie left the gym in a reflective mood. Sally's article had been helpful, but clearly a lot of problems remained. It was obvious from what Coach Mylko had just told him that they could expect no help from the school. So that left matters squarely up to the Orphans—Orphans for sure, Jamie thought cynically. Here in megarich Orkney High with its Olympic-size pool and its Super Bowl stadium, the kids who wanted to play soccer would practically have to beg for every dime they needed.

But Sally's article did give a well-needed boost to the morale of the team, and Coach Huntley arranged for two more practice games. The Orphans lost both by scores of 5–1 and 6–2. Although Jamie was bitterly disappointed, the coach gave no indication of dejection. "Don't go by the score," she remarked after the second game. "The main thing is that we're getting solid experience." She paused. "And now for some good news. I've got so much confidence in all of you that I was able to get us into the conference."

There was a collective gasp from the circle of players at this bombshell, followed by a chorus of excited shouts.

"We're in the conference? That's terrific!" Jamie said. "But uniforms, Coach! We've got no uniforms!"

Coach Huntley smiled. "So that's why you've been calling yourselves the Orphans. Anyway, it's not how we suit up for the game that counts but how we play the game. We'll do OK!"

"Where will we play our home games?" Red Carson asked. "The school won't let us use the football field."

Coach nodded. "I've discussed this with the league officials. Until we get our own field, we'll have to play all our games away. It's a disadvantage, but disadvantages would seem to be a way of life for us."

"Good show!" exclaimed Monty Templeton, his eyes snapping.

"But Coach Huntley," said Charlie Riley, a timbre of frustration in his voice, "we've just got to do something about uniforms, especially now that we're in the conference."

"Speaking of uniforms," contributed Jamie, "I just got an idea. Why don't we have a car wash? At a buck a car we should do all right. We'll need a little publicity, of course. Maybe Sally Reynolds can help us in the *Clarion*."

"Then let's do it," Coach said crisply. "Uniforms will be good for our morale, if nothing else. Meanwhile, I'll be in touch with the conference officials about the schedule. Oh, Jamie, may I see you for a minute before you leave?"

"Sure," he responded as the others drifted off.

Satisfied they were alone, she turned to him. "I'll get right to the point Jamie. You're the captain of this team and you're the one who put the whole thing together.

"First, you know as well as I do that some people in town haven't been exactly crazy about the idea of having a soccer team at our school. Through the years, Orkney High School has stood for two things: football and winning. Now we show up with a makeshift soccer team that has already lost three games and will almost surely lose a lot more. Despite that nice article Sally wrote about us, I can feel the chill in the air."

Jamie nodded. "I know what you mean. Any attention we get means less attention for the Wildcats, although that's not true."

"But that's what they think." She hesitated, "What I have to say now is a little more difficult to express. I happen to believe we have the greatest bunch of kids in the world. There are some people though who may think differently. Already I've heard some stories going around. Some of them are supposed to be funny, I guess, but some are cruel too." She hesitated.

"Go on," he urged.

"You must understand," she continued, "that a few years ago a youngster, say like Sy Romano, with one arm, would never have gone out for a tough, physical-contact sport. Now, not only are such kids insisting on playing, but society is insisting on it too. It just makes sense, provided of course the youngster can carry his own weight on the field."

"Sy does more than that," countered Jamie. "He's the guy who makes our whole halfback line click."

"Right, but it is more than just Sy. We happen also to have a partially deaf boy with a hearing aid. And of course a boy with glasses, although that's not uncommon. Now, three such boys in a big school like Orkney isn't unusual. But they're all on the same team—our team. You begin to realize we have a rather unique team." She stopped and waited.

He frowned. "I never thought of them like that before. They were just all kids. Great kids."

"Exactly the way anyone should think of them. However, you must realize that up until a short time ago none of them was doing anything, as far as sports were concerned. They were, in a sense, rejects. Then soccer came into their lives. That's why I love the game. It's the great equalizer. It gives every kid a chance and doesn't penalize anyone. Understand, Jamie, I think the kids we have are just the greatest. But I wanted you to know there are some stories going around."

Jamie felt anger flare along his nerves. "Why would anyone spend time on such rotten gossip? Just because we might steal some of the thunder from the Wildcats?" He froze. "Not Coach Mylko?"

"Bob Mylko? Not Bob. He can be tough but he plays fair." She slung her tote bag over her shoulder. "Well, that's it, Jamie. And good luck on the car wash."

Jamie was fairly silent during the ride home in Charlie's car. Charlie apparently didn't notice. He never stopped talking. "How about that? She got us into the conference! Man, that's what I need to show my stuff! Competition!" He stopped. "About that car-wash idea of yours—great!" Charlie switched on the radio. "We're on our way, man!"

All of a sudden Jamie felt tired. He leaned back, closed his eyes, and let the music wash over him. His mind went back over the events of the day—to the game they had played that afternoon, to the news about their being accepted into the conference, to the things that Coach Huntley had just told him. Curiously, instead of being depressed, he felt strangely uplifted by what she had said. They were the greatest bunch in the world—all of them.

"Yep, Charlie Riley, we're on our way!"

Think and Discuss

1. Why is the name "Soccer Orphans" appropriate to Jamie's team?
2. Why do the Orphans lose their game against Kenyon?
3. How does the article in the *Clarion* help the Orphans?
- 4. Which words in the sentences below suggest bias?
   a. The Spartans mounted a blistering attack.
   b. Orkney's demoralized defense had been shattered.
   c. After a series of desperate assaults, inexperience and lack of conditioning took their toll.
- 5. Which sentence below shows bias? How?

   Perhaps one of soccer's greatest appeals is that it can be played by men and women of average height and weight. One doesn't have to be a glandular goon to participate.
- Comprehension Skill: Biased writing

Communication Workshop

Talk

Work with a small group. Take turns pretending you are students at Orkney High and tell the rest of the group which games you will attend—football or soccer—and why. Then discuss as a group which of the sports played at your school is your favorite—either to watch or to play.

Speaking/Listening: Group discussion

Write

Pick your favorite sport to play or watch. Write a paragraph that describes some exciting moments during a real or imaginary game, but do not use the name of the sport. Write the name on the back of your paper. Then read your paragraph to your group and see if they can guess which sport you wrote about.

Writing Fluency: Paragraph

How to Study for Tests

Have you ever tried to figure out how much spare time you have each school day? If you're like most students, you spend about eight hours sleeping and about eight hours in school. You also spend a couple of hours eating meals and performing household chores. That leaves you about six hours a day of spare time. If you spend just two of those hours doing your homework and studying for tests, you will still have four hours a day all to yourself, which is quite a bit. And those two study hours will help your schoolwork immensely.

Studying for tests isn't that difficult. By using a few simple techniques, you'll be able to make your studying more efficient and effective. When the teacher announces a test, you should begin studying for it right away. If you wait until the last minute, you won't have sufficient time to review all the material. Be aware that you need to concentrate. Some teenagers study best in a quiet corner all by themselves. Others find that soft music helps them concentrate.

Once you find a place to study, assemble all the materials you will need, such as your textbooks, your class notes, and your homework and test papers. Then try to predict what material will appear on the test. Your class notes will show you the most important points covered in class. Review those points and reread the appropriate sections of the textbooks. When you review a textbook, form test questions in your mind and try to answer them. Many textbooks have questions at the end of each chapter; you should answer these as well. Also carefully read any chapter or unit summaries. Then look at your homework and test papers. If you made any mistakes, review that material again.

If you're having trouble remembering any material, try rereading it just before you go to bed and then reviewing it in the morning. Go to bed early on the night before the test. When you wake up, you'll be ready to go.

The Women's 400 Meters

by Lillian Morrison

Skittish,
they flex knees, drum heels and
shiver at the starting line

waiting the gun
to pour them over the stretch
like a breaking wave.

Bang! they're off
careening down the lanes,
each chased by her own bright tiger.

Would you want to spend your spare time on another planet, in a spooky castle, or chasing a giant gorilla? It's not as difficult as you may think. All you need is some knowledge of movies. As you read to find out more about these strange places and characters, look for opinions and determine if they are supported by facts.

At the Movies

by Jarmila Zemla

Most teens enjoy spending some of their spare time at the movies. And some of the most popular movies today are those in which special effects are an important element.

Although we tend to think of special effects as a recent development in movies, they've been used since the early years of movie making. The 1902 movie *A Trip to the Moon,* for example, included many special effects and lavish sets.

By 1926 there were 20,000 theaters in the United States. This was also the time of German influence on American films. German film makers had made generous use of fantasy and myth in their films, and soon actors like Boris Karloff and films like *Frankenstein, The Mummy,* and *King Kong* were popular. *Flash Gordon* and *Batman* in the 1940s altered the direction back to space science-fiction adventure. In the 1950s and 1960s many Sci-Fi films reacted to the horrors of nuclear war. Most recently, Sci-Fi films have become more fantasy-oriented, relying heavily on special effects.

One creative use of special effects was in the classic 1933 movie, *King Kong.* The giant gorilla that people saw on the screen was really only eighteen inches tall. Up to six models of Kong were used so that movie audiences could thrill to Kong marching down the streets of New York or climbing up the Empire State Building.

The famous scene where the screaming actress Fay Wray is held in the palm of Kong's hand was produced in a unique way. An eight-foot model of Kong's hand and arm was built with moving parts that could be raised or lowered like a crane. Kong's fingers were wrapped around Wray's waist while she was still standing. Then the hand was raised about ten feet into the air with Wray kicking and screaming. The gorilla's fingers were loosened and Wray scrambled to hold on to keep from falling.

Another remarkable fact about Kong was the head section, which was built like the arm and hand with moving parts. The head was made out of wood, metal, and cloth and was covered on the outside by bearskin. Kong's nose was two feet across, and his teeth were up to ten inches long. Three operators stayed inside Kong's head, and with the use of pneumatic levers they were able to move the mouth, lips, eyes, and eyelids for the enraptured audience.

King Kong's success was based on more than special effects; it also had an interesting plot. King Kong lives on one end of Skull Island, an island inhabited by a tribe of natives and prehistoric monsters. A movie crew hears about the monsters and wants to film them. An actress (played by Fay Wray) goes along and has the misfortune of being captured by the natives. She is tied up and offered as the Bride of Kong. When Kong

sees her, he immediately falls in love with her and carries her
off, fighting off prehistoric monsters and the sailors who come
to rescue Fay. Wray is eventually rescued, and Kong is
captured and brought to New York to be displayed as a tourist
attraction. He escapes, finds Wray in her hotel room, and, in a
famous scene, reaches through the open window and grabs
her. He begins to climb, with her, up the Empire State
Building. Military planes are called out, and they fly around
Kong, shooting at him from all sides. Before he falls to his
death, he tenderly places Fay in a safe place—King Kong is
really a tender-hearted creature, after all.

　　Like *King Kong*, *The Invisible Man* created a sensation. At
the beginning of this 1933 film, a man arrives in a small
English village. He wears a heavy overcoat, his face is
wrapped in bandages, and his nose is hidden behind a small
shield. He wears dark glasses over his eyes and thick white

gloves cover his hands. His appearance fills the villagers with curiosity and fear as they try to figure out what lies beneath the mummylike bandages.

But the Invisible Man's chief problem is not his wardrobe. He is a scientist named Jack Griffin who discovered a formula that makes him invisible. He leaves his laboratory for the small village in the hopes that he will discover a cure for his condition. Unfortunately, his experiments do not work, the new chemical he uses drives him mad, and he begins to commit a series of crimes.

The police officials in the village now have a problem of amazing proportions on their hands. Not only is there a criminal loose, but he is insane and invisible. This dilemma is finally solved when Griffin is forced to hide in a barn during a snowstorm. Police surround the barn. Griffin attempts to escape, an easy task for an invisible man, but Griffin's presence is revealed to the police by footprints he leaves in the freshly fallen snow.

Filming *The Invisible Man* presented unique challenges to the special effects team. When Griffin was wrapped up, the actor could easily be photographed. But when he removed his bandages and wore only a suit, special filming techniques had to be used. The film was made in black and white, so the special effects person had an all-black set built. Then its walls and floors were completely covered in black velvet because velvet does not reflect light. Finally, an actor was dressed in a black velvet body suit, tights, gloves, and hood. He then put on a regular suit over the velvet costume. Photographed against the completely black background, all that was visible to the camera was a suit of clothes moving about the room. This film was then superimposed on film of the regular set, with visible actors and furniture. The film combination made an invisible man appear to delighted audiences, inspiring such sequels to the film as *The Invisible Man Returns, The Invisible Woman,* and *Abbott and Costello Meet the Invisible Man.*

Giant gorilllas and invisible men were new creations, but stories of vampires had frightened people long before films were made. Legends about vampires, creatures who leave their graves at night to nip at the necks and drink the blood of their victims, date back at least to ancient Greece.

These legends spread throughout Europe, where stories of vampires and their evil deeds continued for hundreds of years. The 1897 publication of Bram Stoker's book *Dracula* introduced the most famous vampire of all—Count Dracula, who lived in a spooky castle filled with cobwebs, huge staircases, and cold fireplaces.

But movie audiences had to wait until 1931 for the Count to stare at them with the eyes of a hypnotist and say, "Good e-e-evening." The special effects team had to transform the Count into a bat, but credit for the movie's most famous image goes to the make-up artists and costumers who created the Count's remarkably chilling appearance. His pale face has particularly sharp white teeth, which protrude over his lips. His hands are broad, with hairs in the center of his palm. Long fine nails are cut to sharp and menacing points.

The Creature from the Black Lagoon is another amazing being who just wants to be left alone—in the bottom of the swamp. The Creature, half man, half fish, is covered with scales and has gigantic claws where his fingers and toes should be. Scientists discover his existence and try to remove him from his natural habitat. Clearly, the Creature does not much like being disturbed in that way and a battle begins. This film, originally released in 1954, inspired a series of sequels, and the Creature was soon reappearing in *Revenge of the Creature* (1955) and *The Creature Walks Among Us* (1956).

The early Creature movies were produced in a special technique called "3-D." The purpose of this technique was to make objects on the screen look three-dimensional, more lifelike. The characters looked as if they were coming out of the screen at the audience, a wonderful effect for a monster like the Creature. The problem with this technique was that viewers had to wear special 3-D glasses, which did not always work. Sometimes they were uncomfortable, and some viewers even complained about the smell of the plastic glasses. The 3-D revolution was rejected almost as quickly as it began.

New standards for Sci-Fi films were set, however, with *2001: A Space Odyssey.* Costing over $10 million, the movie began a period in which special effects were more important than the story itself. Along with the visual effects, special attention was given to the music.

The story itself is hard to follow. It begins in a prehistoric time with groups of apelike creatures. Suddenly a large, black monolith appears and gives off a humming sound. This marks the dawn of a civilization. The movie then jumps quickly to the near future. A scientist travels to the moon to investigate the discovery of another monolith. Then, in the main portion of the movie, two astronauts are piloting a spaceship to Jupiter. It soon becomes apparent that the computer on board the spaceship is not working. It kills one of the astronauts. Before the other astronaut destroys it, the computer, which talks (although it is not much of a conversationalist), reveals the reason for the mission to Jupiter—to discover the source and power of the monoliths. The film ends with the astronaut dying of old age in a luxury apartment on Jupiter. His body becomes that of a human baby floating in space.

Although often criticized for its illogical plot, *2001: A Space Odyssey* greatly upgraded the technological standards for Sci-Fi films. Experimental techniques were used to create special effects. A galaxy of starbursts was created by dropping dribbles of dye from an eyedropper onto a glass plate.

Star Wars, The Empire Strikes Back, and *Return of the Jedi* make up a trilogy of Sci-Fi films. They feature an innocent farm boy, Luke Skywalker, who travels through strange worlds and is continually encountering conflicts between good and evil. The first conflict begins with a search through space for the beautiful Princess Leia. She has been captured by agents of the evil Galactic Empire. Her trusted robot helper, Artoo-Detoo, delivers a message to the wise old Obi-Wan Kanobi. This sets in motion the climactic battle between Obi-Wan and Lord Darth Vader, the evil side of the Force.

The *Star Wars* films have made huge box office grosses. One reason for their popularity is their realistic quality. The film makers went to great expense for the right locations and effects. Much of the film was shot in Tunisia, which has a desert that gives the impression of a distant planet. Scenes of Luke's hole-in-the-ground house were shot in Matmata, an African town that was built underground and is hundreds of years old. Other scenes were constructed in film studios outside London, England. The spaceships that the heroes and villains seemed to ride in were actually elaborate "toys" made for the movie in California. These "ships" were only about two

feet long and couldn't even fly. Instead, a special camera moved around them. The battle was fought with laser swords that actually were made of many tiny glass beads glued to a rod. A small motor in the sword's handle turned the rod. The glass beads reflected light from a bright lamp placed over the actors.

Laser-beam sword fights, giant gorillas climbing the Empire State Building, and invisible men sneaking around villages may sound incredible, but in the movies, anything is possible.

Meet a Reader

Susie Flores, a seventh grader in Texas, has seen several of the movies discussed in this article. Susie is especially impressed by the special effects in *The Invisible Man:* "It was the hardest effect to do, and the way it was done was very clever." Susie, who "loves computers," is in the Gifted and Talented Program at her school. When she isn't reading poetry or sports stories, Susie can be found playing cornet in the band or participating in volleyball, basketball, or track events.

Comprehension Check

Think and Discuss

1. If you could spend your spare time watching one of the movies described in the article, which one would you choose? Support your answer with factual information about the film.
2. List three important facts about the special effects in the 1933 movie *King Kong*.
3. List the steps involved in the process of filming the special effects of *The Invisible Man*.
● 4. Name at least two kinds of people whose opinion you would trust about the worth of a movie and tell why.
● 5. Both of the following statements are valid opinions. Why?
   a. The movie *2001: A Space Odyssey* created new standards for sci-fi film makers.
   b. One reason for the popularity of *Star Wars* is its realistic quality.
● Comprehension Skill: Fact and opinion

Communication Workshop

Talk

Pretend your class is made up of the most powerful critics in the movie business. Discuss with a small group how you would rate the films described in the article "At the Movies." Award one to four stars, with four being the best. Then discuss your all-time favorite films and compare them to the films mentioned in the article.
Speaking/Listening: Cooperative learning

Write

Write a short review of your favorite film of all time. Be sure to give your opinions of the film and back them up with examples. Read your review to your classmates. Does it make them want to see the film? Why or why not?
Writing Fluency: Film review

Movie Madness

What do you think is going on in these photos from old movies? On a separate sheet of paper, write a caption for each photo to share with your classmates.

LOOKING BACK

See your Thinker's Handbook for tips.

Prewriting

Thinking and Writing About the Section

You have read three persuasive selections in this section about spare time. You can write a persuasive paragraph for a classmate in which you state an opinion from one of the selections and give facts to support that opinion. First copy the chart below. Then fill in the missing information.

Selection	Opinion	Supporting Reasons
The Soccer Orphans	Everyone should go see Soccer Orphans.	1. Soccer is age-old sport. 2. 3.
At the Movies	*King Kong* is a fantastic movie.	1. 2. The special effects are creative. 3.
Tricks of the Trade	You should be very critical of ads.	1. 2. 3. Ads may be full of permissible lies.

Writing

Now write a paragraph in which you state an opinion from the chart and give facts to support it. For more information about persuasive paragraphs, see your Writer's Handbook.

Revising

Read your first draft to a partner. Have you stated your opinion in your topic sentence? Have you used facts to back it up? Did you save your most convincing reason until last? Make changes if necessary. Then proofread and write your final copy.

Presenting

Read your paragraph to a classmate. Does he or she agree with you?

11

Making Choices

Picture yourself curled up in a big, comfortable armchair, reading by firelight. Outside, a wild storm rages; great sheets of rain beat against the windows and ferocious winds howl around the corners. But you're so interested in what you're reading that you don't even notice the storm. What is it that you're reading?

You could be reading the selections in this section about three animals in the wilderness, a mystery in a crumbling English manor, and life on a distant planet. In each of these selections, the characters must make choices that change their lives. What choices do they make?

Recognizing Setting

Look closely at this picture. Look at the deeply wooded wilderness and the wild animals. Close your eyes for a moment. Picture yourself there—alone. How would you describe the setting and how it makes you feel? You could talk about the loneliness, fear, and the sense of isolation you feel because of the wilderness and the dangers lurking there.

Often when you read, you will find that the setting is one of the most important things to understand in a story. The **setting** is when and where a story takes place. In some stories, the setting can determine what happens to the characters and how they behave. The setting can also cause the characters to have problems they wouldn't have had if the setting were different. When you read, look for details—words and phrases—an author uses to describe the setting and try to picture the setting in your mind.

The paragraphs below begin Chapter 1 of *The Incredible Journey*. The paragraphs describe the setting into which three pets will venture. Notice the details that help you picture the setting.

Chapter 1

This journey took place in a part of Canada which lies in the northwestern part of the great sprawling province of Ontario. It is a vast area of deeply wooded wilderness—of endless chains of lonely lakes and rushing rivers. Thousands of miles of country roads, rough timber lanes, overgrown tracks leading to abandoned mines, and unmapped trails snake across its length and breadth. It is a country of far-flung, lonely farms and a few widely scattered small towns and villages, of lonely trappers' shacks and logging camps. Most of its industry comes from the great pulp and paper companies who work their timber concessions deep in the very heart of the forests; and from the mines, for it is rich in minerals. Prospectors work through it; there are trappers and Indians; and sometimes hunters who fly into the virgin lakes in small amphibious aircraft; there are pioneers with visions beyond their own life span; and there are those who have left the bustle of civilization forever, to sink their identity in an unquestioning acceptance of the wilderness. But all these human beings together are as a handful of sand upon the ocean shores, and for the most part there is silence and solitude and an uninterrupted way of life for the wild animals that abound there; moose and deer, brown and black bears; lynx and fox; beaver, muskrat and otter; fishers, mink and marten. The wild duck rests there and the Canada goose, for this is a fringe of the central migratory flyway. The clear tree-fringed lakes and rivers are filled with speckled trout and steelheads, pike and pickerel and whitefish.

Almost half the year the country is blanketed with snow; and for weeks at a time the temperature may stay many degrees below zero; there is no slow growth of spring, but a sudden short burst of summer when everything grows with wild abandon; and as suddenly it is the fall again. To many who live there, fall is the burnished crown of the year, with the crisp sunny days and exhilarating air of the Northland; with clear blue skies, and drifting leaves, and, as far as the eye can see, the endless panorama of glorious rich flaming color in the turning trees.

This is the country over which the three travelers passed, and it was in the fall that they traveled, in the days of Indian summer.

1. The journey takes place in northwestern Ontario. What is this part of Canada like?

   In answering question 1, did you look for details that tell you the setting is a wilderness? This part of Canada is a deeply wooded wilderness filled with wild animals. If you had difficulty answering question 1, reread the first paragraph and note such details as "endless chain of lonely lakes," "unmapped trails," and "lynx and fox" to help you describe the setting.

2. What details does the author give you to show that the setting is one of "silence and solitude"?

   Did you look for details that pointed out that only a few people live there? The setting is one of "silence and solitude" because there are few farms, small towns, and villages. It is populated only by prospectors, trappers, Indians, hunters, and pioneers. If you had difficulty answering, reread and look for details that describe the people who live there and reveal how few people there are.

3. How does the author let you know that this wilderness setting is harsh for most of the year?
4. When does the journey take place?

Practicing Setting

Reread the opening paragraphs. Think about how such a setting could create conflict for the pets.

1. How might starting on a journey in the fall of the year cause problems for the three pets?
2. Think about *all* of the details the author uses to describe the setting. Why might the wilderness setting determine what happens to the animals?

Tips for Reading On Your Own

- Look for details—words and phrases—that describe the setting and picture the setting in your mind.
- Ask yourself how the setting helps determine what happens to the characters and creates problems for them.

What choice could three pets have to make? You'll find out as you meet Bodger, Luath, and Tao. As you read, keep in mind the opening paragraphs you have already read and continue to picture the setting.

The Incredible Journey

by Sheila Burnford

John Longridge lived several miles from one of the small towns in an old stone house that had been in his family for several generations. He was a tall, austerely pleasant man of about forty, a bachelor, and a writer by profession, being the author of several historical biographies. He spent much of his time traveling and gathering material for his books, but always returned to the comfortable old stone house for the actual writing. He liked the house to himself during these creative periods, and for many years had enjoyed an ideal arrangement whereby his domestic wants were cared for by a middle-aged couple, Mrs. Oakes and her husband Bert, who lived in a small cottage about half a mile away. Mrs. Oakes came in every day to look after the house and cook the main meals. Bert was in charge of the furnace, the garden and all the odd jobs. They came and went about their business without disturbing Longridge, and there was complete accord among them all.

On the eve of the incredible journey, towards the end of September, Longridge sat by a crackling log fire in his comfortable library. The curtains were drawn and the firelight flickered and played on the bookshelves and danced on the ceiling. The only other light in the room came from a small shaded lamp on a table by the deep armchair. It was a very peaceful room and the only sound was the occasional crackling from the logs or the rustling of a newspaper, the pages of which Longridge turned with some difficulty, for a slender wheat-colored

Siamese cat was curled on his knee, chocolate-colored front paws curved in towards one another, sapphire eyes blinking occasionally as he stared into the fire.

On the floor, his scarred, bony head resting on one of the man's feet, lay an old white English bull terrier. His slanted almond-shaped eyes, sunk deep within their pinkish rims, were closed; one large triangular ear caught the firelight, flushing the inside a delicate pink, so that it appeared almost translucent. Anyone unaccustomed to the rather peculiar points of bull terrier beauty would have thought him a strange if not downright ugly dog, with the naked, down-faced arc of his profile, his deep-chested, stocky body and whip-tapered tail. But the true lover of an ancient and honorable breed would have recognized the blood and bone of this elderly and rather battered body; would have known that in his prime this had been a magnificent specimen of compact sinew and muscle, bred to fight and endure; and would have loved him for his curious mixture of wicked, unyielding fighter yet devoted and docile family pet, and above all for the irrepressible air of sly merriment which gleamed in his little slant eyes.

He twitched and sighed often in his sleep, as old dogs will, and for once his shabby tail with the bare patch on the last joint was still.

By the door lay another dog, nose on paws, brown eyes open and watchful in contrast to the peacefulness radiated by the other occupants of the room. This was a large red-gold Labrador retriever, a young dog with all the heritage of his sturdy working forebears in his powerful build, broad noble head and deep, blunt, gentle mouth. He lifted his head as Longridge rose from the chair, depositing the cat, with an apologetic pat, on the floor, and carefully moving his foot from under the old dog's head before walking across the room to draw one of the heavy curtains and look out.

A huge orange moon was rising just above the trees at the far end of the garden, and a branch of an old lilac tree tap-tapped in the light wind against the window pane. It was bright enough outside to see the garden in clear detail, and he noticed how the leaves had drifted again across the lawn even in the short time since it had been raked that afternoon, and that only a few brave asters remained to color the flower beds.

He turned and crossed the room, flicking on another light, and opened a narrow cupboard halfway up the wall. Inside were several guns on racks and he looked at them thoughtfully, running his fingers lovingly down the smooth grain of the hand-rubbed stocks, and finally lifted down a beautifully chased and engraved double-barreled gun. He "broke" it and peered down the gleaming barrels; and as though at a signal the young dog sat up silently in the shadows, his ears pricked in interest. The gun fell back into place with a well-oiled click and the dog whined. The man replaced the gun in sudden contrition, and the dog lay down again, his head turned away, his eyes miserable.

Longridge walked over to make amends for his thoughtlessness, but as he bent down to pat the dog the telephone rang so suddenly and shrilly in the quiet room that the cat jumped indignantly off the chair and the bull terrier started clumsily to his feet.

Longridge picked up the receiver, and presently the breathless voice of Mrs. Oakes was heard, accompanied by a high-pitched, whining note in the distance.

"Speak up, Mrs. Oakes—I can hardly hear you."

"I can hardly hear you either," said the breathless voice distantly. "There, is that better? I'm shouting now! What time are you leaving in the morning, Mr. Longridge? What's that? Could you talk louder?"

"About seven o'clock. I want to get to Heron Lake before nightfall," he shouted, noting with amusement the scandalized expression of the cat. "But there's no need for you to be here at that time, Mrs. Oakes."

"What's that you said? Seven? Will it be all right if I don't come in until about nine? My niece is coming on the early bus and I'd like to meet her. But I don't like to leave the dogs alone too long. . . ."

"Of course you must meet her," he answered, shouting really loudly now as the humming noise increased. "The dogs will be fine. I'll take them out first thing in the morning, and—"

"Oh, thanks, Mr. Longridge—I'll be there around nine without fail. What's that you said about the animals? (Oh, you pernickety, dratted old line!) Don't you worry about them; Bert and me, we'll see. . . . tell old Bodger . . . bringing marrow bone. Oh, wait till I give that operator a piece of my mi . . ."

But just as Longridge was gathering strength for a last bellow into the mouthpiece the line went dead. He put the receiver back with relief and looked across the room at the old dog who had climbed stealthily into the armchair and sat lolling back against the cushions, his eyes half closed, awaiting the expected reproof. He addressed him with the proper degree of ferocity, telling him that he was a scoundrelly opportunist, a sybaritic barbarian, a disgrace to his upbringing and his ancestors, "AND"—and he paused in weighty emphasis—"a very . . . *bad* . . . *dog!*"

At these two dread words the terrier laid his ears flat against his skull, slanted his eyes back until they almost disappeared, then drew his lips back over his teeth in an apologetic grin, quivering the end of his disgraceful tail. His parody of sorrow brought its usual reprieve: the man laughed and patted the bony head, then enticed him down with the promise of a run.

So the old dog, who was a natural clown, slithered half off the chair and stood, with his hindquarters resting on the cushions, waving his tail and nudging the cat, who sat like an Egyptian statue, eyes half closed, head erect, then gave a throaty growl and patted at the pink and black bull-terrier nose. Then together they followed the man to the door, where the young dog waited to fall in behind the little procession. Longridge opened the door leading on to the garden, and the two dogs and the cat squeezed past his legs and into the cool night air. He stood under the trellised porch, quietly smoking his pipe, and watched them for a while. Their nightly routine never varied—first the few minutes of separate local investigation, then the indefinable moment when all met again and paused before setting off together through the gap in the hedge at the bottom of the garden and into the fields and woods that lay beyond. He watched until they disappeared into the darkness (the white shape of the bull terrier showing up long after Longridge was unable to distinguish the other two), then knocked his pipe out against the stone step and re-entered the house. It would be half an hour or more before they returned.

Longridge and his brother owned a small cabin by the shores of remote Heron Lake, about two hundred miles away; and twice a year they spent two or three weeks there together, leading the life they loved: spending many hours in companionable silence in their canoe, fishing in spring and hunting in the autumn. Usually he had simply locked up and left, leaving the key with Mrs. Oakes so that she could come in once or twice a week and keep the house warm and aired. However, now he had the animals to consider. He had thought of taking them all to a boarding kennel in the town, but Mrs. Oakes, who loved the assorted trio, had protested vigorously and asserted that she herself would look after them "rather than have those poor dumb animals fretting themselves into a state in some kennel, and probably half starved into the bargain." So it had been arranged that she and Bert would look after the three animals. Bert would be working around the garden, anyway, so that they could be outside most of the time and Mrs. Oakes would feed them and keep her eye on them while she was working in the house.

When he had finished packing, Longridge went into the library to draw the curtains, and seeing the telephone he was reminded of Mrs. Oakes. He had forgotten to tell her to order some coffee and other things that he had taken from the store cupboard. He sat down at the desk and drew out a small memo pad.

Dear Mrs. Oakes, he wrote, *Please order some more coffee and replace the canned food I've taken. I will be taking the dogs (and Tao too of course!)* . . . Here he came to the end of the small square of paper, and taking another piece he continued: *. . . out for a run before I leave, and will give them something to eat, so don't let our greedy white friend tell you he is starving! Don't worry yourselves too much over them—I know they will be fine.*

He wrote the last few words with a smile, for the bull terrier had Mrs. Oakes completely in thrall and worked his advantage to the full. He left the pages on the desk under a glass paperweight; then opened the door in answer to a faint scratch. The old dog and the cat bounded in to greet him with their usual affection, bringing the fresh smell of the outdoors with them. The young dog followed more sedately and stood by, watching aloofly, as the other whipped his tail like a lash against the man's legs, while the cat pressed against him purring in a deep rumble; but he wagged his tail briefly and politely when the man patted him.

The cat walked into the library to curl up on the warm hearth. Later when the ashes grew cold he would move to the top of the radiator, and then, sometime in the middle of the night, he would steal upstairs and curl up beside the old dog. It was useless shutting the bedroom door, or any other door of the house for that matter, for the cat could open them all, latches or doorknobs. The only doors that defeated him were those with porcelain handles, for he found it impossible to get a purchase on the shiny surface with his long monkeylike paws.

The young dog padded off to his rug on the floor of the little back kitchen, and the bull terrier started up the steep stairs, and was already curled in his basket in the bedroom when Longridge himself came to bed. He opened one bright, slanted eye when he felt the old blanket being dropped over him, then pushed his head under the cover, awaiting the opportunity he knew would come later.

The man lay awake for a while, thinking about the days ahead and of the animals, for the sheer misery in the young dog's eyes haunted him.

They had come to him, this odd and lovable trio, over eight months ago, from the home of an old and dear college friend. This friend, Jim Hunter, was an English professor in a small university about two hundred and fifty miles away. As the university owned one of the finest reference libraries in the province, Longridge often stayed with him and was, in fact, godfather to the Hunters' nine-year-old daughter, Elizabeth. He had been staying with them when the invitation came from an English university, asking the professor to deliver a series of lectures which would involve a stay in England of nearly nine months, and he had witnessed the tears of his goddaughter and the glum silence of her brother, Peter, when it was decided that their pets would have to be boarded out and the house rented to the reciprocal visiting professor.

Longridge was extremely fond of Elizabeth and Peter, and he could understand their feelings, remembering how much the companionship of a cocker spaniel had meant when he himself was a rather lonely child, and how he had grieved when he was first separated from it. Elizabeth was the self-appointed owner of the cat. She fed and brushed him, took him for walks, and he slept at the foot of her bed. Eleven-year-old Peter had been inseparable from the bull terrier ever since the small white puppy had arrived on Peter's first birthday. In fact, the boy could not remember a day of his life when Bodger had not been part of it. The young dog belonged, in every sense of the word, heart and soul to their father, who had trained him since puppyhood for hunting.

Now they were faced with the realization of separation, and in the appalled silence that followed the decision Longridge watched Elizabeth's face screw up in the prelude to tears. Then he heard a voice, which he recognized with astonishment to be his own, telling everybody not to worry, not to worry at all—he would take care of everything! Were not he and the animals already well known to one another? And had he not plenty of room, and a large garden? . . . Mrs. Oakes? Why, she would just love to have them! Everything would be simply wonderful! Before the family sailed they would bring the dogs and the cat over by car, see for themselves where they would sleep, write out a list of instructions, and he, personally, would love and cherish them until their return.

So one day the Hunter family had driven over and the pets had been left, with many tearful farewells from Elizabeth and last-minute instructions from Peter.

During the first few days Longridge had almost regretted his spontaneous offer: the terrier had languished in his basket, his long arched nose buried in the comfort of his paws, and one despairing, martyred eye haunting his every movement; and the cat had nearly driven him crazy with the incessant goatlike bleating and yowling of a suffering Siamese; the young dog had moped by the door and refused all food. But after a few days, won over perhaps by Mrs. Oakes's sympathetic clucking and tempting morsels of food, they had seemed to resign themselves, and the cat and the old dog had settled in, very comfortably and happily, showing their adopted master a great deal of affection.

It was very apparent, however, how much the old dog missed children. Longridge at first had wondered where he disappeared to some afternoons; he eventually found out that the terrier went to the playground of the little rural school, where he was a great favorite with the children, timing his appearance for recess. Knowing that the road was forbidden to him, because of his poor sight and habit of walking stolidly in the middle, he had found a short cut across the intervening fields.

But the young dog was very different. He had obviously never stopped pining for his own home and master; although he ate well and his coat was glossy with health, he never maintained anything but a dignified, unyielding distance. The man respected him for this, but it worried him that the dog never seemed to relax, and always appeared to be listening—longing and waiting for something far beyond the walls of the house or the fields beyond. Longridge was glad for the dog's sake that the Hunters would be returning in about three weeks, but he knew that he would miss his adopted family. They had amused and entertained him more than he would have thought possible, over the months, and he realized tonight that the parting would be a real wrench. He did not like to think of the too quiet house that would be his again.

He slept at last, and the dreaming, curious moon peeped in at the window to throw shafts of pale light into the rooms and over each of the sleeping occupants. They woke the cat downstairs, who stretched and yawned, then leaped without visible effort onto the window sill, his gleaming eyes, with their slight cast, wide open and enormous, and only the tip of his tail twitching as he sat motionless, staring into the garden. Presently he turned, and with a single graceful bound crossed to the desk; but for once he was careless, and his hind leg knocked the glass paperweight to the floor. He shook the offending leg vigorously, scattering the pages of Longridge's note—sending one page off the desk into the air, where it caught the upward current of hot air from the wall register and sailed across the room to land in the fireplace. Here it slowly curled and browned, until nothing remained of the writing but the almost illegible signature at the bottom.

When the pale fingers of the moon reached over the young dog in the back kitchen he stirred in his uneasy sleep, then sat upright, his ears pricked—listening and listening for the sound that never came: the high, piercing whistle of his master that would have brought him bounding across the world if only his straining ears could hear it.

And lastly the moon peered into the upstairs bedroom, where the man lay sleeping on his side in a great fourposter bed; and curled against his back the elderly, comfort-loving white bull terrier slept in blissful, warm content.

Chapter 2

There was a slight mist when John Longridge rose early the following morning, having fought a losing battle for the middle of the bed with his uninvited bedfellow. He shaved and dressed quickly, watching the mist roll back over the fields and the early morning sun break through. It would be a perfect fall day, an Indian summer day, warm and mellow. Downstairs he found the animals waiting patiently by the door for their early morning run. He let them out, then cooked and ate his solitary breakfast. He was out in the driveway, loading up his car when the dogs and cat returned from the fields. He fetched some biscuits for them and they lay by the wall of the house in the early sun, watching him. He threw the last item into the back of the car, thankful that he had already packed the guns and hunting equipment before the Labrador had seen them, then walked over and patted the heads of his audience, one by one.

"Be good," he said. "Mrs. Oakes will be here soon. Good-by, Luath," he said to the Labrador, "I wish I could have taken you with me, but there wouldn't be room in the canoe for three of us." He put his hand under the young dog's soft muzzle. The golden-brown eyes looked steadily into his, and then the dog did an unexpected thing: he lifted his right paw and placed it in the man's hand. Longridge had seen him do this many a time to his own master and he was curiously touched and affected by the trust it conveyed, almost wishing he did not have to leave immediately just after the dog had shown his first responsive gesture.

He looked at his watch and realized he was already late. He had no worries about leaving the animals alone outside, as they had never attempted to stray beyond the large garden and the adjacent fields; and they could return inside the house if they wished, for the kitchen door was the kind that closed slowly on a spring. All that he had to do was shoot the inside bolt while the door was open, and after that it did not close properly and could be pushed open from the outside. They looked contented enough, too—the cat was washing methodically behind his ears—the old dog sat on his haunches, panting after his run, his long pink tongue lolling out of his grinning mouth; and the Labrador lay quietly by his side.

Longridge started the car and waved to them out of the window as he drove slowly down the drive, feeling rather foolish as he did so. "What do I expect them to do in return?" he asked himself with a smile. "Wave back? Or shout 'Good-by'? The trouble is I've lived too long alone with them and I'm becoming far too attached to them."

The car turned around the bend at the end of the long tree-lined drive and the animals heard the sound of the engine receding in the distance. The cat transferred his attention to a hind leg; the old dog stopped panting and lay down; the young dog remained stretched out, only his eyes moving and an occasional twitch of his nose.

Twenty minutes passed by and no move was made; then suddenly the young dog rose, stretched himself, and stood looking intently down the drive. He remained like this for several minutes, while the cat watched closely, one leg still pointing upwards; then slowly the Labrador walked down the driveway and stood at the curve, looking back as though inviting the others to come. The old dog rose too, now, somewhat stiffly, and followed. Together they turned the corner, out of sight.

The cat remained utterly still for a full minute, blue eyes blazing in the dark mask. Then, with a curious hesitating run, he set off in pursuit. The dogs were waiting by the gate when he turned the corner, the old dog peering wistfully back, as though he hoped to see his friend Mrs. Oakes materialize with a juicy bone; but when the Labrador started up the road he followed. The cat still paused by the gate, one paw lifted delicately in the air—undecided, questioning, hesitant; until suddenly, some inner decision reached, he followed the dogs. Presently all three disappeared from sight down the dusty road, trotting briskly and with purpose.

About an hour later Mrs. Oakes walked up the driveway from her cottage, carrying a string bag with her working shoes and apron, and a little parcel of tidbits for the animals. Her placid, gentle face wore a rather disappointed look, because the dogs usually spied her long before she got to the house and would rush to greet her.

"I expect Mr. Longridge left them shut inside the house if he was leaving early," she consoled herself. But when she pushed open the kitchen door and walked inside, everything seemed very silent and still. She stood at the foot of the stairs and called them, but there was no answering patter of running feet, only the steady tick-tock of the old clock in the hallway. She walked through the silent house and out into the front garden and stood there calling with a puzzled frown.

"Oh, well," she spoke her thoughts aloud to the empty, sunny garden, "perhaps they've gone up to the school. . . . It's a funny thing, though," she continued, sitting on a kitchen chair a few minutes later and tying her shoelaces, "that Puss isn't here— he's usually sitting on the window sill at this time of the day. Oh, well, he's probably out hunting—I've never known a cat like that for hunting, doesn't seem natural somehow!"

She washed and put away the few dishes, then took her cleaning materials into the sitting room. There her eye was caught by a sparkle on the floor by the desk, and she found the glass paperweight, and after that the remaining sheet of the note on the desk. She read it through to where it said: "I will be taking the dogs (and Tao too of course!) . . .", then looked for the remainder. "That's odd," she thought, "now where would he take them? That cat must have knocked the paperweight off last night—the rest of the note must be somewhere in the room."

She searched the room but it was not until she was emptying an ash tray into the fireplace that she noticed the charred curl of paper in the hearth. She bent down and picked it up carefully, for it was obviously very brittle, but even then most of it crumbled away and she was left with a fragment which bore the initials J. R. L.

"Now, isn't that the queerest thing," she said to the fireplace, rubbing vigorously at the black marks on the tile. "He must mean he's taking them all to Heron Lake with him. But why would he suddenly do that, after all the arrangements we made? He never said a word about it on the telephone—but wait a minute, I remember now—he was just going to say something about them when the line went dead; perhaps he was just going to tell me."

While Mrs. Oakes was amazed that Longridge would take the animals on his vacation, it did not occur to her to be astonished that a cat should go along too, for she was aware that the cat loved the car and always went with the dogs when Longridge drove them anywhere or took them farther afield for walks. Like many Siamese cats, he was as obedient and as trained to go on walks as most dogs, and would always return to a whistle.

Mrs. Oakes swept and dusted and talked to the house, locked it and returned home to her cottage. She would have been horrified to the depths of her kindly, well-ordered soul if she had known the truth. Far from sitting sedately in the back of a car traveling north with John Longridge, as she so fondly visualized, the animals were by now many miles away on a deserted country road that ran westward.

They had kept a fairly steady pace for the first hour or so, falling into an order which was not to vary for many miles or days; the Labrador ran always by the left shoulder of the old dog, for the bull terrier was very nearly blind in the left eye, and they jogged along fairly steadily together—the bull terrier with his odd, rolling, sailorlike gait, and the Labrador in a slow lope. Some ten yards behind came the cat, whose attention was frequently distracted, when he would stop for a few minutes and then catch up again. But, in between these halts, he ran swiftly and steadily, his long slim body and tail low to the ground.

When it was obvious that the old dog was flagging, the Labrador turned off the quiet, graveled road and into the shade of a pinewood beside a clear, fast-running creek. The old dog drank deeply, standing up to his chest in the cold water; the cat picked his way delicately to the edge of an overhanging rock. Afterwards they rested in the deep pine needles under the trees, the terrier panting heavily with his eyes half closed, and the cat busy with his eternal washing. They lay there for nearly an hour, until the sun struck through the branches above them. The young dog rose and stretched, then walked towards the road. The old dog rose too, stiff-legged, his head low. He walked toward the waiting Labrador, limping slightly and wagging his tail at the cat, who suddenly danced into a patch of sunlight, struck at a drifting leaf, then ran straight at the dogs, swerving at the last moment, and as suddenly sitting down again.

They trotted steadily on, all that afternoon—mostly traveling on the grassy verge at the side of the quiet country road; sometimes in the low overgrown ditch that ran alongside, if the acute hearing of the young dog warned them of an approaching car.

By the time the afternoon sun lay in long, barred shadows across the road, the cat was still traveling in smooth, swift bursts, and the young dog was comparatively fresh. But the old dog was very weary, and his pace had dropped to a limping walk. They turned off the road into the bush at the side, and walked slowly through a clearing in the trees, pushing their way through the tangled undergrowth at the far end. They came out upon a small open place where a giant spruce had crashed to the ground and left a hollow where the roots had been, filled now with drifted dry leaves and spruce needles.

The late afternoon sun slanted through the branches overhead, and it looked invitingly snug and secure. The old dog stood for a minute, his heavy head hanging, and his tired body swaying slightly, then lay down on his side in the hollow. The cat, after a good deal of wary observation, made a little hollow among the spruce needles and curled around in it, purring softly. The young dog disappeared into the undergrowth and reappeared presently, his smooth coat dripping water, to lie down a little away apart from the others.

The old dog continued to pant exhaustedly for a long time, one hind leg shaking badly, until his eyes closed at last, the labored breaths came further and further apart, and he was sleeping—still, save for an occasional long shudder.

Later on, when darkness fell, the young dog moved over and stretched out closely at his side and the cat stalked over to lie between his paws; and so, warmed and comforted by their closeness, the old dog slept, momentarily unconscious of his aching, tired body or his hunger.

In the nearby hills a timber wolf howled mournfully; owls called and answered and glided silently by with great outspread wings; and there were faint whispers of movement and small rustling noises around all through the night. Once an eerie wail like a baby's crying woke the old dog and brought him shivering and whining to his feet; but it was only a porcupine, who scrambled noisily and clumsily down a nearby tree trunk and waddled away, still crying softly. When he lay down again the cat was gone from his side—another small night hunter slipping through the unquiet shadows that froze to stillness at his passing.

The young dog slept in fitful, uneasy starts, his muscles twitching, constantly lifting his head and growling softly. Once he sprang to his feet with a full-throated roar which brought a sudden splash in the distance, then silence—and who knows what else unknown, unseen or unheard passed through his mind to disturb him further? Only one thing was clear and certain—that at all costs he was going home, home to his own beloved master. Home lay to the west, his instinct told him; but he could not leave the other two—so somehow he must take them with him, all the way.

Think and Discuss

1. What choice do the three pets make and why?
2. What happens to the note Longridge writes to Mrs. Oakes?
3. What conclusion does Mrs. Oakes draw when she reads the note? Why?
• 4. How has the wilderness setting already affected the physical condition of the three animals?
• 5. How does the setting add danger to the old bull terrier's struggle for survival?

See your Thinker's Handbook for tips.

• Literary Skill: Setting

Talk

Work with a small group to discuss the coincidence that leads to the confusion over the note left by Longridge to Mrs. Oakes. How does she come to think he has taken the animals with him? Why isn't anyone aware the animals are missing?
Speaking/Listening: Group discussion

Write

Look again at the note that Longridge writes to Mrs. Oakes. Then rewrite the note in your own words on a single piece of paper. Use only twenty-three words. Be sure your message is direct and clear and cannot be misunderstood. Read your note to your group and listen to theirs. Discuss how each can be made clearer, even with the few words allowed.
Writing Fluency: Note

Helen Stoner chooses to enlist the aid of the legendary detective, Sherlock Holmes, and in doing so he tries to discover the meaning of the words—"It was the band! the speckled band!" As Holmes goes about the business of solving a crime, you'll discover some of his remarkable character traits.

CLASSIC

THE SPECKLED BAND

by Sir Arthur Conan Doyle

In glancing over my notes of the seventy odd cases in which I have during the last eight years studied the methods of my friend Sherlock Holmes, I find many tragic, some comic, a large number merely strange, but none commonplace; for, working as he did rather for the love of his art than for the acquirement of wealth, he refused to associate himself with any investigation which did not tend towards the unusual, and even the fantastic. Of all these varied cases, however, I cannot recall any which presented more singular features than that which was associated with the well-known Surrey family of the Roylotts of Stoke Moran. The events in question occurred in the early days of my association with Holmes, when we were sharing rooms as bachelors, in Baker Street. It is possible that I might have placed them upon record before, but a promise of secrecy was made at the time, from which I have only been freed during the last month by the untimely death of the lady to whom the pledge was given. It is perhaps as well that the facts should now come to light, for I have reasons to know there are widespread rumours as to the death of Dr. Grimesby Roylott which tend to make the matter even more terrible than the truth.

It was early in April, in the year '83, that I woke one morning to find Sherlock Holmes standing, fully dressed, by the side of my bed. He was a late riser as a rule, and, as the clock on the mantelpiece showed me that it was only a quarter past seven, I blinked up at him in some surprise, and perhaps just a little resentment, for I was myself regular in my habits.

'Very sorry to wake you up, Watson,' said he, 'but it's the common lot this morning. Mrs. Hudson has been awakened, she retorted upon me, and I on you.'

'What is it, then? A fire?'

'No, a client. It seems that a young lady has arrived in a considerable state of excitement, who insists upon seeing me. She is waiting now in the sitting-room. Now, when young ladies wander about the metropolis at this hour of the morning, and wake sleepy people up out of their beds, I presume that it is something very pressing which they have to communicate. Should it prove to be an interesting case, you would, I am sure, wish to follow it from the onset. I thought at any rate that I should call you, and give you the chance.'

'My dear fellow, I would not miss it for anything.'

I had no keener pleasure than in following Holmes in his professional investigations, and in admiring the rapid deductions, as swift as intuitions, and yet always founded on a logical basis, with which he unravelled the problems which were submitted to him. I rapidly threw on my clothes, and was ready in a few minutes to accompany my friend down to the sitting-room. A lady dressed in black and heavily veiled, who had been sitting in the window, rose as we entered.

'Good morning, madam,' said Holmes cheerily. 'My name is Sherlock Holmes. This is my intimate friend and associate, Dr. Watson, before whom you can speak as freely as before myself. Ha, I am glad to see that Mrs. Hudson has had the good sense to light the fire. Pray draw up to it, and I shall order you a cup of hot coffee, for I observe that you are shivering.'

'It is not cold which makes me shiver,' said the woman in a low voice, changing her seat as requested.

'What then?'

'It is fear, Mr. Holmes. It is terror.' She raised her veil as she spoke, and we could see that she was indeed in a pitiable state of agitation, her face all drawn and grey, with restless, frightened eyes, like those of some hunted animal. Her features and figure were those of a woman of thirty, but her hair was shot with premature grey, and her expression was weary and haggard. Sherlock Holmes ran her over with one of his quick, all-comprehensive glances.

"SHE RAISED HER VEIL.."

'You must not fear,' said he soothingly, bending forward and patting her forearm. 'We shall soon set matters right, I have no doubt. You have come in by train this morning, I see.'

'You know me, then?'

'No, but I observe the second half of a return ticket in the palm of your left glove. You must have started early, and yet you had a good drive in a dog-cart, along heavy roads, before you reached the station.'

The lady gave a violent start, and stared in bewilderment at my companion.

'There is no mystery, my dear madam,' said he, smiling. 'The left arm of your jacket is spattered with mud in no less than seven places. The marks are perfectly fresh. There is no vehicle save a dog-cart which throws up mud in that way, and then only when you sit on the left-hand side of the driver.'

'Whatever your reasons may be, you are perfectly correct,' said she. 'I started from home before six, reached Leatherhead at twenty past, and came in by the first train to Waterloo. Sir, I can stand this strain no longer, I shall go mad if it continues. I have no one to turn to—none, save only one, who cares for me, and he, poor fellow, can be of little aid. I have heard of you, Mr. Holmes; I have heard of you from Mrs. Farintosh, whom you helped in the hour of her sore need. It was from her that I had your address. Oh, sir, do you not think you could help me too, and at least throw a little light through the dense darkness which surrounds me? At present it is out of my power to reward you for your services, but in a month or two I shall be married, with the control of my own income, and then at least you shall not find me ungrateful.'

Holmes turned to his desk, and unlocking it, drew out a small case-book which he consulted.

'Farintosh,' said he. 'Ah, yes, I recall the case; it was concerned with an opal tiara. I think it was before your time, Watson. I can only say, madam, that I shall be happy to devote the same care to your case as I did to that of your friend. As to reward, my profession is its reward; but you are at liberty to defray whatever expenses I may be put to, at the time which suits you best. And now I beg that you will lay before us everything that may help us in forming an opinion upon the matter.'

'Alas!' replied our visitor. 'The very horror of my situation lies in the fact that my fears are so vague, and my suspicions depend so entirely upon small points, which might seem trivial to another, that even he to whom of all others I have a right to look for help and advice looks upon all that I tell him about it as the fancies of a nervous woman. He does not say so, but I can read it from his soothing answers and averted eyes. But I have heard, Mr. Holmes, that you can see deeply into the manifold wickedness of the human heart. You may advise me how to walk amid the dangers which encompass me.'

'I am all attention, madam.'

'My name is Helen Stoner, and I am living with my stepfather, who is the last survivor of one of the oldest Saxon families in England, the Roylotts of Stoke Moran, on the western border of Surrey.'

Holmes nodded his head. 'The name is familiar to me,' said he.

'The family was at one time among the richest in England, and the estate extended over the borders into Berkshire in the north, and Hampshire in the west. In the last century, however, four successive heirs were of a dissolute and wasteful disposition, and the family ruin was eventually completed by a gambler, in the days of the Regency. Nothing was left save a few acres of ground and the two-hundred-year-old house, which is itself crushed under a heavy mortgage. The last squire dragged out his existence there, living the horrible life of an aristocratic pauper; but his only son, my stepfather, seeing that he must adapt himself to the new conditions, obtained an advance from a relative, which enabled him to take a medical degree, and went out to Calcutta, where, by his professional skill and his force of character, he established a large practice. In a fit of anger, however, caused by some robberies which had been perpetrated in the house, he beat his native butler to death, and narrowly escaped a capital sentence. As it was, he suffered a long term of imprisonment, and afterwards returned to England a morose and disappointed man.

'When Dr. Roylott was in India he married my mother, Mrs. Stoner, the young widow of Major-General Stoner, of the Bengal Artillery. My sister Julia and I were twins, and we were only two years old at the time of my mother's re-marriage. She had a considerable sum of money, not less than a thousand a year, and this she bequeathed to Dr. Roylott entirely whilst we resided with him, with a provision that a certain annual sum should be allowed to each of us in the event of our marriage. Shortly after our return to England my mother died—she was killed eight years ago in a railway accident near Crewe. Dr. Roylott then abandoned his attempts to establish himself in practice in London, and took us to live with him in the ancestral house at Stoke Moran. The money which my mother had left was enough for all our wants, and there seemed no obstacle to our happiness.

'But a terrible change came over our stepfather about this time. Instead of making friends and exchanging visits with our neighbours, who had at first been overjoyed to see a Roylott of Stoke Moran back in the old family seat, he shut himself up in his house, and seldom came out save to indulge in ferocious quarrels with whoever might cross his path. Violence of temper approaching to mania has been hereditary in the men of the family, and in my stepfather's case it had, I believe, been intensified by his long residence in the tropics. A series of disgraceful brawls took place, two of which ended in the police-court, until at last he became the terror of the village, and the folks would fly at his approach, for he is a man of immense strength, and absolutely uncontrollable in his anger.

'Last week he hurled the local blacksmith over a parapet into a stream and it was only by paying over all the money that I could gather together that I was able to avert another public exposure. He had no friends at all save the wandering gipsies, and he would give these vagabonds leave to encamp upon the few acres of bramble-covered land which represent the family estate, and would accept in return the hospitality of their tents, wandering away with them sometimes for weeks on end. He has a passion also for Indian animals, which are sent over to him by a correspondent, and he has at this moment a cheetah and a baboon, which wander freely over his grounds, and are feared by the villagers almost as much as their master.

'You can imagine from what I say that my poor sister Julia and I had no great pleasure in our lives. No servant would stay with us, and for a long time we did all the work of the house. She was but thirty at the time of her death, and yet her hair had already begun to whiten, even as mine has.'

'Your sister is dead, then?'

'She died just two years ago, and it is of her death that I wish to speak to you. You can understand that, living the life which I have described, we were little likely to see anyone of our own age and position. We had, however, an aunt, my mother's maiden sister, Miss Honoria Westphail, who lives near Harrow, and we were occasionally allowed to pay short visits at this lady's house. Julia went there at Christmas two years ago, and met there a half-pay Major of Marines, to whom she became engaged. My stepfather learned of the engagement when my sister returned, and offered no objection to the marriage but within a fortnight of the day which had been fixed for the wedding, the terrible event occurred which has deprived me of my only companion.'

Sherlock Holmes had been leaning back in his chair with his eyes closed, and his head sunk in a cushion, but he half opened his lids now, and glanced across at this visitor.

'Pray be precise as to details,' said he.

'It is easy for me to be so, for every event of that dreadful time is seared into my memory. The manor house is, as I have already said, very old, and only one wing is now inhabited. The bedrooms in this wing are on the ground floor, the sitting-rooms being in the central block of the buildings. Of these bedrooms, the first is Dr. Roylott's, the second my sister's, and the third my own. There is no communication between them, but they all open out into the same corridor. Do I make myself plain?'

'The windows of the three rooms open out upon the lawn. That fatal night Dr. Roylott had gone to his room early, though we knew that he had not retired to rest, for my sister was troubled by the smell of the strong Indian cigars which it was his custom to smoke. She left her room, therefore, and came into mine, where she sat for some time, chatting about her approaching wedding. At eleven o'clock she rose to leave me, but she paused at the door and looked back.

' "Tell me, Helen," said she, "have you ever heard anyone whistle in the dead of the night?"

' "Never," said I.

' "I suppose you could not possibly whistle yourself in your sleep?"

' "Certainly not. But why?"

' "Because during the last few nights I have always, about three in the morning, heard a low clear whistle. I am a light sleeper, and it has awakened me. I cannot tell where it came from— perhaps from the next room, perhaps from the lawn. I thought that I would just ask you whether you had heard it."

' "No, I have not. It must be those wretched gipsies in the plantation."

' "Very likely. And yet if it were on the lawn I wonder that you did not hear it also."

' "Ah, but I sleep more heavily than you."

' "Well, it is of no great consequence, at any rate," she smiled back at me, closed my door, and a few moments later I heard her key turn in the lock.'

'Indeed,' said Holmes. 'Was it your custom always to lock yourselves in at night?'

'Always.'

'And why?'

'I think that I mentioned to you that the Doctor kept a cheetah and a baboon. We had no feeling of security unless our doors were locked.'

'Quite so. Pray proceed with your statement.'

'I could not sleep that night. A vague feeling of impending misfortune impressed me. My sister and I, you will recollect, were twins, and you know how subtle are the links which bind two souls which are so closely allied. It was a wild night. The wind was howling outside, and the rain was beating and splashing against the windows. Suddenly, amidst all the hubbub of the gale, there burst forth the wild scream of a terrified woman. I knew that it was my sister's voice. I sprang from my bed, wrapped a shawl round me, and rushed into the corridor. As I opened my door I seemed to hear a low whistle, such as my sister described, and a few moments later a clanging sound, as if a mass of metal had fallen. As I ran down the passage my sister's door was unlocked, and revolved slowly upon its hinges. I stared at it horror-stricken, not knowing what was about to issue from it. By the light of the corridor lamp I saw my sister appear at the opening, her face blanched with terror, her hands groping for help, her whole figure swaying to and fro like that of a drunkard.

"HER FACE BLANCHED WITH TERROR."

I ran to her and threw my arms round her, but at that moment her knees seemed to give way and she fell to the ground. She writhed as one who is in terrible pain, and her limbs were dreadfully convulsed. At first I thought that she had not recognized me, but as I bent over her she suddenly shrieked out in a voice which I shall never forget, "O, Helen! It was the band! The speckled band!" There was something else which she would fain have said, and she stabbed with her finger into the air in the direction of the Doctor's room, but a fresh convulsion seized her and choked her words. I rushed out, calling loudly for my stepfather, and I met him hastening from his room in his dressing-gown. When he reached my sister's side she was unconscious, and though he poured brandy down her throat, and sent for medical aid from the village, all efforts were in vain, for she slowly sank and died without having recovered her consciousness. Such was the dreadful end of my beloved sister.'

'One moment,' said Holmes; 'are you sure about this whistle and metallic sound? Could you swear to it?'

'That was what the county coroner asked me at the inquiry. It is my strong impression that I heard it, and yet among the crash of the gale, and the creaking of an old house, I may possibly have been deceived.'

'Was your sister dressed?'

'No, she was in her nightdress. In her right hand was found the charred stump of a match, and in her left a matchbox.'

'Showing that she had struck a light and looked about her when the alarm took place. That is important. And what conclusions did the coroner come to?'

'He investigated the case with great care, for Dr. Roylott's conduct had long been notorious in the country, but he was unable to find any satisfactory cause of death. My evidence showed that the door had been fastened upon the inner side, and the windows were blocked by old-fashioned shutters with broad iron bars, which were secured every night. The walls were carefully sounded, and were shown to be quite solid all round, and the flooring was also thoroughly examined, with the same result. The chimney is wide, but barred up by four large staples. It is certain, therefore, that my sister was alone when she met her end. Besides, there were no marks of any violence upon her.'

'How about poison?'

'The doctors examined her for it, but without success.'

'What do you think that this unfortunate lady died of, then?'

'It is my belief that she died of pure fear and nervous shock, though what it was which frightened her I cannot imagine.'

'Were there gipsies in the plantation at the time?'

'Yes, there are nearly always some there.'

'Ah, and what did you gather from this allusion to a band—a speckled band?'

'Sometimes I have thought that it was merely the wild talk of delirium, sometimes that it may have referred to some band of people, perhaps to these very gipsies in the plantation. I do not know whether the spotted handkerchiefs which so many of them wear over their heads might have suggested the strange adjective which she used.'

Holmes shook his head like a man who is far from being satisfied.

'These are very deep waters,' said he; 'pray go on with your narrative.'

'Two years have passed since then, and my life has been until lately lonelier than ever. A month ago, however, a dear friend, whom I have known for many years, has done me the honour to ask my hand in marriage. His name is Armitage—Percy Armitage—the second son of Mr. Armitage, of Crane Water, near Reading. My stepfather has offered no opposition to the match, and we are to be married in the course of the spring. Two days ago some repairs were started in the west wing of the building, and my bedroom wall has been pierced, so that I have had to move into the chamber in which my sister died, and to sleep in the very bed in which she slept. Imagine, then, my thrill of terror when last night, as I lay awake, thinking over her terrible fate, I suddenly heard in the silence of the night the low whistle which had been the herald of her own death. I sprang up and lit the lamp, but nothing was to be seen in the room. I was too shaken to go to bed again, however, so I dressed, and as soon as it was daylight, I slipped down, got a dog-cart at the Crown Inn, which is opposite, and drove to Leatherhead, from whence I have come on this morning, with the one object of seeing you and asking your advice.'

'You've done wisely,' said my friend. 'But have you told me all?'

'Yes, all.'

'Miss Stoner, you have not. You are screening your stepfather.'

'Why, what do you mean?'

For answer Holmes pushed back the frill of black lace which fringed the hand that lay upon our visitor's knee. Five little livid spots, the marks of four fingers and a thumb, were printed upon the white wrist.

'You have been cruelly used,' said Holmes.

The lady coloured deeply, and covered over her injured wrist. 'He is a hard man,' she said, 'and perhaps he hardly knows his own strength.'

There was a long silence, during which Holmes leaned his chin upon his hands and stared into the crackling fire.

'This is very deep business,' he said at last. 'There are a thousand details which I should desire to know before I decide upon our course of action. Yet we have not a moment to lose. If we were to come to Stoke Moran to-day, would it be possible for us to see over these rooms without knowledge of your stepfather?'

'As it happens, he spoke of coming into town to-day upon some most important business. It is probable that he will be away all day, and that there would be nothing to disturb you. We have a housekeeper now, but she is old and foolish, and I could easily get her out of the way.'

'Excellent. You are not averse to this trip, Watson?'

'By no means.'

'Then we shall both come. What are you going to do yourself?'

'I have one or two things which I would wish to do now that I am in town. But I shall return by the twelve o'clock train, so as to be there in time for your coming.'

'And you may expect us early in the afternoon. I have myself some small business matters to attend to. Will you not wait and breakfast?'

'No, I must go. My heart is lightened already since I have confided my trouble to you. I shall look forward to seeing you again this afternoon.' She dropped her thick black veil over her face, and glided from the room.

'And what do you think of it all, Watson?' asked Sherlock Holmes, leaning back in his chair.

'It seems to me to be a most dark and sinister business.'

'Dark enough and sinister enough.'

'Yet if the lady is correct in saying that the flooring and walls are sound, and that the door, window, and chimney are impassable, then her sister must have been undoubtedly alone when she met her mysterious end.'

'What becomes, then, of these nocturnal whistles, and what of the very peculiar words of the dying woman?'

'I cannot think.'

'When you combine the ideas of whistles at night, the presence of a band of gipsies who are on intimate terms with this old doctor, the fact that we have every reason to believe that the doctor has an interest in preventing his stepdaughter's marriage, the dying allusion to a band, and finally, the fact that Miss Helen Stoner heard a metallic clang, which might have been caused by one of those metal bars which secured the shutters falling back into their place, I think there is good ground to think that the mystery may be cleared along those lines.'

'But what, then, did the gipsies do?'

'I cannot imagine.'

'I see many objections to any such a theory.'

'And so do I. It is precisely for that reason that we are going to Stoke Moran this day. I want to see whether the objections are fatal, or if they may be explained away. But what—!'

The exclamation had been drawn from my companion by the fact that our door had been suddenly dashed open, and that a huge man framed himself in the aperture. His costume was a peculiar mixture of the professional and of the agricultural, having a black top-hat, a long frock-coat, and a pair of high gaiters, with a hunting-crop swinging in his hand. So tall was he that his hat actually brushed the cross-bar of the doorway, and his breadth seemed to span it across from side to side. A large face, seared with a thousand wrinkles, burned yellow with the sun, and marked with every evil passion, was turned from one to the other of us, while his deep-set bile-shot eyes, and the high thin fleshless nose, gave him somewhat the resemblance to a fierce old bird of prey.

'Which of you is Holmes?' asked this apparition.

'My name, sir, but you have the advantage of me,' said my companion quietly.

'I am Dr. Grimesby Roylott, of Stoke Moran.'

'Indeed, Doctor,' said Holmes blandly. 'Pray take a seat.'

'I will do nothing of the kind. My stepdaughter has been here. I have traced her. What has she been saying to you?'

'It is a little cold for the time of the year,' said Holmes.

'What's she been saying to you?' screamed the old man furiously.

'But I have heard that the crocuses promise well,' continued my companion imperturbably.

'Ha! You put me off, do you?' said our new visitor, taking a step forward, and shaking his hunting-crop. 'I know you, you scoundrel! I have heard of you before. You are Holmes the meddler.'

My friend smiled.

'Holmes the busybody!'

His smile broadened.

'Holmes the Scotland Yard jack-in-office.'

Holmes chuckled heartily. 'Your conversation is most entertaining,' said he. 'When you go out close the door, for there is a decided draught.'

'I will go when I have had my say. Don't you dare to meddle with my affairs. I know that Miss Stoner has been here—I traced her! I am a dangerous man to fall foul of! See here.' He stepped swiftly forward, seized the poker, and bent it into a curve with his huge brown hands.

'See that you keep yourself out of my grip,' he snarled, and hurling the twisted poker into the fireplace, he strode out of the room.

'He seems a very amiable person,' said Holmes, laughing. 'I am not quite so bulky, but if he had remained I might have shown him that my grip was not much more feeble than his own.' As he spoke he picked up the steel poker, and with a sudden effort straightened it out again.

'Fancy his having the insolence to confound me with the official detective force! This incident gives zest to our investigation, however, and I only trust that our little friend will not suffer from her imprudence in allowing this brute to trace her. And now, Watson, we shall order breakfast, and afterwards I shall walk down to Doctors' Commons, where I hope to get some data which may help us in this matter.'

It was nearly one o'clock when Sherlock Holmes returned from his excursion. He held in his hand a sheet of blue paper, scrawled over with notes and figures.

'I have seen the will of the deceased wife,' said he. 'To determine its exact meaning I have been obliged to work out the present prices of the investments with which it is concerned. The total income, which at the time of the wife's death was little short of £1,100, is now through the fall in agricultural prices not more than £750. Each daughter can claim an income of £250, in case of marriage. It is evident, therefore, that if both girls had married this beauty would have had a mere pittance, while even one of them would cripple him to a serious extent. My morning's work has not been wasted, since it has proved that he has the very strongest motives for standing in the way of anything of the sort. And now, Watson, this is too serious for dawdling, especially as the old man is aware that we are interesting ourselves in his affairs, so if you are ready we shall call a cab and drive to Waterloo. I should be very much obliged if you would slip your revolver into your pocket. An Eley's No. 2 is an excellent argument with gentlemen who can twist steel pokers into knots. That and a tooth-brush are, I think, all that we need.'

At Waterloo we were fortunate in catching a train for Leatherhead, where we hired a trap at the station inn, and drove for four or five miles through the lovely Surrey lanes. It was a perfect day, with a bright sun and a few fleecy clouds in the heavens. The trees and wayside hedges were just throwing out their first green shoots, and the air was full of the pleasant smell of the moist earth. To me at least there was a strange contrast between the sweet promise of spring and this sinister quest upon which we were engaged. My companion sat in front of the trap, his arms folded, his hat pulled down over his eyes, and his chin sunk upon his breast, buried in the deepest thought. Suddenly, however, he started, tapped me on the shoulder, and pointed over the meadow.

'Look there!' said he.

A heavily timbered park stretched up in a gentle slope, thickening into a grove at the highest point. From amidst the branches there jutted out the grey gables and high roof-tree of a very old mansion.

'Stoke Moran?' said he.

'Yes, sir, that be the house of Dr. Grimesby Roylott,' remarked the driver.

'There is some building going on there,' said Holmes; 'that is where we are going.'

'There's the village,' said the driver, pointing to a cluster of roofs some distance to the left; 'but if you want to get to the house, you'll find it shorter to go over this stile, and so by the footpath over the fields. There it is, where the lady is walking.'

'And the lady, I fancy, is Miss Stoner,' observed Holmes, shading his eyes. 'Yes, I think we had better do as you suggest.'

We got off, paid our fare, and the trap rattled back on its way to Leatherhead.

"WE GOT OFF, PAID OUR FARE."

'I thought it as well,' said Holmes, as we climbed the stile, 'that this fellow should think we had come here as architects, or on some definite business. It may stop his gossip. Good afternoon, Miss Stoner. You see that we have been as good as our word.'

Our client of the morning had hurried forward to meet us with a face which spoke her joy. 'I have been waiting so eagerly for you,' she cried, shaking hands with us warmly. 'All has turned out splendidly. Dr. Roylott has gone to town, and it is unlikely that he will be back before evening.'

'We have had the pleasure of making the Doctor's acquaintance,' said Holmes, and in a few words he sketched out what had occurred. Miss Stoner turned white to the lips as she listened.

'Good heavens!' she cried, 'he has followed me, then.'

'So it appears.'

'He is so cunning that I never know when I am safe from him. What will he say when he returns?'

'He must guard himself, for he may find that there is someone more cunning than himself upon his track. You must lock yourself from him to-night. If he is violent, we shall take you away to your aunt's at Harrow. Now, we must make the best use of our time, so kindly take us at once to the rooms which we are to examine.'

The building was of grey, lichen-blotched stone, with a high central portion, and two curving wings, like the claws of a crab, thrown out on each side. In one of these wings the windows were broken, and blocked with wooden boards, while the roof was partly caved in, a picture of ruin. The central portion was in little better repair, but the right-hand block was comparatively modern, and the blinds in the windows, with the blue smoke curling up from the chimneys, showed that this was where the family resided. Some scaffolding had been erected against the end wall, and the stonework had been broken into, but there were no signs of any workmen at the moment of our visit. Holmes walked slowly up and down the ill-trimmed lawn, and examined with deep attention the outsides of the windows.

'This, I take it, belongs to the room in which you used to sleep, the centre one to your sister's, and the one next to the main building to Dr. Roylott's chamber?'

'Exactly so. But I am now sleeping in the middle one.'

'Pending the alterations, as I understand. By the way, there does not seem to be any very pressing need for repairs at that end wall.'

'There were none. I believe that it was an excuse to move me from my room.'

'Ah! that is suggestive. Now, on the other side of this narrow wing runs the corridor from which these three rooms open. There are windows in it, of course?'

'Yes, but very small ones. Too narrow for anyone to pass through.'

'As you both locked your doors at night, your rooms were unapproachable from that side. Now, would you have the kindness to go into your room, and to bar your shutters.'

Miss Stoner did so, and Holmes, after a careful examination through the open window, endeavoured in every way to force the shutter open, but without success. There was no slit through which a knife could be passed to raise the bar. Then with his lens he tested the hinges, but they were of solid iron, built firmly into the massive masonry. 'Hum!' said he, scratching his chin in some perplexity, 'my theory certainly presents some difficulties. No one could pass these shutters if they were bolted. Well, we shall see if the inside throws any light upon the matter.'

A small side-door led into the whitewashed corridor from which the three bedrooms opened. Holmes refused to examine the third chamber, so we passed at once to the second, that in which Miss Stoner was now sleeping, and in which her sister had met her fate. It was a homely little room, with a low ceiling and a gaping fireplace, after the fashion of old country houses. A brown chest of drawers stood in one corner, a narrow white-counter-paned bed in another, and a dressing-table on the left-hand side of the window. These articles, with two small wickerwork chairs, made up all the furniture in the room, save for a square of Wilton carpet in the centre. The boards round and the panelling of the walls were brown, worm-eaten oak, so old and discoloured that it may have dated from the original building of the house. Holmes drew one of the chairs into a corner and sat silent, while his eyes travelled round and round and up and down, taking in every detail of the apartment.

'Where does that bell communicate with?' he asked at last, pointing to a thick bell-rope which hung down beside the bed, the tassel actually lying upon the pillow.

'It goes to the housekeeper's room.'

'It looks newer than the other things?'

'Yes, it was only put there a couple of years ago.'

'Your sister asked for it, I suppose?'

'No, I never heard of her using it. We used always to get what we wanted for ourselves.'

'Indeed, it seemed unnecessary to put so nice a bell-pull there. You will excuse me for a few minutes while I satisfy myself as to this floor.' He threw himself down upon his face with his lens in his hand, and crawled swiftly backwards and forwards, examining minutely the cracks between the boards. Then he did the same with the woodwork with which the chamber was panelled. Finally he walked over to the bed and spent some time in staring at it, and in running his eye up and down the wall. Finally he took the bell-rope in his hand and gave it a brisk tug.

'Why, it's a dummy,' said he.

'Won't it ring?'

'No, it is not even attached to a wire. This is very interesting. You can see now that it is fastened to a hook just above where the little opening of the ventilator is.'

'How very absurd! I never noticed that before.'

'Very strange!' muttered Holmes, pulling at the rope. 'There are one or two very singular points about this room. For example, what a fool a builder must be to open a ventilator in another room, when, with the same trouble, he might have communicated with the outside air!'

'That is also quite modern,' said the lady.

'Done about the same time as the bell-rope,' remarked Holmes.

'Yes, there were several little changes carried out about that time.'

'They seem to have been of a most interesting character— dummy bell-ropes, and ventilators which do not ventilate. With your permission, Miss Stoner, we shall now carry our researches into the inner apartment.'

Dr. Grimesby Roylott's chamber was larger than that of his stepdaughter, but was as plainly furnished. A camp bed, a small wooden shelf full of books, mostly of a technical character, an arm-chair beside the bed, a plain wooden chair against the wall, a round table, and a large iron safe were the principal things which met the eye. Holmes walked slowly round and examined each and all of them with the keenest interest.

'What's in here?' he asked, tapping the safe.

'My stepfather's business papers.'

'Oh! you have seen inside then?'

'Only once, some years ago. I remember that it was full of papers.'

'There isn't a cat in it, for example?'

'No. What a strange idea!'

'Well, look at this!' He took up a small saucer of milk which stood on the top of it.

"WELL, LOOK AT THIS!"

'No; we don't keep a cat. But there is a cheetah and a baboon.'

'Ah, yes, of course. Well, a cheetah is just a big cat, and yet a saucer of milk does not go very far in satisfying its wants, I daresay. There is one point which I should wish to determine.' He squatted down in front of the wooden chair, and examined the seat of it with the greatest attention.

'Thank you. That is quite settled,' said he, rising and putting his lens in his pocket. 'Hullo! here is something interesting!'

The object which had caught his eye was a small dog lash hung on one corner of the bed. The lash, however, was curled upon itself, and tied so as to make a loop of whipcord.

'What do you make of that, Watson?'

'It's a common enough lash. But I don't know why it should be tied.'

'That is not quite so common, is it? Ah, me! it's a wicked world, and when a clever man turns his brain to crime it is the worst of all. I think that I have seen enough now, Miss Stoner, and, with your permission, we shall walk out upon the lawn.'

I had never seen my friend's face so grim, or his brow so dark, as it was when we turned from the scene of this investigation. We had walked several times up and down the lawn, neither Miss Stoner nor myself liking to break in upon his thoughts before he roused himself from his reverie.

'It is very essential, Miss Stoner,' said he, 'that you should absolutely follow my advice in every respect.'

'I shall most certainly do so.'

'The matter is too serious for any hesitation. Your life may depend upon your compliance.'

'I assure you that I am in your hands.'

'In the first place, both my friend and I must spend the night in your room.'

Both Miss Stoner and I gazed at him in astonishment.

'Yes, it must be so. Let me explain. I believe that that is the village inn over there?'

'Yes, that is the "Crown".'

'Very good. Your windows would be visible from there?'

'Certainly.'

'You must confine yourself to your room, on pretence of a headache, when your stepfather comes back. Then when you hear him retire for the night, you must open the shutters of your window, undo the hasp, put your lamp there as a signal to us, and then withdraw with everything which you are likely to want into the room which you used to occupy. I have no doubt that, in spite of the repairs, you could manage there for one night.'

'Oh, yes, easily.'

'The rest you will leave in our hands.'

'But what will you do?'

'We shall spend the night in your room, and we shall investigate the cause of this noise which has disturbed you.'

'I believe, Mr. Holmes, that you have already made up your mind,' said Miss Stoner, laying her hand upon my companion's sleeve.

'Perhaps I have.'

'Then for pity's sake tell me what was the cause of my sister's death.'

'I should prefer to have clearer proofs before I speak.'

'You can at least tell me whether my own thought is correct, and if she died from some sudden fright.'

'No, I do not think so. I think that there was probably some more tangible cause. And now, Miss Stoner, we must leave you, for if Dr. Roylott returned and saw us, our journey would be in vain. Good-bye, and be brave, for if you will do what I have told you, you may rest assured that we shall soon drive away the dangers that threaten you.'

"GOOD-BYE, AND BE BRAVE."

Sherlock Holmes and I had no difficulty in engaging a bedroom and sitting-room at the Crown Inn. They were on the upper floor, and from our window we could command a view of the avenue gate, and of the inhabited wing of Stoke Moran Manor House. At dusk we saw Dr. Grimesby Roylott drive past, his huge form looming up beside the little figure of the lad who drove him. The boy had some slight difficulty in undoing the heavy iron gates, and we heard the hoarse roar of the Doctor's voice, and saw the fury with which he shook his clenched fists at him. The trap drove on, and a few minutes later we saw sudden light spring up among the trees as the lamp was lit in one of the sitting-rooms.

'Do you know, Watson,' said Holmes, as we sat together in the gathering darkness, 'I have really some scruples as to taking you to-night. There is a distinct element of danger.'

'Can I be of assistance?'

'Your presence might be invaluable.'

'Then I shall certainly come.'

'It is very kind of you.'

'You speak of danger. You have evidently seen more in these rooms than was visible to me.'

'No, but I fancy that I may have deduced a little more. I imagine that you saw all that I did.'

'I saw nothing remarkable save the bell-rope, and what purpose that could answer I confess is more than I can imagine.'

'You saw the ventilator, too?'

'Yes, but I do not think that it is such a very unusual thing to have a small opening between two rooms. It was so small that a rat could hardly pass through.'

'I knew that we should find a ventilator before ever we came to Stoke Moran.'

'My dear Holmes!'

'Oh, yes, I did. You remember in her statement she said that her sister could smell Dr. Roylott's cigar. Now, of course that suggests at once that there must be a communication between the two rooms. It could only be a small one, or it would have been remarked upon at the coroner's inquiry. I deduced a ventilator.'

'But what harm can there be in that?'

'Well, there is at least a curious coincidence of dates. A ventilator is made, a cord is hung, and a lady who sleeps in the bed dies. Does not that strike you?'

'I cannot as yet see any connection.'

'Did you observe anything very peculiar about that bed?'

'No.'

'It was clamped to the floor. Did you ever see a bed fastened like that before?'

'I cannot say that I have.'

'The lady could not move her bed. It must always be in the same relative position to the ventilator and to the rope—for so we may call it, since it was clearly never meant for a bell-pull.'

'Holmes,' I cried, 'I seem to see dimly what you are hitting at. We are only just in time to prevent some subtle and horrible crime.'

'Subtle enough and horrible enough. When a doctor does go wrong he is the first of criminals. He has nerve and he has knowledge. Palmer and Pritchard were among the heads of their profession. This man strikes even deeper, but I think, Watson, that we shall be able to strike deeper still. But we shall have horrors enough before the night is over: for goodness' sake let us have a quiet pipe, and turn our minds for a few hours to something more cheerful.'

About nine o'clock the light among the trees was extinguished and all was dark in the direction of the Manor House. Two hours passed slowly away, and then, suddenly, just at the stroke of eleven, a single bright light shone out right in front of us.

'That is our signal,' said Holmes, springing to his feet; 'it comes from the middle window.'

As we passed out he exchanged a few words with the landlord, explaining that we were going on a late visit to an acquaintance, and that it was possible that we might spend the night there. A moment later we were out on the dark road, a chill wind blowing in our faces, and one yellow light twinkling in front of us through the gloom to guide us on our sombre errand.

There was little difficulty in entering the grounds, for unrepaired breaches gaped in the old park wall. Making our way among the trees, we reached the lawn, crossed it, and were about to enter through the window, when out from a clump of laurel bushes there darted what seemed to be a hideous and distorted child, who threw itself on the grass with writhing limbs, and then ran swiftly across the lawn into the darkness.

'My!' I whispered. "Did you see it?'

Holmes was for the moment as startled as I. His hand closed like a vice upon my wrist in his agitation. Then he broke into a low laugh, and put his lips to my ear.

'It is a nice household,' he murmured, 'That is the baboon.'

I had forgotten the strange pets which the Doctor affected. There was a cheetah, too; perhaps we might find it upon our shoulders at any moment. I confess that I felt easier in my mind when, after following Holmes's example and slipping off my shoes, I found myself inside the bedroom. My companion noiselessly closed the shutters, moved the lamp on to the table, and cast his eyes round the room. All was as we had seen it in the day-time. Then creeping up to me and making a trumpet of his hand, he whispered into my ear again so gently that it was all that I could do to distinguish the words.

'The least sound would be fatal to our plans.'

I nodded to show that I had heard.

'We must sit without a light. He would see it through the ventilator.'

I nodded again.

'Do not go to sleep; your very life may depend upon it. Have your pistol ready in case we should need it. I will sit on the side of the bed, and you in that chair.'

I took out my revolver and laid it on the corner of the table.

Holmes had brought up a long thin cane, and this he placed upon the bed beside him. By it he laid the box of matches and the stump of a candle. Then he turned down the lamp and we were left in darkness.

How shall I ever forget that dreadful vigil? I could not hear a sound, not even the drawing of a breath, and yet I know that my companion sat open-eyed, within a few feet of me, in the same estate of nervous tension in which I was myself. The shutters cut off the least ray of light, and we waited in absolute darkness. From outside came the occasional cry of a night-bird, and once at our very window a long-drawn, cat-like whine, which told us that the cheetah was indeed at liberty. Far away we could hear the deep tones of the parish clock, which boomed out every quarter of an hour. How long they seemed, those quarters! Twelve o'clock, and one, and two, and three, and still we sat waiting silently for whatever might befall.

Suddenly there was the momentary gleam of a light up in the direction of the ventilator, which vanished immediately, but was succeeded by a strong smell of burning oil and heated metal. Someone in the next room had lit a dark lantern. I heard a gentle sound of movement, and then all was silent once more, though the smell grew stronger. For half an hour I sat with straining ears. Then suddenly another sound became audible—a very gentle, soothing sound, like that of a small jet of steam escaping continually from a kettle. The instant that we heard it, Holmes sprang from the bed, struck a match, and lashed furiously with his cane at the bell-pull.

'You see it, Watson?' he yelled. 'You see it?'

But I saw nothing. At the moment when Holmes struck the light I heard a low, clear whistle, but the sudden glare flashing into my weary eyes made it impossible for me to tell what it was at which my friend lashed so savagely. I could, however, see that his face was deadly pale, and filled with horror and loathing.

"HOLMES LASHED FURIOUSLY."

He had ceased to strike, and was gazing up at the ventilator, when suddenly there broke from the silence of the night the most horrible cry to which I have ever listened. It swelled up louder and louder, a hoarse yell of pain and fear and anger all mingled in the one dreadful shriek. They say that away down in the village, and even in the distant parsonage, that cry raised the sleepers from their beds. It struck cold to our hearts, and I stood gazing at Holmes, and he at me, until the last echoes of it had died away into the silence from which it rose.

'What can it mean?' I gasped.

'It means that it is all over,' Holmes answered. 'And perhaps, after all, it is for the best. Take your pistol, and we shall enter Dr. Roylott's room.'

With a grave face he lit the lamp, and led the way down the corridor. Twice he struck at the chamber door without any reply from within. Then he turned the handle and entered, I at his heels, with the cocked pistol in my hand.

It was a singular sight which met our eyes. On the table stood a dark lantern with the shutter half open, throwing a brilliant beam of light upon the iron safe, the door of which was ajar. Beside this table, on the wooden chair, sat Dr. Grimesby Roylott, clad in a long grey dressing-gown, his bare ankles protruding beneath, and his feet thrust into red heelless Turkish slippers.

Across his lap lay the short stock with the long lash which we had noticed during the day. His chin was cocked upwards, and his eyes were fixed in a dreadful rigid stare at the corner of the ceiling. Round his brow he had a peculiar yellow band, with brownish speckles, which seemed to be bound tightly round his head. As we entered he made neither sound nor motion.

'The band! the speckled band!' whispered Holmes.

I took a step forward. In an instant his strange head-gear began to move, and there reared itself from among his hair the squat diamond-shaped head and puffed neck of a loathsome serpent.

'It is a swamp adder!' cried Holmes—'the deadliest snake in India. He has died within ten seconds of being bitten. Violence does, in truth, recoil upon the violent, and the schemer falls into the pit which he digs for another. Let us thrust this creature back into its den, and we can then remove Miss Stoner to some place of shelter, and let the county police know what has happened.'

As he spoke he drew the dog whip swiftly from the dead man's lap, and throwing the noose round the reptile's neck, he drew it from its horrid perch, and, carrying it at arm's length, threw it into the iron safe, which he closed upon it.

Such are the true facts of the death of Dr. Grimesby Roylott, of Stoke Moran. It is not necessary that I should prolong a narrative which has already run to too great length, by telling how we broke the sad news to the terrified girl, how we conveyed her by the morning train to the care of her good aunt at Harrow, of how the slow process of official inquiry came to the conclusion that the Doctor met his fate while indiscreetly playing with a dangerous pet. The little which I had yet to learn of the case was told me by Sherlock Holmes as we travelled back next day.

'I had,' said he, 'come to an entirely erroneous conclusion, which shows, my dear Watson, how dangerous it always is to reason from insufficient data. The presence of the gipsies, and the use of the word "band," which was used by the poor girl, no doubt, to explain the appearance which she had caught a horrid glimpse of by the light of her match, were sufficient to put me upon an entirely wrong scent. I can only claim the merit that I instantly reconsidered my position when, however, it became clear to me that whatever danger threatened an occupant of the room could not come either from the window or the door. My attention was speedily drawn, as I have already remarked to you, to this ventilator, and to the bell-rope which hung down to the bed. The discovery that this was a dummy, and that the bed was clamped to the floor, instantly gave rise to the suspicion that the rope was there as a bridge for something passing through the hole, and coming to the bed. The idea of a snake instantly occurred to me, and when I coupled it with my knowledge that the Doctor was furnished with a supply of creatures from India, I felt that I was probably on the right track. The idea of using a form of poison which could not possibly be discovered by any chemical test was just such a one as would occur to a clever and ruthless man who had had an Eastern training. The rapidity with which such a poison would take effect would also, from his point of view, be an advantage. It would be a sharp-eyed coroner indeed who could distinguish the two little dark punctures which would show where the poison fangs had done their work. Then I thought of the whistle. Of course, he must recall the snake before the morning light revealed it to the victim. He had trained it, probably by the use of the milk which we saw, to return to him when summoned. He would put it through the ventilator at the hour that he thought best, with the certainty that it would crawl down the rope, and land on the bed. It might or might not bite the occupant, perhaps she might escape every night for a week, but sooner or later she must fall a victim.

'I had come to these conclusions before ever I had entered his room. An inspection of his chair showed me that he had been in the habit of standing on it, which, of course, would be necessary in order that he should reach the ventilator. The sight of the safe, the saucer of milk, and the loop of whipcord were enough to finally dispel any doubts which may have remained. The metallic clang heard by Miss Stoner was obviously caused by her father hastily closing the door of his safe upon its terrible occupant. Having once made up my mind, you know the steps which I took in order to put the matter to the proof. I heard the creature hiss, as I have no doubt that you did also, and I instantly lit the light and attacked it.'

'With the result of driving it through the ventilator.'

'And also with the result of causing it to turn upon its master at the other side. Some of the blows of my cane came home, and roused its snakish temper, so that it flew upon the first person it saw. In this way I am no doubt indirectly responsible for Dr. Grimesby Roylott's death, and I cannot say that it is likely to weigh very heavily upon my conscience.'

Comprehension Check

Think and Discuss

1. What is the speckled band? How does the band at first mislead Holmes?
2. Why does Dr. Roylott make alterations to the manor house?
- 3. What is Dr. Roylott's motive in committing the crime?
- 4. Sherlock Holmes is extremely observant. List at least four examples of his powers of observation.
5. Were you able to solve the mystery before Holmes was? If so, at what point did you figure out what was really happening?
- Literary Skill: Character

Communication Workshop

Talk

In order to write a good mystery story, an author must provide clues, both for the characters in the story and for the reader. Work with a partner to make a list of all the evidence that Sir Arthur Conan Doyle provides. Then take turns playing Sherlock Holmes as he talks to Watson about the evidence he has collected or the observations he has made.

Speaking/Listening: Role-playing

Write

Write a paragraph as Sherlock Holmes and use the evidence you have collected to prove Dr. Roylott is guilty. Cite both his motive and the evidence against him. Explain how the evidence points only to him and his guilt. Read your paragraph to your partner and listen to hers or his. Which makes the stronger case against Dr. Roylott?

Writing Fluency: Paragraph

Three Wishes

by Karla Kuskin

Three wishes
Three.
The first
A tree:
Dark bark
Green leaves
Under a bit of blue
A canopy
To glimpse sky through

To watch sun sift through
To catch light rain
Upon the leaves
And let it fall again.
A place to put my eye
Beyond the window frame.

Wish two:
A chair
Not hard or high
One that fits comfortably
Set by the window tree
An island in the room
For me
My own
Place to sit and be
Alone.

My tree
There.
Here my chair,
Me,
Rain, sky, sun.
All my wishes
All the things I need
But one
Wish three:
A book to read.

Room in Brooklyn
Edward Hopper
Charles Henry Hayden Fund 35.66
Courtesy, Museum of Fine Arts, Boston.

Recalling What You Know

Reading the different kinds of stories presented in this section may bring to mind other stories you've read. By recalling what you already know about literature, you can add to your enjoyment and understanding of what you read. Asking yourself a few questions can help you recall the great variety of literature you've read in this book.

1. **Modern realistic fiction** can help you realize that other people share many of the experiences you may encounter. Remember Beth Lambert's lesson in "Philip Hall Likes Me, I Reckon Maybe"? And Jenny's relationship with Grandy in "Jenny Kimura Smith Meets Grandy"? What other stories have you read like these?

2. **Traditional tales** can take you "far away and long ago." Did you enjoy running with Atalanta or soaring to earth with Tonweya? What other myths, legends, and folk tales have you read?

3. **Mysteries** like "The Midnight Visitor" and "The Speckled Band" give you the opportunity to play detective. What mysteries do you like?

4. **Sports and animal stories** can offer pleasant reading and can help you understand yourself. What did you learn about team spirit from "The Soccer Orphans"? Have you ever had a special understanding with a pet, or have you ever lost a pet?

5. **Science fiction** is exciting and full of adventure. Think about "The Samaritan" and get ready to read "The Naming of Names" in the next unit.

Recalling what you already know about different kinds of stories and what they have to offer in the way of interesting people, places, and experiences will enhance your ability to appreciate all kinds of literature.

The Bitterings chose to travel to Mars, but from his first step on Mars, Mr. Bittering is filled with fear—a fear that won't go away. What happens to him when the ability to make choices is taken away? As you read about the strange events on Mars, you can practice your reading techniques.

THE NAMING OF NAMES

by Ray Bradbury

The rocket metal cooled in the meadow winds. Its lid gave a bulging *pop*. From its clock interior stepped a man, a woman, and three children. The other passengers whispered away across the Martian meadow, leaving the man alone among his family.

The man felt his hair flutter and the tissues of his body draw tight as if he were standing at the center of a vacuum. His wife, before him, seemed almost to whirl away in smoke. The children, small seeds, might at any instant be sown to all the Martian climes.

The children looked up at him, as people look to the sun to tell what time of their life it is. His face was cold.

"What's wrong?" asked his wife.

"Let's get back on the rocket."

"Go back to Earth?"

"Yes! Listen!"

The wind blew as if to flake away their identities. At any moment the Martian air might draw his soul from him, as marrow comes from a white bone. He felt submerged in a chemical that could dissolve his intellect and burn away his past.

They looked at Martian hills that time had worn with a crushing pressure of years. They saw the old cities, lost in their meadows, lying like children's delicate bones among the blowing lakes of grass.

"Chin up, Harry," said his wife. "It's too late. We've come over sixty million miles."

The children with their yellow hair hollered at the deep dome of Martian sky. There was no answer but the racing hiss of wind through the stiff grass.

He picked up the luggage in his cold hands. "Here we go," he said—a man standing on the edge of a sea, ready to wade in and be drowned.

They walked into town.

Their name was Bittering—Harry and his wife Cora, Dan, Laura, and David. They built a small white cottage and ate good breakfasts there, but the fear was never gone. It lay with Mr. Bittering and Mrs. Bittering, a third unbidden partner at every midnight talk, at every dawn awakening.

"I feel like a salt crystal," he said, "in a mountain stream, being washed away. We don't belong here. We're Earth people. This is Mars. It was meant for Martians. For heaven's sake, Cora, let's buy tickets for home!"

But she only shook her head. "One day the atom bomb will fix Earth. Then we'll be safe here."

"Safe and insane!"

Tick-tock, seven o'clock sang the voice-clock; *time to get up.* And they did.

Something made him check everything each morning—warm hearth, potted blood-geraniums—precisely as if he expected something to be amiss. The morning paper was toast-warm from the 6 A.M. Earth rocket. He broke its seal and tilted it at his breakfast place. He forced himself to be convivial.

"Colonial days all over again," he declared. "Why, in ten years there'll be a million Earthmen on Mars. Big cities, everything! They said we'd fail. Said the Martians would resent our invasion. But did we find any Martians? Not a living soul! Oh, we found their empty cities, but no one in them. Right?"

A river of wind submerged the house. When the windows ceased rattling, Mr. Bittering swallowed and looked at the children.

"I don't know," said David. "Maybe there're Martians around we don't see. Sometimes nights I think I hear 'em. I hear the wind. The sand hits my window. I get scared. And I see those towns way up in the mountains where the Martians lived a long time ago. And I think I see things moving around those towns, Papa. And I wonder if those Martians *mind* us living here. I wonder if they won't do something to us for coming here."

"Nonsense!" Mr. Bittering looked out the windows. "We're clean, decent people." He looked at his children. "All dead cities have some kind of ghosts in them. Memories, I mean." He stared at the hills. "You see a staircase and you wonder what Martians looked like climbing it. You see Martian paintings and you wonder what the painter was like. You make a little ghost in your mind, a memory. It's quite natural. Imagination." He stopped. "You haven't been prowling up in those ruins, have you?"

"No, Papa." David looked at his shoes.

"See that you stay away from them. Pass the jam."

"Just the same," said little David, "I bet something happens."

Something happened that afternoon.

Laura stumbled through the settlement, crying. She dashed blindly onto the porch.

"Mother, Father—the war, Earth!" she sobbed. "A radio flash just came. Atom bombs hit New York! All the space rockets blown up. No more rockets to Mars, ever!"

"Oh, Harry!" The mother held onto her husband and daughter.

"Are you sure, Laura?" asked the father quietly.

Laura wept. "We're stranded on Mars, forever and ever!"

For a long time there was only the sound of the wind in the late afternoon.

Alone, thought Bittering. Only a thousand of us here. No way back. No way. No way. Sweat poured from his face and his hands and his body; he was drenched in the hotness of his fear. He wanted to strike Laura, cry, "No, you're lying! The rockets will come back!" Instead, he stroked Laura's head against him and said, "The rockets will get through someday."

"Father, what will we do?"

"Go about our business, of course. Raise crops and children. Wait. Keep things going until the war ends and the rockets come again."

The two boys stepped out onto the porch.

"Children," he said, sitting there, looking beyond them, "I've something to tell you."

"We know," they said.

In the following days, Bittering wandered often through the garden to stand alone in his fear. As long as the rockets had spun a silver web across space, he had been able to accept Mars. For he had always told himself: Tomorrow, if I want, I can buy a ticket and go back to Earth.

But now: The web gone, the rockets lying in jigsaw heaps of molten girder and unsnaked wire: Earth people left to the strangeness of Mars, the cinnamon dusts and wine airs, to be baked like gingerbread shapes in Martian summers, put into harvested storage by Martian winters. What would happen to him, the others? This was the moment Mars had waited for. Now it would eat them.

He got down on his knees in the flower bed, a spade in his nervous hands. Work, he thought, work and forget.

He glanced up from the garden to the Martian mountains. He thought of the proud old Martian names that had once been on those peaks. Earthmen, dropping from the sky, had gazed upon hills, rivers, Martian seas left nameless in spite of names. Once Martians had built cities, named cities; climbed mountains, named mountains; sailed seas, named seas. Mountains melted, seas drained, cities tumbled. In spite of this, the Earthmen had felt a silent guilt at putting new names to these ancient hills and valleys.

Nevertheless, man lives by symbol and label. The names were given.

Mr. Bittering felt very alone in his garden under the Martian sun, an anachronism bent here, planting Earth flowers in a wild soil.

Think. Keep thinking. Different things. Keep your mind free of Earth, the atom war, the lost rockets.

He perspired. He glanced about. No one watching. He removed his tie. Pretty bold, he thought. First your coat off, now your tie. He hung it neatly on a peach tree he had imported as a sapling from Massachusetts.

He returned to his philosophy of names and mountains. The Earthmen had changed names. Now there were Hormel Valleys, Roosevelt Seas, Ford Hills, Vanderbilt Plateaus, Rockefeller Rivers, on Mars. It wasn't right. The American settlers had shown wisdom, using old Indian prairie names: Wisconsin, Minnesota, Idaho, Ohio, Utah, Milwaukee, Waukegan, Osseo. The old names, the old meanings.

Staring at the mountains wildly, he thought: Are you up there? All the dead ones, you Martians? Well, here we are, alone, cut off! Come down, move us out! We're helpless!

The wind blew a shower of peach blossoms.

He put out his sun-browned hand, gave a small cry. He touched the blossoms, picked them up. He turned them, he touched them again and again. Then he shouted for his wife.

"Cora!"

She appeared at a window. He ran to her.

"Cora, these blossoms!"

She handled them.

"Do you see? They're different. They've changed! They're not peach blossoms any more!"

"Look all right to me," she said.

"They're not. They're *wrong!* I can't tell how. An extra petal, a leaf, something; the color, the smell!"

The children ran out in time to see their father hurrying about the garden, pulling up radishes, onions, and carrots from their beds.

"Cora, come look!"

They handled the onions, the radishes, the carrots among them.

"Do they look like carrots?"

"Yes . . . no." She hesitated. "I don't know."

"They've changed."

"Perhaps."

"You know they have! Onions but not onions, carrots but not carrots. Taste: the same but different. Smell: not like it used to be." He felt his heart pounding, and he was afraid. He dug his fingers into the earth. "Cora, what's happening? What is it? We've got to get away from this." He ran across the garden. Each tree felt his touch. "The roses. The roses. They're turning green!"

And they stood looking at the green roses.

And two days later Dan came running. "Come see the cow. I was milking her and I saw it. Come on!"

They stood in the shed and looked at their one cow.

It was growing a third horn.

And the lawn in front of their house very quietly and slowly was coloring itself like spring violets. Seed from Earth but growing up a soft purple.

"We must get away," said Bittering. "We'll eat this stuff and then we'll change—who knows to what? I can't let it happen. There's only one thing to do. Burn this food!"

"It's not poisoned."

"But it is. Subtly, very subtly. A little bit. A very little bit. We mustn't touch it."

He looked with dismay at their house.

"Even the house. The wind's done something to it. The air's burned it. The fog at night. The boards, all warped out of shape. It's not an Earthman's house any more."

"Oh, your imagination!"

He put on his coat and tie. "I'm going into town. We've got to do something now. I'll be back."

"Wait, Harry!" his wife cried.

But he was gone.

In town, on the shadowy step of the grocery store, the men sat with their hands on their knees, conversing with great leisure and ease.

Mr. Bittering wanted to fire a pistol in the air.

What are you doing, you fools! he thought. Sitting here! You've heard the news—we're stranded on this planet. Well, move! Aren't you frightened? Aren't you afraid? What are you going to do?

"Hello, Harry," said everyone.

"Look," he said to them. "You did hear the news, the other day, didn't you?"

They nodded and laughed. "Sure. Sure, Harry."

"What are you going to do about it?"

"Do, Harry, do? What *can* we do?"

"Build a rocket, that's what!"

"A rocket, Harry? To go back to all that trouble? Oh, Harry!"

"But you *must* want to go back. Have you noticed the peach blossoms, the onions, the grass?"

"Why, yes, Harry, seems we did," said one of the men.

"Doesn't it scare you?"

"Can't recall that it did much, Harry."

"Idiots!"

"Now, Harry."

Bittering wanted to cry. "You've got to work with me. If we stay here, we'll all change. The air. Don't you smell it? Something in the air. A Martian virus, maybe; some seed, or a pollen. Listen to me!"

They stared at him.

"Sam," he said to one of them.

"Yes, Harry?"

"Will you help me build a rocket?"

"Harry, I got a whole load of metal and some blueprints. You want to work in my metal shop on a rocket, you're welcome. I'll sell you that metal for five hundred dollars. You should be able to construct a right pretty rocket, if you work alone, in about thirty years."

Everyone laughed.

"Don't laugh."

Sam looked at him with quiet good humor.

"Sam," Bittering said. "Your eyes—"

"What about them, Harry?"

"Didn't they used to be gray?"

"Well, now, I don't remember."

"They were, weren't they?"

"Why do you ask, Harry?"

"Because now they're kind of yellow-colored."

"Is that so, Harry?" Sam said, casually.

"And you're taller and thinner—"

"You might be right, Harry."

"Sam, you shouldn't have yellow eyes."

"Harry, what color eyes have *you* got?" Sam said.

"My eyes? They're blue, of course."

"Here you are, Harry," Sam handed him a pocket mirror. "Take a look at yourself."

Mr. Bittering hesitated and then raised the mirror to his face.

There were little, very dim flecks of new gold captured in the blue of his eyes.

"Now look what you've done," said Sam a moment later. "You've broken my mirror."

Harry Bittering moved into the metal shop and began to build the rocket. Men stood in the open door and talked and joked without raising their voices. Once in a while they gave him a hand on lifting something. But mostly they just idled and watched him with their yellowing eyes.

"It's suppertime, Harry," they said.

His wife appeared with his supper in a wicker basket.

"I won't touch it," he said. "I'll eat only food from our deep-freeze. Food that came from Earth. Nothing from our garden."

His wife stood watching him. "You can't build a rocket."

"I worked in a shop once, when I was twenty. I know metal. Once I get it started, the others will help," he said, not looking at her, laying out the blueprints.

"Harry. Harry," she said, helplessly.

"We've got to get away, Cora. We've *got* to!"

The nights were full of wind that blew down the empty moonlit sea meadows past the little white chess cities lying for their twelve-thousandth year in the shallows. In the Earthmen's settlement, the Bittering house shook with a feeling of change.

Lying abed, Mr. Bittering felt his bones shifted, shaped, melted like gold. His wife, lying beside him, was dark from many sunny afternoons. Dark she was, and golden-eyed, burnt almost black by the sun, sleeping, and the children metallic in their beds, and the wind roaring forlorn and changing through the old peach trees, the violet grass, shaking out green rose petals.

The fear would not be stopped. It had his throat and heart. It dripped in a wetness of the arm and the temple and the trembling palm.

A green star rose in the east.

A strange word emerged from Mr. Bittering's lips.

"Iorrt. Iorrt." He repeated it.

It was a Martian word. He knew no Martian.

In the middle of the night he arose and dialed a call through to Simpson, the archaeologist.

"Simpson, what does the word *Iorrt* mean?"

"Why that's the old Martian word for our planet Earth. Why?"

"No special reason."

The telephone slipped from his hand.

"Hello, hello, hello, hello," it kept saying while he sat gazing out at the green star. "Bittering? Harry, are you there?"

The days were full of metal sound. He laid the frame of the rocket with the reluctant help of three indifferent men. He grew very tired in an hour or so and had to sit down.

"The altitude," laughed a man.

"Are you *eating,* Harry?" asked another.

"I'm eating," he said, angrily.

"From your deep-freeze?"

"Yes!"

"You're getting thinner, Harry."

"I'm not!"

"And taller."

"Liar!"

His wife took him aside a few days later. "Harry, I've used up all the food in the deep-freeze. There's nothing left. I'll have to make sandwiches using food grown on Mars."

He sat down heavily.

"You must eat," she said. "You're weak."

"Yes," he said.

He took a sandwich, opened it, looked at it, and began to nibble at it.

"And take the rest of the day off," she said. "It's hot. The children want to swim in the canals and hike. Please come along."

"I can't waste time. This is a crisis!"

"Just for an hour," she urged. "A swim'll do you good."

He rose, sweating. "All right, all right. Leave me alone. I'll come."

The sun was hot, the day quiet. There was only an immense staring burn upon the land. They moved along the canal, the father, the mother, the racing children in their swim suits. They stopped and ate meat sandwiches. He saw their skin baking brown. And he saw the yellow eyes of his wife and his children, their eyes that were never yellow before. A few tremblings shook him but were carried off in waves of pleasant heat as he lay in the sun. He was too tired to be afraid.

"Cora, how long have your eyes been yellow?"

She was bewildered. "Always, I guess."

"They didn't change from brown in the last three months?"

She bit her lips. "No. Why do you ask?"

"Never mind."

They sat there.

"The children's eyes," he said. "They're yellow, too."

"Sometimes growing children's eyes change color."

"Maybe *we're* children, too. At least to Mars. That's a thought." He laughed. "Think I'll swim."

They leaped into the canal water, and he let himself sink down and down to the bottom like a golden statue and lie there in green silence. All was water—quiet and deep, all was peace. He felt the steady, slow current drift him easily.

If I lie here long enough, he thought, the water will work and eat away my flesh until the bones show like coral. Just my skeleton left. And then the water can build on that skeleton—green things, deep water things, red things, yellow things. Change. Change. Slow, deep, silent change. And isn't that what it is up *there?*

He saw the sky submerged above him, the sun made Martian by atmosphere and time and space.

Up there, a big river, he thought, a Martian river, all of us lying deep in it, in our pebble houses, in our sunken boulder houses, like crayfish hidden, and the water washing away our old bodies and lengthening the bones and—

He let himself drift up through the soft light.

Dan sat on the edge of the canal, regarding his father seriously.

"Utha," he said.

"What?" asked his father.

The boy smiled. "You know. *Utha's* the Martian word for 'father.' "

"Where did you learn it?"

"I don't know. Around. *Utha!*"

"What do you want?"

The boy hesitated. "I—I want to change my name."

"Change it?"

"Yes."

His mother swam over. "What's wrong with Dan for a name?"

Dan fidgeted. "The other day you called Dan, Dan, Dan. I said to myself, 'That's not my name. I've a new name I want to use.' "

Mr. Bittering held to the side of the canal, his body cold and his heart pounding slowly. "What is this new name?"

"Linnl. Isn't that a good name? Can I use it? Can I, please?"

Mr. Bittering put his hand to his head. He thought of the silly rocket, himself working alone, himself alone even among his family, so alone.

He heard his wife say, "Why not?"

He heard himself say, "Yes, you can use it."

"Yaaa!" screamed the boy. "I'm Linnl, Linnl!"

Racing down the meadowlands, he danced and shouted.

Mr. Bittering looked at his wife. "Why did we do that?"

"I don't know," she said. "It just seemed like a good idea."

They walked into the hills. They strolled on old mosaic paths, beside still pumping fountains. The paths were covered with a thin film of cool water all summer long. They kept their bare feet cool all the day, splashing as in a creek, wading.

They came to a small deserted Martian villa with a good view of the valley. It was on top of a hill. Blue marble halls, large murals, a swimming pool. It was refreshing in this hot summertime. The Martians hadn't believed in large cities.

"How nice," said Mrs. Bittering, "if we could move up here to this villa for the summer."

"Come on," he said. "We're going back to town. There's work to be done on the rocket."

But as he worked that night, the thought of the cool blue marble villa entered his mind. As the hours passed, the rocket seemed less important.

In the flow of days and weeks, the rocket receded and dwindled. The old fever was gone. It frightened him to think he had let it slip this way. But somehow the heat, the air, the working conditions—

He heard the men murmuring on the porch of his metal shop.

"Everyone's going. You heard?"

"All going. That's right."

Bittering came out. "Going where?" He saw a couple of trucks, loaded with children and furniture, drive down the dusty street.

"Up to the villas," said the man.

"Yeah, Harry. I'm going. So is Sam. Aren't you, Sam?"

"That's right, Harry. What about you?"

"I've got work to do here."

"Work! you can finish that rocket in the autumn, when it's cooler."

He took a breath. "I got the frame all set up."

"In the autumn is better." Their voices were lazy in the heat.

"Got to work," he said.

"Autumn," they reasoned. And they sounded so sensible, so right.

"Autumn would be best," he thought. "Plenty of time, then."

No! cried part of himself, deep down, put away, locked tight, suffocating. No! No!

"In the autumn," he said.

"Come on, Harry," they all said.

"Yes, in the autumn. I'll begin work again then."

"I got a villa near the Tirra Canal," said someone.

"You mean the Roosevelt Canal, don't you?"

"Tirra. The old Martian name."

"But on the map—"

"Forget the map. It's Tirra now. Now I found a place in the Pillan Mountains—"

"You mean the Rockefeller Range," said Bittering.

"I mean the Pillan Mountains," said Sam.

"Yes," said Bittering, buried in the hot, swarming air. "The Pillan Mountains."

Everyone worked at loading the truck in the hot, still afternoon of the next day.

Laura, Dan, David carried packages. Or, as they preferred to be known, Ttil, Linnl, and Werr carried packages.

The furniture was abandoned in the little white cottage.

"It looked just fine in Boston," said the mother. "And here in the cottage. But up at the villa? No. We'll get it when we come back in the autumn."

Bittering himself was quiet.

"I've some ideas on furniture for the villa," he said after a time. "Big, lazy furniture."

"What about your encyclopedia? You're taking it along, surely?"

Mr. Bittering glanced away. "I'll come and get it next week."

They turned to their daughter. "What about your New York dresses?"

The bewildered girl stared. "Why, I don't want them any more."

They shut off the gas, the water; they locked the doors and walked away. Father peered into the truck.

"Gosh, we're not taking much," he said. "Considering all we brought to Mars, this is only a handful!"

He started the truck.

Looking at the small white cottage for a long moment, he was filled with a desire to rush to it, touch it, say good-by to it, for he felt as if he were going away on a long journey, leaving something to which he could never quite return, never understand again.

Just then Sam and his family drove by in another truck.

"Hi, Bittering! Here we go!"

The truck swung down the ancient highway out of town. There were sixty others traveling the same direction. The town filled with a silent, heavy dust from their passage. The canal waters lay blue in the sun, and a quiet wind moved in the strange trees.

"Good-by town!" said Mr. Bittering.

"Good-by, good-by!" sang the family, waving to it.

They did not look back again.

Summer burned the canals dry. Summer moved like flame upon the meadows. In the empty Earth settlement, the painted houses flaked and peeled. Rubber tires upon which children had swung in back yards hung suspended like stopped clock pendulums in the blazing air.

At the metal shop, the rocket frame began to rust.

In the quiet autumn Mr. Bittering stood, very dark now, very golden-eyed, upon the slope above his villa, looking at the valley.

"It's time to go back," said Cora.

"Yes, but we're not going," he said quietly. "There's nothing there any more."

"Your books," she said. "Your fine clothes. Your *lles* and your fine *ior uele rre.*"

"The town's empty. No one's going back," he said. "There's no reason to, none at all."

The daughter wove tapestries and the sons played songs on ancient flutes and pipes, their laughter echoing in the marble villa.

Mr. Bittering gazed at the Earth settlement far away in the low valley. "Such odd, such ridiculous houses the Earth people built."

"They didn't know any better," his wife mused. "Such ugly people. I'm glad they've gone."

They both looked at each other, startled by all they had just finished saying. They laughed.

"Where did they go?" he wondered. He glanced at his wife. She was golden and slender as his daughter. She looked at him, and he seemed almost as young as their eldest son.

"I don't know," she said.

"We'll go back to town maybe next year, or the year after, or the year after that," he said, calmly. "Now—I'm warm.

How about taking a swim?"

They turned their backs to the valley. Arm in arm they walked silently down a path of clear-running spring water . . .

Five years later a rocket fell out of the sky. It lay steaming in the valley. Men leaped out of it shouting.

"We won the war on Earth! We're here to rescue you! Hey!"

But the American-built town of cottages, peach trees, and theaters was silent. They found a flimsy rocket frame rusting in an empty shop.

The rocket men searched the hills. The captain established headquarters in an abandoned building. His lieutenant came back to report.

"The town's empty, but we found native life in the hills, sir. Dark people. Yellow eyes. Martians. Very friendly. We talked a bit, not much. They learned English fast. I'm sure our relations will be most friendly with them, sir."

"Dark, eh?" mused the captain. "How many?"

"Six, eight hundred, I'd say, living in those marble ruins in the hills, sir. Tall, healthy. Beautiful women."

"Did they tell you what became of the men and women who built this Earth settlement, Lieutenant?"

"They hadn't the foggiest notion of what happened to this town or its people."

"Strange. You think those Martians killed them?"

"They look surprisingly peaceful. Chances are a plague did this town in, sir."

"Perhaps. I suppose this is one of those mysteries we'll never solve. One of those mysteries you read about."

The captain looked at the room, the dusty windows, the blue mountains rising beyond, the canals moving in the light, and he heard the soft wind in the air. He shivered. Then, recovering, he tapped a large fresh map he had thumb-tacked to the top of an empty table.

"Lots to be done, Lieutenant." His voice droned on and on quietly as the sun sank behind the blue hills. "New settlements. Mining sites, minerals to be looked for. Bacteriological specimens taken. The work, all the work. And the old records were lost. We'll have a job of remapping to do, renaming the mountains and rivers and such. Calls for a little imagination.

"What do you think of naming those mountains the Lincoln Mountains, this canal the Washington Canal, those hills—we can name those hills for you, Lieutenant. Diplomacy. And you, for a favor, might name a town for me. Polishing the apple. And why not make this the Einstein Valley, and further over. . . . Are you *listening*, Lieutenant?"

The lieutenant snapped his gaze from the blue color and the quiet mist of the hills far beyond the town.

"What? Oh, *yes*, sir!"

Comprehension Check

Think and Discuss

1. What happens when Bittering's ability to make choices is taken away?
2. Something happens on Earth that causes Bittering's fear to grow. Reread page 526 to find out what happens.
3. Why is Bittering frightened about moving up to the villas?
4. What does Bittering feel about Earth people at the end of the story?
5. How many years pass before the rocket men arrive? Skim page 535 to find out.

• Study Skill: Reading techniques

Communication Workshop

Talk

Discuss with a small group why the story is called "The Naming of Names." What happens to the Martian names when the Earth people arrive? What happens to the Earth people's language and names as the story progresses? Whose names win in the end? Why do you think the power to determine what things are named, or called, is so important to a group of people?

Speaking/Listening: Cooperative learning

Write

Write a paragraph to explain why you think this story is entitled "The Naming of Names." Use examples from the story to support your explanations. Read your paragraph to your group and listen to some of theirs. Who has a particularly interesting idea about the story's title?

Writing Fluency: Paragraph

LOOKING BACK

See your Thinker's Handbook for tips.

Prewriting

Thinking and Writing About the Section
You have read three stories in this section that tell about choices characters make and what eventually happens to them. You can write a summary paragraph for your teacher to tell about the most important ideas in one of the stories. First copy the chart below. Then fill in the missing information.

Story	Character(s)' Choice	Outcome
The Incredible Journey	Animals decide to travel through wilderness to find owner.	
The Speckled Band	Helen decides to seek help from Sherlock Holmes.	
The Naming of Names	Bitterings choose to go to Mars.	

Writing

Use the information in the chart to write a summary paragraph about one of the stories. Use only the important ideas of the story in your paragraph. For more information on summary paragraphs, use your Writer's Handbook.

Revising

Read your first draft to a partner. Did you begin with a topic sentence that states the main idea? Did you use only important ideas? Make changes if necessary. Then proofread for spelling and punctuation errors. Write your final copy.

Presenting

Give your paragraph to your teacher. Offer to collect other paragraphs on the same story and make a bulletin board display for your teacher.

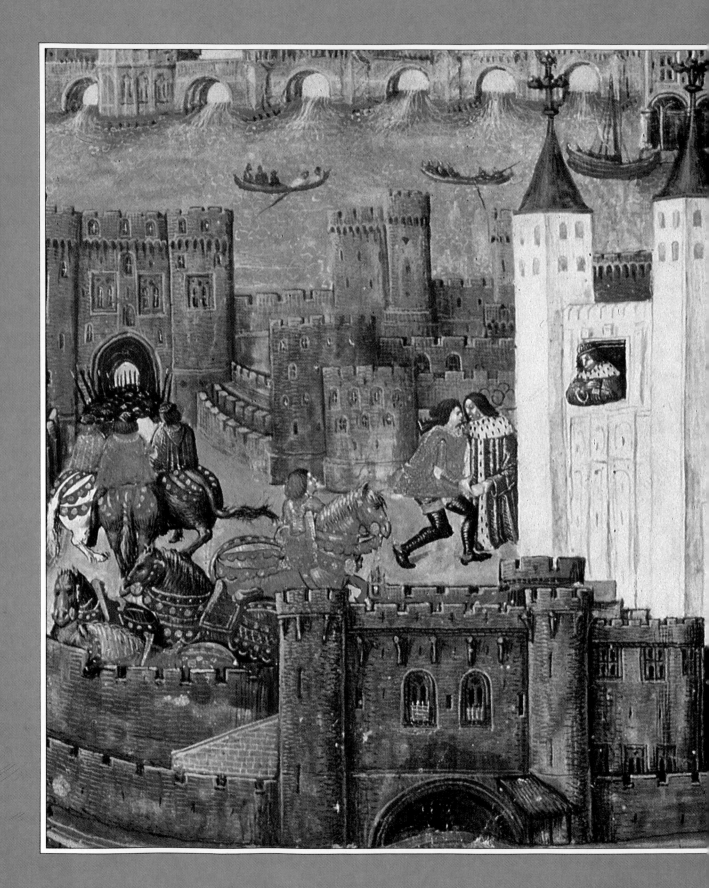

12

A Far Other Time

When your homework is piling up and you just don't seem to have any time to call your own, do you ever wish that you'd been born in some far other time when life was simpler?

Well, you can take time out from the twentieth century, because time travel *is* possible. The selections you are about to read will take you to a fascinating far other time—the Middle Ages. You will visit village gardens, misty lakes, and mossy towers and travel in the company of knights, ladies, and wandering minstrels.

Patterns of Organization

Have you ever wondered what life was really like in some far other time? One way you can find such information is from textbooks. And one way to remember and understand what you read in textbooks is to figure out how the author organized the information.

In textbooks, lessons as well as the paragraphs in them can be organized in different ways. Some of these ways are by sequence, cause and effect, and comparison. You already know that organization by **sequence** shows events in the order in which they happened. You also know that **causes and effects** can be discovered by asking "What happened?" and "Why did it happen?" And **comparisons** tell how things are alike or different.

Using Your Reading Skills

The paragraphs on the opposite page are from the geography textbook, *People on Earth*. As you read the paragraphs, keep in mind what you have just read about patterns of organization.

1. What time period is covered in these paragraphs? What does the order in which the events are discussed tell you about the organization?

   The time period is A.D. 476 to A.D. 1000. Since the events are presented in the order in which they happened, this should tell you that the information is organized by sequence.

2. Which paragraph tells why feudalism developed and what effects it had on the local leaders and the farmers? What pattern of organization does the author use in that paragraph?

   The answers to these questions are found in the first paragraph, in which the author uses a cause and effect pattern of organization.

3. What two kinds of organization does the author use in the third paragraph?
4. What kind of organization does the author use to describe how life in A.D. 1000 was different from life in A.D. 500?

THE FALL OF ROME / THE RISE OF EUROPE (A.D. 476–1000)

After the fall of the Roman Empire, Europe experienced a long period when warlike tribes invaded the settled farming areas. Only strong local leaders could protect the farmers from the tribal invaders who burned and stole. The leaders built castles, and the farmers swore them allegiance. **Feudalism** developed. Under this system, the leaders became lords. In return for protection, the farmers lost their liberty and became **serfs,** or slaves. Soils that had formerly been part of a shifting agricultural system were now worked year after year. The soils lost their fertility. For about 500 years, there was no surplus food in Europe, little safety, and little trade.

By about A.D. 1000, most tribal raids had stopped. Christianity had civilized the tribes. The strongest feudal lords had become kings. Around their small but growing kingdoms, the beginnings of nation-states formed. The language spoken by the king and his court was put into writing by court scribes. It became the official language in all the territory that the king conquered.

As raiding stopped, people felt more secure. Trade increased. Farmers learned to use animal fertilizers. Food became more available. People learned skills other than farming. Some became craftsmen or tradesmen. Towns grew up. Some towns grew up around the king's castle. Some grew up along routes of trade at such places as river crossings or the beginnings of mountain passes. Some grew up around centers of worship. Great cathedrals were built. They were symbols of the people's faith and of their skills as builders.

Townspeople gave allegiance to the king. But they were free. They were not serfs. The seeds of democracy started in the towns, which became more or less self-governing. In northern and western Europe, a league of merchant towns formed to protect and promote trade. It was called the **Hanseatic League.** These towns promoted trade fairs throughout Europe. They developed systems of banking and money exchange.

Some other common patterns of organization are main idea and supporting details, problem and solution, and question and answer. **Main idea** gives the most important idea about a topic and includes **details** that support that idea; **problem and solution** states a problem and suggests ways of solving it; and **question and answer** asks a question and then offers possible answers. By activating your knowledge of these patterns of organization as well as your other reading skills you can better understand textbook lessons. Noticing the pattern of organization will also help you take notes, outline, and make a report as well as be able to answer the textbook questions and do better on tests.

Practicing Textbook Reading

Read the paragraphs from *People on Earth* on the next page and use what you know about paragraph organization to answer the questions below.

1. Look at the first sentence of each paragraph and note how they reflect the organizational pattern of the entire page. What pattern is it? How do you know?
2. List three effects that contact with the Muslim culture had on Europe.
3. What influence did merchants have on the arts and learning?
4. What caused the shift in world power from Italy and the Muslim Empire to the Atlantic kingdoms?

Tips for Reading on Your Own

- When you read textbooks, recall what you already know about patterns of paragraph and lesson organization.
- Remember that the most common types of organization are sequence, cause and effect, comparison, and main idea and supporting details.
- When you figure out how information has been organized, use the organization to help you take notes, write an outline, write a report, answer the questions in the textbook, or study for a test.

Contacts with Other Lands

After the end of the Roman Empire, there was little learning in Europe. Most of the Latin and Greek writings had been destroyed by the invading tribes. But Christian monks had preserved and recopied some texts. Scholars studied these texts.

Some scholars also went to the cities in the Muslim lands, such as Córdoba in southern Spain. There the learning of the Greeks and Romans had been translated into Arabic. There Muslim scholars were making great advances in medicine, mathematics, and geography. In those days, the Muslims were like the Romans had been before. The Muslims controlled a large, flourishing empire.

In one other way, Europe also became aware of Muslim culture. That was through the **Crusades.** These were expeditions led by the Christian kings to capture Jerusalem and the Holy Land from the Muslims. The crusaders did not achieve their goal, but they marveled at the wealth and comfort in the Muslim cities. They wanted the silks and spices from eastern Asia that the Muslims introduced to them. Kings and their courts in Europe began to demand these kinds of luxuries.

Trade with the Muslims began to grow. The middlemen in this trade were the merchants in the cities of Italy. These merchants sent their vessels to the eastern end of the Mediterranean to Muslim ports. The Italian cities became prosperous. Wealthy merchants promoted the arts and scientific learning. In the north, the Hanseatic League cities also prospered. They also promoted the work of scientists and artists.

People began to dream of a water route to Asia. They wanted to bring the Asiatic goods directly to Europe. The Spanish and the Portuguese learned much as they fought to drive the Muslims out of their lands. The year the last Muslims left Spain was the year Columbus made his first voyage to the Americas. Shortly after 1500, a Spanish expedition sailed around the world.

Europe now had the ships and the knowledge of navigation. Wealthy kings and queens could finance voyages. The race for gold, for spices, for riches, and for colonies began. It was joined by all the Atlantic-facing kingdoms. Wealth and power passed from the Italian cities to the kingdoms facing the Atlantic. The Muslim Empire weakened as European kingdoms began to prosper.

Lessons 3 and 4 from Eastern Hemisphere, *a social studies text, will take you to a far other time. You'll visit a farming village in the year 1200 and you'll see how that way of life changed. Use what you know about patterns of organization to help you understand the period of time covered and the changes that took place.*

The Middle Ages

In the Early Middle Ages, English villagers thought little about being part of a national group. Ties were to the village and local region. By the 1500s, ties to the national group were stronger.

The English villages of Wotton, Underwood, and Ludgershall in Buckinghamshire, England, in 1575.

Lesson 3   Life in Medieval England

In the year 1200 most English people lived in small farming villages. To get a sense of what life was like, imagine walking through a village on a warm autumn day.

Village Life

As you walk down the main street, you see that it's not much of a street at all. It's just a dirt path where people walk from house to house and from houses to fields. The center of the village is an open, green area with a little pond at one side. A few cows are grazing on the green grass, and some ducks swim in the pond.

All around you, on either side of the green, are the farmers' houses. The farmers are called **peasants**. Mostly, the peasants' houses are built of wooden posts and mud-plaster walls. All of them have thatched roofs and dirt floors. Here and there a farm woman is sweeping her floor dirt out into the green.

Religion and the church were very important in the lives of medieval Europeans. The church was the center of village life as the drawing below shows. People prayed there, were married in the church, and were buried in the churchyard. Everyone belonged to the church, and all the holidays were religious celebrations. The strong religious beliefs of medieval Europeans contributed to the crusades of the Middle Ages. The crusades were religious wars aimed at winning from the Arabs the land where Jesus lived and taught.

Many of the houses are quite long, forty-five feet or more. The peasant family lives at one end of the house, and the animals sleep at the other end. During the winter this arrangement helps keep everyone warm.

The long houses belong to families who work the most land in the village fields. Often this is fifteen to thirty acres. Villagers who work very little land live in smaller houses. These villagers often do other jobs in the village such as baking, herding, woodcutting, and blacksmithing. The blacksmith works with iron to make and fix tools.

At the far end of the village green you can see a small, stone church. Like most European villagers, these villagers are Christians. The parish priest lives next to the church in a stone house. The priest leads religious services on Sundays, helps the farmers when they are ill, and conducts special ceremonies at times of birth and death and marriage.

The only other large building in sight belongs to the lord of the village. The lord is a member of the country's ruling

The drawings on this page and the next were made in the 1300s. They show English peasants at work.

class. He oversees work in the fields. He makes rules for the village. He acts as a judge when someone is accused of breaking the rules. He is also supposed to protect the villagers in time of trouble. For their part, the villagers work the lord's fields and pay rent on the land that they work for themselves.

The lord's home is larger than the peasants' and is made of stone. The lord receives and entertains guests in the building's large, main hall. He also holds the village court in that room. Storage rooms for food and supplies are found in the cellars. The lord and his family sleep on the second floor. On special occasions the lord and his lady drink from silver cups and wear fine, silk clothing. Yet, the lord does not live well by our standards. His house is cold and drafty. The only heat comes from fireplaces. And like everyone else in the village, he and his family get along without running water and other conveniences we take for granted.

Knights and Their Lords

Lords such as the one just described were granted their power and their land by more important members of the ruling class—by kings and by more important nobles. A very powerful lord (one called baron, duke, or earl to show his social position) might control many villages. The king was simply a very powerful lord.

In return for power and land, the lord of a village owed military service to the more powerful noble. We know these horse-riding, armor-covered soldiers as **knights** (nīts). The knights were called into service whenever nobles began to fight over land or power. Most knights owed about forty days of service out of each year.

Although it sounds as if kings and nobles spent lots of time fighting, they really did not. They spent most of their time overseeing the life and work of the villages under their control. In fact, the most powerful lords lived much as the knights in the village you saw. They owned fine clothing and fine jewelry, but they lived the lives of country people.

Below, two knights fight on horseback. These were the kinds of warriors who went on the crusades. The First Crusade, which began in 1096, was a success, and Europeans ruled a kingdom there until 1291. Seven other crusades followed over the next 200 years, but none were successful in conquering land. They were successful, however, in making Europeans more aware of the Arab world and what it had to offer. The Arabs gave much to Europe through trade and in the exchange of ideas.

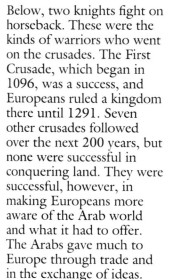

Checking Up

1. Why do you suppose thirteenth-century English farmers lived in villages rather than on farms separated from one another?

2. Who was the one wealthy person in this village?

3. What were the sources of his wealth and power?

4. Did people live as you thought they did during this time? Why or why not?

Lesson 4   The Growth of Trade and Towns

In the Early Middle Ages (from about A.D. 600 to 1000) Europe was a land of rural villages like the ones described in Lesson 3. The population was small. There were few towns and nothing that we would call a large city. Europe was mostly covered with dense forests.

In the Later Middle Ages (from about A.D. 1000 to 1350) all of this began to change. The European population grew much larger. Towns grew into real cities. Europeans went out from their homelands to trade—and fight—with people who lived to the south and far to the east.

A street in a medieval French town. The street is lined with shops. From left to right: a tailor, a furrier, a barber, and a druggist.

Population Growth in Medieval Europe (France, Germany, Italy, and the British Isles)

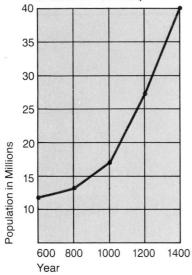

Population in Millions (y-axis: 10, 15, 20, 25, 30, 35, 40)

Year (x-axis: 600, 800, 1000, 1200, 1400)

Who's Who

Marco Polo was probably the most famous medieval trader and traveler. He was the son of an Italian merchant. In the late 1200s Marco Polo traveled east by ship and by camel with his father and uncle. Three and one-half years later they reached China.

Marco Polo stayed in China for more than a decade. He traveled widely throughout Asia. When he returned to Europe, he described what he had seen in a book. His book was used as a guide for centuries.

A Growing Population

The graph at left shows how much the population of several European countries grew during the Later Middle Ages. Many historians think this took place because Europeans found ways to produce more food. One way was by using more iron tools. Farmers used iron axes to cut the great forests. They used iron shovels and hoes to drain swamplands. Once these fertile lands were ready for use, the farmers used heavy plows made partly of iron to till the soil. In this way each farmer was able to plow more land and harvest more food. The increased amount of food, in turn, was capable of supporting a larger population.

Europeans also got more food by fishing. In earlier times, fishing had been limited to waters close to shore. During the Later Middle Ages, though, fishermen began venturing farther into the Atlantic. Fish became a major source of food— especially for people living in towns.

The Growth of Trade

As food production increased, trade increased as well. One kind of trade was local. Farmers took their extra food into nearby towns. They sold it and bought some of the goods made in the towns. They also used the money to pay rent to their lords. This kind of trade had always gone on in Europe, but it increased as farmers began to grow more food than they needed for just themselves.

The other sort of trade was carried on over long distances. (See the map on page 551.) Europeans began to trade with the Islamic countries and, through the Muslims, with countries such as India and China. Europeans traded leather, furs, salt, grain, iron, timber, and slaves to the south and east. In return they got spices, fine cloth, oranges, almonds, raisins, figs, and more.

Eventually people in Europe came to depend on the goods they got in overseas trade. Trade in spices provides an example. Spices such as pepper, cinnamon, and ginger were highly valued in Europe. People at the time had no refrigerators. As a result, they used a lot of salt to preserve foods. Spices covered the taste of foods preserved in this way. Many Europeans liked the spices when they were used on fresh

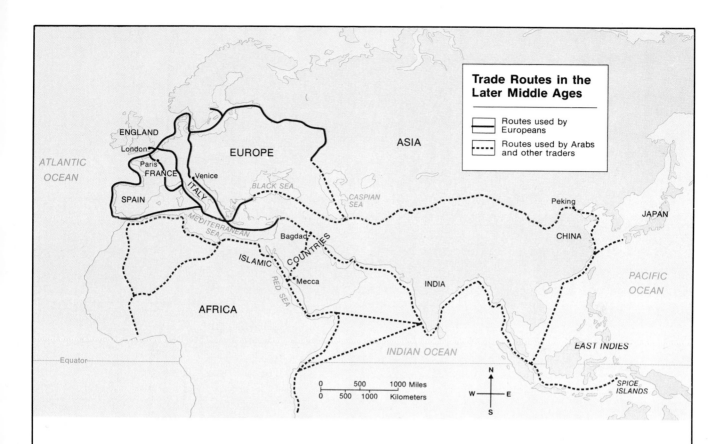

food too. Gradually, more and more people depended on spices. People with money were willing to pay a lot for spices, and so merchants who dealt in these goods made a great deal of money.

More Towns and Cities

At the same time trade was growing in Europe, more and more Europeans came to live in the towns and cities. Many of the new townspeople had been peasants. They moved to the cities to find jobs that paid more money.

Italian towns grew fastest because they were closest to the Islamic world. Italian cities during this period became very rich on the trade they controlled. Venice was the greatest of the trade centers, but cities such as London and Paris, which were farther north in Europe, also grew large.

As towns and cities grew, a new class of people arose in Europe—a middle class made up mainly of city people. They became more and more important in each nation because

Does this map indicate that many European traders ventured outside of Europe? What is the evidence?

This painting of medieval Venice shows Marco Polo sailing east with his father and uncle.

they could read and write and because they knew all about money and taxes. In many countries, kings came to rely on middle-class people to run their governments.

Some city people came to have more power and wealth than others. At the top were rich merchants. They controlled much of the sea trade, and they ran city government. They lived in large houses very much as lords did. Craft workers had less wealth and power. They lived in small houses above or behind their shops. They banded together in organizations called **guilds** (gildz). The guilds protected their jobs and trained young men in each trade. Craft workers took

great care and pride in the things they made. Least powerful among the city people were workers who did odd jobs of all kinds. They had no guilds and, thus, no protection. Often they rioted against the rich people who ran the city. City society remained much the same throughout the Middle Ages and long afterward.

Skilled workers during the Middle Ages had to belong to guilds. A guild controlled the number of people who could practice a craft and the quality of goods produced. In order to qualify as a master-craftsman, a person had to serve an apprenticeship of seven years, pay a fee to the guild, and give proof of his skill. The mason and the carpenter above are displaying their skills before a guild official. The fifteenth-century painting above left is of Cloth Merchants' Street in Bologna, Italy.

Checking Up

1. How did the increased use of iron lead to population growth in Europe during the Middle Ages?

2. Why were spices important to Europe in the Middle Ages?

3. Would you rather have lived in a city as a craft worker or in a village as a peasant during the Middle Ages? Why?

Comprehension Check

See your Thinker's
Handbook for tips.

Think and Discuss

1. What time periods are covered in Lessons 3 and 4 and how did life change in those time periods? What patterns of organization helped you answer the question?
2. In Lesson 3, you "walked" through a medieval village. List three details that describe the village and three details that describe the people who lived there.
3. How is a lord's home different from a peasant's home and from a modern home? What pattern of organization helped you answer the question?
4. Answer question 1 under **Checking Up** on page 553.
5. What new class of people arose in European cities? Why were they important?

• Study Skill: Textbook reading

Communication Workshop

Talk

Imagine that through your school's Time Machine Exchange Program a teenager from medieval England will soon be arriving to visit. Work with a partner to discuss the differences between travel in medieval times and in the twentieth century. What do you think a medieval teenager would ask about how to ride a bicycle or drive a car? How can you explain either process so he or she can understand? Take turns being the modern teenager and try to explain either process to the medieval teenager.
Speaking/Listening: Role-playing

Write

Prepare for the medieval teen's visit by writing a paragraph to explain how to ride a bike or drive a car. Be sure to include each step of the process so your explanation will be clear. Read your paragraph to the class and listen to theirs. Who explained the process in a particularly interesting way?
Writing Fluency: Paragraph

The Song of Wandering Aengus

by William Butler Yeats

I went out to the hazel wood,
Because a fire was in my head,
And cut and peeled a hazel wand,
And hooked a berry to a thread;
And when white moths were on the wing,
And moth-like stars were flickering out,
I dropped a berry in a stream
And caught a little silver trout.

When I had laid it on the floor
I went to blow the fire aflame,
But something rustled on the floor,
And some one called me by my name:
It had become a glimmering girl
With apple blossom in her hair
Who called me by my name and ran
And faded through the brightening air.

Though I am old with wandering
Through hollow lands and hilly lands,
I will find out where she has gone,
And kiss her lips and take her hands;
And walk among long dappled grass,
And pluck till time and times are done
The silver apples of the moon,
The golden apples of the sun.

In ancient tales, every knight who came riding through the green wood seemed to be on a difficult quest. The knight you are about to meet is no different; he takes on a quest that seems impossible. Is he foolish to pursue it? As you read, think about the author's purpose and how her style—her choice of words and use of images—captures the flavor and feeling of a far other time.

The Knight and the Naiad of the Lake

by Barbara Leonie Picard

Early one summer morning, while the sun was still low in the sky, a young knight was riding by a small lake which was known to the people of those parts as the Lake of the Naiad,[1] for it was said that an immortal being, with the shape of a lovely woman, dwelt in its depths, and might sometimes be seen flashing through the waters or standing on the grassy margin. It was said, too, that in the lake there was a palace with towers and pinnacles, fair gardens of water-blossoms and freshwater shells, and that in this palace the Naiad lived.

But none of this the young knight knew, for he was a stranger to that place, passing through in search of adventures worthy of his newly-won knighthood. He was happy as he rode along. His horse was a fine and noble animal, his armour shone in the morning sunlight and his helmet glittered like gold, his sword was trusty and his purse was full, and he had no care in all the world, and only the hope and eager expectation of the many strange and wonderful and lovely things that life would have to offer him.

---

1. Naiad (ni'yad)

    As he rode by, he suddenly caught sight of a young woman sitting among the yellow irises on a tiny islet only a few yards from the shore of the lake, where grew a single willow tree which dipped its silver leaves in the water. He reined in his horse and watched her for a moment, and then he rode forward to the very edge of the lake and dismounted. He spoke to her and she answered him courteously enough.

"Fair lady," he said, "what is your name?"

"I am the Naiad of the Lake."

"And may I ask where is your home?" inquired the knight.

"I dwell in the lake," said the Naiad. "In the depths of the lake I have a palace, there have I dwelt for ever, and there shall I dwell for evermore."

"Fair lady," said the knight, "I am very young, and though my heart is brave and I think that when the time comes I shall not fail, I am as yet untried in deeds of courage and I have no lady whose favours I may wear at the jousting and whose beauty I may praise to other men. Will you be my lady and take me for your faithful knight, to wear your favours worthily and to lay my good deeds at your feet?"

She gave a little ripple of mocking laughter that was like the tinkle of water lapping on the pebbles of a shore. "You must be very young indeed, Sir Knight, to ask such a thing of me, the Naiad of the Lake."

"If you grant my request," he said, "I will serve you truly, and ask no more of you than your smiles at my successes."

"You are rash and overbold," she said. "Begone before I grow angry."

"I will ask no more of you than only your blessing on my future," he begged.

Her voice was as cold as the lake in December and as hard as ice. "You are young," she said, "but you are only a man, and one day you will grow old and die. I am deathless and ever beautiful, and yet you dare to ask to be my knight. Begone."

But the knight knelt down on the shore of the lake and pleaded with her, and at all his entreaties she grew more angry and more scornful.

"Then is there no hope for me?" he asked at last.

"None," she said. And then suddenly she smiled as though she had thought of something, and again she gave her mocking laugh that was like the tinkle of water lapping on the pebbles of a shore. "Yes, there is hope," she said. "Seven hundred years ago I lost a ring. I dropped it at the bottom of the lake and it was swallowed by a fish. A fisherman, from his little boat, caught the fish. From that day to this I have not seen my ring, but I should be glad to possess it again. Find the ring and bring it here to me and I will be your lady and take you for my knight."

The young knight was overjoyed and could hardly find words to express his gratitude at the honour she had done him. But she sat on her islet among the irises and laughed at him, for she thought that he could never find the ring.

"How shall I know the ring when I see it?" he asked.

"You cannot fail to recognize it," said the Naiad, "for it shines like green fire. But hold it up to the sun and the fire turns red, and hold it over the water and it will become blue."

"And if you are not here when I return?" he asked.

"I shall be here, somewhere in the lake," she laughed. "Only call to me and I will come."

The knight rose to his feet. "I will find your ring, Naiad of the Lake," he said, "though it take me many years, and I will bring it here to you and claim you as my lady."

The Naiad laughed again. "You may have more than that," she said. "Bring me my ring and I will not only have you for my knight, but I will take you to live with me in my beautiful palace in the depths of the lake, in honour and joy for ever."

Proud and happy, the young knight mounted his horse. "I shall not fail you," he said. "I will find your ring and return it to you and claim my reward. Until then, farewell, Naiad of the Lake."

And he rode away, followed by her mocking laughter as she slipped back into the water, and a short way off, when he turned round to see her for the last time, there was no longer anyone on the little islet, only the yellow irises and the willow tree that dipped its silver leaves in the lake. But he could still hear her laughter that was like the tinkle of water lapping on the pebbles of a shore.

From that day on the knight thought of nothing but his quest. He sought the ring and nothing else. He passed by fame and glory and riches, friendship and affection, and sought only the ring. His companions named him the Steadfast Knight, but more in mockery than in admiration, for they thought that he was foolish to seek so hard for something that he might never find. But their scorn and their entreaties were of no avail and he never wavered in his determination to find the ring and return it to the Naiad of the Lake. And it was in this hope that he spent all his inheritance, all his time, and all his youth.

He sought the ring over the whole world. In towns and villages, in castles and in hovels, on mountains and in valleys he searched. He travelled to all the wise men of the east to ask their help, and when they failed him, he went by night to the witches and the wizards of the north. He asked of the ring from every man and woman that he met, whether of high or low degree, and some of them answered him politely, and others with rudeness and mockery, and many thought him mad. And every now and then, now in one part of the world, now in another, he would meet with someone who had news of the ring. Perchance a peasant who had heard his father speak of it, or a witch who saw it in her crystal ball, and once he met a very old woman who had for a moment held it in her hands, when she was young and fair. But in all his travels he could find no one to tell him what had become of it.

And so the years passed and the knight grew old, and still he had not found what he sought. He was tired, he was aged, his riches were all spent, but still he travelled on, determined that he would not give up the search while he yet lived.

And then one day, in the fiftieth year of his quest, as he rode along a little-used track that had once been a prosperous highway, the poor, skinny old horse that was all the mount he could afford to own, stumbled a little and began to limp.

"It is another stone in his hoof," thought the knight wearily, and stiffly he dismounted, and taking the horse's foot in his hands, tried to dislodge the stone with his dagger.

His old eyes were no longer as sharp as they once had been, but they caught a glint of green as the stone fell from the hoof on to the dust of the roadway. He picked it up and turned it round, and it flashed green fire; he held it to the sun and it glowed crimson; a ditch ran along on either side of the road, he held it over the muddy water and it sparkled blue light. There was no longer any doubt about it. It was the Naiad's ring. He slipped it on to one of his fingers and it flashed there, mocking his bony old hands.

He mounted his horse again, and turning its head, started on the long journey back to the Lake of the Naiad.

When the knight reached the lake for the second time in his life, it was evening, and he came on foot. He had sold his old horse to buy food for the last stages of his journey. He leaned on a staff he had cut himself from the hedges, and his scabbardless sword clanked dismally against his rusty armour which felt so heavy to his tired limbs. The lake looked as it had been when he had seen it last. Even the little islet had not changed. The irises still bloomed and the willow tree still dipped its silver leaves in the water.

On the shore of the lake opposite the islet, the knight stopped. "I am here," he thought. "This is my goal. I shall call to the Naiad of the Lake and give her the ring," and he smiled to himself. But because he was thirsty, first he took off his helmet and knelt down, and cupping his hands he bent over the water to drink. As

he did so, he caught sight of his reflection as if in a mirror. He saw his thin white hair, his lined and haggard face, his tired and hollow eyes, and paused. "I am old," he said to himself, " and she is ever young and ever beautiful. What would she want with a knight as old and as ugly as I? It would not be fair to claim my reward. Let her have her ring, I shall not call to her." And he rose, and taking off the ring he flung it away from him as far as he could, and like a flash of blue fire, it dropped into the lake. Then the knight picked up his helmet and his staff, and carrying them, turned and walked sadly away. "I may be allowed to spend the rest of my days in peace," he thought.

But he had not gone many slow paces when he thought he heard a sound behind him. He paused. Was that the laughter of the Naiad of the Lake, or was it only the tinkle of water lapping on the pebbles of the shore? He listened and it seemed as though he heard a voice calling him.

"Sir Knight, Sir Knight."

He turned round. The sun was setting across the lake and it dazzled his old eyes so that he had to shade them with his hand. In the gold and crimson light it seemed to him that he could see a figure where he had stood, a few moments earlier. "It is not the sunlight on the water," he thought, "it is something more. It is the Naiad of the Lake."

"Sir Knight, come back."

He went to the margin of the lake and stood beside her and heard her speak to him. "Why did you go without calling me?"

"I am old," he said. "What would you, deathless and ever lovely, want with an aged knight like myself?"

He felt her hand in his. "Look into the water."

He looked into the lake at his feet and saw them both reflected there, standing side by side. And he saw himself young and straight, his hair and his eyes as bright as they had been on that first day when he had ridden that way, and his armour shone in the sunlight like gold.

"You have brought me my ring and my promise is yet to be kept. My palace waits for you in the depths of the lake. Come with me and we shall live there together in joy and eternal youth for ever."

He smiled, and with her hand in his, stepped into the lake and walked onwards into the golden water until it covered his head.

Meet the Author

Barbara Leonie Picard, who grew up in Sussex, England, remembers editing a weekly magazine when she was about nine or ten: "Each issue was limited to a single copy written in an exercise book; and every feature in the magazine—including a readers' competition, a serial, and the illustrations—were solely the work of the editor."

Miss Picard first began writing original fairy tales for her own amusement. The pastime enabled her to combine her interests in language, mythology, folk culture, and literature. Her first stories were published in 1949, and since then Miss Picard has published retellings of myths and legends of many lands in addition to several collections of fairy tales and full-length novels. Her novel, *One Is One* was a runner-up for the Carnegie Medal in 1965.

Viewed through the mists of time, the image of the gallant young warrior being dubbed a knight on the field of battle takes on the golden, mythical glow of Camelot and the Round Table. Was becoming a knight really so romantic? As you read this social studies lesson to find out, think about the author's purpose.

Training to Be a Knight

The Page's Training

To be a knight required that you start young, for you had many things to learn, not simply about warfare but about courtesy as well. The son of a knight might be taken from the care of his mother as early as seven years of age and sent off to the castle of some powerful nobleman to begin his training as a page. Every kind of menial job was his: fetching and carrying, running errands, helping the lady of the household in all her many duties, learning to come when he was called and to wait patiently when there was nothing for him to do. As he grew older, his day filled. He might be taught to play some musical instrument, to compose verse, and to wait on table. He learned the use of arms—the sword, the lance, the axe, on which his life would someday depend—and he practiced wrestling, leaping, running, and vaulting into the saddle without touching the stirrup while in full armor. All this training prepared him for the next step: to become a squire, at about the age of fourteen.

The Squire's Tasks

And now there were still other details of service to learn and perform. As a squire he had to know how to carve every sort of meat at the table and to know the correct word for each type of carving. A deer was *broken*, a swan was *lifted*, a hen was *despoiled*, a duck was *unbraced*, and a peacock was *disfigured*. He had to know every aspect of the hunt, with the right words to describe a *skulk* of foxes, a *sounder* of swine, or a *pride* of lions; he had to be familiar with the care and repairing of armor, with the management of hounds, with the mews where the hawks were trained. As squire of the bedchamber he must help his lord undress, comb his hair, prepare his bed, and even "drive out the dog and cat, giving them a clout."[1] As squire of the body he must keep his lord's weapons and armor in good condition, replacing worn leather and burnishing away rust; as squire of the stables he must groom and exercise horses and learn how to train a war-horse; as squire of the table he must cut bread, pour beverages, and serve properly with a napkin over his arm.

Knightly Ideals

In all the squire's tasks it was never forgotten that he was not just a servant. He was an apprentice, preparing to take his place in the order of knighthood. Much more than bodily fitness and a readiness to serve were required of the young man who would be a knight. He had to learn manners and attitudes and above all, the meaning of honor. Honor had grown out ot the military and feudal

1. Quoted by Jay Williams, *Knights of the Crusades,* New York: American Heritage Publishing Co., 1962.

side of knighthood. Virtue, which had come from knighthood's religious roots, was equally important for the would-be knight.

But there were courtly virtues too, which brought manners into being. These expressed themselves chiefly in the changing attitudes toward women. The young squire not only swore to defend womankind but he chose a lady whose token he wore and to whom he vowed to be faithful. When at last he received his weapons and was allowed to fight in tournaments, it was under the eye of his lady that he fought, and for her glory.

The Tournament

The tournament was the most popular of games and was a kind of high point in the career of the young man aiming for his spurs and belt. In it can be seen all the aspects of chivalry: elaborate ritual and fine show, courage, honor, championship of ladies, and knightly virtue.

When a tourney was given, it was often used as the occasion for the arming of a group of young squires or for the bestowing of knighthood. It might represent, then, the bow of a young man in the world of arms through his appearance in a mock battle, where it could be seen whether he displayed the proper courage and bearing.

The tournament might last several days, and each evening would be full of dancing and feasting—at any rate for those who could still walk and had teeth enough left to chew with. It was usually divided into two types of event: the joust, or duel with lances between two horsemen; and the melee, or sham battle between two companies of knights.

Heraldic Origins

An important addition to chivalry which may possibly have come from the Saracens was the heraldic badge, or blazon. Certainly it began to be widely used during the Crusades and especially after the introduction of the closed helmet, which prevented a man's face being seen. Distinctive designs were painted on the shield so that the knight could be recognized, and in later times these designs were sewn on his surcoat and the trappings of his horse. Beginning as a personal badge, they became by degrees hereditary badges to be handed down in his family; a man who bore such a blazon on his shield could be known not only for *who* he was but for *what* he was as well—a member of the knightly caste.

By the Way
The joust was fought in this agreed pattern: first mounted combat with lances, followed by a duel on foot, then surrender on bended knee.

Shelley

Keyes

Comprehension Check

Think and Discuss

1. Do you think the Steadfast Knight was foolish to pursue his quest? Why or why not?
2. Did the ending of the story surprise you? Why or why not?
• 3. What is the author's purpose in the first selection? Give three examples of her choice of words and of imagery that support her purpose and capture the medieval setting.
4. "The Knight and the Naiad of the Lake" is a fairy tale about the quest of a knight. After reading the textbook lesson, "Training to Be a Knight," do you think knighthood was really as romantic as it is often thought to be? Why or why not?
• 5. What is the author's purpose in "Training to Be a Knight"? Support your answer with two examples.
• Comprehension Skill: Author's purpose

Communication Workshop

Talk

Have a small group discussion about how well you could perform a squire's chores and learn the correct terms for carving and for describing groups of animals. Knights had to learn terms that described groups of people as well as animals. Some examples are "a melody of harpists," "a sentence of judges," and "an eloquence of lawyers." Discuss how each term says something about the habits or characteristics of the group it describes.
Speaking/Listening: Cooperative learning

Write

The list below contains examples of groups of modern-day people. Be a modern knight and, on a separate sheet of paper, complete the examples by adding descriptive terms. Read your terms for each group to the class and listen to theirs. Compare the terms you chose for each group of people.

a _(riot)_ of comedians   a(n) _____ of joggers

a(n) _____ of plumbers   a(n) _____ of students

Writing Fluency: Descriptive terms

Looking for Meaning

When archeologists study ruins from other times, they are able to learn about the people who constructed them and about the conditions at that time. One way they do this is by asking questions. For example, an archeologist might be digging up a ruined cottage from the Middle Ages. The only sections remaining might be parts of the outside walls and a chimney. An archeologist can figure out what the cottage looked like and even reconstruct it by asking questions such as these: Where did the people sleep? What did they eat? How many rooms did this cottage probably have?

Like an archeologist, as a good reader you can usually figure things out by asking good questions. If a sentence is unclear, stop and ask yourself what it really means. Take the sentence apart and make sure you understand each part. Here is a sentence that might be unclear to you: "In Chaucer's time, audiences gathered to hear bards narrate tales of chivalry." Some questions you might ask about this sentence are: When was Chaucer's time? What are bards? What does "chivalry" mean? By answering these questions, you will discover that the sentence means: "In the Middle Ages, people got together to hear poets tell stories about knights."

Remember how archeologists are able to reconstruct cultures by digging for answers. You can do the same thing in your reading—all you have to do is ask questions.

In a far other time, a young minstrel travels the king's highway in search of his famous father, Roger the Minstrel. "The road is home to the minstrel," Roger had told him. But there are twists and turns of the road that Adam doesn't suspect. Discover the exciting adventure that awaits Adam on the road through the king's forest.

ADAM OF THE ROAD

by Elizabeth Janet Gray

In the summer of 1294, eleven-year-old Adam Quartermayne set out on the roads of England with his father and his beloved spaniel, Nick. Along the way they stopped at an inn, where Adam played his harp and sang, Roger told a tale, and even Nick entertained the merchants and travelers by doing tricks.

But then Nick was stolen by the minstrel Jankin, and Adam, in pursuit of them, became separated from Roger in a crowded market town. Word had it that Jankin was going to the fair at Winchester, so Adam decided to go there. Along the way, he encountered a familiar face—Daun William, a merchant he had met back at the inn, who kindly offered to let Adam ride with Oswald, one of his two servants. So they set off through the forest, riding close together—Daun William first, then a servant leading a pack horse, then Oswald, with Adam perched behind.

It was a little mysterious to ride through the king's forest, where the trees, oak and ash and elm and beech, grew so tall, and the undergrowth was thick with fern and briar. Now and then they saw the river shining in the sunshine; now and then they saw one of the king's fallow deer standing motionless and startled in the sun-splotched shade. The birds kept their late August silence, but sometimes there was a bit of yellow and gray flitting among the leaves or a flash of wings across the road. Most of the time Adam saw only the trees that came up close to the road's edge—not cut back two hundred feet on each side as the law decreed—and heard only the steady plop-plop of their own horses' hoofs. It made him drowsy after a while.

Suddenly there was a shout, and an arrow came zinging in front of them to bury its head in a tree not three feet away from Daun William. The next moment an arrow zinged behind Adam and stuck quivering in the tree nearest him. Daun William's horse, the most spirited of the five, promptly reared up on his hind legs, while the others plunged and backed against each other in fright and confusion. Amid a great crashing in the undergrowth, four men rode shouting out of the woods.

"Robbers!" thought Adam. "Robbers. This is happening to *me*."

One, the leader, wore full armor. From head to toe he was encased in chain mail that caught the sun and gave it back in a hundred winking bits. He was a knight—that Adam knew from his spurs and the crest on his helm—but he had gone to some pains to conceal his armorial bearings. His horse had no trappings; his own surcoat was plain black; even his shield had been painted over with black. Only his crest betrayed him: a gilded leopard that reared itself from the top of his steel helm. Perkin[1] would know, thought Adam, what family bore a leopard on its crest. He had a sword with a jeweled pommel that caught the sunshine, and he carried a lance leveled menacingly at the surprised and shocked merchant.

1. Perkin is Adam's friend at school.

One of the others with him was a squire, with sword and buckler, and a dagger in his belt. The other two were yeomen in green with a long bow and a quiverful of peacock-tipped arrows apiece. The knight's visor was closed and nothing of his face was to be seen, but these three others had hard, leathery faces with small mean eyes.

Daun William had a sword, but he was too busy persuading his horse to return its forefeet to the ground even to unsheathe it. Each of his servants had a long knife at his belt, but what were two slightly dull knives against such an assortment of lances, swords, daggers, and arrows, all very sharp and plainly intended for use?

Adam peeped cautiously over Oswald's shoulder and wondered what was going to happen next.

"This is an outrage!" burst out the merchant angrily. "Sir knight, whoever you are, call off your men and let us go on our way."

The knight made no answer. The eyes of everybody almost unwillingly turned to the two packhorses and their very large, very bulging, very heavy saddle-bags crammed with goods to be sold at Giles's Fair in Winchester.

The knight nodded, and the squire without a word yanked off the merchant's sword and threw it clattering to the ground, tied his hands behind him and handed the reins of his horse to one of the yeomen to hold.

"Help!" bellowed the merchant with a burst of noise that amazed Adam. "Help! Ho! Robbers! Ho!"

The servants took it up, and for a moment the woods echoed with their clamor. They made so much noise that Adam more than half expected a troop of horsemen to come galloping to their rescue. Nothing of the kind happened. The robber knight and his men silenced the other three speedily and none too gently by stuffing their mouths with their own hoods. Adam, just before they reached him, steadied himself with his hand on Oswald's shoulder, and stretching out his neck like a rooster, screeched a final, "Help! Robbers! Ho!"

In that instant it occurred to Adam that he was still free. He slid down from the horse, bent low, and ran under his belly. A man lunged at him and grabbed his harp. With a quick twist Adam slid the thong off his shoulder. He stuck out his foot, hooked it around the man's ankle and jerked. When he felt the man topple and heard him fall, Adam turned and plunged headlong into the underbush. Briars tore at his clothes and bushes scraped his cap off. Shielding his face with his arm, he bent over and ran close to the ground as fast as he could put one foot before the other, plowing through the thick leafy growth and dodging around trees.

He heard shouts behind him. An arrow sang over his head. He doubled back, tripped over a root, and saw as he fell a beech tree arching its branches like a green tent above his head. The next second he was up again, thinking with his feet and hands, with his knees and elbows. Before his mind had caught up, he was climbing into that beech tree, swiftly, silently, like a cat, up into the sun-mottled tangle of leaves and branches. Just as he stretched himself out flat on a big limb, he saw a piece of dead wood that had lodged in a cleft. He seized it, and flung it out into the air to fall with a snap and a rustle into the bushes twenty feet away. In that moment, one of the yeomen, following close on Adam's trail, stopped, and without looking up, turned in the direction of the noise he had heard and the ferns that he saw stirring suspiciously.

Adam lay on his branch with his hot cheek against the smooth warm wood and panted softly. An ant, its pathway blocked, ran over his face and he blew it off, but silently. The loudest sound in the world just then, he thought, was the noise of his own beating heart.

The leaves, which were thick enough to hide him, also kept him from seeing what was happening. He heard footsteps as the two yeomen hunted for him, footsteps crashing nearer, then going away again, then returning right to his tree. He thought he was surely lost now, but the man had only come to get his arrow. "The boy must have gone to earth like a fox," Adam heard him call.

Presently Adam heard the sound of horses' hoofs. He raised his head and strained his ears to listen. They were departing at a walk, all of them, the riders and the led horses.

Now there was silence in the wood again, except for a squirrel chattering. Adam sat up astride his limb. His face was red and throbbing, and streaming with perspiration. He wiped it with his sleeve, pushed his hair off his hot wet forehead, and slowly swung himself down from the tree. Now that the danger was over, he discovered what that scramble had cost him, where his clothes were torn and where his flesh, how his shoulder ached and his knee bled.

The road, when he limped out onto it again, bore record of the struggle in a mass of hoof-prints and scattered leaves and twigs. Daun William's sword, badly rusted, lay broken on the ground. The scabbard, which had been a pretty thing, was gone.

On the other side of the road a path went into a forest. Here were more footprints. This must be the way he had taken them, that black robber knight. Adam stood and looked up that path to where it curved and vanished. Determination rose slowly like a tide within him, and set his wide mouth in a straight line.

Robbers. Stopping a good merchant who was going about his business without harming anybody! A knight, who had vowed to be chivalrous and protect the weak! Somebody ought to go after him. The sheriff or the bailiff or somebody. Besides, they had *his* harp.

With a wag of his head Adam set off resolutely down the road to find the sheriff.

The sound of horses' hoofs behind him made him scramble off the road again to hide behind a big clump of ferns in the ditch.

When he saw that it was only a couple of chapmen with their small trunks fastened behind their saddles, he jumped out and called to them:

"Hi! Stop! There's been a robbery and I want to find the sheriff!"

At the word robbery they turned pale, whipped up their horses, and galloped away, leaving Adam standing in the road looking indignantly after them.

After that Adam saw nobody till he left the wood behind. Then the first person whom he came on was a young shepherd, who was eating his dinner under a hedge with his dog sitting up watchfully beside him and his flock grazing in the field before him. Because Adam spoke the northern dialect and the shepherd an extreme southern one, they had trouble at first in understanding each other. The shepherd thought that Adam wanted something to eat and offered him some bread and salt herring.

Adam sat down crosslegged on the ground beside the strong young man with the kindly brown eyes, and had first a drink of clear cold water from the stone jug, then, a little hesitantly, some of the fish and bread. There seemed to be plenty of it, and he was very hungry. Between mouthfuls, gesticulating with his hands and going back to find other expressions for words the shepherd did not understand, he told his story.

"I want to find the sheriff," he finished. "If we go back quickly enough, maybe we can catch the robber knight and rescue poor Daun William so he can take his things to the Fair after all."

"I don't know where the sheriff is," answered the shepherd. "But Sir Adam Gurdon is bailiff. He'll be your man. Sir Adam will know. He's lord of the manor here. This is his demesne land and his flock, and I'm his shepherd. The village over yonder belongs to him. You'll see the manor house beyond the church. Go tell him what you saw, and don't let the steward put you off. It's harvest time, and he'll be in a tizzy over it."

Adam thanked the shepherd for his dinner and got up to go. "Have you seen a minstrel pass this way?" he asked.

"There's many a minstrel passes this way. I don't pay much heed to them. A lass in the village told me there was one by with a dog that could walk on his hind legs like a little man—"

"When was that?" Adam interrupted eagerly.

"I don't remember. Two-three days ago."

"Was it a red spaniel?"

"Bless you, lad, I didn't see him. The lass said she wished she had one like him, but I gave her a kitten instead—pure white it were, with blue eyes and one black paw. Eh, she was pleased. Liked it better than a dog, she said."

The wind blew softly over the field and stirred the bracken around a rock. A bird perched on a sheep's back to look for ticks, and the sheep went on cropping the short grass without noticing it. Adam felt drowsy after his dinner, and this would have been a good place to lie down and sleep for a while, but he had tarried too long already. He set off at a brisk pace in the direction the shepherd showed to him.

He passed the fields that were being harvested and saw what must have been the whole village, men, women, and children, out working in the sun. Some cut the grain with long scythes; some followed behind and bound it into sheaves; some piled the sheaves into great wagons. Franklins with rods in their hands walked among them seeing that they were doing the job thoroughly and that all of the grain went into the wagons. It was the lord's fields they were harvesting now, putting in the days of "boon work" that each villein was required to give to his lord. Across the road Adam saw the fields that belonged to the villeins waiting

to be harvested. They were laid out in strips, with unplowed land between them to separate one man's holdings from another's. The breeze sweeping over the golden grain made paths and swirls in it.

The village itself was deserted, except for a few mothers and babies and lame folk. The houses and the cottages, each in its garden, clustered together along both sides of the road, while the fields and the meadows and the pasture land and woodland spread out all around them as far as the eye could see. Beyond the church, as the shepherd said, was the lord's gateway, and beyond that, sitting on a bit of a hill where it could overlook the village and the land that belonged to it, was the manor house.

It was not easy for a boy with torn clothes and no cap to convince the lord's servants, in the height of the busy harvest season, that he had important business with the lord of the manor. Without his harp Adam could not even claim a minstrel's right of entrance.

Determinedly, he stood his ground with each one he met, with porter and with usher and with steward, and he found that if he repeated the words "robber knight" often enough and clearly enough he did eventually get passed on from one man to the next in order.

It was mid-afternoon and the church bells were ringing for evensong before he finally won through to Sir Adam, who was in his counting room conferring with his reeve about the harvest. The reeve had a notched tally-stick, on which he was figuring this year's yield, and the knight had a parchment roll on which was written last year's score, and between the two they were growing each minute more mixed up and cross.

"Well, what is it, boy?" snapped Sir Adam. He was a powerfully built young man, much less handsome than his own shepherd, but with the habit of authority.

"Please, Sir Knight, are you the bailiff?" said Adam respectfully.

"Yes," answered the knight. "I am. What then?"

"Can you catch robbers and put them in a dungeon?"

"Yes," Sir Adam smiled, as if he had not quite meant to, "I can. Have you got some robbers?"

"Yes," said Adam, copying the knight's style, which he admired, "I have. At least, we can get them if you hurry. They're up the Farnham Road in the forest. They took Daun William of Dover and his packhorses and his servants, but I got away. There were five of them, and the leader is a knight. He has painted over the charge on his shield, but his crest is a leopard."

Sir Adam and his reeve exchanged looks. Both stiffened to attention.

"What did I tell you?" said Sir Adam to the reeve. "That's de Rideware without a doubt. I've suspected him this long time. You're sure of the crest, boy?"

"A leopard rampant," repeated Adam firmly.

Sir Adam began to snap out orders. "Call Walter. Tell him to bring my hauberk and sword. Have Gerald get horses. You go yourself and collect me men with cross-bows. We ride at once."

The manor house, which had been sleepy in the afternoon sunshine, began to ring with the sound of running feet, of quick commands, and clattering metal. Sir Adam's squire of the body brought his coat of chain mail and helm, his shield and sword and spurs. His squire of the stable brought his horse, with trappings on which were blazoned, as on his surcoat and shield, the Gurdon arms. No hiding of his bearings for Sir Adam! From all directions men came running, some with long bows and some with the more powerful cross-bows.

In an amazingly short time a band of men was ready to ride out. At its head was Sir Adam, and beside him—oh, wonder and joy!—was Adam son of Roger, on a brown palfrey to show him the way.

Behind them were several squires, and the reeve, and then the archers. As they rode through the village, the people, home from the fields, crowded to the roadside to watch them pass and several of the young men ran for their bows and followed on foot.

Adam rode along in a state of high glory, wishing with all his heart that Roger could see him now, that Hugh and Godfrey could see him, and Perkin, and Jill and John Ferryman![2] He watched for his friend the shepherd as they went by the pasture, and made up for all the others who were not there by standing up in his stirrups and waving violently to the shepherd.

Into the forest they rode, and everyone whom they met stepped off the road into the ditch to let them pass. It took much less time to get back to the place where the robbers had jumped out of ambush than it had taken Adam to go from there to the village.

"We're almost there," said Adam. "Look, that's the tree where I hid—over there—and now you can see where the road is all cut up with hoof-prints, and there's where they went into the wood."

Without pausing, Sir Adam turned into the path. "Fall back, boy," he ordered, "and ride in the midst of the men. You're too exposed here."

Adam regretfully fell back. Still, he comforted himself, he was lucky to be here at all. He told the squires about Roger and Jankin and Nick, and how he lost his harp.

"We'll get it back for you," said one, "and then you can show us what kind of minstrel you are."

The path led deeper and deeper into the forest. Sometimes they had to bend over to keep from being scraped off their horses by boughs of trees. They rode silently. Even Adam stopped chattering after a while, and felt his heart beating faster. Any minute, he

---

2. Hugh and Godfrey and Jill and John Ferryman are friends Adam has made in his travels.

thought uncomfortably, an arrow might zing through the air before his nose, or nearer.

They came to a park where the trees were sparser and the ground beneath them was cleared of undergrowth. A whole herd of fallow deer moved calmly here, scarcely even troubling to look up when the silent band of men rode past. Then the path forked, and Sir Adam took the left-hand branch. The squires nodded to one another. "He knows," said one. "He's been looking for a chance to catch de Rideware."

Before long they came to Rideware Hall, a stout stone house protected by a wall and a moat. Adam hardly knew what he expected when he saw the moat: a siege possibly, certainly a fight, and perhaps even hot lead pouring down from the top of the wall. What happened was that they found an ordinary plank bridge—not a drawbridge at all—across a stagnant and scummy bit of water shallow enough to wade. Sir Adam rode over and pounded on the door in the wall with his mailed fist.

After some delay it was opened by an agitated-looking porter.

"Sir Robert is not at home," he declared over and over, but the bailiff only pushed him aside, and the others crowded after him.

When Squire Walter leaned forward and said something in a low voice, Sir Adam, turning in his saddle, commanded:

"Surround the house. There may be a postern door."

Adam heard some of the men behind him obediently wheel their horses, but his eyes and ears were all for what was going on in front of him. They were in a muddy courtyard now, where various wooden sheds were built against the thick outside wall. Some chickens fled squawking with spread wings before them, and from a pen in one corner came the excited barking of several dogs. A monkey tied to a post scrambled up it and chattered shrilly from the top. The hall itself was a stone building jutting out from the wall opposite the entrance, with narrow pointed windows, and a rather impressive flight of stone steps leading to a stout wooden door banded with iron hinges ending in a fleur-de-lis design. This door now opened, and a pale, thin lady in a green gown with wide sleeves stood at the top of the steps.

"Sir Robert is away," said she in a thin reedy voice. "If he were here, he would resent this intrusion."

Her words were disdainful, but she looked frightened and sad. Adam felt sorry for her, and so, evidently, did Sir Adam, for he answered her gently enough as he dismounted and strode up the steps, "I have reason to believe that he is here. I must ask you to stand aside and let me enter."

His squires followed him with their hands on their swords, and after them, alternately craning his neck to look over shoulders and ducking his head to look under elbows, went Adam. Lady de Rideware gave way without further argument, and they all marched unchallenged into the hall.

It was dark inside, for the wooden shutters had been closed. The first thing was to get them open. In the light that came bit by bit, Adam saw a long room with rough stone walls. The hearth was in the center, heaped with cold ashes and half-burned logs. Down both sides ran rough board tables and benches, and at the sight of these Adam drew in his breath. They were strewn with heaps of beautiful brocades and velvets and silks, and with little bags and boxes of rare spices. In that gray, chilly, musty hall the brilliant scarlets and blues and golds of the merchant's wares made a rare show of color, and the rich fragrance of the spices rose above the dank smell of the dirty rushes on the floor. On the benches, bound and gagged, sat the merchant of Dover and his two servants, showing in their eyes and joyful squirmings their sudden relief from fright and anger.

Confusion followed. Sir Adam ran up the stairs at one end of the hall to the solar above, looking for the missing knight; others searched in the chamber below, and in the buttery and the cellar. In the excitement of the search, they forgot to free the prisoners, who beat on the floor with their feet and uttered muffled squeals to call attention to themselves. Adam took his own knife out of his wallet and with some difficulty managed to hack away the bonds first of the merchant and then of the two servants.

"He escaped through the postern when he heard you coming," cried Daun William. "Don't waste time looking for him here."

At the same moment a shout from outside drew everyone to the windows.

"They've found his trail," shouted Sir Adam. "Walter, you and Hubert stay here and see the merchant and his goods safely out on the road again. Keep Rauf and Harry with you, in case of trouble. Simon! Gerald! The rest of you! With me!"

Stamping and clanking, they were gone. The clatter of horses' hoofs in the courtyard was followed by shouts and the thudding of hoofs on the grass on the other side of the moat. Walter and Hubert, the squires, and Rauf and Harry, the yeomen, watched from the windows with undisguised disappointment the departure of the rest of the band without them.

"They'll get him this time," said Walter, turning away at last. "Caught red-handed. He'd better run if he wants to keep his head on his shoulders."

Lady de Rideware had vanished. Daun William and his men were folding up the goods and repacking the saddlebags, groaning over the silks mussed and the spices spilt. It would be at best a lengthy process to get all those things back again into the proper bags in the proper order, and Daun William's nerves were in no condition to make short work of it. He fussed over the folding and refolding of each piece; he changed his mind three times about the particular box of spice and length of velvet that he would give to Sir Adam as a thank-offering. The squires tried to hurry him up, but soon, seeing that they only made him more nervous and therefore slower than ever, they gave it up and amused themselves by practicing with Rauf's cross-bow, using the shabby canopy over the knight's seat at the high table as a target.

Adam prowled about looking for his harp which he found at last among the rushes under a table. Except for a piece chipped off one corner, it was unharmed. He tuned it lovingly and plucked the strings.

"It's a lucky thing there's a moon tonight," said Squire Hubert, casting a resentful glance at the merchant who, standing in a long ray of late sunshine, still folded and unfolded and refolded lengths of material, "or we'd never get home. I wonder if they've caught de Rideware yet."

"They'll come back this way when they do, surely," said Walter. "Since we aren't with them we may as well be here as anywhere. What songs do you know, boy?"

Adam perched on one end of the table, and swinging his legs in time to the music, he harped and sang:

> "Trolly, lolly, lolly, lo,
>   Sing trolly, lolly, lo,
>   My love is to the green wood gone,
>   Now after will I go,
>   Sing trolly, lolly, lolly, lo."

It was a catchy tune that Roger had taught him. They took it up, the two young squires and the yeomen. On the second round, Adam changed it:

> "The robber knight's to the green wood gone,
>   Now after we will go."

To their surprise Daun William joined in with,

"Sing trolly, lolly, lolly, lo."

The packing was finished.
"Sing trolly, lolly, lolly, lo," squeaked Oswald, three bars behind everyone else.

The robbers were caught and Adam resumed his search for his father and his dog. Several months—and many adventures—later, the three were joyfully reunited. Adam stood tall and proud as he greeted Roger; he had learned that the road is truly home to the minstrel.

Meet the Author

Elizabeth Janet Gray was awarded the Newbery Medal for *Adam of the Road* in 1943. The book grew out of her interest in medieval romances and minstrels' tales. In her Newbery acceptance speech, Elizabeth Gray said, "In *Adam of the Road* I was, first and foremost, telling a story of the adventures of a boy and his dog and his father on the roads of England when liberty was young, but beyond that I hoped that it might suggest to the children who read it that people in the olden days were as real as we are and had much the same problems, and that each individual's courage and laughter, his wisdom and honesty and kindness, are important to the world about him for happiness and for freedom."

LOOKING BACK

See your Thinker's Handbook for tips.

Prewriting	**Thinking and Writing About the Section**

You have read about many aspects of medieval life in this section. You can write a persuasive paragraph for a classmate stating your opinion about the quality of life in medieval times. First copy the chart and then fill in the missing information.

Life in the Middle Ages	
Positive	1. minstrels 2. 3. 4.
Negative	1. highwaymen 2. 3. 4.

Writing	Now use information from the chart to write your paragraph. State your opinion of life in medieval times in a topic sentence and give facts from the chart as reasons to support your opinion. For more information on persuasive paragraphs, see your Writer's Handbook.
Revising	Read your first draft to a partner. Did you state your opinion clearly in a topic sentence and then give facts and reasons for support? Did you use words such as *for example?* Make changes if necessary and proofread. Write your final copy.
Presenting	Read your paragraph to a classmate. Is he or she convinced by your paragraph? Which facts and reasons are particularly convincing?

Books to Read

Adorable Sunday by Marlene Fanta Shyer. Charles Scribner's Sons, © 1983.

How could an exciting career as a young model in TV commercials ever stop being fun? Sunday discovers the realities—the ups and downs—of that so-called glamorous life.

Canyon Winter by Walt Morey. Dutton, © 1972.

When fifteen-year-old Peter Grayson survives a plane crash, he knows he's stranded in the wilderness. Luckily, he follows a buck deer and finds a log cabin, a hermit, and three animal friends. In his six months with the hermit, Pete learns to love and appreciate all wildlife and the wilderness that supports it.

Castle by David Macaulay. Houghton Mifflin, © 1977.

Follow the step-by-step process of the engineering and construction of a thirteenth-century Welsh castle and adjoining village. Excellent detailed drawings illustrate every aspect of this procedure.

Anno's Medieval World by Mitsumasa Anno. Philomel Books, © 1979.

"The earth is flat," or so thought most people in the Middle Ages. Find out how citizens of medieval times felt as new ideas threatened their way of life.

Student's Handbooks

This handbook answers the kinds of questions that you might ask when you are writing your **Looking Back** assignments in this book as well as when you are doing other writing assignments. It is divided into four parts, one part for each step of the writing process: prewriting, writing, revising, and presenting. The handbook also explains four types of writing: narrative, descriptive, explanatory, and persuasive/analytical.

Prewriting

1. I know the topic I'm going to write about, but how can I organize my ideas and narrow my topic?

There are many ways to organize ideas. One way is to use a chart, such as the one on page 55. Another good way to narrow a topic is to use a web, or cluster diagram. This is a visual way to show how a main topic, subtopics, and details are related to one another. To make a cluster diagram, first write the main topic and circle it. Then write related topics around it. Circle them and draw lines to connect them to the main topic. Last, list details related to the subtopics. Notice in the cluster diagram below that *disaster cake* and *turkey bomb* are narrower than *poor cooks* and narrower still than *Carrie and Warren* and *Characters Whose Traits Lead to Important Incidents*.

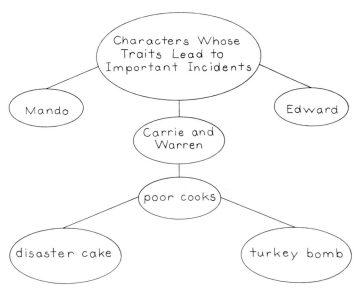

2. When I'm given a writing assignment, what is my first task?

When you are asked to write, your first task is to determine your purpose for writing and your audience. Your audience is the people whom you want to read your work. It may be your teacher, your classmates, a friend, a writing partner, your family, or perhaps even someone you don't know. To determine your purpose, ask yourself, "What *type* of writing am I being asked to do?" Study the following chart to help you better understand your purpose for writing.

Type of Writing	Purpose	Examples
narrative	• to tell about something that happened to you, to someone you know, or to a character in a story you have read • to tell about something and how you felt about it • to tell the events in the order in which they happened	• narrative paragraph • personal narrative • friendly letter • short story • play
descriptive	• to paint a picture in words by using sensory details, figures of speech, and spatial order to help readers see, hear, feel, taste, and smell what you describe • to describe similarities and differences	• descriptive paragraph • comparison-contrast paragraph • character study • poem
explanatory	• to tell how something is made or done • to entertain or to give information in an interesting way	• explanatory paragraph • how-to report • feature story
persuasive/ analytical	• to state an opinion and give supporting reasons in order to convince others to share your opinion • to collect facts, analyze them, and reach a conclusion • to interpret a literary work	• persuasive paragraph • summary paragraph • research report • literary response essay

Writing

1. Sometimes when I sit down, I just can't get started. What should I do then?

There are several ways to get started. Here are some suggestions.

Review Your Notes Look through your Prewriting notes for a single fact or idea that you can use to get your piece going. Suppose you're writing a report about training for certain professions and your notes tell you that it is more difficult to get into veterinary school today than it is to enter medical school. That's a surprising fact. So perhaps your report starts out, "If you want to be a veterinarian, you'd better be prepared to make better grades than classmates who want to be doctors who treat people."

Psych Yourself Up You've seen athletes preparing for a match. They perform calisthenics, deep breathing, and often their own personal exercises. You can do the same thing to prepare to write. Perhaps you can make a ritual out of sharpening your pencils and arranging your paper and research tools. Or maybe you could pick a word at random, like *morose*, or *juxtapose*, and quickly write three sentences using the word. Develop a routine that works for you—that helps you psych yourself up.

Just Start Finally, just begin getting the words down on paper. Imagine that each line you write awakens two million more cells in your brain, which in turn send new ideas to your writing.

2. What is a first draft?

A first draft is just that—the first time your ideas come to life on the paper. You will have time to give them more form and substance later on, but you have to have something to work with. If you don't like everything you write, don't worry. Circle any sentence or paragraph that you *do* like and get on with your writing.

Revising

1. I have just written my first draft. What do I do next?

It is helpful to pause, read over your first draft, and "listen" to yourself. Think about your main point. Is it clear? Will it make sense to your audience? Also think about the overall direction your writing is taking. Does your draft reflect the criteria for the specific type of writing you are doing? The chart below offers some information on what makes a specific type of writing good.

Type of Writing	How to Make it Good
narrative	• keep to one main idea • tell the events in time order • use signal words such as *first, next, then,* and *last* to make the order clear
descriptive	• keep to one main idea • choose words that help your reader see, feel, hear, smell, and taste what you describe • be sure the details support the main idea • use spatial order—describe your topic from a particular position, such as top to bottom—to organize your paragraph
explanatory	• begin with a topic sentence that tells what you intend to explain • follow the topic sentence with details that support the main idea • tell the steps in order • use examples to clarify or illustrate the steps • use signal words such as *first* and *next,* or *for example* to connect your ideas
persuasive/ analytical	• keep your audience in mind in order to choose ideas and language that will appeal to them • state your opinion in your topic sentence • use facts and reasons to support your opinion • use signal words such as *for example, in addition,* and *most important* to connect your reasons • draw conclusions based on facts • put the most persuasive reasons last

2. What should I do when I revise?

First, revise your content. Get together with a partner, a small group, your teacher, or a friend, and have them listen as you read your first draft. Ask for comments on what is good about your writing and how it could be made better. Take notes on what people say and use them to help you make changes.

3. How do I make changes?

There are four kinds of changes to make when you revise— adding, taking out, reordering, and proofreading. They are explained below. Remember that you can use the information you gathered in Prewriting as well as your notes as you work through these changes.

Adding Information Reread your draft and check to see if you left out any important information, such as a major fact in a research report or a crucial descriptive phrase in a character study.

Taking Out Unnecessary Information Check to see that you have kept to your topic. If you are writing about island vacation spots and find you have included two paragraphs about your recent vacation in the mountains, take this information out.

Moving Words, Sentences, and Paragraphs The process of revising gives you a chance to improve the sequence of your information. The steps in building a kite must be explained in time order. Your most important reason to support an opinion must come at the end of a paragraph, not buried in the middle. Use scissors and tape to cut and rearrange parts of pages.

Proofreading Your final task in revising is to check your paper for mistakes in spelling, punctuation, capitalization, and form. Use the proofreading marks at the top of the next page to help you make these changes.

Proofreader's Marks

≡	Make a capital.	∧	Add something.
/	Make a small letter.	ℓ	Take out something.
⊙	Add a period.	⌐→	Move something.
∧	Add a comma.	¶	New paragraph.
⌄	Add quotation marks.	⟨sp⟩	Correct spelling.

4. How can I be sure I've done a thorough job of revising?
You can use this Revision Checklist to check yourself.

Revision Checklist

Content
- Does each paragraph have a clear main idea?
- Do all the sentences in each paragraph keep to the main idea?
- Are the events, steps, or reasons in the correct order? Should some information be rearranged?
- Is each sentence as clear and concise as I can make it?
- Have I chosen words that say exactly what I mean?
- Have I removed information that doesn't keep to the topic?
- Is there any information missing that I should add?
- Have I used language appropriate for my purpose and audience?
- Are all my facts and figures correct?

Mechanics
- Is each sentence capitalized and punctuated correctly?
- Are all the sentences complete? Are there any fragments or run-ons?
- Is each word spelled correctly?
- Do the subjects and verbs agree?
- Have I kept the correct verb tense throughout?
- Is each paragraph indented?
- Is there a special form for this kind of writing? If so, have I followed that special form?
- Is my handwriting as clear as I can make it?

Presenting

1. What are some ways I can present my writing to others?

There are many ways to share your writing. Here are some suggestions.

<u>Read Aloud</u> When your final version of a piece of writing has been finished, read it aloud to your classmates, parents, or a friend. Oral reading gives you a sense of how your writing sounds.

<u>Publish Your Work</u> Some magazines and newspapers publish young people's writing. Your school may also have a newspaper that is looking for student contributions. Offer your work for publication in one of these areas. Ask your teacher to help you do this.

<u>Illustrate and Display Your Work</u> Choose a piece of descriptive writing and draw realistic illustrations to accompany it. Or, decide on your favorite opinion piece and make up a cartoon, such as you might see on the editorial page, to go with it. When you have illustrated two or three pieces of your work, mount them on a bulletin board or a posterboard.

2. How can our class work together to present our writing?
Here are some ways your class can work together.

Start a Class Newspaper Follow these steps:
a. Choose a small group to be in charge of the newspaper.
b. As a class, think of a name for your newspaper. Decide when you will print your first issue and how often you will publish.
c. Discuss the types of news stories, features, cartoons, and other information you want to print and ask for contributions from class members.
d. Work in teams to revise and proofread all pieces.
e. Print and distribute your newspapers inside and outside your school.

Start a Class Library Examine the books in your room. Are any of these books written by someone you know? Probably not. But you can change that situation quickly! Start a class project that will make your writing and your classmates' writing available to everyone. Learn how to make bound books. Then start a class library.

Write Books for Others With the help of your teacher, find other classes in your school or community that would like to exchange their writing with your class. For example, you might write books for second graders and arrange to edit their writing.

Make a Class Mural Arrange your editorials or research reports on large sheets of paper taped together. Include drawings and photographs that illustrate your topics.

Invite a Published Writer to Your Class There are writers in every community. Invite a published writer—book, magazine, or newspaper—to discuss his or her work with your class. Arrange to have your guest listen to works written by members of your class.

This handbook can help you with the assignments in *Time Was . . .* , as well as in your other classes and in your life outside of school. It can help you think about the tasks you are asked to do before, during, and after you do them. The handbook also includes several activities that may help you think in new ways.

Tips to Help You Think

Task 1: Understanding Content

To better understand what you read, *reflect* on such questions as these:

- Does what I'm reading make sense to me? If not, do I need to stop and reread?

- Can I figure out why these characters are acting the way they are?

- Can I identify this character's goal or problem and the attempts to solve it?

- Can I make a prediction about what will happen next?

- How can I paraphrase this difficult passage?

- Can I state the main point or central issue of this selection?

- Would it help me to list causes and effects, or to note the sequence of events in this selection?

- How is this information like or different from what I have read before?

- What main points do I need to include to summarize this article?

- What major characters, goals, and events must I describe to summarize this story?

Task 2: Answering Questions

To *answer* questions, think about *asking* yourself questions:

- Do I understand what this question is saying?

- Is this question asking for one or more than one answer?

- What other questions can I ask myself in order to lead up to this question?

- Would brainstorming help me get started?

- What process, or strategy, should I use in order to arrive at the answer to this question?

Examples of Questions	Strategies for Answering
What is the topic? List three facts.	recall information stated in the selection
What events lead to the solution? What details support the main idea?	gather and pull together several pieces of information
What conclusion can you draw? What can you infer from the facts?	make inferences about the selection from clues and common sense
Why is the character honorable? Why is this a good title? Do you like the selection? Why or why not?	evaluate and analyze the information and add examples or reasons

Task 3: Communicating Ideas

When you work with a partner or a small group, keep these questions in mind:

• Do we have a clear idea about what we are to do?

• How should we organize ourselves—should we each take a job or should we work in committees?

• What procedure do we need to use to complete the task—should we generate questions, role-play, or complete steps in order?

• Do we need to set short-term goals or steps?

• Could we make our information clearer by putting it into a chart or web?

• Do we need to take notes on our ideas?

• Are we focused on the task or are we wandering away from it?

• Are we asking one another to clarify ideas?

• Can we restate in our own words what others are saying so we know we are communicating successfully?

• Have we completed our task? Have we done what we set out to do?

Activities for You to Enjoy

Activity 1: Solving Problems

One way to solve problems is to evaluate the information you have. Think about such questions as the following as you read the problems described on this page. Then tell what could be done.

• Do I have a clear idea of the central issue in this situation?

• Would it help me to list known facts?

• Can I predict other problems that may arise?

• How can I figure out what might be the result for each solution I suggest?

• What solutions can I think of to solve these problems?

You have taken in a friendly Zorcan who has escaped from a civil war on Zorc. His name is Rebak and he wants to go to school with you. He looks different from most humans but this is no problem because people in your school do not attach any value to people's looks. He must, however, be able to do competent work in one or more sports, classes, and outside activities.

Rebak has long strong legs and human-type feet. His arms look something like flippers, but have very tiny fingers. In human terms, he has very poor eyesight, but excellent hearing. His sense of touch is extraordinary and he can taste and smell about as you do.

Rebak learned English in a very few days and has told you he speaks seven intergalactic languages fluently. He is also a good mimic; after watching an evening of TV, he was able to imitate three major TV stars perfectly. He does not have much mechanical aptitude; Zorc is so advanced technologically that everything is done for the inhabitants. The Zorc society has no system of numbers, for they believe everything is "one." They place a high value on storytelling and plays.

Which of the following would you encourage Rebak to get involved in at school? Which would you advise him not to do? Why?

Classes: math, shop, French, science, history, literature
Sports: football, track, basketball, volleyball, swimming
Outside activities: drama club, video club, cooking club, hiking club, photography club

Activity 2: Solving Problems (Scientific Method)

Another way to solve problems is to use the scientific method. Review the following steps in the scientific method. Then read the problem and describe what you will do by following the scientific method.

- Identify and state the problem.

- Gather the known facts.

- Find additional facts that pertain to the problem.

- Write a hypothesis—an idea that tries to explain the problem.

- Conduct observations or experiments to gather data.

- Analyze the data and draw conclusions.

You work in the school cafeteria during lunch hours, clearing trays and tables. You have noticed an interesting phenomenon. On some days the students eating lunch seem to have a high energy level before they eat and after they have finished. On other days they seem much more tired after they have finished. The energy level does not seem to be connected to the time of week; you have seen low energy on Tuesdays and Fridays, and the same is true for high energy. The phenomenon does not seem to be connected to the class from which students have come. On a high energy day, gym-class students are just as peppy as students coming from English class. You have noticed that students often have more energy on a day when fresh fruits and vegetables are offered for lunch. On the other hand, they seem to have less energy on days when heavy, starchy meals have been served. You also wonder about the amount of food that is eaten—could this make any difference? You decide to find out what causes the high energy level.

Activity 3: Analyzing Data

One way to analyze data, whether the information is in print or pictured, is to think it through very carefully. Read the following questions and use them to help you decide what you think each picture shows and what uses it has.

- Does this picture make sense to me?

- Can I figure out what it could be by looking closely at it?

- Do I have enough data to describe it? Am I seeing the total picture?

- Would identifying one picture help me draw conclusions about what the other pictures are?

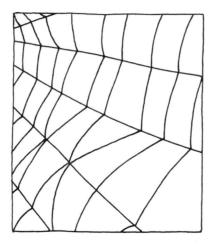

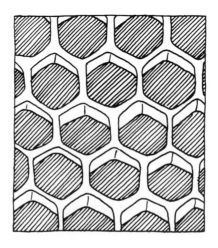

Activity 4: Determining Relevance of Information

One way to determine relevance of information is to figure out if it is relevant—essential to your task—or irrelevant—not essential or helpful. Read the following questions and use them to solve the case.

• Can I identify the task?

• Would it help me to list all of the clues?

• Can I trace where each clue might take me in order to figure out if it is relevant or not?

• Can I list all the clues that are not relevant?

• Can I list the clues that are relevant and tell why?

You are the famous mystery writer Agatha Chrystal. You have been called to the scene of a bank robbery. The people in the bank have given you the following information. Two robbers entered the bank through the front door in the middle of the banking day. They wore stocking caps over their heads. Both were short and wore ordinary clothing. One talked with a foreign accent and the other did not talk at all. They went to a teller at the far corner of the bank, an area which is not covered as often by the closed circuit security system. The robber who spoke demanded $5,000 in a paper sack. When the teller had handed over the money, the robber again spoke: "C'mon Vicky . . . er, Steve, let's go!"

Which of the following clues might lead you, Agatha Chrystal, to solve the case? Why? Which would not be of much use? Why?

the height of the robbers
the foreign accent of one robber
the time of day of the robbery
the entry of the robbers through the front door
the fact that one robber did not speak at all
the stocking cap masks
the request for a paper bag to carry the money
the avoidance by the robbers of the security camera
one robber's calling the other "Vicky, er, Steve"

On the next few pages are some of the strategies you've learned to help you figure out the meaning and pronunciation of words.

Phonics: Short Vowel Sounds
Strategy 1: I can use what I know about **short vowel sounds.**

> Say the words. Listen to the vowel sounds. What kind of letters are before and after the vowel printed in dark type in each word?
>
> | Short *a* | Short *e* | Short *i* | Short *o* | Short *u* |
> |-----------|-----------|-----------|-----------|-----------|
> | clan | press | flinch | shock | pun |
> | adhere | decade | incorrect | toxic | ungrateful |
> | elastic | connection | transistor | despondent | rustic |
> | distract | assent | drastic | pentagon | handcuffs |

Vocabulary and Skill Application

Use your word study strategy to figure out which word belongs in each sentence. Choose the word that has the same short vowel sound as the word in parentheses and makes sense.

1. If I hear music while I am studying, I become _____. (clan)
   a. confused   b. tapestry   c. distracted

2. March straight ahead, then _____ to the left. (flinch)
   a. pivot   b. discourage   c. trudge

3. The windows were closed and covered with _____. (pun)
   a. shutters   b. shades   c. destructive

4. The building was shaped like a _____. (shock)
   a. prominent   b. pentagon   c. square

5. We needed the _____ of the group to change the rules. (press)
   a. consensus   b. decade   c. approval

6. She couldn't hear the speaker above the _____ of the crowd. (clan)
   a. noisiness   b. telegraph   c. clamor

7. Ice cream may be a great _____ to a dieter. (press)
   a. attraction   b. temptation   c. domestic

8. Because many plants are _____, be careful about what your pets eat. (shock)
   a. dangerous   b. toxic   c. recognition

Phonics: Long Vowel Sounds
Strategy 2: I can use what I know about **long vowel sounds.**

Say these words. Listen to the long vowel sounds. Which letter or
letters stand for the vowel sound in each word?

Long *a*	Long *e*	Long *i*	Long *o*	Long *u*
aged	me	aside	abode	prune
citation	beam	confining	global	annually
remainder	feeble	plight	associate	blueprint
causeway	flimsy	pry	foam	menu

Vocabulary and Skill Application

Use your word study strategy to figure out which word belongs
in each sentence. Choose the word that has the same vowel sound
as the word in parentheses and makes sense.

1. The clerk was very helpful and treated me with a great deal of
   _____. (me)
   a. courtesy   b. politeness   c. capacity
2. From the air, astronauts' views of the earth are _____.
   (abode)
   a. hostess   b. global   c. extensive
3. Some people think most TV programs contain too much blood
   and _____. (aside)
   a. violence   b. confining   c. injury
4. The play was a _____ because the star forgot his lines. (aged)
   a. disaster   b. remainder   c. failure
5. We couldn't see the house through the dense _____. (aged)
   a. vegetation   b. citation   c. forest
6. We read the _____, then decided to eat elsewhere. (prune)
   a. listing   b. menu   c. presume
7. The store's _____ said, "No offer is too low." (abode)
   a. momentum   b. slogan   c. advertisement
8. I understood the word after the teacher _____ it. (aside)
   a. explained   b. tidal   c. defined
9. I'll be able to drive in my _____ year of high school. (me)
   a. second   b. feeble   c. senior
10. The robber _____ the police for only two hours before she was
    caught. (prune)
    a. eluded   b. baffled   c. perused

Phonics: R-Controlled Vowel Sounds
Strategy 3: I can use what I know about **r-controlled vowel sounds.**

Say these words. Listen to the vowel sounds. What letter comes after the vowel printed in dark type in each word?

fa**r**ce	he**r**mit	mi**r**th	bo**r**edom	bu**r**den
ma**r**gin	ete**r**nal	vi**r**tues	o**r**nery	scu**rr**y
impa**r**t	conce**r**n	fi**r**mament	refo**r**m	tu**r**pentine

---

Vocabulary and Skill Application

Use your word study strategy to figure out which word belongs in each sentence. Choose the word that has the same vowel sound as the word in parentheses and makes sense.

1. The boat sprang a leak and was soon _____ by water. (hermit)
   a. submerged   b. eternal   c. covered

2. The ability to laugh when things go wrong is one of my teacher's greatest _____. (mirth)
   a. thirteen   b. talents   c. virtues

3. Leave space for comments along the _____ of your paper. (farce)
   a. arsenal   b. margin   c. edge

4. They watched the squirrels _____ up the tree. (burden)
   a. scamper   b. scurry   c. turtle

5. When small children don't get enough sleep they may wake up feeling mean and _____. (boredom)
   a. ornery   b. accord   c. grumpy

6. I am _____ to dogs, but I like cats too. (farce)
   a. attracted   b. partial   c. impart

7. My hamster doesn't like to be held—it keeps _____ until I put it back in its cage. (mirth)
   a. squirming   b. wiggling   c. girth

8. Sometimes it's hard to decide what is best to plant on _____ land. (hermit)
   a. barren   b. concern   c. fertile

9. The new rules were agreed upon by a _____ of those at the meeting. (boredom)
   a. number   b. transform   c. majority

10. The ground is always wet in a _____ area. (farce)
    a. varnished   b. marshy   c. swampy

Phonics: Vowel Sounds

Strategy 4: I can use what I know about **vowel sounds.**

Say these words. Listen to the vowel sounds. What letters stand for the vowel sound in each word?

best**ow**ing	j**oi**nt	**au**dible	r**oo**st	p**ou**t
unbekn**ow**n	unsp**oi**led	m**au**l	bedr**oo**m	dev**our**
crowded	depl**oy**	**aw**kwardly	falseh**oo**ds	**ou**ght
cauliflower	destr**oy**	squ**aw**l	f**oo**tlights	th**ou**ghtful

Vocabulary and Skill Application

Use your word study strategy to figure out which word belongs in each sentence. Choose the word that has the same vowel sound as the word in parentheses and makes sense.

1. No one is certain how many _____ there are in our solar system. (joint)
   a. asteroids   b. deploy   c. planets

2. Although I like most vegetables, one of my all-time favorites is _____. (crowded)
   a. artichokes   b. follow   c. cauliflower

3. People pay a lot of money for _____ Abraham Lincoln signatures. (audible)
   a. maul   b. actual   c. authentic

4. Some theaters have _____ in different colors to shine on the stage. (falsehoods).
   a. woodpecker   b. footlights   c. spotlights

5. The army had to retreat because it was completely _____. (pout)
   a. outnumbered   b. devour   c. exhausted

6. The contents of the packages were _____ to everyone at the party. (bestowing)
   a. important   b. unbeknown   c. below

7. When the tide came in, it _____ the sandcastle we'd taken all day to build. (deploy)
   a. damaged   b. royal   c. destroyed

8. He has a _____ understanding of how many kinds of machines work. (pout)
   a. deep   b. profound   c. vouch

Structure: Syllabication
Strategy 5: I can use what I know about **syllabication**.

A. When a word ends with a consonant followed by **–le**, divide before the consonant: bri·dle.

B. When a word has two consonants betwen two vowels, divide between the two consonants: wis·dom.

C. When a word has one consonant between two vowels, first try dividing before the consonant. The first vowel sound will be long: ma·son. If you don't know the word, then divide the word after the consonant. The first vowel will be short: cam·el.

Vocabulary and Skill Application

Use your word study strategy to choose the word that fits each sentence. Choose the word that is syllabicated in the same way as the word in parentheses and makes sense.

1. The dog stepped on Tim's glasses and got a _____ in his foot. (cam·el)
   a. piece   b. fragment   c. needle

2. The injured dog had to _____ when he walked. (bri·dle)
   a. proceed   b. limp   c. hobble

3. The dog's leg didn't _____ him from being friendly. (wis·dom)
   a. hamper   b. prevent   c. stop

4. He liked to swim as a puppy and learned to swim ten _____. (ma·son)
   a. lengths   b. miles   c. meters

5. He liked to play in the yard but the _____ made him sneeze. (wis·dom)
   a. flowers   b. pollen   c. tulips

Structure: Prefixes and Suffixes
Strategy 6: I can use what I know about **prefixes and suffixes.**

> **A.** Add the prefix **il–**   il + *legal* = **il***legal*
> **B.** Add the prefix **en–**   en + *close* = **en***close*
> **C.** Add the prefix **out–**   out + *number* = **out***number*
> **D.** Add the prefix **re–**   re + *fresh* = **re***fresh*

> **A.** Add the suffixes **–ation, –ize, –or, –ship** without changing the root word:
> *consider* + **ation** = *consider***ation**
> *equal* + **ize** = *equal***ize**
> *govern* + **or** + **ship** = *govern***orship**
> **B.** Drop the **e** and add the suffix **–ation:**
> *repute* + **ation** = *reput***ation**
> **C.** Change the **y** to **i** and add the suffix **–ize:**
> *apology* + **ize** = *apolog***ize**

Vocabulary and Skill Application
For each underlined word, list the root word, prefix, and/or suffix.
1. He liked to <u>criticize</u> my handwriting as being <u>illegible</u>.
2. The people wanted to <u>recolonize</u> the island under the <u>protectorship</u> of the mainland government.
3. Viewers of the marathon were <u>enraptured</u> to see the underdog <u>outdistance</u> all her competitors.
4. The murderer could not resist the <u>temptation</u> to <u>reappear</u> at the scene of the crime.
5. The <u>enactor</u> of the seat belt law could <u>envision</u> a decrease in the number of highway deaths.
6. The <u>accusation</u> of his assistant destroyed the mayor's popularity.

See also Skill Lesson, "Understanding Multiple Affixes," pages 450–451.

Structure: Meaningful Word Parts

Strategy 7: I can use what I know about **meaningful word parts.**

Look at these word parts. What do they mean?
mal (bad, badly; poor, poorly)   micro (very small)
spir (breathe)   trans (over, across, through)

Vocabulary and Skill Application

Complete each sentence by choosing the word that fits. Use the underlined context words for clues.

1. A machine that is <u>working poorly</u> is _____.
   a. broken   b. malfunctioning   c. microcopier
2. The man was just passing <u>through</u> and couldn't stay long. He was a _____ guest at the hotel.
   a. transient   b. strange   c. inspiring
3. The new X-100 computer's _____ is the <u>smallest</u> one ever made.
   a. component   b. screen   c. microchip
4. The salty fluid that literally "<u>breathes</u>" from your skin is called _____.
   a. transmigration   b. sweat   c. perspiration

Etymology

Strategy 8: I can use what I know about **word histories.** See Skill Lesson, "Learning About Etymologies," on pages 312–313.

Word Study: Dictionary
Strategy 9: I can use the dictionary to find pronunciations and meanings of words.

together	toil

a hat	**i** it	**ou** out	**ng** long	**ə** stands for:
ā age	**ī** ice	**u** cup	**sh** she	a in about
ä far	**o** hot	**u̇** put	**th** thin	e in taken
e let	**ō** open	**ü** rule	**ᴛʜ** then	i in pencil
ē equal	**ô** order	**ch** child	**zh** measure	o in lemon
ėr term	**oi** oil			u in circus

toil[1] (toil), *n.* hard work; labor: *succeed after years of toil.* See **work** for synonym study. —*v.i.* **1** work hard. **2** move with difficulty, pain, or weariness: *They toiled up the steep mountain.* [<Old French *toellier* drag about <Latin *tudiculare* stir up <*tudicula* olive press <*tudes* <mallet] —**toil′er,** *n.*
toil[2] (toil), *n.* Often, **toils,** *pl.* net or snare: *The thief was caught in the toils of the law.* [<Middle French *toile* <Latin *tela* web <*texere* to weave]

Vocabulary and Skill Application
Write your answers to the following questions.
1. What shows the first and last words on a page?
2. What shows how the letters sound?
3. What do you call the word you are looking for?
4. In each of the following sentences, which entry tells you what **toil** means:
   a. Her years of <u>toil</u> were finally rewarded.
   b. The bird fought against the <u>toils</u> in which it was caught.
5. What tells you the part of speech?
6. What is the run-on for **toil**[1]?
7. What is the synonym for **toil**[1]?
8. How would you find another synonym for **toil**[1]?
9. What information is shown in brackets?

Context
Strategy 10: I can use what I know about **context.**

See Skill Lesson, "Using Context to Figure Out Unfamiliar Words" on pages 74 and 75; "Using Context to Find Appropriate Word Meaning" on pages 170 and 171.

Glossary

How to Use the Pronunciation Key

After each entry word in this glossary, there is a special spelling, called the **pronunciation**. It shows how to say the word. The word is broken into syllables and then spelled with letters and signs. You can look up these letters and signs in the **pronunciation key** to see what sounds they stand for.

This dark mark (′) is called the **primary accent**. It follows the syllable you say with the most force. This lighter mark (′) is the **secondary accent.** Say the syllable it follows with medium force. Syllables without marks are said with least force.

Full Pronunciation Key

ə stands for:						
a in about	**a**	hat, cap	**i**	it, pin	**p**	paper, cup
e in taken	**ā**	age, face	**ī**	ice, five	**r**	run, try
i in pencil	**ä**	father, far			**s**	say, yes
o in lemon			**j**	jam, enjoy	**sh**	she, rush
u in circus	**b**	bad, rob	**k**	kind, seek	**t**	tell, it
	ch	child, much	**l**	land, coal	**th**	thin, both
	d	did, red	**m**	me, am	**ŦH**	then, smooth
			n	no, in		
	e	let, best	**ng**	long, bring	**u**	cup, butter
	ē	equal, be			**u̇**	full, put
	ėr	her, learn	**o**	hot, rock	**ü**	rule, move
			ō	open, go		
	f	fat, if	**ô**	order, all	**v**	very, save
	g	go, bag	**oi**	oil, toy	**w**	will, woman
	h	he, how	**ou**	house, out	**y**	young, yet
					z	zoo, breeze
					zh	measure, seizure

The contents of the Glossary entries in this book have been adapted from *Scott, Foresman Intermediate Dictionary*, Copyright © 1983 Scott, Foresman and Company and *Scott, Foresman Advanced Dictionary*, Copyright © 1983 Scott, Foresman and Company.

A

a·bode (ə bōd′), *n.*, place of residence; dwelling; house or home.

a·broad (ə brôd′), *adv.* outside one's country; in or to a foreign land or lands: *The diplomat lived abroad much of his life.*

a·bun·dance (ə bun′dəns), *n.* an overflowing quantity or amount; great plenty.

ac·co·lade (ak′ə lād), *n.* recognition of merit; praise in recognition of an accomplishment; award.

ac·quire (ə kwīr′), *v.t.,* **-quired, -quir·ing. 1** get by one's own efforts or actions: *acquire an education.* **2** come into the possession of: *acquire land.*

ad·here (ad hir′), *v.i.,* **-hered, -her·ing. 1** stick fast; remain firmly attached; cling *(to).* **2** hold closely or firmly; cleave *(to): In spite of objections the manager adhered to the plan.*

ad·ja·cent (ə jā′snt), *adj.* lying near or close; adjoining; next: *The house adjacent to ours has been sold.*

ad·lib or **ad lib** (ad lib′), *v.,* **-libbed, -lib·bing,** *adj.,* —*v.t., v.i.* make up words or music as one goes along; improvise; extemporize. —*adj.* made up on the spot; improvised.

af·fect (*v.* ə fekt′; *n.* af′ekt), *v.t.* have an effect on; act on; influence or change: *Nothing you say will affect my decision.*

af·fec·tion (ə fek′shən), *n.* feeling of warm liking and tender attachment; fondness; love: *His constant nagging destroyed her affection for him.*

a·flame (ə flām′), *adv., adj.* **1** in flames; on fire. **2** in a glow; glowing. **3** eager; enthusiastic; excited.

a·ged ‘(ā′jid), *adj.* having lived a long time; old: *an aged woman.*

a·gil·i·ty (ə jil′ə tē), *n.* the ability to move with speed or ease; nimbleness.

al·ler·gy (al′ər jē), *n., pl.* **-gies. 1** an unusual reaction of body tissue to a particular substance, differing in symptoms according to the substance, which may be a food, pollen, hair, or cloth. Hay fever, asthma, headaches, and hives are common signs of allergy. **2** INFORMAL. a strong dislike: *an allergy for work.*

a·mend·ment (ə mend′mənt), *n.* change made or offered in a law, bill, or motion by addition, omission, or alteration of language. The Constitution of the United States has over twenty amendments.

a·mi·a·ble (ā′mē ə bəl), *adj.* having a good-natured and friendly disposition; pleasant and agreeable.

a·miss (ə mis′), *adv.* in a wrong way; wrongly.

a·nach·ro·nism (ə nak′rə niz′əm), *n.* **1** error in fixing a date or dates; erroneous reference of an event, circumstance, or custom to a wrong, especially an earlier date. **2** anything out of keeping with a specified time, especially something proper to a former age but not to the present. [<Greek *anachronismos* < *ana-* back + *chronos* time]

an·a·lyt·ic (an′l it′ik), *adj.* concerned with or based on the breaking up of anything complex into its various simple elements.

a·nat·o·my (ə nat′ə mē), *n., pl.* **-mies.** science of the structure of animals and plants based upon dissection, microscopic observation, etc.

an·nu·al (an′yü əl), *adj.* coming once a year: *A birthday is an annual event.* —**an′nu·al·ly,** *adv.*

an·tag·o·nize (an tag′ə nīz), *v.t.,* **-nized, -niz·ing.** make an enemy of; arouse dislike in: *Your unkind remarks antagonized people who had been your friends.*

an·tiq·ui·ty (an tik′wə tē), *n., pl.* **-ties. 1** great age; oldness. **2** times long ago, especially the period from 5000 B.C. to A.D. 476.

a·pol·o·gy (ə pol′ə jē), *n., pl.* **-gies.** words of regret for an offense or accident; acknowledgment of a fault or failure, expressing regret and asking pardon.

ap·pa·ri·tion (ap′ə rish′ən), *n.* **1** a supernatural sight or thing; ghost or phantom. **2** the appearance of something strange, remarkable, or unexpected.

ap·pren·tice (ə pren′tis), *n., v.,* **-ticed, -tic·ing.** —*n.* **1** person learning a trade or art, especially one bound by a legal agreement to work for an employer for a certain length of time in return for instruction. **2** beginner; learner.

ap·pren·tice·ship (ə pren′tis ship), *n.* **1** condition of being bound by an agreement to learn a trade or art. **2** time during which one works for an employer in return for instruction.

a·ris·to·crat·ic (ə ris′tə krat′ik), *adj.* **1** of or connected with a class of people having a high position in society because of birth or title: *the aristocratic class.* **2** stylish or grand: *an aristocratic air.*

ar·mor (är′mər), *n.* a covering, usually of metal or leather, worn to protect the body in fighting. —*v.t., v.i.* cover or protect with armor. Also, BRITISH **armour.** [< Old French *armeüre* < Latin *armatura* < *armare* to arm.] —**ar′mor·like′,** *adj.*

ar·o·mat·ic (ar′ə mat′ik), *adj.* sweet-smelling; fragrant; spicy.

ar·se·nal (är′sə nəl), *n.* place for storing or manufacturing military weapons and ammunition.

as·cot (as′kət, as′kot), *n.* necktie with broad ends, resembling a scarf, tied so that the ends may be laid flat, one across the other.

affection

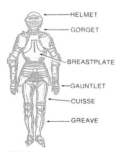

armor
of the 1400s, weighing about 65 pounds (29.5 kg.)

HELMET
GORGET
BREASTPLATE
GAUNTLET
CUISSE
GREAVE

a hat	oi oil	ə stands for
ā age	ou out	a in about
ä far	u cup	e in taken
e let	ù put	i in pencil
ē equal	ü rule	o in lemon
ėr term	ch child	u in circus
i it	ng long	
ī ice	sh she	
o hot	th thin	
ō open	ŦH then	
ô order	zh measure	

a·skew (ə skyü′), *adv., adj.* out of the proper position; turned or twisted the wrong way.

as·sault (ə sôlt′), *n.* **1** a vigorous attack made with blows or weapons. **2** a sudden and violent attack.

as·sign (ə sīn′), *v.t.* **1** give as a share, task, duty, etc.; allot: *The teacher has assigned the next ten problems for today.* **2** designate or appoint (to a post or duty): *We were assigned to collect tickets at the door.* [< Latin *assignare* < *ad-* to, for + *signare* to mark < *signum* mark]

as·ter·oid (as′tə roid′), *n.* any of numerous minor planets which revolve about the sun, chiefly between the orbits of Mars and Jupiter.

ath·lete (ath′lēt′), *n.* person trained to do physical exercises of agility and strength, especially one who participates or competes in games requiring physical skill and stamina. [< Greek *athlētēs* < *athlein* compete for a prize < *athlon* prize]

ath·let·ic (ath let′ik), *adj.* of, like, or suited to an athlete. —**ath·let′i·cal·ly,** *adv.*

auc·tion·eer (ök′shə nir′), *n.* person whose business is conducting a public sale in which each thing is sold to the person who offers the most money for it.

au·da·cious (ô dā′shəs), *adj.* having the courage to take risks; recklessly daring; bold: *an audacious pilot.* —**au·da′cious·ly,** *adv.*

au·di·ble (ô′də bəl), *adj.* that can be heard; loud enough to be heard.

aus·tere (ô stir′), *adj.* **1** stern in manner or appearance; harsh: *a silent, austere man.* **2** severe in self-discipline; strict in morals: *The Puritans were austere.* **3** severely simple: *The tall, plain columns stood against the sky in austere beauty.* **4** grave; somber; serious. —**aus·tere′ly,** *adv.*

au·then·tic (ô then′tik), *adj.* **1** worthy of acceptance, trust, or belief; reliable: *an authentic account of the incident.* **2** genuine; not copied; real: *A comparison of signatures showed that the letter was authentic.* —**au·then′ti·cal·ly,** *adv.*

au·thor·i·za·tion (ô′thər ə zā′shən), *n.* legal right; official permission; sanction.

av·a·lanche (av′ə lanch), *n.* **1** a large mass of snow and ice, or of dirt and rocks, loosened from a mountainside and descending swiftly into the valley below. **2** anything like an avalanche: *an avalanche of questions.* [< French]

aw·ful (ô′fəl), *adj.* **1** causing fear; terrible: *an awful storm.* **2** filling with awe; impressive: *The mountains rose to awful heights.* **3** INFORMAL. very bad, great, ugly, etc.: *an awful mess.* —*adv.* INFORMAL. very: *I was awful mad.*

awk·ward (ôk′wərd), *adj.* not graceful or skillful in movement; clumsy; ungainly: *The seal is very awkward on land, but graceful in the water.* —**awk′ward·ly,** *adv.* —**awk′ward·ness,** *n.*

B

bach·e·lor (bach′ə lər), *n.* man who has not married; an unmarried man.

bac·ter·i·o·log·i·cal (bak tir′ē ə loj′ə-kəl), *adj.* of or having to do with bacteriology.

Bad·lands (bad′landz′), *n.pl.* **1** rugged, barren region in SW South Dakota and NW Nebraska in which erosion has produced unusual land formations. **2 badlands,** any similar region.

baf·fling (baf′ling), *adj.* puzzling; confusing; perplexing: *This puzzle is baffling.*

bail·iff (bā′lif), *n.* **1** assistant to a sheriff, who makes arrests, etc. **2** the chief magistrate in certain towns in England.

bar·ri·o (bär′ē ō), *n., pl.* **-ri·os. 1** (in Spanish-speaking countries) a district of a city or town. **2** section of a city inhabited chiefly by Spanish-speaking people. [< Spanish < Arabic *barrī* outside]

bass[1] (bās), *n.* **1** the lowest male voice in music. **2** singer with such a voice.

bass[2] (bas), *n., pl.* **bass·es** or **bass.** any of various North American freshwater or saltwater fishes with spiny fins, used for food.

ba·zaar or **ba·zar** (bə zär′), *n.* **1** a marketplace consisting of a street or streets full of small shops and booths. **2** place for the sale of many kinds of goods. [< Persian *bāzār*]

beam (bēm), *n.* **1** a large, long piece of timber, ready for use in building. **2** any of the main horizontal supports of a building or ship. **3** side of a ship, or the sideward direction at right angles to the keel, with reference to wind, sea, etc. The weather beam is the side toward the wind. **4** the widest part of a ship. **5 on the beam,** INFORMAL. just right.

be·drag·gled (bi drag′əld), *adj.* **1** wet and hanging limp. **2** soiled or stained as if dragged in the dirt.

be·lief (bi lēf′), *n.* **1** thing believed; what is held to be true or real. **2** religious faith; creed: *What is your belief?*

be·siege (bi sēj′), *v.t.,* **-sieged, -sieg·ing. 1** surround by armed forces in order to compel surrender; lay siege to: *For ten years the Greeks besieged the city of Troy.* **2** crowd around.

avalanche
(def.1)

be·stow (bi stō′), *v.t.* **1** give (something) as a gift. **2** confer an honor on: *The king bestowed knighthood on the victor.*

bet·ter·ment (bet′ər mənt), *n.* a making better; improvement: *to work for the betterment of living conditions.*

bi·og·ra·phy (bī og′rə fē, bē og′rə fē), *n., pl.* **-phies,** an account of a person's life.

blanch (blanch), *v.t.* make white or pale: *Old age blanched his hair.* —*v.i.* turn white or pale: *blanch with fear.*

blue·print (blü′print′), *n.* **1** a photographic print of white lines on a blue background or blue lines on a white background, used chiefly in copying building plans, mechanical drawings, maps, etc. **2** a detailed plan for any enterprise.

bo·na fide (bō′nə fīd′; bō′nə fī′dē), *adj.* **1** in good faith; without deceit or fraud. **2** done in good faith; genuine. [< Latin]

bo·nan·za (bə nan′zə), *n.* **1** a rich mass of ore in a mine. **2** any rich source of profit. [< Spanish, literally, fair weather, prosperity]

bore·dom (bôr′dəm, bōr′dəm), *n.* weariness caused by dull, tiresome people or things.

bow (bou), *n.* the forward part of a ship, boat, or aircraft.

bran·dish (bran′dish), *v.t.* wave or shake threateningly; flourish.

bra·zen (brā′zn), *adj.* having no shame; shameless; impudent. —**bra′zen·ly,** *adv.*

breadth (bredth, bretth), *n.* **1** distance from side to side of a surface; width. **2** freedom from narrowness in outlook; largeness (of mind, view, etc.): *A tolerant person usually has breadth of mind.*

broth (brôth, broth), *n., pl.* **broths** (brôŦHz, broths). a thin soup made from water in which meat, fish, or vegetables have been boiled.

bur·den (bėrd′n), *n.* **1** something carried; load (of things, care, work, duty, or sorrow). **2** a load too heavy to carry easily; heavy load: *Your debts are a burden that will bankrupt you.* —*v.t.* **1** put a burden on; load. **2** load too heavily; weigh down; oppress: *She was burdened with worries.*

burn (bėrn), *v.* **burned** or **burnt, burn·ing,** *n.* —*v.* **1** be on fire; be very hot; blaze; glow: *The campfire burned all night.* **2** become injured, scorched, etc., by fire, heat, or acid. See synonym study below. **3** be very excited or eager: *burning with enthusiasm.* **4** use to produce heat: *Our furnace burns oil.* **5** to sunburn: *The sun burned her face.*

burn up, a consume: *A large car burns up the gasoline.* **b** INFORMAL. make angry. —*n.* **1** injury caused by fire, heat, or acid; burned place. **2** a sunburn. [combination of Old English *beornan* be on fire and Old English *bærnan* consume with fire] —**burn′a·ble,** *adj.*

Syn. *v.* **2 Burn, scorch, sear** mean to injure or be injured by fire, heat, or acid. **Burn,** the general word, suggests any degree from slight injury to destruction. **Scorch** means to burn the surface enough to discolor it. **Sear** means to burn or scorch the surface enough to dry or harden it.

C

cant (kant), *n.* a sloping, slanting, or tilting position. —*v.i.* **1** tilt, pitch on one side, or turn over. **2** have a slanting position or direction.

ca·pac·i·ty (kə pas′ə tē), *n., pl.* **-ties.** amount of room or space inside; largest amount that can be held by a container, in a space, etc.

car·di·o·vas·cu·lar (kär′dē ō vas′kyə-lər), *adj.* of, having to do with, or affecting both the heart and the blood vessels.

cas·u·al (kazh′ü əl), *adj.* **1** without plan or method; careless: *a casual answer, a casual glance.* **2** informal in manner; offhand: *casual manners, casual living.* —**cas′u·al·ly,** *adv.*

cause·way (kôz′wā′), *n.* a raised road or path, usually built across wet ground or shallow water.

ce·leb·ri·ty (sə leb′rə tē), *n., pl.* **-ties.** a famous person; person who is well known or much talked about.

cha·grin (shə grin′), *n.* a feeling of disappointment, failure, or humiliation. —*v.t.* cause to feel chagrin.

chas·ten (chā′sn), *v.t.* **1** punish in order to correct or strengthen. **2** cause to be more humble and modest.

chest·nut (ches′nut, ches′nət), *n.* **1** any of a genus of trees belonging to the same family as the beech, that bears sweet, edible nuts in prickly burs. **2** nut of any of these trees. **3** a reddish brown. INFORMAL. a stale joke or story.

chiv·al·ry (shiv′əl rē), *n.* **1** qualities of an ideal knight in the Middle Ages; bravery, honor, courtesy, protection of the weak, respect for women, generosity, and fairness to enemies. **2** rules and customs of knights in the Middle Ages.

chord[1] (kôrd), *n.* combination of two or more musical notes sounded together, usually in harmony.

a hat	oi oil	ə stands for
ā age	ou out	a in about
ä far	u cup	e in taken
e let	u̇ put	i in pencil
ē equal	ü rule	o in lemon
ėr term	ch child	u in circus
i it	ng long	
ī ice	sh she	
o hot	th thin	
ō open	ŦH then	
ô order	zh measure	

chord[2] (def. 1)
AB and AC are **chords.**

coil
a coil of rope

concave lenses
A, concave surface
B, double concave
C, concave and convex

chord[2] (kord), *n.* **1** a line segment connecting two points on a curve. **2** cord (def. 3). **3** string of a harp or other musical instrument. **4** emotion or feeling: *touch a sympathetic chord.* **5** a main, horizontal part of a bridge support.

cin·na·mon (sin′ə mən), *n.* spice made from the dried, reddish-brown inner bark of a laurel tree of the East Indies.

clam·or (klam′ər), *n.* a loud noise or continual uproar; shouting. —*v.i.* make a loud noise or continual uproar; shout.

clan (klan), *n.* **1** group of related families that claim to be descended from a common ancestor. **2** group of people closely joined together by some common interest.

close[1] (klōz), *v.,* **closed, clos·ing,** *n.* —*v.* **1** bring together; shut: *Close the door.* **2** stop up; fill; block: *close a gap.* **3** bring to an end; finish: *close a debate.* —*n.* an end; finish.
close down, shut completely; stop.
close in, come near and shut in on all sides.
close out, sell in order to get rid of.
close up, shut completely.

close[2] (klōs), *adj.,* **clos·er, clos·est,** *adv., n.* —*adj.* **1** with little space between; near together: *close teeth.* **2** fitting tightly; narrow: *They live in very close quarters.* —*adv.* near; closely. —*n.* an enclosed place.

coil (koil), *v.t.* wind around and around in circular or spiral shape: *The snake coiled itself up.* —*n.* anything wound around and around in circular or spiral shape: *a coil of rope.*

com·mem·o·rate (kə mem′ə rāt′), *v.,* **-rat·ed, -rat·ing.** preserve or honor the memory of: *a stamp commemorating the landing of the Pilgrims.*

com·mit (kə mit′), *v.t.,* **-mit·ted, -mit·ting.** do or perform (usually something wrong): *commit a crime.*

com·pact (*adj.* kəm pakt′, kom′pakt) **1** firmly packed together; closely joined: *Cabbage leaves are folded into a compact head.* **2** having the parts neatly or tightly arranged within a small space: *a compact portable TV set.* **3** using few words; brief and well organized.

com·part·ment (kəm pärt′mənt), *n.* a separate division or section; part of an enclosed space set off by partitions.

com·pas·sion (kəm pash′ən), *n.* feeling for another's sorrow or hardship that leads to help; sympathy; pity. [< Latin *compassionem < compati* suffer with < *com-* with + *pati* suffer]

com·pen·sate (kom′pən sāt), *v.i.,* **-sat·ed, -sat·ing.** balance by equal weight, power, etc.; make up *(for)*: *Skill sometimes compensates for lack of strength.*

com·pete (kəm pēt′), *v.i.,* **-pet·ed, -pet·ing. 1** try hard to obtain something wanted by others; be rivals; contend. See **contend** for synonym study. **2** take part (in a contest): *Will you compete in the final race?*

com·pet·i·tive (kəm pet′ə tiv), *adj.* relating to, characterized by, or based on an effort to obtain something wanted by others: *a competitive examination for a job.* —**com·pet′i·tive·ly,** *adv.* —**com·pet′i·tive·ness,** *n.*

con·cave (kon kāv′, kon′kāv, kong′kāv), *adj.* hollow and curved like the inside of a circle or sphere; curving in.

con·dole (kən dōl′), *v.i.,* **-doled, -dol·ing.** express sympathy; grieve; sympathize: *Their friends condoled with them at the funeral.* [< Latin *condolere < com-* with + *dolere* grieve, suffer]

con·du·it (kon′dü it, kon′dit), *n.* **1** channel or pipe for carrying liquids. **2** a flexible length of tubing or duct generally used to carry liquids or cover wire.

con·fec·tion (kən fek′shən), *n.* a sweet edible such as candy, cake, pastry, candied fruit, ice cream, etc.

con·fine (kən fīn′), *v.t.,* **-fined, -fin·ing.** keep within limits; restrict: *She confined her reading to biography.*

con·sen·sus (kən sen′səs), *n.* general agreement; opinion of all or most of the people consulted.

con·spire (kən spīr′), *v.,* **-spired, -spir·ing.** —*v.i.* **1** plan secretly with others to do something unlawful or wrong; plot. **2** act together: *All things conspired to make her birthday a happy one.* —*v.t.* plot (something evil or unlawful). [< Latin *conspirare,* originally, breathe together < *com-* with + *spirare* breathe] —**con·spir′er,** *n.* —**con·spir′ing·ly,** *adv.*

con·tempt (kən tempt′), *n.* the feeling that a person, act, or thing is mean, low, or worthless; scorn; despising; disdain: *We feel contempt for a cheat.*

con·tend (kən tend′), *v.i.* **1** work hard against difficulties; fight; struggle: *The first settlers in America had to contend with sickness and lack of food.* **2** take part in a contest; compete: *Five runners were contending in the first race.* See synonym study below. **con·tend′er,** *n.*
Syn. *v.i.* **2 Contend, compete** mean to take part in a contest for something. **Contend** suggests struggling against opposition: *Our team is contending for the championship.* **Compete** emphasizes the rivalry involved and the prize to be won: *Only two of us are competing for the cup.*

con·tin·u·ous (kən tin′yü əs), *adj.* without a stop or break; connected; unbroken; uninterrupted: *a continuous line, a continuous sound, continuous work.* —**con·tin′u·ous·ly,** *adv.*

con·trap·tion (kən trap′shən), *n.* INFORMAL. device or gadget.

con·tri·tion (kən trish′ən), *n.* **1** sorrow for one's sins or guilt; being contrite; penitence. **2** deep regret.

con·ven·ience (kən vē′nyəns), *n.* **1** comfort; advantage: *Electricity is a modern convenience.* **2** thing that saves trouble or work.

con·viv·i·al (kən viv′ē əl), *adj.* **1** fond of eating and drinking with friends; jovial; sociable. **2** of or suitable for a feast or banquet; festive.

co·or·di·na·tion (kō ôrd′n ā′shən), *n.* **1** harmonious adjustment or working together: *Poor coordination in the hands makes drawing difficult.* **2** an acting together in a smooth way: *A good batter has good coordination.*

co·quette (kō ket′), *n.* woman who tries to attract men; a flirt.

cord (kôrd), *n.* **1** a thick string; very thin rope. **2** anything resembling a cord, such as an electrical extension cord. **3** nerve, tendon, or other structure in an animal body that is somewhat like a cord, such as the spinal cord; chord.

cor·rob·o·rate (kə rob′ə rāt′), *v.t.,* **-rat·ed, -rat·ing.** make more certain; confirm; support: *Eyewitnesses corroborated my testimony in court.*

coun·te·nance (koun′tə nəns), *n.* **1** expression of the face: *an angry countenance.* **2** face; features: *a noble countenance.*

coun·ter·clock·wise (koun′tər-klok′wīz′), *adv., adj.* in the direction opposite to that in which the hands of a clock go; from right to left.

coun·ter·feit (koun′tər fit), *v.t.* copy (money, handwriting, pictures, etc.) in order to deceive or defraud; forge: *He was arrested for counterfeiting twenty-dollar bills.*

cour·te·sy (kėr′tə sē), *n., pl.* **-sies.** polite behavior; thoughtfulness for others; civility.

cre·du·li·ty (krə dü′lə tē, krə dyü′lə tē), *n.* a too great readiness to believe; a tendency to be easily deceived.

crev·ice (krev′is), *n.* a narrow opening resulting from a split or crack.

cri·sis (krī′sis), *n., pl.* **-ses** (-sēz′). **1** a deciding event: *a crisis in a person's career.* **2** state of danger or anxious waiting: *a health crisis, a monetary crisis.*

crit·ic (krit′ik), *n.* **1** person who makes judgments of the merits and faults of books, music, pictures, plays, acting, etc. **2** person who disapproves or finds fault; faultfinder.

cu·li·nar·y (kyü′lə ner′ē, kul′ə ner′ē), *adj.* of or having to do with cooking or the kitchen.

cur·i·ous (kyůr′ē əs), *adj.* **1** eager to know: *a curious student.* **2** too eager to know; prying: *curious about other people's business.* **3** strange or unusual: *a curious old book.* [< Latin *curiosus* inquisitive, full of care] —**cur′i·ous·ly,** *adv.* —**cur′i·ous·ness,** *n.*

D

debt·or (det′ər), *n.* person who owes something to another: *Years ago debtors were often sent to prison.*

de·but or **dé·but** (dā′byü), *n.* a first public appearance: *a young actor's debut on the stage.*

dec·ade (dek′ād), *n.* **1** period of ten years. **2** group, set, or series of ten. [< Middle French *décade,* ultimately < Greek *deka* ten]

de·cel·e·rate (dē sel′ə rāt′), *v.t., v.i.,* **-rat·ed, -rat·ing.** decrease the velocity (of); slow down. —**de·cel′e·ra′tion,** *n.*

de·cline (di klīn′), *n.* **1** a losing of power, strength, value, etc.: *the decline of the Roman Empire.* **2** a falling to a lower level; sinking; lessening: *a decline in prices.*

de·crep·it (di krep′it), *adj.* broken down or weakened by old age; old and feeble.

de·duc·tion (di duk′shən), *n.* **1** reaching of conclusions by reasoning; inference. A person using deduction reasons from general laws to particular cases. EXAMPLE: All animals die; this cat is an animal; therefore, this cat will die. **2** thing deduced; conclusion.

de·fense (di fens′), *n.* **1** something that guards against attack or harm. **2** a guarding against attack or harm; defending or protecting.

de·fi·ant (di fī′ənt), *adj.* openly resisting; standing up against authority. —**de·fi′ant·ly,** *adv.*

de·fine (di fīn′), *v.t.,* **-fined, -fin·ing.** **1** make clear the meaning of; explain: *A dictionary defines words.* **2** make clear; make distinct: *The shadow defined the shape of the building.*

de·lir·i·ous (di lir′ē əs), *adj.* **1** temporarily out of one's senses due to fever, insanity, etc. **2** wandering in mind; raving. —**de·lir′i·ous·ly,** *adv.*

de·mesne (di mān′, di mēn′), *n.* house and land belonging to a feudal lord and used by him.

a hat	oi oil	ə stands for
ā age	ou out	a in about
ä far	u cup	e in taken
e let	ů put	i in pencil
ē equal	ü rule	o in lemon
ėr term	ch child	u in circus
i it	ng long	
ī ice	sh she	
o hot	th thin	
ō open	ŦH then	
ô order	zh measure	

countenance
The general was a man of stern **countenance.**

destructive
A house is being battered by a **destructive** hurricane.

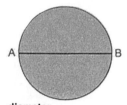

diameter
Line AB is a **diameter**.

dimples

de·mure (di myůr′), *adj.*, **-mur·er, -mur·est. 1** artificially proper; assuming an air of modesty; coy: *a demure smile.* **2** reserved or composed in demeanor; serious and sober. **—de·mure′ly,** *adv.*

de·note (di nōt′), *v.t.*, **-not·ed, -not·ing.** be the sign of; indicate: *A fever usually denotes sickness. The symbol* × *denotes multiplication.*

de·ploy (di ploi′), *v.t.* spread out, extend, or place, especially in a planned position: *deploy offensive missiles.*

de·spite (di spīt′), *prep.* in spite of; regardless of: *We went for a walk despite the rain.*

de·spond·ent (di spon′dənt), *adj.* having lost heart, courage, or hope; discouraged; depressed. **—de·spond′ent·ly,** *adv.*

de·struc·tive (di struk′tiv), *adj.* destroying; ruinous; causing destruction: *Earthquakes are destructive. Termites are destructive insects.* **—de·struc′tive·ly,** *adv.*

di·am·e·ter (dī am′ə tər), *n.* **1** a line segment passing from one side through the center of a circle, sphere, etc., to the other side. **2** the length of such a line segment; measurement from one side to the other through the center; width; thickness: *The diameter of the earth is about 8000 miles.*

di·gest (də jest′, dī jest′), *v.t.* change or break down (food) in the mouth, stomach, and intestines into materials which the body can assimilate, store, or oxidize and use as nourishment.

di·lem·ma (də lem′ə), *n.* situation requiring a choice between two possibilities, which are or appear equally unfavorable; difficult choice.

dim·ple (dim′pəl), *n., v.,* **-pled, -pling.** *—n.* **1** a small hollow or indented place formed in the surface of some part of a person's body, especially in the act of smiling. **2** any small, hollow place. *—v.t.* make or show dimples in. *—v.i.* form dimples.

dis·con·so·late (dis kon′sə lit), *adj.* **1** without hope; forlorn; unhappy: *disconsolate over the death of a friend.* **2** cheerless; gloomy; dejected: *disconsolate over the loss of the game.* **—dis·con′so·late·ly,** *adv.*

dis·cord (dis′kôrd), *n.* **1** disagreement of opinions and aims. **2** combination of two or more tones not in harmony with each other. **3** a clashing of sounds.

dis·dain (dis dān′), *v.t.* regard or treat with contempt; scorn. *—n.* a feeling of scorn or contempt.

dis·lodge (dis loj′), *v.t.,* **-lodged, -lodg·ing.** drive or force out of a place, position, etc.: *She used a crowbar to dislodge a heavy stone.*

dis·pel (dis pel′), *v.t.,* **-pelled, -pel·ling.** drive away and scatter; disperse: *dispel one's fears.*

dis·pute (dis pyüt′), *v.t.,* **-put·ed, -put·ing. 1** argue about; debate; discuss: *The lawyers disputed the case before the judge.* **2** call in question; argue against.

dis·tract (dis trakt′), *v.t.* turn aside or draw away (the mind, attention, etc.): *Noise distracts my attention from study.*

do·mes·tic (də mes′tik), *adj.* **1** of the home, household, or family affairs: *domestic problems, a domestic scene.* **2** attached to home; devoted to family life. [< Latin *domesticus* < *domus* house] **—do·mes′ti·cal·ly,** *adv.*

do·mi·cil·i·ate (dom ə sil′ē āt), *v.i.,* **-at·ed, -at·ing.** reside; dwell; settle in a place of residence.

dor·mi·to·ry (dôr′mə tôr′ē, dôr′mə tōr′ē), *n., pl.* **-ries.** a building with many sleeping rooms. Colleges often provide dormitories where students live and study

dra·mat·ic (drə mat′ik), *adj.* **1** seeming like a play; full of action or feeling; exciting. **2** striking; impressive: *a dramatic combination of colors.* **—dra·mat′i·cal·ly,** *adv.*

dras·tic (dras′tik), *adj.* **1** acting with force or violence; vigorous. **2** vigorously effective; severe. **—dras′ti·cal·ly,** *adv.*

draught (draft), *n., v.t., adj.* draft.

du·al (dü′əl, dyü′əl), *adj.* consisting of two parts; double; twofold: *The car for student drivers had dual controls.* **—du′al·ly,** *adv.*

E

ear·nest (ėr′nist), *adj.* strong and firm in purpose; eager and serious. **—ear′nest·ly,** *adv.*

ef·fect (ə fekt′), *n.* whatever is produced by a cause; something made to happen by a person or thing.

ef·fi·cien·cy (ə fish′ən sē), *n., pl.* **-cies. 1** ability to produce the effect wanted without waste of time, energy, etc. **2** a productive and effective operation: *Friction reduces the efficiency of a machine.*

e·las·tic (i las′tik), *adj.* having the quality of returning to its original size, shape, or position after being stretched, squeezed, bent, etc.: *Rubber bands, sponges, and steel springs are elastic.* *—n.* **1** tape, cloth, cord, etc., woven partly of rubber. **2** a rubber band.

e·lec·tro·cute (i lek′trə kyüt), *v.t.,* **-cut·ed, -cut·ing.** kill or be killed by the passage of a high voltage of electricity through the body.

el·e·va·tion (el′ə vā′shən), *n.* **1** a raised place; high place: *A hill is an elevation.* **2** height above sea level: *The elevation of Denver is 5300 feet.*

el·i·gi·ble (el′ə jə bəl), *adj.* fit to be chosen; properly qualified; desirable: *Pupils had to pass all subjects to be eligible for the team. He was an eligible candidate for office.*

em·ber (em′bər), *n.* piece of wood or coal still glowing in the ashes of a fire.

em·pha·sis (em′fə sis), *n., pl.* **-ses** (-sēz′). special force put on particular syllables, words, or phrases: *A speaker puts emphasis on important words by stressing them.*

en·co·mi·um (en kō′mē əm), *n., pl.* **-mi·ums, -mi·a** (-mē ə). a formal expression of high praise.

en·coun·ter (en koun′tər), *v.t.* **1** meet unexpectedly: *I encountered an old friend on the train.* **2** meet with (difficulties, opposition, etc.). —*n.* **1** an unexpected meeting. **2** a meeting face to face.

en·cy·clo·pe·di·a (en sī′klə pē′dē ə), *n.* **1** book or set of books giving information on all branches of knowledge, usually with its articles arranged alphabetically. **2** book treating one subject very thoroughly, usually with its articles arranged alphabetically. Also **cyclopedia** or **encyclopaedia.** [<New Latin *encyclopaedia* < Greek *enkyklopaideia,* for *enkyklios paideia* well-rounded education]

en·light·en (en līt′n), *v.t.* give truth and knowledge to; free from prejudice, ignorance, etc.; inform; instruct.

en·rap·ture (en rap′chər), *v.t.,* **-tured, -tur·ing.** fill with great delight.

en·vi·sion (en vizh′ən), *v.t.* picture in one's mind: *envision oneself as famous.*

es·pi·o·nage (es′pē ə nij, es′pē ə-näzh), *n.* the systematic use of spies or other secret agents by one country to gain military secrets, strategic information, etc., of other countries.

e·ter·nal (i tėr′nl), *adj.* **1** without beginning or ending; lasting throughout all time; timeless. **2** always and forever the same. **3** seeming to go on forever.

e·ven·tu·al·i·ty (i ven′chü al′ə tē), *n., pl.* **-ties.** a possible occurrence or condition; possibility: *We hope for rain, but we are ready for the eventuality of a drought.*

ex·cru·ci·at·ing (ek skrü′shē ā′ting), *adj.* causing great suffering; very painful; torturing. —**ex·cru′ci·at′ing·ly,** *adv.*

ex·pec·ta·tion (ek′spek tā′shən), *n.* **1** a looking forward to; anticipation. **2** good reason for expecting something: *They have expectations of inheriting money from a rich uncle.*

ex·pel (ek spel′), *v.t.,* **-pelled, -pel·ling. 1** drive out with much force; force out; eject: *When we exhale we expel air from our lungs.* **2** put (a person) out; dismiss permanently: *A student who cheats may be expelled from school.*

ex·plor·a·to·ry (ek splôr′ə tôr′ē, ek-splōr′ə tōr′ē), *adj.* **1** of or having to do with exploration. **2** having to do with a search through, over, or into, for purposes of discovery.

F

fal·low (fal′ō), *adj.* pale yellowish-brown.

false·hood (fôls′hùd), *n.* **1** a false statement; lie. **2** something untrue.

fan·tas·tic (fan tas′tik), *adj.* **1** very odd; wild and strange: *The firelight cast weird, fantastic shadows on the walls.* **2** very fanciful; incredible; strange beyond belief. —**fan·tas′ti·cal·ly,** *adv.*

fan·ta·sy (fan′tə sē, fan′tə zē), *n., pl.* **-sies. 1** play of the mind; product of the imagination; fancy. **2** picture existing only in the mind. **3** a wild, strange fancy. Also, **phantasy.**

farce (färs), *n.* **1** a play full of ridiculous happenings, absurd actions, and unreal situations, meant to be very funny. **2** a ridiculous mockery; absurd pretense; sham: *The trial was a mere farce.*

fear·less (fir′lis), *adj.* without fear; afraid of nothing; brave; daring. —**fear′less·ly,** *adv.* —**fear′less·ness,** *n.*

fer·tile (fėr′tl), *adj.* **1** able to bear seeds, fruit, young, etc. **2** able to produce much; producing crops easily: *Fertile soil yields good crops.*

feu·dal (fyü′dl), *adj.* of or having to do with feudalism. —**feu′dal·ly,** *adv.*

feu·dal·ism (fyü′dl iz′əm), *n.* the social, economic, and political system of western Europe in the Middle Ages. Under this system vassals gave military and other services to their lord in return for protection and the use of the land.

fit·ful (fit′fəl), *adj.* going on and then stopping for a while; irregular: *a fitful sleep.* —**fit′ful·ly,** *adv.*

fleur-de-lis (flėr′də lē′, flėr′də lēs′), *n., pl.* **fleurs-de-lis** (flėr′də lēz′). **1** design or device used in heraldry to represent a lily (originally supposed to represent an iris). **2** the coat of arms of the royal family of France. **3** the iris flower or plant. [<Middle French, lily flower]

flim·sy (flim′zē), *adj.,* **-si·er, -si·est.** lacking material strength; not solid or substantial; light and thin; slight; frail: *The flimsy grocery bag tore.*

flinch (flinch), *v.i.* **1** withdraw or hold back from difficulty or danger; shrink. **2** react by wincing: *I flinched when the doctor gave me a shot.*

flum·mox (flum′əks), *v.t.* INFORMAL. bring to confusion; bewilder.

a hat	oi oil	ə stands for
ā age	ou out	a in about
ä far	u cup	e in taken
e let	ù put	i in pencil
ē equal	ü rule	o in lemon
ėr term	ch child	u in circus
i it	ng long	
ī ice	sh she	
o hot	th thin	
ō open	ᴛH then	
ô order	zh measure	

fleur-de-lis

fracas
Their argument ended in a **fracas.**

gaff (def. 2)

gaunt
The guitar player was pale and **gaunt.**

foot·lights (fút′līts′), *n.pl.* row of lights at the front of a stage.

fore·stall (fôr stôl′, fōr stôl′), *v.t.* **1** prevent by acting first: *The owner forestalled a strike by starting to negotiate early with the union.* **2** act sooner than; get ahead of: *by settling the deal over the telephone, she had forestalled all her competitors.*

forte[1] (fôrt, fōrt), *n.* something a person does very well; strong point: *Golf is her forte.*

forte[2] (fôr′tā), in music: —*adj.* loud; strong. —*adv.* loudly; strongly.

fort·night (fôrt′nīt, fôrt′nit), *n.* two weeks. [Middle English *fourtenight* fourteen nights]

fra·cas (frā′kəs), *n.* a noisy quarrel or fight; uproar; brawl.

frag·ment (frag′mənt), *n.* **1** piece of something broken, part broken off. **2** an incomplete or disconnected part: *fragments of a conversation.*

fray (frā), *v.t.* cause to separate into threads; make ragged or worn along the edge. —*v.i.* become frayed; ravel out or wear through.

fur·ri·er (fėr′ē ər), *n.* **1** dealer in furs. **2** person whose work is preparing furs or making and repairing fur coats, etc.

G

gaff (gaf), *n.* **1** a strong hook on a handle or barbed spear for pulling large fish out of the water. **2** spar or pole used to extend the upper edge of a fore-and-aft sail. **3 stand the gaff,** SLANG. hold up well under strain or punishment.

gan·grene (gang′grēn′, gang grēn′), *n.* death and decay of tissue when the blood supply of a part of a living person or animal is cut off by injury, infection, or freezing.

gaunt (gônt, gänt), *adj.* very thin and bony; with hollow eyes and a starved look: *Sickness had made him gaunt.*

gen·darme (zhän′därm), *n., pl.* **-darmes** (-därmz). A member of the police in France and several other European countries who has had military training. [<Old French *gens d'armes* men of arms]

ge·ra·ni·um (jə rā′nē əm), *n.* **1** any of a genus of cultivated or wild plants, usually having deeply notched leaves and showy white, pink, red, or purple flowers. **2** the flower of any of these plants.

glut·ton (glut′n), *n.* **1** a greedy eater; person who eats too much. **2** person who never seems to have enough of something.

gnat (nat), *n.* any of various small, two-winged flies. Most gnats suck blood and give bites that itch.

gon·er (gô′nər, gon′ər), *n.* INFORMAL. person or thing that is dead, ruined, or past help.

gong (gông, gong), *n.* a large piece of metal shaped like a bowl or saucer which makes a loud noise when struck.

gran·ule (gran′yül), *n.* **1** a fine grain or particle. **2** a small bit.

grid·i·ron (grid′ī′ərn), *n.* a football field.

grime (grīm), *n.* dirt rubbed deeply and firmly into a surface: *the grime on the coal miner's hands.*

gross (grōs), *adj., n., pl.* **gross·es,** *v.* —*adj.* with nothing taken out; whole; entire. Gross receipts are the money taken in before costs are deducted. —*n.* the whole sum; total amount. —*v.t.* make a gross profit of; earn a total of: *gross $20,000 per year.*

grudge (gruj), *n.* feeling of anger or dislike against because of a real or imaginary wrong; ill will.

guild (gild), *n.* **1** association or society formed by people having the same interests, work, etc., for some useful or common purpose: *the hospital guild of a church.* **2** (in the Middle Ages) an association of merchants in a town or of persons in a particular trade or craft, formed to keep standards high, promote their business interests, protect themselves, etc. Also, **gild.** [<Scandinavian (Old Icelandic) *gildi*]

gun·wale (gun′l), *n.* the upper edge of the side of a ship or boat. Also, **gunnel.** [<*gun* + *wale* a plank; because formerly used to support the guns]

H

hag·gard (hag′ərd), *adj.* looking worn from pain, fatigue, worry, hunger, etc.; careworn; gaunt.

ham·per (ham′pər), *v.t.* hold back; obstruct in action; hinder; restrain.

heir (er, ar), *n.* **1** person who receives or has the right to receive someone's property or title after the death of its owner; person who inherits property. **2** person who inherits anything; person who receives or has something from a predecessor.

hem·i·sphere (hem′ə sfir), *n.* **1** one half of a sphere or globe formed by a plane passing through the center. **2** half of the earth's surface: *the Western Hemisphere, the Eastern Hemisphere.*

he·ral·dic (he ral′dik), *adj.* of or having to do with the science and art of designing and using coats of arms.

hold·out (hōld′out′), *n.* INFORMAL.
1 person or group that refuses to accept terms, submit, or comply with a trend, order, etc. **2** refusal to accept terms, submit, or comply.

host·ess (hō′stis), *n.* woman who receives and entertains guests socially.

hu·man·i·tar·i·an (hyü man′ə ter′ē ən), *adj.* helpful to humanity; devoted to the welfare of all human beings.

hyp·no·tist (hip′nə tist), *n.* person who places another person into a condition resembling a deep sleep in which the subject has little will and acts according to the suggestions of the person who brought about the condition.

I

i·dyll or **i·dyl** (ī′dl), *n.* **1** a short poem or piece of prose describing some simple and charming scene or event, especially one connected with domestic or country life. **2** a simple and charming scene.

il·leg·i·ble (i lej′ə bəl), *adj.* very hard or impossible to read; not plain enough to read: *illegible handwriting.*

il·lu·sion (i lü′zhən), *n.* **1** appearance or feeling that misleads because it is not real; thing that deceives by giving a false idea. **2** a false impression or perception; optical illusion: *The highway gave the illusion of becoming narrower in the distance.*

I·ma·ri (i mä′rē), brightly colored, elaborately decorated porcelain from the province of Hizen, Japan. [<*Imari,* a port in Japan]

im·mense (i mens′), *adj.* extremely large; huge; vast: *An ocean is an immense body of water.*

im·part (im pärt′), *v.t.* **1** give a part or share of. **2** communicate; tell.

im·pec·ca·ble (im pek′ə bəl), *adj.* free from fault; flawless: *impeccable manners, an impeccable appearance.* —**im·pec′ca·bly,** *adv.*

im·pen·e·tra·ble (im pen′ə trə bəl), *adj.* **1** that cannot be pierced or passed: *The thorny branches made a thick, impenetrable hedge.* **2** impossible to explain or understand. **3** not open to ideas, influences, etc.: *an impenetrable mind.*

im·plode (im plōd′), *v.i, v.t.,* **-plod·ed, -plod·ing.** burst or cause to burst inward.

im·pov·er·ished (im pov′ər isht), *adj.* very poor; lacking the necessary resources.

in·cor·rect (in′kə rekt′), *adj.* containing errors or mistakes; wrong; faulty. —**in′cor·rect′ly,** *adv.*

in·cred·i·ble (in kred′ə bəl), *adj.* hard to believe; seeming too extraordinary to be possible; unbelievable: *incredible*

bravery. *Many old superstitions seem incredible to us.* —**in·cred′i·bly,** *adv.*

in·di·vid·u·al (in′də vij′ü əl), *n.* **1** person. See **person** for synonym study. **2** one person, animal, or thing. —*adj.* **1** single; particular; separate: *an individual question.* **2** having to do with or peculiar to one person or thing: *individual tastes.* —**in′di·vid′u·al·ly,** *adv.*

in·ex·or·a·ble (in ek′sər ə bəl), *adj.* not influenced by pleading or entreaties; relentless; unyielding: *The forces of nature are inexorable.* —**in·ex′or·a·bly,** *adv.*

in·flec·tion (in flek′shən), *n.* **1** a change in the tone or pitch of the voice: *We usually end questions with a rising inflection.* **2** a variation in form to express mood, etc.

in·fur·i·ate (in fyur′ē āt), *v.t.,* **-at·ed, -at·ing.** fill with wild, fierce anger; make furious; enrage.

in·sane (in sān′), *adj.* not sane; mentally ill; crazy. —**in·sane′ly,** *adv.*

in·sec·ti·cide (in sek′tə sīd), *n.* substance or agent for killing insects.

in·sep·ar·a·ble (in sep′ər ə bəl), *adj.* constantly together. *inseparable companions.*

in·sol·u·ble (in sol′yə bəl), *adj.* **1** that cannot be dissolved: *Fats are insoluble in water.* **2** that cannot be solved; unsolvable: *an insoluble situation.*

in·sure (in shur′), *v.t.,* **-sured, -sur·ing.** arrange for money payment in case of loss of (property, profit, etc.) or accident or death to (a person).

in·ter·cept (in′tər sept′), *v.t.* take or seize on the way from one place to another: *intercept a letter, intercept a football.*

in·tru·sion (in trü′zhən), *n.* act of coming unasked and unwanted; a trespass on the property of another.

in·vest (in vest′), *v.t.* lay out or use (money) for something that is expected to produce a profit in the form of interest, benefit, income, etc.: *She invested her money in stocks, bonds, and land.*

ir·ri·ta·tion (ir′ə tā′shən), *n.* something that annoys, causes anger, provokes: *Their interruptions were an irritation to me.*

Is·lam (is′ləm, i släm′), *n* **1** the religion of the Moslems, based on the teachings of Mohammed as they appear in the Koran. It holds that there is only one God, Allah, and that Mohammed is his prophet. **2** the countries inhabited by Moslems or under Moslem rule. [<Arabic *islām* submission (to the will of God)]

Is·lam·ic (is slam′ik, i släm′ik), *adj.* of or having to do with Islam.

illusion
an optical illusion.
The parallel vertical lines appear to go apart and come together because of the slanted lines.

impeccable
Their attire was
impeccable.

J

joint (joint), *n.* **1** the place at which two things or parts are joined together. **2** part of the stem of a plant.

jot (jot), *v.t.,* **jot·ted, jot·ting.** write briefly or in haste: *The clerk jotted down the order.*

joust (joust, just, jüst), *n.* **1** combat between two knights on horseback, armed with lances, especially as part of a tournament. **2 jousts,** *pl.* a tournament. —*v.i.* fight with lances on horseback. Knights used to joust with each other for sport. [<Popular Latin *juxtare* be next to <Latin *juxta* beside] —**joust′er,** *n.*

K

kelp (kelp), *n.* **1** a large, tough, brown seaweed. **2** ashes of seaweed, used as a source of iodine.

kink (kingk), *n.* **1** a twist or curl in thread, rope, hair, etc. **2** pain or stiffness in the muscles of the neck, back, etc.

knight (nīt), *n.* **1** (in the Middle Ages) a man raised to an honorable military rank and pledged to do good deeds. After serving as a page and squire, a man was made a knight by the king or a lord. **2** (in modern times) a man raised to an honorable rank because of great achievement or service. A British knight uses the title *Sir* before his name. EXAMPLE: Sir John Smith or Sir John. —*v.t.* raise to the rank of knight. [Old English *cniht* boy]

knight

L

lac·quer (lak′ər), *n.* varnish consisting of shellac dissolved in alcohol or some other solvent, sometimes tinged with coloring matter, used for coating metals, wood, etc. —*v.t.* coat with lacquer.

land·scape (land′skāp), *n.* **1** view of scenery on land. **2** landforms of a region.

lar·yn·gi·tis (lar′ən jī′tis), *n.* inflammation of the voice box (larynx), usually accompanied by hoarseness.

lav·en·der (lav′ən dər), *adj.* pale purple.

lav·ish (lav′ish), *adj.* **1** very free or too free in giving or spending; extravagant: *A very rich person can be lavish with money.* **2** more than enough; given or spent very freely or too freely: *lavish gifts.* —**lav′ish·ly,** *adv.* —**lav′ish·ness,** *n.*

leg·is·la·ture (lej′ə slā′chər), *n.* group of persons that has the duty and power of making laws for a state or country.

lei·sure·ly (lē′zhər lē, lezh′ər lē), *adj., adv.* without hurry; taking plenty of time.

less (les) *adj.* **1** smaller in size, degree, etc.; slighter: *of less width, less importance.* **2** not so much; not so much of: *less rain, less money.*
➡ **less, lesser.** Both are used as comparatives (of *little*), *less* more usually referring to size or quantity: *less time, less food; lesser,* a formal word, referring to value or importance: *a lesser writer.*

less·er (les′ər), *adj.* **1** less; smaller. **2** less important of two: *the lesser of two evils.* ➡ See **less** for usage note.

lim·pid (lim′pid), *adj.* clear or transparent: *limpid water, limpid eyes.*

lin·guist (ling′gwist), *n.* **1** an expert in languages. **2** person skilled in a number of languages.

list·less (list′lis), *adj.* seeming too tired to care about anything; not interested in things; not caring to be active. —**list′less·ly,** *adv.* —**list′less·ness,** *n.*

M

ma·gen·ta (mə jen′tə), *n.* **1** a purplish-red dye. **2** a purplish red.

ma·jor·i·ty (mə jôr′ə tē, mə jor′ə tē), *n., pl.* **-ties. 1** the largest number; greater part; more than half the whole number. **2** a larger party or group opposed to a minority, as in voting or other action.

mal-, *combining form.* bad or badly; poor or poorly: *Malodorous = smelling bad. Maladjusted = poorly adjusted.* [<Latin *malus* bad]

mal·func·tion (mal′fungk′shən), *n.* an improper functioning; failure to work or perform. —*v.i.* function badly; work or perform improperly. [<Latin *malus* bad + *functionem* perform]

mal·treat (mal trēt′), *v.t.* treat badly or cruelly: *maltreat animals.* —**mal·treat′ment,** *n.* [<Latin *malus* bad + Old French *traitier* to handle]

mar·gin (mär′jən), *n.* edge or border: *the margin of a lake.*

marsh (märsh), *n.* low land covered at times by water; soft wet land.

mar·shal (mär′shəl), *n.* officer of various kinds, especially a police officer. A United States marshal is an officer of a federal court whose duties are like those of a sheriff.

mar·tial (mär′shəl), *adj.* **1** of war; suitable for war: *martial music.* **2** of or having to do with the military.

ma·son (mā′sn), *n.* person whose work is building with stone or brick. [<Old French *maçon* <Late Latin *machionem*]

maul (môl), *v.t.* beat and pull about; handle roughly.

max·i·mum (mak′sə məm), *n., pl.* **-mums** or **-ma,** *adj.* —*n.* the largest or highest amount: greatest possible

amount; highest point or degree. —*adj.*
largest or highest; greatest possible:
The maximum score on the test is 100.

me·di·e·val (mē'dē ē'vəl, med'ē ē'vəl),
adj. **1** of, having to do with, or
belonging to the Middle Ages (the years
from about A.D. 500 to about 1450).
2 like that of the Middle Ages. Also,
mediaeval. [<Latin *medium* middle +
aevum age]

mem·o·ry (mem'ər ē), *n., pl.* **-ries.**
1 person, thing, or event that is
remembered. **2** all that a person
remembers; what can be recalled to
mind: *examine one's memory carefully.*
[<Old French *memorie* <Latin *memoria*
< *memor* mindful. Doublet of MEMOIR.]

men·ace (men'is), *n., v.,* **-aced, -ac·ing.**
—*n.* something that threatens; threat: *In
dry weather forest fires are a menace.*
—*v.t.* threaten: *Floods menaced the
valley towns with destruction.*
—**men'ac·ing·ly,** *adv.*

me·ni·al (mē'nē əl, mē'nyəl), *adj.* suited
to or belonging to a servant who does
the humblest and most unpleasant tasks.

men·u (men'yü, mā'nyü), *n.* **1** list of the
food served at a meal; bill of fare. **2** the
food served. [<French, small, detailed
<Latin *minutum* made small.]

mer·chant (mèr'chənt), *n.* **1** person who
buys and sells commodities for profit,
now especially on a relatively large
scale. **2** storekeeper; retail shopkeeper.
[<Old French *marchëant,* ultimately
<Latin *merx, mercis* wares]

mere (mir), *adj.* nothing else than; only;
simple: *The cut was a mere scratch.*

me·squite (me skēt'), *n.* a deep-rooted
tree or shrub of the pea family, common
in the southwestern United States and in
Mexico, that often grows in dense
clumps or thickets.

micro-, *combining form.* **1** small; very
small; microscopic: *Microorganism = a
microscopic organism.* **2** one millionth of
a —: *Microfarad = one millionth of a
farad.* **3** that magnifies small —:
*Microphone = instrument that
magnifies small sounds.* [<Greek
mikros small]

mi·cro·chip (mī'krō chip'), *n.* a small
chip or piece of electrical material, often
silicon, which holds a computer circuit
or other electronic circuit. [<Greek
mikros small + Old English *cippian* cut]

mi·cro·phone (mī'krə fōn'), *n.*
instrument for magnifying or transmitting
sounds by changing sound waves into
an electric current. Microphones are
used in broadcasting, telephony, etc.
[<Greek *mikros* small + *phōnē* sound]

mi·cro·scope (mī'krə skōp'), *n.* an
optical instrument consisting of a lens or
combination of lenses for magnifying
things that are invisible or indistinct to
the naked eye.

mi·cro·sec·ond (mī'krō sek'ənd), *n.*
unit of time equal to one millionth of a
second. [<Greek *mikros* small + Latin
secunda second division of an hour into
sixty parts]

mid·point (mid'point'), *n.* the middle
part of anything; midway point: *the
midpoint of a journey.*

mile·age (mī'lij), *n.* **1** miles covered or
traveled: *Our car's mileage last year
was 10,000 miles.* **2** miles traveled per
gallon of gasoline: *Do you get good
mileage with your car?*

min·is·tra·tion (min'ə strā'shən), *n.*
help; aid: *ministration to the poor,
ministration to the sick.*

mi·nor·i·ty (mə nôr'ə tē, mī nôr'ə tē),
n., pl. **-ties. 1** the smaller number or
part; less than half. **2** a smaller party or
group opposed to a majority, as in
voting or other action.

mirth (mèrth), *n.* merry fun; merriment;
gladness or gaiety usually accompanied
by laughter.

mis·er·y (miz'ər ē), *n., pl.* **-er·ies.** a
miserable, unhappy state of mind.

mock (mok), *v.t.* **1** laugh at scornfully;
make fun of; ridicule. **2** imitate; copy.
—*adj.* not real; copying; sham; imitation:
a mock battle.

mock·er·y (mok'ər ē), *n., pl.* **-er·ies** a
making scornful fun; ridicule; derision.

mod·er·ate (mod'ər it), *adj.* **1** kept or
keeping within proper bounds; not
extreme: *moderate expenses.* **2** not
violent, severe, or intense; calm:
moderate in speech. **3** not very large or
good; fair; medium: *a moderate profit.*
—**mod'er·ate·ly,** *adv.*

mod·est (mod'ist), *adj.* **1** not displaying
or calling attention to one's own self.
2 moderate: *a modest request.* **3** not
expensive or showy: *a modest little
house.* —**mod'est·ly,** *adv.*

mole¹ (mōl), *n.* a spot or slight lump on
the skin, usually brown.

mole² (mōl), *n.* **1** any of a family of small,
dark mammals that live underground
most of the time and feed on insects,
worms, etc. **2** a person who works hard
in a position of secrecy, especially a
person who penetrates a spy
organization in order to discover its
plans and identify its members:
*Information from a mole led to the
arrest of the secret agent.*

mo·men·tum (mō men'təm), *n., pl.*
-tums, -ta (-tə). **1** quantity of motion of
a moving body, equal to the product of
its mass and velocity; force with which a
body moves: *A falling object gains
momentum as it falls.* **2** driving force
resulting from movement: *The runner's
momentum carried him far beyond the
finish line.*

mon·arch (mon'ərk), *n.* king, queen,
emperor, empress, etc.; ruler.

a hat	oi oil	ə stands for
ā age	ou out	a in about
ä far	u cup	e in taken
e let	u̇ put	i in pencil
ē equal	ü rule	o in lemon
ėr term	ch child	u in circus
i it	ng long	
ī ice	sh she	
o hot	th thin	
ō open	ᴛʜ then	
ô order	zh measure	

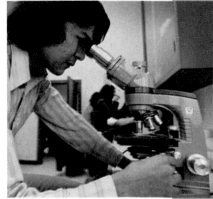

microscope

mole² (def. 1)
about 7 in. (18 cm.)
long with the tail

mon·o·lith (mon′l ith), *n.* **1** a single large block of stone. **2** monument, column, statue, etc., formed of a single large block of stone.

mul·ti·ple (mul′tə pəl), *adj.* of, having, or involving many parts, elements, relations, etc.; many and various: *a person of multiple interests.*

mur·al (myu̇r′əl), *n.* picture or decoration, usually of extensive size, painted or placed on a wall. [<Latin *muralis* < *murus* wall]

mus·cle (mus′əl), *n.* a body tissue composed of fibers, each of which is a long cell. The fibers can tighten or loosen to move parts of the body.

mus·cu·lar (mus′kyə lər), *adj.* **1** having to do with the muscles; influencing the muscles: *muscular structure, muscular contraction.* **2** having well-developed muscles; strong: *a muscular arm.*

Mus·lim or **Mus·lem** (muz′ləm), *n.* person who believes in and follows the teachings of Mohammed. Also, **Moslem.** [<Arabic *muslim* one who submits]

mu·ti·ny (myüt′n ē), *n., pl.* **-nies,** *v.,* **-nied, -ny·ing.** —*n.* open rebellion against lawful authority, especially by sailors or soldiers against their officers. *v.i.* take part in a mutiny; rebel.

mu·tu·al (myü′chü əl), *adj.* done, said, felt, etc., by each toward the other; given and received: *mutual promises, mutual dislike.* —**mu′tu·al·ly,** *adv.*

N

nano-, *combining form.* one billionth of a: *Nanosecond = one billionth of a second.* [<Greek *nanos* dwarf]

na·no·sec·ond (nā′nō sek′ənd, nan′ō-sek′ənd), *n.* one billionth of a second.

no·ble (nō′bəl), *adj.,* **-bler, -blest,** *n.* —*adj.* high and great by birth, rank, or title; aristocratic: *a noble family, noble blood.* —*n.* person high and great by birth, rank, or title: *Most of the nobles were loyal to the king.* [<Old French < Latin *noblis* renowned, well-known < *gnoscere* to come to know]

no·bly (nō′blē), *adv.* in a noble manner.

noc·tur·nal (nok tèr′nl), *adj.* **1** of the night: *Stars are a nocturnal sight.* **2** in the night: *a nocturnal visitor.* **3** active in the night: *The owl is a nocturnal bird.*

node (nōd), *n.* **1** knot, knob. **2** (in botany) part of a stem that normally bears a leaf or leaves.

non·cha·lant (non′shə lənt, non′shə-länt′), *adj.* without enthusiasm; coolly unconcerned; indifferent: *It was hard to remain nonchalant during all the excitement.* —**non′cha·lant·ly,** *adv.*

nos·tal·gia (no stal′jə), *n.* a painful or wistful yearning for one's home, country, city, or for anything far removed in space or time.

nour·ish (nèr′ish), *v.t.* make grow, or keep alive and well, with food; feed; nurture: *Milk nourishes a baby.*

nour·ish·ment (nèr′ish mənt), *n.* **1** food. **2** a nourishing.

O

oil·cloth (oil′klôth′, oil′kloth′), *n., pl.* **-cloths** (-klôtɦz′, -kloths′). **1** cloth made waterproof by coating it with paint or oil, used to cover shelves, tables, etc. **2** piece of this cloth.

or·ner·y (ôr′nər ē), *adj.* INFORMAL. **1** mean or irritable in disposition. **2** of a mean kind: *an ornery remark.* —**or′ner·i·ness,** *n.*

or·ni·thol·o·gy (ôr′nə thol′ə jē), *n.* branch of zoology dealing with the study of birds. [<Greek *ornithos* bird + English *-logy*]

o·ver·come (ō′vər kum′), *v.t.,* **-came** (-kām′), **-come, -com·ing. 1** get the better of; win the victory over; conquer; defeat: *overcome one's faults, overcome all difficulties.* **2** make weak or helpless; overwhelm: *overcome by weariness, overcome with joy.*

o·ver·see (ō′vər sē′), *v.t.,* **-saw** (-sô′), **-seen** (-sēn′), **-see·ing.** look after and direct (work or workers); superintend; manage.

P

page (pāj), *n., v.,* **paged, pag·ing.** —*n.* **1** person employed by a hotel, club, legislature, etc., to run errands, carry parcels, deliver messages, etc. **2** youth who attends a person of rank. **3** youth who was preparing to be a knight. —*v.i.* act as a page; be a page. [<Old French, perhaps ultimately <Greek *paidos* child, boy]

pal·pi·ta·tion (pal′pə tā′shən), *n.* **1** a very rapid beating of the heart; throb. **2** a quivering; trembling.

pang (pang), *n.* **1** a sudden, short, sharp pain: *the pangs of a toothache.* **2** a sudden feeling: *A pang of pity moved his heart.*

par·a·lyze (par′ə līz), *v.t.,* **-lyzed, -lyz·ing. 1** affect with a lessening or loss of the power of motion or feeling: *The patient's arm was paralyzed.* **2** make powerless or helplessly inactive; cripple: *Fear paralyzed my mind.*

par·ish (par′ish), *n.* **1** district that has its own church and clergy. **2** people of a parish. **3** members of the congregation of a particular church. **4** (in Louisiana) a county. [<Old French *paroisse* < Late Latin *parochia* < Late Greek *paroikia*, ultimately < *para-* + *oikos* dwelling.

par·tial (pär′shəl), *adj.* not complete; not total; *a partial eclipse of the sun.*
—**par′tial·ly,** *adv.*

par·tic·i·pate (pär tis′ə pāt), *v.i.,* **-pat·ed, -pat·ing.** have a share; take part: *The teacher participated in the children's games.*

pas·sion (pash′ən), *n.* **1** a very strong or violent feeling or emotion, such as great haste and fear. **2** a very strong liking: *She has a passion for music.*

pas·tor (pas′tər), *n.* minister or member of the clergy having charge of a church or congregation; spiritual guide.

pa·tri·ot·ic (pā′trē ot′ik), *adj.* **1** loving one's country. **2** showing love and loyal support of one's country.
—**pa′tri·ot′i·cal·ly,** *adv.*

pau·per (pô′pər), *n.* **1** a very poor person. **2** person supported by charity or public welfare.

ped·a·gogue (ped′ə gog, ped′ə gôg), *n.* teacher of children; schoolmaster.

ped·i·gree (ped′ə grē′), *n.* **1** list of ancestors of a person or animal. **2** line of descent; ancestry; lineage.

pen·du·lum (pen′jə ləm, pen′dyə ləm), *n.* weight so hung from a fixed point that it is free to swing to and fro through a regular arc under the influence of gravity. The movement of the works of a tall clock is often timed by a pendulum.

pen·e·trate (pen′ə trāt), *v.t.* **-trat·ed, -trat·ing. 1** enter into or pass through: *The bullet penetrated this wall and two inches into the one beyond.* **2** soak or spread through; permeate: *The odor penetrated the whole house.*

pen·ta·gon (pen′tə gon), *n.* **1** a plane figure having five sides and five angles. **2 the Pentagon,** a five-sided building in Arlington, Virginia, that is the headquarters of the Department of Defense of the United States.

per·ish (per′ish), *v.i.* be destroyed; die: *Soldiers perish in battle. Flowers perish when frost comes.*

per·mis·si·ble (pər mis′ə bəl), *adj.* that can be allowed; not forbidden.
—**per·mis′si·bly,** *adv.*

per·pet·u·al (pər pech′ü əl), *adj.* **1** lasting forever; eternal: *the perpetual hills.* **2** never ceasing; continuous; constant: *a perpetual stream of visitors.*
—**per·pet′u·al·ly,** *adv.*

per·sist (pər sist′, pər zist′), *v.i.* **1** continue firmly; refuse to stop or be changed. **2** say or ask again and again.

per·son (pėr′sən), *n.* man, woman, or child; human being. See synonym study below. **Syn. Person, individual** mean a human being. **Person** is the common word: *She is a nice person.* **Individual** emphasizes the person's singleness.

pe·ruse (pə rüz′), *v.t.,* **-rused, -rus·ing. 1** read, especially thoroughly and carefully. **2** examine in detail, in order to learn; look at with attention.

phys·i·cal (fiz′ə kəl), *adj.* of the body; bodily: *physical exercise.*
—**phys′i·cal·ly,** *adv.*

pi·az·za (pē az′ə), *n.* a large porch along one or more sides of a house; veranda.

pike[1] (pīk), *n.* a long wooden shaft with a sharp-pointed metal head; spear. Foot soldiers used to carry pikes.

pike[2] (pīk), *n.* a sharp point, pointed tip, or spike, such as the head of an arrow or spear.

pike[3] (pīk), *n., pl.* **pikes** or **pike. 1** any of a family of large, slender, freshwater fishes of the Northern Hemisphere, having spiny fins and a long, pointed head, such as a muskellunge and pickerel. **2** any of certain similar fishes, such as the pike perch.

pike[4] (pīk), *n.* **1** turnpike; main highway: *cruise along the pike.* **2 come down the pike,** INFORMAL. appear; show up.

pin·na·cle (pin′ə kəl), *n.* **1** a high peak or point of rock, ice, etc. **2** the highest point: *at the pinnacle of one's fame.* **3** a slender turret or spire. [Latin *pinna* point or wing]

pit·tance (pit′ns), *n.* **1** a small allowance of money. **2** a small amount or share.

piv·ot (piv′ət), *n.* shaft, pin, or point on which something turns. —*v.i.* turn on or as if on a pivot.

plague (plāg), *n.* **1** highly contagious, epidemic, and often fatal bacterial disease that occurs in several forms, one of which is bubonic plague. **2** any epidemic disease; pestilence.

plight (plīt), *n.* condition or situation, usually bad: *in a sad plight.*

pneu·mat·ic (nü mat′ik, nyü mat′ik), *adj.* **1** filled with air; containing air, especially compressed air: *a pneumatic tire.* **2** worked by air, especially compressed air: *a pneumatic drill.*

poise (poiz), *n.* **1** self-possessed composure, assurance, and dignity: *She has perfect poise and never seems embarrassed.* **2** the way in which the body, head, etc., are held.

pole·cat (pōl′kat′), *n.* **1** a small, dark-brown, carnivorous European weasel which can emit a very disagreeable odor. **2** skunk.

a hat	oi oil	ə stands for
ā age	ou out	a in about
ä far	u cup	e in taken
e let	u̇ put	i in pencil
ē equal	ü rule	o in lemon
ėr term	ch child	u in circus
i it	ng long	
ī ice	sh she	
o hot	th thin	
ō open	ᴛʜ then	
ô order	zh measure	

pentagon (def. 1)

plight

proportion
She was tiny in **proportion** to the dog.

prosaic
Washing dishes is a **prosaic** task.

po·lit·i·cal (pə lit′ə kəl), *adj.* **1** of or concerned with the science and art of government: *political parties.* **2** having to do with citizens or government. **3** of politicians or their methods: *a political slogan.* **4** of or having to do with government or a government; governmental: *political districts.* —**po·lit′i·cal·ly,** *adv.*

pol·len (pol′ən), *n.* a fine, yellowish powder consisting of grains or microspores, that are released from the anthers of flowers to fertilize the pistils. [<Latin, fine flour]

pom·mel (pum′əl, pom′əl), *n.* **1** part of a saddle that sticks up at the front. **2** a rounded knob on the hilt of a sword, dagger, etc.

pop·u·late (pop′yə lāt), *v.t.,* **-lat·ed, -lat·ing.** live in; inhabit: *This city is densely populated.*

pout (pout), *v.i.* **1** thrust or push out the lips, as a displeased or sulky child does. **2** show displeasure.

pre·ma·ture (prē′mə chur′, prē′mə tur′, prē′mə tyur′), *adj.* before the proper time; too soon.

pre·mi·um (prē′mē əm), *n.* **1** a reward, especially one given as an incentive to buy. **2** unusual value: *Our teacher puts a premium on neatness and punctuality.*

pre·side (pri zīd′), *v.i.,* **-sid·ed, -sid·ing.** hold the place of authority; have charge of a meeting.

pre·sume (pri zum′), *v.,* **-sumed, -sum·ing.** —*v.t.* take for granted without proving; suppose: *The law presumes innocence until guilt is proved.*

pre·vail (pri vāl′), *v.i.* **1** be the stronger; win the victory; succeed: *prevail against an enemy. Reason prevailed over emotion.* **2** be effective.

pro·duce (prod′üs, prod′yüs; prō′düs, prō′dyüs), *n.* farm products, especially fruits and vegetables.

pro·fes·sion·al (prə fesh′ə nəl), *adj.* **1** following an occupation as one's career: *a professional soldier, a professional writer.* **2** earning a living from something that others do for pleasure: *a professional ballplayer.* **3** undertaken or engaged in by professionals rather than amateurs: *a professional ball game.* —*n.* person who earns a living from something that others do for pleasure.—**pro·fes′sion·al·ly,** *adv.*

pro·found (prə found′), *adj.* **1** very deep: *a profound sigh, a profound sleep.* **2** deeply felt; very great: *profound despair.* **3** going far deeper than what is easily understood; having or showing great knowledge or understanding: *a profound book, a profound thinker, a profound thought.* —**pro·found′ly,** *adv.*

pro·hi·bi·tion (prō′ə bish′ən), *n.* **1** act of forbidding or preventing. **2** law or order that bans or outlaws something.

pro·long (prə lông′, prə long′), *v.t.* make longer; extend in time or space; stretch, lengthen, or protract.

prom·i·nent (prom′ə nənt), *adj.* **1** well-known or important; distinguished: *a prominent citizen.* **2** that catches the eye; easy to see: *A single tree in a field is prominent.* —**prom′i·nent·ly,** *adv.*

pro·pel (prə pel′), *v.t.,* **-pelled, -pel·ling.** drive or push forward; force ahead: *propel a boat by oars.*

pro·por·tion (prə pôr′shən, prə-pōr′shən), *n.* **1** relation in magnitude; size, number, amount, or degree of one thing compared to another. **2 proportions,** *pl.* **a** size; extent. **b** dimensions.

pro·pos·al (prə pō′zəl), *n.* **1** what is suggested; a plan; scheme. **2** offer of marriage.

pro·sa·ic (prō zā′ik), *adj.* matter-of-fact; ordinary; not exciting. —**pro·sa′i·cal·ly,** *adv.*

pros·per·ous (pros′pər əs), *adj.* **1** doing well; successful. **2** favorable; helpful: *prosperous weather for growing wheat.* —**pros′per·ous·ly,** *adv.*

pros·trate (pros′trāt), *v.,* **-trat·ed, -trat·ing,** *adj.* —*v.t.* lay down flat; cast down: *The captives prostrated themselves before the conqueror.* —*adj.* **1** lying flat with face downward. **2** lying flat: *I stumbled and fell prostrate on the floor.*

pro·vi·sion (prə vizh′ən), *n.* **1** care taken for the future; arrangement made beforehand. **2** that which is made ready; stock, especially of food. **3 provisions,** *pl.* supply of food and drinks.

prune (prün), *v.t.,* **pruned, prun·ing. 1** cut out useless or undesirable parts from. **2** cut undesirable twigs or branches from (a bush, tree, etc.): *prune fruit trees.* **3** cut off or out: *Prune all the dead branches.*

pry[1] (prī), *v.,* **pried, pry·ing,** *n., pl.* **pries.** —*v.* look with curiosity; peep: *pry into the private affairs of others.* —*n.* an inquisitive person.

pry[2] (prī), *v.,* **pried, pry·ing,** *n., pl.* **pries.** —*v.* **1** raise, move, or separate by force, especially by force of leverage: *pry up a stone, pry the top off a bottle.* **2** get with much effort: *We finally pried the secret out of her.* —*n.* lever for prying.

psalm·o·dy (sä′mə dē, säl′mə dē, sal′mə dē), *n., pl.* **-dies. 1** act, practice, or art of singing psalms or hymns. **2** psalms or hymns.

pug·na·cious (pug nā′shəs), *adj.* having the habit of fighting; fond of fighting; quarrelsome. —**pug·na′cious·ly,** *adv.*

pul·pit (pul′pit), *n.* platform or raised structure in a church from which the minister preaches.

pun (pun), *n.* a humorous use of a word where it can have different meanings, or of two or more words with the same or nearly the same sound but different meanings; play on words: *"We must all hang together, or we shall all hang separately"* is a famous pun by Benjamin Franklin.

pyr·a·mid (pir′ə mid), *n.* **1** a solid figure having a polygon for a base and triangular sides which meet in a point. **2** thing or things having the form of a pyramid: *a pyramid of stones.*

Q

quake (kwāk), *v.i.,* **quaked, quak·ing.** **1** shake or tremble from cold, anger, etc.: *quake with fear.* **2** rock violently: *The earth quaked.*

quest (kwest), *n.* **1** a search or hunt: *She went to the library in quest of something to read.* **2** expedition of knights: *There are many stories about the quests of King Arthur's knights.*

queue (kyü), *n.* **1** braid of hair hanging down from the back of the head. **2** a line of people, automobiles, etc.: *There was a long queue in front of the theater.*

R

ram·pant (ram′pənt), *adj.* **1** passing beyond restraint or usual limits; unchecked: *The vines ran rampant over the fence. The mob ran rampant through the town.* **2** angry; excited; violent. **3** (in heraldry) standing up on the hind legs. —**ram′pant·ly,** *adv.*

rash (rash), *adj.* **1** too hasty and careless. **2** characterized by undue haste: *a rash promise.* —**rash′ly,** *adv.* —**rash′ness,** *n.*

rasp (rasp), *v.i.* make a harsh, grating sound: *The file rasped as she worked.* —*v.t.* utter with a grating sound: *rasp out a command.*

re·cede (ri sēd′), *v.i.,* **-ced·ed, -ced·ing.** **1** go or move backward. **2** slope backward: *a chin that recedes.* **3** withdraw: *recede from an agreement.*

re·cep·tion (ri sep′shən), *n.* **1** act of taking in or of accepting. **2** a gathering to receive and welcome people.

re·cip·ro·cal (ri sip′rə kəl), *adj.* **1** in return: *Although she gave me a present, she expected no reciprocal gift from me.* **2** mutual: *reciprocal distrust.*

rec·og·ni·tion (rek′əg nish′ən), *n.* **1** acknowledgment: *We insisted on complete recognition of our rights.* **2** a formal acknowledgment conveying approval or appreciation.

rec·on·cile (rek′ən sīl), *v.t.,* **-ciled, -cil·ing.** **1** make friends again. **2** settle (a disagreement or difference).

re·form (ri fôrm′), *v.t.* make better; improve by removing faults. —*v.i.* become better: *They promised to reform if given another chance.* —*n.* a change intended to improve conditions; improvement: *The new government made many needed reforms.*

re·main·der (ri mān′dər), *n.* the part left over; the rest; the balance of.

re·peal (ri pēl′), *v.t.* do away with; withdraw; annul: *Prohibition was repealed in 1933.*

re·plen·ish (ri plen′ish), *v.t.* fill again; provide a new supply for; renew: *replenish one's wardrobe. You had better replenish the fire.*

re·prieve (ri prēv′), *n.* **1** delay in carrying out a punishment, especially of the death penalty. **2** the order giving authority for such delay. **3** temporary relief from any evil or trouble.

rep·tile (rep′tǝl, rep′tīl), *n.* any of a class of cold-blooded vertebrates that breathe by means of lungs, move by creeping or crawling, and usually have skin covered with dry horny plates or scales. Snakes, lizards, turtles, alligators, and crocodiles are reptiles. [< Late Latin, neuter of *reptilis* crawling < Latin *repere* to crawl]

rep·u·ta·ble (rep′yə tə bəl), *adj.* having a good reputation; well thought of; in good standing. —**rep′u·ta·bly,** *adv.*

re·sume (ri züm′), *v.t.,* **-sumed, -sum·ing.** **1** begin again; go on: *Resume reading where we left off.* **2** get or take again: *Those standing may resume their seats.*

re·tire·ment (ri tīr′mənt), *n.* the act of giving up an office, occupation, etc., especially at the end of an active career: *Our teacher planned an early retirement.*

re·triev·al (ri trē′vəl), *n.* act of calling back; recovery: *the retrieval of information from the storage of a computer.*

re·veal (ri vēl′), *v.t.* make known; disclose; divulge: *reveal a secret.*

rind (rīnd), *n.* the firm outer covering of oranges, melons, cheeses, etc.

ri·ot (rī′ət), *n.* a wild, violent public disturbance; disturbance; confusion; disorder. —*v.i.* behave in a wild, disorderly way.

roost (rüst), *n.* bar, pole, or perch on which birds rest or sleep. —*v.i.* sit as birds do on a roost; settle for the night.

a hat	oi oil	ə stands for
ā age	ou out	a in about
ä far	u cup	e in taken
e let	u̇ put	i in pencil
ē equal	ü rule	o in lemon
ėr term	ch child	u in circus
i it	ng long	
ī ice	sh she	
o hot	th thin	
ō open	ŦH then	
ô order	zh measure	

pyramid (def. 1)
two types of pyramids

rampant (def. 3)
lion rampant

ro·tate (rō′tāt), *v.i.*, **-tat·ed, -tat·ing.** move around a center or axis; turn in a circle; revolve.

rou·tine (rü tēn′), *n.* a fixed, regular method of doing things; habitual doing of the same things in the same way: *the daily routine of working and sleeping.*

rug·ged (rug′id), *adj.* **1** covered with rough edges; rough and uneven: *rugged ground.* **2** able to do and endure much. —**rug·ged·ness,** *n.*

rus·tic (rus′tik), *adj.* **1** belonging to or suitable for the country; rural. **2** simple; plain: *rustic, unassuming ways.*

rus·tler (rus′lər), *n.* INFORMAL. cattle thief.

S

sal·va·tion (sal vā′shən), *n.* **1** person or thing that saves from danger or difficulty. **2** the preservation from destruction or failure.

sane (sān), *adj.*, **san·er, san·est.** **1** having a healthy mind; not crazy; rational. **2** having or showing good sense; sensible. [< Latin *sanus* healthy] —**sane′ly,** *adv.*

scan·dal (skan′dl), *n.* a shameful action, condition, or event that brings disgrace or shocks public opinion: *unearth a scandal in the government.*

scath·ing (skā′ᴛʜing), *adj.* bitterly severe; withering: *a scathing remark, scathing criticism.* —**scath′ing·ly,** *adv.*

sculp·ture (skulp′chər), *n.* **1** art of making figures by carving, modeling, casting, etc. Sculpture includes the cutting of statues from blocks of marble, stone, or wood, casting in bronze, and modeling in clay or wax. **2** sculptured work; piece of such work.

scur·ry (skér′ē), *v.i.*, **-ried, -ry·ing.** run quickly; scamper; hurry.

scythe (sīᴛʜ), *n.* a long, thin, slightly curved blade on a long handle, for cutting grass, etc. —**scythe′like′,** *adj.*

se·cre·cy (sē′krə sē), *n.*, *pl.* **-cies.** **1** condition of being secret or of being kept secret. **2** ability to keep things secret. **3** tendency to conceal; lack of frankness.

sed·i·ment (sed′ə mənt), *n.* **1** matter that settles to the bottom of a liquid. **2** (in geology) earth, stones, etc., deposited by water, wind, or ice: *When glaciers melt, they leave sediment behind.*

se·lect (si lekt′), *v.* pick out; choose: *Select the book you want.* —*adj.* **1** picked as best; chosen specially: *A few select officials were admitted to the conference.* **2** choice; superior: *That store carries a very select line of merchandise.* **3** careful in choosing; particular as to friends, company, etc.: *She belongs to a very select club.*

sen·ior (sē′nyər), *adj.* **1** the older (designating a father whose son has the same given name): *John Parker, Senior.* **2** higher in rank or longer in service: *the senior member of a firm, a senior judge.*

sen·ti·men·tal (sen′tə men′tl), *adj.* **1** having or showing much tender feeling: *sentimental poetry.* **2** likely to act from feelings rather than from logical thinking. —**sen′ti·men′tal·ly,** *adv.*

se·quel (sē′kwəl), *n.* **1** that which follows; continuation. **2** a complete story continuing an earlier one about the same people.

sev·er (sev′ər), *v.t.* cut apart; cut off: *sever a rope.* —*v.i.* part; divide; separate: *The rope severed and the swing fell down.*

sheath (shēth), *n.*, *pl.* **sheaths** (shēᴛʜz, shēths). case or covering for the blade of a sword, knife, etc.

shut·ter (shut′ər), *n.* a movable cover for a window.

si·dle (sī′dl), *v.i.*, **-dled, dling. 1** move sideways. **2** move sideways slowly so as not to attract attention.

sim·pli·fy (sim′plə fī), *v.t.*, **-fied, -fy·ing.** make simple or simpler; make plainer or easier.

sin·is·ter (sin′ə stər), *adj.* **1** showing ill will; threatening: *a sinister look.* **2** bad; evil; dishonest. **3** disastrous; unfortunate.

skel·e·ton (skel′ə tən), *n.* **1** the framework of bones and cartilage in vertebrates that supports the muscles, organs, etc. **2** frame: *the steel skeleton of a building.*

skew·er (skyü′ər), *n.* **1** a long pin of wood or metal stuck through meat to hold it together while it is cooking. **2** something used like a long pin.

skil·let (skil′it), *n.* a shallow pan with a long handle, used for frying.

slack[1] (slak), *adj.* **1** not tight or firm; loose: *a slack rope.* **2** careless: *a slack housekeeper.* **3** slow: *The horse was moving at a slack pace.* **4** not active; not brisk; dull: *Business is slack at this season.* **5** gentle or moderate. —*n.* **1** part that hangs loose: *Pull in the slack of the rope.* **2** a dull season; quiet period; lull. **3** a stopping of a strong flow of the tide or a current of water. —*v.t.* **1** make slack; let up on. —*v.i.* be or become slack; let up. [Old English *slæc*] —**slack′ly,** *adv.* —**slack′ness,** *n.*

slack[2] (slak), *n.* dirt, dust, and small pieces left after coal is screened; small or refuse coal.

slo·gan (slō′gən), *n.* word or phrase used by a business, club, political party, etc., to advertise its purpose; motto: *"Service with a smile" was the store's slogan.*

sculpture
a **sculpture** by Michelangelo

slum (slum), *n.* Often, **slums,** *pl.* a run-down, overcrowded part of a city or town. Poverty, dirt, and unhealthy living conditions are common in the slums.

smol·der (smōl′dər), *v.i.* burn and smoke without flame: *The campfire smoldered for hours after the blaze died down.* Also, **smoulder.**

snug (snug), *adj.,* **snug·ger, snug·gest,** *v.,* **snugged, snug·ging,** *adv.* —*adj.* **1** comfortable and warm; sheltered: *The cat has found a snug corner behind the stove.* **2** compact, neat, and trim: *The cabins on the boat are snug.* **3** well-built; seaworthy: *a snug ship.* **4** fitting closely: *That coat is a little too snug.* **5** small but sufficient: *snug income.* **6** hidden; concealed: *The fox lay snug as the hunters passed by.* —*v.t.* make snug. —*v.i.* nestle; snuggle. *adv.* in a snug manner. [probably <Low German] —**snug′ly,** *adv.* —**snug′ness,** *n.*

so·lic·i·tude (sə lis′ə tüd, sə lis′ə tyüd), *n.* anxious care; anxiety; concern.

sol·i·tar·y (sol′ə ter′ē), *adj.* **1** alone or single; only: *A solitary rider was seen in the distance.* **2** individual; separate: *a solitary example.*

sound[1] (sound), *n.* **1** that which is or can be heard. **2** noise, tone, note, etc., whose quality indicates its source or nature: *the sound of music.* —*v.* **1** make a sound or noise: *sound an alarm.* **2** seem; appear: *That excuse sounds peculiar.* **3** make known; announce. **4 within sound,** near enough to hear.

sound[2] (sound), *adj.* **1** free from disease; healthy. **2** free from injury or decay: *a sound ship.* **3** free from error or logical defect: *a sound argument.*

sound[3] (sound), *v.* **1** measure the depth of (water, etc.) by letting down a weight fastened to the end of a line. **2** Often, **sound out.** try to find out the views or feelings of.

sound[4] (sound), *n.* **1** a narrow channel of water joining two larger bodies of water, or between an island and the mainland. **2** air bladder of a fish.

span (span), *n.* **1** part between two supports. **2** distance between two supports: *The arch had a fifty-foot span.*

spasm (spaz′əm), *n.* **1** a sudden, abnormal, involuntary contraction of a muscle or muscles. **2** any sudden, brief fit or spell of unusual energy or activity.

spec·u·late (spek′yə lāt), *v.i.,* **-lat·ed, -lat·ing. 1** think carefully; reflect; consider: *The philosopher speculated about time and space.* **2** guess; conjecture.

spell (spel), *n.* **1** period or time of anything: *a spell of coughing, a spell of hot weather.* **2** INFORMAL. a brief period: *rest for a spell.*

spon·ta·ne·ous (spon tā′nē əs), *adj.* caused by natural impulse or desire; not forced or compelled; not planned beforehand: *Both sides burst into spontaneous cheers at the skillful play.*

stag·nant (stag′nənt), *adj.* **1** not running or flowing: *stagnant air, stagnant water.* **2** foul from standing still.

stal·wart (stôl′wərt), *adj.* **1** strongly built; sturdy; robust. **2** strong and brave; valiant. **3** firm; steadfast.

stan·dard·ize (stan′dər dīz), *v.t.,* **-ized, iz·ing.** make something conform in size, shape, weight, quality, strength, etc.: *The parts of an automobile are standardized.* —**stan′dard·i·za′tion,** *n.*

star·va·tion (stär vā′shən), *n.* a suffering from extreme hunger; a weakness due to lack of food.

sub·merge (səb mėrj′), *v.,* **-merged.** —*v.t.* **1** put under water; cover with water: *land submerged by a flood.* **2** cover; bury: *His talent was submerged by his shyness.* —*v.i.* **1** sink under water; go below the surface: *The submarine submerged.* **2** sink out of sight. [<Latin *submergere* < *sub-* under + *mergere* to plunge]

sub·mis·sion (səb mish′ən), *n.* **1** a yielding to the power, control, or authority of another; submitting: *The defeated general showed his submission by giving up his sword.* **2** obedience; humbleness: *They bowed in submission to the queen's order.*

sub·tle (sut′l), *adj.,* **-tler, -tlest. 1** delicate; thin; fine: *a subtle odor of perfume.* **2** so fine or delicate as to elude observation or analysis: *subtle distinctions.* **3** faint; mysterious: *a subtle smile.*

suc·ces·sive (sək ses′iv), *adj.* coming one after another; following in order.

suit·or (sü′tər), *n.* man courting a woman.

sul·len (sul′ən), *adj.* **1** silent because of bad humor or anger: *The sullen child refused to answer my question.* See synonym study below. **2** gloomy; dismal: *The sullen skies threatened rain.* [<Middle English *soleine,* ultimately < Latin *solus* alone] —**sul′len·ly,** *adv.* —**sul′len·ness,** *n.* Syn. **1** Sullen, **sulky, glum** mean silent and bad-humored or gloomy. **Sullen** suggests an ill-natured refusal to talk or be cooperative because of anger or bad humor or disposition: *It is disagreeable to have to sit at the breakfast table with a sullen person.* **Sulky** suggests moody or childish sullenness because of resentment or discontent: *Dogs sometimes become sulky because they are jealous.* **Glum** emphasizes silence and low spirits because of some depressing condition or happening: *She is glum about the results of the election.*

a hat	oi oil	ə stands for
ā age	ou out	a in about
ä far	u cup	e in taken
e let	ů put	i in pencil
ē equal	ü rule	o in lemon
ėr term	ch child	u in circus
i it	ng long	
ī ice	sh she	
o hot	th thin	
ō open	ŦH then	
ô order	zh measure	

tête-à-tête, adv.
They dined **tête-à-tête.**

toxic
This mushroom is **toxic.**

su·per·im·pose (sü′pər im pōz′), *v.t.,* **-posed, -pos·ing.** put or lay one object on top of something else; overlay.

su·pine (sü pīn′), *adj.* **1** lying flat on the back. **2** lazily inactive; listless. —**su·pine′ly,** *adv.*

sup·press (sə pres′), *v.t.* **1** keep in; hold back; keep from appearing: *She suppressed a yawn. Each nation suppressed news that was not favorable to it.* **2** keep secret; refrain from disclosing or divulging: *suppress the truth.*

sus·te·nance (sus′tə nəns), *n.* food or provisions; nourishment: *The lost campers went without sustenance for two days.*

swel·ter·ing (swel′tər ing), *adj.* extremely and unpleasantly hot.

syb·a·rite (sib′ə rīt′), *n.* person who cares very much for luxury and pleasure.

syb·a·rit·ic (sib′ə rit′ik), *adj.* luxurious; voluptuous.

T

tack·le (tak′əl), *n., v.,* **-led, -ling.** —*n.* equipment; apparatus; gear. Fishing tackle means the rod, line, hooks, etc., used in catching fish. —*v.t.* **1** try to deal with: *a difficult problem to tackle.* **2** lay hold of; seize or attack.

talk·a·tive (tô′kə tiv), *adj.* having the habit of talking a great deal; fond of talking.

tap·es·try (tap′ə strē), *n., pl.* **-tries,** **1** fabric with pictures or designs woven in it, used to hang on walls, cover furniture, etc. **2** a picture in tapestry. [< Old French *tapisserie* < *tapisser* to cover with a carpet < *tapis* carpet < Greek *tapēs*]

taut (tôt), *adj.* tightly drawn; tense: *a taut rope.*

tax·i·der·mist (tak′sə dėr′mist), *n.* an expert in preparing the skins of animals and stuffing and mounting them so that they look alive.

tel·e·graph (tel′ə graf), *n.* apparatus, system, or process for sending coded messages over wires by means of electrical impulses.

tempt (tempt), *v.t.* **1** make or try to make (a person) do something wrong by the offer of some pleasure or reward: *Hunger tempted them to steal food.* **2** appeal strongly to; attract: *That candy tempts me.*

temp·ta·tion (temp tā′shən), *n.* **1** a tempting. **2** a being tempted: *"Lead us not into temptation."* **3** thing that tempts.

ter·ror·ize (ter′ə rīz′), *v.t.,* **-ized, -iz·ing. 1** fill with great fear. **2** rule or subdue by threat or violence. —**ter′ror·i·za′tion,** *n.*

tête-à-tête (tāt′ə tāt′), *n.* a private conversation between two people. [< French, head to head]

the·o·ret·i·cal (thē′ə ret′ə kəl), *adj.* **1** planned or worked out in the mind, not from experience; based on supposition, not on fact. **2** dealing with fancy as opposed to fact. —**the′o·ret′i·cal·ly,** *adv.*

thigh (thī), *n.* part of the leg between the hip and the knee.

thwart (thwôrt), *n.* **1** seat across a boat, on which a rower sits. **2** brace between the gunwales of a canoe.

tim·bre (tim′bər, tam′bər), *n.* the quality in sounds, regardless of their pitch or volume, by which a certain voice, instrument, etc., can be distinguished from other voices, instruments, etc. Because of differences in timbre, identical notes played on a violin, an oboe, and a trumpet can be distinguished from one another.

toil[1] (toil), *n.* hard work; labor: *succeed after years of toil.* —*v.i.* **1** work hard. **2** move with difficulty, pain, or weariness. *They toiled up the steep mountain.* —**toil′er,** *n.*

toil[2] (toil), *n.* Often, **toils,** *pl.* net or snare: *The thief was caught in the toils of the law.*

tox·ic (tok′sik), *adj.* **1** of poison; caused by poison: *a toxic illness.* **2** poisonous: *toxic plants.*

trans·form (tran sfôrm′), *v.t.* **1** change in form or appearance. **2** change in condition, nature, or character.

trous·seau (trü′sō, trü sō′), *n., pl.* **trous·seaux** (trü′sōz, trü sōz′), **trous·seaus.** a bride's outfit of clothes, linen, etc. [< French, originally, bundle]

tur·pen·tine (tėr′pən tīn), *n.* **1** mixture of oil and resin obtained from various cone-bearing trees. **2** an oil distilled from this mixture. Turpentine is used in mixing paints and in medicine, etc.

ty·ran·nic (tə ran′ik, tī ran′ik), *adj.* cruel; unjust; like a tyrant: *Hitler's actions were tyrannic.*

U

un·be·known (un′bi nōn′), *adj.* not known: *He arrived unbeknown to anyone.*

un·bid·den (un bid′n), *adj.* **1** not bidden; not invited: *an unbidden guest.* **2** without being ordered; not commanded.

un·de·ni·a·ble (un′di nī′ə bəl), *adj.* that cannot be denied or disputed; certain. —**un′de·ni′a·bly,** *adv.*

un·grate·ful (un grāt′fəl), *adj.* not grateful; not thankful; unappreciative: *an ungrateful child.* —**un·grate′ful·ly,** *adv.*

V

vac·u·um (vak′yü əm, vak′yüm), *n., pl.* **vac·u·ums** or **vac·u·a** (vak′yü ə), *adj., v.* —*n.* **1** an empty space without even air in it. **2** an enclosed space from which almost all air or other matter has been removed. **3** an empty space; void. [< Latin, neuter of *vacuus* empty]

var·nish (vär′nish), *n.* a thin, transparent liquid that gives a smooth, glossy appearance to wood, metal, etc., often made from resinous substances dissolved in oil or alcohol. —*v.t.* put varnish on.

veg·e·ta·tion (vej′ə tā′shən), *n.* plant life; growing plants: *There is not much vegetation in deserts.*

ve·ran·da or **ve·ran·dah** (və ran′də), *n.* a large porch or gallery along one or more sides of a house.

ves·tige (ves′tij), *n.* a slight remnant; trace; mark: *Ghost stories are vestiges of a former widespread belief in ghosts.*

vig·il (vij′əl), *n.* a staying awake for some purpose; a watching; watch: *All night the mother kept vigil over the sick child.*

vi·gnette (vin yet′), *n.* **1** a literary sketch; short verbal description. **2** any scene or view of small, pleasing, and delicate dimensions.

vin·tage (vin′tij), *n.* type or model of something which was fashionable or popular during an earlier season: *a hat of the vintage of 1940.* —*adj.* **1** of outstanding quality; choice: *vintage wines.* **2** dating from long ago; out-of-date; old-fashioned: *a vintage automobile.*

vir·tu·al (vėr′chü əl), *adj.* being something in effect, though not so in name; for all practical purposes; actual; real: *The battle was won with so great a loss of soldiers that it was a virtual defeat.* —**vir′tu·al·ly,** *adv.*

vir·tue (vėr′chü), *n.* **1** moral excellence; goodness. **2** a particular moral excellence: *Justice and kindness are virtues.*

vi·rus (vī′rəs), *n.* **1** any of a group of disease-producing agents composed of protein and nucleic acid, smaller than any known bacteria and dependent upon the living tissue of hosts for their reproduction and growth. Viruses cause rabies, polio, chicken pox, the common cold, and many other diseases. **2** a poison produced in a person or animal suffering from an infectious disease. [<Latin, poison]

vis·i·bil·i·ty (viz′ə bil′ə tē), *n., pl.* **-ties.** **1** condition or quality of being seen or exposed to view. **2** condition of light, atmosphere, etc., with reference to the distance at which things can be clearly seen.

vol·can·ic (vol kan′ik), *adj.* of or caused by a volcano; having to do with volcanoes: *a volcanic eruption.* —**vol·can′i·cal·ly,** *adv.*

vol·ca·no (vol kā′nō), *n., pl.* **-noes** or **nos. 1** an opening in the earth's crust through which steam, ashes, and lava are expelled in periods of activity. **2** a cone-shaped hill or mountain around this opening, built up of the material thus expelled. [< Italian < Latin *Vulcanus* Vulcan]

vouch (vouch), *v.i.* be responsible; give a guarantee *(for): I can vouch for the truth of the story. The principal vouched for the student's honesty.*

W

waft (waft, wäft), *v.t.* carry over water or through air: *The waves wafted the boat to shore.* —*v.i.* float: *the boat wafted slowly on the surface.*

wheez·y (hwē′zē), *adj.,* **wheez·i·er, wheez·i·est.** inclined to breathe with difficulty and with a whistling sound: *a wheezy old dog.* —**wheez′i·ly,** *adv.*

wis·dom (wiz′dəm), *n.* **1** knowledge and good judgment based on experience. **2** wise conduct; wise words. **3** scholarly knowledge.

wiz·ard (wiz′ərd), *n.* **1** man supposed to have magic power; magician; sorcerer. **2** INFORMAL. a very clever person; expert: *be a wizard at math.* [Middle English < *wys* wise]

wretch·ed (rech′id), *adj.* **1** very unfortunate or unhappy. **2** very unsatisfactory; miserable: *a wretched hut.* **3** very bad: *a wretched traitor.* —**wretch′ed·ly,** *adv.* —**wretch′ed·ness,** *n.*

Z

zer·o (zir′ō), *n.* **1** the figure or digit 0; naught. **2** point marked with a zero on the scale of a thermometer, etc. [< Italian < Arabic *sifr* empty]

a hat	oi oil	ə stands for
ā age	ou out	a in about
ä far	u cup	e in taken
e let	u̇ put	i in pencil
ē equal	ü rule	o in lemon
ėr term	ch child	u in circus
i it	ng long	
ī ice	sh she	
o hot	th thin	
ō open	ᴛʜ then	
ô order	zh measure	

volcano

Page 314: Slightly adapted from pp. 9–25 of *Young Man in a Hurry* by Jean Lee Latham. Copyright © 1958 by Jean Lee Latham. Reprinted by permission of Harper & Row, Publishers, Inc.

Page 330: Adaptation of "The Samaritan" by Richard Harper. Copyright © 1963 by Richard Harper. Reprinted by permission.

Page 340: "The Road Not Taken" by Robert Frost from *The Poetry of Robert Frost* edited by Edward Connery Lathem. Copyright 1916, © 1969 by Holt, Rinehart and Winston. Copyright 1944 by Robert Frost. Reprinted by permission of Holt, Rinehart and Winston, Publishers.

Page 364: Table, "Leading Uses of Home Computers," source: Gallup Organization. Reprinted by permission of American Institute of Public Opinion.

Page 370: Abridgment and adaptation of pp. 52–71, 150–155 and 206–217 in *Jenny Kimura* by Betty Cavanna. Reprinted by permission of William Morrow & Company.

Page 386: Adaptation from *Let the Balloon Go* by Ivan Southall. Copyright © 1968 Ivan Southall. Reprinted by permission of Associated Book Publishers Ltd. (Methuen Children's Books.)

Page 402: Adapted from "The Story of Atalanta" from *Two Queens of Heaven: Aphrodite, Demeter* by Doris Gates. Copyright © 1974 by Doris Gates. Reprinted by permission of Viking Penguin, Inc.

Page 406: Adapted from *Tonweya and the Eagles and Other Lakota Indian Tales* retold by Rosebud Yellow Robe. Text copyright © 1979 by Rosebud Yellow Robe Frantz. Reprinted by permission of the publisher, Dial Books for Young Readers.

Page 433: "Windy Nights," by Robert Louis Stevenson, from *A Child's Garden of Verses*.

Page 443: Adapted from *The School on Madison Avenue: Advertising and What It Teaches* by Ann E. Weiss. Copyright © 1980 by Ann E. Weiss. Reprinted by permission of the author.

Page 452: Adaptation from *The Soccer Orphans* by William MacKellar. Copyright © 1979 by William MacKellar. Reprinted by permission of Dodd, Mead & Company, Inc. and McIntosh and Otis, Inc.

Page 464: "The Women's 400 Meters" from *The Sidewalk Racer and Other Poems of Sports and Motion* by Lillian Morrison. Copyright © 1968, 1977 by Lillian Morrison. By permission of Lothrop, Lee & Shepard Company (A Division of William Morrow & Company).

Page 481: From *The Incredible Journey: A Tale of Three Animals* by Sheila Burnford with illustrations by Carl Burger. Copyright © 1960, 1961 by Sheila Burnford. By permission of Little, Brown and Company, in association with The Atlantic Monthly Press and David Higham Associates Limited.

Page 521: Text of "Three Wishes" from *Near the Window Tree* by Karla Kuskin. Copyright © 1975 by Karla Kuskin. Reprinted by permission of Harper & Row, Publishers, Inc.

Page 523: "The Naming of Names" by Ray Bradbury. Copyright 1949 by Ray Bradbury, renewed © 1977 by Ray Bradbury. Reprinted by permission of Don Congdon Associates, Inc.

Pages 541 and 543: From *People on Earth: A World Geography* by D. Drummond and R. Drummond, pp. 336–338. Copyright © 1983 by Scott, Foresman and Company.

Page 544: From *Eastern Hemisphere: Europe, Asia, Africa, and Oceania: Scott, Foresman Social Studies*, grade 7, pp. 161–169, by Dr. Joan Schreiber et al. Copyright © 1986 by Scott, Foresman and Company.

Page 555: "The Song of Wandering Aengus" by William Butler Yeats from *Collected Poems of William Butler Yeats*. Reprinted by permission of A. P. Watt Ltd. for Michael Yeats and Macmillan (London) Ltd.

Page 556: "The Knight and the Naiad of the Lake" from *The Faun and the Woodcutter's Daughter* by Barbara Leonie Picard. Reprinted by permission of the author.

Page 562: Excerpt from "Barbara Leonie Picard" from *Third Book of Junior Authors* ed. by Doris De Montreville and Donna Hill, p. 228. Copyright © 1972 by The H. W. Wilson Company, New York. By permission of The H. W. Wilson Company.

Page 563: Adaptation from "To Be a Knight" by Jay Williams. Copyright © 1962 American Heritage Publishing Co., Inc. Reprinted from Horizon Caravel *Knights of the Crusades* by Jay Williams, 1962.

Page 568: From *Adam of the Road* by Elizabeth Janet Gray. Copyright 1942, renewed © 1969 by Elizabeth Janet Gray. Reprinted by permission of Viking Penguin Inc.

Page 585: Excerpt from *Newbery Medal Books: 1922–1955*, ed. by Bertha Mahony Miller and Elinor Whitney Field. Copyright 1955 by The Horn Book, Inc. Reprinted by permission.

Artists

Section 1: William Burlingham, 18–19; Joe Van Severen, 20; Dan Siculan, 23, 24, 25, 26, 28, 29, 33; Chuck Slack, 47, 48, 50, 52, 54

Section 2: Cynthia Maniates, 63, 67, 71; Scott Foresman Photo Studio, 84; Joe Van Severen, 74

Section 3: Richard Berival, 136, 145; Jim Carleton, 141; Betty Maxey, 123, 126, 129, 130–131, 132, 134; Joe Van Severen, 135

Section 4: Terry Sirrell, 183

Section 6: Larry Frederick, 269; Robert Korta, 248, 250, 253, 255, 258; Joe Van Severen, 265, 267

Section 7: Stephan Clay, 331, 335, 339; Mark McMahon, 340

Section 8: Cheryl Arnemann, 371, 373, 376, 379; Robert Trammel, 358

Section 9: Michael Conway, 386, 391, 396; Ben Otero, 414, 417, 419, 420, 424, 429; Helen Nelson Reed, 403; Robert Trammel, 384

Section 10: Ben Otero, 453, 459; Scott Foresman Photo Studio, 439, 440

Section 11: Michael Conway, 478; Ben Otero, 524, 530; Helen Nelson Reed, 476–477

Section 12: Nathan Greene, 568, 576, 582; Helen Nelson Reed, 556–557, 561

Freelance Photography

Michael Goss, 203, 205, 207, 209, 211, 212, 213, 228, 229, 230, 231, 234, 235, 236

Pictures

Pages 9, 10, 16: From MR. MYSTERIOUS AND COMPANY by Sid Fleischman with illustrations by Eric Von Schmidt, Copyright © 1962 by Albert S. Fleischman. By permission of Little, Brown and Company, in association with The Atlantic Monthly Press; Page 37: Dan Morrill; Page 38: Cindy Charles; Pages 43, 46: Deng Ming-Dao. Courtesy Jade Snow Wong; Page 44: Alex Selkirk; Pages 56–57: Copyright © 1973 by Saul Steinberg; Page 76: Steve Lissau; Page 79: James Thurber drawing reprinted from AN AMERICAN BESTIARY by Mary Sayre Haverstock, Harry N. Abrams, Inc. Page 80: Joseph A. Di Chello, Jr.; Page 81: Leonard Freed/Magnum Photos; Page 82: © Long Photography, Inc. 1985; Page 87: Alain Gauthier; Page 89: Ernst Haas/Magnum Photos; Page 92: Wide World Photos; Pages 93, 94: UPI/Bettmann Newsphotos; Page 102: Focus On Sports; Page 105; Wide World Photos; Pages 106, 110–113: Courtesy Ruth Gruber; Pages 115, 119: Courtesy Michael Naranjo & Laurie Engel Naranjo; Page 121: Myrtle Todes; Page 147: The Illustrated London News Picture Library; Page 149: Reprinted by permission of the American Library Association; Pages 150–151: The Metropolitan Museum of Art, Wolf Fund, 1906. Catherine Lorillard Wolfe Collection; Page 158: Runk/Schoenberger from Grant Heilman Photography; Page 159: Photri; Page 160: Jay M. Pasachoff; Page 164: Courtesy Nova Scotia Information Service; Page 169: (top left) Reprinted from AUDUBON, the magazine of the National Audubon Society; © 1978 by Clarence Brown; Page 169: (top right) Reprinted from AUDUBON, the magazine of the National Audubon Society; © 1976 by Roy Wilson; Page 170: Bob Glaze/Artstreet; Pages 173–175: © The Cousteau Society, Inc. 930 W. 21st St., Norfolk, VA 23517; Page 176: Douglas P. Wilson; Pages 179, 180: David Doublet; Page 181: Michael O'Neill; Page 186: © Wolfgang Kaehler; Page 188: (top) Jeff Foott/TOM STACK & ASSOCIATES; Page 188: (center) Joe Branney/TOM STACK & ASSOCIATES; Page 188: (bottom) © Wolfgang Kaehler; Page 189: (top) Robert Perron/Photo Researchers; Page 189: (center) Martin Rogers/FPG; Page 189: (bottom) Kenneth Murray/Photo Researchers; Page 191: (left) Alan Pitcairn from Grant Heilman Photography; Page 191: (center) David R. Frazier; Page 191: (right) Bohdan Hrynwych/Southern Light; Page 192: (left) Karen Donelson/TOM STACK & ASSOCIATES; Page 192: (right) W. Grenfell/TOM STACK & ASSOCIATES; Page 193: (left) Karen Donelson/TOM STACK & ASSOCIATES; Page 193: (center) Kevin Schafer/TOM STACK & ASSOCIATES; Page 193: (right) Robert Reiff/FPG; Pages 194, 195 (top), 195 (center), 196: Steve Lissau; Page 195: (bottom) Edmund Nagele/FPG; Pages 198–199: Reprinted by permission of DODD, MEAD & COMPANY, INC. from THE INSIDE–OUTSIDE BOOK OF NEW YORK by Roxie Munro. Copyright © 1985 by Roxie Munro; Page 200: Milton Greene, from THE MARCEL MARCEAU COUNTING BOOK by George Mendoza, Doubleday & Company; Pages 214, 219: Museum of Fine Arts, Boston; Page 225: Detail, Masanobu: Interior view of Nakamura Theater in Edo, 18th century. Art Institute of Chicago, Clarence Buckingham Collection; Pages 238–239: "Double Portrait of Israhel van Meckenem and His Wife Ida" by

printed by permission.

Israhel van Meckenem. National Gallery of Art, Washington. Rosenwald Collection; Pages 242–243: Nic Nicosia, "Near (Modern) Disaster #8," Courtesy Texas Gallery, Houston; Page 244: (left) Philadelphia Commercial Museum; Page 263: Tokyo National Museum; Pages 274, 278, 290: From THE PICTURES OF J. R. R. TOLKIEN. by J.R.R. Tolkien. Copyright © 1979 by George Allen and Unwin (Publishers) Ltd. Reprinted by permission of Houghton Mifflin Company. Page 293: Photograph by Snowdon, Camera Press, London; Page 295: Reprinted by permission of the American Library Association; Pages 296–297: Baron Wolman; Pages 307, 309, 311: Andy Hayt/SPORTS ILLUSTRATED; Pages 314, 320, 328: I. N. Phelps Stokes Collection, New York Public Library, Astor, Lenox & Tilden Foundations; Page 324: Museum of the City of New York; Page 327: Courtesy Macmillan Publishing Company; Page 349: Library of Congress; Page 353: (left) Painting by Charles Wilson Peale. Courtesy Mount Vernon Ladies' Association; Page 353: (right) Library of Congress; Page 356: Painting by John Trumbull. Yale Unversity Art Gallery; Page 360: Wide World Photos; Page 363: Reprinted from June 10, 1985 issue of BUSINESS WEEK by special permission, © 1985 by McGraw-Hill, Inc.; Page 365: Courtesy Digital Equipment Corporation; Pages 382–383: From THE CIRCUS IN AMERICA by Charles Philip Fox & Tom Parkinson; Page 400: Courtesy Macmillan Publishing Company; Pages 406, 409, 412: Jerry Pinckney; Page 411: Courtesy E. P. Dutton, Inc.; Page 433: Dan Morrill; Page 435: Reprinted by permission of the American Library Association; Pages 436–437: Art Pahlke; Page 438: Miguel/The Image Bank; Page 439: (bottom) Robert Amft; Page 441: P. Miller/The Image Bank; Page 442 (surfer): Steve Lissau; Page 464: G. Gove/The Image Bank; Page 465: The National Film Archive; Page 467: Museum of Modern Art/ Film Stills Archive; Page 469: From the collection of the Memory Shop; Page 470: Museum of Modern Art/Film Stills Archive; Page 472: © Lucasfilm Ltd. (LFL) 1980. All rights reserved. Courtesy of Lucasfilm Ltd.; Page 474 (top), 474 (bottom left): Museum of Modern Art/Film Stills Archive; Page 474: (bottom right) MGM/USA; Pages 538–539: British Library Board; Page 544: The Huntington Library, San Marino, CA; Pages 546–547, 548: British Library Board; Page 549: Bülloz; Page 552: The Bodleian Library, Oxford. M. S. Bodley 264, fol. 218r; Page 553: (left) Scala/Art Resource; Page 553: (right) British Library Board; Page 563: British Museum Trustees; Page 564: Bibliotheque Nationale; Page 565: William A. Norman; Page 567: David Warren/Shostal Associates; Page 585: Courtesy Elizabeth Gray Vining; Page 587: Reprinted by permission of the American Library Association. Page 598: U.S.D.A.; Page 601: Library of Congress; Page 602(t): NOAA; Page 604(t): "Farmers Attacking Officials at the Springfield Arsenal under Daniel Sharp's Leadership in 1786," American History Division, The New York Public Library, Astor, Lenox & Tilden Foundations; Page 604(b), "The Old Guitarist," Pablo Picasso, 1903, Helen Birch Bartlett Memorial Collection, Courtesy of the Art Institute of Chicago; Page 606: The British Library; Page 607(b): John H. Gerard; Page 610(t): John Tenniel illustration from Lewis Carroll's ALICE'S ADVENTURES IN WONDERLAND; Page 610(b): Paul Mathews; Page 612: Alinari/Art Resource; Page 614(t) "Notorious Gentlemen," Culver Pictures, Inc.; Page 615: Hugo Brehme/Rapho/Photo Researchers, Inc.

Cover Artists
Leo and Diane Dillon